Frommer's®

Turkey

4th Edition

by Lynn A. Levine

Here's what the critics say about Frommer's:

"Amazingly easy to use. Very portable, very complete."

—*Booklist*

"Detailed, accurate, and easy-to-read information for all price ranges."
—*Glamour Magazine*

"Hotel information is close to encyclopedic."

—*Des Moines Sunday Register*

"Frommer's Guides have a way of giving you a real feel for a place."
—*Knight Ridder Newspapers*

WILEY

Wiley Publishing, Inc.

About the Author

Lynn A. Levine has contributed to a number of Frommer's titles, including *Frommer's Italy from $70 a Day* and *Frommer's Southeast Asia*. Her work has appeared in the *Boston Globe, Elle, MSNBC/Newsweek Budget Travel, Travel Holiday,* and the *UN Chronicle*. She is a communications consultant for UNICEF and also runs the website www.talking turkey.com.

Published by:

Wiley Publishing, Inc.

111 River St.
Hoboken, NJ 07030-5774

ISBN-13: 978-0-471-78556-9
ISBN-10: 0-471-78556-3

Editor: Stephen Bassman
Production Editor: Katie Robinson
Cartographer: Guy Ruggiero
Photo Editor: Richard Fox
Production by Wiley Indianapolis Composition Services

Front cover photo: Whirling dervishes.
Back cover photo: Sculpture fragment of Nike (goddess of Victory) in Ephesus.

For information on our other products and services or to obtain technical support, please contact our Customer Care Department within the U.S. at 800/762-2974, outside the U.S. at 317/572-3993 or fax 317/572-4002.

Wiley also publishes its books in a variety of electronic formats. Some content that appears in print may not be available in electronic formats.

Manufactured in the United States of America

5   4   3   2

Contents

(5) Short Hops from Istanbul: Around the Sea of Marmara & the North Aegean   152

(6) The Central & Southern Aegean Coasts   182

(7) The Turquoise & Mediterranean Coasts   246

(8) Cappadocia & the Interior   320

9 Ankara 358

Appendix A: Turkey in Depth 380

Appendix B: A Glossary of Useful Turkish Phrases 417

Index 426

List of Maps

Acknowledgments

Special thanks are in order for a handful of incredibly wonderful and supportive individuals. Thanks to Sirma, Sila, Ilgin Aydin, Suha, Süleyman, and Hakan for their professional assistance and personal friendship. Each has been instrumental in supporting my work on this guide and in introducing me to the soul of Turkey. Thanks to Mustafa, the best roommate ever. Special thanks to Credo Tours for use of the sofa.

An Invitation to the Reader

In researching this book, we discovered many wonderful places—hotels, restaurants, shops, and more. We're sure you'll find others. Please tell us about them, so we can share the information with your fellow travelers in upcoming editions. If you were disappointed with a recommendation, we'd love to know that, too. Please write to:

Frommer's Turkey, 4th Edition
Wiley Publishing, Inc. • 111 River St. • Hoboken, NJ 07030-5774

An Additional Note

Please be advised that travel information is subject to change at any time—and this is especially true of prices. We therefore suggest that you write or call ahead for confirmation when making your travel plans. The authors, editors, and publisher cannot be held responsible for the experiences of readers while traveling. Your safety is important to us, however, so we encourage you to stay alert and be aware of your surroundings. Keep a close eye on cameras, purses, and wallets, all favorite targets of thieves and pickpockets.

Other Great Guides for Your Trip:

Frommer's Europe

Pauline Frommer's Europe

Frommer's Europe from $85 a Day

Frommer's Road Atlas Europe

Frommer's Star Ratings, Icons & Abbreviations

Every hotel, restaurant, and attraction listing in this guide has been ranked for quality, value, service, amenities, and special features using a star-rating system. In country, state, and regional guides, we also rate towns and regions to help you narrow down your choices and budget your time accordingly. Hotels and restaurants are rated on a scale of zero (recommended) to three stars (exceptional). Attractions, shopping, nightlife, towns, and regions are rated according to the following scale: zero stars (recommended), one star (highly recommended), two stars (very highly recommended), and three stars (must-see).

In addition to the star-rating system, we also use seven feature icons that point you to the great deals, in-the-know advice, and unique experiences that separate travelers from tourists. Throughout the book, look for:

Finds	Special finds—those places only insiders know about
Fun Fact	Fun facts—details that make travelers more informed and their trips more fun
Kids	Best bets for kids, and advice for the whole family
Moments	Special moments—those experiences that memories are made of
Overrated	Places or experiences not worth your time or money
Tips	Insider tips—great ways to save time and money
Value	Great values—where to get the best deals

The following **abbreviations** are used for credit cards:

| AE | American Express | DISC | Discover | V | Visa |
| DC | Diners Club | MC | MasterCard | | |

Frommers.com

Now that you have the guidebook to a great trip, visit our website at **www.frommers.com** for travel information on more than 3,000 destinations. With features updated regularly, we give you instant access to the most current trip-planning information available. At Frommers.com, you'll also find the best prices on airfares, accommodations, and car rentals—and you can even book travel online through our travel booking partners. At Frommers.com, you'll also find the following:

- Online updates to our most popular guidebooks
- Vacation sweepstakes and contest giveaways
- Newsletter highlighting the hottest travel trends
- Online travel message boards with featured travel discussions

What's New in Turkey

If thoughts of a slow international economy and ongoing insurgencies in Afghanistan and Iraq are holding you back, rest assured: Turkey has more than gracefully weathered the storm. The nation's economic growth rivals that of China's, while tourism is up, up, up, for the first time in several years. So, in spite of somewhat inflated prices in comparison to previous years, Turkey still presents itself as one of the best, safest, *easiest*, and all-around rewarding destinations in the region.

PLANNING YOUR TRIP For complete planning information, see chapter 2. The Turkish government opened a new **Tourism Office** in D.C. at 2525 Massachusetts Ave. NW, Suite 306, Washington, DC 20008 (© **202/612-6800;** fax 202/319-7446; tourismdc@aol.com).

You can also check out two useful websites for insider information: **www.mymerhaba.com**, a site maintained by a group of expats in Istanbul, and at **www.gatetoturkey.com**, the companion site to the airport magazine, *The Gate*. For the more ambitious, Tömer, the language school attached to Ankara University, has initiated its first Online Turkish Learning Center at **www.turkish-center.com**.

Visitor Information, Entry Requirements & Money Visas for **Americans** now cost $26 on entry. Visas may be purchased at the visa window next to the immigration counters.

But the big news is that with solid economic growth rivaling that of China's, Turkey finally has reached the level of stability where lopping six zeros off the national currency would not send the country into convulsions. As of January 2005, the Yeni Turk Lirası, or "New Turkish Lira," equals the previous 1,000,000 "old" Turkish Lira. As of January 2006, only new YTL currency are in circulation.

Getting Around With the arrival of **Onur Air** (www.onurair.com.tr) and more recently, **Flyair** (www.flyair.com.tr), Turkish Airlines no longer has a monopoly on domestic flights, or on your wallet. Onur and Flyair fly from Istanbul to Ankara, Kayseri, Antalya, and İzmir, in addition to points east. Expect one-way fares for both airlines to level off at around 75YTL ($55).

ISTANBUL For complete coverage of Istanbul, see chapter 4.

Getting Around The Zeytinburnu-to-Eminönü Tramway has been extended from Eminönü to Beşiktaş, making jaunts across the Galata Bridge between Sultanahmet and Karaköy (and points beyond) much easier on the feet. Note that you have to exit the train, cross the platform, and change trains at Eminönü on your way to Sultanahmet.

Visitor Information The **British Consulate** is back in its original location at Mesrutiyet Caddesi 34, Tepebşı (Beyoglu) (© **0212/334-6400;** fax 0212/334-6401), in a brand-new building—but this time behind a *very* secure high wall.

Safety Perhaps it's indicative of economic growth, or of increased tourism creating more opportunity, but Istanbul seems to be experiencing a new level of petty crime. And it's seeped into the otherwise pastoral neighborhood of Sultanahmet, where previously, crimes were committed by glorified gigolos with a wink and a smile. Not so now. Men walking alone are now at high risk of being mugged in dark byways, and contents of purses are routinely disappearing. It seems as though the Big Bad City has arrived in the quiet, leafy green neighborhoods of Istanbul's Old City. Take all the precautions you would take visiting any major international metropolis.

Where to Stay Boutique hotels, the darling of carpet-sellers-turned-hoteliers, are popping up like mushrooms in Sultanahmet with prices akin to truffles. Kind of diminishes the cache, which is why I recommend sticking to honest originals like the **Ayasofya Konakları** (p. 79), which just underwent a complete upgrade (they used to be called pensions, not mansions), and its sister property, the **Yeşil Ev** (p. 92), which recently added air-conditioning to all its rooms. Meanwhile, the **Hotel Empress Zoe** (p. 80) added four suites with gardens. I've also added the new **Hotel Erguvan** (p. 80), because it's managed to keep its prices lower than the other boutique wannabes. It's also quite lovely. But the main solution to the problem of where to stay is to shift your center over to the other, increasingly vibrant, part of the city just across the Golden Horn. **Ansen 130** (p. 82) is an all-suite hotel that would be just as welcomed on Thompson Street in New York's SoHo as in Istanbul's Beyoğlu district. And the Marmara Istanbul has become so popular that to keep up with demand, the owners opened the second, even more stylish Marmara Pera, in the heart of Beyoğlu's revival.

Where to Dine **Doğa Balık** (p. 93) has earned a position as one of Istanbul's best fish restaurants. But I love this place because their selection of over 30 mezes is the best I've ever had. The vegetable and seafood salads are outstanding, while the organic greens (try the "goat food") will make you moan with pleasure. Go figure.

After Dark Istanbulers really love their views. And so do we. The latest hot vista is visible from **360 Istanbul** (p. 147), a panoramic bar and restaurant located practically in the steeple of St. Antoine. The 180-degree views are just as stunning from one of the bars, fish restaurants, and tearooms on the lower level of the Galata Bridge. Sit close to the middle, to avoid views of shoreline sea scum.

What to See & Do in Istanbul The future of Istanbul is no longer exclusively in its past. With the opening of the **Istanbul Museum of Modern Art** (p. 128), the city is clearly looking forward. And in the same spirit of renewal, a group of developers and preservationists bought up an entire neighborhood of turn-of-the-20th-century homes, restored them to their original state of grandeur, and named the whole project **Fransiz Sokağı (French Street).** Only French restaurants, boutiques, and people selling French stuff need apply for a permit to open a business here.

AROUND THE SEA OF MARMARA & THE NORTH AEGEAN For complete information on this region, see chapter 5.

Çanakkale **TJ's Tours** (© 0286/814-3121; www.anzacgallipolitours.com) recently arrived on the scene to break the monopoly that Hassle Free has held on tours of Troy and Gallipoli (p. 170). TJ's can also provide accommodations in their hostel or in their upgraded Eceabat Hotel.

Where to Stay The formerly dowdy **Akol** (© 0286/217-9456) has been completely renovated, and is now worthy of its four stars (p. 167).

The family-run **Anzac Hotel** (© **0286/ 217-7777**) has also undergone a complete overhaul, so that now all rooms have air-conditioning, satellite TV, and high-speed Internet, against a background of Italian walnut (p. 167). Attached to TJ's Tours is the shiny new **Eceabat Hotel** (© **0286/814-3121**), a brand-new pension with three-star amenities. It's located on the shores of the Gallipoli Peninsula opposite Çanakkale, making it just a bit more convenient to the battlefields of Gallipoli.

THE CENTRAL & SOUTHERN AEGEAN COASTS For complete information on this region, see chapter 6.

İzmir The city center known as Pasaport is now connected to the Gulf of İzmir via an expansive **seafront promenade** (p. 183). Crowning the project is the restoration of an old customs house designed by Gustave Eiffel that now houses a new entertainment and shopping center called **Konak Pier** (p. 190).

Çeşme The **Sisus Hotel** (© **30-2810-300330** in Greece) is the newest addition to Dalyan Marina, combining style and serenity in one smart little hotel (p. 199). Over in Çeşme town, the **Pırıl Hotel** (© **0232/712-7574**) is no longer the jewel in the rough it was when I first stayed (p. 198). Instead, it's transformed itself into a five-star luxury property good enough for the smart set disillusioned with Bodrum.

Meanwhile, over in the historically characteristic village of Alaçatı, visitors to Çeşme can hole up in the shuttered stone **Alaçatı Taş Hotel** (© **0232/716-7722**), with its multilingual staff and backyard swimming pool (p. 195).

Visitors can take advantage of the ancient site of Didyma with an overnight at the 150-year-old stone house–turned B&B; a room at the **Medusa House** (© **0256/811-0063**) will allow you to enjoy a leisurely, tourist-free consultation with the ancient oracles (p. 219).

Bodrum While those in the know think they're smarter than everyone else for heading out to the hotels on the Bodrum Peninsula, the guests of the **Butterfly Hotel** (© **0252/313-8358**) are as smug as can be. This new luxury boutique property is a former home converted into a six-room diamond only a hop, skip, and a jump from the waterfront and twin harbors (p. 238).

THE TURQUOISE & MEDITERRANEAN COASTS For complete information on this region, see chapter 7.

Kas The **Gardenia Hotel** (© **0242/ 836-2368**) is a nice, new, and affordable hotel with vistas to die for. It's also within walking distance of restaurants and shops (p. 294).

CAPPADOCIA & THE INTERIOR For complete information on this region, see chapter 8.

Where to Stay Adding to the glut of boutique caves in the region is the sumptuously adorned **Sacred House** (© **384/ 341-7102**), named as such because the hotel occupies the space of a former church (p. 329). The panoramic rooftop lounge and restaurant serves Armenian-leaning food. Meanwhile, to keep up with the pack, **Esbelli Evi** (© **0384/341-3395**) now boasts four luxurious and self-contained cave house suites, each with its very own private grassy garden sheltered behind a high stone wall (p. 328).

Where to Dine You can't miss this quintessentially Turkish bar/cafe/restaurant; **Alaturca** (© **0384/271-2176**) takes up a two-story building in the town center— including the bean-bag-strewn lawn outside for whiling the time away (p. 336).

ANKARA For complete information on this region, see chapter 9.

What to See The crown jewel of the cult of Atatürk resides, rightfully, within

Atatürk Mausoleum (Anıtkabir) (p. 369), a sprawling memorial to a great man. So it was right and good that the new Atatürk Museum was inaugurated, complete with light and sound dioramas, oil portraits, and republican memorabilia.

The trend in Turkey toward historic preservation has reached the neighborhood around the Ankara fortress. Most notable is the completion of the **Rahmi M. Koç Museum** (✆ 0312/309-6800), a new tribute to science and engineering housed in the most impressive Çengelhan, a 16th-century caravansary and merchant trading post (p. 373).

Where to Stay Visitors to Ankara hoping to find five-star amenities without selling out to the big-name franchises now choose the **Gordion Hotel** (✆ 0312/427-8080), the new and manageably sized boutique property located in the heart of the diplomatic and business center (p. 367).

The 150-room **Swissôtel Ankara,** Yıldızevler Mahallesi, 21 Sokak No. 2 (✆ 0312/409-3000; fax 0312/409-3399; www.ankara.swissotel.com), is a new property that opened in May 2006 near the government and ambassador buildings in Çankaya, with lots of standard luxury amenities, tech-savvy conference facilities, and an extensive wellness center. Double rooms go for 122€–366€ ($100–$300). Keep your eyes peeled for some nice incentives throughout 2006.

1

The Best of Turkey

Just call Turkey the comeback kid. Having been stuck in the doldrums of terrorism, the Gulf War, the August 1999 earthquake, the September 11th terrorist attacks, and the current war in Iraq, Turkey's tourism industry is finally reaping much-deserved rewards. But it's a fine line between rewards and highway robbery. On the one hand, a restructuring of the Turkish economy has translated into a whopping 9% growth in GDP in the past 5 years. Business is booming, the middle class is spending money, and foreigners seem to be descending on Turkey as if it were going out of business. On the other hand, the class of entrepreneurs making their living solely off of tourism seems to have come together and decided to make up for the combined past seasons' losses in one fell swoop. The result is that Turkey is no longer the bargain it was a mere 2 years ago. Hotels that once quoted prices in U.S. dollars switched to the symbol of the € (representing a 21% increase); in Istanbul, Cappadocia and in other popular regions, even this decrease in value has been compounded by further increases. For visitors wielding euros, Turkey is still very much an affordable destination. But for Americans paying in the pathetic dollar, Turkey is anything but a good value. So now you ask, is it worth it?

Absolutely. But you'll need to find the right balance. Traveling off-season will give you the strongest bargaining power. But you may also have to settle for less than top-of-the-line luxury in your accommodations, avoid the tourist traps, and forego that sunrise balloon ride over Cappadocia. If you do, I guarantee that you'll soon see why people who know just can't get enough of Turkey.

The magic of Turkey bubbles over in its history, culture, gastronomy, humanity, exotic nature, and commerce. Turkey bills itself, and rightfully so, as the "Cradle of Civilization," boasting more Greek ruins than Greece and more Roman archaeological sites than all of Italy. Turkey is also a major custodian of sacred sites revered by Christians, Jews, and Muslims alike, and of invaluable remnants of early Greek civilization, Byzantine majesty, and Ottoman culture and artistry. But, while most tourist brochures zone in on archaeological ruins and artistic masterpieces, few devote the appropriate space to the magnificence of Turkey's Mediterranean, its self-indulgent pleasures (imagine basking in a mineral mud bath), or the wide array of choices available for nature lovers and sports enthusiasts. Turkey is a singularly unique country, still unspoiled and innocent, and pleasantly surprised by the fact that visitors come from far and wide to witness its way of life. It's all rather disarming to travelers who've visited other parts of the world, where crowds of rubbernecking, Bermuda shorts–wearing, camera-sporting arrivals elicit exclamations of "damned tourists." Turks welcome their guests with a genuineness of spirit and boundless generosity that defies superlatives. This from a population in which 80% of the people can't afford meat and where the native language provides no word for "bitter." Truly, until you experience Turkish hospitality, you've barely broken the surface of what generosity can be.

Turkey is so densely packed with riches of every kind that the most difficult decision will be what *not* to see. I found it difficult to write this book without making it sound like a press release, because the country is so superlative and the culture so contrary to what you'd expect. You'll soon see for yourselves why nobody leaves Turkey with a lukewarm impression. Face it; there's no way to see it all. So this book attempts to sort through the absolute essentials of a first-time visit, providing an introduction to a country and culture you will surely want to revisit.

1 The Most Unforgettable Travel Experiences

- **Taking a *Hamam:*** The Turkish bath, rising out of the Islamic requirement of cleanliness, is not just practical, it's a minivacation. A good *hamam* experience includes the proper traditional ambience and a heavy-handed scrubbing. For historical value and pomp, you can't beat the **Çemberlitaş Hamamı** (p. 120), or for luxury, the one at Istanbul's **Ritz-Carlton** (p. 85), which comes with the hefty charge of 40€ ($50) for private access for non-guests on weekdays; 52€ ($63) on weekends (fee includes use of the fitness center, swimming pool, sauna, Jacuzzi and *hamam*). The lounge area of the men's section in the **Yeni Kaplıca** (p. 163) in Bursa and the **Talya Hotel** (p. 312) in Antalya are fabulously decorated with some of the most gorgeous wood details; you'll feel like royalty. The Queen Mother of all luxury *hamams,* however, is the sky-lit and picture-windowed marble *hamam* at the **Ada Hotel** (p. 241) in Türkbükü, outside of Bodrum, *by candlelight.*

- **Sharing Tea with the Locals:** Tea is at the center of Turkish culture; no significant negotiation takes place without some. But more than commerce, tea stops the hands of time in Turkey; it renews the bonds of friends and family. Having tea is inevitable, as is the invitation to share a glass with a total stranger. Accept the invitation: There's more in the glass than just a beverage.

- **Soaking in a Thermal Pool:** Sometimes Turkey seems like one big open-air spa; chemically rich waters bubble up from below while frigid spring water rushes down from above. The **Çeşme Peninsula** seems like one big hot bath, and a whole slew of brand-new luxury facilities are willing to accommodate (see "Highlights of the Çeşme Peninsula," in chapter 6). In the Sacred Pool of Hierapolis at the **Pamukkale Thermal** (p. 227), you swim amid the detritus of ancient civilizations as sulfur bubbles tingle your skin. Bursa's **Çelik Palas Hotel** (p. 160) has a domed pool hot enough to make your knees weak. Down the road at the **Kervansaray Termal Hotel** (p. 161), the pools of running water are enclosed in a 700-year-old original *hamam.*

- **Discovering the Covered Bazaar:** Nobody should pass through Turkey without spending a day at the mother of all shopping malls. The atmosphere crackles with the electricity of the hunt—but are you the hunter or the hunted? The excitement is tangible, even if you're on the trail of a simple pair of elf shoes or an evil-eye talisman. It's the disciplined shopper who gets out unscathed. See "Shopping" in chapter 4.

- **Riding the Ferry Across the Dardanelles:** Wars were fought for control of these straits. And thanks to a long line of steadfast Turks, you and I can

Turkey

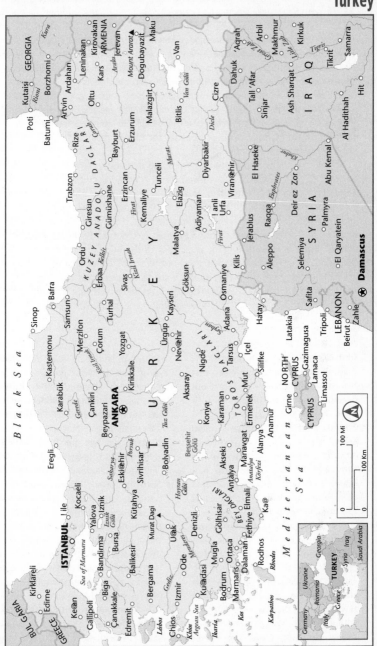

Midnight Express: Fact or Fiction?

The 1978 movie *Midnight Express,* directed by Alan Parker and scripted by Oliver Stone, elicits strong resentment in Turkey for the portrayal of Billy Hayes, who, in spite of a well-publicized crackdown on drug smuggling, took a dumb risk and lost. The movie, which won the director an Oscar, is a hideously graphic (and mostly fictional) account of human rights violations in a Turkish prison. The truth is that the *real* Billy Hayes acknowledges the inaccuracy of many of the scenes in the movie; he was in a low-security prison, and no guard was killed in order for him to escape. Actually, the Turkish government released him.

The name of the movie derives from the midnight train service from Istanbul to Edirne, which, at the time, briefly traveled through Greek territory. During the 1960s and 1970s, the Turkish government reacted to international criticism (particularly from the U.S.) of its harsh sentencing guidelines with a discreet and diplomatic trick. Foreigners convicted of drug-related offenses were divested of their passports and released during appeal. Then they were quietly ushered onto the Midnight Express train, where, once in Greece (and with the complicity of Greek guards on the train), they hopped off the train and were jailed until they could obtain new passports from their consulates. The Turks were thus able to maintain a hard-line stance without jeopardizing diplomatic relations.

---

sit back and enjoy the breezes, the high cliffs, and the fortresses that helped win the battle—and leave our passports back at the hotel. See "Gallipoli (Gelibolu)" in chapter 5.

- **Cruising the Turquoise Coast:** Words just don't do this justice. Aboard a wooden *gulet* (traditional broad-beamed boat), you drift past majestic mountains, undiscovered ruins, and impossibly azure waters, as the sun caresses your skin from sunrise to sunset. In this environment the morning aroma of Nescafe takes on an almost pleasant quality when enjoyed on deck, anchored just offshore a pine-enclosed inlet. By 9am you're diving off the rail and cursing the day it all has to end. See "All About the Blue Voyage" on p. 40.

- **Paragliding over Ölüdeniz:** There's no better place in the world than the surging summit of Babadağ for this wildly exhilarating and terrifying sport. For 15 brief minutes, you're flying high above the magnificent turquoise waters of Ölüdeniz with the mountains in the foreground. The safety factor? Not to be underestimated, but hey, that nice body of water should help break your fall. See "Fethiye & Ölüdeniz" in chapter 7.

- **Settling into Turkish Style:** As nomads, the Turks communed on home-woven cushions and kilims in their tents. The Ottomans continued the tradition of *şark* (Oriental) seating, and now every tourist destination thinks that's what we want. They're right. We want kilims, saddles, cushions, and low copper tables. The best ones are cozy and atmospheric: the poolside *şark* at the **Montana Pine Resort** (p. 276); the open-air *şark* shaded by trees at **Yaka**

Park (p. 269); or the natural air-conditioning of the platform *şarks* of **Hidden Paradise Restaurant** at Saklıkent Gorge, where the ice-cold waters of a mountain spring rush underneath (see "Fethiye & Ölüdeniz" in chapter 7).

• **Ballooning over Cappadocia:** Watch this surreal landscape change character right before your eyes: In a matter of minutes, the sun rises over the cliffs, valleys, and ravines, and colors morph from hazy blue to orange, pink, and finally yellow. The capper? A post-flight champagne breakfast. See "Exploring the Region" in chapter 8.

• **Spending the Night in a Cave:** The ceilings are low, the light is dim, and there are niches in the wall for your alarm clock—this is the troglodyte life as the Cappadocians lived it for thousands of years. Some of these "cave hotels" are rudimentary, others extravagant; but all are cool in summer, warm in winter, and as still as the daybreak. Among the best: **Esbelli Evi** (p. 328) and **Yunak Evleri** (p. 329), both in Ürgüp, and **Gamirasu** (p. 330) in Ayvalı.

2 The Best Small Towns

• **Bergama:** The soul of this village is the marketplace. Donkeys and their owners are parked next to stalls of fresh produce. Carpets hang from the awnings of old village houses around the Red Basilica to create a bit of shade from the hot sun. And only a few hundred yards away is Pergamum, one of the finest archaeological sites of antiquity. See "Bergama" in chapter 5.

• **Alaçatı:** A hilltop mound of windmills and 800-year-old Selçuk barrel-houses guard the entrance to the tiny Aegean village of Alaçatı. So close to the sea, and yet so far . . . See "Highlights of the Çeşme Peninsula" in chapter 6.

• **Şirince:** Originally a sanctuary for Greeks in the dying days of Ephesus, this dense hillside of preserved houses enclosed within a landscape of grape orchards is the perfect antidote to an overdose of archaeological sites. A bottle of local wine enjoyed amid the atmosphere of a former schoolhouse helps the medicine go down, too. See p. 204.

• **Gümüşlük:** The chance to walk on water—or nearly so—thanks to the sunken city walls of ancient Myndos;

what more could one want? How about an undiscovered enclosed bay, a sandy beach, and characteristic waterfront fish shacks. See "Bodrum" in chapter 6.

• **Karmylassos/Kayaköy:** Haunting panoramas of lives interrupted blanket the hillside of this once-thriving Greek settlement, abandoned during the 1924 population exchange between Turkey and Greece. Rather than reinhabit the houses—now crumbling and roofless—local Turkish residents have settled in the rolling and fertile plains of the surrounding valley. See p. 268.

• **Kalkan:** An influx of expatriates has put this little merchant village on the map. Now it's a chic and quirky tourist center—but the popularity has only resulted in improvement. The more old timber houses that are restored, the longer the roster of fabulous rooftop terraces and sea views. See "Kalkan" in chapter 7.

• **Kaleköy:** Also known as Simena, this seaside village clings to the side of the rock more efficiently than its sunken neighbors. With only 300 inhabitants living practically on top of one another, the town is too small to even have a street; a haphazard nonsystem of paths weaves around the village houses. There's no such thing as trespassing—it's just blissfully simple. See "Kaş" in chapter 7.

- **Güzelyurt:** A Cappadocian village where the livestock outnumber the residents, Güzelyurt provides a perfectly hospitable, off-the-beaten-track getaway. All of the features that draw you to Cappadocia—underground cities, rock-cut houses, and monastery complexes hidden in the nearby valley—are found within the confines of the village. See "The Ihlara Valley" in chapter 8.

- **Ayvalı:** The smell of apricots permeates the village as the harvest blankets the roofs of the flat-topped, semi-troglodyte houses. Down in the valley is an almost eerie grouping of cave facades that retain the curvy lines of the smooth cave surfaces. At sunset, the sound of drums in the distance and the image of village women baking the evening meal's bread in ancient rock ovens create an unforgettable vision of rural life. See p. 326.

3 The Best Ruins & Archaeological Sites

- **Pergamum:** Pergamum was once one of the most influential societies in the ancient world. Only traces of its greatness remain—but high atop the hillside, the acropolis still sings the songs of the wind through its broken pillars. The theater is the most extraordinary remnant of this forgotten society, clinging stubbornly to the side of a hill that overlooks a fruitful and expansive plain. See "Bergama" in chapter 5.

- **St. John's Basilica** (Selçuk): Most of the marble or cut-stone ruins you'll see in Turkey are ankle-high, a shadowy evocation of what once was. That's why the preserved redbrick walls of St. John's Basilica create such a pleasantly unexpected surprise. This holy site retains the soul of its original purpose; pilgrims gather around the presumed saint's tomb in an unabashed atmosphere of goodwill. See p. 204.

- **Ephesus:** Ephesus is among the best-preserved ancient sites in the Mediterranean, rivaled only by Pompeii. Frankly, it's humbling to see how efficiently life functioned before the advent of mechanized whatnots. In ancient times an important port city, the now-landlocked Ephesus (the shore is presently 5km/3 miles away) was an advanced society with a clear-cut hierarchy and an economic base, and the extensive archaeological remains are here to prove it. The partially reconstructed Library of Celsus, the newly excavated portions of the terraced housing, and the strangely evocative Public Latrine are just a few of the highlights of this sprawling, marble-strewn site. See "Ephesus" in chapter 6.

- **Ancient Theatre** (Hierapolis): The acoustics are as great down in the pit as they were 3,000 years ago. The extreme upper tiers overlook the great expanse of ancient Hierapolis—and now, thanks to UNESCO, unobstructed views of Pamukkale's whitening terraces. See "Pamukkale & Hierapolis" in chapter 6.

- **Temple of Apollo** (Didyma): It'll be love at first sight at the monumental gate of the enormous, heroic, and unexpectedly intact Temple of Apollo. Mosey on across the street to get a glimpse of the sacred settlement—including the Sacred Way connecting the site with Miletus—currently under excavation. See "Kuşadası" in chapter 6.

- **Lycian Tombs:** How did they get there? And why? Expertly carved into inaccessible vertical cliffs to resemble a classical temple, the Lycian sarcophagi are mysterious and dramatic, with their Gothic headdresses perched above the ghosts of royalty. The best spots to see them? Dalyan, Kaunos, Myra, and while boating the pristine waters of Kekova. See chapter 7.

- **Yazılıkaya:** The stony lineup of cone-headed deities at this sacred Hittite shrine is undeniably more impressive in person than in pictures. The true mystery is, who was the first to discover Chamber B, a room of enigmatic carved reliefs inconspicuously hidden inside a jagged chasm in the rock? See p. 378.

4 The Best Museums, Mosques & Churches

- **Blue Mosque** (Istanbul): This landmark mosque assumes a stance of authority over Sultanahmet Park. Just under the dome, hundreds of stained-glass windows sparkle like jewels until you are convinced that you're in the presence of a celestial being. The blue of the mosque actually changes to yellow, orange, and red, depending on the time of day and the entrance you choose to use. See p. 103.

- **Ayasofya** (Istanbul): When faced with the dome of this masterpiece, it's tempting to mimic the actions of Mehmet the Conqueror almost 600 years ago and drop to your knees in a gesture of utter humility. The sensation is increased by the low level of filtered light that finds its way in, temporarily blinding you to everything except the source of illumination. See p. 99.

- **Topkapı Palace** (Istanbul): Perspective check—this was once somebody's *house*. Actually, it was the home of a whole lot of people—up to 5,000 at a time, all in the service of one man. The sultan surrounded himself with the most beautiful women in the world. He collected the most precious treasures of the East. He assembled the most sacred relics of the Muslim faith under this roof. Six hundred years of Ottoman history,

and it's all behind these grand ornamental gates. See p. 109.

- **Ephesus Museum** (Selçuk): Not all of the treasures of Ephesus were smuggled out of the country to end up in Western museums. There's certainly enough here to keep you busy for a while; the explanations are succinct and the labeling clear. Now you'll finally know the story behind those omnipresent souvenir statues of the little guy with the huge erection. See p. 202.

- **Bodrum Underwater Archaeology Museum:** The only one of its kind, the Underwater Archaeology Museum displays the vast findings from the discovery of a pre-14th-century shipwreck. All the more amazing, because when divers stumbled on it, all they were looking for were a few sponges. See p. 235.

- **Underground Cities of Derinkuyu & Kaymaklı:** In Cappadocia, not everyone got a room with a view—at least not if your life was at stake. These multilevel cave cities, thought to date back to the 2nd century B.C., have supported up to 20,000 people at once in times of danger and religious persecution (though some speculation puts the number closer to 60,000). Clamber through the surprisingly intricate warren of passageways and living quarters where entire villages thrived in safety and darkness for months at a time. But claustrophobics beware—it's very dark and sometimes very snug. See p. 343.

- **Open-Air Museums of Zelve & Göreme:** When you live amid a landscape composed primarily of porous volcanic tufa, it doesn't take long before you realize, "Hey, I could make a great house out of this stuff." In Göreme you'll see cave churches decorated with stunning medieval frescoes; the ingenious structures at Zelve are more a window into daily living, troglodyte-style. See p. 327 and 333.

- **Museum of Anatolian Civilizations** (Ankara): It's rare that a museum has the material to catalog a culture's backbone from beginning to end—but here, it happens. Looking for prehistoric cave paintings of Cappadocia's volcanoes? Got it. How about detailed archives of commerce from 2000 B.C.? Got that, too. Hittite wedding ceremonies? A Phrygian chariot trampling? Fertility statuettes? Yup, yup, yup. See p. 370.

5 The Best Beaches

Most of Turkey's best beaches have been snatched up by big hotel chains—leaving less than stellar public alternatives for the nonpaying riffraff. Hotels sometimes charge a day fee for use of the beach, or maybe just the use of a lounge chair—as little as 2€ ($2.50) a day. The bonus: Hotels have snack bars, watersports, and clean toilets; and for the most part, the beaches have been left in their natural states.

- **Alaçatı Bay** (Çeşme Peninsula): The actual stretch of beach is small, but the beach opens up to an enormous bay blessed with lofty winds—paradise for windsurfers. The high winds are attributed to the sizable stretch of water and the absence of anything obstructing it. The beach is backed by hills, hills, and more hills, all topped by dry, barren brush. See "Highlights of the Çeşme Peninsula" in chapter 6.

- **Pırlanta Beach** (Çeşme Peninsula): Pırlanta, which means "diamond" in Turkish, describes the creamy whiteness of this sandy stretch of the peninsula. The beach is long and wide and faces the open Aegean. It's also easily accessible by *dolmuş* (minivan-type public transportation) from Çeşme's town center. See "Highlights of the Çeşme Peninsula," in chapter 6.

- **Altınkum Beach** (Çeşme Peninsula): The golden-colored sand from which the beach takes its name is located in a relatively hard-to-find spot at the southernmost tip of the peninsula. Luckily, this only serves to keep this public park blissfully empty and undervisited. Because this beach faces the open sea, the water is a refreshing few degrees cooler than elsewhere on the peninsula. See "Highlights of the Çeşme Peninsula" in chapter 6.

- **Ayayorgı Beach** (Çeşme Peninsula): Not a beach per se, but a few narrow concrete piers jutting out over the water. Nevertheless, Ayayorgı is a charming spot, hidden in an overgrowth of orange and olive groves and open to a small and intimate cove. See "Highlights of the Çeşme Peninsula" in chapter 6.

- **Ölüdeniz Beach** (Ölüdeniz): The posters just don't do it justice. On one end is the great expanse of Belcekız Beach, enclosed by the brittle silhouette of Babadağ and the landing pad for paragliders sporting jet-propulsion packs. And on the beach is the jaw-dropper, the Blue Lagoon made real: still waters in no less than three shades of turquoise. See "Fethiye & Ölüdeniz" in chapter 7.

- **Butterfly Valley** (Fethiye): After reaching the Blue Lagoon—the holy grail of Turkish beaches—it seems odd to want to go elsewhere. But the Fethiye area abounds with stunning scenery. If you can tear yourself away from the main event, take the 30-minute boat ride to Butterfly Valley, a sandy paradise hewn out of a soaring gorge. See "Fethiye & Ölüdeniz" in chapter 7.

- **Martı Resort Deluxe Hotel** (Içmeler): Nestled between two peaceful pine hills and boxed in by a series of curvaceous islands, the beach at the Martı creates the sensation of being lost at sea. The cove is known by a few savvy *gulet* captains who lay anchor offshore, though close enough to cast an admiring gaze along the broad-beamed hull. See "Marmaris & the Datça Peninsula" in chapter 7.

- **Iztuzu Beach** (Dalyan): Strict rules of conduct here; Iztuzu Beach is a national preserve and breeding ground for the Caretta Caretta, or loggerhead turtle. But at night, after the crowds have gone home, you can sit in complete darkness and watch the lights move out to sea, or listen to the sounds of home life glide over the river from a nearby fishing village. Just don't wander too close to the waterline, and on behalf of the turtles, stay away from the off-limits areas. See "Dalyan & Kaunos" in chapter 7.

- **Kaputaş Beach** (near Kalkan): Hundreds of years ago a huge chasm opened up the side of the mountain face and spilled its contents out to sea. The gorge has dried up, but what's left is Kaputaş Beach, a small, sandy patch 400 steps down from the highway that feels like the middle of nowhere. From here, it's just a short swim to some nearby phosphorescent caves. See "Kalkan" in chapter 7.

- **Patara Beach** (near Kalkan): Eighteen kilometers (11 miles) of beach backed by dunes and marshlands—need I say more? The Mediterranean rises to the challenge in the summer, when it turns a deep shade of blue. Watch out for the winds, though, which probably managed to submerge an entire ancient city in sand in no time at all. See "Kalkan" in chapter 7.

- **Konyaaltı** (Antalya): The newly developed waterfront in center-city Antalya breathes new life into a seaside resort that risked second-rate status. Miles of pebble beaches, waterfront promenades, meandering lawns, cafes, and activities make this one of Turkey's most coveted destinations. Bodrum, look out! See "Antalya" in chapter 7.

6 The Best Splurge Hotels

- **Çirağan Palace** (Istanbul; ✆ **800/ 426-3135** in the U.S., 800/363-0366 in Canada, 0800/868-588 in the U.K., 800/623-578 in Australia, 0800/446-368 in New Zealand, or 0212/258-3377 in Istanbul): More than just Istanbul's poshest hotel, the Çirağan Palace is a destination in its own right. The grandeur of the lobby—tinted by light coming through the stained glass and imbued with the fragrance of fresh roses—hardly prepares you for what's to come. Expect regal gardens, a delicious Bosphorus-side pool, big fluffy beds, flawless service, and an automated phone system that puts AT&T's to shame. Make sure you splurge for that sea view, or all bets are off. See p. 87.

- **Four Seasons Hotel** (Istanbul; ℂ **800/332-3442** in the U.S., or 0212/638-8200): Nothing drives home the magnitude of this hotel's history than to watch a former political prisoner once incarcerated here break down and cry in the hallway. Some original tile and marble details were preserved and reused in the renovation, and you might encounter the rough etchings of an inmate's name in one of the columns. But these days the unqualified opulence and comfort of this grand hotel couldn't be further from its bread-and-water past. Keep your eyes peeled for the much-delayed inauguration of the Bosphorus branch of this wonderful hotel, now scheduled for 2007. See p. 76.

- **Kısmet Hotel** (Kuşadası; ℂ **0256/ 618-1290**): To get the full effect of the Kısmet, go for the gusto and book a suite, preferably with a balustraded balcony. The next morning, watch the waters of the Aegean change color with the rising sun through your sliding glass door, without ever lifting your head off the pillow. See p. 221.

- **Ada Hotel** (Türkbükü, Bodrum Peninsula; ℂ **0252/377-5915**): If you're looking for the quintessential Turkish elegance, the Ada Hotel's got it, and more. Characteristic, stylish, romantic and utterly memorable, all rolled into a boutique experience on the hillside above the trendy yet serene outpost of Türkbükü. See p. 241.

- **The Marmara Otelı** (Bodrum; ℂ **0252/313-8130**): Deluxe, sleek, and breathtakingly situated—the Marmara sometimes feels more like an art gallery than a hotel, though infinitely more inviting. From your perch above Bodrum on a grassy lawn, you can mull over what Philippe Starck would think of the hotel. In your spare time, slink an hour in the hotel spa's saltwater flotation tank. See p. 240.

- **Hillside Su** (Antalya; ℂ **0242/249-0700**): The over-the-top design concept may lead to snow blindness, but what a way to go. It's sleek, stark, savvy, and razor sharp in its wit. And it comes with all of the necessary holiday trimmings, to architectural specifications, of course. See p. 311.

7 The Best One-of-a-Kind Places to Stay

- **Sultanahmet Palace Hotel** (Istanbul; ℂ **0212/458-0460**): A traditional *hamam* takes the place of a modern bathroom in every room of this hotel, with a supply of bathroom accouterments the Canyon Ranch would be proud of. Reserve one of the suites so that when the lights fade, you can open the drapes and watch sea gulls circle above the lights of the Blue Mosque. See p. 78.

- **Club Caravanserail** (Kuşadası; ℂ **0256/614-4115**): Staying in an old Selçuk or Ottoman inn doesn't mean you have to settle for badly whitewashed walls or monastery-level

accommodations. At this elegant inn, the parquet floors shine and the stone steps leading to the upper floor are steep and cumbersome enough to be totally original. See p. 220.

- **Villa Mahal** (Kalkan; ℂ **0242/844-3268**): They call it the Pool Room, but it's closer to a honeymoon suite. This free-standing circular room is removed from the main buildings—which provides a modicum of privacy, if you don't count the walls made entirely of glass. The room has its very own hilltop terrace and private pool. Makes me *almost* want to get married. See p. 287.

- **Aboard a *Gulet*** (the Turquoise Coast): The blazing August sun gives way to a mild summer night, and you wake up at dawn on the rear deck of the *gulet* with the rest of your shipmates, covered in fresh morning dew. The next night you'll know to bring a blanket and slather on some mosquito repellent; but there's nothing like sleeping under the stars, in a cove along the shores of the Mediterranean. See "All About the Blue Voyage" on p. 40.

- **Gamirasu Hotel** (Ayvalı; ☏ **0384/ 341-5825**): The sound of drums at sunset and the fragrance of freshly baked bread wafting from the communal cave ovens are your only companions at this secluded village hotel. Truly a diamond in the rough of the valley, the Gamirasu is a welcome lesson in the simpler things in life. See p. 330.

8 The Best Stuff to Bring Home

- **Carpets & Kilims:** No matter how lame your bargaining skills, it's still cheaper than Bloomingdale's—and boy, do they look good unrolled under (or on) your coffee table. Turkey's tribal carpets and kilims represent a cultural tradition that goes back for centuries. The symmetrical designs we're most accustomed to are found in rugs from **Kayseri** (see "Kayseri" in chapter 8) and Hereke— the latter traditionally boasts the most exquisite silk-on-silk showpieces.

- **Ottoman Books & Rare Prints:** The Ottomans were masters of calligraphy, embellishing the page with dust from sapphires, lapis lazuli, gold, and other gems. Miniatures generally represent scenes from the life of a sultan and his family, with colorful shades to give the page life. One of the most valuable of originals or reproductions is the *tugra,* the sultan's elaborately ornate and personal seal. The **Sahaflar Çarşısı** in Istanbul is the best place to find these treasures, as are the streets near **Tünel** in Beyoğlu. See "Shopping" in chapter 4.

- **Turkish Delight:** This gummy, marshmallowy treat made of dried nuts, fruits, syrup, and cornstarch is a national favorite. I personally hate the stuff, but to each his own. It's known as *lokum* in Turkish—a word also used to refer to a voluptuous woman. The best *lokum* is available at **Hacı Bekir** in Istanbul (see "Shopping" in chapter 4), but you can find it at the Egyptian Bazaar or in practically every *pastane* or souvenir shop.

- **Pottery & Ceramics:** These arts thrived under the Ottomans, whose skilled craftsmen perfected the coral red and cobalt blue of the İznik tile. No one has ever been able to reproduce the intensity of these colors, until now. The only authentic reproductions come out of the **İznik Foundation**'s workshop and showroom in İznik (see "Bursa" in chapter 5), which has a branch in Istanbul (see "Shopping" in chapter 4). Ordinary but equally stunning porcelain designs on white clay come from Kuthaya (the painting is done at private workshops), and are sold throughout Turkey. Just make sure you don't get skinned.

- **Turkish Textiles:** Check the manufacturer's label on your fine linens, terrycloth supplies, and cotton T-shirts. I bet you didn't realize it, but Turkey exports a huge amount of textiles, supplying the raw materials for well-known retailers such as OP, Calvin Klein, Walt Disney, and XOXO. **Bursa** and **Pamukkale** are both famous for the quality of their

The Best Turkey Websites

The **World Wide Web** makes it simple to do additional research before you leave home. These sites provide a range of information, from destination overviews to up-to-date listings on everything from restaurants, hotels, and local events, as well as valuable links to other sites:

- **www.kultur.gov.tr** is the official site of the Turkish Ministry of Culture, and an excellent source for information and links to the country's major arts events.
- **www.tourismturkey.org** is the website of the Ministry of Tourism.
- **www.turkishdailynews.com** and **www.turkishpress.com**, the sites for Turkey's two English-language dailies, allow you to plug into real-time issues.
- **www.mymerhaba.com** is for ex-patriots by ex-patriots, but we like to eavesdrop on them, too.
- **www.thegate.com** is the local magazine you're most likely to pick up in the airport (it's free). The online version mirrors the print edition with current info on Istanbul, plus a "Turkey from A to Z" link.

goods; many Istanbul residents head to one of these towns to stock up on plush towels and terrycloth robes. (Good-quality pieces can be had for under 7YTL/$5.) Bursa is also famous for its silks. See "Bursa" in chapter 5, and "Pamukkale & Hierapolis" in chapter 6.

- **Copper:** Turks use copper for everything, probably because it looks so good (particularly the white copper). Tea servers with triangular handles pass you by countless times a day; the wide copper platters that double as tables represent typical Turkish style. Those shiny white bowls you see in a *hamam* are copper, too. For the best prices and widest selection, head to **Çadırcılar Caddesi,** near the Grand Bazaar (see "Shopping" in chapter 4), or **Bakırcılar Çarşısı,** near the citadel in Ankara (see "Shopping" in chapter 9).
- **Gold & Silver:** The price by weight is the same, but with labor so cheap you're bound to get a deal. Shopping

thoroughfares glitter with the stuff—some of it attractive, some of it hideous. The **Istanbul Handicrafts Center** (see "Shopping" in chapter 4) has an atelier where an artisan crafts his own work. In **Ürgüp** (see "Ürgüp" in chapter 8), many of the pieces have local precious stones. Museum gift shops are also great sources of unique jewelry.

- **Leather:** The quality and workmanship of Turkish leather is so superior it even fools the Italian experts. Istanbul is the capital of Turkish leather, with shops concentrated in the Grand Bazaar and in select shops of Sultanahmet. See "Shopping" in chapter 4.
- **Foodstuffs:** The exoticism of the East is in full bloom at Istanbul's **Egyptian Spice Bazaar,** where you can find over five different types of saffron at prices that will ensure you take home a sample of each. Specialty stores and *şarcüteris* (small groceries selling deli-style meats and cheeses) in the **Fish**

Market in Beyoğlu marinate a variety of delectable little morsels in sealed jars ready-made to take home. Although this isn't Tuscany, you won't know it by the quality of the olive oil; head over to the local supermarket, **Migros,** and stock up on a few bottles. The smoothest and most delicious is bottled by Komili. See "Shopping" in chapter 4.

- **Meerschaum Pipes:** Carved from the magnesium silicate found primarily in Eskişehir, these ivory-colored pipes are hollowed out and polished to mimic playful or grotesque images. The pipes are sold in most souvenir shops and make fun, frolicsome showpieces.

2

Planning Your Trip to Turkey

You've decided to experience for yourself the beauty, history, and hospitality of this culturally rich and complex country. What do you need to know before you go? All the basics are outlined in this chapter: the when, why, and how of traveling to, in, and around Turkey.

1 The Regions in Brief

Turkey really is where it all began. Although Greece gets the credit for having sown the seeds of Western civilization, for the most part it did it (with a good bit of help, too) on what is now Turkish soil. In Turkey, not only do you bear witness to the ancient nomadic civilizations with minor credits in the Old and New Testaments, but you also have the opportunity to experience the absurdly rich cultural and historical mosaic laid by the ancient, Greek, Persian, Selçuk, Byzantine, and Ottoman empires. Turkey is also the quintessential destination for sybarites: As an eastern Mediterranean country, it gives you the pearly sands of Iztuzu Beach, the turquoise waters of Lycia, the ski slopes of Uludağ, the thermal springs of Bursa and Çeşme, and a profound connection with history.

Turkey forms a natural bridge between two continents, occupying the westernmost point of Asia while attached to Europe by way of Thrace (the northwesterly region separated from the Asian continent by the Bosphorus Straits, the Sea of Marmara, and the Dardanelles). Turkey is surrounded by four seas: the Black Sea to the north separating Turkey from Russia, the Ukraine, and Romania; the Aegean to the west; the Mediterranean to the south; and the Sea of Marmara. European borders are shared with Bulgaria and Greece, with whom it still has maritime disputes; and in many resort towns along the Turkish coastline, you can skip a stone to the nearest Greek island. To the east and south, Turkey shares borders with Georgia, Armenia, Iran, Iraq, and Syria.

Persistent concerns about the political stability in the eastern and southeastern regions of Turkey, combined with a rudimentary tourist infrastructure, have discouraged all but the most intrepid tourists from venturing to these scenic and historically significant regions. For this reason, this guidebook does not include the regions of the southeast and east. (Editorial and space constraints require the exclusion of the Black Sea Coast as well.) Instead, this guidebook focuses on the bang-for-your-buck absolute musts for a first-time visit to Turkey's western half. Inevitably, the first time won't be your last.

ISTANBUL & ENVIRONS
Many people go to Istanbul expecting an Eastern, exotic, even forbidden city. While it's true that Istanbul is undeniably Asian in the way it operates, most visitors are surprised to find a familiar and infinitely inviting European metropolis. Home to three mighty empires and coveted by others for its strategic hold over

access in and out of the Black Sea, Istanbul is truly the original *Jewel in the Crown.* The city itself has one foot in Europe and the other in Asia—the only place in the world where a ferry can transport you to a different continent every 15 minutes. The grandeur of the Blue Mosque and the Ayasofya, the opulence of Dolmabahçe Palace, the echo of intrigue behind the walls of Topkapı, and the soulful wail of the muezzin's call to prayer from one of the hundreds of graceful minarets all have the power to transport you to another era, an exotic culture, and another way of living.

But Istanbul, like any complex and important international city, is more than just the sum of its monuments. The outdoor tables of the Kumkapı district come to life with singing and dancing, fresh sea bass, and fried calamari, while craftsmanship and commerce vie for business almost everywhere you turn. Lush tea gardens, dingy back-alley coffeehouses, streets teeming with men and women in various layers of modern or Islamic dress, the crush of low-income weekenders lazing along the Golden Horn, and the bustle of the jewel-encrusted upper crust in the expensive and exclusive shops of Nişantaşı—all are genuine and undisputable facets of this complex city. Two months, let alone 2 days, would never be enough to discover it all.

Istanbul is surrounded by water and served by multiple ferry and hydrofoil services. It is reasonable to use Istanbul as a base for 1- or 2-day excursions to Bursa, Gallipoli, and Troy (see below), while closer to home are the beach towns of the Black Sea and the popular getaways of the Princes' Islands.

AROUND THE SEA OF MARMARA & THE NORTH AEGEAN COAST

Any army with visions of presiding over Seraglio Point seems to have camped out in this region. Attached to the base of Mount Uludağ sits the city of **Bursa,** whose eminence as the first capital of the Ottoman Empire earned the city a host of **monumental tombs.** Seeing the final resting place of such a density of dead sultans is not the only reason to go there, however. Bursa is important for its Selçuk and early Ottoman architecture, and is famous for its natural **thermal springs;** no visit to the town would be complete without taking a dip in a hot mineral pool or mud bath.

A pilgrimage to the silent cliffs of the **Gallipoli Peninsula** is especially poignant for Australians and New Zealanders, who sent their boys off to one of the bloodiest campaigns of World War I. Here Turkish and Anzac (Australian and New Zealand Army Corps) units dug into trenches, exchanged cigarettes, and fought to the death. The charming fishing and port town of **Çanakkale** is primarily used as a base for excursions to Gallipoli, and fills up beyond capacity with beer-drinking backpackers from down under every year on April 25 for the multiple, daylong memorial services commemorating Anzac Day.

Troy is Troy. Everybody says it's disappointing but nobody ever passes it by. That's the dilemma—where else can you get this close to Homer's *Iliad,* to Agamemnon, to Achilles, and to Warner Brothers' own rendition of the Trojan Horse?

The principal Hellenistic center and later a thriving Roman province, **Pergamum** (also accepted as Pergamon in written documentation), enjoyed an era of prosperity that endured for almost 400 years. Just on the outskirts of modern-day **Bergama,** Pergamum boasts one of Turkey's finest archaeological sites in the **Acropolis,** with its **Temple of Athena,** the remnants of the **great library,** the **Altar of Zeus,** the spectacular hillside **theater,** and the **Agora.** The **Asklepion** was the world's first medical center, using groundbreaking techniques in healing such as bathing, dieting, exercise, and dream therapy. Down the road is the crumbling but impressive **Red Basilica,** originally a temple honoring Serapis (known in Egypt as Osiris), later to become a Byzantine church and one of the seven churches of Asia Minor mentioned by St. John in the Book of Revelation.

THE CENTRAL & SOUTHERN AEGEAN COASTS

İzmir, the third-largest city in Turkey and the most important port on the Aegean, is typically a stopover on the way in or out of the airport, or as a base for visits to Ephesus and Pamukkale. If you've planned a day in town, take a picturesque seaside walk along the **Kordon** in Alsancak or mill around **Konak Square** to see the ornate architecture of the **clock tower**—the symbol of İzmir.

Only an hour away is the **Çeşme Peninsula,** site of expansive sandy beaches, scenic coves, historic ruins, and the many thermal springs from which it takes its name. The charming little seaside town of Çeşme is essentially the last sane stop before getting on the hedonistic highway of the Turquoise and Mediterranean coasts.

Kuşadası is the first in a long line of boisterous beach resort towns and a required stop on the cruise ship circuit because of its convenient proximity to Ephesus. Because there is nothing of significant historical value in Kuşadası, much of the local travel business is geared toward getting you out of town; and, the archaeological ruins of **Didyma, Miletus,** and **Priene** are an easy day trip away. If you do stick around, a few noteworthy beaches in and around town offer an array of watersports options as well as several enchanting tea gardens within the **castle** walls.

No trip to Turkey is complete without a firsthand look at the breathtaking **limestone travertines of Pamukkale,** restored to their original luster through the efforts of UNESCO. Although it is no longer possible to shed your footwear and stroll along the snow-white terraces, the sheer magnitude of this enormous calcium formation is astounding. The Romans seem to have always established cities near curative waters, and the remains of the city of **Hierapolis,** along with its baths, acropolis, and theater, are all located on-site.

The most important Roman center in the Asian Provinces and one of the best preserved antique civilizations in the world, **Ephesus** is the most frequented tourist destination in all of Anatolia. Visitors flock here for the **Library of Celsus,** the **Marble and Arcadian Ways,** and the **Great Theatre,** along with an impossible legacy left to the ancient city through centuries of Greek, Roman, and Byzantine daily life.

The town of **Selçuk** is usually snubbed by visitors to Ephesus, and the few who do stop in usually make a beeline for the archaeological findings in the **Ephesus Museum,** the **House of the Virgin Mary,** and the mysterious remains of the **Temple of Artemesion. St. John's Basilica,** built by Justinian in the 6th century in honor of John, who came to Ephesus in the company of the Virgin Mary, should be included on every faith tour to Turkey; the **Isabey Mosque,** exemplifying Muslim acceptance of the Christian and Jewish prophets, is also worth a visit. A side trip to the former Greek winemaking village of **Şirince** offers another view of typical Turkish life, and the nearby beaches of **Pamucak** are there for anyone going through beach withdrawals.

After 10 years of merciless tourism, the whitewashed hillside and unspoiled bays that make up **Bodrum** are still revered by the Turks as *the* place to vacation. It's the original disembarkation point for the romanticized *Mavi Yolculuk* or **Blue Voyage,** a watery retreat with no distractions but pine cliffs, still expanses of water, and endless days of blissful tranquillity.

Beyond the infamous and cutting-edge nightlife of Bodrum's center, Bodrum offers the ruins of the ancient **Mausoleum,** one of the Seven Wonders of the World (though now a sad shadow of its former self) and the **Underwater Archaeological Museum,** the only museum in the world of its kind and keeper of the oldest known shipwreck, dating to the 14th century B.C. The museum is housed in the **Castle of St. Peter,** a 15th-century fortress built by the Knights of St. John. The castle is perched above the twin bays of Bodrum, presenting breathtaking views from every vantage point. It is also here that the tours for daily and weekly boat excursions pick up momentum.

THE TURQUOISE & MEDITERRANEAN COASTS

The Aegean meets the Mediterranean at the tip of the Datça Peninsula, the rugged and mountainous outpost west of Marmaris. The Blue Voyage continues in the craggy inlets and crystalline waters around **Datça, Hisarönü, Türünç, Içmeler,** and **Marmaris,** in short daylong versions or full weeklong *gulet* cruises (the traditional broad-beamed boat), departing from **Netsel Marina,** arguably the best marina in the eastern Mediterranean.

If you've skipped the Blue Voyage, be sure to at least plan a day trip along the **Dalyan River** to see the enigmatic **Lycian rock-cut tombs,** to walk along the protected beaches of **Iztuzu** where the loggerhead turtles lay their eggs, and to mingle with the goats in the ancient city of **Kaunos.**

Not just a turnaround port for cruises back to Marmaris, **Fethiye** and its surroundings make up one of the most enchanting spots on the Mediterranean. A stroll past the marina promenade reveals the ancient city of **Telmessos,** with its limestone **rock tombs,** its

amphitheater, and the old city, characterized by narrow streets and squares lined with shops, coffeehouses, and restaurants. The surrounding area is also a paradise for nature lovers and athletes alike. An 8km (5-mile) drive through mountainous terrain brings you to **Ölüdeniz Beach,** set below the splendor of **Babadağ,** which provides paragliders with the perfect conditions for a wondrous flight. Down the beach are the pristine waters of the **blue lagoon** from which *Ölüdeniz* (dead sea) takes its name. A detour off the road between Ölüdeniz and Fethiye brings you to the abandoned Greek village of **Kayaköy,** a haunting reminder of the population exchange of 1923. The untouched **Butterfly Valley,** accessible only by boat, is a nature lover's dream, where during the months of April and May the bright red Tiger butterfly breaks free of its cocoon. **Saklıkent Gorge** is another wonder of natural design, with torrents of icy water carving an extraordinary path through the rock. The ancient historic sites along this part of the coast, including **Tlos, Xanthos, Letoon,** and **Patara,** which boasts an unbroken 13km (8-mile) sandy beach, are some of the richest and best preserved in the region.

Often mistaken for a fishing village, **Kalkan** is a glossy seaside village nestled at the foot of the Taurus Mountains. Nearby **Kaputaş Beach** is a breathtaking result of a gorge in the making, and the beaches of **Patara** are only 20 minutes away.

When all of the tourists left for Kalkan, the charming fishing village of **Kaş** was left much the way it was before the tourists chewed it up and spit it out. The tourist infrastructure has remained, and you will find a quiet town dotted with a few **Lycian tombs,** a 6th-century-B.C. **amphitheater,** and lots of pleasant shopping. Kaş is also the departure point for active excursions like kayaking, mountain biking, diving, and canyoning, as well as the must-do day trip to the sunken city of

Kekova, which makes stopovers at the ancient village of **Simena,** now a fishing village of some 300 inhabitants. The nearby town of **Demre** lies shoulder to shoulder with the ancient Lycian city of **Myra,** and it was here that the bishop of Myra left his legacy and came to be known as **St. Nicholas.** The ancient site of **Olympos,** with its "fire-breathing" **Chimaera,** lies halfway between Kaş and Antalya, and few take the time to follow the oleander-laden and winding road down from the highway to this waterfront outpost.

Eastward, beyond the rocky coves of Lycia, are the pearly sand beaches of Turkey's Turquoise Coast. **Antalya** is the Mediterranean coast's main port city, as well as Turkey's principal holiday resort. The citadel walls of the **Kaleiçi** district enclose a typically Ottoman residential neighborhood, providing a majestic backdrop to the marina below. Nearby are the ancient ruins of **Termessos,** easily visited as a day excursion from anywhere along the Gulf of Antalya.

CAPPADOCIA & THE INTERIOR

Arriving into **Cappadocia** is as much like getting a part as an extra in *Lost in Space* as you can get. The phallic **"fairy chimneys"** were formed by thousands of years of rugged winds and rain, and in fact, the same type of erosion continues today. In **Üchisar, Göreme,** and **Ürgüp,** not only can you ogle the **rock caves** from afar, but you also actually sleep in one. In the valleys of Cappadocia, you can visit some of the hundreds of incredible **frescoed chapels** and **cave churches** from the Iconoclastic and Byzantine eras. The troglodyte cities of **Derinkuyu** and **Kaymaklı** present a sobering image of persecution, where Christians, along with their livestock, hid hundreds of feet below ground, and where a detour down a dark tunnel will teach you just how *dark* dark can really be.

Beyond the wonder of Cappadocia is the industrial town of **Kayseri,** holding particular interest for scholars of Selçuk art and architecture.

ANKARA

The capital of Turkey since 1923 and the administrative center of the country, Ankara is nothing if not clean, modern, and efficient. Lacking in the kind of history that attracts visitors to Istanbul, Ankara merits at least a trip to **The Museum of Anatolian Civilizations,** one of the best museums of its kind, displaying a comprehensive collection of treasures from the beginning of the history of man as we know it. The **Atatürk Mausoleum** is Turkey's equivalent of the Kennedy Memorial, honoring a forward-thinking man without whom modern Turkey would now be a Greek colony. Left over from an earlier era are the **Column of Julian,** the **Temple of Augustus,** and the **Roman Baths.** A visit to the old **citadel** or dinner within the castle walls should be part of any itinerary in Ankara.

Ankara is also an excellent base for excursions to **Hattuşaş,** home to the great Hittite kingdom for more than a thousand years, and the nearby sanctuary of **Yazılıkaya.**

2 Visitor Information, Entry Requirements & Money

Everyone's first stop for comprehensive information on Turkey as well as visa requirements should be the Turkish Embassy website specific to your country (**www.turkey.org** or www.tourismturkey. org in the U.S.; see the listings below). The Embassy also administers a "consulate online" at **www.e-konsolosluk.net.**

The Turkish Ministry of Culture (**www. kultur.gov.tr**) has an excellent website that contains cultural information, events, regional resources, and current-events articles. Two other great sites for current information are www.gatetoturkey.com, which also puts out *The Gate* magazine available in Istanbul airports, and www.mymerhaba.com, created by expats for expats living in Turkey.

In the U.S., the **Turkish Government Tourist Office** has a presence in both New York and Washington, D.C.: at 821 United Nations Plaza, New York, NY 10017 (*©* **212/687-2195**) and at 2525 Massachusetts Ave., Suite 306 (*©* **202/ 612-6800**), where you can stock up on maps, brochures, ferry schedules to Greece, and access to practical information via an interactive computer database (open Mon–Fri 9am–5pm).

TURKISH EMBASSIES & CONSULATES

IN THE U.S.   For residents of Washington, D.C., Maryland, Virginia, West Virginia, and the Bahamas: Turkish Embassy, 2525 Massachusetts Ave. NW, Washington, DC 20008 (*©* **202/612- 6700**; fax 202/612-6744; Consular Section: *©* 202/612-6741; fax 202/319- 1639; www.turkey.org).

For residents of Alabama, Arkansas, Louisiana, Missouri, New Mexico, Oklahoma, Tennessee, and Texas: Turkish Consulate, 1990 Post Oak Blvd., Suite 1300, Houston, TX 77056 (*©* **713/622- 5849**; fax 713/623-6639).

For residents of Alaska, Arizona, California, Colorado, Hawaii, Idaho, Montana, Nevada, Oregon, Utah, Washington State, Wyoming, and the Pacific Islands: Turkish Consulate, 6300 Wilshire Blvd., Suite 2010, Los Angeles, CA 90048 (*©* **323/655-8832**; fax 323/655-8681; www.turkiye.net/lacg).

For residents of Illinois, Indiana, Iowa, Kansas, Michigan, Minnesota, Mississippi, Nebraska, North Dakota, Ohio, South Dakota, and Wisconsin: Turkish Consulate, 360 Michigan Ave., Suite 1405, Chicago, IL 60601 (*©* **312/263- 0644**; fax 312/263-1449).

For residents of Connecticut, Delaware, Florida, Georgia, Kentucky, Maine, Massachusetts, North Carolina, New Hampshire, New Jersey, New York, Pennsylvania, Rhode Island, South Carolina, Vermont, and Puerto Rico: Turkish Consulate, 821 United Nations Plaza, New York, NY 10017 (*©* **212/949-0160**; fax 212/983- 1293).

IN CANADA   Turkish Embassy, 197 Wurtemburg St., Ottawa, ON K1N 8L9 (*©* **613/789-4044**; fax 613/789-3442; www.turkishembassy.com). Also, Turkish Embassy Tourism Section, 360 Albert St., Suite 801, Ottawa, ON K1N 8L9 (*©* **613/789-4044**; fax 613/789-3442).

IN AUSTRALIA & NEW ZEALAND Turkish Embassy, Canberra, 60 Mugga Way, Red Hill, ACT 2603 (*©* **02/6295- 0227**; fax 02/6239-6592; www.turkish embassy.org.au).

IN THE U.K.   Turkish Embassy, 43 Belgrave Sq., London SW1X 8PA (*©* **020/7393-0202**; fax 020/7393-0066; www.turkishembassylondon.org). The Turkish Consulate General is at Rutland Lodge, Rutland Gardens, Knightsbridge SW7 1BW (*©* **020/7589-0360**; fax 020/7584-6235). The Turkish Culture and Tourism Office is at 170–173 Piccadilly, London W1J 9EJ (*©* **020/7629- 7771**; fax 020/7491-0773; www.goto turkey.co.uk).

ENTRY REQUIREMENTS

An entry visa is required for citizens of the U.S. (US$26 for a single entry for stays up to 3 months, or $87 for multiple entries valid for up to 5 years for stays as long as 3 months at a time), Canada (US$60 or 45€ on arrival valid for 90 days and multiple entries), the U.K. (£36 for multiple entries up to 3 months, or £70 for up to 2 years), and Australia (US$20 on arrival), while a valid passport is sufficient for citizens of New Zealand.

It's unnecessary to acquire an entry visa prior to departure, as visas can easily be obtained upon arrival. Visa windows are conveniently located adjacent to the immigration line at the port of entry; simply proceed to the visa counter *before* you get in the immigration line, and have your money ready. Visas obtained on entry can be paid in cash in U.S. dollars or in euros; U.K. residents can pay in pounds. Depending on your nationality, visas are valid for 3 months; visas for multiple entry within a 90-day period are also available for a higher fee. Consult your local embassy website for details.

EMBASSIES IN ANKARA **United States,** Atatürk Bulv. 110, Kavaklıdere (© 0312/455-5555); **Canada,** Cinnah Cad. 58, Çankaya (© 0312/409-2700); **United Kingdom,** Şehit Ersan Cad. 46/A, Çankaya (© 0312/455-3344); **Australia,** Uğur Mumcu Caddesi 88/7, Gaziosmanpaşa (© 0312/459-9500); **New Zealand,** Iran Cad. 13/4, Kavaklıdere (© 0312/467-9054).

CONSULATES IN ISTANBUL The **United States,** Istinye Mahallesi, Kaplıacalar Mevkii 2 (© 0212/335-9000); **Canada,** Istiklal Caddesi 373/5 (© 0212/251-9838); **United Kingdom,** 34 Meşrutiyet Cad., Tepebaşı (© 0212/334-6500); **Australia,** AskerocağI Caddesi 15, Şişli (© 0212/243-1333).

CUSTOMS

ON ENTRY The Turkish government has established a list of items that may be brought into the country duty-free. In addition to personal effects, travelers are permitted: one video player; one pocket computer; one portable radio/tape player; one pair of binoculars (no night vision allowed); one camera and five rolls of film; one typewriter; personal sporting equipment; necessary medical items; gifts not exceeding US$300; spare car parts; and various other relatively improbable items for the average tourist. (A complete list is available through the Turkish Embassy website.) Sharp instruments and weapons may not be brought into the country without special permission (diving and camping knives included). Obviously, the importation, buying, selling, and consumption of marijuana and other narcotics is *strictly* forbidden. You shouldn't need to watch *Midnight Express* to figure that one out (see "*Midnight Express:* Fact or Fiction?" in chapter 1, "The Best of Turkey").

The Turkish Embassy's official consular advisory requires that antiques or other valuables such as video cameras, laptops, and even cellphones be registered in your passport upon entry into Turkey to ensure that they leave with you when your journey is over, but judging by the cheerful wave-through by border officials, it seems that this enforcement of this practice is less than completely stringent.

ON EXIT For valuables purchased during your stay, be prepared to provide receipts or other proof of purchase—particularly for that 4"×6" prize silk Hereke—to avoid problems with Turkish Customs when you leave and to aid in declarations in your home country. Forget about having your carpet salesman lie on the official Certificate of Origin, because the U.S. immigration police are prepared to consult their little carpet blue book if you try to slip through without paying up. Be aware that the authentic 16th-century porcelain soup tureen that you bought or those authentic ancient coins attached to your new necklace are either fake or unable to make the journey with you; it is illegal to take antiquities or anything of historical value out of the country. To enforce this, the Turkish government requires that anything dating to the end of the 19th century be authenticated by a museum official before its exportation can even be considered. It is also illegal to carry out tobacco seeds and plants, or hides, skins, or clothing made from wild animals. For items dating prior to the 20th century, permission plus a

What Things Cost in Istanbul	YTL	US$
Daytime taxi from airport to Sultanahmet	16.00	12.00
Nighttime taxi from airport to Sultanahmet	27.00	20.00
Bus from airport to town	7.00	5.00
Double at Çirağan Palace with sea view	700.00–15,200.00	516.00–11,250.00
Double at Sarı Konak	95.00–143.00	70.00–106.00
Dinner for one at the Four Seasons	68.00	50.00
Dinner for one at a *köftecisi* (meatball restaurant)	10.00	7.50
Bosphorus cruise on public ferry	3.50	2.50
Bosphorus cruise with tour group on public or private ferry	54.00	40.00
Ticket on tram	1.20	0.85
Admission to Topkapı Palace and all exhibits	33.00	24.00
Taxi from Sultanahmet to Taksim	8.00	6.00
Bus from Sultanahmet to Taksim	1.20	0.85
Glass of tea at Meşale tea gardens	2.00	1.50
Glass of tea in a carpet shop in the Arasta Bazaar	free	free

handwritten annotation: FREE DAY IN ISTANBUL

One 9"×12" wool-on-wool carpet (See "*Caveat Emptor!* Carpet-Buying Tips" in chapter 4, "Istanbul," for advice on buying carpets.) can cost from 540YTL to 1,620YTL ($400–$1,200) and way up.

handwritten annotation: COST OF CARPET COSTS

certificate of authenticity from a museum official is needed. Minerals require special documentation obtainable from the General Directorate of Mining Exploration and Research in Ankara (© **312/287-3430;** in Turkish only: www.mta.gov.tr).

MONEY

On January 1, 2005, the Turkish Central Bank lopped six zeros off a currency that saw phenomenal inflation in the past decade or so. But those were the old days. With a national economic growth rate rivaling that of China's, Turkey's economy is stronger than it's ever been. Meanwhile, those millionaire banknotes of yesteryear

have been replaced with the New Turkish Lira, or Yeni Türk Lirası (YTL). Banknotes come in denominations of 1, 5, 10, 20, 50, and 100 YTL, while coins, called the New Kurus, or Yeni Kurus (YKr), come in 1, 5, 10, 25, and 50 kurus pieces (1YTL = 100YKr). There is also a 1YTL coin. As of this writing, US$1 = 1.35YTL; conversely, 1YTL = 74¢. Prices quoted in U.S. dollars in this book are based on this rate of exchange.

Until about 2 years ago, local prices were frequently quoted in U.S. dollars. But the weakness in the dollar has prompted a shift to the euro, which has resulted, for Americans at least, in a remarkable loss of value. Hotel rooms previously costing US$80 per night now cost 80€, or US$99, with no commensurate upgrade in services.

Note: Since most hotels in Turkey list prices in euros, this book will do the same; the dollar/euro is exchanged in this book based on a rate of US$1 = 0.82€, or conversely, 1€ = US$1.22. The British pound, where applicable, is converted at a rate of £1 = US$1.77 (or US$1 = 56p).

Although I have tried to be as accurate as possible in quoting prices in this book, please be aware that there are a number of things working against me. Obviously, the fluctuation of exchange rates plays an enormous role. But equally capricious is the erratic nature of on-the-spot price quotes and market demand. Recent shocks in petroleum prices have also resulted in titanic increases in the cost of transportation in Turkey. Finally, don't be surprised if prices change after this book goes to print.

ATMs

For years, the easiest way to get money away from home has been from an ATM. Unfortunately, a recent innovation by U.S.-based banks has been to charge a commission of around 3% on withdrawals *in addition to the 4YTL ($3) transaction fee*. On principle, I'll probably just carry around cash, but for those of you willing to succumb to endless, creative bank fees, all cities and major tourist destinations in Turkey have bank machines on the Cirrus (© 800/424-7787; www.mastercard.com) and PLUS (© 800/843-7587; www.visa.com) networks. Among the most reliable of the local banks are **Akbank, Türk Iş Bankası, Garanti Bankası, Yapı Kredi Bankası,** and **Ziraat Bankası.** Ask whether you need a new personal identification number (PIN), as most ATMs in Turkey accept numbered passwords only, and some limit their input to four digits.

Also, be aware that the ATMs are often fickle or empty, so always carry around alternatives in the form of cash or traveler's checks for emergencies.

TRAVELER'S CHECKS

In Turkey, as in many other European countries, local merchants are loathe to accept traveler's checks, as banks charge large fees to cash them out. Banks tend to charge high commissions or hide the commission in lower rates, as do the exchange offices around town. Hotels are most amenable to exchanging your traveler's checks, but hotel exchange rates are notoriously unfavorable. What's that saying? "You gotta spend money to spend money." Or something like that.

CREDIT CARDS

Credit cards are another safe way to carry money. Be sure to let the bank holding your credit card know that you will be using the card abroad; this will save you the unexpected inconvenience of having your charge denied—a more frequent occurrence now that banks have become more proactive in combating credit card theft. Be aware that bank merchants routinely add 6% to 8% onto the price of an item paid for with plastic, but recently, these institutions have begun itemizing this fee as a separate charge on your statement. Check with your credit card provider regarding its policies on overseas purchases to make sure that if you are renting a car, you won't be surprised to be shelling out a $45 commission to the credit card merchant to use its card. Keep in mind that added fees may be offset by the competitive rates of exchange used by the issuing bank, and often worth the convenience. You can also withdraw cash advances from your credit card at any bank, though check with your credit card provider before you go, because some have cash-advance limits as low as $500 per month. Remember, however, that you'll start paying *hefty* interest on the advance the moment you receive the cash, and you won't receive frequent-flier miles for a cash advance taken on an airline credit card.

3 When to Go

After more than 3 years of crushing silence, Turkey's tourism industry has recovered and is moving at a nice clip, thank you very much. If you're looking for bargains, the window of opportunity has passed. For the inconvenience of traveling on full flights, staying in hotels booked to capacity, and paying top dollar for almost everything (except that the dollar sign has changed to the euro, leaving Americans with no increase in value), visitors will be greeted by a country positively overflowing with optimism for a more prosperous future.

Turkey's Average Daytime Temperature (°F/°C)

	Jan	Feb	Mar	Apr	May	June	July	Aug	Sept	Oct	Nov	Dec
Antalya												
Temp (°F)	50	52	55	61	68	77	82	82	77	68	59	54
Temp (°C)	10	11	13	16	20	25	28	28	25	20	15	12
İzmir												
Temp (°F)	48	50	52	61	68	77	82	81	73	64	59	50
Temp (°C)	9	10	11	16	20	25	28	27	23	18	15	10
Istanbul												
Temp (°F)	41	43	45	54	61	70	73	73	68	61	54	46
Temp (°C)	5	6	7	12	16	21	23	23	20	16	12	8
Ankara												
Temp (°F)	32	34	41	52	61	68	73	73	64	55	46	36
Temp (°C)	0	1	5	11	16	20	23	23	18	13	8	2

Nevertheless, the seasonal ebbs and flows of tourism in Turkey follow some general patterns. Prices peak during high season, which loosely refers to July and August, and the first half of September, when the azure coastlines teem with sun-and-fun seekers. It can get excruciatingly hot during these months, especially in Antalya, conveniently providing the excuse for a beachside or cruising vacation. Sightseeing is good any time of year, but keep in mind that in the summer, the white stone and marble of archaeological sites heat up considerably by 10 or 11am, while most museums close earlier in winter.

During the "shoulder season" months of April, May, mid- to late September, and October, prices are slightly lower, crowds are fewer, and the heat (however dry) does not have you scampering off a restaurant terrace or out of a tea garden for the relief of an air-conditioned dining room. You might even need a sweater for the early morning chill or late evening breezes, especially in Istanbul and on the steppes. June is the perfect summer month to shop for a bargain in Turkey, when many hotels experience an ebb in visitors yet the weather cooperates nicely. Cappadocia is a great destination for rafting in the spring as well as for the autumn colors, while hiking, biking, and camping around the coastal villages are great spring or fall diversions.

In the winter the coastal towns shut down like a submarine before a descent. Cappadocia takes on an otherworldly wonderland aspect covered with a dusting of snow, but icy conditions may ruin

Muslim Holy Month of Ramadan

One of the five obligations required by Islam is the observation of **Ramadan** (Ramazan in Turkish, but the former is more popularly used, even in Turkey), the Muslim holy month of fasting. For one full lunar month (Sept 23–Oct 22 in 2006; Sept 12–Oct 11 in 2007), Muslims are prohibited during daylight hours from eating, drinking, smoking, or succumbing to sexual thoughts or activity. Instead, they adapt to an altered schedule, rising before daylight for breakfast or *sahur,* and then going back to bed. The fast is broken at sundown with an early evening meal, or *iftar.* Because of the extended daylight hours in summertime, this 30-day marathon is particularly arduous, but even in the wintertime, the sleep deprivation, hunger, thirst, and nicotine withdrawal are admirable displays of determination.

Ramadan evenings include festivities and fun. In Istanbul the **Hippodrome** is transformed into a street fair lined with imitation typical wooden houses, where you can buy books, *gözleme* (a crepe filled with cheese, spinach, or both), and *kebaps* (kabobs), or sit at one of the teahouses.

There are some small considerations for potential visitors. In exchange for all of this cultural overload, expect a slight alteration in the way people and places operate: Restaurants that are normally open might be closed; shops that are normally closed might be open; menu items that are normally available might be unavailable due to the general lack in demand. Also bothersome are the drummers who systematically wander the streets waking Muslims (and everybody else) for **sahur, or the predawn meal**. If sleep isn't something you compromise on, then consider yourselves forewarned.

a horseback-riding trek. Also, the hilltops of the Gallipoli Peninsula can get very wet and windy, so a pilgrimage to the battlegrounds may be best planned for the summertime.

TURKEY CALENDAR OF EVENTS

Islam follows the lunar calendar, which is shorter than the Gregorian calendar by 11 days. The result is that Muslim religious holidays fall on different dates each year. The dates for religious holidays listed here are accurate for 2006 and 2007.

January

Camel Wrestling Festival, Selçuk. Did you know that as the temperature drops, a camel's aggression level rises? This event, scheduled erratically in January or February, provides a natural, if not inhumane, tension release as much for the poor beasts as for the testosterone-heavy locals nervously betting against the odds. The camels' mouths are bound to prevent biting, and 14 rope bearers stand by in case the scene starts to get out of hand. The last one to remain standing or in the ring wins. Sometime in January or February; dates vary.

March

Festival of Victory, Çanakkale. This festival celebrates the Turks' successful defense of the Dardanelles against invading British warships during World War I. Performances by the traditional Ottoman army *mehter* band, with its imposing cacophony of cymbals, horns, and percussion, can only suggest the terror instilled by the approaching Ottoman army. March 18.

April

International Film Festival, Istanbul. This festival lasts 2 weeks, from the last Saturday of March to mid-April, offering movie buffs the rare opportunity to view Turkish movies with English subtitles. For schedules and tickets, contact travel agencies in Istanbul (© 0212/334-0700; www.istfest.org). Early April.

National Sovereignty and Children's Day, Istanbul and Ankara. This day celebrates the anniversary of the first Grand National Assembly, which met in Ankara in 1920 and was later decreed by Atatürk as Children's Day. The day is marked by parades and processions by schoolchildren. Banks and public offices are closed. April 23.

Anzac Day, Çanakkale. A trip to the Gallipoli Peninsula has become a sort of pilgrimage for Australians and New Zealanders indoctrinated into the folklore of the failed Allied invasion of the Straits. Memorial ceremonies begin at dawn, and are staggered throughout the morning. Keep in mind that Çanakkale is bursting at the seams with down-unders who, although solemn and respectful by day, let loose in the bars at night. April 24 and 25.

International Music Festival, Ankara. Home of the country's first conservatory, symphonic orchestra, opera, ballet, and theater, Ankara shows the world its importance as a major cultural center each year during this international event. There are orchestral performances, chamber music, and Turkish contemporary artists playing traditional and folk music from all over the world. For schedules and tickets, contact the Sevda-Cenap & Music Foundation, Tunali Hilmi Sok.

114–26 (© 0312/427-0855; www.ankarafestival.com). Late April to mid-May.

May

Festival of Culture and Art, Selçuk and Ephesus. The best part about this local festival is the use of the Great Theatre at Ephesus as a venue for some of the concerts and theatrical presentations. First week of May.

Youth & Sports Day. Atatürk arrived in Samsun on this day in 1919, which signifies the beginning of the Independence War. Students nationwide participate in athletic games, gymnastic events, and parades. May 19.

Fatih Festivities, Istanbul. This festival commemorates the conquest of Byzantium in 1453 by Sultan Fatih Mehmet with local celebrations. May 29.

June

Aspendos Opera and Ballet Festival. Live performances in the spectacular (now open-air) Theatre of Aspendos, the best-preserved theater of antiquity. For information, call © 0312/309-1409 or fax 0312/310-7248. June through July.

Istanbul International Music Festival. This world-class festival features big names in opera and ballet. Ironically, one of the festival's favorite operatic presentations is Mozart's *Abduction from the Seraglio,* often staged in Topkapı Palace. For schedules and tickets, contact the Istanbul Foundation for Culture & the Arts (© 0212/293-3133; www.istfest.org). Mid-June to mid-July.

Kırkpınar Oil Wrestling Tournaments, Edirne and in villages around the country. This revered national sport involves the fittest of Turkish youth and astonishing amounts of olive oil to prevent the opponent from getting a good grip. The event is usually accompanied by a colorful market and fair. Late June/early July.

July

Cabotage Day. This maritime festival commemorates the establishment of Turkey's sea borders. Major ports with marinas usually celebrate with yacht races and swimming competitions. For more information, contact the tourist information office of the town you will be visiting. July 1.

International Jazz Festival, Istanbul. Performances are held at various locations around the city. For schedules, dates, and tickets, contact the Istanbul Foundation for Culture & the Arts (© 0212/293-3133; www.istfest.org).

Folklore and Music Festival, Bursa. One of Turkey's best folk-dancing events of the year, this festival features dance groups from around the country, lasts 1 week, and includes concerts and crafts displays. For more information and specific dates, contact the Bursa Foundation of Culture, Art and Tourism (© 0312/427-1853) or the Bursa Tourism Information Office (© 0224/251-1834).

August

Assumption of the Virgin Mary, Ephesus. A special Mass conducted by the archbishop of İzmir celebrates the Assumption at the house of Mary. August 15.

Zafer Bayramı (Victory Day). This national holiday commemorates the decisive victory over the invading Greek armies during the War of Independence in 1922. Parades run through the main streets, and if you go soon, you may still brush elbows with some surviving vets. August 30.

International Mountain Biking Festival, Cappadocia. The Delta Bike Club celebrates the marriage of bicycles and monastic pathways with their annual mountain festival. The setting offers unbeatable peaks and valleys formed of ancient volcanic tuffa, and various levels of difficulty (© 0312/223-6027; www.deltabisiklet.com). End of August.

October

International Arts Biennale, Istanbul. The Istanbul Foundation for Culture and Arts puts on this major visual arts event organized around a current political or philosophical theme. Artists are selected from over 45 countries, whose innovative exhibitions are displayed in venues like the Yerebatan Cistern, Dolmabahçe Cultural Center, and even commuter ferries. Third week in October.

Cumhuriyet Bayramı (Republic Day). This event celebrates the proclamation of the Republic of Turkey in 1923. Parades, public speeches, and fireworks displays are just a few of the organized events, but the Turks do their own celebrating as well. October 29.

Şeker Bayramı (or Ramadan Baramı) is a 3-day celebration punctuating the end of Ramadan. The evening revelry reaches its peak during the last 3 evenings. Presents and sweets are given to the children (*şeker* means sugar in Turkish), and the Turkish Delight industry makes a killing. October 23 to October 25, 2006; October 12 to October 14, 2007.

November

Yachting Week, Marmaris. A star-studded international boating crowd gathers here to set sail for the Aegean or the Mediterranean. For information, call © 0252/455-3636, or fax 0252/455-3650. First week in November.

Anniversary of Atatürk's Death. Turkey comes to a grinding halt at exactly 9:05am, when the population pays its respects to the father and founder of the Republic. Rather than a moment of silence, the streets and waterways echo with the blare of car horns and foghorns. Atatürk-related activities are planned for the day, such as conferences, speeches, and exhibitions, in addition to a memorial concert at the Atatürk Cultural Center's opera house. November 10.

December

Festival of St. Nicholas, Demre. Santa Claus actually lived on the Mediterranean, as bishop of Myra in the 4th century. A festival and symposium are held at the Byzantine church that honors old St. Nick. Early December.

Mevlana Festival, Konya. Whirling dervishes believe that spiritual union with God is achieved through the *sema,* a trance-inducing dancing rite. The mystical ballet is shared with the public during this December festival, providing a window into one of Turkey's most precious cultural treasures. Book your tickets early, either through a travel agent or by contacting Konya's Tourism Information Office (✆ **332/351-1074**). The week leading up to December 17.

Kurban Bayramı. In the Koranic version of an old favorite, it was Abraham's son Ismael, not Isaac, who was spared the knife. Kurban Bayramı celebrates Abraham's willingness to sacrifice his son, with 4 days of feasting and a death sentence to an alarming number of sheep the likes of which one only sees around Thanksgiving. In fact, the 4-day festival of sacrifice is the culmination of the Hajj (holy pilgrimage), and much of the meat is given to the poor. December 31, 2006, to January 3, 2007; December 20 to December 23, 2007.

4 Insurance

Check your existing insurance policies and credit card coverage before you buy travel insurance. You may already be covered for lost luggage, canceled tickets or medical expenses. The cost of travel insurance varies widely; you can get estimates from various providers through **InsureMyTrip.com**.

TRIP-CANCELLATION INSURANCE

Trip-cancellation insurance helps you get your money back if you have to back out of a trip, if you have to go home early, or if your travel supplier goes bankrupt. Allowed reasons for cancellation can range from sickness to natural disasters to the State Department declaring your destination unsafe for travel. (Insurers usually won't cover vague fears, though, as many travelers discovered who tried to cancel their trips in Oct 2001 because they were wary of flying.) In this unstable world, trip-cancellation insurance is a good buy if you're getting tickets well in advance—who knows what the state of the world, or of your airline, will be in 9 months? Insurance policy details vary, so read the fine print—and especially make sure that your airline or cruise line is on the list of carriers covered in case of bankruptcy. For more information, contact one of the following recommended insurers: **Access America** (✆ 866/807-3982; www.accessamerica.com); **Travel Guard International** (✆ 800/826-4919; www.travelguard.com); **Travel Insured International** (✆ 800/243-3174; www.travelinsured.com); and **Travelex Insurance Services** (✆ 888/457-4602; www.travelexinsurance.com).

LOST-LUGGAGE INSURANCE On

domestic flights, checked baggage is covered up to $2,500 per ticketed passenger. On international flights (including U.S. portions of international trips), baggage is limited to approximately $9.07 per pound, up to approximately $635 per checked bag. If you plan to check items more valuable than the standard liability, see if your valuables are covered by your homeowner's policy, get baggage insurance as part of your comprehensive travel-insurance package, or buy Travel Guard's "BagTrak" product. Don't buy insurance at the airport, as it's usually overpriced. Be sure to take any valuables or irreplaceable items with you in your carry-on luggage, as many valuables (including books, money, and electronics) aren't covered by airline policies.

If your luggage is lost, immediately file a lost-luggage claim at the airport, detailing the luggage contents. For most airlines, you must report delayed, damaged, or lost baggage within 4 hours of arrival. The airlines are required to deliver luggage, once found, directly to your house or destination free of charge.

CAR-RENTAL INSURANCE   If you hold a private auto insurance policy, you probably are covered in the United States, but not abroad, for loss or damage to the car, and liability in case a passenger is injured. The credit card you used to rent the car also may provide some coverage.

Car-rental insurance probably does not cover liability if you caused the accident. Check your own auto insurance policy, the rental company policy, and your credit card coverage for the extent of coverage: Is your destination covered? Are other drivers covered? How much liability is covered if a passenger is injured? (If you rely on your credit card for coverage, you may want to bring a second credit card with you, as damages may be charged to your card and you may find yourself stranded with no money.)

Car-rental insurance costs about $20 a day.

5 Health & Safety

STAYING HEALTHY

There are no severe health risks in travel to Turkey, nor are vaccinations required. It's still a good idea to use common sense in traveling to less developed areas. **Food poisoning and diarrhea** are probably the most prevalent illnesses associated with travel to Turkey. Although water from the tap is chlorinated and generally safe to drink, even the locals drink bottled water. Resist the temptation to drink fresh running spring water, even if you see people lined up filling empty bottles. (*Please* take my word on this.) Avoid nonpasteurized dairy products and shellfish during the hot summer months, and maintain a healthy suspicion of street vendors. In the event that you become ill, drink plenty of (bottled) water and remember that diarrhea usually dissipates on its own. Pepto Bismol (bismuth subsalicylate) can often prevent symptoms, but if the problem becomes truly inconvenient, pharmacists are generally sympathetic and bilingual,

and will be able to provide an effective remedy. (**Ercefuryl** works wonders.)

Although the persistence and tenaciousness of Turkish **mosquitoes** might cause you to suffer, it is unlikely that malaria will. The high-risk areas are southeastern Anatolia and the Cukurova/ Amikova areas, regions that because of political unrest are not covered in this book. Keep in mind that you're more likely to catch deadly mosquito-borne diseases in your own backyard than abroad. If you are experiencing symptoms, seek prompt medical attention while traveling as well as for up to 3 years after your return. Don't forget to pack a proven insect repellent (especially for those nights camped out on the deck of the *gulet*).

Rabies is unfortunately alive and well in parts of Turkey, but it's highly unlikely that this will affect visits to the popular tourist destinations. The population of stray dogs and cats shouldn't be too much of a concern because apart from their being grungy, the worst thing about them is that they're cute and irresistible. Carry a package of wet wipes for quick cleanups or, more-sound advice, stay away from the animals altogether. For outdoor adventure travelers going to rural destinations, consult your doctor for pre-exposure immunization.

WHAT TO DO IF YOU GET SICK AWAY FROM HOME

Any local consulate can provide a list of area doctors who speak English. If you do get sick, you may want to ask the concierge at your hotel to recommend a local doctor; even his or her own. This will probably yield a better recommendation than any information number would. Local doctors advertise their services through discreet signs near their offices, and most speak English. If you can't find a doctor who can help you right away, try the emergency room of one of the private hospitals listed under "Fast Facts: Turkey," later in this chapter.

THE SAFE TRAVELER

Most first-time travelers to Turkey are somewhat apprehensive about safety issues. The Western media hasn't exactly painted a rosy picture of Turkey—or of Muslims, for that matter. The first thing to realize is that Turkey is the model for democratic secularism in the Middle East, and although predominantly Muslim, is merely fanatic about maintaining a separation of church and state. So business goes on as usual, with Turks drinking alcohol (or not), going to mosque (or not), and living life pretty much the same as you and me. Furthermore, as Islam preaches tolerance and acceptance, you

may be surprised to feel more comfortable being Jewish in Istanbul than in, say, Columbus, Ohio.

Terrorism is on everybody's mind when considering a trip abroad, but in Turkey, where Turks have 20 years of experience fighting terrorists, flare-ups are now the exception rather than the rule. The only time you will get a glimpse of the existence of anything out of the ordinary is in the metal detectors at the entries of some five-star hotels or when traveling by domestic airline. Before boarding, each passenger must single out and identify his or her baggage out of the lineup of luggage at the foot of the aircraft. (With any luck, no orphaned bags will be left over.)

Theft is a concern when staying home as much as when traveling. Just display as much caution in Istanbul's covered bazaar as you would on the Times Square subway platform in Manhattan. And don't be deceived by the relative, idyllic quiet of Istanbul's Sultanahmet neighborhood, as professional thievery is reaching new heights. Of course, it only takes one jerk to ruin your vacation. Typically, you're a target if you look like a tourist and carelessly fumble through your wallet in crowded areas like the train station or the ferry depot. Have your money ready beforehand and keep your handbag zipped up tight and your eyes open. Don't walk anywhere alone at night (this warning includes men). Beware of anyone who brushes up against you, even seemingly pious women in chadors (full-length veils) and adorable little kids straight out of *Oliver Twist.* Don't leave any valuables in your hotel room unless it's in the room safe. Hang onto your passport.

6 Specialized Travel Resources

TRAVELERS WITH DISABILITIES

A disability shouldn't stop anyone from traveling—but that doesn't mean you should expect wheelchair access to 2,000-

year-old rock pits. Although ramps have begun to appear in select Turkish hotels and museums, don't expect the going to be easy. Turkish hospitality being what it is, it's the odd tour guide or group leader who won't bend over backward to accommodate your individual needs.

Many travel agencies offer customized tours and itineraries for travelers with disabilities. **Flying Wheels Travel** (© 507/451-5005; www.flyingwheelstravel.com) offers escorted tours and cruises that emphasize sports and private tours in minivans with lifts. **Accessible Journeys** (© 800/846-4537 or 610/521-0339; www.disabilitytravel.com) caters specifically to slow walkers and wheelchair travelers and their families and friends.

Organizations that offer assistance to travelers with disabilities include **Moss-Rehab** (www.mossresourcenet.org), which provides a library of accessible-travel resources online; the **Society for Accessible Travel and Hospitality** (© 212/447-7284; www.sath.org; annual membership fees: $45 adults, $30 seniors and students), which offers a wealth of travel resources for all types of disabilities and informed recommendations on destinations, access guides, travel agents, tour operators, vehicle rentals, and companion services; and the **American Foundation for the Blind** (© 800/232-5463; www. afb.org), which provides information on traveling with Seeing Eye dogs.

For more information specifically targeted to travelers with disabilities, the community website **iCan** (www.icanonline.net/channels/travel/index.cfm) has destination guides and several regular columns on accessible travel. Also check out the quarterly magazine *Emerging Horizons* ($14.95 per year, $19.95 outside the U.S.; www.emerginghorizons.com); **Twin Peaks Press** (© 360/694-2462), offering travel-related books for travelers with special needs; and *Open World Magazine,* published by the Society for Accessible Travel and Hospitality (see above; subscription: $18 per year, $35 outside the U.S.).

GAY & LESBIAN TRAVELERS

The fact that homosexuality is legal in Turkey is an interesting result of centuries of segregation of the sexes, veneration of female virtue, and lazy afternoons spent in the *hamam* (Turkish bath). Nevertheless, we're talking about a fairly conservative culture, so discretion is advisable, even if Turkish men are into more public displays of affection with each other than with their wives.

The International Gay & Lesbian Travel Association (IGLTA) (© 800/448-8550 or 954/776-2626; www.iglta.org) is the trade association for the gay and lesbian travel industry, and offers an online directory of gay- and lesbian-friendly travel businesses; go to their website and click on "Members."

Many agencies offer tours and travel itineraries specifically for gay and lesbian travelers. **Above and Beyond Tours** (© 800/397-2681; www.abovebeyondtours.com) is the exclusive gay and lesbian tour operator for United Airlines. **Now, Voyager** (© 800/255-6951; www.nowvoyager.com) is a well-known San Francisco–based gay-owned and -operated travel service. **Olivia Cruises & Resorts** (© 800/631-6277 or 510/655-0364; www.olivia.com) charters entire resorts and ships for exclusive lesbian vacations and offers smaller group experiences for both gay and lesbian travelers.

Gay.com Travel (© 800/929-2268 or 415/644-8044; www.gay.com/travel or www.outandabout.com), is an excellent online successor to the popular *Out & About* print magazine. It provides regularly updated information about gay-owned, gay-oriented, and gay-friendly lodging, dining, sightseeing, nightlife, and shopping establishments in every important destination worldwide. It also offers trip-planning information for gay and lesbian travelers for more than 50 destinations, along various themes, ranging from Sex & Travel to Vacations for Couples.

The following travel guides are available at many bookstores, or you can order them from any online bookseller: *Frommer's Gay & Lesbian Europe* (www.frommers. com), an excellent travel resource to the top European cities and resorts; *Spartacus International Gay Guide* (Bruno Gmünder Verlag; www.spartacusworld. com/gayguide) and *Odysseus: The International Gay Travel Planner* (Odysseus Enterprises Ltd.), both good, annual, English-language guidebooks focused on gay men; and the *Damron* guides (www. damron.com), with separate, annual books for gay men and lesbians.

SENIOR TRAVEL

Always mention the fact that you're a senior when you first make your travel reservations. For example, many hotels offer seniors' discounts. Don't be shy about asking for discounts, but always carry some kind of identification, such as a driver's license, that shows your date of birth.

Members of **AARP** (formerly known as the American Association of Retired Persons), 601 E St. NW, Washington, DC 20049 (© **888/687-2277**; www. aarp.org), get discounts on hotels, airfares, and car rentals. AARP offers members a wide range of benefits, including *AARP: The Magazine* and a monthly newsletter. Anyone 50 or older can join.

Many reliable agencies and organizations target the 50-plus market. **Elderhostel** (© **877/426-8056**; www.elder hostel.org) arranges study programs for those age 55 and over (and a spouse or companion of any age) in the U.S. and in more than 80 countries around the world. Most courses last 5 to 7 days in the U.S. (2–4 weeks abroad), and many include airfare, accommodations in university dormitories or modest inns, meals, and tuition. **ElderTreks** (© **800/741-7956**; www.eldertreks.com) offers small-group tours to off-the-beaten-path or adventure-travel locations, restricted to travelers 50 and older. **INTRAV**

(© **800/456-8100**; www.intrav.com) is a high-end tour operator that caters to the mature, discerning traveler (not specifically seniors), with trips around the world that include guided safaris, polar expeditions, private-jet adventures, and small-boat cruises down jungle rivers.

Recommended publications offering travel resources and discounts for seniors include the quarterly magazine *Travel 50 & Beyond* (www.travel50andbeyond. com); *Travel Unlimited: Uncommon Adventures for the Mature Traveler* (Avalon); *101 Tips for Mature Travelers,* available from Grand Circle Travel (© **800/221-2610** or 617/350-7500; www.gct.com); *The 50+ Traveler's Guidebook* (St. Martin's Press); and *Unbelievably Good Deals and Great Adventures That You Absolutely Can't Get Unless You're Over 50* (McGraw-Hill).

STUDENT TRAVEL

If you're planning to travel outside the U.S., you'd be wise to arm yourself with an **International Student Identity Card (ISIC),** which offers substantial savings on rail passes, plane tickets, and entrance fees. It also provides you with basic health and life insurance and a 24-hour help line. It's also the only officially acceptable form of student identification, good for cut rates on Turkish State Railways, Turkish Maritime Lines, museums and archaeological sights, as well as rail passes, plane tickets, and other discounts. The card is available for $22 from **STA Travel** (© **800/781-4040,** and if you're not in North America there's probably a local number in your country; www.sta.com or www.statravel.com), the biggest student travel agency in the world. If you're no longer a student but are still under 26, you can get an **International Youth Travel Card (IYTC)** for the same price from the same people, which entitles you to some discounts (but not on museum admissions). (*Note:* In 2002 STA Travel

Tips Important Tips for Women Travelers

Rule number one: Scrupulously avoid contact with anyone using a Westernized name. It's hard to believe, but in the major tourist areas of Turkey, particularly in the streets of Sultanahmet, an entire industry thrives on the acquisition and manipulation of emotions. This time, I'm not referring to carpet sales, but to something much more inestimable. Foreign women, receptive, even eager for new and exotic experiences, are just ripe for the picking, and although less than attractive ones can be particularly vulnerable, any single girl with cash in the bank and foreign nationality is a target.

Sultanahmet is filled with professional "gigolos" practiced in the art of courtship and persuasion. One will generously show a girl around town, take her to perfect hidden corners of the city, hold doors open for her, pay every bill, and rapidly sweep her off her feet. He will operate under the guise of success; perhaps he will drive you around in a Mercedes. The better ones come armed with scripts; the statements "You foreigners don't know how to trust anyone!" and "You foreigners think that we (Turks) are all thieves and barbarians" effectively disarm even the most remotely liberal.

Inevitably the topic of how bad things are economically will be carefully broached: How he can't pay his bills, how worried he is over his debts, and how any moment the authorities will repossess his furniture. Some invent elaborate stories of woe and before you know it, the woman is offering, no—insisting, that he accept her help. And, because foreign passports command top dollar on the black market, it's not unheard of for passports to mysteriously go missing.

Some seducers even take this kind of behavior to its limits by pursuing the game as far as the wedding contract. But the most deplorable of the lot have been known to forge the marriage certificate with the assistance of those in the neighborhood even less scrupulous than themselves.

bought competitors **Council Travel** and **USIT Campus** after they went bankrupt. It's still operating some offices under the Council name, but it's owned by STA.)

Travel CUTS (© **800/667-2887** or 416/614-2887;   www.travelcuts.com)

offers similar services for both Canadians and U.S. residents. Irish students should turn to **USIT** (© **01/602-1600;** www. usitnow.ie).

7 Getting There

Partnerships among international airlines have blurred the lines of air travel, and changing market demands force airlines to continually adapt or change their services. Check with your travel agent or with the airlines directly for specific services.

BY PLANE
FROM THE UNITED STATES & CANADA Turkish Airlines (© **800/ 874-8875;** www.turkishairlines.com) in partnership with **American Airlines** (© **800-433-7300;** www.aa.com) and **Delta Airlines** (© **800/241-4141;**

But this kind of behavior doesn't represent all of Turkey, and overall, women traveling alone in Turkey are treated with an almost exaggerated courtesy. In some cases, a woman will be in a better position to experience the openness of the Turkish people than if traveling en masse. With all of this warmth and hospitality, it's difficult to know how to temper one's instincts toward friendliness without affirming the general opinion among the more conservative class of Turks that all Western women are prostitutes. Even an innocent greeting or seemingly harmless camaraderie can be misinterpreted, so it's important to find a balance between polite formality and the openness that North American, European, and Australian women find so normal.

Practically speaking, no matter how modern the country may seem on the surface, don't be surprised if you're the only female in a restaurant. Eateries often have an *aile salonu* (family salon), an unintimidating dining area provided for men, women, couples, and anyone else not wishing to dine among groups of smoking, drinking, mustached Turks.

However Westernized Istanbul has become, wearing cutoff cheek-revealing shorts and a spandex midriff top is in bad taste. In the resort areas of the Aegean and Mediterranean seas, the economy of tourism seems to have won out over the local mores, but bathing topless is still insensitive. In Anatolia the sight of bare legs can cause a stir, so be sure to cover up on those long drives into the interior. In Istanbul, especially in the more modern neighborhoods, dress is modern, even racy, but when visiting the more traditional neighborhoods like Sultanahmet or Fatih, modesty will at least broadcast a different message to those likely to leer. Chances are you'll be visiting at least one mosque, and to enter, your shoulders, legs, and head must be covered. It's a nice idea to carry around a scarf, but all mosques provide some type of head covering.

www.delta.com) offer the only direct nonstop service to Istanbul from the U.S. Delta provides direct service from Atlanta and New York. Turkish Airlines flies direct to Istanbul from New York and Chicago, with access to connecting flights from other U.S. cities on American Airlines. These airlines are just the tip of the iceberg; most major international airlines flying to Istanbul offer flights from U.S. cities much too numerous to inventory, either as part of their own network or in partnership with an American airline. Choosing one involves a change of planes in the airline's home country, but this slight inconvenience is often accompanied by cheaper, more comparable fares.

Air France (© 800/237-2747; www.airfrance.com), **Alitalia** (© 800/223-5730; www.alitalia.com), **Austrian Airlines** (© 800/843-0002; www.austrianair.com), **British Airways** (© 800/247-9297; www.british-airways.com), **Iberia** (© 800/574-8742; www.iberia.com), **Northwest** (© 800/255-2525; www.nwa.com), and **Lufthansa** (© 800/645-3880; www.lufthansa.com) all provide service to Istanbul. In addition, Lufthansa flies to Ankara and Antalya, and Austrian Airlines flies to Ankara.

More often than not, Turkish Airlines will provide the connecting flights to other Turkish destinations.

There is no direct service to Turkey from Canada. **Air France, Alitalia, British Airways, Delta, KLM/Northwest,** and **Lufthansa** all provide connecting service out of Toronto. From Montreal, flights are available on **Air France, Alitalia, British Airways, Delta, Iberia, Northwest,** and **Lufthansa** (© 800/563-5954). Vancouver is serviced by **British Airways, KLM/Northwest** (via Seattle), and **Lufthansa.**

FROM THE UNITED KINGDOM
The only nonstop service to Istanbul out of London is provided by **British Airways** (© 0845/77-333-77) and **Turkish Airlines** (© 20/7766-9300), which also flies nonstop from Manchester (© 161/489-5287). **Air France** (© 0845/082-0162), **Alitalia** (© 0870/544-8259), **Austrian Airlines** (© 0845/601-0948), **KLM/Northwest** (© 08705/074-074), **Lufthansa** (© 0845/7737-747), and **Olympic** (© 8706/060-460) offer connecting service through their home ports, providing service from many other major cities in the U.K. as well. There are also charter airline options. **Onur Air,** Şenlikkoy Mahallesi Çatal Sok. 3 Florya (© **0212/663-9176;** www.onurair.com.tr), offers service from several U.K. cities into Dalaman, Bodrum, İzmir, and Antalya via Istanbul; and from various cities throughout Europe.

FROM AUSTRALIA & NEW ZEALAND There are few choices for connecting flights to Turkey. In partnership with Turkish Airlines, **Qantas** (© 13-13-13 in Australia; 64-9/357-8900 in Auckland) will get you from Sydney, Auckland, and Brisbane, connecting you to a Turkish Airlines flight into Istanbul. **Olympic Airways** (© 612/9251-2044 in Australia) has overnight flights from Sydney and Melbourne via Athens. Other flights from Sydney are offered on

British Airways (© 1300/767-177 in Australia, or 0800/274-847 in Auckland), **Singapore Airlines** (© 612/9350-0100), **KLM/Northwest** (© 008/221-714), and **Lufthansa** (© 1300/655-727). From New Zealand, Singapore Airlines flies out of Auckland and New Plymouth; from Australia, British Airways flies out of Brisbane and Melbourne; and Lufthansa services Brisbane.

BY TRAIN

Direct trains depart daily from Bucharest and Budapest and take about 27 and 40 hours, respectively—and that's without any border delays. It is your responsibility to obtain visas where required (either transit or tourist, depending on your travel plans) for every border that you will cross. If you're coming from Greece, the procedure is a bit more convoluted. Trains leave regularly for Alexandroupolis, but there is no direct train connection to Turkey once you get there. The best option would be to get to the nearest train station in Turkey, but it's a lot easier to catch the bus to Istanbul from the Alexandroupolis train station. Depending on how long you get hung up at the border, it can take anywhere from 6 to 8 hours to get to Istanbul.

Of course, the **Orient Express** is still an option (© **866/674-3689** in the U.S., 0845/077-2222 in the U.K., 1-800/000-395 in Australia, and 09/379-3708 in New Zealand). Departing from Paris once a year in late summer and passing through Zurich, Innsbruck, Vienna, Budapest, and Bucharest, the journey takes 4 days and costs a meager $6,500.

BY CAR

Renting a car in Turkey is so economical that driving to Turkey makes little sense. But some people just insist on the comfort of their own vehicle, so be prepared for the red tape of sorting out multiple transit visas and 4 days of hard driving. There are two traditional routes to take, the "northern" one through Belgium, Germany, Austria, Hungary, Romania, and Bulgaria, and the "southern" one through Belgium, Germany, Austria, and Italy with a car ferry connection to Turkey. Drivers planning to stay longer than 3 months must have an **International Driving Permit (IDP),** which also comes in handy in out-of-the-way places where the local police can't decipher your national version. You'll also be required to provide proof of third-party insurance at the Turkish border.

BY FERRY

Long-distance and short-hop passenger ferries service the central and eastern Mediterranean, connecting various ports in Turkey with Italy and Greece. For example, ferryboat service connects **Bodrum** with Cos and Rhodes; **Marmaris** with Rhodes; **Kuşadası** with Samos, and **Çeşme** with Chios (for details, see individual sections). Ferry service also connects Ayvalik (near Çanakkale) and Lesbos. For those of you toying with the idea of day-tripping it to

Greece (after all, it's sooooo close), keep in mind that after the ride over and the long lines through customs, you'll have precious little chance to venture beyond the port.

FROM ITALY   Marmara Lines (**www. marmaralines.com**) currently makes the crossing between Brindisi and Çeşme two times a week from June to September. The Brindisi–Çeşme crossing takes about 30 hours and passage costs from about 80€ ($100) for a Pullman seat inside to 265€ ($325) for a double outside berth on an upper deck with toilet and shower, depending on the season and ferry line you travel. Port taxes are an additional 25€ ($30) and apply to both passengers and vehicles.

Marmara Lines also runs ferry service between Ancona and Çeşme from March through October; prices range from 145€ ($175) for a seat (5€/$6 more will get you a bunk bed in a four-person, inside, lower berth) to 350€ ($430) for luxury accommodations. Prices are about 80€ ($100) per person higher in August.

8 Package Tours & Escorted Tours

With so many options spread out over such large distances, the options for travel to Turkey seem to be limited only by your individual travel style.

Independent travelers tend to prefer package tours that, while not necessarily spontaneous, provide competitive prices on airfare and hotel accommodations. Some people love escorted tours; they let you relax and take in the sights while a bus driver fights traffic for you; they spell out your costs upfront; and they take you to the maximum number of sights in the minimum amount of time with the least amount of hassle. With few exceptions, most operators offering escorted tours will offer air/hotel packages, arrange land-only trips, customize a tour, or add

on short stays or *gulet* excursions (if not already included) on request. These days, the travel industry competition is stiff, causing the lines of delineation between the two to become slightly blurred. With increased personal service in mind, many escorted tours are offering customized options, while many traditional packagers are offering escorted land packages.

ESCORTED TOURS

If you do choose an escorted tour, ask a few simple questions before you buy: What is the cancellation policy? How busy is the schedule? What is the size of the group? What is included in the price? Think strongly about purchasing travel insurance from an independent agency,

All About the Blue Voyage

The *Mavi Yolculuk* or "Blue Voyage" emerged in the late 1920s, when Cevat Şakir Kabaağaçlı, a dissident political writer who had been exiled to Bodrum, began offering visiting friends the idyllic experience of cruising around the Gulf of Gökova. Today cruising along the Turkish Mediterranean is one of the highlights of any trip to Turkey. And in some cases, it's the only way to visit the small fishing villages and islands of the southwestern coast. But to do it right, you should plan in advance and know your options.

The traditional Turkish sea excursion is either by *gulet* or yacht cruiser, the majority of which depart from Marmaris or Bodrum. Hiring a **private yacht** (or bareboat charter) is a popular choice for those with sailing proficiency and a taste for independence and adventure. Captained yachts are also available as an option. The *gulet*, a wooden broad-beam boat that evolved from a fishing vessel, typically accommodates 8 to 12 people and comes equipped with many modern conveniences.

In addition to chartering the entire *gulet*, it is also possible to charter a cabin on an individual basis. This last option, however, is riddled with pitfalls, not the least of which can be safety concerns. Generally, the *gulets* used for individual cabin charters didn't make the first cut for that season, thanks to torn cushions, faded decks, clogged toilets, smelly cabins, and a boat that should have been sent out to pasture long ago. Many tour operators and yacht agents have responded by acquiring and chartering out their own *gulets*, so check at the time of booking to make sure you'll be on one of these more recent acquisitions. If your booking agent can't or won't give you specific information about the boat you'll be on, be prepared for the worst, and negotiate a discount in advance if the *gulet* you were promised gets substituted at the last minute.

especially if the tour operator asks you to pay upfront. *One final caveat:* Because escorted-tour prices are based on double occupancy, the single traveler is usually penalized.

Many of the companies offering escorted tours to Turkey offer ambitious itineraries; it's important to select a tour with a pace that's right for you.

CULTURAL TOURS

Turkey is, essentially, one big open-air museum, and it would be difficult not to have a learning experience while traveling in such a historically rich country. For their Turkey trips, **Intrepid Travel** (in the U.S. ℰ **877/847-8192;** www.intrepid travel.com) manages to effectively combine authentic experiences with an optimal cultural overview.

If you're looking for luxury without compromising the authenticity of your Turkish experience, **INCA** (ℰ **510/420-1550;** www.incafloats.com) provides nature and cultural adventures.

Using a local travel agent can make anybody a bit skittish, but expert in the region is the English-proficient **Credo Tours** (ℰ **90-212/254-8175** in Istanbul; fax 90-212/237-9670; www.credo.com. tr), inspiring nothing but confidence

Weeklong *gulet* cruises commonly depart from Marmaris on Sunday mornings (boarding Sat nights) and last 1 week, although it's also possible to sail from Fethiye, Bodrum, or anywhere else your heart desires. (There may be a transport fee.) A typical weeklong Blue Voyage will run you anywhere from 340YTL to 1,080YTL ($250–$800) per person, with as much as 70% added on for a single supplement. Meals are usually included, but all drinks, even water, are extra (but available and reasonably priced onboard). Boats may come equipped with air-conditioning, but even on a private and comparatively luxurious boat, the generator, and thus the air-conditioning, gets shut down at night.

Although most Turkish boat operators offer their services directly to the public, every travel agent and his brother has a friend in the boat business. The problem is wading through all of the brokerage options, especially when the ship's captain lists his boat with multiple agencies. The best way to ensure quality in booking your *gulet* or yacht cruise is to use a reputable local tour broker. Be an informed buyer and get a detailed description of the boat, keeping in mind that vessels need a complete renovation at least every 5 years. Also, decide whether a hose attachment to the sink faucet is sufficient, or whether you require a separate cabin shower. Finally, flush toilets (as opposed to the hand-pump type) are considered a luxury.

But look, it's not all bad news. There's really no way to ruin a week of tooling around turquoise waters with a culturally and linguistically diverse passenger list. Hold your nose and just dive in.

with their quick, efficient, and competitively priced service. Faxes and e-mails are answered within 24 hours, and there is no request that is too unusual.

If you're planning to drag along unwilling offspring, try booking through **Thomson Family Adventures** (© 800/262-6255 or 617/864-4803; fax 617/497-3911; www.familyadventures.com) for kid-friendly trips without adult compromise. Thomson takes an added interest in your children, establishing departure dates according to the school calendar, and they provide fun educational activities prior to departure.

Depending on your commitment to the educational aspect of your vacation, you may want to connect with one of the outfitters geared specifically toward this type of travel. **IST Cultural Tours** (© 800/833-2111), organizes painstakingly researched tours for the traveler who's looking for a more in-depth cultural experience, and a partnership with the History Channel ensures a high level of quality. **Far Horizons** (© 800/552-4575; www.farhorizon.com) offers eight archaeological tours for small groups, including a 10-day voyage by sea. Tours hook up with local professionals like archaeologists, scientists, and experts as guides. **The Smithsonian** (© 202/357-4700; www.si.edu) has land and sea "study tour" voyages available to members.

BOAT TRIPS (AKA THE BLUE VOYAGE)   Club Voyages, 43 Hooper Ave., Atlantic Highlands, NJ 07716 (© **888/842-2122** or 732/291-8228; fax 732/291-4277), bent over backward to accommodate my absurd itinerary, and I've later learned that this individualized attention is due not only to a love of and commitment to the trade and to Turkey, but because owners/operators Pat and Kemal are sincerely caring people. They specialize in high-end quality private charters with or without crew, with the possibility of land tour add-ons or land-only packages.

Blue Voyage Tours & Travel (© **800/818-8753** or 414/392-0146; www.bluevoyage.com) has all the *gulet* charter options, as well as a three-cabin boat they've added to their fleet. Depending on availability, the boats can be chartered for as few as 2 days and for as little as 470€ ($575) per day if you're willing to travel in May or October.

For reliable contacts within Turkey, contact **Credo Tours** (in Istanbul © **90-212/254-8175;** fax 90-212/237-9670; www.credo.com.tr), **Aegean Yachting** (© **90-252/316-1517;** fax 90-252/316-5749), or **Gino Group** (© **90-252/412-0676;** fax 90-252/412-2066).

You can go the extra nautical mile on a Blue Voyage by signing up with a reputable sailing school. **Gökova Yachting,** based in Netsel Marina in Marmaris (©/fax **0252/413-1089;** http://sailturkey.org) is the only licensed international sailing school where students can advance through the five levels of sailing proficiency from beginner to racer. Yacht master Cumhur (Jim) Gökova presides over one of the newest fleets in the Mediterranean, and also handles bookings directly. Tuition is 600€ ($730) per

person per week, and covers one proficiency level of instruction.

CULINARY TOURS   Only a true foodie can appreciate the rewards of planning a vacation with a special emphasis on the eating habits of a country. In Turkey, where much of the language and expressions refer back to the kitchen, there's no better way to get to the heart of this culture. Kathleen O'Neill's **Culinary Expeditions in Turkey** (© **415/437-5700** in the U.S.; fax 925/210-1337; www.turkishfoodandtravel.com), provides a gateway to the tradition, hospitality, and gastronomy of Turkey through "eating expeditions" that focus on the food of Turkey's eastern Mediterranean, either in the region of Gaziantep or cruising along the Turquoise coast.

ACTIVE VACATIONS   Gorp Travel (© **877/440-4677;** www.gorp.com) offers the most variety of choices, with excursions organized around trekking, watersports, and cycling. Gorp is also one of many U.S. booking agents for **The Imaginative Traveler** (© **800/225-2380;** www.imaginative-traveller.com), the U.K.'s leading adventure tour company.

Wildland Adventures (© **800/345-4453;** www.wildland.com) gears its off-the-beaten-track hiking and cultural trips toward ensuring distinctive accommodations and plenty of downtime. **Argeus,** based in Ürgüp, Istiklal Cad. 13 (© **0384/341-4688;** fax 0384/341-4888; www.argeus.com.tr), is the most qualified local company for tailor-made tours and packages in Cappadocia, and the exclusive representatives for REI activities in Turkey. Guides are knowledgeable and enthusiastic. The price for a regular day tour is 100€ ($120) per person for two people—a bit hefty in comparison to the lower-end outfitters, but with Argeus, there are no shopping detours and all museum fees are included.

Meanwhile, **Middle Earth Travel,** Gaferli Mah. Cevizler Sokak, Göreme (© **0384/271-2559;** www.middleearth travel.com), targets the hardiest of independent adventure travelers, with 6-day and 2-week treks into the Kaçkar Mountains, an 8-day climb up Mount Ararat, volcano climbs, and organized expeditions along the Lycian Way and St. Paul's Trail (see chapter 7).

Clients of **Cappadocia Tours** based in Ürgüp (© **0384/341-7485;** fax 0384/ 341-7487; www.cappadociatours.com) leave Turkey with a deeper attachment to the country thanks to a grass-roots approach that moves beyond the museums. In addition to the must-sees of Cappadocia, they also lead safari tours into the mountains, to waterfalls, and to off-the-beaten-track villages and little-explored underground cities.

SPA VACATIONS

It's obvious by the glossy brochure published by the Ministry of Tourism that Turkey recognizes the value of the country's natural thermal resources. But it's only recently that entrepreneurs have stepped up to the plate with suitably deluxe facilities that provide alternatives to the medicinal or blue-collar environments of some of the country's older centers. At the top of the list is Istanbul's Ritz-Carlton (p. 85), with its deluxe menu of signature treatments and ultimate spa packages.

In the hot springs–rich peninsula of **Çeşme** (see chapter 6, "The Central & Southern Aegean Coasts"), a luxury thermal spa is now the rule rather than the exception. The **Altın Yunus** was the first, and now five-star properties with thermal-rich waters include the **Süzer** and the new **Sheraton Çeşme,** which gears its high-tech thermal center to nothing more ambitious than treatments for pure pleasure. The **Sheraton Voyager** in Antalya features a high-tech wellness center (p. 312).

Two other traditional centers for thermal treatments are **Bursa** (see chapter 5, "Short Hops from Istanbul: Around the Sea of Marmara & the North Aegean") and **Pamukkale** (see chapter 6).

In Bodrum **The Marmara Oteli** (p. 240) converted five of their rooms into a center geared toward complete self-indulgence. The spa offers stone therapy, a "fat attack" sea mud body pack, and the ultimate endorphin high: 60 minutes of weightless relaxation in their state-of-the-art flotation tank.

EXCURSIONS INTO EASTERN TURKEY

For the first time in more than 20 years, eastern Turkey is enjoying an extended period of calm, and slowly but surely, destinations that previously came with State Department warnings are appearing in tour brochures. Make no mistake, however, as far as creature comforts go, it's still the Wild West out east. Alas, publisher's directives about page limits constrain me from elaborating on such wondrous destinations as **Zeugma, Antioch, Mt. Nemrut,** and **Lake Van.** Instead, I can highly recommend **Credo Tours** (© **90-212/254-8175;** fax 90-212/237-9670; www.credo.com.tr) for your foray into Turkey's eastern and southeastern provinces.

Another reputable outfitter experienced in the east is **Fez Travel** (© **90-212/516-9024;** fax 90-212/638-8764; www.feztravel.com), run by a group of Australians who made a name for themselves with a hop-on-hop-off circuit of Turkey's hot spots. These trips, top-heavy with Australian backpackers, are geared more toward the budget end of travel. Meanwhile, many tour operators based in Göreme, in Cappadocia, run overnight bus tours to Mount Nemrut, mostly utilized by backpackers.

9 Getting Around

BY CAR

Driving in Turkey can be extremely frustrating, if not downright fatal. Obviously the worst-case scenario is that you get hit by an oncoming bus (not as rare as you might think), while the minor inconvenience of getting stuck behind a farm tractor going 24kmph (15 mph) can make the most passive driver go postal. Any way you look at it, getting around Turkey by car is an extreme sport. My best advice is: Drive defensively; expect the unexpected; leave your road rage at home; get used to blowing your horn to announce your presence; never get overconfident; and remember that all accidents must be reported to the police (dial ✆ 155 and sit tight).

Travelers with heart problems shouldn't be either drivers or navigators; my advice is to take the bus and keep the curtains closed at all times. But if you have the spirit, driving through Turkey is a great way to travel independently with the utmost of freedom. If you're used to driving in cities like New York, London, or anywhere in Italy, driving through Turkey should be a walk in the park. Did I also mention that it is really fun?

The road conditions have improved dramatically in recent years (except along the eastern coast of the Mediterranean, beginning around Antalya), but in general, never let your guard down. Advisories suggest that you stay off the roads at night, but because headlights announce the presence of oncoming traffic (when in use), driving on those hairpin mountainous roads is probably safest after dark, although this won't help much when confronted with a herd of goats in your lane. Be sure to fill up the tank at every opportunity, because the likelihood that you will find any fuel other than diesel is inversely related to the distance that you drive away from civilization.

Among the behaviors I have witnessed from Turkish drivers: 1) right-hand turns from the left lane and left-hand turns from the right lane, 2) minibuses stopping without warning to pick up passengers, 3) vehicles backing up on off-ramps, 4) impatient drivers driving the wrong way in your lane because they didn't want to sit in traffic, and 5) drivers that pass you while you're in the process of passing someone else *on a two-lane highway.* And it takes a rock-hard constitution to withstand the gale-force winds caused by the all-too-close-for-comfort proximity of a never-ending stream of oncoming buses. Be prepared to use part of the shoulder (if there is one) to avoid getting hit by oncoming traffic.

Avis (✆ 800/230-4898, or in Canada 800/272-5871; www.avis.com) has locations in all major cities, at most airports, and at select hotels and resorts. If you reserve a car before you go, you can take advantage of their **On Call** program (✆ 800/297-4447 *in advance of your trip* for access numbers in Turkey; have your confirmation or reservation number ready), which provides 24-hour, toll-free assistance for physicians, lost baggage, prescriptions from home, and mechanical problems. **National Car Rental** (✆ 800/227-7368;** www.nationalcar.com) has outlets pretty much everywhere, too, with rates comparable to those of Avis. Other options are **Budget** (✆ 800/527-0700, or in Canada 800/268-8900; www.budget.com), with limited outlets in Turkey, and **Sixt** (✆ 0216/318-9040 in Turkey; www.sunrent.com), with 20 locations throughout Turkey.

The ubiquitous local mom-and-pop companies offer satisfactory vehicles for competitive prices, if you don't mind renting models you've never heard of. A compact manual can be had for as little as 40YTL ($30) a day with unlimited mileage and insurance included, and if you're really nice, you can probably get an airport transfer thrown in for good

A Note on Distances

The concept of precision is a foreign one in Turkey. "Not far" is a relative term and "just over there" indicates a point in the distance as the crow flies. Similarly, when comparing the travel literature on distances between towns, you'll notice a glaring absence of consistency. Please note that although all distances in this book have been confirmed using official maps and brochures, it is a fact that even distances reported by official agencies may be incorrect. Therefore, I plead for mercy for some of the mileages that I quote.

measure. These private rates are also a plus when you consider that it will cost you at least 55YTL ($40) to fill up the tank, but make sure everything on the car works, especially the horn, the turn signals, and the radio.

BY PLANE

After one too many 12-hour hauls on a non-air-conditioned bus with unrelenting piped-in ethnic music and the pungent odors of lemon cologne and BO, you may prefer to spend your next full day of travel waiting around an airport cafe rather than in a bus seat. **Turkish Airlines** (© 800/874-8875 in the U.S., 207-766-9300 in London, 0212/663-6300 in Istanbul; www.turkishairlines.com) provides regular domestic service within Turkey, with major hubs in Istanbul, Ankara, and İzmir. The recent arrival of **Onur Air** (in Istanbul © 0212/663-9176; www.onurair.com.tr) and **Flyair** (in Istanbul © 0212/444-4359; www.flyair.com.tr) has created some healthy competition in Turkey's domestic air transportation industry. Onur Air flies from Istanbul to Ankara, İzmir, Antalya, and Kayseri, to name just a few destinations, while Flyair flies from Istanbul to İzmir and Bodrum. One-way domestic fares on Onur Air or Flyair will cost around 80YTL ($60), while passage on Turkish Airlines will cost you slightly more, around 107YTL ($79). You can book flights last-minute at one of the airline offices or through an officially recognized travel agent. These days, with

flights into Istanbul consistently full, it's a good idea to plan ahead. Although it's still possible to fly last-minute, try to book your domestic seats as much in advance as possible, especially if your travel falls during one of the *bayrams* (religious holidays).

Those with more of a jet-setting mentality can charter domestic flights through **Marinair** (© 0212/663-1829; www.bonair.com.tr), providing service from Istanbul to Bodrum/Türkbükü, Çeşme, Dalaman, Göcek, and Kaş. Travel time is approximately 1½ hours, and fares hover around 3,375YTL to 4,050YTL ($2,500–$3,000).

BY TRAIN

In the years leading up to World War I, Turkey's railroads developed thanks to the "generosity" of German and British government-supported ventures sucking up to an as-yet neutral potential ally. These entrepreneurs recognized the value of old stone, making not-so-convenient detours in the track-laying to valuable archaeological sites. The result was a uselessly meandering system highly efficient at carting away priceless archaeological finds, enriching both foreign museums and the pockets of these "part-time engineers." The Pergamum Altar is now in the Pergamon Museum in Berlin; King Priam's treasures were whisked out of Troy, passing through Berlin's Hermitage Museum and on to Moscow's Pushkin Museum; while many treasures from the Temple of Artemis are now housed in the

British Museum. The only exception to an across-the-board recommendation to stick to the buses is with regard to the night train from Istanbul to Ankara. Although the bus is faster by about 3 to 4 hours, skyrocketing bus fares are making the train the choice of many. Besides cheaper fares, a bunk on the sleeper car will have you arriving fresh and ready to go on arrival (minus the shower; the cars come with sink only). For information on timetables and fares, log on to **www. tcdd.gov.tr**.

BY BUS

Traveling by bus brings up images of greasy-haired, guitar-toting rebels lifted from the pages of a Jack Kerouac novel. Turkey has taken the grungy image of bus travel and brought it to new heights of comfort and respectability. There are several categories of bus travel: municipal buses, the local *dolmuş*, long-distance buses, and short-distance minibuses.

In big cities like Istanbul, Ankara, İzmir, and Antalya, **municipal buses** provide a cheap way to get around, if you can actually figure out how. Destinations are posted on the windshield, but it's always a good idea to ask the driver if he's going your way before getting on. Getting on in the middle of a bus route can be confusing, but there's always the ubiquitous good Samaritan there to steer you in the right direction. In Istanbul the modern green buses are for commuters with debit tokens only, while the used-up old orange buses are for everybody else; tickets can be purchased from the cashier onboard.

Another popular and economic way of getting around is the **dolmuş**, essentially a minivan with passenger seats. The best description of these little group taxis is in the translation: *dolmuş* in English means "stuffed." The *dolmuş* follows a set route, stopping and starting to pick up passengers until no one else will fit in it. The main stops are posted on the windshield

and you pay according to the distance that you go, usually under 1YTL (75¢). This system works well in and around small towns; drivers will politely honk as they drive to see if you want to get on, and routes are direct to the places you want to go. *Dolmuşes* do run on Sunday, so don't let those crafty taxi drivers convince you otherwise.

In major metropolitan areas such as Istanbul, the process is a bit more complicated, even for the locals. The best way to avoid an inner-city trip to nowhere is to board at one of the *dolmuş* stands marked by a blue "D" and take it to the final destination. Fares are usually posted, and rarely exceed 70YKr per ride (about 55¢). It's also acceptable to pay the driver before you get off, so you can enjoy a bit of spontaneity as well. *Dolmuşes* stop running in the early evening, so in the outlying areas, make sure you've got a way back to the hotel.

Long-distance buses are an integral part of the Turkish culture, probably because there are often few alternatives for intercity travel other than renting a car.

The major bus companies in Turkey (*Note:* Phone numbers beginning with 444 are national toll-free numbers and can be dialed from anywhere in Turkey) are **Ulusoy** (© 444-1888; www.ulusoy otobus.com), **Varan** (© 0212/251-7474; www.varanturizm.com), **Kamil Koç** (© 444-0562; www.kamilcoc.com.tr), **Uludağ** (© 0212/245-2795; www. uludagturizm.com.tr), **Metro** (© 444-3455) and **Pamukkale** (© 444-3535; www.pamukkaleturizm.com.tr), with the first two costing nearly double the other companies. Less expensive newcomers, offering fares as much as 7YTL to 14YTL ($5–$10) lower depending on your destination, may also be a good option. All have counters at the local bus station (*otogar*) as well as offices conveniently located around town. You may want to buy your tickets in advance if the *otogar* is

Tips   ## Don't Let Taxi Drivers Take You for a Ride

There is a certain amount of control you give up when entering a taxi in a strange city. Your safest bet is to have your hotel concierge phone for the taxi rather than you flagging it down. (In Istanbul, under no circumstances should you hire a taxi off the street in front of the Ayasofya.) Some hotels and taxi companies have agreements that award the company repeat business in exchange for honesty and accountability at no extra charge to the passenger. Still, the risk that absolute ignorance of a location will be rewarded with a circuitous route is fairly high. Knowing in advance that there's nothing you can do about it is usually enough to let you sit back and relax. But there still are a few things to look out for to avoid being scammed.

Check to see that the meter is running, and that the correct rate applies. The less expensive day rate (*gunduz* alternately flashes with the metered fare) applies from 7am to midnight, but crafty taxi drivers will push the night (*gece*) rate button to increase the fare. If you've caught a driver in the act, threaten to summon the police, or get out of the cab.

Beware of the "bait and switch" routine, whereby the driver takes your 10YTL banknote (worth about $7) and accuses you of having given him a 1YTL note (worth about 70¢). You can avoid this by holding on to the banknote until you've received your change. Also, note that 1YTL notes are blue-toned and 10YTL notes are orange.

For longer distances or drives outside of the city limits, taxis usually have a list of set rates. Be sure you've discussed these in advance, as you may be able to negotiate a discount (though it's doubtful). A final word: Don't get into a cab expecting bad things to happen. Just be a smart customer.

---

a considerable distance from the town center or if you plan to stick to a time schedule. Better bus companies offer free minibus service between the ticket office and the *otogar*.

If you're on a more relaxed timetable, it's just as easy to show up at the *otogar;* with competition stiff for your business, the bus companies that provide service to your destination will find you. If you have time, it doesn't hurt to shop around, because the seat the agent is trying to sell you may not be on the first bus to leave for your destination.

If you're like me, you believe it should take approximately 3 hours to cover 322km (200 miles). Not so on the bus, as most of the major highways in Turkey are the two-lane variety, and are enforced with excruciatingly low speed limits that large hulking masses have trouble maintaining. Gauge at least 40% more time on the bus than what you figure it would take you to get there by car, and keep the curtains drawn so you can't see how slow you're actually going.

Roughly, you can expect to pay about 5YTL to 10YTL ($4–$7) for every hour of travel. Water and soft drinks are served on the bus; if you're lucky, you'll get a little kid-size breakfast cake to tide you over until the next feeding. A sprinkle of cologne is part of the Turkish culture, but better the brand that smells of baby oil and talcum powder than the one that stinks like Lemon Pledge. Rest stops are made at erratic intervals, but there's usually enough time at one of the pickup and drop-off points for a quick dash to the Turkish toilet. (Let the man onboard know you'll be right back!)

Except on rare occasions (and in my case, total cluelessness), unacquainted men and women do not sit together on the bus. My grievance with this tradition is more practical than unprogressive: old Turkish ladies tend to be hefty and spill out onto the adjacent seat, while it is common practice for Turkish mothers to save a bus fare by seating her 6-year-old son on her lap for the 6-hour trip. On longer trips, pay for two seats (and two snack cakes). You'll be glad you did.

10 Tips on Accommodations

Hotels in Turkey are classified by a government-designated star system that apparently was established in the Neolithic era, so booking a five-star hotel in Turkey doesn't necessarily guarantee the comfort and amenities of an equivalently rated establishment in a major city like Istanbul. Roughly, stars are awarded for the presence of amenities like fitness centers or conference space, so a worn-out old five-star with moldy bathroom tile might rate higher than a brand-new sky-lit gem with nothing to offer but basic clean rooms, stunning balconies, and a pool.

Unless stated otherwise, all rates quoted in the hotel reviews in this book include breakfast and tax. Many hotels rely exclusively on solar power, which sounds great until you get in a cold shower at sunrise. This is increasingly rare, however, as many establishments are installing backup generators for "24-hour hot water." Power outages are an unavoidable part of daily life, and because the water supply operates on an electric pumping system, there will be no water for the duration of the outage, usually only a couple of hours. In the sweaty heat of the summer, this is where the neighborhood *hamam* comes in handy.

Typical hotel rooms in Turkey seem to have more rooms with twin beds, so unless you specify that you want a double "French" bed, you and your partner will feel like a couple out of a 1950s sitcom. Fitted sheets seem to be an anomaly in Turkey, so if you're a restless sleeper, expect to get a view of the mattress in the morning. Ask for an extra sheet if there's nothing between you and the blanket, as bed-making habits in Turkey vary from hotel to hotel. And not even the Four Seasons Hotel in Sultanahmet will spare you from the startling blare of the neighborhood's muezzin at sunrise. TVs are generally a standard feature in rooms, but even a TV with a satellite hookup will limit you to BBC World, CNN, and endless hours of cycling tournaments. Local programming is at least captivating, with reruns of *Guys and Dolls* or *The Terminator* in Turkish. Another interesting media feature in the room is a built-in radio with centrally piped-in music. There is generally a choice of up to three channels, and if you don't like the music, I discovered that calling down to the reception desk for special requests was effective.

Another standard characteristic of hotels rated three stars or lower (Turkish rating) is the "Roman shower"—essentially a showerhead on the wall and a drain in the floor. In some cases, you'll get a square enamel stall basin and a shower curtain, and practiced proficiency with the hand-held showerhead will eventually ensure the least amount of leakage on the bathroom floor. Be aware, too, that an ongoing problem of not just the older hotels is the rapidity in which a clear drain will get clogged. I've kept recommendations of these hotels to the exceptional minimum.

During the in-between seasons, many hotels, operating with heating systems programmed to run during the winter months only, may leave you out in the cold. In the absence of central heat, many special-category hotels simply provide standing electric heaters. If you're prone to cold, make sure your hotel offers heat.

All hotels provide laundry and dry-cleaning services, seeing to it in the process that they make a huge profit on the transaction. Depending on the establishment, expect to pay anywhere from 3€ to 7€ ($3.50–$8.50) per item for ordinary laundry. At under 4€ ($5) a load, a local laundromat is a cheap alternative, as long as you don't mind borrowing the hotel iron. Another service offered by all five-star hotels is babysitting, arranged by the hotel through reputable outside agencies.

Also, it is imperative to note that except in rare cases (like full occupancy, which is happening a lot lately), the room rates provided in the listings are "rack rates," fictional prices that are almost never quoted—not even to the most desperate last-minute walk-in. It is more likely than not that a rate will adjust itself anywhere from 10% to 50% (or more!) at the time of booking, depending on the season and how hungry the owner is. This doesn't mean that hoteliers have become market hagglers; it simply means that the prices listed for hotels are inextricably tied to the market. Parents with kids will be pleased to learn that children 6 and under, and in some cases 12 and under, stay free.

In order to increase business, hotels in Turkey make rooms available at absurdly low rates to travel agents so that they will provide them with business on a regular basis. Ironically, a recent, yet not yet pervasive, development has been for hotels to undercut these agents with their own web rates. Therefore, it is up to the buyer to do the legwork. But buyer beware: not all travel sites advertising cheap hotels on the Web are equally reputable, so I recommend that you stick to the local travel agencies recommended in this guide (or those recommended to you by friends and relatives). For a list of charming hotels beyond those recommended in this guide, log onto **www.nisanyan.net** (run by the owners of the Nisanyan houses in Şirince; see chapter 6) and use the "search hotel" function. Be aware, however, that all of the hotels listed on this site pay a subscription fee and therefore may not be as wonderful in person. A great resource for locating affordable hotels is **www. hostelworld.com**, which lists youth hostels, tours, and tips for working abroad.

When you make your reservation, ask if the hotel is renovating; if it is, request a room away from the renovation work or stay elsewhere. Many hotels now offer nonsmoking rooms; if smoke bothers you, by all means ask for one.

Finally, somebody has to get the best room in the house (and somebody has to get the worst). My advice is to book early and confirm what you're getting in advance. Many hotels in Turkey have one standard room rate, good even for a high floor with a breathtaking view of the Mediterranean. Corner rooms can provide an added bonus as well, as they are usually larger and quieter. Superior rooms or junior suites are a great way to pamper yourself, and with the strength of the dollar and current tourist bargaining power, staying in one doesn't have to break the bank. Avoid rooms on the street as they tend to be noisy; paradoxically, the hotels will book you in these first, as they are considered to be superior to those in the rear. Finally, be wary of partnerships between hotels and carpet shops, or worse, carpet dealers masquerading as hoteliers—rare, but yet another way for these guys to get your undivided attention.

11 Recommended Books & Films

Turkey's past is so densely packed with history's most critical eras that if you don't do your homework before you go, you'll wind up simply wandering through pretty piles of rocks and stone.

BOOKS

At the very least, pick up a copy of *A Traveller's History of Turkey* (Interlink Books, 1998), by Richard Stoneman, a readable overview of Turkey's history from A to Z that will fit in your back pocket. Take it with you, as Stoneman provides a handy reference of ancient sites in the appendix.

A Short History of Byzantium (Vintage Books, 1998), John Julius Norwich's condensed version of a three-volume epic, actually entertains while faithfully covering the life of one of the most enduring empires on Earth. *Ottoman Centuries: The Rise and Fall of the Turkish Empire* (William Morrow & Co., 1988), by Lord Kinross, has established itself as the definitive guidebook on Turkey during the Ottoman Empire. In a thoroughly readable prose, Kinross leads you through history while providing the contexts for understanding Turkey today. Another book by Kinross is *Atatürk, the Rebirth of a Nation* (titled *Atatürk: A Biography of Mustafa Kemal, Father of Modern Turkey* in the U.S. and currently out of print), also respected as *the* handbook on the man who single-handedly reconstructed a nation. Also see Andrew Mango's more recent *Atatürk* (John Murray Pubs, 2004).

Constantinople: City of the World's Desire, 1453–1924 (Griffin Trade Paperback, 1998), by Philip Mansel, provides an accurate and colorful history of the Ottoman Empire while sprinkling the pages with attention-grabbing little morsels of lesser-known trivia. *Turkey Unveiled: A History of Modern Turkey* (Overlook Press, 1999) was written by Hugh and Nicole Pope, two journalists working for the *Wall Street Journal* and *Le Monde,* respectively. In *Turkey Unveiled,* the Popes give us insights on the most divisive issues of Turkey today. A more recent analysis of modern problems and trends in Turkey written from a Western insider's point of view is provided by Stephen Kinzer, former Istanbul bureau chief of the *New York Times,* in *Crescent and Star: Turkey Between Two Worlds* (Farrar Straus & Giroux, 2001).

Keep your eyes peeled in used-book stores both at home and in Turkey for old versions of George Bean's series, *Lycian Turkey, Aegean Turkey, Turkey's Southern Shore,* and *Turkey Beyond the Meander* (last published by John Murray Ltd., 1989–90), which comprise the masterwork collection of archaeological guidebooks on Turkey, but are unfortunately out of print. Filling the void is the new and improved printing of Dr. Ekrem Akurgal's *Ancient Civilizations and Ruins of Turkey* (Net Turistik Yayınlar San. Tic. A.Ş. Istanbul, 2001), first printed in 1969 and currently the definitive guidebook to archaeological sites in Turkey.

Walking is a great way to see rural Turkey, and Kate Clow shows you the way in her books. *The Lycian Way* (Upcountry Ltd., 2000) is a detailed mapping out of the ancient footpaths and roads between Fethiye and Antalya, with details on the history, archaeological sites, and wildlife along the way. She's even considerate enough to let us know how out-winded we can expect to get. A collection of 20 maps is included, so although the full trek would take at least 4 to 6 weeks, you can use this guidebook for a less ambitious day trip. For information on the trail, log on to **www.lycian way.com**. Also, check out *St Paul Trail* (Upcountry Ltd., 2004), which is just as detailed, with color photos and maps chronicling the way taken by St. Paul on his missionary journeys through Asia Minor.

World War I buffs will want to show up on the battlefields at Gallipoli armed with a copy of Tim Travers *Gallipoli 1915 (Battles & Campaigns)* (Tempus Publishing, 2004). Aussies should hunt down a copy of *Gallipoli* (Macmillan Australia, 2001), by Les Carlyon and available in Australia.

Coverage of terrorist actions committed by militant Muslims has prejudiced much of the Western world against anything Islamic, causing many tourists to Turkey to be unnecessarily apprehensive. *Teach Yourself Islam* (NTC Publishing Group, 1994), by Ruqaiyyah Maqsood, gets to the soul of the religion by providing explanations of beliefs and analyzing the purposes behind the rituals in a straightforward and absorbing manner. *What Went Wrong* (Oxford University Press, 2001), a balanced and scholarly work by Bernard Lewis, guides readers through the transformation of Islam from a cultural, scientific, and economic powerhouse to a significantly tarnished underdog. Finish off this reading list with *What's Right With Islam* (Harper San Francisco, 2004), in which Feisal Abdul Rauf argues how the violence perceived by the West to be at the heart of terrorism has, in fact, nothing to do with religion and everything to do with economics and politics.

Jeremy Seal's *A Fez of the Heart: Travels Around Turkey in Search of a Hat* (Harvest Books, 1996) and Mary Lee Settle's *Turkish Reflections* (Touchstone Books, 1992) are two excellent travelogues that have established themselves as de facto reads for anyone interested in Turkey. *Turkish Reflections,* although accused of being outdated, succeeds in providing an accurate portrayal of the Turkish people and vivid images of the physical landscape. Interesting little snippets of trivia are sprinkled throughout the text and are especially entertaining as supplements to a historical perspective, but as a read, may be more suitable for post-voyage reminiscences. In *A Fez of the Heart,* Jeremy Seal succeeds in capturing the sights and smells of his destinations while ostensibly on the hunt for the legacy left by the fez. Seal tosses in bits of history while you're not looking and throws in unexpected episodes of hilarity that will garner you unwanted attention in public places.

For Orhan Pamuk, *Istanbul: Memories and the City* (Alfred A. Knopf, 2005) is a personal reflection on life growing up in the "melancholy" of an Istanbul in transition. Descriptions of faded apartment buildings, and the tension between tradition and convention are as much a self-portrait as a window into the city at the crossroads of civilization.

For a modern woman's view of what it's like to work, live, and travel in Turkey, pick up the recently compiled and released *Tales From the Expat Harem: Foreign Women in Modern Turkey* (Citlembik, 2005; to be published in the U.S. in 2006). It's a compilation of essays, stories, and travelogues by various non-Turkish women.

In fiction, obviously, the most insightful reads will be those books written by native Turks, and in recent years, several Turkish authors have created mesmerizing works of fiction set within a vivid Turkish reality. Orhan Pamuk made quite a splash in the United States; his novels *The White Castle* (Vintage, 1998), *The Black Book* (Harvest Books, 1996), *The New Life* (Vintage, 1998) and the *New York Times* literary prize winners *Snow* (Vintage, 2005) and *Istanbul: Memories of a City* (Knopf, 2005) can easily be found in bookstores. Irfan Orga's *Portrait of a Turkish Family* (Hippocrene Books, 1989) is a poignant account of a simple Turkish family caught between the Ottoman Empire and Atatürk's Republic. Journalist and leading satirist Aziz Nesin spent much of his life in prison, where he penned a large portion of his highly biographical essays. The University of Texas Center for Middle Eastern Studies has put some of his works online, which provide colorful images of growing up in a traditional Turkish family at the beginning of the 20th century (http://menic.utexas.edu/menic/cmes/pub/iboy/iboy.html; you may have to key in each successive link individually).

FILMS

The Turks rigorously resent the unfair characterization of Turkish people in the 1978 film *Midnight Express* (see "*Midnight Express:* Fact or Fiction?" in chapter 1, "The Best of Turkey"), a movie that has been accused of encouraging prejudices in Westerners. They point out that the movie was financed by Greek cinema magnate Kirk Kerkorian and filmed using actors of predominantly Greek and Armenian origin—two nations notorious for their bad blood with Turkey. Nevertheless, it's a movie classic, it did win an Oscar, and it *was* set in Istanbul.

Gallipoli (1981), with a young, spellbinding Mel Gibson, is a movie classic that brings the World War I battle down to a human level. This movie is a mustsee for anyone making the trip to the battlegrounds.

FAST FACTS: Turkey

American Express Amex has yet to establish a strong presence in Turkey. Türk Express is the official representative of Amex Travel Related Services in Turkey, at Cumhuriyet Cad. 91/1 Elmadağ in the Hilton Hotel (℘ **0212/230-1515**). American Express also provides a toll-free access number within Turkey for Global Assist (℘ **312/935-3601**).

ATM Networks Banks on the Cirrus or PLUS network include Akbank, Garanti Bankası, Yapı Kredi Bankası, and Ziraat Bankası. See also the section on ATMs under "Visitor Information, Entry Requirements & Money" earlier in this chapter.

Business Hours The reality is that if there are customers, the shops will stay open. Official hours of operation for shops are Monday through Saturday 9:30am to 1pm and 2 to 7pm, but I've yet to find a store closed at lunchtime, and increasingly, shops are opening on Sunday afternoons. Visitors to Istanbul take note that the Grand Bazaar and the Egyptian Spice Market are both closed on Sunday. Museums and palaces are generally open Tuesday through Sunday from 9:30am to 5 or 5:30pm, while the closing day for palaces is Tuesday, Thursday, or both. Banks are open Monday through Friday from 8:30am to noon and 1:30 to 5pm. Government offices are open Monday through Friday 8:30am to 12:30pm and 1:30 to 5:30pm.

Driving Rules Seat belts are compulsory, and the driving age is 18. Helmets are compulsory for motorcycles; motoring offenses result in an on-the-spot fine. In case of an accident, leave the vehicle where the incident occurred and call the police (℘ **155**).

Drugstores The sterile-looking, well-lit store with the word *Eczane* on the facade is a pharmacy, and will cater to most of your emergency drug needs. Pharmacists are also capable of diagnosing and addressing minor injuries and illnesses. You can even ask for a product by its brand name. (For example, Bayer

Aspirin has a corner on the Turkish headache market.) Pharmacies are open Monday through Saturday from 9am to 7pm, but not to worry: There is at least one open in every district at night and on Sundays, the location of which is posted in the window of every other drugstore in the neighborhood—in Turkish. Have your hotel send someone over to pick up whatever you need.

Electricity The standard is 220 volts, and outlets are compatible with the round European two-prong plug. Laptops are generally self-regulating, but check with your manufacturer before plugging in. You may be able to leave your hair dryer at home, as most hotel rooms come equipped with at least a weak one.

Emergencies For fire dial © **110**; for general first-aid emergencies (ambulance included) dial © **112**. For other health services or to call for a private ambulance in Istanbul: International Hospital Ambulance (© **0212/663-3000**); Istanbul Health Services (European side © **0212/247-0781**; Asian side © **0216/302-1515**). In Ankara call Bayındır Hospital Ambulance (© **0312/287-9000**), or call Özel Ambulans Servisi (© **0312/425-1565**).

Holidays The official holidays are New Year's Day (Jan 1), Independence and Children's Day (Apr 23), Youth and Sports Day (May 19), Victory Day (Aug 30), and Republic Foundation Day (Oct 29). Banks, public offices, and schools are closed for these national holidays. Although a secular state, most Turks also celebrate Şeker Bayramı, a 3-day celebration punctuating the end of the feast of Ramadan (Oct 23–25, 2006; Oct 12-14, 2007), and Kurban Bayramı (Dec 31, 2006-Jan 3, 2007; Dec 20-23, 2007), a 4-day feast honoring Abraham's willingness to sacrifice his son to God. All Islamic holidays follow a lunar calendar and thus fall on different dates every year: Banks, governmental offices, and most shops are closed on these days.

Internet Access Most hotels now provide free Internet as part of the hotel's services. ISDN lines are also becoming standard equipment in better hotels. Wireless access is even becoming quite prevalent. If you and 20 other people are relying on the hotel computer, there's still bound to be an Internet cafe nearby. They're still dirt-cheap—a fact that almost makes up for the excruciatingly slow transfer of data. An hour of Internet use costs anywhere from 1.75YTL to 11YTL ($1.25–$8), depending on where you are. For dinosaur dial-up users, AOL's local access number in Istanbul is © **0212/234-6100.** AT&T Business Internet Services can be accessed at © **0212/399-0001** and 0212/3990050. Both charge supplementary connection fees.

Language In tourist areas, English, French, and German are widespread, but that doesn't absolve you of the responsibility of learning a few much-appreciated basics such as "please," "thank you," "how much," and "where's the toilet." See appendix B, "A Glossary of Useful Turkish Phrases," for Turkish translations.

For the linguistically challenged, it may not be so unusual to encounter some minor language barrier outside of main tourist areas (including, surprisingly enough, established restaurants), but the inherent willingness of the Turks to help combined with a little sign language and a lot of laughs will almost always do the trick.

Legal Aid Foreigners and tourists get the benefit of the doubt in most every run-in with the law, but there are some things you just can't talk your way out of. For real trouble, contact your embassy or consulate for assistance and ask for their list of private law firms catering to English-speaking foreigners.

Liquor Laws For a predominantly Muslim country, it might be surprising that alcohol is even sold in Turkey. The truth is, the drinking of alcohol is not an issue: Some do, some don't. Beer, wine, and spirits are readily available in restaurants, bars, and liquor stores, and theoretically you have to be at least 18 to purchase or consume them. Bars stay open until the people go home.

Mail The PTT (post office), hard to miss with its black and yellow signs, offers the usual postal services, in addition to selling tokens *(jeton)* and phone cards for the phone booths located in and around the post office and in most public places. Postcards cost 50YKr (35¢) to Europe and 95YKr (70¢) to all other continents. The PTT also has currency exchange and traveler's check services; in major tourist areas PTT kiosks are strategically located for emergency money needs. For express deliveries or shipping packages, the PTT operates an *acele posta servisi* (or APS), but for your own sense of security, you'd better stick with the old reliable UPS or DHL.

Maps The tourist information office should be your first stop in every destination for local maps, which are detailed and free. The only difference between the free maps and the commercial ones, available in bookstores and tourist boutiques, is that the latter are usually illustrated with icons of important sites, so you don't inadvertently stroll by the Blue Mosque without realizing it.

Newspapers & Magazines *Turkish Daily News* and the *Turkish Press* are Turkey's only nationally published English-language papers providing local, national, and international news. Both have websites (www.turkishdailynews.com and www.turkishpress.com). The national paper, *Zaman*, also has an English-language website (www.zaman.com). In the larger cities, the *International Herald Tribune, USA Today,* and Britain's *Financial Times* are widely available, although they're generally light on local news. The *Guide Istanbul* is a good resource for events in town (free in most five-star hotels), with interesting features and essential local listings. *Cornucopia* is a more upscale English-language glossy featuring articles on Turkish art, history, and culture, while Turkish Airlines' *Skylife* and the airport's own *Gate1* shouldn't be overlooked for monthly exhibits and performances as well as features on destination-related topics.

Pets In a country where an overwhelming percentage of the population has difficulty affording even the basic necessities, it's not surprising that domesticated animals are an anathema. Most Turks are unaccustomed to having any direct contact with household pets. Some react with fear, and others, influenced by stiff requirements of cleanliness called for by Islam, find dogs unclean and will dramatically avoid any physical contact with one. As a result, traveling with Fido can be a real challenge: Many (but not all) hotels have strict no-pet policies, passage on a passenger ferry will require your remaining in the garage (bring a portable kennel or Sherpa bag), and major bus companies prohibit dogs onboard (but offer the luggage compartment!). Both Turkish Airlines and Delta allow pets in cargo and onboard (with restrictions), and the only thing you'll need is an international certificate of health from your veterinarian. There are no specific rabies requirements for entry into Turkey but there certainly are for the return, so make sure your pet's vaccinations meet U.S. requirements.

Police Dial © **155** in the case of theft or in the event of a car accident, as you will need to fill out a police report for administrative and/or insurance purposes.

Smoking A local saying goes something like this: "Eat like a Turk, smoke like a Turk," which roughly translates to "don't expect anyone to comply with non-smoking laws." In theory, smoking is prohibited on public transportation, in movie theaters, in airports, and the like. But realizing the hardships of driving a bus, bus companies allow the drivers to smoke. This is a good time to work on tolerance, and remember to pack Visine and to sit upwind at outdoor cafes.

Taxes The value-added tax (VAT or sales tax) in Turkey is called the KDV; it's 18% on all goods and services, unless you're in the market for a refrigerator or washing machine, in which case the VAT is 26%. (Ultraluxury goods are taxed at 40%, while the government adds 1% on things like butter and milk, and 8% on nonbasic foodstuffs.) Ask the shop in which you've purchased goods to provide you with the special VAT Refund Invoice, which must then be validated at the Customs Office at the airport prior to departure.

Telephones Telephones are operated with *jetons* or prepaid phone cards, both available at the post office (PTT). Phone cards are available in 30, 60, or 100 units, the latter costing about 6.75YTL ($5) and getting you approximately 5 minutes on the phone to the U.S. The Smart Card telephone system (50 units cost about 4YTL/$3; also available at the post office) operates using a superior system, but distribution of public telephones is still too limited to be very convenient.

The following access numbers will connect you with a U.S. operator for credit card or collect calls: AT&T (© **00/800-12277**); MCI (© **00/800-11177**); and Sprint (© **00/800-14477**).

The dialing codes for calling your home country are 001 for the United States and Canada, 0044 for the United Kingdom, 0061 for Australia, and 0064 for New Zealand.

Dial local calls by using the seven-digit phone number; if dialing out of town, you must include 0 plus the city code. When calling a cellphone (identifiable by the 0531, 0532, 0533, 0534, 0535, 0536, and so on exchanges), you must include the zero. When dialing any number in Turkey from abroad, drop the zero. Istanbul has two city codes: 216 for the Asian side and 212 for the European side.

Time Zone Turkey is 7 hours ahead of Eastern Standard Time, so when it is noon in New York, it is 7pm in Istanbul.

Tipping Indispensable as a supplement to an already low wage, gratuities are a way of life in Turkey, and are often expected for even the most minor service. Try to keep small notes handy and follow these guidelines: give the bellhop 50 kurus to 1YTL (35¢–75¢) per bag; leave at least an additional 10% of the restaurant bill for your waiter; reward your tour guide with 14YTL to 27YTL ($10–$20) for a job well done; thank the captain of your *gulet* with about 68YTL ($50); and give your masseur/masseuse 4YTL ($3) *before* the rubdown.

Tipping

Shows of appreciation are also expected from your chambermaid, your barber or hairdresser, and an usher who has shown you to your seat.

Toilets   There are two types of waste repositories in Turkey, the traditional toilet and the Turkish toilet, that dreaded porcelain contraption in the floor. Traditional toilet bowls are equipped at the rear with a tube for running water operated by a faucet located on the wall to the right of the tank, allowing for quick cleanups after every use. Many Turks and Europeans swear the Turkish toilet is hygienically superior; but having stepped in more unidentifiable liquids than I care to remember, I'm not convinced. In any case, you'll be thankful for those footrests and might even master the art of avoiding backsplash. The floor-level faucet and bucket are also for quick wash-ups (probably the reason the floor is wet); in both cases, toilet paper is for drying. Flushing the toilet paper is sometimes hazardous to the life of the plumbing, but generally when this is the case, there will be a sign above the tank requesting that you dispose of it in the nearby wastebasket. My advice? Lift your skirts high, hang on to the cuffs of your pants, and *always* carry tissues.

Water   Water is an integral part of Turkish culture; when the French were perfecting the art of camouflaging fermenting bodily odors with perfume, the sultans were basting in spring water in a sky-lit marble chamber aided by a handful of naked members of the harem. Today, water runs freely in public fountains where local villagers come to refill empty 2-liter bottles. The hosing down of the sidewalks is a daily occurrence, as are the ritual cleansings at the architecturally wondrous ablution fountains found outside every mosque. In a word: Turks are squeaky clean. But the reality is that the water you bathe in is not necessarily the water you want to drink. Take it from someone with an iron constitution—it will *definitely* slow you down. Drink bottled water and wash fruits thoroughly before eating.

Suggested Turkey Itineraries

This chapter gives you a rough outline of what you can reasonably see in 1 or 2 weeks in Turkey. Here I make all the tough decisions for you (most of the time; you'll need to choose between Ephesus and Cappadocia). If the idea of letting someone else plan your entire trip is a buzz kill for you (and I can't blame you), you still might peruse this chapter to see my recommendations for exactly *how much* you can see here in this amount of time.

1 The Best of Turkey in 1 Week

Frankly, 1 week isn't enough time to explore very much of anything anywhere, let alone Istanbul, the seat of three former world empires. And that doesn't include the 2 days spent on international travel (assuming you had to cross an ocean to get here). Because all of Turkey's major sights are scattered to the four corners of the country—and getting from one to the next will involve either a flight, a long car or bus ride, or both—a scant 7 days will force you to make some hard choices, and you'll have to hustle at high speed during what traditionally should be "downtime." With 1 week, expect to have barely enough time to cover the basics of Istanbul and one other destination. Because boat captains now regularly offer 3- and 4-day "Blue Cruises," you just may be able to squeeze in one of these, although if you do, you'll surely be compromising any hopes of experiencing the heart and soul of Turkey by sequestering yourself on the (albeit magnificent) coastal seas.

That said, an oft-asked question is "Should I go to Ephesus or Cappadocia?" It's a true dilemma: Go to Ephesus, the ancient port city and home to early Christianity's most venerated icons—or head to Cappadocia, where all weird and wonderful rock formations *not* carved by nature were hollowed out for sheer secular and profane necessity. My answer is usually in the form of a question: "Why do you want to go to Ephesus?" Weed out the underlying sense of biblical enormity, and it's just another major archaeological must-see, right? So if the appeal is purely archaeological, and if you've been to Rome or seen Pompeii, then I'd have to tout Cappadocia as unique enough to win hands down. Happily, with more than just 1 week (or high energy and lots of commitment), you can actually do both. So, depending on your interests and the answer to my question above, below are suggestions for both a 1- and 2-week itinerary. **Start:** *On foot from Sultanahmet.*

Day ❶: Arrive, off and running in Istanbul

Most transatlantic flights arrive in **Istanbul** 🟊🟊🟊 in the late morning, so after you check in to your hotel and have a quick nap and a shower, it's time to head out. Spend the first afternoon getting acquainted with the old city of Sultanahmet, beginning with a good orientation point, the **Hippodrome** 🟊 (p. 106). You might duck into a local **tea garden** for a bite to eat (avoid the touristy ones closest to the Hippodrome). Then go directly to the Sultanahmet Mosque, better known as the **Blue Mosque** (p. 103). Follow this up with a walk through the imposing **Ayasofya** (p. 99), stopping along the way for a quick peek into the **Haseki Sultan Hamamı** (p. 121), now a beautifully restored space used by the Ministry of Tourism as a fixed-priced carpet shop (see "Shopping" in chapter 4). Next stop is the ancient underground **Yerebatan Cistern** (p. 120) across the street at Yerebatan Caddesi. If you haven't yet run out of daylight, scoot over to the **St. Savior in Chora** church (p. 119) for some of the finest Byzantine mosaics anywhere—and plan to stay for dinner (**Asitane** restaurant is located in the Kariye Hotel adjacent to the museum; see p. 97).

Day ❷: Topkapı Palace and the Grand Bazaar

Begin Day 2 fresher and better prepared for an exhausting morning poking around **Topkapı Palace** (p. 109), and don't you dare skip out on the **Treasury** (p. 111)—although if you're pressed for time or money, you can definitely skip the tour of the **Harem**, which departs at regular intervals. Instead, head back to the first courtyard, where you'll find access to the **Istanbul Archaeology Museum** (p. 107). Few visitors take the time to visit this impressive collection of ancient and even famous artifacts (for example, **The Treaty of Kadesh,** signed by Pharaoh Ramses and the Hittite King), but I *highly* recommend this one, and add that everyone I've ever sent here has thanked me for the tip. When you finally do exit the palace grounds, turn right immediately outside the main gate out along **Soğukçeşme Sokağı** for a walk through a typical 19th-century Ottoman neighborhood. Go down the hill and pick up the tram at the nearby Gülhane stop (you'll have to cross the main avenue to

get the correct tram) and take it to the Bayezit stop near one of the entrances to the **Grand Bazaar** (p. 104). If you ever get out, there's a sound-and-light show in **Sultanahmet Park** under the Blue Mosque on summer nights at 9pm (the language of the display rotates daily), after which you can grab dinner at one of the numerous rooftop restaurants mentioned in chapter 4, "Istanbul."

Day ❸: A Day on the Bosphorus, and an Ottoman Band

Set out early in the morning for a daylong cruise up the **Bosphorus** (p. 129), allowing yourself at least an hour to explore the **Egyptian Spice Bazaar** (p. 133) and neighboring **Yeni Cami** (p. 124) before you board at the nearby ferry docks. If you're concerned about time, take a half-day guided sightseeing tour, which includes a stop at the Egyptian Bazaar, an informed description of the sights along the Asian and European shores, and a visit to **Rumeli Castle** (p. 130), which wraps up around lunchtime. If you take the guided tour, spend the remainder of the afternoon walking the length of Istanbul's main artery, in **Istiklal Caddesi** (p. 66) and poking in and around the back streets of **Beyoğlu.** If possible, arrange this afternoon exploration around the 3pm performance of the mighty **Mehter Band** in the **Military Museum** up in Harbiye (walking distance from Taksim Square or a short taxi ride; see p. 128). (If you miss the 3pm English performance, the whole thing repeats in Turkish at 3:30pm.) Then, if you allow yourself one unexpected itinerary stop in Istanbul, make it this: From the Military Museum, take a taxi up to the modern and trendy seaside village of **Ortaköy** (just above the Çiragan Palace), where you'll find restaurants, cafes, and sidewalk vendors under the Bosphorus bridge (p. 64). Reward yourself with a relaxing dinner at one of the many places on the quay, or head back to Beyoğlu for a meal at one of the classic *meyhanes* (taverns) of the *balıkpazarı* (fish bazaar).

For the rest of your week in Turkey, you're faced with the big question: "Ephesus or Cappadocia?" I'm outlining a plan for both:

PLAN A:

Day ❹: The Ancient Site of Ephesus

Take a domestic flight to İzmir, and using either Selçuk or Kuşadası as your base, spend the day visiting the archaeological site of **Ephesus** ✹✹✹, the **Ephesus Museum** ✹✹✹, the **Temple of Artemis** ✹, **St. John's Basilica** ✹✹✹ and the **House of the Virgin Mary** ✹✹✹. If you have your own car, have dinner up in the village of **Şirince** ✹✹.

See the "Ephesus" section, beginning on p. 207, for all listings.

Day ❺: Pamukkale's Travertine Terraces

You'll need a whole day for a visit to **Pamukkale** ✹✹, which should include a visit to the **travertines** ✹✹ and the archaeological site of **Hierapolis** ✹✹, plus a dip in the effervescent **Sacred Pool** ✹✹✹. If you've got your own wheels, stop along the way at the impressive ruins of **Aphrodisias** ✹✹.

See the "Pamukkale & Hierapolis" section, beginning on p. 224, for all listings.

Day ❻: Three Greek Sites

Dedicate the day to exploring the more neighboring ancient sites of **Priene** ✹✹, **Miletus** ✹✹, and **Didyma** ✹✹ (p. 218, 219, and 219) on a leisurely drive down to **Bodrum** ✹✹✹.

Day ❼: Bodrum and Beyond

On your last day in Turkey, you'll have to decide whether you want to relax on a beach or maintain your holiday in the fast lane. Either way, you should schedule a visit to the **Underwater Archaeology**

Museum ✹✹✹, located in the conspicuous and imposing **St. Peter's Castle** ✹✹✹. And although there's not much left of the supposedly wondrous **Mausoleum of Halicarnassus,** you'll have to do some impressive tap-dancing to explain to your friends why you didn't go. (It'll be quick, I promise.) Do both of these things early, to leave plenty of time to drive out to **Gümüşlük** ✹✹, the as-of-yet unspoiled waterside village and site of submerged ancient ruins. There's a tiny beach there too, although better beaches are located all along the peninsula, particularly around Yalıkavak and Turgutreis. (If you prefer a beach closer to home, head over to the crowded resort beaches at Gümbet, the bay adjacent to downtown Bodrum.)

See the "Bodrum" section, beginning on p. 230, for all listings.

Or you might be tempted by the landscape of Cappadocia:

PLAN B:

Day ❹: Cappadocia's Fairy Chimneys and Monastic Caves

Take an early domestic flight to **Cappadocia** ✹✹✹. If you're arriving in Kayseri, it's about an hour's drive into any of the towns in the region. Rent a car and begin your visit in the rock-cut monastery of **Zelve Valley** ✹, being careful not to slip during one of the more challenging cave climbs (climbing not obligatory). Depart Zelve, following signs for the **open-air museum of Göreme** ✹✹✹, with its frescoed churches and fairy chimneys. Follow the road into the modern section of the village, and have a bite to eat at the Orient Restaurant. Spend some time in the bazaar behind the *otogar*, then head out for a visit to the rock city of **Üçhisar** ✹✹✹. Climb up to the top of the fortress for a splendid panoramic view of the entire region, second only to a sunrise balloon ride, do some shopping at the base of the fortress, then head back to your hotel for some old-fashioned Turkish conversation and a glass of tea.

See chapter 8, "Cappadocia & the Interior," for all listings.

Day ❺: Cappadocia's Underground Cities

Set out early in the morning for the **underground cities** ❀❀❀ of Kaymaklı and Derinkuyu, where you will work up an appetite ascending and descending hundreds of underground steps. Drive the short distance to Belisırma, one of the access points for entry into the **Ihlara Valley** ❀. Before setting out on your hike, stop at one of the combination restaurant-and-camping sites for a rustic riverside lunch. After lunch, head over to the village of **Güzelyurt** ❀, wander through the valley, and poke through the village's own underground city. Finish up with dinner at the open buffet at the Kaya Hotel in Üçhisar, unless your hotel offers dinner on the premises.

See chapter 8, "Cappadocia & the Interior," for all listings.

Day ❻: Cappadocia: Land of Beautiful Horses

Experience the **valleys of Cappadocia** ❀❀❀ firsthand with a horseback-riding tour or a hike through the valleys. Have lunch at the Greek House in Mustafapaşa and spend the rest of the day around **Avanos** hunting for ceramics or shopping in Ürgüp for carpets, traditional keepsakes, or silver. Try to manage your time so that you're in town for the 9pm showing of the **Whirling Dervishes** at the 12th-century caravansary.

See chapter 8, "Cappadocia & the Interior," for all listings.

Day ❼: Ankara: Pre- and Post-Republican

Take this day to drive to and visit **Ankara**, from where you can arrange to fly home via Istanbul. Begin your time in Ankara around the ancient **citadel** ❀, starting with the remarkable **Museum of Anatolian Civilizations** ❀❀❀ (which also has a great gift shop). A few steps up the hill opposite the entrance to the fortress is the restored **Çengelhan,** the 16th-century caravansary now housing the **Rahmi Koç Science Museum.** Spend an hour wandering around the inside of the citadel, then head left outside the entrance you came in through and work your way through the copper, antiques, and carpet shops on the steeply cobbled streets heading to the daily market on **Çıkrıkçılar Caddesi.** From the bottom of Çıkrıkçılar Caddesi you will find yourself back in the heart of Ulus. From here, take a taxi to the Atatürk Mausoleum and Museum at **Anıtkabir** ❀❀. Once finished, have dinner at one of the restaurants off of Tünalı Hilmi, then call it a day.

See chapter 9, "Ankara," for all listings.

2 The Best of Turkey in 2 Weeks

Follow the suggestions for the 1-week itinerary for the first week. Then assess how much time and energy you want to put into travel and what your travel goals are. Outdoor activities, historic ruins, and extraordinary natural sites converge **along the coast between Antalya and Fethiye,** which is where I recommend you spend the remainder of your stay. If you're arriving from "Plan B" (Cappadocia), you can start your Turquoise Coastal Tour in Antalya (the drive takes about 5½ hours from Cappadocia; you can also fly via Istanbul) and follow these suggestions beginning with day 14 and working backward. Or fly into Dalaman beginning at the top, in Fethiye. In either case, you'll lose a day, unfortunately, either at the airport or on the road.

Day ❽: Fly & Drive to Fethiye

Assuming you have any time left over after your travels, spend the day wandering around the old city of **Fethiye,** shopping, eating, and taking a *hamam* break. Visit the **Roman theater** and the rock-cut **Lycian tombs** ✪✪ of ancient Telmessos. Have dinner at Meğri Restaurant in the center of the old town, and then have a drink at Türkü Evi, a characteristic Turkish pub.

See the "Fethiye & Ölüdeniz" section, beginning on p. 263, for listings.

Days ❾ & ❿: Blue Waters and Stunning Scenery

Take a few hours in the National Park area (**Ölüdeniz, or the Blue Lagoon** ✪✪✪), where you can swim in the lagoon that graces the cover of every tourism brochure on Turkey's Mediterranean. From the waterfront of **Belcekız Beach** ✪✪✪, hop on one of the few daily boat taxis for the half-hour trip to **Butterfly Valley** ✪✪✪, where you can either test out another beach or hike back toward the head of the gorge and the waterfalls. If you abhor crowds (and have a car or scooter), drive up past the ghost village of Kayaköy to the secluded and stunning **Gemiler Beach** ✪✪✪. On the way back, stop off at Kayaköy ✪✪✪ for a haunting sunset, then grill your own wild boar in the garden restaurant of Cin Bal. On day 10, take the "**12-Island Tour**" ✪✪, a daylong minicruise to watery caves and breathtaking coves where you can swim ashore for a close-up view of abandoned ruins or, if you've had enough of beautiful blue waters, take this opportunity to visit the 18km (11-mile) gorge of **Saklıkent** ✪✪.

See the "Fethiye & Ölüdeniz" section, beginning on p. 263, for listings.

Days ⓫, ⓬, ⓭ & ⓮: The Lovely Lycian Coast

Leave Fethiye early to allow time to explore the ruins of **Xanthos** ✪✪ and **Patara** ✪✪ (and perhaps spend a few hours on **Patara Beach** ✪✪ on your way east). There are a number of points along the coast that are worthy of a stopover; these are generally limited by the location of your hotel. I recommend an overnight in either **Kaş** ✪✪, Olympos or, if you can hold out for a late arrival after a full day of exploration, in Antalya. Places to stop along the way? **Kekova Bay** ✪✪✪, where ancient Lycian tombs tumble into the sea. Take a boat taxi over to the idyllic village of **Kale** ✪✪ (ancient Simena) for a lunch of fresh fish with your feet dangling in the reeds, and a short walk up to the castle. **Olympos** ✪ is another one of my favorite destinations, located on the outskirts of the small beachfront village of **Çıralı** ✪✪. It's also a good starting place for a short walk along the **Lycian Way.** An afternoon picnic and stroll through ancient Roman ruins are even more delightful than imaginable at **Phaselis** ✪✪✪, where a pine tree forest meets a particularly lovely trio of harbors. Finish up in **Antalya** ✪✪, either with some last-minute shopping in the meandering streets of **Kaleiçi,** in the **Antalya Museum** ✪✪✪, or curled up on a cushion at one of the choice beach clubs now lining the pebbled waterfront of **Konyaaltı** ✪✪✪.

See chapter 7, "The Turquoise & Mediterranean Coasts" for all listings.

4

Istanbul

Rarely will a visit to Turkey exclude the burgeoning, chaotic, confused, messy, muddled, and glorious wonder that is **Istanbul** ⚘⚘⚘. Istanbul is home to a layering of civilization on civilization, of empire built on empire. It's as momentous as Rome, as captivating as Paris, and as exotic as Bangkok (this last is potentially a bad thing).

A city that straddles Europe and Asia, Istanbul is a symbol of greatness, coveted historically by everyone from Xerxes all the way down the historical dateline through World War I, when Russia was green with envy over the possibilities of what free passage through the Bosphorus Straits could do for its economy. Even today, foreign commerce gets a free ride as hundreds of thousands of sometimes oversize and hazardous ships stream up and down this epic waterway.

The traditions inherited from 2,500 years of history are most evident in the Old City, known as Old Stamboul or Sultanahmet. A stroll through this historic peninsula will reveal ancient Roman hippodromes, peristyles, and aqueducts, the greatest excesses of the Byzantine Empire, the mystique and power of the Ottoman Empire, and the relentless hassling by the merchant class. As a religious center (heart of the Greek Orthodox Church as well as the Islamic faith for centuries), Istanbul is the custodian of one of the world's most important cultural heritages and home to some of the world's most opulent displays of art and wealth. Early Greek civilization left us the building blocks for Rome and Byzantium, which swathed these earlier foundations in rich mosaics and left its mark in monuments such as the Hippodrome and Ayasofya. Even Fatih Mehmet II was astounded at the beauty of the city he had finally conquered. The Ottoman dynasty redirected the city's fortunes into the imperial majesty of undulating domes and commanding minarets, and the sumptuousness of Topkapı Palace.

Across the Golden Horn is the modern heart of the city, heir to the future of the country, pulsating with all the electricity of a cutting-edge international metropolis. Although the political capital sits safely in the heartland, this part of Istanbul projects itself into the world as Turkey's ambassador of art, entertainment, music, and education.

Today Istanbul is home to 14+ million of the 65 million people living in Turkey, many of whom are poor village folk who've migrated to the big city out of economic need. Over brunch, the residents of the more prosperous neighborhoods along the Bosphorus revile the poor wedged into the squalid back streets of Galata, while the religious fundamentalists of the Fatih neighborhood stare out through their veils in disapproval. All of the contradictions of a complex society in transition converge in Istanbul; the city is a microcosm of the tug-of-war between East and West and the "haves" and the "have-nots." Many of these have-nots develop get-rich-quick schemes to capitalize on the traffic brought in by the city's monumental past. It's a cold, calculating, and cruel world out there, but with a little mental preparedness, one that can be easily overcome. In Rome, preadolescent gypsies prey on tourists; in New York, it's the street dice men; and in Istanbul, it's anybody multilingual in Sultanahmet.

Yet, however nonrepresentative Istanbul is of Turkey as a whole, however unscrupulous the merchants can be, and however disinterested much of the population may be over the city's fantastic roots, Istanbul is so exotic, wonderful, complex, and utterly monumental, that once seen, it's impossible to break free from its spell.

1 Orientation

ARRIVING

BY PLANE

Istanbul's **Atatürk International Airport** (② 0212/663-6400; www.ataturkairport. com) opened its doors in February 2000 next to the old and outdated Atatürk International Airport (now serving domestic flights), in Yeşilköy. The airport boasts a 24-hour pharmacy, a clinic, and a kids' playroom (freeing you up to shop or get a massage). New arrivals must first obtain an entry visa at the windows adjacent to the immigration booths; remember to have the appropriate fee ready (see "Visitor Information, Entry Requirements & Money" in chapter 2, "Planning Your Trip to Turkey"). I repeat: *there is no need to obtain a visa prior to your arrival in Turkey.*

There are two tourist information desks; several car-rental desks (including Avis, Sixt, Hertz, Budget, Europcar, and National); Türkiye Iş Bankası for on-the-spot money changing; and an ATM compatible with the Cirrus, PLUS, Visa, and MasterCard networks, all located on the lower level.

The best way to get to the city center from the airport is by taxi. A taxi into Sultanahmet should cost around 16YTL ($12) and a ride into Taksim around 20YTL ($15), depending on traffic and whether or not you got the scenic route. If you're on a budget, take advantage of the newly completed train connection between the airport (downstairs next to the international arrivals terminal; 1.15YTL/85¢) and Zeytinburnu, where you can connect above ground to the tramway into Sultanahmet (or the Grand Bazaar, or Eminönü; 1.15YTL/85¢). Alternatively, **Havaş** operates a shuttle bus every 30 minutes from just outside the airport exit to the Taksim neighborhood (daily 6am–11pm). Be sure not to get off at Aksaray, the seedy first stop. The fare from the airport to Taksim is 8YTL ($6) and the ride takes approximately 30 minutes, but it's still a short taxi or a haul up a load of steps to the tramway from the drop-off point to your hotel.

Because many hotels offer free airport pickup and transfer back to the hotel for stays of 3 days or longer, check to see if you will even need to navigate the public transport options outside the airport terminal before your departure.

For return tips to the airport from Sultanahmet, you can now reserve a seat on one of the regularly scheduled minivan shuttle departures for 5YTL ($3.50). Signs advertising the service are posted in most budget hotels; if you don't see a sign, ask your receptionist to call for you.

BY TRAIN

Sirkeci Station (② 0212/511-5888) has been serving train passengers arriving (and departing) Istanbul from European cities for over a century, and has served as a model

Frommer's Favorite Istanbul Experiences

- **Experiencing the *Hamam* (Turkish Bath):** Go for broke and sign up for the skin sloughing and massage.
- **Hearing a Performance of the Ottoman Mehter Band:** The underappreciated Military Museum in Harbiye puts on two half-hour daily performances of what was once the avant-garde of the fearless and brutal Ottoman army.
- **Having a Drink in the Courtyard of the Old Prison Walls:** The former house of nightmares is now the gardens of the Four Seasons Hotel, where you can relax over a *rakı* (aniseed-flavored spirit) and admire the lookout towers.
- **Eating Your Way Through Ortaköy:** The neighborhood is particularly vibrant on a summer evening, with the lights twinkling beneath the Bosphorus Bridge. The streets behind the mosque are a food fair of Turkish fast food, or choose a spot at one of the many popular cafes.
- **Soaking Up the Atmosphere at the Pierre Loti Café:** The views of the Golden Horn from this hilltop make the trip to Pierre Loti worth the detour. Take a walk through the picturesque cemetery adjacent to the cafe.
- **Immersing Yourself in the History of the Pera Palas Hotel:** A drink in the legendary Orient Bar, a ride in one of the very first elevators, a visit to room no. 411, and a walk through the venerated Atatürk Room will transport you to another century. The patisserie is worth a stop, too, and for 8YTL ($6), you can have your very own key to Agatha Christie's former room.
- **Taking a Tour Through Dolmabahçe Sarayı:** The members of the tour group are almost as entertaining as the tour itself. The great equalizer has to be the plastic blue booties mandatory for admittance into the

for railway stations throughout central Europe. A tram stop is immediately outside the station entrance; ask your hotel if there is a tram stop located nearby.

The **Haydarpaşa Station** in Kadıköy on the Asian side (© 0216/336-0470) is the end of the line for trains arriving from Anatolia; there's a ferry landing just outside the station with service to Eminönü, Karaköy, Yenikapı, Avcılar, and Bakırköy.

VISITOR INFORMATION

In addition to offices at the airport (© 0212/663-0793) and in Sirkeci Train Station (© 0212/511-5888), you may stumble upon a tourist information office in one of the many tourist hubs around town. The location in Sultanahmet Meydanı (© 0212/518-1802) is pretty handy, as are the ones in the Hilton Hotel Arcade (© 0212/233-0592), in Beyazit Meydanı (near the Grand Bazaar; © 0212/522-4902), and at the Karaköy Seaport (© 0212/249-5776). If you're out and about and need help, contact the passably multilingual Tourism Police at © 0212/527-4503.

All of the airlines with a presence in Turkey can be found on Cumhuriyet Caddesi in Taksim, except for the odd exceptions such as KLM or El Al, which have offices in

palace, but a look at the palace's crystal staircase and superb *hamam* will remind you of the delineation between the haves and the have-nots.

- **Wandering the Streets Behind the Egyptian Spice Market:** It's just as much fun outside as it is inside the market, where purveyors of produce set their prepared foods out on the streets for the local lunch crowd. Bring wet wipes.
- **Hunting the Labyrinthine Corridors of the Grand Bazaar:** When the salesman turns away from you in disgust, you've learned the bottom price for that item. Find another stall selling the same thing and conclude the transaction in the old-fashioned Turkish way: with a handshake and a *"güle güle"* (goodbye).
- **Crossing the Galata Bridge on Foot from Karaköy to Eminönü:** Fishermen line the railings above, while dinner (or tea, or backgammon) is served below as the majestic and inspiring silhouettes of the Süleymaniye, Rüstem Paşa, and Yeni Camii loom in the distance. If you wait till after sunset, you get to see the seagulls circling the minarets.
- **Taking a Cruise Up the Bosphorus:** This time-honored boat trip crosses from Europe to Asia and back again every 15 minutes. Float in the wake of Jason and the Argonauts, Constantine the Great, and others, and imagine the battles that took place between these shores.
- **Dining at Asitane:** Overload on *kebaps* (kabobs) and *köfte* (meatballs). All the restaurants bill themselves as "Ottoman," but few of them can actually boast of having translated the recipes from the kitchens of Topkapı.
- **Noshing Waterside at Eminönü:** For 12 to 14 hours a day, fresh fish is grilled quayside and presented for a spectacular 1.15YTL (85¢) by a gracious man in traditional costume. Grab your sandwich and step aside; the condiments are to the right on the railing.

Nişantaşı. Contact numbers in Istanbul for the major airlines are: **Air Canada** (© 0212/334-2920 or 0212/252-6544), **American Airlines** (© 0212/219-8223), **British Airways** (© 0212/234-1300), **Delta Airlines** (© 0212/310-2000), **KLM** (© 0212/368-3333), **Qantas** (© 0212/219-8223), and **Turkish Airlines** (© 444-0849 toll-free or 0212/663-6300 at the airport, © 0212/252-1106 in Taksim).

CITY LAYOUT

Istanbul is the only city in the world on two continents, split down the middle by the mighty Bosphorus Straits. To the east of the waterway is the **Asian side,** a predominantly residential retreat with little of the chaos of its European counterpart. The modern business district of Taksim and the historic peninsula of the Old City occupy the **European side** of the Bosphorus, separated by the picturesque **Golden Horn** estuary and connected by a number of bridges and by ferry. While the major sightseeing draw is over in the Old City, you should plan to give at least equal time to the modern heart of Istanbul, essential in gaining a balanced picture of the many facets of the city, and of Turkey.

⟨Value Airport Transport on the Cheap

Many hotels are now offering free pickup at the airport for stays over 3 days. Check to see if yours is one of them.

HOW TO FIND AN ADDRESS   Addresses in Turkey name the major thoroughfare followed by a logical walk-through of the smaller avenues until you get to the actual street address. Of course, in villages, where there are no major thoroughfares, you'll see a lot of the word *mahallesi,* which means, roughly, neighborhood. For example, if you're trying to find the Hotel Avicenna, located at Mimar Mehmet Ağa Caddesi, Amiral Tafdil Sok. 31–33, Sultanahmet/Istanbul, isolate the Sultanahmet neighborhood on the map of Istanbul and look for Mimar Mehmet Ağa Caddesi, one of the main streets. Next, look for a cross street by the name of Amiral Tafdil Sokağı and you will find the hotel at numbers 31–33. (In this case, the hotel takes up two old Ottoman houses.) In many cases, there is another number after the street address following a *"/"* which specifies the floor on which a place is located—usually in the case of apartments, Internet cafes, and other entities not located on the ground floor. Another handy word is *karşısı,* which means *across from,* as in *Isabey Camii karşısı Serin Sokak, Selçuk* (across from the Isabey Mosque on Serin St., in Selçuk).

Free maps are available at any tourist information office. Also available for purchase in bookstores are maps with clear and easily identifiable main attractions, but the smaller streets are left nameless, if included at all. None of the maps mentioned above are 100% accurate, but you may not even notice because signs are posted everywhere for museums, hotels, and restaurants, and there will be plenty of people on the street offering to give you a hand. Asking directions is part of the local culture and a great way to get local tips.

ISTANBUL'S NEIGHBORHOODS IN BRIEF

European Side

Yes, Virginia, Istanbul is in Europe. This fact is more than obvious in the modern, pulsating heart of the city known as Taksim Square and in the sprawl of surrounding neighborhoods. Technically, the entire district is called **Beyoğlu,** although colloquially it refers to the neighborhood formerly known as **Pera** (the turn-of-the-20th-century corner of the city that is today centered around the Pera Hotel). But Beyoğlu can also (confusingly) refer to the neighborhoods of **Karaköy, Galata, Tünel, Taksim, Nişantaşı,** and **Çukurçuma,** to name just a few. So as not to confuse my readers with a short description of every corner of Istanbul,

it's important to know that neighborhoods generally bear the name of a major landmark, and that neighborhood delineations are not that clearcut. All you need to know is that today, Beyoğlu attracts artists, diplomats, expat journalists, and just plain commuters along its streets full of gentrified cafes, restaurants, bars, discos, and brightly lit pastry shops. It's also helpful to know that if Beyoğlu is the heart and soul of modern Istanbul, then **Istiklal Caddesi** is its lifeline. This hectic shopping street bisects the district from Taksim to Tünel, where the street disappears amid narrower streets heading downhill past the Galata Tower and down to Karaköy,

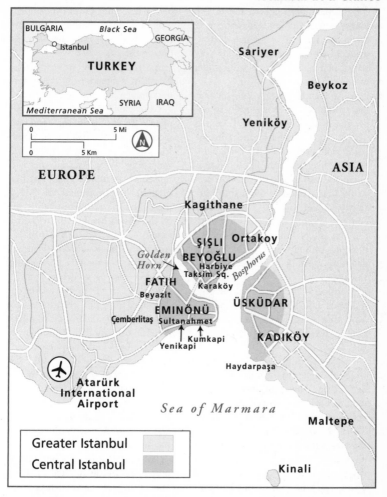

the Golden Horn, and the Galata Bridge. But I'm getting ahead of myself. Let's start at the very beginning.

Proudly standing at the head of Istiklal Caddesi is **Taksim Square.** Popular culture thrives here, a magnet for radicals with no other outlet, including a subculture of transvestites, recently made popular by various television personalities, in the neighborhoods around the square. Nightclubs, seedy bars, and Internet cafes take up a

good amount of local real estate, or at least whatever the high-rise hotels left undeveloped. Standing at the center of **Taksim Square** is a statue of Atatürk and the founding fathers of Turkey, representing on one side the War of Independence and on the other the Republic. The Atatürk Cultural Center (Atatürk Kültür Merkezi) mars the skyline looking more like a condenser of an air-conditioning unit than the grand opera house that it is. In addition to the

State Opera and Ballet, the AKM houses the Symphony Orchestra and the State Theatre Company. Performances by outside companies are presented here along with art exhibitions in the galleries.

A concentration of full-service, high-rise hotels targeting businesspeople makes the area around Taksim a perfect place for bustle and convenience, not to mention the availability of a proper cappuccino. The location is also connected to a transportation network that includes the cable car/tramway along Istiklal Caddesi that connects Taksim Square with Tünel, the very short funicular at Tünel, a plethora of municipal buses, and a daunting network of *dolmuşes* (minivan-type public transportation). Unfortunately, the area also attracts the indigents and pilferers of Istanbul, so leave your valuables in the hotel and stick to the main avenues after the sun goes down.

Istiklal Caddesi ends at **Tünel,** which also refers to the one-stop funicular called Tünel; to make matters worse, both the upper and lower entrances of the funicular are called Tünel. To avoid confusion, I refer to the area around the upper entrance as Tünel and the lower as Karaköy. If you decide to take the funicular up or down, you'll be missing one of Istanbul's more characteristic neighborhoods—known as **Galata.** Galata historically referred to the fortified area between the Atatürk and Galata bridges and extended up from the shoreline to the Galata Tower. Istanbul's earliest settlements were found in and around Galata, today a hodgepodge of steeply sloping streets radiating from the tower. Where Karaköy and Galata merge, you'll find a wealth of architectural monuments left by the European communities that thrived

here during the Ottoman period, as well as a small community of street urchins and—on the fringes—at least one brothel.

At the bottom of the hill is **Karaköy,** a functionally messy transport hub and essentially home to a guild of plumbing and electricity suppliers. Recent additions (and well-received upgrades) include the Istanbul Modern, as well as the tea gardens and waterpipe cafes located near the museum's entrance. The northern/modern neighborhoods of Beyoğlu meet the city's southern/historic sister on the **Galata Bridge,** which spans the estuary of the **Golden Horn.** The structure is in its umpteenth incarnation and serves not only as a thoroughfare but also as a destination. The lower level of the bridge was recently developed to house restaurants, bars, and even backgammon cafes, offering the visitor yet another irresistible viewfilled venue. On the southern shore of the Golden Horn is the **Old City,** which refers to the open-air museum enclosed within the **ancient city walls.** It encompasses the districts of Eminönü and Fatih, whose names are also attached to neighborhoods within the districts.

For visitors, the neighborhood and port of **Eminönü** (located in the district of the same name), which borders the Golden Horn along the northeastern shore of the historic peninsula, is synonymous with the Egyptian Spice Bazaar. But for a glimpse of the true color of this wild and wonderful city, visitors would do well to explore the frenetic passageways around the bazaar. (Head uphill behind the market long enough and you're sure to arrive at the Grand Bazaar.)

Sirkeci extends eastward from Eminönü to the streets around the train station, top-heavy with electronics, bookstores, office supply stores, and fast-food joints. The advantage of staying in Sirkeci is that if you're getting around by taxi, you won't have to sit in as much traffic, plus the main attractions of Sultanahmet are only a few minutes' walk away. The downside? A nighttime stroll may be met with inquiries as to how much you charge. (Men get "You want woman?" instead.)

Up the hill from Sirkeci is the neighborhood of **Sultanahmet,** centered around the Blue Mosque and the Aya-sofya, two massive edifices challenging each other from opposite ends of Sultanahmet Park. The streets south of the Blue Mosque heading down toward the **Cankurtaran** train stop are oddly neglected, given that here is where you will find the truest representation of the progress the city has made in recent years. (It's also ripe for robbings, so try to walk back here in groups.) Real estate is being snapped up at a brisk rate, and dilapidated shacks are being transformed into wonderful little special-category pensions that offer a family-style Turkish welcome.

The main avenue of **Divanyolu** (whose name changes to Yeniçeriler Caddesi and then Ordu Caddesi) bisects the Old City and heads west from Sultanahmet Park past the **Grand Bazaar.** The road splits at the intersection of Aksaray; the tramway, which follows Divanyolu, continues along the southernmost avenue (Millet Caddesi), while the northern fork becomes the major thoroughfare Adnan Menderes Bulvarı.

The western region of the historic peninsula, which roughly extends west of Aksaray, is known as **Fatih,** a neighborhood known for its religiously fervent character and recognizable for the chadors, floor-length cotton robes, and skullcaps worn by its residents. Here, it's not uncommon for a restaurant to withhold alcoholic beverages from the locals or ban them altogether. Progressive Istanbulers cringe at the mention of your staying in this neighborhood, but cultural immersion aside, the Fatih district is extremely spread out and farther than you need to go to base yourself—not to mention there's not a decent hotel in sight.

To end this tour at the very beginning, I'm going to bring you back to Taksim. Bordering the Bosphorus above Taksim is **Beşiktaş,** a splendid waterside tract where the last sultans chose to build their homes. Several five-star hotels in the area are trying to duplicate the royal experience and are damn near succeeding. From the Çira-ğan Palace north to the Bosphorus Bridge begins a parade of destinations for the beautiful and not so beautiful people, with a popular stopover at **Ortaköy,** a vibrant seaside landing with a festive atmosphere that's pervasive year-round. A number of fishing villages transformed into bourgeois residential neighborhoods follow the Bosphorus road north of Ortaköy, including **Bebek, Arnavutköy,** and **Emirgan;** you can visit these by hopping on a local bus or sightsee from the bow of a Bosphorus ferry.

Asian Side

The Asian side is a quiet and predominantly upper-class residential area

---

Fun Fact **Did You Know?**

Beşiktaş, meaning "cradle stone," is named after the crib in which Jesus was born, which was thought to have been brought here by early Christians.

interspersed with a smattering of architecturally notable mosques and synagogues. The tree-lined shopping section along **Bağdat Caddesi** attracts a local clientele, but frankly has nothing exceptional to offer a foreigner accustomed to a cosmopolitan afternoon out. **Üsküdar** covers a lot of territory worthy of a student of architecture; otherwise, stick to the already impressive structures on the European side. **Beylerbeyı Sarayı,** the summer palace of the sultans, commands the right banks of Üsküdar above the Bosphorus Bridge, and just up the hill at **Çamlıca** is an incomparable view of the Bosphorus.

2 Getting Around

BY PUBLIC TRANSPORTATION

THE BUS   Metropolitan buses in Istanbul are frequent, comprehensive, and economical. The final destination of the bus is indicated above the front windshield, with a selection of major stops listed on the side of the bus next to the entrance, not much help if you aren't familiar with the basic layout of the city. Always check with the driver before getting on to make sure the bus is going in the direction you need, and once boarded, ask your neighbor frequently when to get off. Some of the more useful major hubs are at Eminönü, Taksim, and Beşiktaş. Tickets are sold at the major hubs or on the bus—if you're lucky enough to get one with a "cashier" onboard. At press time, one ride cost about 1.35YTL ($1).

One of the most useful bus routes is the no. 14, which runs between Taksim and Sultanahmet approximately every 35 minutes (service on Sun only runs from about 10:55am–5pm). The bus stop in Sultanahmet is located on Sultanahmet Parkı, across from the tourist information office.

THE *DOLMUŞ*   The main *dolmuş* stands are located in Taksim, Sirkeci, and Aksaray, and connect to points all over the city. *Dolmuşes* are often more direct than metropolitan buses and cheaper than taxis, cutting down on time and leaving more money in your pocket. When boarding, tell the driver your destination, and ask how much it will be *(ne kadar?).* For shorter distances, 2YTL to 3YTL ($1–$2) should cover it. The driver will drop you off at your destination, but if you want to get off sooner, say *"Inmek istiyorum, lütfen,"* the short version of "I want to get off" with a "please" stuck on the end.

Transport Made Easy with the Akbil

Istanbul's metropolitan transportation, although not streamlined, is getting better. Buses, the tramway, the metro, and seabuses (not the ferries, which are privately owned) have been outfitted to accept the "Akbil," a refillable contraption that fits into a button on the turnstiles. Akbils are available for purchase at booths displaying the Akbil logo in Taksim Square, Eminönu[um], and Aksaray for the initial outlay of around 2.75YTL ($2). For extended visits, a modest per-ride savings is a bonus to the convenience, saving you up to 1.25YTL (90¢) each time you use it, and when you're ready to leave, you can return the Akbil for your original deposit. Pre-loaded Akbils can also be purchased for a day (4YTL/$2.90), weekly (20YTL/$570), bi-weekly (35YTL/$26) or monthly (60YTL/$44).

THE TRAMWAY When the tram from Eminönü to Zeytinburnu was built and inaugurated in 1991, the planners had overlooked one very important detail: money collection. Passengers rode for free for 1 year while the system installed booths and printed tickets. The system has grown up quite a bit since then; the City recently extended the tramway from Eminönü to Beşiktaş. For visitors staying in Sultanahmet, the tram can be your best friend, connecting the Egyptian Spice Bazaar (stop: Eminönü) and the buses of Eminönü with Sirkeci Train Station (stop: Sirkeci), Sultanahmet (stop: Sultanahmet), and the Grand Bazaar (stop: Çemberlitaş or Beyazit) for 1.35YTL ($1) per ride. Token *(jeton)* booths are located at the entrance to the turnstiles; akbils can be refilled in Eminönü or Taksim.

Another tramway makes the walk along Istiklal Caddesi shorter, connecting Taksim and Tünel just when your feet are ready to fall off. This aboveground streetcar costs 1.35YTL ($1) and makes stops in front of the Hüseyn Ağa Camii, at Galatasaray High School/Flower–Fish Market, and in Beyoğlu at Nutru Sokak (in front of the Turkiye Iş Merkezi). (*Note:* At press time, the tramway is suspended due to road construction).

THE METRO/UNDERGROUND Istanbul's subway isn't very ambitious, but then again, this isn't a city you recklessly start digging up. More akin to an underground funicular, the subway known as Tünel connects the neighborhood of the same name at the end of Istiklal Caddesi with Karaköy and the Galata Bridge for 1.35YTL ($1). Tünel trains run Monday through Saturday from 7am to 9pm and Sunday from 7:30am to 9pm. From Karaköy you can catch a bus going to Eminönü on the other side, or walk the span of this scenic bridge to connect with the tramway (or simply wander around the back streets of Eminönü and Sirkeci).

A new and modern underground was recently completed, connecting Taksim with its northern suburbs. Because there's *always* traffic on these roads, hopping on the metro will not only save money, but also time. The metro runs from Taksim to Levent (Akmerkez is only a short cab ride away), making stops in Osmanbey (walking distance to Nişantaşı), Şişli/Meçidiyeköy (commercial center), and Gayrettepe (more commerce). The metro is open from around 6:30am until midnight and costs 1.35YTL ($1) per ride.

The metro extension connecting the airport to town is now complete, providing access at Yenikapı (just outside the airport) to Aksaray via a roundabout route via the *otogar* (bus station). (If you're destination is Sultanahmet, exit the metro at ground level, transfer to the tramway, which is but a short walk away, and hop on any train marked EMINÖNÜ.) Eventually, the line will provide a direct connection between Aksaray, Galata, and Taksim.

THE FERRY & SEABUS Commuter ferries and seabuses shuttle passengers across the Bosphorus between Europe and Asia, as well as to the nearby Princes' Islands. Some of the more useful crossings are between Eminönü and Kadıköy; Eminönü and Karaköy; Karaköy and Kadıköy; Beşiktaş and Üsküdar; Beşiktaş and Kadıköy; and Karaköy and Haydarpaşa, this last crossing indispensable for transfers to the train and points east.

The ferry that takes the time-honored cruise up the Bosphorus leaves from Eminönü, making stops at Beşiktaş (near Dolmabahçe Palace and the Çirağan Palace) on its crisscross pattern up the channel. Fares and daily departure times (4YTL/$3; departing 10:35am and 1:35pm; confirm times, as they may change) are posted on or near the ticket window.

Tips   **Take a Quick Cruise**

For a do-it-yourself Bosphorus cruise, ferries depart from Eminönü Pier #3 at 10:35am and 1:35pm daily for the 2-hour excursion to the final stop at Anadolu Kavağı. Return ferries depart from Anadolu Kavağı at 3 and 5pm, but a time-saving option is to get off at the last stop, have lunch in one of the touristy but atmospheric fish restaurants on the quay, and take a bus back to Taksim. A one-way ticket on the ferry costs 4.50YTL/3.30 (7.50YTL/$5.55 round-trip).

Long-distance ferries or the faster seabuses provide transportation to the Princes' Islands (from Eminönü and Kabataş) and to points along the southern coast of the Marmara Sea. If you're interested in traveling by car to cities along the Marmara region (for example, Bursa, Çanakkale, İzmir, and points south), the easiest and quickest way is to take a car ferry or seabus from Yenikapı to Yalova (then drive to Bursa, a 50-min. trip) or from Yenikapı to Bandırma (then drive to Çanakkale or İzmir, and so on, a trip of about 1 hr., 45 min.). For information on fares and schedules for the seabuses, contact **Istanbul City Ferry Lines**, Şehir Hatları Vapurları (✆ **0212/244-4233**). For seabuses, consult the **Istanbul Deniz Otobüsleri** website (in Turkish and English) at **www.ido.com.tr** or in Istanbul call their automated information line at ✆ **0212/516-1212** (or contact the port offices directly: Bostancı ✆ 0216/410-6633, Kabataş ✆ 0212/249-1558, Kadıköy ✆ 0212/336-8819, Karaköy ✆ 0212/251-6144, and Yenikapı ✆ 0212/517-9696).

BY CAR

You have to be an extremely aggressive driver (and not just a little crazy) to drive in Istanbul. Novices will tempt an already high incidence of theft, wonder at the ignorance of fellow drivers, curse the absence of available parking, and spend too much vacation time sitting in traffic wondering which street to take. Best to avoid the hassle and instead take advantage of the cheap—if not a little less than streamlined—public transportation options.

If you do decide to disregard better judgment and good counsel, be aware that parking in Istanbul is a nightmare, with very little on-street parking and with signs written in Turkish. Aside from the day lot next to the Mosaic Museum on the fringes of Sultanahmet, forget about parking in the Old City or around Taksim unless you're a guest of one of the five-star hotels, which have spaces available in their parking garages for nominal fees. In less central areas, some side-street lots are manned with guards with a red label on their sleeves. Pay them and they will "guard" your car while you're away; or opt for a more freelance approach, where some indigent promises to keep an eye on your car for a tip. If you get towed, the fee to recover your car is about 67.5YTL ($50)—but good luck finding it, since there are more than four car pounds around the city and not a traffic cop in sight.

Apart from the car-rental counters at the airport (see "By Plane" under "Arriving" earlier in this chapter), the major car-rental companies in Istanbul are **Avis** (✆ **800/230-4898** in the U.S.; 800/272-5871 in Canada, 0216/474-1800 toll-free locally, or in the Hilton Hotel Arcade, Taksim 0212/246-5256); **Budget,** Cumhuriyet Caddesi, Taksim (✆ **800/527-0700** in the U.S., 800/268-8900 in Canada, or 0212/253-9200); and **Ekin/Hertz,** Cumhuriyet Cad. 295, Harbiye (✆ **800/654-3131** in the

U.S. or 0212/233-1020 locally). Local car-rental companies have offices concentrated on Divanyolu Caddesi in Sultanahmet and around Taksim, and tend to be a bit cheaper than the tried and true ones—a definite plus, considering a tank of gasoline can run you up to 110YTL ($80). Be sure to run a quick check of the car before departing—check the turn signals and the brakes, locate the gas cap release, and confirm your insurance coverage.

BY TAXI

Taxis are plentiful in Istanbul and are more likely to hail you than vice versa. Avoid taxis that congregate around the main tourist spots like Topkapı Palace, Ayasofya, and at the cruise ship landing in Karaköy—these are the ones adept at confusing tourists with the number of zeros on banknotes. Better to have your hotel call a cab for you, the agreement being that the hotel will continue giving the taxi stand business only as long as the drivers remain aboveboard. Similarly, when out and about, pop into the nearest hotel and have the receptionist call a taxi for you. A taxi from Sultanahmet to Taksim will cost between 6.75YTL and 14YTL ($5–$10), depending on traffic and distance, while nighttime rates are always highest. For more, see "Don't Let Taxi Drivers Take You for a Ride," in chapter 2.

FAST FACTS: Istanbul

American Express Amex has yet to establish a strong presence in Turkey, with only one general office in Istanbul for customer service at the Akbank in Elmadağ on Cumhuriyet Cad. 153 (© 0212/233-0080). Amex does provide a toll-free number within Turkey for Global Assist (© 0312/935-3601). Türk Express is the official representative of Amex Travel Related Services in Turkey, at Cumhuriyet Cad. 91/1 Elmadağ in the Hilton Hotel (© 0212/230-1515).

Babysitters Most of the larger hotels provide some type of child-care service for a fee, be it an on-site nanny or a babysitter referral.

Climate Istanbul has seen temperatures ranging from 0°F to 104°F (18°C to 40°C), but it's unlikely that you'll encounter such extremes. Summer lasts roughly from mid-June to mid-September. The city sees a sloshy 27 inches of rain annually, mostly between October and March. In spite of the cold temperatures that sweep in from the Black Sea in winter, large accumulations of snowfall are a rarity, although light dustings do occur.

Consulates The new **American Consulate** is now located at Istinye Mahallesi, Kaplıcalar Mevkii 2 (© 0212/335-9000). The **British Consulate** is back in its original, pre-terrorist bombing location at Mesrutiyet Caddesi 34, Tepebşı (Beyoglu) (© 0212/334-6400; fax 0212/334-6401).

Courier Services The post office (PTT) offers an express mail service *(acele posta servisi)*, while you may feel safer with old reliables such as DHL (© 0212/478-1000), Federal Express (© 0212/549-0404), TNT (© 0216/425-1700), or Sky Net (© 0212/253-6348). UPS has an office at Küçük Ayasofya Cad. Aksakal Sok. 14, Sultanahmet (© 0212/517-4102).

Dentist If Istanbul's new tooth hospital (© 0212/327-4020; www.dentistanbul. com) in Beşiktaş can't solve your oral problems, then the new American Hospital in Nişantaşı (✆ **0212/231-4050**) and the International Hospital in Yeşılyurt (✆ **0212/663-3000**) provide emergency dental services in an English-speaking atmosphere. Log onto http://istanbul.usconsulate.gov/visa/doctlist.html.

Emergencies Local emergency numbers are: fire ✆ **110,** police ✆ **155,** and ambulance ✆ **112.** Emergencies may also warrant a call to Medline (✆ **0212/ 282-0000,** 24 hr. a day), a private company equipped to deal with any medical crisis, including ambulance transfers (cost varies according to distance), lab tests, and home treatment (40YTL/$30). The International Hospital (see "Hospitals" below) also provides ambulance services.

Hospitals For the best local emergency care, put yourself in the hands of one of the reputed *private* hospital facilities: the American Hospital, Güzelbahçe Sokağı Nişantaşı (✆ **0212/231-4050** or 0212/311-2000); Florence Nightingale Hospital, Abidei Hürriyet Cad. 290, Şişli (✆ **0212/224-4950**); the International Hospital, Çinar Oteli Yanı, Yeşılköy (✆ **0212/663-3000**); the German Hospital, Sıraselviler Caddesi 119, Taksim (✆ **0212/293-2150**); and the Balat Jewish Hospital, Hisarönü Cad. 46–48, Fatih (✆ **0212/524-1156** or 0212/635-9280) are just a few of the establishments with reliable English-speaking staff. Don't forget that payment is required at the time of treatment.

Laundry Drop your duffel bag off at Star Laundry on Yeni Akbıyık Caddesi 18, Sultanahmet (✆ **0212/638-2302**), and start fresh for only 1.75YTL ($1.30) per kilo (2.2 lb.). The attendant will separate your whites and colors to boot. On the other side of the Golden Horn, there are a couple of laundry/dry cleaners near the Pera Palas Hotel, but the prices don't warrant circumventing the hotel service.

Newspapers & Magazines Taksim and Beyoğlu are the neighborhoods with the highest concentration of foreigners, and thus the most newsstands and bookstores carrying foreign-language publications. The *International Herald Tribune,* the *Guardian,* and the *Financial Times* are widely available in Istanbul, as are *Time* and *Newsweek.* The *Guide Istanbul* contains essential listings for tourists and is available at newsstands or provided free at some hotels. The *Turkish Daily News,* Turkey's English-language newspaper, gives a basic rundown of the day's headlines. The *Turkish Press* is more widely available along the Mediterranean Coast. If you have Internet access, log on to www.turkish dailynews.com, www.turkishpress.com, or www.zaman.com, the bilingual website of the Turkish language national paper.

Pharmacies Pharmacists in Turkey are qualified to provide some medical services beyond filling prescriptions, such as administering injections, bandaging minor injuries, and suggesting medication. During off hours, call the Chamber of Pharmacists (✆ **0212/6336-9964** or dial ✆ **118**), or go to the nearest pharmacy for postings (in Turkish) to find out which one in your neighborhood is handling the current 24-hour rotation. (One pharmacy is always open according to a rotating schedule.)

Restrooms Public restrooms are located all around town, in addition to those in public buildings such as museums. "Toilet money" in Istanbul costs about 30YKr (20¢), which occasionally includes a bonus handful of toilet paper. Flushing the toilet paper can sometimes be hazardous to the plumbing; when this is the case, you will usually see a sign above the tank requesting that you dispose of it in the nearby wastebasket.

Taxes There is a flat 18% VAT (value-added tax) incorporated into the price of everything you buy, although a few five-star hotels tack this onto their room rates.

3 Where to Stay

For someone new to Istanbul, one of the first questions you will ask yourself is "where should I make my base?" In previous editions, I unreservedly directed my readers to Sultanahmet, where old dilapidated homes converted into "Special Category" hotels created the perfect gateway to an authentic past. There have been three very important developments in the past few years. First, hotel rooms that used to cost 40€ ($50) now charge 80€ ($100) and up, for absolutely no added value. Admittedly this is primarily a disadvantage for those paying in U.S. dollars, but on principle I refuse to pay upwards of 80€ ($100) for a room that once cost me 16€ ($20). Let me put this further into perspective: The luxury five-star Hotel Ceylan Inter-Continental (reviewed below) has Internet rates as low as 133€ ($160). Second, given the enormous profit margins that a hotel can bring in, it seems as if everyone has gotten in on the act—transforming a market of family-run houses into a sea of mass-produced soulless "boutique hotels." Finally, and most disappointingly, the hassling by carpet salesmen and their ilk has reached new levels; last time I stayed in town several hotel guests opted for the safety of the hotel lobby rather than brave the irritating and stressful storm of harassment. It is therefore with a heavy heart that I recommend this neighborhood only with the admonition to book through a reputable agent, stay vigilant (for formal and informal crime), or preferably, base yourself in Beyoğlu, where hotels are managed by people schooled in hotel management (and not carpet sales), and the food and nightlife are better anyway.

The price of your hotel room generally includes breakfast and tax, although a few higher-priced hotels tack these on top of the room rate. The price categories listed in this section are to be used mainly as guidelines due to the market-driven nature of the industry. It's not uncommon, for example, for a room listed at 205€ ($250) a night to sell for significantly less through an agency. For this reason you may find fewer options under the "Inexpensive" or "Moderate" headings below.

In general, agency rates can be as much as 75% less than the rack rate, and even after the agency commissions are tacked on, you can still get a better rate than if you booked it yourself. Meanwhile, many hotels are offering special rates via the Internet that undercut even the agents, so it's important to do the legwork if you're looking to get the best rate.

For those game enough to hole up on the less-convenient-to-everything Asian side, there are two pretty amazing options that promise to mitigate the trouble of getting there and getting around. The first is the brand-new luxury boutique **Sumahan Hotel,** in Çengelköy. It's deluxeness rivals that of the Çiragan, and more amenable given that the latter's best rooms are booked more than a year in advance. The hotel provides three shuttles per day to the Kabataş docks (just below Dolmabahçe Palace). There are also commuter boats from the waterfront near the centrally located Eminönü two times daily.

The posh and luxuriously restored **Bosphorus Palace Hotel** (previously and popularly known as the Bosphorus Pasha), Yalıboyu Cad. 64, 34676, near the Beylerbeyi Palace (*©* **0216/422-0003;** fax 0216/422-0012; www.bosphoruspalace.com) is another time-honored option on the Asian side. The **Radisson SAS Bosphorus Hotel** (*©* **0212/310-1500**), Çiragan Cad. 46, 34349, on the banks of the Bosphorus Strait, opened in January 2006, and posts prices that range from a moderate 135€ ($165) to an extravagant 650€ ($790) per night.

Meanwhile, keep your eyes open for the arrival of the **new Four Seasons Bosphorus,** scheduled for 2007, which promises to provide flawless hospitality to the waterfront around Ortaköy.

EMINÖNÜ: SIRKECI & EMINÖNÜ
MODERATE

Hotel Yaşmak Sultan   This hotel, with its formulaic accommodations and Ottoman facade, will nevertheless make you grateful to the travel gods when you arrive tired, laden with luggage, and covered in plane grit. It's not on the same level as the Eresin Crown, but neither are its prices. The rooms are clean and simple and include such comforts as satellite TV and 24-hour room service. They also cater to nonsmokers, families, and people with disabilities, providing appropriate facilities or services upon request. Hotel amenities rival those at deluxe hotels and include a well-equipped fitness center, a newly renovated dry sauna, and a petite Turkish bath with marble arches and ceramic tiles.

Ebusuud Cad. 18–20, 34410 Sirkeci/Istanbul. *©* 0212/528-1343. Fax 0212/528-1348. www.hotelyasmaksultan. com. 84 units. 100€ ($122) double; 150€ ($180) suite. Rates lower Nov–Mar. AE, MC, V. Underground parking garage. **Amenities:** Restaurant; bar; fitness room; Turkish bath; sauna; 24-hr. room service; babysitting, laundry service; dry cleaning; elevator. *In room:* A/C, satellite TV, minibar, hair dryer, safe, bathtub, pillow menu.

EMINÖNÜ: IN & AROUND SULTANAHMET
VERY EXPENSIVE

Eresin Crown Hotel 🐦🐦   With its business center, conference facilities, and fully equipped meeting room, the stately Eresin Crown hopes to attract business trippers hoping to accomplish some sightseeing after-hours. Rooms are well appointed but a bit sterile, simply adorned with pale yellow and beige tones, window seats, plaster friezes, and kilims. Each has a Jacuzzi (those in the six suites have special massage mechanisms). During the building of the Eresin, Byzantine floor mosaics, marble columns, and a cistern were uncovered, artifacts later identified as belonging to the women's quarters of Justinian's palace. Altogether, the hotel recovered, registered, and now exhibits 49 historically significant museum pieces dating to the Hellenistic and Byzantine times, giving this hotel a "boutique museum" quality. From its enormous rooftop terrace, the Eresin also boasts one of the most magnificent panoramic views of Old City in Sultanahmet.

Küçük Ayasofya Cad. 40, 34400 Sultanahmet/Istanbul. *©* 0212/638-4428. Fax 0212/638-0933. www.eresin sultanahmet.com.tr. 59 units. 275€–325€ ($335–$400) double; 400€–600€ ($490–$730) suite. AE, MC, V. **Amenities:** 2 restaurants; 2 bars; business center; 24-hr. room service; laundry service; dry cleaning; elevator. *In room:* A/C, satellite and cable TV, minibar, hair dryer, safe.

Four Seasons Hotel 🐦🐦🐦   For the journalists and intellectual dissidents sentenced to a prison term in this building, a period of incarceration was something to brag about—and it still is, albeit for different reasons. After a long period of neglect, this Turkish neoclassical building located in the heart of Sultanahmet was converted from

Eminönü Hotels & Restaurants

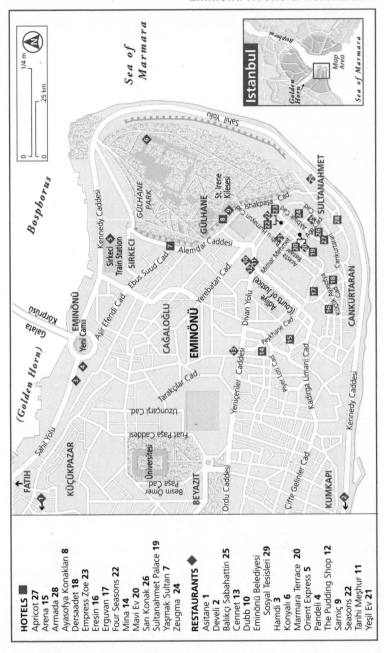

HOTELS ■
Apricot **27**
Arena **15**
Armada **28**
Ayasofya Konakları **8**
Dersaadet **18**
Empress Zoe **23**
Eresin **16**
Erguvan **17**
Four Seasons **22**
Mina **14**
Mavi Ev **20**
Sarı Konak **26**
Sultanahmet Palace **19**
Yaşmak Sultan **7**
Zeugma **24**

RESTAURANTS ◆
Asitane **1**
Develi **2**
Balkçı Sabahattin **25**
Cennet **13**
Dubb **10**
Eminönü Belediyesi
   Sosyal Tesisleri **29**
Hamdi **3**
Konyalı **6**
Marmara Terrace **20**
Orient Express **5**
Pandeli **4**
The Pudding Shop **12**
Sarnıç **9**
Seasons **22**
Tarihi Meşhur **11**
Yeşil Ev **21**

a prison into a five-star hotel, with much of the original marble and tile recycled into its present-day, elegant design. The saffron exterior is a bit severe, but the contrast within couldn't be greater. Rooms have elegant furniture all purchased locally; the architect even stayed true to tradition by applying paint as they did in the Ottoman palaces—with a spatula. The opulent and luxurious bathrooms, all with separate toilet cabin, present a formidable amount of competition for time spent sightseeing, and the king-size beds are amazingly comfy. Plus, almost all of the rooms have views of something fabulous.

Tevkifhane Sok. No. 1, 34110 Sultanahmet/Istanbul. © 800/332-3442 in the U.S., or 0212/638-8200. Fax 0212/638-8210. www.fshr.com. 65 units. High season 300€–425€ ($370–$520) double; 490€–700€ ($600–$850) suite. B&B rates are higher; rates lower Nov–Mar. AE, DC, MC, V. Complimentary valet parking. **Amenities:** Restaurant; 2 bars; fitness room; Jacuzzi; sauna; shopping arcade; 24-hr. room service; laundry service; dry cleaning; nonsmoking rooms; elevator. *In room:* A/C, satellite TV w/pay movies, minibar, hair dryer.

EXPENSIVE

Arena Hotel ✹ *Finds*   Located in an unpolished corner of Sultanahmet just steps behind the Hippodrome, the Arena Hotel is truly a diamond in the rough. The three-story hotel occupies a restored Ottoman house that has remained in the same generation for over 80 years, retaining traditional touches such as family heirloom furnishings and "grandmother Gül's caftan" in the lobby's salon. The rooms reflect the good taste of a bygone era, and feature gleaming wood floors and classic Turkish rugs. There are two suites, each with a balcony, the only two tubs in the house and a flatscreen TV. Better yet, there's an intimate little *hamam* on the basement level and a charming and reasonably priced restaurant with an alfresco extension in a trellised courtyard.

Küçükayasofya Mah. Şehit Mehmet Paşa Yokuşu Üçler Hamam Sok. 13–15, 34400 Sultanahmet/Istanbul. © 0212/458-0364. Fax 0212/458-0366. www.arenahotel.com. 27 units. 150€ ($180) double; 200€ ($245) suite. Special Internet rates according to availability. AE, DC, DISC, MC, V. Limited hotel parking on street. **Amenities:** Restaurant; Turkish bath for 10€ ($12) extra; 24-hr. room service; laundry service; dry cleaning; elevator. *In room:* A/C, satellite TV, minibar, hair dryer, safe.

Mavi Ev (Blue House) ✹   If the Blue House weren't actually painted blue, one would think the name came from the fact that the hotel is practically attached at the hip to the Blue Mosque, a stone's throw away. This hotel is a fine example of modern Turkish elegance, with its tile floors, carpets, stained glass, and understated details. Most of the rooms have stall showers, while suites have Jacuzzis. The rooftop restaurant (and bar) is especially noteworthy, if not for the food, then for the back-door viewing of the sound-and-light displays above the Blue Mosque (summer months only). The entire effect is enchanting, and you couldn't get a better view of the domes if you were standing right on top of them.

Dalbastı Sok. 14, 34400 Sultanahmet/Istanbul. © 0212/638-9010. Fax 0212/638-9017. www.bluehouse.com.tr. 27 units (25 with shower). 140€ ($170) double; 250€ ($305) suite. 15% discount for payment in cash. MC, V. Public parking for 1.65€ ($2) per day across the street. **Amenities:** Restaurant; bar; 24-hr. room service; laundry service; dry cleaning; elevator. *In room:* A/C, cable TV, minibar, hair dryer.

Sultanahmet Palace Hotel ✹   Designed in the style of a garden villa, this enchanting hotel offers visitors the best opportunity for temporary immersion into the life of an Ottoman subject, on a smaller scale, of course. This hotel features Byzantine-style hand-carved moldings above Roman terra-cotta flooring, a grand marble central staircase below a stunning half-cylinder stained-glass dome, courtyards and terrace fountains, and breathtaking views in summer of the Marmara Sea from the from the breakfast terrace. The Blue Mosque creates a fourth wall in the street-side rooms, a view so impressive that you won't mind the brutal dawn awakening. Rooms on the top floor are disappointingly small, so when reserving, try to nab a second-floor room or one of the suites, which have tiny wrought-iron balconies. In place of a shower or tub, each room comes with its own tricky but spectacular marble clad mini-*hamam* (large-size visitors and creatures of habit should avoid this hotel). Unfortunately though, a glitch in the heating system prevents them from producing any steam. A showerhead is provided, but less adventurous travelers may find the setup a bit off-putting, especially since water sprays everywhere, and remains until housekeeping arrives.

Torun Sok. 19, 34400 Sultanahmet/Istanbul. © 0212/458-0460. Fax 0212/518-6224. www.sultanahmetpalace.com. 36 units. Nov–Mar 135€ ($163) double, 285€ ($235) suite. AE, MC, V. Free parking next door. **Amenities:** Restaurant; 24-hr. room service; laundry service; dry cleaning; elevator. *In room:* A/C, satellite TV, minibar, hair dryer, Turkish bath.

MODERATE

Ayasofya Konakları ⍣   In the 1980s, the State-run Turkish Touring and Automobile Club set off a craze for historic preservation when it restored a handful of clapboard Ottoman mansions on a blissfully quiet, cobblestone street of Sultanahmet. Back then, the collection of pension-style rooms saw a veritable stampede of illustrious visitors. After more than 20 years and commensurate wear and tear (plus a new manager), the pension has grown into its stately skin: Rooms have been restored and upgraded, and many have benefited by a number of additional comforts (including air-conditioning and TV). The *konakları* also enjoy one of the city's most characteristic settings, sandwiched between the imperial outer wall of Topkapı Palace and the Ayasofya, and encompass open-air garden and terrace cafes, and an expansive garden that surrounds a wonderful *orangerie* decorated with an original Roman "holy water room."

Soğukçeşme Sok., 34400 Sultanahmet/Istanbul. © 0212/513-3660. Fax 0212/514-0213. www.ayasofyapensions. com. 64 units. 85€ ($105) double; 100€ ($122) for rooms with a view of the Ayasofya); 160€ ($195) suite. 30% discount Nov 1–Dec 21 and Jan 8–Mar 31. AE, MC, V. **Amenities:** Restaurant (see review for Sarnıç in "Where to Dine" later in this chapter); 2 bars; 24-hr. room service; laundry service; dry cleaning.

Dersaadet Oteli ⍣   In Turkish, Dersaadet means "place of felicity and beauty"— an appropriate designation for this handsome jewel fashioned in the style of a 19th-century Ottoman house. The gleaming parquet floors and the deep wooden details lend a grace to the simplicity of the rooms, most of which have a view of the Marmara Sea and Asian side, and even the smallest room in the house has a graciousness about it. A couple of the bathrooms have showers and sinks arranged in a small space like a puzzle, but all units are different, so ask ahead what to expect, or go for broke and simply opt for the recently renovated honeymoon-worthy Penthouse Suite. The two rooftop terraces, one a covered garden patio and the other an open brick and mosaic terrace, offer stunning views of the Blue Mosque and Marmara Sea.

Kapıağası Sok. No. 5, 34400 Sultanahmet/Istanbul. © 0212/458-0760. Fax 0212/518-4918. www.dersaadethotel. com. 16 units. 85€ ($105) double; 140€–220€ ($170–$270) suite. 10% discount for payment made in cash. Free airport pickup for stays of 3 nights or more. MC, V. Free parking in adjacent lot. **Amenities:** Bar; 24-hr. room service; laundry service; dry cleaning; elevator. *In room:* A/C, satellite TV, minibar, hair dryer.

Fehmi Bey   With so much "boutique hotel" competition in the neighborhood these days, it's only because Fehmi Bey recently renovated its rooms that I decided to give it a second look. Now, rooms are much better aesthetically, with upgraded bathrooms and polished original wooden floors. But except for a handful of extraordinarily large rooms, most are claustrophobic, making me question the value of this hotel in a season of high demand. I suggest booking one of the three deluxe corner rooms (nos. 103, 203, and 303), which have equally ample bathrooms. A "family room" is actually two rooms, one of which has a foldout sofa bed for kids. Otherwise, you can't beat the location (steps from everything), plus the hotel offers the added bonus of a sauna and business center. As almost all hotels in the neighborhood, this one also boasts an incredible rooftop terrace; there's also a nice little garden.

Ucler Sokak 15, 33340 Sultanahmet/Istanbul. © **0212/638-9083.** Fax 0212/518-1264. www.fehmibey.com. 34 units. 90€ ($110) double; 100€–130€ ($122–$160) suite. AE, MC, V. **Amenities:** Rooftop restaurant (summers only); bar; sauna; elevator; 24-hr. room service; laundry service; screening room; business center; secretarial services. *In room:* A/C, satellite TV, safe.

Hotel Armada ★ Located on the outer edges of Sultanahmet, the Hotel Armada is a true four-star hotel that makes a good choice for groups. (Individuals who decide to stay here should realize that it's a short yet uphill walk to all major sights.) It boasts an expansive lobby cafe, an atmospheric bar, and one of the best rooftop terraces anywhere in the neighborhood. Rooms are decorated in "Ottoman style" simplicity, with wooden chair rails, decorative painted flowers, and subdued fabrics. The bathrooms are small but functional, with a negligible amount of wear and tear around the edges. A buffet breakfast is served in a delightful penthouse atrium adjacent to the terrace (the restaurant dining room), and the fish restaurants of Kumkapı are within walking distance (as is Balıkçı Sabahattin restaurant; see "Where to Dine" later in this chapter). Weekend guests may want to request a room away from the evening entertainment activities to insulate themselves from the late-night echoes through the marble staircases.

Ahırkapı Sok. (just behind Cankurtaran), 34400 Sultanahmet/Istanbul. © **0212/638-1370.** Fax 0212/518-5060. www.armadahotel.com.tr. 110 units. 75€–85€ ($90–$105) double. Breakfast 9€ ($11). Rates are exclusive of VAT. AE, DC, MC, V. Parking. **Amenities:** 2 restaurants; 2 bars; 24-hr. room service; laundry service; dry cleaning; elevator. *In room:* A/C, satellite TV, minibar, hair dryer, safe.

Hotel Empress Zoe ★ This hotel, designed and hand-painted by the owner Anne's Greek brother-in-law, is a master creation drawing from Byzantium and Anatolia, with a little bit of Santa Fe thrown in for good measure. The hotel overlooks the crumbling remnants of the oldest *hamam* in the city, and from the rooftop terrace, the only obstruction is the Marmara Sea. Access to the rooms is via a narrow circular iron staircase—good to know if traveling light wasn't on this trip's agenda. If you do hurt your back on the way up, you'll be pleased to find extremely comfortable beds when you make it to your room. Because the hotel combines three separate houses (the most recent addition creates an annex of four garden suites), it benefits from a number of secluded courtyards and panoramic terraces. The rooftop bar is warmly draped in deeply colored Turkish kilims and blankets, and there's a fireplace for those crisp winter evenings.

Akbıyık Cad. Adliye Sok. 10, 34400 Sultanahmet/Istanbul. © **0212/518-2504.** Fax 0212/518-5699. www.emzoe. com. 19 units. 70€–100€ ($85–$122) double; 100€–140€ ($122–$170) suite. 10% discount for payment by cash or traveler's checks. MC, V. **Amenities:** 3 bars; nonsmoking rooms. *In room:* A/C, hair dryer, safe.

Hotel Erguvan ★ This is one of those new boutique hotels I spoke about earlier. The four-story building located just below the ancient retaining wall of the Hippodrome is fresh and welcoming. Rooms retain either the original parquet or laminate, and an unobjectionable vanilla-pudding-colored paper covers the walls. Half of the rooms have bathtubs, which is a rarity on this side of town and every window in the place is double-glazed, whether it needs it or not (it really doesn't, unless you haven't gotten the hang of sleeping through that dawn call to prayer). The manager made a point of mentioning that the building was reconstructed in compliance with Istanbul's new earthquake code, a fact I'm not sure made me feel better or not. Pay an additional 15€ ($18) and you'll get a sea-view room.

Aksakal caddesi 3, 34400, Sultanahmet/Istanbul. ℂ 0212/458-2784. Fax 0212/458-2788. www.erguvanhotelistanbul. com. 22 units. 70€ ($85) double. 10% discount if paid in cash. Free pickup from airport for stays of 3 days or longer. MC, V. **Amenities:** Rooftop restaurant and bar in summer only; Internet point; wireless; 24-hr. room service; laundry; dry-cleaning; elevator. *In room:* A/C, cable TV, minibar, hair dryer, wireless, safe.

Hotel Mina ⟨ੈ *(Value)* The facilities are pristine and four-star level, including the bathrooms, which all come equipped with tubs and high-quality fixtures. The bulk of the rooms are a bit on the small side, so try to book early for one of the more roomy accommodations. The location couldn't be better: Steps off Divanyolu, it's practically on top of the Grand Bazaar and only a 5-minute walk to the Hippodrome. The top-floor restaurant enjoys amazing views of the Marmara Sea and port activity.

Pierloti Caddesi Dostluk Yurdu Sokak 6, 34400 Cağaloğlu/Istanbul. ℂ 0212/458-2800. Fax 0212/458-2808. 44 units. 80€ ($98) double; 100€ ($122) suite. MC, V. **Amenities:** Restaurant; 24-hr. room service; laundry service; dry cleaning; elevator. *In room:* A/C, cable TV, minibar, hair dryer, safe.

Sarı Konak Hotel ⟨ੈ⟨ੈ *(Finds)* It's easy to see why visitors choose to stay in this small family-run establishment. Bahattin and his son Umit roll out the red carpet for everyone. The rooms are simple but charming; the bathrooms are spotless and functional; and air-conditioning comes in half the rooms—the other half have ceiling fans. TVs were recently installed in the majority of the rooms, including the new suite, which also has high-speed Internet access and a Jacuzzi. The terrace cafe has stunning views of both the Blue Mosque and the Marmara Sea, and the stylish white cushioned banquettes make this spot all the more alluring. Breakfast is something to look forward to, for what better way to start a day than with homemade jam, fresh flowers, and the soothing trickle of the garden courtyard's water fountain against the backdrop of an ancient Byzantine wall?

Mimar Mehmet Ağa Cad. 42–46, 34400 Sultanahmet/Istanbul. ℂ 0212/638-6258. Fax 0212/517-8635. www.sari konak.com. 17 units. 59€–89€ ($72–$109) double; 129€–169€ ($157–$206) suite. Rates reflect seasonal fluctuations. AE, MC, V. **Amenities:** 2 bars; 24-hr. room service; laundry service; dry cleaning; elevator. *In room:* A/C.

Zeugma Hotel ⟨ੈ The theme at this small, middle-end boutique hotel housed in a restored 19th-century Ottoman house is ancient Rome, with reproductions of mosaics discovered at the site of Zeugma decorating the walls. Bacchus presides in the lobby-level lounge (which doubles as the breakfast room); meanwhile, a small top-floor terrace looks out proudly over his restaurant (breakfast is served here in summer). The best rooms are those on the top floor, as they get the sea views and Jacuzzis; otherwise, all the rooms are essentially the same: clean, bright, and functional, with cabin showers and parquet flooring. Windows are double-glazed to keep out the sounds of nighttime revelers across the street, but I'd play it safe and reserve a room in the back.

Akbıyık Cad. 35, 34400 Sultanahmet/Istanbul. ℂ 0212/517-4040. Fax 0212/516-4333. www.zeugmahotel.com. 10 units. 50€ ($62) single; 70€–90€ ($85–$110) double. DC, MC, V. **Amenities:** Restaurant/wine bar; 24-hr. room service; laundry service; dry cleaning; free Internet in lobby. *In room:* A/C, cable TV, minibar, hair dryer.

INEXPENSIVE

Apricot Hotel ⟨ੈ *(Value)* The Apricot Hotel is the perfect example of why inexpensive doesn't have to mean cheap. Hakan, the owner, is bucking the trend of inflated neighborhood prices by supplying a clean, bright, family-style atmosphere at fixed prices. At 3 years old, accommodations are still relatively fresh: Beds are comfortable, pillows are thick and fluffy, and the plumbing actually works like a charm, cranking out scalding water in a heartbeat. Also, windows are double-glazed. Hakan, a licensed tour guide, spends his spare time scheming over the details that would make his hotel better, like a book exchange, daily newspaper delivery, weekly roof-barbecues, and fragrant spurts of air freshener. The hotel receives a number of walk-ins (somehow always groomed), so book early; rooms don't stay vacant for long.

Akbıyık Cad. 75, 34400 Sultanahmet/Istanbul. ©/fax **0212/638-1658.** www.apricothotel.com. 18 units. 35€ ($42) single; 44€–55€ ($54–$67) double. 1 free airport transfer on request. No credit cards. **Amenities:** Bar. *In room:* A/C, satellite TV, minibar.

BEYOĞLU
VERY EXPENSIVE

Ansen 130 *Finds*   It seems as though upgraded rooms in Istanbul are just flying off the shelves. Go figure. Ansen 130, inserted in a restored 19th-century architectural jewel, fills this need by offering 10 positively cavernous rooms that any bachelor looking for an apartment would kill for. Light wood and laminate dominate the decor, which is punctuated with more beige and a bit black in the sofa, bedspread, and electronics. Bathrooms have pleasantly chunky hardware, and there's a kitchenette with everything you'll need for a long or short stay except for the groceries. Ansen 130 has a ground-level bar that is popular even among nonguests, a cigar/wine bar next door, and a restaurant that's made Istanbul's top 15.

Meşrutiyet Caddesi, Ansen 130, 34430 Tepebaşı. © **0212/245-8808.** Fax 0212/245-7179. www.ansensuite.com. 10 units. 205€–295€ ($250–$360). See website for weekly and monthly rates. MC, V. **Amenities:** Restaurant; 2 bars; meeting room for 20; 24-hr. room service; laundry; dry-cleaning; elevator. *In room:* A/C, satellite TV, kitchenette w/minibar, wireless and Ethernet Internet, hair dryer, safe.

Ceylan Inter-Continental   In 1996 the Istanbul Sheraton morphed into the Ceylan Inter-Continental, making way for yet another luxury five-star hotel. Unfortunately, the existing concrete-and-glass monolith exterior didn't change its shape in the process. But structures like these are meant to please the eye from the inside, and that it does. The central glass-and-marble staircase sets the stage for just the right amount of pomp for the hotel's "international clientele." Choosing among the sunken Palm Terrace, the elegant Tea Lounge, and the high-storied City Lights Bar presents a difficult dilemma for an afternoon break or a late-night drink. The rooms are plush and elegant, with an armchair, desk, and loveseat to create a homey feel. That Ricky Martin and the Rolling Stones slept here elevate this hotel to six stars in my mind (all for as low as 133€ ($162) if you book via the Internet). And it's all just a few steps away from the bustle of Taksim Square.

Asker Ocagı Cad. No. 1, Taksim/Istanbul. © **0212/231-2121** or 800/327-0200 in the U.S., 0181/847-2277 in the U.K., 008/221-335 in Australia, or 0800/442-215 in New Zealand. Fax 0212/231-2180. www.interconti.com. 390 units. 315€ ($384) standard double; 900€ ($1,100) and up suite. Breakfast (18€/$22) and tax extra. AE, MC, V. Garage parking. **Amenities:** 3 restaurants; 3 bars; patisserie; outdoor pool; state-of-the-art health club; Turkish bath; Jacuzzi; sauna; tanning salon; shopping arcade; salon; 24-hr. room service; laundry service; dry cleaning; nonsmoking rooms; elevator. *In room:* A/C, satellite and cable TV and in-room movies, dataport, minibar, hair dryer, safe, bathtub.

Lares Park   In the concrete jungle that is Taksim, the last thing you'd expect to find is a modern, luxury hotel that manages to compete with the neighboring heavy-hitters without compromising Ottoman tradition. They didn't spare any expense on

Beyoğlu Hotels & Restaurants

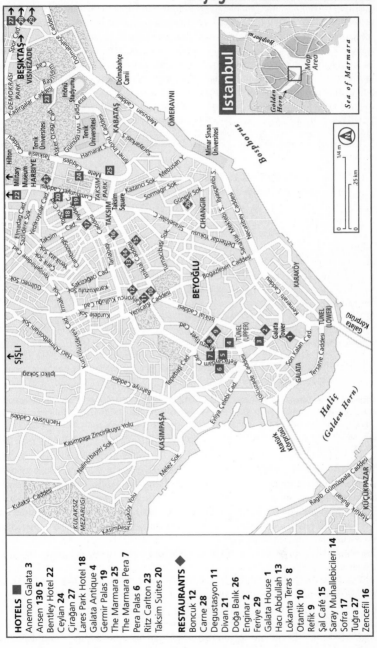

HOTELS ■

Anemon Galata **3**
Ansen 130 **5**
Bentley Hotel **22**
Ceylan **24**
Çırağan **27**
Lares Park Hotel **18**
Galata Antique **4**
Germir Palas **19**
The Marmara **25**
The Marmara Pera **7**
Pera Palas **6**
Ritz Carlton **23**
Taksim Suites **20**

RESTAURANTS ◆

Boncuk **12**
Carne **28**
Degustasyon **11**
Divan **21**
Doğa Balık **26**
Enginar **2**
Feriye **29**
Galata House **1**
Hacı Abdullah **13**
Lokanta Teras **8**
Otantik **10**
Refik **9**
Şal Café **15**
Saray Muhallebicileri **14**
Sofra **17**
Tuğra **27**
Zencefil **16**

quality—bathroom towels are pleasingly plump—and a standard unit gives you plenty of room to move around. But that's not the best part. The health club is a haven of relaxation, with patio-style lounge chairs set around a large indoor area with swimming pool, Jacuzzi, and juice bar. There's also a fitness center and tempting Turkish bath, and you don't have to pay a cent extra to use any of it. The location right smack in the center of a vibrant commercial center is far enough away from the minarets of Sultanahmet to permit an uninterrupted night's sleep.

Topçu Cad. 23, 80090 Taksim/Istanbul. © 0212/254-5100. Fax 0212/256-9249. www.laresparkhotel.com. 179 units. 110€ ($134) single; 130€ ($160) double; 165€ ($200) suite. Rates slightly lower Nov–Mar excluding Christmas and New Year's Day. AE, MC, V. **Amenities:** Restaurant; bar; cafe/patisserie; indoor swimming pool; fitness room; Turkish bath; Jacuzzi; sauna; business center; 24-hr. room service; laundry service; dry cleaning; elevator. *In room:* A/C, satellite TV w/pay movies, minibar, hair dryer, safe.

The Marmara Istanbul ☆☆☆   The Marmara is an excellent choice for those traveling for business or pleasure, particularly for its towering location above central and bustling Taksim Square. In fact, the hotel got so popular that they opened a second one, **The Marmara Pera,** down the street. The Taksim Square hotel's got everything necessary for an exclusive and pampered visit to Istanbul, including spacious bathrooms and spectacular views. The recently renovated Club Floor specifically pampers business travelers with 24-hour floor supervision, complimentary breakfast, and in-room fax and coffee service. The Pera property, meanwhile, in spite of its 200 rooms, feels like a boutique property, as spaces are kept to manageable scale and the decor is understatedly trendy.

Taksim Sq., Taksim/Istanbul. © 0212/251-4696. Fax 0212/244-0509. www.themarmara.com. 410 units. 190€–283€ ($230–$345) double; 180€–210€ ($220–$255) Club Floor; 310€–820€ ($380–$1,000) business and executive suites. Special weekend packages available. AE, MC, V. Ticketed parking lot below. **Amenities:** 3 restaurants; 3 bars; cafe/patisserie; outdoor swimming pool; state-of-the-art health club; Jacuzzi; sauna; shopping arcade; salon; 24-hr. room service; laundry service; dry cleaning; nonsmoking rooms; executive floor; elevator. *In room:* A/C, satellite TV, dataport, minibar, hair dryer, safe, bathtub.

Meşrutiyet Caddesi, Derviş Sok. 1, Tepebası/Istanbul. © 0212/251-4646. Fax 0212/249-8033. www.themarmarahotels. com. 200 units. 172€–190€ ($210–$230) city view double; 180€–190€ ($220–$230) sea view double; 245€ ($300) suite. AE, MC, V. **Amenities:** Rooftop restaurant; rooftop pool; bar; fitness center; business center; wireless Internet; four meeting rooms; laundry; dry-cleaning; elevator. *In room:* A/C, satellite TV, wireless and dataport, minibar, hair dryer, safe, bathtub.

Pera Palas Hotel   With its glory days in the past, a stay at the Pera Palas is more of a trip in a time machine than an attempt at making history. Built in 1892 as lodging befitting the exclusive passengers of the Orient Express, the hotel has an appropriately star-studded guest list: Agatha Christie wrote *Murder on the Orient Express* in room no. 411; Atatürk made room no. 101 (now a museum) his home in the days preceding the Gallipoli campaign; and Jacqueline Kennedy Onassis, Greta Garbo, Edward VIII, Josephine Baker, and Mata Hari all made stops here—their names adorn the rooms in which they stayed.

The Pera Palas reflects the Francophilia that had taken hold over the Ottoman Empire in the latter half of the 19th century, and in spite of some musty odors, retains much of the charm of a Parisian salon. Accordingly, the rooms are more authentic than deluxe, and only one-third of them come furnished with air-conditioning. But if character is more important to you than glitz, stay here. Beware the extras: Laundry and minibar items cost a small fortune, while coffee in the Orient Bar will run you close to 5.75€ ($7).

Fun Fact   A Mystery Worthy of Agatha Christie Herself

There has been much ado over **Agatha Christie's "mysterious" 11-day disappearance**, especially when it stands to substantiate the factual basis of a movie script *and* boost the profits of a historic hotel. The 1979 Warner Bros. movie *Agatha,* which makes reference to 11 missing days in the life of the author, was met with criticism by those who accused the movie studio of having fabricated the author's disappearance. In response, the movie studio hired a medium to get to the bottom of those 11 days. In a spiritual session, the medium, Tamara Rand, was "advised" by the late author that the answer to the mystery could be found in room no. 411 of the Pera Palas Hotel, where as a repeat guest between 1926 and 1932, Christie penned *Murder on the Orient Express.* In a much-hyped event, representatives of the film company and a group of reporters assembled in room no. 411 while a remote connection was established with Ms. Rand, who led them to a rusty old key hidden beneath the floorboards. Presumably, the key was to the author's diary and would reveal the answers to those 11 days. The key never left the premises, because the hotel and studio executives were unable to reach an agreement on compensation. (The hotel's chairman asked for $2 million plus 15% of the film's profits "for restoration of the hotel" in exchange for the key.) Rumors persisted about Christie's whereabouts, eventually putting her in a nearby hotel in the arms of Dashiell Hammett. That the author makes no mention of these 11 days in her autobiography has over the years only fueled the fire. In spite of the uproar caused by the recovery of her abandoned car and several cryptic notes she sent before her "disappearance," the truth may be less racy. It seems that she simply checked into a health spa in Yorkshire on December 4, 1926, under the surname of her husband's lover.

Meşrutiyet Cad. 98–100, 80050 Tepebaşı/Istanbul. © 0212/251-4560. Fax 0212/251-4089. www.perapalas.com. 145 units. 220€ ($270) double; 380€ ($465) suite. AE, DC, DISC, MC, V. Independent parking garage nearby. **Amenities:** Restaurant; 2 bars; 24-hr. room service; laundry service; dry cleaning; elevator. *In room:* A/C, satellite TV, minibar, hair dryer.

Ritz-Carlton Istanbul ✹✹✹   The modern glass monolith that houses the Ritz-Carlton has marred the skyline above Dolmabahçe Palace for years, eliciting criticism at almost every turn. But the hotel's opulence and luxury make it forgivable. The hotel strives for a niche alongside that of the other high-priced hotels, such as the Çirağan Palace (p. 87), by establishing membership clubs to its cigar bar and health center. The hotel also offers the most exclusive spa and treatment services, such as exotic massage treatments or premier health center and fitness packages for 2,420€ ($2,950) per year. Standard rooms are spacious, with large picture windows that let in lots of light, and suites that benefit from lovely parquet flooring and splendid views of the Bosphorus. Also, the beds are wonderfully high and fluffy. Bathrooms are equally deluxe, with bathtubs and separate showers, heated towel warmers, scales, handmade tiles, and designer soaps. Separate from the hotel's amenities are a privately owned movie theater (reservations required), a shopping arcade, an outlet of the Divan Patisserie, and a chic post-movie cafe. The *hamam* is the most luxurious in town.

Elmadağ Askerocağı Cad. 15, 80200 Şişli/Istanbul. ✆ 0212/334-4444. Fax 0212/334-4455. www.ritzcarlton.com. 244 units. 350€–512€ ($425–$625) double; 595€–760€ ($725–$925) suite. AE, DC, MC, V. Indoor parking garage. **Amenities:** 2 restaurants; 3 bars; indoor swimming pool; health club; spa; Turkish bath; Jacuzzi; sauna; concierge; tour desk; car-rental desk; shopping arcade; salon; 24-hr. room service; massage; babysitting; laundry service; dry cleaning; nonsmoking rooms; executive floor; elevator. *In room:* A/C, satellite TV, dataport, minibar, hair dryer, safe, bathtubs.

Taksim Suites 🏆🏆🏆 *Finds*   Philippe Starck would be proud of the "Zen-like" simplicity of these brand-new luxury designer suites, all of which come completely outfitted with state-of-the-art European kitchens, Jacuzzis, top-of-the-line sound systems, and modem lines for Internet connections. Although I did spot a few suspiciously IKEA-like standbys like CD holders and bedside tables, the glass vanities, steel basins, curved asymmetrical headboards, and pure whites and beiges (except in the Miyako Suite, which is upholstered in black) more than compensate. Windows are noiseproof, making the views of Taksim Park even more enjoyable, especially from the two-bedroom, penthouse suite, where remote-controlled blinds open and close to allow for views from the bathtub. The sense of sublime comfort is complete with free use of the on-site washer and dryer, but admittedly, more guests will appreciate the fitness room, sauna, and free Internet access (for those not carrying their own laptops).

Cumhuriyet Cad. 49 (corner of Topçu Cad.), 80090 Taksim/Istanbul. ✆ 0212/254-7777. Fax 0212/256-2021. www.taximsuites.com. 14 suites (including 2 penthouses). Nightly rate 180€–200€ ($220–$245) suite, 300€ ($365) penthouse. Weekly rate 800€–850€ ($975–$1,035) suite, 1,500€ ($1,830) penthouse. Monthly rates also available. AE, DC, MC, V. **Amenities:** Fitness room; Jacuzzi; sauna; concierge; 24-hr. room service; laundry service; dry cleaning; elevator. *In room:* A/C, satellite TV/VCR, fax, dataport, kitchen, fridge, coffeemaker, hair dryer, iron, safe.

EXPENSIVE

Bentley Hotel 🏆🏆🏆 *Finds*   Off the tourist radar yet only a 10-minute walk to Taksim is this tribute to minimalist Milanese design. The Bentley has already fast become a favorite of the fashionista and publishing crowd, thanks to a combination of high-tech amenities, great aesthetics, and convenient proximity to the trendy New York SoHo-like section of Nişantaşı. Each of the seven floors contains two standard rooms, two ample singles, and two suites (one a corner), while the two penthouse suites enjoy the additional bonus of a private, semi-wraparound terrace. All rooms are decorated with a sleek and spare palette of white, beige, and black, offering top-quality electronics, Internet connections, and even an espresso machine. The lobby bar is even appealing enough for nonguests, and a mezzanine restaurant overlooking the glass-facade lobby can accommodate even larger parties.

Halaskargazi Cad. 75 (opposite the Military Museum), 80220 Harbiye/Istanbul. ✆ 0212/291-7730. Fax 0212/291-7740. www.bentley-hotel.com. 14 units. 165€–205€ ($200–$250) double; 245€ ($300) suite; 330€ ($400) penthouse. AE, DC, MC, V. **Amenities:** Restaurant; bar; fitness room; sauna; concierge; 24-hr. room service; laundry service; dry cleaning; elevator. *In room:* A/C, satellite TV/VCR, CD player, fax, dataport, minibar, coffeemaker, hair dryer, safe.

Germir Palas Hotel 🏆   Wooden wainscoting, faux Chippendale sofas, and Parisian-style cityscapes of Istanbul make stepping into the brand-new Germir Palas like stepping back in time to 19th-century Paris. The hotel's eye-catching and elegant style is a direct result of the Germir family's other enterprise: As owners of a textile business, they've coordinated warm floral wallpaper with leafy green and beige fabrics to create a warm and welcoming atmosphere. Rooms are comparatively small, so if possible, book one of the seven corner rooms, which are slightly bigger but sacrifice the view. Bathrooms are spacious and all come equipped with full bathtubs. The lobby-level brasserie-style bar is a great meeting place; the hotel also offers two base-ment-level conference rooms.

Cumhuriyet Cad. 17, 80090 Taksim/Istanbul. ℂ 0212/361-1110. Fax 0212/361-1070. www.germirpalas.com. 49 units. 150€ ($185) double. AE, MC, V. **Amenities:** Restaurant; bar; concierge; tour desk; car-rental desk; 24-hr. room service; massage; babysitting; laundry service; dry cleaning; nonsmoking rooms; elevator. *In room:* A/C, satellite TV, minibar, hair dryer, safe, bathtub.

INEXPENSIVE

Anemon Galata ⚘   Thanks to the restoration of this 19th-century neighborhood gem, the revival of Galata is clearly in high speed. The building enjoys a front row seat to the intimate neighborhood plaza at the base of the commanding Galata Tower. The hotel itself offers sophisticated old-world style and in-room architectural features such as original crown moldings and ceiling frescoes. Wall-to-wall carpeting (which I barely tolerate) and staid decor in the rooms do the building less than full justice, but the up side of all that sound-sucking upholstery is that you certainly won't hear the neigh-bors. For the best views, pick a room on the third floor or above. The hotel truly impresses from the rooftop restaurant, however, where proximity to the tower and views of the city make this an excellent option for an evening stopover.

Büyükhendek Cad. 11, 80020 Kuledibi/Istanbul. ℂ 0212/293-2343. Fax 0212/292-2340. www.anemongalata.com. 30 units. 125€–150€ ($150–$180) double. AE, MC, V. **Amenities:** Restaurant; bar; concierge; 24-hr. room service; laundry service; dry cleaning; elevator. *In room:* A/C, satellite TV, minibar, hair dryer, safe.

Galata Antique Hotel   A clean, inexpensive option in this part of town is hard to find, but the Galata Antique, located just down the street from the British embassy and a few steps away from the entrance to Tünel and Istiklal Caddesi, provides a friendly and convenient one. The building was designed by the French architect Val-laury in 1881, and still retains some 19th-century charm in its caged elevator and carved wooden arches. The rooms are tasteful, elegant, and new, and the bathrooms, although recently redone with fresh tile, are fractionally disappointing due to the sparse sink and shower setups. The entrance to the hotel sits in the middle of a flight of exterior steps, so the Galata Antique may not be appropriate for everyone. How-ever, the central location is ideal.

Meşrutiyet Cad., Nergis Sok. 10, 80090 Beyoğlu/Istanbul. ℂ 0212/245-5944. Fax 0212/245-5947. www.galata antiquehotel.com. 27 units. 100€ ($122) double; 140€ ($170) suite. MC, V. **Amenities:** Bar; concierge; 24-hr. room service; laundry service; dry cleaning; elevator. *In room:* A/C, satellite TV, minibar, hair dryer.

ALONG THE BOSPHORUS
VERY EXPENSIVE

Çirağan Palace Hotel Kempinski Istanbul ⚘⚘⚘ *Kids*   Residence of the last Ottoman sultans, the hotel that you see today is actually two buildings: the faithfully restored stone-and-marble sultan's palace (housing 12 VIP suites) and the modern five-star deluxe hotel, both standing majestically on the shores of the Bosphorus and presiding over a collection of sculpted lawns, marble gates, a waterside swimming pool, and even a putting green. Hard to believe that a little over a decade ago, the Çirağan was a burned-out shell of its current and former splendor. The guest list reads like a who's who of international royalty, but these days, not even royalty rates the royal treatment. Instead, people like you, me, and Sarah Ferguson get stuck with dreary and noisy park-facing rooms. (Also, avoid rooms at the center of the hotel, which fill with restaurant smoke and food odors through vents.) My advice? Book the best room you can afford; otherwise, you may be disappointed.

Çırağan Cad. 84, 80700 Beşiktaş/İstanbul. ② **800/426-3135** in the U.S., 800/363-0366 in Canada, 0800/868-588 in the U.K., 800/623-578 in Australia, 0800/446-368 in New Zealand, 0212/258-3377 in Istanbul. Fax 0212/259-6686. www.ciraganpalace.com. 316 units. 315€–395€ ($384–$480) park-view double; 425€–970€ ($518–$1,185) sea-view double; 835€–4,920€ ($1,020–$6,000) hotel suite; 985€–9,225€ ($1,200–$11,250) palace suite (some with park view). Breakfast and tax extra. Double weekend rates available. AE, DC, MC, V. **Amenities:** 3 restaurants (see review for Tuğra on p. 96); numerous bars; indoor and outdoor swimming pools; putting green; health club; fitness room; Turkish bath; Jacuzzi; sauna; concierge; car-rental desk; shopping arcade; salon; 24-hr. room service; babysitting, laundry service; dry cleaning; nonsmoking rooms; palace section; elevator. *In room:* A/C, satellite TV w/pay movies, dataport, minibar, hair dryer, safe.

NEAR THE AIRPORT

Airport Hotel Located on the grounds of Istanbul's Atatürk Airport, this is a sure-fire way to make sure you don't miss that flight. Not surprisingly, the hotel attracts lots of business travelers—the business center and executive meeting rooms make sure of that—but even the most sun-kissed vagabond will enjoy breakfast views of the runway. Rooms are pleasingly bright, airy, and unusually spacious, and offer high-tech amenities like TVs that show flight details and Internet access. The hotel also offers rooms at hourly rates (for naps on long layovers and such) and a well-appointed fitness room for those crack-of-dawn workouts.

Atatürk Havalimanı Dış Hatlar Terminali, Yeşilköy/İstanbul. ② **0212/465-4030.** Fax 0212/465-4730. www.airport hotelistanbul.com. 85 units. 106€ ($130) double air side; 123€–140€ ($150–$170) land side. AE, MC, V. **Amenities:** Bar, fitness room; 24-hr. room service; laundry service; dry cleaning; elevator. *In room:* A/C, satellite TV w/pay movies, minibar, hair dryer, safe.

4 Where to Dine

For the most part, 90% of the restaurants and eateries in the neighborhood of Sultanahmet are sadly lacking, and although you can forgive an eatery a less than stellar meal at lunchtime, I for one can't forgive the extortion. Instead, I recommend you sample the honest home cooking at the various innocuous *lokantas* (dives with steam tables), particularly along Pierloti Caddesi, between the Hippodrome and Cağaloğlu and in the working streets around the Grand Bazaar. In a pinch, head over to Buhara 93 (Şifa Hamamı Sokak 15A; ② **0212/518-1511**) for some pretty good, cheap basic Turkish fare, and pizza that I've come to know and love. For dinner, spring for a taxi (about 6.75YTL/$5) and venture beyond the confines of the tourist trap for one of Beyoğlu's more genuine restaurants or *meyhanes* (traditionally male-dominated taverns or pubs serving food and drink). The restaurants of Beyoğlu and Taksim are more consistent in that they serve a regular stream of locals and businessmen rather than rely entirely on the tourist industry. A bit farther up the Bosphorus in Beşiktaş and Etiler are the five-star restaurants that attract Turkish jet-setters and consulate personnel, for the most part providing a wide selection of fresh-fish specialties, excellent service, and spectacular views.

The neighborhood of Kumkapı on the fringes of Sultanahmet capitalizes on the fish market across the highway, a year-round carnival crammed with typical tavernas. Don't walk there alone, though, as these are the streets that attract the worst petty thieves.

Restaurant dining rooms resemble ghost town eateries in the summer, but if you just continue up the steps, you'll see why. Istanbul is a city of rooftop terraces, and summer dining is almost exclusively enjoyed high above the city accompanied by warm breezes and breathtaking panoramas.

Dressing for dinner in Turkey requires the same amount of good judgment as anywhere in the Western world. Although a jacket and tie (or black dress for women) would be perfectly appropriate for a Saturday evening meal at an upscale restaurant or hotel dining room, a pair of pressed pants and a nice shirt will also do the trick in any listing indicating "dress smart." Leave the beachwear for the beach (including Bermuda shorts, cutoffs, and tank tops), and you should avoid any unnecessary faux pas.

EMINÖNÜ: SIRKECI & EMINÖNÜ

MODERATE

Pandeli Lokantası *Overrated* TURKISH   Pandeli is one of those neighborhood traditions that lives on more for its location and longevity than for anything particularly outstanding about the restaurant. Pandeli was opened in 1901 by a Greek of Turkish descent and has become a local institution ever since its arrival on the upper level of the Egyptian Spice Bazaar. It's a popular place among businessmen on expense accounts as much as for bazaar shoppers looking for a place to eat. Steak is a big item on the menu, and the lentil soup is noteworthy, but aside from the caviar, the menu selections are rather uninspiring. If you nab a table in the main room facing the ancient blue İznik tiles and windows overlooking the bazaar, you can watch the human traffic come and go.

Mısır Çarşısı 1, Eminönü (immediately inside the entrance to the Egyptian Bazaar). ℘ 0212/522-5534. Main courses 6.75YTL–12YTL ($5–$9). MC, V. Mon–Sat 11am–4pm.

INEXPENSIVE

Eminönü Belediyesi Sosyal Tesisleri *Finds* TRADITIONAL TURKISH   The security guards sporadically stationed at the gated entrance aren't exactly an inviting presence, but this is indeed one of the neighborhood's finds. It's actually a combined tea garden and restaurant, placed strategically on an outdoor terrace that makes up part of the ancient Byzantine fortress wall. There's a small building situated at the back of the grounds, containing a dining room serving traditional Turkish meals. And because it's owned by the Municipality—presumably the reason for the guards—this destination is bone dry (no alcohol). I recommend this place regularly for anyone looking for an authentic, atmospheric, and hassle-free meal at the right price.

Ahırkap[id] Iskele Sokak 1, Cankurtaran (near the Armada Hotel, under the train tracks at the Dede Efendi entrance to the neighborhood from the sea road). ℘ 0212/458-5415. Main courses 6.75YTL–12YTL ($5–$9). MC, V. Daily 11am–midnight.

Hamdi Et Lokantası *Value* KEBAPS   Hamdi's southeastern *kebaps* will never come close to Develi's, but this is a good alternative to the overpriced mediocrity of Pandeli Lokantası only steps from the entrance to the Spice Market. The restaurant's popular terrace views of the Galata Tower and Golden Horn add to the convenience of the location, and you can move to the cozy *şark* (Oriental-style seating area) for your after-dinner cup of coffee or tea. Specialties of the house include the *erikli kebap,* minced meat from a suckling lamb where all of the fat has been cooked out, and the showcase *testi kebap,* a stew of diced meat, tomatoes, shallots, garlic, and green pepper cooked over an open fire and served tableside by breaking the terra-cotta pot (minimum 10 people, advance orders required). Hamdi caters to vegetarians with the vegetable *kebap,* spiced with parsley and garlic; don't pass up the *yuvarlama,* a flavorful yogurt soup with tiny rice balls served only at dinnertime.

Tahmis Cad. Kalçin Sok. 17 (set back behind the bus depot), Eminönü. ℂ 0212/528-0390. Reservations required for dinner. Dress smart. Appetizers and main courses 5.50YTL–11YTL ($4–$8). MC, V. Daily 11am–midnight. Closed 1st day and last 3 days of Ramadan.

Orient Express Cafe ⊛ (Finds) TURKISH/OTTOMAN   Located next to track no. 1, the Orient Express restaurant—a real find—is proof that you don't have to pay an arm and a leg for white tablecloths, good food, and nostalgia. The elegant niches with their large stained-glass window insets and the handsome clapboard ceiling take you back at least a century, although the decorator would have done well to scrap the enormous *Shining Time Station* oil-on-canvas on the wall.

The limited but satisfying menu relies heavily on lamb, with a tender lamb shoulder as the pride of the chef. Craving eggplant, I ordered the *beğendili kebap*, cubes of flavorful beef atop a bed of eggplant purée (or was that ambrosia?). The crème caramel was a formidable substitute to an empty coffer of rice pudding, and the service was black-tie and flawless.

Sirkeci Train Station, Sirkeci. ℂ 0212/522-2280. Appetizers 5.50YTL–8YTL ($4–$6); Main courses 10YTL–18YTL ($7.50–$13). MC, V. Daily noon–11pm.

EMINÖNÜ: IN & AROUND SULTANAHMET
VERY EXPENSIVE
Seasons Restaurant ⊛⊛ MEDITERRANEAN   Rated no.1 in Zagat's "Best of Europe" since the book first came out, this restaurant at The Four Seasons continues to be a favorite, not only for expats and foreign visitors, but for Istanbulers as well. There are menus for breakfast, lunch, and dinner, each adapted to seasonal offerings approximately every 3 months. The *izgara levrek madalyon* (medallions of grilled sea bass) seems to be a recurrent theme, served with a ragout of vegetables, yellow tomatoes, a beet reduction, and chive essence; you can also find Oriental-leaning dishes such as wok-fried Japanese soba noodles with sweet chile, bok choy, and shiitake mushrooms, or the seared scallops with shrimp rolls and ginger. A popular event is the Sunday brunch buffet (70YTL/$52 per person), a display of excess that attracts a clique of Istanbul's food and beverage connoisseurs.

Four Seasons Hotel, Tevkifhane Sok. 1, Sultanahmet. ℂ 0212/638-8200. Reservations required. Dress smart. Appetizers 14YTL–24YTL ($10–$18); main courses 19YTL–28YTL ($14–$21) and up for selections off the daily "Gourmet Menu." AE, DC, MC, V. Daily 6:30–11am, noon–3pm, and 7–11pm.

EXPENSIVE
Balıkçı Sabahattin ⊛⊛⊛ (Finds) FISH   There are no menus here, which is fine because not one member of the staff speaks English (or French, or German, or Italian), a minor inconvenience that's part of the charm of the place. Even Jean Paul Gaultier was recently able to enjoy an anonymous meal here, the staff is so clueless. The formula seems to work: Balıkçı Sabahattin is part of a small empire that includes the Hotel Armada, Allafranga, and the Kalkan Han in Kalkan.

First to arrive in the procession of courses are the mezes (appetizers), which include a mushroom yogurt "dip" and an intriguingly tasty smoked eggplant purée. For the main course, you will be offered a choice of grilled sea bass, a bubbling casserole of "red fish," or some other seasonal catch. Drinks and dessert are included (hopefully a scoop of their tahini ice cream), and what you can't finish you can feed to one of the hungry kittens milling about. When the weather chills up (or if you came too late for an outdoor table), meals are served inside a restored old Ottoman house on the fringes of Sultanahmet.

Cankurtaran, Sultanahmet (behind Armada Hotel). © 0212/458-1824. Appetizers 5.50YTL–15YTL ($4–$11); fish 25YTL–35YTL ($19–$26). V. Daily noon–3pm and 7–10:30pm.

Dubb Indian Restaurant and Gallery ✦ INDIAN

The owner of this inventive restaurant grew to love the cuisine of India while based there for his carpet-exporting business. Returning to Istanbul, he discovered a way to combine the two unrelated activities in Dubb, an Indian restaurant housed in a beautifully restored Ottoman house doubling as a gallery for his most prized collection of Turkish carpets and kilims. The house is composed of four intimate levels, each painstakingly preserved and decorated, with a rooftop terrace view that makes you feel like the Ayasofya landed on your plate. The traditional Indian recipes are skillfully executed, while the portions are more representative of Turkish dishes than of the meager portions we've all come to expect from Indian cuisine. Try the tandoori chicken and the spinach purée with feta cheese, and wash it all down with one of four types of flavored *lassi* (yogurt drink).

Incili Çavuş Sok. 10, Sultanahmet. © 0212/513-7308. Main courses 11YTL–24YTL ($8–$18). MC, V. Daily noon–midnight.

Sarniç (Moments FRENCH/TURKISH

The setting for this restaurant, an old Roman cistern tucked away behind the Ayasofya, is nothing less than dramatic. The flickering light of 500 candles bounces off the iron grillwork, the lofty brick domes, and the stone pillars, while the crackling of the fire in the massive stone chimney (an inauthentic but effective addition) supplies more romance than a girl can handle. It's hard to believe that only a few years ago, before the Turkish Touring and Automobile Association bought and restored it, the cistern served as a greasy old auto repair shop.

The menu, created by the longtime chef who cut his teeth at the now defunct Sheraton Hotel, marries traditional French entrees like beef bourguignon with standard Turkish grills. But while the service is good and the ambience is great, my experience there was (twice) reminiscent of a large institutional wedding (except for the marinated beef salad, which was truly memorable). Perhaps then, it is a hit-or-miss thing.

Soğukçeşme Sok., Sultanahmet. © 0212/512-4291. Reservations required. Dress smart. Appetizers 10YTL–38YTL ($7.50–$28); Main courses 18YTL–50YTL ($13–$37). AE, MC, V. Daily noon–midnight; lunch available for groups only.

MODERATE

Konyalı Topkapı Sarayı Lokantası TRADITIONAL TURKISH/OTTOMAN

With such a prestigious location and a star-studded guest book that includes Jackie Kennedy, Mohammed Ali, and Richard Nixon, who'd have thought that Konyalı was a franchise operation with over 10 outlets in Istanbul? But what was once good enough for the queen is little more than a convenient if stunningly sited stopover for a short walk through history.

Diners at Topkapı are expecting the recipes they've read about in the guidebooks, but other than exorbitant prices, Konyalı offers nothing more than the usual lineup of stews, *kebaps*, and eggplant dishes. Diners should pass up the a la carte dining room and opt for the cafeteria-style cafe section, where you can enjoy the same views of the Marmara Sea without the prices and pretension. Tipping its hat to a mostly tourist clientele, there's also a bureau de change on the premises.

Topkapı Palace, Sultanahmet. © 0212/513-9696. A la carte main courses (in restaurant, not the cafeteria) 19YTL–31YTL ($14–$23). AE, MC, V. Wed–Mon 10am–5pm.

Marmara Terrace Restaurant ✦ (Moments NOUVELLE TURKISH

What distinguishes a good restaurant from a great one? How about a front-row seat to the (muted) sound-and-light show over the massive domes of the Blue Mosque? With a show like the one at this rooftop terrace restaurant, the chef doesn't really have to work too hard to draw a crowd. Regrettably, the terrace is only opened on appropriately balmy evenings June through September; the rest of the time, there's a lovely enclosed street-side cafe or an indoor lobby-level dining area. The appetizer of mixed mezes is the tastiest and most innovative sampler you'll eat during your stay in Turkey, consisting of carrot rolls with yogurt, seafood with smoked salmon and shrimp, cold vegetables, and Ottoman spring rolls with cheese and potatoes. Traditional main courses are pre-pared with a flare, such as the juicy lamb chops or the Ottoman-style *köfte*. There's also a fresh catch of the day, preferably prepared on the outdoor grill, but leave room for the desserts, as the chef succeeds in creating delectable Turkish favorites without drowning them in syrup. During the off season, the same menu is available in the lobby-level restaurant, or weather permitting, in the garden cafe, where you can dine to the sound of *fasıl* music.

In the Mavi Ev (Blue House), Dalbastı Sok. 14, Sultanahmet. © 0212/638-9010. Reservations suggested. Main courses 15YTL–22 ($11–$16). AE, MC, V. Daily noon–11pm. Restaurant moves from the roof terrace to the lobby level off season.

Yeşil Ev ⚘ FRENCH/TURKISH   Located in a rebuilt historic Ottoman mansion, the Yeşil Ev restaurant takes full advantage (in the summertime) of the luxurious set-ting provided by the garden and grand fountain. The Ottoman/French menu includes a decent duck a l'orange, the one-time selection of choice for the visit of France's prime minister, but although reputed as one of the top restaurants in Istanbul, meals here sometimes get mixed reviews. The elegant *orangerie* is open in good weather only (in winter for groups of eight or more), and on a balmy summer's eve, you won't even notice the check.

Kabasakal Cad. 5, Sultanahmet. © 0212/517-6785. Dress smart. Appetizers 6.75YTL–22YTL ($5–$16); main courses 16YTL–28YTL ($12–$21) (and up for prawns and fish). AE, MC, V. Daily noon–11pm.

INEXPENSIVE

Cennet (Kids) (Value) GÖZLEME/MANTI   Salty crepes and Turkish ravioli—these are the specialties of the house, filled with cheese, meat, and even potato. Along with eggs for breakfast, there's a typical selection of mezes and meat dishes. The food is adequate enough, but the real reasons to stop here are the traditional Turkish decor, the low seating, and the round, aproned women sitting cross-legged in the middle of the floor rolling out dough. The waitstaff dresses in the costumes of earlier centuries, and visi-tors are encouraged to don one of the spare outfits—puffy sultans' hats and all—for the duration of dinner. There's live music, and yes, it's a bit touristy, but hey, are you here to *avoid* this kind of thing?

Divanyolu Cad. 90, Çemberlitaş. © 0212/513-1416. Main courses 5YTL–8YTL ($3.70–$6). MC, V. Daily 9am–11pm.

The Pudding Shop (Overrated) TURKISH   In its heyday, The Pudding Shop was an obligatory stop on the "hippie trail," a starting point for restless vagabonds from the West on their way through the exotic East. With its anti-establishment clientele, it wasn't long before it gained the reputation of ground zero for drug dealings and other unsavory business propositions. Today The Pudding Shop fades into history alongside the other fast-food restaurants on Divanyolu Caddesi, with fluorescent backlit menu displays and stacks of ex-pat publications. When the turnover is high, the traditional Turkish fare is worthy of the joint's original popularity, but when in doubt, stick to the eggplant dishes and avoid things that tend to overcook. Or do a comparison with Can's cafeteria-style *lokanta* next door.

Divanyolu Cad. 6 (across from the tram), Sultanahmet. © 0212/522-2970. Main courses 4YTL–19YTL ($3–$14). MC, V. Daily 8:30am–10pm or later.

Tarihi Meşhur Sultanahmet Köfteçısı ★★ *Kids* *Value* KÖFTE This little, quality dive on the main drag has been around longer than Turkey has been a republic, and after one bite it's easy to see why. It's hard to imagine a simple meatball as delectable as the ones made here, but if you're not convinced, there's not much in the way of an alternative. (They also served lamb *şiş* for 6.75YTL/$5, but here, it's beside the point.) Side dishes are limited to white beans or a shepherd's salad (tomato, cucumber, onions, and chile). Top the meal off with the *irmik helvası*, a modestly sweet semolina comfort food beloved by Turks.

Divanyolu Cad. 12/A, Sultanahmet. © 0212/513-1438. *Köfte* 4.75YTL ($3.50). No credit cards. Daily noon–10pm.

BEYOĞLU: AROUND TAKSIM SQUARE
MODERATE

Divan Lokantası ★ *Value* NOUVELLE TURKISH While tourists are inundating *Tuğra* (the Çirağan's five-star restaurant) for authentic Ottoman cuisine, Divan Lokantası is considered by locals as the only restaurant in town where the food doesn't taste foreign. What Divan calls "World Cuisine" is just another way of saying that they're constantly updating traditional recipes and newer innovations, creating a superb dining experience enriched by the sound of classical music in the background. Last I checked, you could delight in goat trotters on croutons, a hard-to-find menu item traditional to the Beykoz region, or the more Anatolian *anali kızlı*, poached lamb and veal patties with a bulgur and tomato concasse.

Divan Oteli, Cumhuriyet Cad. 2, Elmadag. © 0212/231-4100. Reservations required. Dress smart. Appetizers 8YTL–12YTL ($6–$9); main courses 19YTL–40YTL ($14–$29). AE, DC, MC, V. Mon–Fri noon–3:30pm and 7–11:30pm; Sat 7pm–midnight.

Doğa Balık ★★ People's eyes light up at the mention of this highly popular restaurant positioned on the rooftop (top floor in winter) of the Zurich Hotel in the newly arrived expat-heavy neighborhood of Cihangir. But the view is almost besides the point here. The very freshest fish of the season is served here: amply sized bonito (palamut) or turbot (kalkan) costing upwards of 30YTL ($22) per kilo. However delectable is the fish, the real attraction here is the overwhelming selection of mezes. There are 30 varieties of wholesome forest greens all guaranteed to make you moan with pleasure: from nettles, to feverfew, to purslane, to "goat food." Don't miss the non-green mezes, in particular the *mercemek köfetsi* (lentil balls), and the monkfish salad. Indeed, load up on the appetizers and skip the main course.

Akarsu Yokusu Caddesi 44–46, Cihangir (follow Siraselviler Caddesi down from Taksim square and turn left when you reach the mosque). © 0212/293-9143. Vegetable mezes 6YTL ($4.50); fish mezes 12YTL ($8.80); fish 12YTL ($9) and up (by weight). MC, V. Daily noon–1:30am.

Hacı Abdullah TRADITIONAL TURKISH Politicians, businessmen, families, and out-of-towners have been coming to Istanbul's first licensed restaurant for over a century. The recipes reflect the best of traditional Turkish cuisine, serving substantial stews, whole artichokes baked with vegetables in olive oil, and their signature dish, the lamb shank with eggplant. Lining the walls are enormous glass jars filled with fruit compotes made on the premises and incorporated into the chef's proud desserts, such as quince marinated in syrup or the sweetbread custard topped with figs, apricot, pistachio, and coconut. For those wishing to celebrate with a glass of wine, Hacı Abdullah unfortunately serves no alcohol.

Sakizağacı Cad. 17, Beyoğlu. ⓒ 0212/293-8561. Reservations suggested. Appetizers 5.50YTL ($4); main courses 8YTL–30YTL ($6–$22). AE, MC, V. Daily noon–10:30pm; later on weekends.

INEXPENSIVE

Şal Café Bar ⓕ ⓕinds TURKISH   When all of the other tourists are wasting their time at the "Authentic Turkish Night" shows around town, you can sit in Şal Café and gloat. *This* is authentic Turkish nightlife, supported by the fact that you will be the only foreigner in sight. Try the *saç kavurma,* a delectable beef or lamb stew prepared in an earthenware pan, or the *ezme,* a spicy raw beef spread. The small space fills up with locals, who, having eaten, get up and dance in the narrow aisle between the musicians and the kilim-covered tables and banquettes. For now, it's a rare sighting if another foreigner shows up, but once this book hits the stands, it'll be just a matter of time until this place becomes a tourist trap.

Istiklal Cad., Büyükparmakkapı Sok. 18A, Beyoğlu/Taksim. ⓒ 0212/243-4196. Appetizers 5.50YTL ($4); main courses under 11YTL ($8). AE, MC, V. Mon–Fri 4pm–1:30am; Sat–Sun 2pm–2am.

Saray Muhallebicileri ⓥalue PATISSERIE/KEBAPS   People have been flocking to Saray Muhallebicileri since its establishment in 1949, and a look in the window will tell you why. The colorful array of desserts lures you off the street and into this patisserie, although with such a huge choice and exceedingly low prices, it'll be difficult to rule out any one thing. Rice-pudding addicts should definitely not pass up this opportunity, although the chocolate pudding is irresistible as well. This is also a good place to try the *tavukgögsü,* a sweet gummy pudding made with chicken that would be less difficult to avoid in another less-tempting establishment. Saray also serves a selection of *kebaps,* but who cares?

Istiklal Cad. 102–104, Beyoğlu. ⓒ 0212/292-3434. *Kebaps* 4.75YTL ($3.50); desserts 1.75YTL ($1.30). No credit cards. Daily 6am–1:30am.

Sofra ⓕⓕ ⓥalue TRADITIONAL TURKISH   Having made a name for itself in London, this British-based chain of Turkish restaurants waited for the right climate to open a branch on native soil. It may have been the exposure to the tastes of foreign palates that elevates traditional recipes to a more creative level: the *imam bayıldı* (stuffed eggplant) comes chopped in cubes along with some unexpectedly tasty chickpeas; cinnamon sticks appear as a garnish. Other uncommon items are the *midya tava* (fried breaded mussels) and *sucuk izgara* (mild sausage). Don't miss the sun-dried apricots filled with clotted cream and sprinkled with almond and pistachio crumbs. Warm weather invites diners to the spectacular roof terrace, which enjoys views of Taksim from underneath the hotel's neon sign. But even when sequestered indoors, the decor of snazzy glass plates, red textured walls, and wrought iron keep it from feeling claustrophobic.

Tarlabaşı Bulv. 36, Beyoğlu (inside the Cartoon Hotel). ⓒ 0212/238-5201. Reservations required. Dress smart. Appetizers 5.50YTL–11YTL ($4–$8); main courses 11YTL–16YTL ($8–$12); fish sold by weight. MC, V. Daily noon–3pm and 7–11pm.

Zencefil SOUPS/SALADS   Billed as a vegetarian cafe (in spite of the chicken with leeks on the menu), this spot serves up wholesome fare worthy of its healthy designation. Homemade bread with herb butter accompanies every meal, which might be a big healthy salad, an ample slice of quiche, or Indian stew with exotic spices and vegetables. Menus have been skillfully translated into English, which is useful, because pumpkin pie probably isn't in your basic Turkish dictionary, and it's too good to miss. Zencefil will be moving to a new location across the street at an undetermined date in the future; if it's not where we say it is, just look across the street.

Kurabiye Sok. 3, Taksim. (C) **0212/244-4082**. Main courses 5.50YTL–9.50YTL ($4–$7). No credit cards. Mon–Sat 9am–11pm.

BEYOĞLU: TÜNEL & GALATA
INEXPENSIVE

Boncuk ✿✿ *Value* TURKISH/ARMENIAN Located on a side street off the Fish Market, this small rustic *meyhane* is the one restaurant on this saturated stretch of restaurants that is consistently full. Boncuk serves delicacies such as fried brains (mmm . . .) and stuffed spleen, but thankfully there's a variety of more recognizable hot and cold mezes like *kızır*, flavorful and spicy bulgur balls, and *topik*, an Armenian specialty made of chickpea paste around a nucleus of onions and currents. Because availability is seasonal, try not to be too disappointed when the waiter informs you that your choice is not on the menu that day.

Nevizade Sok. 19, Beyoğlu. (C) **0212/243-1219**. Appetizers 5.50YTL–8YTL ($4–$6); main courses 6.75YTL ($5) and up for fish. No credit cards. Daily noon–midnight.

Degustasyon Lokantası ✿✿ *Value* MEZES/TURKISH An unexpected oasis in the midst of the confusion of the *balıkpazarı* (the fish market in Beğoğlu), Degustasyon serves a huge selection of mezes, and not just the usual selection of eggplant purée (which is phenomenal) and ezme/pepper paste. Here you'll get some Armenian recipes, such as the fava loaf, thrown in with Turkish traditional dishes. It's just as full of life as the other nearby *meyhanes*, but slightly classier. And obviously, in deference to the location, the restaurant serves a good selection of fish.

Balıkpazarı, Beyoğlu. (C) **0212/292-0667**. Appetizers 5.50YTL–9.50YTL ($4–$7). Main courses 9.50YTL–18YTL ($7–$13) and up for fish. MC, V. Daily 11am–1am or later.

Enginar TURKISH BISTRO Enginar cafe is like a shiny new penny on this scrappy stretch of street, making it obvious that more people should take care of the neighborhood's heritage. As with much of the history of Galata, no one knows for sure what the first building that stood on the sight was; but turn the clock back 100 years and envision these bright "new" stones (additions to foundations that could date back 400 years) as an Italian bank, then later as a Jewish coffeehouse, and most recently as an Akbank location. With its attractive lighting and interior resembling an old warehouse, Enginar is a chic and quiet place for a drink, and the food, seemingly simple by the looks of the menu, is quite good, too, although the portions are miniscule. Try their vegetable crepe for a lighter lunch, or the sesame chicken salad.

Şah Kapısı Sok. 4/A, Galata (continue straight down Istiklal Cad. to the Galata Tower; the cafe is on your right). (C) **0212/293-9697**. Appetizers and main courses 6.75YTL–14YTL ($5–$10). MC, V. Daily 10:30am–12:30am.

Galata House ✿ *Finds* GEORGIAN Hidden along the steep slopes of Galata's historic streets, this little gem of a restaurant, the brainchild of an architect/city planner and his wife, occupies a row house that served as the British jail at the beginning of the 1900s. The coziness of the dining rooms—three small salons and an outdoor upper balcony—belie the building's earlier purpose, except for the few preserved squares of plaster etched by prisoners during periods of extreme boredom. At first, the menu selections appear Turkish but arrive with an unexpected twist of flavor: chicken and pea salad with yogurt and dill, chicken with saffron and walnut, and lamb stew with tarragon—and the result is a light and pleasant alternative to heaps of *kebaps*. Potential visitors should take note, however, of the steep incline of the streets in this neighborhood (wear rubber soles!), and that this particular street is often unlit.

Galata Kulesi Sok. 61, Galata (down the street from the staircase to Galata Tower). ℭ **0212/245-1861.** Appetizers and main courses 11YTL–15YTL ($8–$11). MC, V. Tues–Sun noon–midnight.

Otantik *(Kids* TRADITIONAL ANATOLIAN   For a special night out, Turks head to their favorite *et* or *balık* (meat or fish) restaurant, ready to splurge for dishes they themselves rarely cook at home. Finally, someone realized how delicious these "poor man" home-style recipes are, compiling a menu that includes *hıngal* (potato dumplings served with yogurt), *otantik yuvarlama çorba* (spicy lentil-based vegetable soup), and *keşkek* (a familiar-tasting dish of cream of wheat with pieces of chicken), along with various types of *gözleme* (filled pancake), *pilav*, and *kebaps* at extremely fair prices. The restaurant has four floors, each with its own traditional style, and the room in the fourth-floor annex sits right over the inner atrium of the Beaux Arts Çiçek Pasajı.

Istiklal Cad. 170 (next to the entrance to the Çiçek Pasajı). ℭ **0212/293-8451.** Appetizers and main courses 6.75YTL–11YTL ($5–$8). No credit cards. Daily 8am–midnight.

Refik *⊛* BLACK SEA SPECIALTIES   Tucked into a back street in Beyoğlu, Refik is unassuming, even unimpressive, from the outside. But this little restaurant has been an institution in the neighborhood since its inception in 1954. Success lies equally with the unfailing quality of the ingredients and the pride that goes into the preparation. The earliest shifts arrive at 6am to start the preparations for a menu that is distinct to the Black Sea region, and therefore, heavy on dishes with black cabbage.

The *hamsibuğulama* (fish steamed in season) along with the *arnavut ciğeri* (sautéed Albanian liver and onions) are house specialties, as is the *kara lahana dolması* (stuffed cabbage). Mezes change seasonally, and in the summer, tables spill onto the narrow street. Bonus: A ventilation system sucks the cigarette smoke up and away from diners.

Sofyalı Sok. 10–12, Tünel. ℭ **0212/243-2834.** Reservations required. Appetizers 5.50YTL ($4); main courses 9.50YTL ($7); fish sold by weight. AE, DC, MC, V. Daily noon–10:30pm.

ALONG THE BOSPHORUS
VERY EXPENSIVE

Tuğra *⊛⊛⊛* OTTOMAN   This place has created a legend for itself with its innovative synthesis of foods from the entire Ottoman Empire. Tuğra is the epitome of fusion food, so much so that its Turkish clientele comments that the traditional Ottoman dishes taste unfamiliar. It's possible to drop upwards of 200YTL ($150) per person on the special degustation menu and a few gin and tonics, a hefty price tag for the illustrious reputation of its landlord, the Çırağan Palace. If you don't drink and you order a la carte, you can at least expect an exceptional dining experience without the heart failure.

Çırağan Palace Hotel Kempinski Istanbul, Çırağan Cad 84, 80700 Beşiktaş. ℭ **0212/258-3377.** Reservations required. Dress smart. Appetizers 27YTL–34YTL ($20–$25) (93YTL/$69 for caviar); main courses 43YTL–71YTL ($32–$53); 6-course degustation menu (excluding tax and drinks) is 145YTL ($107). AE, DC, MC, V. Daily 7–11pm.

MODERATE

Carne *⊛⊛* *(Finds* MEDITERRANEAN   This sleek and chic spot across from the more boisterous cafes of Ortaköy is a welcome newcomer, and one of the few spots you can get a kosher meal. Black and beige banquettes, white table runners, and low-hanging lamps create an intimately romantic atmosphere, geared toward clients willing to have a go at the cappuccino pumpkin soup (admittedly an acquired taste). Leaning heavily on classic ingredients of the Mediterranean, Carne puts out mouthwatering dishes such as oven-baked chicken stuffed with apricot or grilled rack of lamb with smoked eggplant, bell pepper, rosemary, and lamb glaze *served in a tulip*. The list of appetizers does little to leave room for the main course, as who can resist a plate of salmon tartar or falafel served with your choice of humus or tomato sauce? For those with religious dietary restrictions, Carne is kosher.

Muallim Naci Cad. 41/10, Ortaköy. ℂ 0212/260-8425. Reservations suggested for dinner. Appetizers 6YTL–14YTL ($4.50–$10); main courses 8YTL–23YTL ($6–$17). MC, V. Daily noon–midnight.

Feriye Restaurant ✿✿ HISTORICAL TURKISH/OTTOMAN   Lesser princes and dignitaries were relegated to this stunning auxiliary palace, which has been renovated and converted into a luxurious restaurant and cultural center. Summertime is definitely the season for this spot, as the tables move out to the seaside terrace, creating a spectacular dining experience little more than an arm's length from scores of jellyfish. The seafood dishes are worth mentioning, if not only for the festivity of the occasion, than for the medallions of swordfish topped with a seafood ragout. Carnivores will not be disappointed by a menu reflecting the tastes of an empire that spanned the Middle East all the way to the Asiatic Sea; try the breast of chicken stuffed with pistachios and see what I mean. Twinkling Bosphorus views and nighttime sea breezes are romance at its best, while Feriye is equally popular during its Sunday brunch service.

Feriye Sarayı, Çırağan Cad. 124, Ortaköy (above the Çırağan Palace on the right). ℂ 0212/227-2216. Reservations required. Main courses 20YTL–65YTL ($15–$48). AE, MC, V. Daily 12:30–3pm and 7pm–midnight.

OFF THE BEATEN TRACK
EXPENSIVE

Körfez ✿✿✿ CREATIVE CUISINE/SPECIALTY FISH   A memorable meal is never just about great food, which is a given at Körfez. Here, the success of the restaurant is directly related to the tone set by the chef and owner, Ömer, who manages to infuse a sense of family-style, casual elegance, without compromising time and labor-intensive recipes. Part of the romance is the setting, an intimate waterside summer patio tucked into a small cove on the Asian side of the Bosphorus, with unexpectedly tranquil views of the floodlit fortress of Rumeli and the Bosphorus Bridge. In winter, dinner is served in a dining room that could easily be mistaken for the Captain's private cabin, which also benefits from a complete wall of windows. Getting there is half the fun: Ömer dispatches the restaurant's private skiff to the docks near Rumeli Hisarı on the European side. Some of Körfez's more teasing dishes are the signature salt-baked fish, a more complex grouper in a spicy Asian sauce, bonito "sushi," mackerel burgers with raisins and pistachios, and *levrek buğlama* (sea bass in a broth with shiitake mushrooms, ginger, tomato, and thyme).

Körfez Cad. 78, Kanıca (on the Asian side across from Rumeli Hisarı). ℂ 0216/413-4314. Reservations required in summer, year-round for shuttle boat transfer. Appetizers and main courses 50YTL–90YTL ($37–$67). MC, V. Mon 7pm–midnight; Tues–Sun noon–midnight.

MODERATE

Asitane ✿✿✿ ⓥ𝑎𝑙𝑢𝑒 OTTOMAN   Clearly, it was good to be the sultan, if he indeed ate at all like I do when I visit Asitane. Taking recipes directly from records of meals at Topkapı Palace, the chef of Asitane has succeeded in re-creating the ingenuity of the Ottoman cooks (and I'm not talking about that stuff drying out in the steam plates around town). The *etli elma dolması* (apple stuffed with lean diced lamb, rice, currants, pistachio, and rosemary) still makes my mouth water—the only regrettable thing is that I'll probably never eat it again, because the menu changes each season. There's a menu in honor of Fatih Sultan Mehmet (the Conqueror) May through June, while vegetarian main-course selections are on the menu year-round.

In the Kariye Oteli. Kariye Camii Sok. 18 (adjacent to the Church of St. Savior in Chora), Edirnekape. ℂ 0212/534-8414. Reservations suggested. Dress smart. Main courses 16YTL–26YTL ($12–$19). AE, DISC, MC, V. Daily noon–midnight.

Develi Restaurant 🟊🟊🟊 SOUTHEASTERN TURKISH KEBAP HOUSE Develi's success may have translated into a blossoming of sister locations around the country, but no matter how good the others may be, this Develi maintains a level of consistency and fabulousness worthy of more than what a simple star rating will allow. For their regional specialties, they follow outstanding recipes from the Gaziantep region of southeastern Turkey—this translates roughly as *blisteringly spicy.* Adventurous eaters should order the fiery *çig köfte,* beefy meatballs combined with every spice in the book, rolled up into flat little meatballs served raw in a soothing lettuce leaf. Other notable menu items include the *muhamara,* a delectable purée of bread, nuts, and chickpeas; the *findik lahmacun,* a thin-crust pizza made Turkish-style with chopped lamb; or the lamb sausage and pistachio *kebap.* Leave room for the *künefe,* a warm slab of baklava dough oozing cheese, dipped in syrup, and covered with crushed pistachio nuts. The rooftop terrace is stupendous in the summer, and there's a non-smoking room for indoor wintry evenings.

Balıkpazarı. Gümüşyüzük Sok. 7, Samatya. ℂ 0212/529-0833. Reservations required. Dress smart. Main courses 8.75YTL–20YTL ($6.50–$15). MC, V. Daily noon–midnight. From the Koca Mustafapaşa Train Station, look for the sign for Develi Otopark on the right; follow the sign and look for the fish market and the restaurant. From Sultanahmet, follow directions to airport and keep your eyes peeled for the Develi sign on the right. Park near the archway, then walk through and past the fish stalls, walk right then left; Develi is immediately on your right up a few steps.

5 What to See & Do in Istanbul

Istanbul is a city that has successfully incorporated a rich past into a promising future—no small feat considering the sheer magnitude of history buried under those cobblestone streets. Three of the greatest empires in Western history each claimed Istanbul as their capital; as a result, the city overflows with extraordinary sites all vying for equal time. Conveniently, all of the top sights are located on or immediately around Sultanahmet Park, but that by no means is an indication that there's nothing worth seeing outside of that neighborhood.

SUGGESTED ISTANBUL ITINERARIES

IF YOU HAVE 1 DAY   Stick to the Sultanahmet district; begin your tour chronologically at the Hippodrome, and work your way through the centuries with a visit to the Ayasofya, the Yerebatan Cistern, and the Blue Mosque. Spend the afternoon exploring the treasures of Topkapı Palace, and if there's any time left, take the tram to the Eminönü to see the Egyptian Spice Market. From there, walk up the hill to the Grand Bazaar (closed Sun), where you'll have but a few short hours to hone your bargaining prowess. (*Tip:* You can save some time by heading to the cistern first; this way you won't get stuck in the backlog of people waiting to get in to Topkapı Palace.)

IF YOU HAVE 2 DAYS   Save the visit to Topkapı Palace for the second day and give yourself ample time to enjoy the first day's itinerary. If you have time, take a taxi to St. Savior in Chora, or, if you're short on time, head to the Mosaic Museum. End the afternoon at a *hamam* and spend the evening in the bar or tea garden of your choice. After the second day's visit to Topkapı, head straight to the Istanbul Archaeology Museum in the first courtyard. After a much-needed coffee break, take a bus to the Military Museum in time for the 3pm performance of the Mehter Band, then walk back to Taksim and continue along the length of Istiklal Caddesi with a long stop in the Flower Arcade and Fish Market. Finish off the evening in one of the *meyhanes* of Beyoğlu.

IF YOU HAVE 3 DAYS   Follow the 2-day itinerary for Days 1 and 2, then set out early on Day 3 for a daylong cruise up the Bosphorus, allowing yourself at least an hour to explore the Egyptian Spice Bazaar and neighboring Yeni Cami and Rüstem Paşa Mosque before you board at the nearby ferry docks. If you're concerned about time, take a half-day guided sightseeing tour, which wraps up around lunchtime; it includes a stop at the Egyptian Spice Bazaar, an informed description of the sights along the Asian and European shores, and a visit to Rumeli Castle. If you've opted for the do-it-yourself Bosphorus cruise, disembark in Sariyer, stop off for a peek in the Sadberk Hanım Museum, then take a bus back to Dolmabahçe Palace for the guided tour. Spend your last evening in the neighborhood shops, followed by a hearty Turkish meal.

THE TOP SIGHTS

Ayasofya 🏛🏛🏛   For almost a thousand years, the Ayasofya was a triumph of Christianity and the symbol of Byzantium, and until the 16th century, maintained its status as the largest Christian church in the world. The cathedral is so utterly awesome that the Statue of Liberty's torch would barely graze the top. Erected over the ashes of two previous churches using dismantled and toppled columns and marble from some of the greatest temples around the empire, the Ayasofya (known in Greek as the Hagia Sophia and in English as St. Sophia, or Church of the Holy Wisdom), was designed to surpass in grandeur, glory, and majesty every other edifice ever constructed as a monument to God. Justinian began construction soon after his suppression of the Nika Revolt, indicating that combating unemployment was high on the list as well. He chose the two preeminent architects of the day: Anthemius of Tralles (Aydın) and Isidorus of Miletus. After 5 years and 4 months, when the construction of the Ayasofya was completed in A.D. 537, the emperor raised his hands to heaven and proclaimed, "Glory to God who has deigned to let me finish so great a work. O Solomon, I have outdone thee!" Enthusiasm for this feat of architecture and engineering was short-lived, because 2 years later, an earthquake caused the dome to collapse. The new dome was slightly smaller in diameter but higher than the original, supported by a series of massive towers to counter the effects of future earthquakes. Glass fittings in the walls were employed to monitor the weight distribution of the dome; the sound of crunching glass was an early warning system indicating that the weight of the dome had shifted. Several more earthquakes caused additional damage to the church, requiring repairs to the dome (among other sections), which was increased in height thanks to the support provided by the addition of flying buttresses (additional buttresses were added at two later dates).

In 1204 the Ayasofya was sacked and stripped down to the bare bones by the Crusaders, a desecration that robbed the church of precious relics and definitively divided the Greek Orthodox and Roman Catholic churches.

Istanbul Attractions

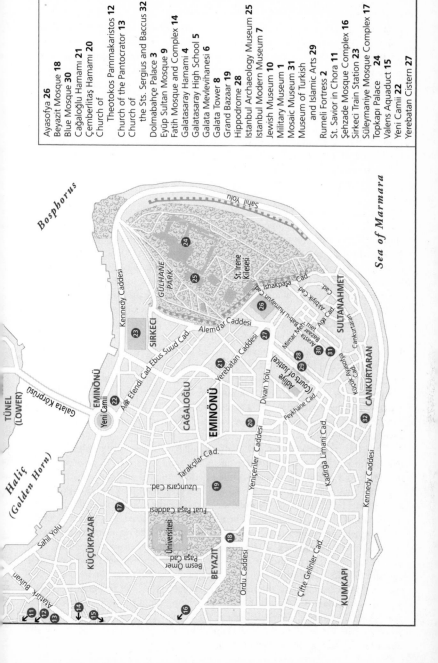

Ayasofya **26**
Beyazit Mosque **18**
Blue Mosque **30**
Cağaloğlu Hamamı **21**
Çemberlitaş Hamamı **20**
Church of
 Theotokos Pammakaristos **12**
Church of the Pantocrator **13**
Church of
 the Sts. Sergius and Baccus **32**
Dolmabahçe Palace **3**
Eyüp Sultan Mosque **9**
Fatih Mosque and Complex **14**
Galatasaray Hamamı **4**
Galatasaray High School **5**
Galata Mevlevihanesi **6**
Galata Tower **8**
Grand Bazaar **19**
Hippodrome **28**
Istanbul Archaeology Museum **25**
Istanbul Modern Museum **7**
Jewish Museum **10**
Military Museum **1**
Mosaic Museum **31**
Museum of Turkish
 and Islamic Arts **29**
Rumeli Fortress **2**
St. Savior in Chora **11**
Şehzade Mosque Complex **16**
Sirkeci Train Station **23**
Süleymaniye Mosque Complex **17**
Topkapi Palace **24**
Valens Aquaduct **15**
Yeni Camii **22**
Yerebatan Cistern **27**

Fun Fact **I Wish I May, I Wish I Might**

According to legend, when construction of the Ayasofya reached the height of a man, the construction team set out to get a bite to eat, leaving their tools under the watch of a small boy. An angel appeared and urged the boy to fetch the men so that they could return to the work of building God's house. When the boy told the angel that he promised not to leave the tools unattended, the angel promised to keep an eye on everything until his return. After leaving the site and thus breaking his promise, the boy was never allowed to return, and the angel continues to wait for him. Go to the entrance of the basilica proper, to the left of the Imperial Door; legend has it that the angel grants a wish to all those who successfully complete a 360-degree circle with their thumb in the hole of this wish-worn column.

After Mehmet II penetrated the city in 1453, his first official stop was to this overwhelming symbol of an empire that he had conquered, and with his head to the ground, he invoked the name of Allah, and declared the great house of worship a mosque. In the years that followed, several adjustments were made to the building, including the covering over of the frescoes and mosaics, due to the prohibition of Islam against the representation of figures. (The Iconoclastic movement of the 8th and 9th centuries had similarly disavowed the use of figural depictions and icons, during which many of the frescoes and mosaics were defaced, destroyed, or cemented over; any figural representations seen today date to after this period). A single wooden minaret was erected (and later replaced by Mimar Sinan during restorations in the 16th c.), and three additional minarets were added at a later date. The altar was shifted slightly to the right to accommodate a *mihrab* (the niche in a mosque oriented toward Mecca), and an ablution fountain, along with a kitchen, was erected in the courtyard.

Ayasofya was converted from a mosque into a museum by Atatürk in 1935, after a painstaking restoration led by Thomas Whitmore of the Byzantium Institute of America. Mosaics and icons that were previously defaced or whitewashed were rediscovered and restored.

While this enduring symbol of Byzantium still has the power to instill awe after so many additions and reconstructions (including tombs, schools, and soup kitchens during its tour of duty as a mosque), the exterior's original architecture is marred by large and boxy buttresses; you'll get more of a representation of the intent of Justinian's original from the inside. On your way in, notice the stone cannonballs lining the gravel path of the outer courtyard. These are the actual cannonballs used by Mehmet the Conqueror in his victorious 1453 battle for the city. The main entrance to Ayasofya leads to the **exonarthex** ⋆, a vaulted outer vestibule that was reserved for those not yet baptized. The **narthex** ⋆⋆, or inner vestibule, glistens with Justinian's original gold mosaics embellished with floral and geometric patterns. The most central of the nine doors leading into the nave of the church, called the **Imperial Gate** ⋆, is topped by a **mosaic** ⋆⋆⋆ of the Christ Pantocrator holding a book with the inscription "Peace be with you. I am the Light of the World." He is surrounded by roundels portraying the Virgin Mary, the angel Gabriel, and a bearded emperor, believed to represent Leo VI asking for forgiveness for his four marriages.

Through the Imperial Gate is a sight that brought both emperors and sultans to their knees: a soaring **dome** ✿✿✿ that rises 56m (184 ft.) in height (about 15 stories) and spans a width of approximately 31m (102 ft.). Light filters through a crown formed by 40 windows and ribs, glittering with the gold mosaic tiles that cover the entire interior of the dome. At its decorative peak (including the side aisles, semi-domes, inner walls, and upper galleries), Ayasofya's interior mosaics covered more than 4 acres of space. Eight calligraphic discs, four of which are the largest examples of calligraphy in the Islamic world, ornament the interior and bear the names of Allah and Mohammed (above the apse); the four successive caliphs, Ali, Abu Bakr, Osman, and Omar (at each of the four corners of the dome); and Ali's sons Hasan and Huseyin (in the nave). The main nave, side aisles, apse, and semi-domes are covered with mosaics and frescoes, depicting religious and imperial motifs or floral and geometric designs. Up in the southern gallery are some of the best mosaics in the church, including the **Deesis** ✿✿✿ (a composition depicting Christ, his mother, and St. John the Baptist), considered to be one of Byzantium's most striking mosaics, in spite of the missing lower two-thirds. This mosaic is one of the oldest, dating to the 14th century. Opposite the Deesis is **the tomb of Henrico Dandalo,** the blind Venetian doge whose success in diverting the Fourth Crusade to Constantinople resulted in his capture of the city in 1204. At the far end of the gallery near the apse are two additional mosaics: one depicting **Empress Zoë** ✿✿ with her third husband, Constantine IX Monomachus (see "Face Off in the Corner" below), separated by a figure of Christ, and a mosaic portrait of **Emperor John II Comnenus,** his wife, Empress Eirene, and their son, Prince Alexius (extended onto the panel on the wall to the right).

Exit the church through the small Vestibule of Warriors in the inner narthex opposite the ramp to the upper gallery. Previously used as an entrance, this is now an exit, so you're forced to turn around and view the mosaic lunette depicting an enthroned **Virgin Mother and Child** ✿✿✿, flanked by Constantine proffering a model of the city and Justinian offering a model (inaccurate) of the Ayasofya. (A mirror has been placed above the current exit to alert you to the mosaic behind you.)

Sultanahmet. ☎ 0212/522-1750. Admission 15YTL ($11). Tues–Sun 9am–5pm.

Blue Mosque (Sultan Ahmet Camii) ✿✿✿   This grand bubble of masonry, one of the great and defining features of Istanbul's skyline, was constructed between 1609 and 1617 by Sultan Ahmet I, who was not only driven by a desire to leave behind an imperial namesake mosque, but was also determined to build a monument to rival the Ayasofya. So great was the Sultan's ambition that he had one unfortunate architect executed before finally choosing Mehmet Ağa, probably a student of Sinan, who came up with a plan commonly accepted as impossible to build. The design is a scheme of

---

Fun Fact **Face Off in the Corner**

Empress Zoe had a lot of clout in the early part of the second millennium. First she had this glorious golden mosaic, found at the end of the upper gallery, crafted in her honor, depicting Christ between herself and her first husband. When her husband died in 1034, she ordered the tiles of his face along with the inscription replaced to accommodate her second husband, repeating the procedure for the third.

successively descending smaller domes that addresses the problem of creating a large covered interior space. The overall effect is one of such great harmony, grace, and power that it's impossible to walk away from this building unaffected.

There are several legends associated with the construction of the **six minarets.** One says that the sultan's desire for gold minarets—*altın* in Turkish—was understood as *altı,* or six. Whatever the reasoning, the construction challenged the preeminence of the mosque in Mecca, which at the time also had six minarets. The ensuing scandal, both in and out of Istanbul, resulted in the sultan's ordering the construction of a seventh minaret at the Kaa'ba.

The mosque was completed after just over 6½ years of work and to this day remains one of the finest examples of classical Ottoman architecture. The original complex included a soup kitchen, a *medrese* (Muslim theological school), a primary school, a hospital, and a market. A ***türbe,*** or mausoleum, stands at the corner of the grounds near the Hippodrome and Sultanahmet Park, and houses the remains of the Sultan Ahmet I, his wife, Kösem, and three of his sons. It also contains some fine examples of calligraphy on cobalt blue İznik tile.

In order to control the visiting mobs and protect the sanctity of the interior, tourists and visitors (nonworshippers) are required to use the entrance off the **Hippodrome,** beneath the symbolic chain that required even the sultan to bow his head when he arrived on horseback. The ablution fountains here indicate that this is actually the main entrance. If you plan your visit during the morning hours when the sun is still angled from the east, the first effect once inside will be one of blindness as the light penetrates the stained glass, creating an illusion of false darkness. As your eyes adjust, the swirling blues, greens, reds, and yellows from the tile and stained glass increase the impression of immensity and grandeur. The abundant use of decorative tile represents the pinnacle of **İznik tile** ⟨☆☆☆⟩ craftsmanship, evident in the rich yet subtle blues and greens in traditional Ottoman patterns of lilies, tulips, and carnations. The overall dominance of blue prompted the mosque's early visitors to label it the Blue Mosque, a name that sticks to this day.

Lateral half **domes** resting on enormous elephantine **columns** ⟨☆☆⟩ (actually called elephant foot pillars) enhance the sense of open space, but critics contend that the pillars are too overbearing and cumbersome. The elegant **medallions** ⟨☆⟩ facing the *mihrab* bear the names of Allah and Mohammed; the ones opposite are decorated with the names of the first four caliphs who ruled the Islamic world.

Sultanahmet. Free admission. Daily 9am–6pm. Avoid visiting during prayer times.

Grand Bazaar (Kapalı Çarşısı) ⟨☆☆☆⟩   The mother of all tourist traps, the Grand or Covered Bazaar is a vivid illustration of all that's gone wrong with the free market. The bazaar is a vast collection of over 2,600 shops (last count), 24 *hans* (privately owned inns or marketplaces), 65 streets, 22 gates, 2 *bedestens* (covered markets), restaurants, mosques, fountains, and teahouses. With over 500 goldsmiths each paying

---

Fun Fact **Did You Know?**

A broken or chipped İznik tile can get up to 27,000YTL ($20,000) at auction while an original in good condition sold at Sotheby's years ago for 810,000YTL ($600,000). Approximately 21,000 tiles were used to decorate the Blue Mosque.

Tips **Two Cafes in the Grand Bazaar**

Need a shot of caffeine? **Fez Café** ((C) **0212/527-3684;** Halıcılar Cad. 62) and **Café Ist** ((C) **0212/527-9353;** Tarakçılar Caddesi), both located in the Grand Bazaar, are open Monday through Saturday 8:30am to 7pm, and offer sanctuary from endless cups of Nescafe with a wide selection of coffees, flavored teas, and fresh-squeezed juices.

---

anywhere from 6,750YTL to 10,800YTL ($5,000–$8,000) per month in rent, it's easy to see why sales tactics are so aggressive. And like any of the world's major commercial centers, it attracts a disproportionate number of ruthless businessmen.

A free market gone awry, the bazaar used to operate on an Eastern mentality that factors a personal exchange into the process of buying and selling. (Although this can be a lovely way to get to know the people, buying a 14YTL ($10) item shouldn't require so much effort.) Innocent Westerners who are inexperienced or too embarrassed by the thought of bargaining (particularly Americans, who are less likely to bat an eye at a 38YTL/$28 T-shirt), naively fork over whatever it costs, ruining it for the rest of us. The result is that bargaining in the Grand Bazaar is falling into disuse and trinkets like those colorful hanging glass lamps are out of my price range. Nevertheless, if you show interest in an item, the price will more than likely be flexible. Etiquette requires that once you negotiate and agree on a price for something, it's rude to back out of the deal, but if we follow the rule of Grand Bazaar law, all's fair in shopping and war.

So how to explain wandering the corridors for 6 hours? Call it an addiction. Although anything but pleasant, it's still a mandatory stop on any itinerary in Istanbul. A good plan of attack is to enter via the **Nuruosmaniye Gate** (take a minute to admire the Nuruosmaniye Mosque, the first example of baroque-style architecture in Turkey), adorned with a marble fountain commemorating the fire of 1954 in which one-third of the bazaar went up in flames. This main drag is **Kalpakçilar Caddesi** *☞*, the glittering main thoroughfare lined on either side with shops of silver and gold. Turn right onto **Kolancılar** and follow it into the **İç Bedesten (Old Bazaar)** *☞* for a dazzling collection of antiques, jewelry, and copperware. Turn right again and follow **Ağa Sokağı** out of the bazaar into **Çuhacılar Hanı,** a beautiful courtyard amid shops of antique silver and gold jewelry. On your way down the passage to the *han,* notice the chaos of the open-air **Stock Exchange,** packed shoulder to shoulder with cellphone-wielding financiers.

To the north of the bazaar just beyond the exterior gates is a scattering of more *hans,* less-frequented workshops with retail outlets that are infinitely more charming than those inside. Because much of the merchandise is made on the premises, prices can be lower than in the main bazaar area.

The **Silk Bazaar (Sandal Bedesten)** *☞*, the oldest section of the bazaar (it was built 10 years after the İç Bedesten, but burned down twice before being rebuilt in stone), and the **Cervahir Bedesten** couldn't be farther apart these days; while Cervahir's quality silver and jewelry can be found in Barney's New York shop windows, the Sandal Bedesten traded in its namesake silk for acrylic and sweats.

Free admission. Best entrances through the Beyazıt Gate (across from the Beyazıt stop on the tramway along Divanyolu) and the Nuruosmaniye Gate (from the Çemberlitaş tramway stop on Divanyolu, follow Vezirhanı Caddesi to the arched entrance to the mosque grounds, which lead to the bazaar). Maps of the bazaar are available at newsstands for 9.50YTL ($7). Mon–Sat 8:30am–7pm.

Hippodrome ⋆ Watching the modestly clothed couples with their children strolling through the park on a Sunday afternoon, it's hard to imagine the centuries of rowdy chariot races, ostentatious royal celebrations, and bloody massacres that took place on these lawns. During the month of Ramadan, the trees above the park are strung with white lights, and temporary tents and imitation Ottoman houses full of fast food are set up along the perimeter, while a pink-and-blue fiberglass elephant ride for toddlers wipes away any remaining stains of the Hippodrome's complex past.

The first track was built in A.D. 203 by Septimus Severus out of the ruins of the city that he had conquered. Modeled on the Circus Maximus in Rome, the Hippodrome was enlarged by Constantine in 324 through the help of supporting vaults and hefty stone walls on the southern portion of the tract. The lower areas (down the hill at the obelisk end of the park) were used as stables and quarters for the gladiators.

Forty rows of seats accommodated up to 100,000 people, agitated supporters divided into merchant guilds, that over time degenerated into political rivalries. These factions were known as the Blues, Greens, Reds, and Whites. The Blues and Greens put aside their disagreements to demonstrate against the emperor in 532, which resulted in a riot with protesters screaming "Nika!"(Greek for victory). In what would become known as the Nika Revolt, much of the imperial palace and the original church of Ayasofya were destroyed. Justinian eventually regained control of his throne and ordered the massacre of some 30,000 to 40,000 people. With the arrival of the Fourth Crusade, the Hippodrome fell into disuse, eventually serving as a marble quarry for the Ottomans after their conquest of the city.

At the height of its splendor, the Hippodrome was crowned with a vast collection of trophies, statues, and monuments, either crafted by local artisans or lifted from the far corners of the empire.

At the southern end of the park is the **Magnetic Column** ⋆⋆, also known as the Walled Obelisk, the Plaited Column, the Colossus, and the Column of Constantine. This column was erected in the 10th century under Constantine VII Porphyrogenitus and was faced with plaques of gilded bronze and brass plates. At one time this obelisk was used to support a pulley system for raising and lowering awnings to protect the spectators from the sun. In 1204 the bronze and brass plates were removed and smelted by the Crusaders to mint coins.

Farther along is the **Serpentine Column** ⋆⋆, a squat spiral standing 25% lower than its original 8m (26 ft.). The column was originally erected outside the Temple of Apollo at Delphi by the 31 Greek city-states to commemorate their victory over the

---

⟨*Tips* Avoid Local Shop "Commissioners"

The dregs of Turkish society mill around the entrances to the major sites in Sultanahmet (Blue Mosque, Ayasofya, Topkapı, and the Hippodrome), lying in wait to pounce on you and a percentage of anything you buy. Avoid walking into a carpet shop accompanied by a local—a simple, naive act that tacks up to 60% on to the cost of your item. Shop owners stay one step ahead by printing business cards for their commissioners, who then coax unwitting tourists into "their shop." (Also, see "Important Tips for Women Travelers" in chapter 2.)

Persians, and later brought to the city by Constantine. Made of melded bronze, the column represents three intertwining serpents, and was crowned by three gold serpents' heads supporting a gold bowl, said to have been cast from the shields of the fallen Persian soldiers. The heads were lost until one resurfaced during the restoration of the Ayasofya, now in the Archaeological Museum. A second head was discovered and, like many ancient Turkish monuments, slithered its way to the British Museum in London.

The **Obelisk of Tutmosis III** ✿✿✿ is easily one of the most astounding feats of engineering in the city. This 13th-century-B.C. solid block of granite weighing over 60 tons was brought to Istanbul by Emperor Theodosius I from its place in front of the Temple of Luxor at Karnak, in Egypt. The four sides of granite are covered from top to bottom with hieroglyphics celebrating the glory of the pharaoh and the god Horus. The monument was placed in the square in A.D. 390, but *two-thirds* of the original was lost during transport. This portion, standing over 20m (65 ft.) high, was erected in under 30 days, on a Roman base depicting bas-reliefs of Theodosius's family, friends, and triumphs at the races.

At the northern end of the Hippodrome is the **Fountain of Wilhelm II (Alman Çeşmesi)** ✿✿, crafted in Germany and assembled in Istanbul to commemorate the emperor's visit to the city in 1895. Notice the initials of both the German monarch and Sultan Abdülhamid on the interior of the dome, inlaid with glittering golden mosaics.

The Hippodrome's crowning monument, long a distant memory of its original grandeur atop a disappeared imperial loggia, was a monumental **statue of four bronze horses.** In the Fourth Crusade's looting of the city in 1204, the monument was carried away to grace the facade of the Basilica of St. Marco in Venice. (Today, the ones on the facade are fake; the real ones are being protected from the elements in the Basilica of St. Marco's museum.)

At Meydanı (Horse Plaza), Sultanahmet. Always open.

Istanbul Archaeology Museum (Arkeoloji Müzesi) ✿✿   The Istanbul Archaeology Museum is housed in three buildings just inside the first court of Topkapı Palace and includes the Museum of the Ancient Orient and the Çinili Köşk. These museums, opened officially in 1891, owe their very existence to Osman Hamdi Bey, a 19th-century Turkish painter, archaeologist, curator, and diplomat, who fought for the Antiquities Conservation Act to combat the rampant smuggling of antiquities out of Turkey.

The Istanbul Archaeological Museum houses over one million objects, the most extraordinary of which are the sarcophagi that date back as far as the 4th century B.C. The museum excels, however, in its rich chronological collection of locally found artifacts that shed light on the origins and history of the city.

Near the entrance is a **statue of a lion** representing the only piece saved from the clutches of British archaeologists from the Mausoleum of Halicarnassus. In the halls to the left is a collection of sarcophagi found at Sidon (ancient Syria) representing various architectural styles influenced by outside cultures including Egypt, Phoenicia, and Lycia. The most famous is the **Alexander Sarcophagus** ✿✿✿, covered with astonishingly advanced carvings of battles and the life of Alexander the Great, discovered in 1887 and once believed to have been that of the emperor himself. The discovery that the occupant was in fact Sidonian King Abdalonymos may have initially been disappointing, but it hasn't diminished the impact of this great ancient work of art.

Found in the same necropolis at Sidon is the stunningly preserved **Sarcophagus of the Crying Women** ✸✸✸, with 18 intricately carved panels showing figures of women in extreme states of mourning. Don't miss the monumental **Lycian tomb** ✸✸✸, carved in a style befitting a great king and just as impressive in this exhibit as on the hills of Lycia.

On the mezzanine level is the exhibit *Istanbul Through the Ages* ✸✸, a rich and well-presented exhibit that won the museum the Council of Europe Museum Award in 1993. To put the exhibit into perspective, the curators have provided maps, plans, and drawings to illustrate the archaeological findings, displayed thematically, which range from prehistoric artifacts found west of Istanbul to 15th-century Byzantine works of art. The recovered **snake's head** ✸ from the Serpentine Column in the Hippodrome is on display, as is the 14th-century bell from the Galata Tower. The upper two levels, closed as of this writing, house the Troy exhibit and displays on the evolution of Anatolia over the centuries, as well as sculptures from Cyprus, Syria, and Palestine.

The newly renovated and reopened **Museum of the Ancient Orient** ✸✸✸ is an exceptionally rich collection of artifacts from the earliest civilizations of Anatolia, Mesopotamia, Egypt, and the Arab continent. The tour begins with pre-Islamic divinities and idols taken from the courtyard of the Al-Ula temple, along with artifacts showing ancient Aramaic inscriptions and a small collection of Egyptian antiquities. Although the individual exhibits are modest in size, the recent upgrade rivals Ankara's archaeological museum for organization and presentation.

Uncovered in the region of Mesopotamia and on display is an **obelisk of Adad-Nirari III** inscribed with cuneiform characters. Of particular significance is a series of colored **mosaic panels** ✸✸ showing animal reliefs of bulls and dragons with serpents' heads from the monumental Gate of Ishtar, built by Nebuchadnezzar, King of Babylonia. A pictorial representation on a **Sumerian devotional basin** of girls carrying pitchers of water whose contents are filling an underground source relates to the ancient Mesopotamian belief that the world was surrounded by water, a belief that has provoked questions over the origins of the biblical Great Flood.

With nothing dating more recent than the 1st century A.D., it's a real challenge to find something in this museum that is not of enormous significance. But two of the highlights are easily the fragments of the 13th-century-B.C. **sphinx** ✸ from the Yarkapı Gate at Hattuşaş (sadly underappreciated in its positioning against a passage wall) and one of the three known tablets of the **Treaty of Kadesh** ✸✸, the oldest recorded peace treaty signed between Ramses II and the Hittites in the 13th century B.C., inscribed in Akkadian, the international language of the era. (The Istanbul Archaeological Museum houses two; the third is in the Staatliche Museum in Berlin.)

Across from the Archaeology Museum is the **Çinili Köşk,** a wonderful pavilion of turquoise ceramic tiles whose facade displays eye-catching blue and white calligraphy. The mansion was originally built by Mehmet the Conqueror as a hunting pavilion, and now more appropriately houses the Museum of Turkish Ceramics. The museum, which is closed more often than not, contains a modest collection of Anatolian and Selçukian tiles, not the least of which is the 14th-century *mihrab* from the Ibrahim Bey mosque in Karaman in central Anatolia. Other highlights include some fine samples from İznik and Kütahya, the two most important production centers for pottery, porcelain, and ceramics during the Ottoman period.

Topkapı Palace (to the right of and behind St. Irene). (℃) **0212/520-7740**. Admission 5.50YTL ($4); includes the Museum of the Ancient Orient and the Çinili Köşk. Tues–Sun 9am–5pm.

Museum of Turkish and Islamic Arts   Ibrahim Paşa, swept into slavery by Turkish raids in Greece, became the beloved and trusted boyhood friend of Süleyman the Magnificent. Educated and converted to Islam and eventually appointed grand vizier, Ibrahim Paşa was the sultan's only companion at mealtime, earning him the favored title *serasker sultan* (commander in chief). He also earned the sultan's sister's hand in marriage.

The palace was a gift from the sultan and was built by Sinan. From this very special palace on the Hippodrome, the sultan's family and friends had front-row seats for festivities in the square. Roxelana, the sultan's wife, managed to dispose of her rival in one of her infamous intrigues, by convincing the sultan that his grand vizier had become too big for his britches.

The palace now houses the changing exhibitions of the Museum of Turkish and Islamic Arts, a fine collection of calligraphy, peace treaties, several examples of the sultan's official seal or *tuğra,* and an insightful ethnographic section depicting the lifestyles of nomads and city-dwelling Ottomans.

Ibrahim Paşa Sarayı, on the Hippodrome, Sultanahmet. ℂ **0212/518-1805.** Admission 4YTL ($3). Tues–Sun 9am–5pm.

Topkapı Palace (Topkapı Sarayı) ✸✸✸   Residence of the sultans, administrative seat of the Ottoman Empire for almost 400 years, and the source of legend on life in the harem, Topkapı Palace should be up at the top of the list for anyone interested in the vast and exotic world behind the seraglio walls. It's impossible to rush through the palace, so you should allot at least a half-day and be prepared to encounter a few bottlenecks throughout the enclosed exhibition halls, especially in the Holy Relics Room where the ardent faithful, in their religious fervor, tend to obstruct the display cases. Built by Mehmet the Conqueror over the ruins of Constantine's Imperial Palace, Topkapı Palace occupies one of the seven hills of the city at the tip of the historic peninsula overlooking the sea. Since it is easily the most valuable real estate in the city, it doesn't take a brain surgeon to see why this spot was preferable to the original palace situated on an inland tract where the university stands today. Mehmet II began construction of the palace 9 years after his conquest of the city, where the sultans reigned continually until 1855, when Abdülmecid moved the imperial residence up the Bosphorus to Dolmabahçe Palace.

Entrance to the grounds is through the Gate of Augustus at the end of the Babuhümayun Caddesi (also called the Bab-ı Hümayün Gate), behind the Ayasofya, named for the square outside the gate that in Byzantine times was a busy crossroads called the Forum of Augustus. Serving as the entrance through which the public would access the grounds, the gate would often display the decapitated heads of uncooperative administrators or rebels as a warning to all who entered. Just outside the gate is the **Ahmet III Fountain** ✸✸, built by Mehmet Ağa in 1729 atop an ancient source of water as a gift to Sultan Ahmet. A poem by the sultan is inscribed in the stone, inviting passersby to "drink the water and pray from the House of Ahmet."

⟮*Fun Fact* **Did You Know?**

Whenever a sultan ordered the execution of someone abroad, he would require that the head be brought back to him as proof. The heads were dipped in wax to preserve them for the long—and sometimes hot—ride home.

Tips **A Cafe Near the Gates of the Topkapi**

Just outside of the main gate to Topkapı Palace is the **Dösim outdoor cafe** and tea garden (open in summer). It's attached to the Dösim gift shop, which must account for the reasonable prices.

The first courtyard, known as the **Court of the Janissaries,** is a public park of gardens and trees, just as it was in earlier days. Along the center path are the remains of a 5th-century Roman cistern. (You can save this for the way out.)

The diagonal path to the left leads to the stunning **Hagia Eirene (St. Irene)** ☆☆☆, the second-largest Byzantine church after Ayasofya, and a church that predates the arrival of Constantine's conquest of the city. The first temple on the site was dedicated to the goddess Aphrodite, then enlarged by Constantine and later reconstructed by Justinian after its near destruction (along with that of the Ayasofya) in the Nika Revolt. Excavation between 1946 and 1950 indicates that a series of buildings existed connecting the church with the Ayasofya, and the fact that both churches were completed and rededicated at about the same time indicates that these houses of worship were in some way part of a complex. The buildings were later demolished to make room for construction of the palace walls. Rumor has it that Mehmet the Conqueror's Italian consort convinced him to store the house porcelain there, where she could then secretly go and pray, but for the record, the Ottomans used the church as an arsenal. Hagia Eirene is closed to the public but is used as a venue for concerts and recitals during the International Istanbul Music Festival in the summertime. The church may be opened on special request (© **0212/520-6952**).

The ticket booths to the palace are located on the right side of the courtyard. Proceed to the Ortakapı (middle gate), known as the **"Gate Of Salutation"** ☆, roughly translated from the Arabic (Turkish version) *Babüsselâm.*

Added by Süleyman the Magnificent in 1524, this gate signaled to all but the sultan to dismount before proceeding into the palace. On either side of the gate are two octagonal towers that essentially served as death row for those who fell out of favor; after a prisoner's execution, the body would be left outside the gate. To the right of the gate (facing), is a marble fountain where the executioner would wash the blood off his hands before reentering the palace.

Begin your visit with the **Palace Kitchens** ☆☆, a complex comprised of a string of lofty chambers topped by a series of chimney-domes, a narrow inner courtyard, and a smaller string of rooms. The largest in the world, the kitchens at one time employed over 1,000 servants working day and night to serve the 5,000 residents of the palace, a number that swelled to 15,000 during Ramadan. At the far end is the original wooden kitchen that survived a 16th-century fire; Sinan, who reconstructed the kitchens, added the massive conical chimneys and enlarged the original space. Suspended from the iron bars in the ceiling were the cauldrons, raised or lowered over the fire pits below according to the desired intensity of the flame. The kitchens are now used to exhibit the palace's rich collection of **porcelain** ☆ numbering close to 12,000 pieces, not all of which are displayed. Topkapı houses the third-most-important collection of porcelain in the world, after Beijing and Dresden, while the palace's collection of celadons surpasses that of Beijing because the Chinese destroyed all of theirs during the Cultural Revolution. Besides these 4th- and 5th-century celadons are pieces from the Sung and Yuan dynasties (9th–13th c.), pieces from the Ming Dynasty (14th and 17th c.), and porcelain from the Ching Dynasty (16th–20th c.). Many of these treasures found their way to Istanbul as gifts exchanged between the Ottomans, Chinese, and Persians as symbols of solidarity toward the maintenance and protection of the roads. There's also a rich collection of silver, particularly coffee services, candelabras, and mirrors (ornamented on the backside because of the proscription requiring the reflective side to be lain face down), and a display of Venetian glass and Bohemian crystal. The Ahmet III Fountain outside the main entrance is reproduced here in a stunning mass of silver, but there are examples of collectibles on a less grandiose scale as well.

Following a direct path along the length of the palace grounds, proceed to the **Gate of Felicity (Babüssaade)** ✸, also known as the Gate of the White Eunuchs. For 400 years, enthronement ceremonies were held at the entrance to this gate, today used as a backdrop for the annual presentation of Mozart's *Abduction from the Seraglio* during the International Istanbul Music Festival. Decapitated heads found their way above this gate as well. Only the sultan and the grand vizier were allowed past this gate into the third courtyard (while the Valide Sultan used a back gate for entrances and exits), the private quarters of the palace. Immediately inside the Gate of Felicity and acting as a visual barrier to the private quarters beyond is the **Throne Room** ✸, a pavilion used by the sultan as an audience chamber to receive (or affront) visiting ambassadors. Notice the interlocking marble used in the construction of the arched doorway; this design technique reinforced the archway and protected it against earthquakes.

Directly to the right is the Seferliler Quarters, now housing the **Palace Clothing Exhibition** or Imperial Wardrobe. Because the sultan's clothing was considered to be holy, a sultan's wardrobe would be wrapped up and preserved in the palace. This opulent display of silk, brocade, and gold-threaded clothing is only a small portion of the whole collection and includes enormously baggy costumes (to give the sultan the visual advantage of size), along with caftans and other garments showing influences from around the empire.

Past the Palace Clothing Exhibition is the Fatih Pavilion, containing a recently restored exhibition of the **Treasury** ✸✸✸, one of the greatest collections of treasures in the world. In 400 years a sultan can amass a great quantity of wealth, supplied through spoils of war, gifts from neighboring kings and queens, and the odd impulse buy. The rooms were off-limits to everyone but the sultan, and in his absence, any visitor was required to be accompanied by at least 40 other men.

Room no. 1 of the Treasury is a collection of Ottoman objects and **ceremonial thrones** ✸✸✸, including one in pure gold, weighing in at 550 pounds, presented to Murat III in 1585 by the Egyptian governor; an ebony throne crafted for Süleyman the Magnificent; and a jewel-encrusted throne, presented to Mahmut I by Nadir Shah of India.

The eye is immediately drawn to the jewel-studded mother-of-pearl and tortoise-shell throne of Sultan Ahmet I, crafted by the master of inlay, Mehmet Ağa, the same man commissioned by the sultan to build the Blue Mosque. (Rumor has it that during his 1995 visit, Michael Jackson requested permission to sit in one of the thrones; however, his request was denied.) Also of note in room no. 1 is the **sword** belonging to Süleyman the Magnificent, with his name and title inscribed on the blade.

Room no. 2 of the Treasury displays a collection of medals, and non-Ottoman objects and gifts (or plunder) received through the spoils of war. Immediately to the left of the exterior door is a **holy relic** ✸—a piece of St. John the Baptist's skull and

---

(*Fun Fact* **Better Safe Than Sorry**

Sultans preferred to eat off celadon china, because the pigments changed color when put in contact with poisons.

---

a section of his forearm, enclosed within a solid gold model. Other highlights include figurines crafted in India from seed pearls, and in the same case, a miniature tree of life and a vessel presented as gifts to the tomb of Mohammed.

The focus of room no. 3 is a pair of shoulder-high **candlesticks** ✦ crafted of solid gold and caked with several thousand brilliants/diamonds and weighing over 105 pounds each. In a world absent of electricity, candlesticks like these would be placed on either side of the *mihrab* to provide light for the reading of the holy book. This pair was presented to the tomb of Mohammed in Medina and brought back to Istanbul after World War I. The rest of the exhibit in room no. 3, an overwhelming collection of jade, rock crystal, zinc, emeralds, and other precious gems, displays Ottoman objects made by artists and craftsmen for the sultans throughout the centuries.

Room no. 4 is the Treasury's *pièce de résistance,* a breathtaking view into the wealth of the Ottoman Empire. The famous **Topkapı Dagger** ✦ is here, weighted down by a row of emeralds and diamonds in the hilt and on the cover. This dagger was the protagonist in the 1964 film *Topkapı* (with Peter Ustinov), an amusing film about a plot to rob the Palace Museum. The actual dagger was intended as a gift from Sultan Mahmud I to Nadir Shah to warn him of an impending conspiracy on his life, but was returned by the couriers following a bloody revolution in which the shah was killed.

You'll notice a group of people hovering around a case at the far end of room no. 4, displaying the 86-caret **Spoon Maker's Diamond** ✦✦, or Kaşıkd[cd]ı Diamond, the fifth-largest diamond in the world glittering in a setting of 49 smaller diamonds. The diamond was actually discovered in the 17th century in a city dump by a local peddler who sold it to a jeweler for pennies.

The exhibit finishes with a stunning collection of "lesser" diamonds and gems, plus the **gold and jewel–encrusted chain mail** ✦✦ of Sultan Mustafa III. Also of note is the **ceremonial sword** ✦, attributed to either Caliph Osman (7th c.) or Osman Gazi (13th c.), and used in any sultan's inauguration, usually in front of Eyüp Sultan Mosque.

Another piece of note is the **golden cradle** ✦✦ in which newborn sons were presented to the sultans, as well as an **emerald pendant** ✦ with 48 strings of pearls originally sent by Sultan Abdülhamid I as a gift to the tomb of the Prophet Mohammed in Mecca. The pendant was returned to Istanbul after Mecca was no longer within the borders of the empire.

Exit the courtyard down the stairs to the right through a long passage. To the right and parallel to the sea is the second terrace, affording one of the best views in the city. Imagine the days of seaside attacks on the palace walls as you watch the maritime traffic go by. During Byzantine times, a chain, composed of links .8m (2½ ft.) long, was forged to span the Golden Horn and prevent enemy ships from accessing the waterway.

This fourth courtyard was the realm of the sultan, and a stroll around the gardens will reveal some lovely examples of Ottoman kiosk architecture. Near the center of the upper level of the courtyard is the **Mustafa Paşa Kiosk,** the oldest building in the complex, which served as the physician's quarters and as a wardrobe for the sultan needing to effect swift changes during state functions. From the picture window overlooking the gardens, the sultan was known to observe wrestling matches, and even join in every now and again.

Perched on the upper terrace at the northernmost corner of the palace complex is the **Baghdad Kiosk** 𝕲, magnificently sited to take best advantage of the views of the Golden Horn. The kiosk is decorated with priceless İznik tiles, both inside and out. In addition to the tiles, the interior space is embellished with stained glass and crowned by a dome decorated with a traditional Ottoman motif in gold leaf. The kiosk served the sultan in colder weather; occupants of the kiosk were warmed by the central brazier.

The **circumcision rooms,** rarely opened to the public, are also located in the fourth courtyard.

Backtrack through the passage and up the steps into the third courtyard. To the right past the Museum Directorate is the **Dormitory of the Pages of the Imperial Treasury,** formerly used to display decorative calligraphy from the Koran as well as jeweled Koran sets. At press time the dormitory was closed. At the far corner of the third courtyard is the **Holy Relic Section** 𝕲𝕲𝕲, the largest collection in the world of this type, containing the personal belongings of the Prophet Mohammed, the caliphs, and even the unexpected **staff of Moses** 𝕲. The items on display were brought back to Istanbul by Selim the Grim in 1517, following his conquest of the holy cities of Mecca and Medina, and after declaring himself caliph. Since the Kaa'ba was restored annually, pieces of the mosque were regularly kept as ornamentation for mosques. This collection was off-limits to anyone but the most favored members of the sultan's family, and was only open to public viewing in 1962. The domed space is ornamented with İznik tiles and quotations from the Koran along with a priceless set of rain gutters, an intricately carved door, and an old set of keys taken from the Kaa'ba. Directly opposite the entrance are the **four sabers** belonging to the first four caliphs, and the first-ever copy of the **Koran** 𝕲, documented on deerskin.

To the right is the **Mohammed Chamber** 𝕲𝕲𝕲, fronted by a booth in which an *imam* (religious guide) has been reciting passages from the Koran continually for the past 500 years. This tradition was started by Mehmet II and sets the stage for the collection of holy relics within. The **golden cloth** 𝕲 that once covered the black stone in the central courtyard of the Kaa'ba in Mecca now hangs in this exhibit, as a new one is richly prepared each year. Considered a gift falling from the heavens, the stone prompted Abraham to build a temple on the spot, attracting worshippers from all faiths for several hundred years. The display cases are hidden behind religious fervent communing with the spirit of the prophet through **relics** 𝕲𝕲 of his hair, a tooth, his footprints, and even soil from his grave. The **Holy Mantle,** the most sacred item in the collection, is contained in a **gold coffer** 𝕲𝕲 and sequestered in an inaccessible area of this room behind a grilled door.

Tips Topkapı Palace Lunch Break

After touring the Treasury, you've reached the halfway point and a good place to stop for lunch or drinks. The expansive **Konyalı restaurant** (𝄐 **0212/ 513-9696**) includes indoor and outdoor dining rooms, as well as an outdoor cafeteria-style snack bar (see "Where to Dine" earlier in this chapter).

Turkish and Iranian miniatures as well as portraits of Ottoman sultans are exhibited in the rooms next to the one containing the Holy Relics. While the original collection amounts to a total of 13,000 specimens, this exhibit comes nowhere near this number. The main draw is the collection of portraits (both copies and originals) modeled after those painted by some of the Renaissance's most celebrated artists (Veronese, Bellini). Lacking any record of the physiological characteristics of the first 12 sultans, the Ottomans had the ones painted by the Venetians brought back to Istanbul in 1579.

In the center of the courtyard is the **Ahmet III Library,** constructed in the 16th century of white marble and recently restored and opened to the public. The bookcases are inlaid with ivory and contain about 6,000 volumes of Arab and Greek manuscripts. The stained glass is from the early 17th century; the platform divan seating is typically Ottoman, and the carpets are over 500 years old.

Return to the second courtyard, where along the right side you will come upon the **Imperial Armory,** a collection of arms and objects acquired during the various military campaigns. Mehmet the Conqueror's sword is here, as is Süleyman the Magnificent's, but it's the unattributed 2.5m (8-ft.) one that really impresses.

Before entering the Harem, take a peek into the **Imperial Council Hall,** or **Divan** ⍟, constructed during the reign of Süleyman the Magnificent. State affairs were conducted here while the sultan eavesdropped from the grate above, which leads directly to the Harem. From this concealed position, the sultan could interrupt proceedings with a motion to his grand vizier and call for a private conference whenever the need arose. His wife, Roxelana, would often secretly attend these sessions, a privilege that ended in several unfortunate fatalities.

To visit the **Harem** ⍟⍟ you must purchase a ticket for one of the tours near the Carriage Gate entrance next to the Divan; your tour time will be indicated on your ticket. Tours depart on the half-hour and last about 30 minutes. Buy your ticket to the Harem at the beginning of your visit to the palace because when the tour buses arrive, the wait on both the ticket and entry lines can be very long. Of the 400 rooms, only around 20 are on the tour, with explanations that are not always audible or, for that matter, intelligible. Nonetheless, the tour is worth taking.

The Harem has three main sections: the outer quarters of the Black Eunuchs charged with guarding the Harem; the inner stone courtyard for the concubines; and the apartments facing the sea reserved for the sultan, his mother, favorite concubines, and future heirs to the throne. The tour begins at the Carriage Gate, where the sultan's mother and wives would be whisked away unseen by outsiders during exits and entrances. Past the first Guard Room is a long courtyard lined with cells that served as the Barracks of the Black Eunuchs. The upper levels were reserved for the younger eunuchs, with the lower cells housing the older ones. Winding through the maze of additions, the tour comes to the quarters of the concubines, unheated and often unsanitary rooms around a claustrophobic stone courtyard. The only way out was to be one of the very lucky few chosen by the mother for the sultan; the others were servants to the sultan, or to the girls higher up on the hierarchy. At its most crowded, the Harem housed over 800 concubines. Even if the sultan rotated every night, the numbers were against those girls, and although some were given to the harems of state officials or grand viziers, many died virgins (but who knows what really went on in there . . .).

In contrast, the **Apartment of the Valide Sultan** ⍟⍟, sandwiched between the girls' quarters and her son's, is a domed wonder of mother-of-pearl, ivory, tortoise

Fun Fact The Forbidden City

The word *harem,* Arabic for "forbidden," conjures up images of bellybuttons, grapes, and palm trees, and of limitless pleasure, unless you're the one fanning the sultan. The reality was closer to a deluxe prison, a stifling hierarchy of slaves, concubines, and wives from which only a few ever emerged. It was even common practice for a new sultan to drown the concubines of his predecessor, to eliminate the possibility that one might be carrying a child with designs on the throne. The mystery enshrouding these enclosed walls was never truly lifted, and even concubines who survived kept silent.

The institution of the harem was established by Süleyman the Magnificent in 1587 following a fire in the palace in Beyazit, when the cunning Roxelana convinced him to transfer his residence over to Topkapı. Muslims are exceedingly private people, and these enclosed and restricted quarters served to maintain the "curtain" over the feminine members of his extended family.

shell, gold leaf, porcelain tiles, and frosted glass. The apartment consisted of a bedroom, a dining room, a chamber for prayer, and an office around a courtyard.

The **sultan's private bath** *⚶*, furnished with the usual *hamam* gear but infinitely more lush, has a guarded mesh gate so that the sultan could relax without the fear of being disturbed or assassinated. The sultan's apartments are close by, and the visit continues with the **Imperial Reception Hall** *⚶⚶*, where celebrations or evenings of entertainment took place while musicians played discreetly from the mezzanine. While the sultan presided from his throne, the women adhered to a strict hierarchy, with the most important women seated at the center of the platform.

One of the few rooms preserving the luster of its creator is the grand domed **Private Chambers of Murat III** *⚶⚶*, built by Sinan in 1578. The walls are covered with a classic blue İznik tile with red highlights, a prototype that was never duplicated. A frieze of calligraphy runs the perimeter of the room, and elegant panels of flowers and plums surround a bronze fireplace. The room is also called the Fountain Room because of the marble fountain that was kept running to mask conversations not intended for prying ears.

The **Reading Room** used by Ahmet I is a small but well-positioned library that affords distracting views of the convergence of the three waterways: the Golden Horn, the Marmara Sea, and the Bosphorus.

The **Fruit Room** is more of a breakfast nook added by Sultan Ahmet III to his private chambers. One look and it's not hard to figure out how this room got its name. The room is enveloped in fruit and floral overkill, but evidently the sultan's attentions were focused on the Harem pool out the window.

The next stop on the Harem tour is at the twin apartments of the crown prince, better known as **The Cage** *⚶*. In the early years of the empire, a crowned prince was well prepared to fulfill his destiny as a leader, beginning his studies in these rooms and later moving on to actual field experience in one of the provinces. When the practice of fratricide was abandoned, brothers of the sultan were sequestered in these rooms, where they either went crazy or languished in the lap of luxury—or both. The opulence of the stained glass and the tile work and the mother-of-pearl inlaid cabinets belie the chambers' primary function as a jail cell, which supports a recent discovery that the actual cage was located in another part of the Harem. The tour guides continue to perpetuate the myth by billing these two rooms as the bona fide cage.

The Harem tour comes to an end at the **Courtyard of the Favorites** ✸✸, surrounded by a charming building recalling the medieval residences of Florence. The apartments on the upper floors were reserved for the members of the Harem the sultan liked best, enjoying open space and sea views as far as the Princes' Islands. The circular spot in the center of the courtyard was covered with a tent for shaded outings, and the grooves served as water channels for cooling.

The exit to the second courtyard is through the **Golden Road,** a narrow stone corridor that was the crown prince's first taste of the world beyond the stifling confines of the Harem.

Sultanahmet, entrance at the end of Babuhümayun Cad., behind the Ayasofya. ℭ **0212/512-0480.** Admission to the palace 12YTL ($9); separate admission for both the Treasury and the Harem 10YTL ($7.50) each. Wed–Mon 9am–5pm (Harem closes at 4pm).

BYZANTINE SIGHTS (OR BYZANTIUM WASN'T BUILT IN A DAY)

Church of Theotokos Pammakaristos (Joyous Mother of God Church, now the Fethiye Camii)
This church was built in 1292 by John Comnenus, probably related to the royal family, and his wife Anna Doukaina. Later additions and renovations were made, including the construction of a side chapel in 1315 to house the remains of Michael Glabas, a former general, and his family. In 1456 the church became the seat of the Greek Orthodox Patriarchate and remained so until 1568. Five years later Murat III converted the church into a mosque and renamed it in honor of his conquest over Georgia and Azerbaijan. To accommodate the requirements of prayer, most of the interior walls were removed to create a larger inner space.

The interior of the church/mosque contains the restored remains of a number of mosaic panels, which, while not as varied as those at the Kariye Camii, serve as another resource for understanding 14th-century Byzantine art. In the dome is a representation of the Pantocrator surrounded by prophets (Moses, Jeremiah, Zephaniah, Micah, Joel, Zechariah, Obadiah, Habakkuk, Jonah, Malachi, Ezekiel, and Isaia). In the apse Christ Hyperagathos is shown with the Virgin and St. John the Baptist. The Baptism of Christ survives intact to the right of the dome.

From the Kariye Camii, follow Draman Cad. (which becomes Fethiye Cad.); turn left onto Fethiyekapısı Sok. (just before the road bends sharply to the right). Admission 2YTL ($1.50). Thurs–Tues 9am–5pm. Ayasofya Museum Directorate at ℭ **0212/635-1273.**

Church of the Pantocrator (Zeyrek Camii)
This former monastery church is one of the most important historic landmarks of the Byzantine period; however, because the structure is in a sad state of neglect, a detour here can only be recommended in tandem with a stroll through the narrow streets of the Zeyrek neighborhood. Dedicated to St. Saviour Pantocrator, the building is actually a composite of two churches and a chapel, making it the second-largest church in Istanbul after Ayasofya. The monastery was founded by Empress Eirene, wife of John II Comnenus, who completed the south church prior to her death in 1124. She was also the first to be buried here (her sarcophagus was moved in the 1960s to the Archaeological Museum, but now resides in the exonarthex of the Ayasofya). The northern church was added by the emperor (her husband) after Eirene's death, and dedicated to Virgin Eleousa, the Merciful or Charitable. Nothing remains of its original ornamentation. The emperor also had the churches connected through the jerry-rigging of a chapel

between the north and south church, which also required the demolition of part of the exterior walls of the two buildings. The *minbar* (pulpit), added when the church was converted into a mosque in the 15th century, is composed of recycled fragments of Byzantine sculpture.

Although the building preserves some of its original decoration (marble pavement, door frames in the narthex, marble apse), it's almost impossible to get a sense of the interior, as each section has been blocked off by wooden partitions.

From Atatürk Bulv., follow Itfaiye Cad. and take the first street to the right. Open at prayer times only.

Galata Tower and the Galata Neighborhood   The neighborhood of Galata, located on a steep hump of land north of the Golden Horn and historic peninsula, actually sits on the earliest foundations of the city, dating, as far as present-day archaeologists can tell, to Greek and Roman times. The district developed into its present form in the 13th century, when Eastern Roman Emperor Michael VIII Palaeologus granted the Genoese permission to settle here. The district became a magnet for merchants from all over Europe: Italians, Germans, Armenians, Jews, and Austrians, all re-creating their own micro-universe. A stroll up and down the steep cobbled streets will reveal schools, private residences, churches, synagogues and Ottoman-era warehouses. (There are also the ruins of a *mikva* or Jewish bathhouse in dire need of restoration opposite the former private mansion of the Camondo banking family, now the Galata Residence.)

The decline of Galata and its subsequent revitalization are both relatively recent phenomena. With the turn-of-the-20th-century flight of the wealthy merchant class to Istanbul's tonier neighborhoods, Galata deteriorated into a magnet for poor rural migrant families and a location of no fewer than three thriving brothels. In the 1990s, the nation's trend for historic preservation arrived in Galata with an ambitious architectural revitalization project that created an inviting public square and a couple of charming and characteristic outdoor tea gardens at the base of the tower. In the past 4 or 5 years, the trend has caught fire, as local real estate gets snapped up by artists, ex-pat journalists, and private developers and turned into galleries, cafes, hotels, and private homes. For a do-it-yourself walking tour, pick up a copy of John Freely's *Galata,* available at the Galata House (restaurant) and the bookstores listed under "Shopping" later in this chapter.

The origins of Galata Tower date back to the 5th or 6th century, but the tower that stands today is a 14th-century reconstruction by the Genoese, built in appreciation of Michael VIII Palaeologus, who granted special permission to allow them to settle the area of Galata. One condition of the agreement was that the Genoese were prohibited from putting up any defensive walls, a ban that they unceremoniously ignored.

The Galata Tower has been used as a jail, a dormitory, a site for rappelling competitions, and a launching pad in the 17th century when Hezarfen Ahmet Çelebi attached wings to his arms and glided all the way to Üsküdar. The tower rises 135m (450 ft.) above sea level and stands 60m (200 ft.) high, with walls that are more than 3.5m (12 ft.) thick. From the summit of the tower, you can see the Golden Horn, the Bosphorus, and the Marmara Sea, a view infinitely more splendid in the evenings when the city takes on a spectacularly romantic glow. The tower is used as a restaurant and nightclub for a traditional **Turkish folkloric** show (Ⓒ **0212/293-8180**).

Şişane. Ⓒ **0212/245-1160.** Historic gate daily 9am–1am (no access during the folklore show). Elevator to the top 8YTL ($6).

700 Years of Turkish Jews

Jews visiting Turkey inevitably ask for a tour of a local synagogue, and as the default working temple in the heart of Galata, Neve Shalom is usually the first and only stop. While interesting to see (particularly after sustaining recurring terrorist attacks), a visit to Neve Shalom is far from the Holy Grail of Jewish sites in Istanbul. It's also not necessarily guaranteed, since a pre-visit request accompanied by a faxed copy of your passport is the *minimum* requirement for entry. I'd recommend instead the **Jewish Museum of Turkey**, located in the restored 19th-century Zulfaris Synagogue. The museum represents the vision of the Quincentennial Foundation (named for the 500-year anniversary of the Jewish expulsion from Spain) and show-cases the peaceful coexistence of Jews and Turks in Turkey. The foundation's vision came to fruition in 2001 with this anthology of Jewish presence in Turkey beginning with the Ottoman conquest of Bursa, through Sultan Beyazit's invitation to those expelled from Spain, to the present day. The museum/synagogue is located at Karaköy Meydanı, Perçemli Sok. (© **0212/ 292-6333;** facing the lower entrance to the Tünel funicular, Perçemli Sokak is the first alley to your right; the museum is at the end of the street on your right). The museum is open Monday through Thursday 10am to 4pm, and Friday and Sunday from 10am to 2pm. Admission is 5YTL ($3.70).

Küçük Ayasofya Camii (Church of the Saints Sergius and Bacchus) ✧ *Finds*
Started in A.D. 527 by Justinian in the first year of his reign, this former church represents an important stage in the process of Byzantine building, particularly in the support of the dome atop an octagonal base. The church took its name from two martyred Roman soldiers later elevated to the status of patron saints; the edifice later assumed the name of "Little Ayasofya" due to its resemblance to the Ayasofya in Sultanahmet Park, which was started in 532. The church was converted into a mosque in the 16th century by the chief eunuch under Beyazit II, who is buried in the garden. We know from the ancient historian Procopius that the interior of the church was covered in marble and mosaics; however, none of this remains. Opposite the entrance to the mosque is a *medrese* that encloses an uncharacteristically serene and leafy garden. An on-site eatery as well as teahouses share the arcade with a number of bookshops and **calligraphy boutiques,** and genuine finds offering samples at some of the most competitive prices in the city.
Lower end of Küçük Ayasofya Cad. Open at prayer times only.

Mosaic Museum   In 1933 excavators discovered a series of mosaics below what is now the Arasta Bazaar, identified as the floor of a peristyle courtyard (open court with porticos) of Constantine's Great Palace. After more mosaics were unearthed in the 1950s, only then did the city fully grasp the scope of the find, and much to the chagrin of the owners of 16 of the shops, a museum was built to enclose the site. Although the collection is not as momentous as that of the Chora, this museum is worth an hour of your time, representing an earlier artistic era absent of religious motifs, showing instead hunting scenes and scenes from mythology.

Entrance at Torun Sok. Across from the entrance to the Sultanahmet Palace Hotel; accessible through Arasta Bazaar to the southeast of Blue Mosque. ✆ 0212/518-1205. Admission 4YTL ($3). Tues–Sun 9am–4:30pm.

St. Savior in Chora (Kariye Müzesi; formerly the Kariye Camii) ✿✿✿   Much of what remained in the coffers of the Byzantine Empire was invested in the embel-lishment of this church, one of the finest preserved galleries of **Byzantine mosaics** ✿ as well as a detailed account of early Christian history. The original church was built in the 4th century as part of a monastery complex outside the city walls (*chora zonton* means "in the country" in Greek), but the present structure dates to the 11th century. The interior restoration and decoration were the result of the patronage of Theodore Metochites, Grand Logothete of the Treasury during the reign of Andronicus II Pale-ologos, and date to the first quarter of the 14th century. His benevolence is depicted in a dedicatory panel in the inner narthex over the door to the nave, which shows Metokhites presenting the Chora to Jesus.

When the church was converted into a mosque in the 16th century, the mosaics were plastered over. A 19th-century architect uncovered the mosaics but was ordered by the government to re-cover those in the section of the prayer hall. American archae-ologists Whittemore and Underwood finally uncovered these masterpieces during World War II, and although the Chora became a museum in 1947, it is still often referred to as the Kariye Camii.

In total there are about 50 mosaic panels, but because some of them are only par-tially discernible, there seems to be disagreement on the exact count. Beginning in the exonarthex, the subjects of the mosaic panels fall into one of four themes, presented more or less in chronological order after the New Testament. Broadly, the themes relate to the cycle of the life of Christ and his miracles, stories of the life of Mary, scenes from the infancy of Christ, and stories of Christ's ministry. The panels not included in these themes are the devotional panels in the exonarthex and the narthex, and the three panels in the nave: *The Dormition of the Virgin, Christ,* and the *Virgin Hodegetria.*

The **Paracclesion** (burial section) is decorated with a series of masterful frescos completed sometime after the completion of the mosaics and were presumably exe-cuted by the same artist. The frescoes reflect the purpose of the burial chamber with scenes of Heaven and Hell, the Resurrection and the Life, and a stirring **Last Judg-ment** with a scroll representing infinity above a River of Fire, and a detail of Jesus sav-ing Adam and Eve's souls from the devil.

Camii Sok., Kariye Meydanı, Edirnekapı. ✆ 0212/631-9241. Admission 10YTL ($7.50). Thurs–Tues 9:30am–6:30pm. *Dolmuşes* leave from under the roadway arch near the Beyazit mosque (destination Karagümlük; get off at the Kariye "Camii").

Valens Aqueduct (Bozdoğan Kemeri)   Now nothing more than a scenic overpass for cars traveling down Atatürk Bulvarı, the Valens Aqueduct or "Arcade of the Gray Falcon" was started by Constantine and completed in the 4th century by Valens. Justinian II had the second tier added; even Mehmet the Conqueror and Sinan had a hand in its restoration and enlargement. The aqueduct connects the third and fourth hills of Istanbul and had an original length of about .8km (½-mile). Water was transported under various rulers to the Byzantine palaces, city cisterns, and then to

Topkapı Palace, and the aqueduct served in supplying water to the city for a total of 1,500 years.

Bridging Atatürk Bulv. between Aksaray and the Golden Horn.

Yerebatan Cistern (Yerebatan Sarnıcı) ⚘⚘   Classical music echoing off the still water and the seductive lighting make your descent into the "Sunken Palace" seem like a scene out of *Phantom of the Opera*. The only thing missing is a rowboat, which was an actual means of transportation before the boardwalk was installed in what is now essentially a great underground fishpond and stunning historical artifact. The cistern was first constructed by Constantine and enlarged to its present form by Justinian after the Nika Revolt using 336 marble columns recycled from the Hellenistic ruins in and around the Bosphorus. The water supply, routed from reservoirs around the Black Sea and transported via the Aqueduct of Valens, served as a backup for periods of drought or siege. It was left largely untouched by the Ottomans, who preferred running, not stagnant, water, and eventually used the source to water the Topkapı Gardens. The cistern was later left to collect silt and mud until it was cleaned by the Municipality and opened to the public in 1987. The water is kept clean and aerated thanks to a supply of overgrown goldfish that are replaced every 4 years or so.

Follow the wooden catwalk and notice the "column of tears," a pillar etched with symbols resembling tears. (An identical pattern is visible on the columns scattered along the tramway near the Universite stop, where the old Byzantine palace was once located.) At the far end of the walkway are two Medusa heads, one inverted and the other on its side; according to mythology, placing her this way caused her to turn herself into stone. Another superstition is that turning her upside down neutralizes her powers. Possibly, the stones were just the right size as pedestals.

Yerebatan Cad. diagonal from St. Sophia, Sultanahmet. 📞 **0212/522-1259**. Admission 10YTL ($7.50). Wed–Mon 9am–5pm.

HISTORIC *HAMAMS* (TURKISH BATHS)

The number of *hamams* in Istanbul mushroomed in the 18th century when the realization hit that they were big business. Mahmut I had the Cağaloğlu Hamamı built to finance the construction of his library near the Ayasofya, but later that century new constructions were limited because the *hamams* were using up the city's resources of water and wood. Only about 20 *hamams* have survived, the most visited of which are the palatial **Çemberlitaş Hamamı,** Vezirhan Cad. 8 (off Divanyolu at the Column of Constantine; 📞 **0212/522-7974;** 33YTL ($25) bath, massage, and *kese* [a scrubbing using an abrasive mitt], including tip; 18YTL ($13) bath only; daily 6am–midnight with separate sections; MasterCard and Visa accepted), which was based on a design by Sinan, and the 18th-century **Cağaloğlu Hamamı,** Yerebatan Caddesi at Ankara Caddesi (📞 **0212/522-2424;** $24 bath and *kese* and 49YTL ($36) if you add the "special massage"; daily 7am–10pm for men, 8am–8pm for women), which allegedly saw the bare bottoms of Franz Liszt, Edward VIII, Kaiser Wilhelm, and Florence Nightingale, and even had a part as an extra in *Indiana Jones and the Temple of Doom.*

The **Tarihi Galatasaray Hamamı,** Sütterazi Sok. 24, Beyoğlu (from Istiklal Caddesi in front of the Galatasaray High School, it's the second street to the left of the gate; 📞 **0212/249-4342;** 34YTL ($25) combined massage and *kese;* daily 5am–midnight for men, 8am–8pm for women), was built by Beyazit II as part of the Galata Sarayı school complex. The men's section is generally accepted as gay.

My, what an inefficient way to fish.

Ring toss, good. Horseshoes, bad.

Faster! Faster! Faster!

We take care of the fiddly bits, from providing over 43,000 customer reviews of hotels, to helping you find our best fares, to giving you 24/7 customer service. So you can focus on the only thing that matters. Goofing off.

travelocity®
You'll never roam alone.™

Moments A Cafe Near the Eyüp Sultan Mosque

If you've made it all the way to Eyüp to visit the mosque, take a short detour to **Pierre Loti,** Gümüşsuyu Balmumcu Sok. 1 ((✆ **0212/581-2696),** the cafe of legend and a spectacular spot for serene views of the Golden Horn. The legend goes that French naval officer Julien Viaud fell in love with Aziyade, a married Turkish woman, during his first visit to Istanbul around 1876. The young woman would sneak out of her husband's harem when he was away for the chance to spend a few fleeting moments in the arms of her lover at his house in the hills of Eyüp. After an absence from Turkey of 10 years, Viaud returned to find Aziyade had died soon after his departure. Viaud gained fame during his lifetime, and his stories are romantic accounts much like the one of legend. This cafe, on the hill of Eyüp, was a favorite of his, and for reasons unknown, became known as Pierre Loti Kahvesi. Eyüp's historic cemetery is on the hill next to the cafe. The cafe is open daily 8am to midnight; no food or alcohol is served here; avoid weekends, when nary an empty table will be your reward for the ride up.

Probably the most spectacular *hamam* in Istanbul is the **Haseki Sultan Hamamı,** in Sultanahmet Parkı. Built by Sinan in 1557 on a symmetrical plan that provided two separate sections of identical domed halls, the *hamam* was decommissioned in later years when it was found that the elongated layout resulted in too much heat loss. The Haseki Sultan Hamamı is now a beautifully restored exhibition center for Dösim (see "Shopping" later in this chapter) and is used for textile and carpet displays.

MONUMENTAL MOSQUES & TOMBS

The **Şehzade** (meaning "Crowned Prince"), Külliyesi, Atatürk Bulvarı, just south of the aqueduct (no phone; free admission; open dawn–dusk), was the first sultanic mosque and one of Sinan's early masterpieces that earned him the title of master builder, or *mimar.* Commissioned by Süleyman in 1543, the mosque and complex was dedicated to his favorite son, Prince Mehmet, who died of smallpox at age 21. The sarcophagus was specially crafted out of wood lattice with ivory inlay—there is no other example like it in the empire—while the tomb is decorated with tiles, stained glass, and domes covered in arabesques. The tomb and complex are built on the site that marks the exact center of Old Istanbul, a fact that probably influenced the architect's decision to create an effect of perfect symmetry. From the outside, the roof looks like a graceful cascade of domes while the four central semi-domes serve to buttress and support the load of the central dome. For many years the Şehzade remained the largest building in Istanbul, but even before the mosque was completed, Süleyman ordered the construction of another grander mosque as a monument to his reign.

Beyazit Mosque (Beyazit Camii) One of the oldest mosques in the city and the oldest surviving imperial mosque, Beyazit Camii was built between 1501 and 1506 using materials taken from Theodosius's Forum of Tauri, on which it was built.

Again, the architect of Beyazit Camii looked to the Ayasofya, employing a central dome buttressed by semi-domes and a long nave with double arcades, although the mosque is half the size of the church. The Beyazit Mosque also borrows elements from the Fatih Mosque, imitating the system of buttressing and the use of great columns

Steam Heat: Taking the *Hamam*

In characteristic socially conscious fashion, the Selçuks were the ones to adopt the Roman and Byzantine tradition of public bathing and treat it like a public work. Lacking baths or running water at home, society embraced the *hamam*, which evolved into not only a place to cleanse body and soul, but a social destination as well. Even the accouterments of the *hamam* took on symbols of status: wooden clogs inlaid with mother of pearl, towels embroidered with gold thread, and so on. Men gathered to talk about politics, sports, and women, while the ladies kept an eagle eye out for suitable wives for their sons.

Hamams were generally designed with separate sections for men and women, and anyone caught trespassing on the wrong side would be sentenced to death. Today it's not uncommon to find a co-ed *hamam*, except that insensitive (and flaccid) members of the opposite sex can detract from the experience, although most do cover up. Better to stick to a *hamam* that provides alternating times for the two sexes.

The utility of the *hamam* has evolved and fallen out of daily use, probably because the neighborhood ones have a reputation for being dirty, and the historic ones come with a hefty admission charge. But when experienced sparingly and in the right spirit, a visit to a *hamam* can be a cleansing one—for both mind and body.

The main entrance of a Turkish bath opens up to a **camekan**, a central courtyard lined with changing cubicles surrounding an ornamental marble fountain. Visitors are presented with the traditional *pestamal,* a checkered cloth worn like a sarong (up higher for women). Valuables are secured in a private locker, provided for each customer, although it's a good idea to leave the best of it at home.

The experience begins past the cooling section (and often the toilets), into the steam room, or **hararet.** For centuries architects worked to perfect the design of the *hararet:* a domed, octagonal (or square) room, often with marvelous oculi to provide entry for sunlight, and with intricate basins at

alongside the dome. Thanks to Sultan Beyazit II's patronage, the Ottomans found a style of their own, which served as a bridge to later classical Ottoman architecture. The sultan, who died in 1512, is buried at the back of the gardens.

Yeniçeriler Cad., across from the Beyazit tramway stop. No phone. Free admission. Dawn–dusk.

Eyüp Sultan Mosque (Eyüp Sultan Camii)   The holiest site in Istanbul as well as one of the most sacred places in the Islamic world, the Eyüp Sultan Mosque was erected by Mehmet the Conqueror over the tomb of Halid bin Zeyd Ebu Eyyûb (known as Eyüp Sultan), the standard-bearer for the Prophet Mohammed as well as the last survivor of his inner circle of trusted companions. It is popularly accepted that while serving as commander of the Arab forces during the siege of 668 to 669, Eyüp was killed and buried on the outskirts of the city. One of the conditions of peace after the Arab siege was that the tomb of Eyüp be preserved.

various intervals and a heated marble platform, known as the **naval stone**, in the center. Often the *hamam* is covered with elaborately crafted and ornately designed tiles.

Hamam protocol goes like this: As you lie on the platform, a half-naked attendant (woman attendants wear panties, men wear pestamals; your attendant may be male or female) will soap you up and give you a scrubbing using an abrasive mitt *(kese)* aimed at removing the outer layer of dead skin and other organic detritus. Many first-time visitors have questions about how much clothing to take off; in segregated *hamams* it's customary and acceptable to strip, although I personally would opt for a bathing suit when confronted with a male masseur.

In hotel *hamams,* you're guaranteed a new mitt; not so in local ones, although the Çemberlitaş Hamamı now offers a pretty package containing a mitt and olive-oil soap for an additional 6.75YTL ($5). The massage is next—although techniques vary in intensity, you may want to instruct your masseur or masseuse to go easy to avoid having your kneecaps pummeled into a slab of marble. Finally you'll be instructed to move over to one of the low marble basins, where your attendant will wash your hair, using a lovely engraved copper *tas* (bowl) for rinsing. If you've been nice (and tipped in advance, if allowed), you may even get a relaxing facial massage. You'll receive a definitive tap on the shoulder followed by "You like?"—an indication that your session is over. At this point you are most likely dehydrated and sleepy, which is when the purpose of that **cold room** with the lounge chairs becomes evident. Refreshments are available and the price list is usually displayed nearby. You can go back into the *hararet* as often as you like, but an hour total in the *hamam* is usually more than enough.

The experience can be delightful and highly utilitarian during those hot summer days when a power outage has cut the water pumps off. Sign up for "the works" at least once and you'll forever reminisce about how you spent an hour in a room with a bunch of naked ladies (or men—or both).

The burial site was "discovered" during Mehmet the Conqueror's siege on the city, although the tomb is mentioned in written accounts as early as the 12th century.

A little village of tombs mushroomed on the spot by those seeking Eyüp Sultan's intervention in the hereafter, and it's still considered a privilege to be buried in the nearby cemeteries. The Girding of the Sword ceremony was traditionally held here. In this Ottoman enthronement rite, Osman Gazi's sword was passed on, maintaining continuity within the dynasty as well as creating a connection with the Turk's early ideal of Holy War.

Eyüp is a popular spot animated by the small bazaar nearby, crowds relaxing by the spray of the fountains, and little boys in blue-and-white satin celebrating their impending circumcisions. Unfortunately, it's a natural magnet for beggars as well. The baroque mosque replaces the original that was destroyed in the earthquake of 1766, but the real attraction here is the *türbe,* a sacred burial site that draws masses of pilgrims waiting in line to stand in the presence of the contents of the solid silver sarcophagus or meditate in prayer. Dress appropriately if you're planning to go in: no shorts, and heads covered for women. The line moves quickly in spite of the bottleneck inside the tomb; take a few moments to sense the power of the site.

Eyüp. Meydanı, off of Camii Kebir Cad. and north of the Golden Horn Bridge. No phone. Free admission. Daily 9am–6pm.

Fatih Mosque and Complex (Fatih Camii ve Külliyesi)   A visit to this mosque is more of a pilgrimage to its illustrious permanent resident, Fatih Mehmet the Conqueror, than to the building and complex, which were constructed over the rubble of the original that collapsed in the earthquake of 1766. The *medreses* (schools) founded by the sultan are the only surviving sections of a complex that included a caravansary, a hospital, several *hamams,* the kitchens, and a market, which combined to form a university that instructed up to 1,000 students at any given time. Wanting a monument more spectacular than that of Ayasofya, the sultan cut off the hands of the architect, Atık Sinan (not Süleyman's Sinan), when the Fatih Mosque failed to surpass the height of the church, despite its position atop the fourth of the seven hills of Istanbul. The tombs of Mehmet II and his wife are located in front of the *mihrab* wall.

Enter on Fevzipaşa Caddesi, Fatih. No phone. Free admission. Dawn–dusk.

The New Queen Mother's Mosque (Yeni Valide Camii, or just plain Yeni Camii)   Begun by Valide Safiye, mother of Mehmet III, in 1597, the foundations of this mosque were laid at the water's edge in a neighborhood slum whose inhabitants had to be paid to move out. Designed by the architect Da'ud Ağa, a pupil of Sinan, the Yeni Camii has become a defining feature of Istanbul's skyline.

The building of the mosque dragged on for over 40 years due to water seepage, funding problems, embezzlement, and the death of the sultan, which temporarily shut down operations completely. The mosque was completed by another queen mother, Valide Sultan Turhan Hattice, mother of Mehmet IV, who is buried in the valide sultan's tomb in the courtyard. Also buried in the tomb of Turhan Hattice are sultans Mehmet IV, Mustafa II, Ahmet III, and Mahmut I.

Eminönü. No phone. Free admission. Dawn–dusk.

Süleymaniye Mosque and Complex (Süleymaniye Camii ve Külliyesi) 🏆🏆
Perched on one of the seven hills of Istanbul and dominating the skyline, this complex is considered to be Sinan's masterpiece as much as the grand monument to Süleyman's reign.

Sinan returned to the Byzantine basilica model for the construction of the mosque with an eye to the Ayasofya. Critics have contended that this was an unsuccessful

---

Tips Catch the Ottoman Mehter Band Outdoors

That must-see **Ottoman Mehter Band** that I tout so much (p. 128) no longer requires that you head over to the Military Museum in the middle of your day. There's now a performance every Friday, an hour and a half prior to noon prayers, right in front of the Eyüp Sultan Mosque. After the music and a visit to the mosque complex, hop onto the brand new **cable car** for the 2-minute ride up to the top of Pierre Loti Hill.

Tips A Sweet Shop Near the Spice Bazaar

Wandering around the spice bazaar, you can really work up an appetite. Across the Galata Bridge at the Karaköy seaport is the humble (and famous) **Güllüoğlu** (© 0212/244-4567) sweet shop, where you'll find the best *börek*—a cheese- or meat-filled pastry that's feathery and delicious. They also keep their glass cases full of baklava.

---

attempt to surpass the engineering feats of the church, but more than likely this was a conscious move on the part of the sultan to create a continuity and a symbolic connection with the city's past. As the Ayasofya was analogous to the Temple of Solomon in Jerusalem, so was the Süleymaniye, as the name Süleyman is the Islamic version of Solomon. After the project was completed, Sinan recounts in his "biography of the Construction," how the sultan humbly handed the keys over to him and asked him to be the one to unlock the doors, acknowledging that the masterpiece was as much the architect's as his own.

The complex includes five schools, one *imaret* (kitchens and mess hall, now a restaurant for groups), a caravansary with stables, a hospital, *hamams,* and a cemetery. The construction of the mosque and complex mobilized the entire city, employing as many as 3,000 workers at any given time, and the 165 ledgers recording the expenses incurred in the building of the mosque are still around to prove it. The great sultan is buried in an elaborate tomb on the grounds, as is his wife Hürrem Sultan (Roxelana). Süleyman carried the tradition of symbolism to his grave with a system of layered domes copied from the Dome of the Rock in Jerusalem. In the garden house next to the complex is the **tomb of Sinan,** where he spent the last years of his life. The tomb was designed by the master architect himself and is inspiring in its modesty and simplicity.

From the Grand Bazaar, cross the park of the university and follow the domes. Free admission. Daily 9:30am–4:30pm.

PALACES OF THE SULTANS

While the power and prestige of a new and modern Europe were increasing, the Ottoman Empire was on its last leg. To create an image of a prosperous and Westernized empire, Sultan Abdülmecid had the Dolmabahçe Palace constructed on European models and abandoned Topkapı Palace and what he considered to be the symbol of an old order. With the official residence of the Ottoman Empire now on the northern shores of the Bosphorus, it wasn't long before members of the court and government officials began to build mansions in the area. More palaces sprang up, and the official shifting of power from south of the Golden Horn to Beşiktaş was complete. If the royal palaces fail to convince you of the Ottoman Empire's extravagance during its final economic decline, they will surely convince you of its opulence.

Beylerbeyi Palace (Beylerbeyi Sarayı)   Beylerbeyi, built under Sultan Abdülaziz by another member of the talented Balyan family of architects in the European style of Dolmabahçe, was the second palace to be built on the Bosphorus and served as a summer residence and guest quarters for visiting dignitaries during their visits to the city. The shah of Iran and the king of Montenegro were guests here as well as the French Empress Eugénie, who admired the palace so much that she had the design of the windows copied on the Tuilleries Palace in Paris. It's a bit dusty, and not as grand

---

Fun Fact Bridge over Troubled Water

In 1501 Sultan Beyazit II invited Leonardo da Vinci to construct a bridge across the Golden Horn at the mouth of the Bosphorus—a technical feat deemed impossible until then. The master submitted a plan so revolutionary that it was deemed unbuildable. (Three years later, the sultan made the same proposal to Michelangelo, but Pope Julius II refused to let him go, and he politely declined.)

---

as Dolmabahçe, but worth a visit if you're on the Asian side and looking for a diversion.

Beylerbeyi, which replaced Abdülmecid's previous palace, was completed in 1865 on a less extravagant scale than the one on the European shores, employing only 5,000 men to build it. Although less grand and weathered by time, Beylerbeyi has some features worthy of a visit, not least of all the terraced garden of magnolias at the base of the Bosphorus Bridge. The monumental staircase to this marble palace is fronted by a pool and fountain which served as much to cool the air as to look pretty, and the floors are covered with reed mats from Egypt that act as insulation against dampness. The grounds contain sumptuous pavilions and kiosks, including the Stable Pavilion, where the imperial stud was kept.

Ironically, Abdülhamid II spent the last 6 years of his life admiring Dolmabahçe from the other side of the Bosphorus, having been deposed and kept under house arrest here until his death in 1918.

Take a ferry to Üsküdar and then a bus to Çayırbaşı. © 0216/321-9320. Entrance/tour 5.50YTL ($4), camera fee 10YTL ($7.50). Tues–Wed and Fri–Sun 9:30am–4pm.

Çirağan Palace   From the first wooden summer mansion built on the spot in the 16th century to the grand waterfront palace that stands today, the Çirağan Palace was torn down and rebuilt no less than five times. Now a palace of deluxe suites for the adjacent Hotel Kempinski Istanbul, the palace takes its name from the hundreds of torches that lined these former royal gardens during the festivals of the Tulip Age in the latter part of the 18th century.

The foundations were laid in 1855 when Sultan Abdülaziz ordered the construction of a grand palace to be built as a monument to his reign. The architect, Nigogos Balyan, ventured as far as Spain and North Africa to find models in the Arab style called for by the sultan. The fickle Abdülaziz moved out after only a few months, condemning the palace as too damp to live in.

Murad V (who in 1876 deposed his uncle Abdülaziz), Abdulhamid II, and Mehmed V were all born in the palace, while Murad V spent the final 27 years of his life imprisoned in the palace while his brother (who deposed him shortly after Murad V bumped his uncle) kept a watchful eye on him from the Yıldız Palace next door.

After Murad V's death, the Parliament took over the building but convened here for only 2 months because of a fire in the central heating vents that spread and reduced the palace to a stone shell in under 5 hours. (Some of the original doors were given as gifts by Abdülaziz to Kaiser Wilhelm and can now be seen in the Berlin Museum.) In 1946 the Parliament handed the property over to the Municipality, which for the next 40 years used it as a town dump as well as a soccer field. In 1986 the Kempinski Hotel Group saved the shell from yet another demise, using the palace as a showcase of suites for its luxury hotel next door. Since its opening, the Çirağan has laundered the pillowcases of princes, kings, presidents, and rock stars, carrying on at least a modern version of a royal legacy of the original.

The palace grounds spread along 390m (1,300 ft.) of coastline and can only be visited as part of a stop-off at the main hotel, preferably from the seaside garden terrace, which provides ample views of the Palace Sea Gate, the Palace Garden Gate, and the main building itself. A cluster of secondary palaces that now serve mainly as schools are located outside the hotel's perimeter, while the one called "Feriye" has been restored as an elegant restaurant and cinema complex (see "Where to Dine" earlier in this chapter).

Çirağan Cad. © 0212/258-3377.

Dolmabahçe Palace (Dolmabahçe Sarayı) 🖈

Extending for almost .8km (½ mile) on a tract of landfill on the shores of the Bosphorus is Dolmabahçe Palace (appropriately translated as "filled garden"), an imperial structure that for the first time looked to Western models rather than to the more traditional Ottoman style of building. The architect of Dolmabahçe was Garabet Balyan, master of European forms and styles amid a long line of Balyan architects.

At a time of economic reform when the empire was still known as "The Sick Man of Europe," Sultan Abdülmecid II sank millions into a palace that would give the illusion of prosperity and progressiveness. The old wooden Beşiktaş Palace was torn down to make room for a more permanent structure, and the sultan spared no expense in creating a house to rival the most opulent palaces of France. While many of his subjects were living without the basics, the sultan was financing the most cutting-edge techniques, tastefully waiting until the end of the Crimean War to move in, even though the palace was completed much earlier than that.

The result is a sumptuous creation consisting of 285 rooms, four grand salons, six galleries, five main staircases, six *hamams* (of which the main one is pure alabaster), and 43 toilets. Fourteen tons of gold and 6 tons of silver were used to build the palace. The extensive use of glass, especially in the Camlı Köşk conservatory, provides a gallery of virtually every known application of glass technology of the day. The palace is a glittering collection of Baccarat, Bohemian, and English crystal as well as Venetian glass, which were used in the construction of walls, roofs, banisters, and even a crystal piano. The chandelier in the Throne Room is the largest one in Europe at 4.5 tons, a bulk that created an engineering challenge during installation but that has withstood repeated earthquake tests. The extravagant collection of objets d'art represents just a small percentage of items presented to the occupants of the palace over the years, and much of the collection is stored in the basement awaiting restoration.

Tours to the palace and harem accommodate 1,500 visitors per day per section, a stream of gaping onlookers shod in blue plastic hospital booties distributed at the entry to the palace to ensure that the carpets stay clean. Tours leave every 20 minutes and last 1 hour for the Selâmlik and around 45 minutes for the Harem. If you're short on time, choose the Selâmlik.

Dolmabahçe Cad. © 0212/236-9000. Admission and guided tour to the Selâmlik (Sultan's Quarters) 12YTL ($9), admission and guided tour to the Harem 8YTL ($6), camera fee 12YTL ($9), video camera 18YTL ($13). Tues–Wed and Fri–Sun 9am–4pm.

EXPLORING MODERN-DAY ISTANBUL

Istanbul is positively pulsating with the energy of what . . . a new century? This is no more visible than in Taksim, the city's beating heart, and the surrounding neighborhood, which is experiencing a resurgence. The imprint of time has left its mark on the neighborhoods of Beyoğlu, Tünel, Galata, and Karaköy, where you can stroll past the turn-of-the-19th-century ambassadorial palaces and barracks, restored 16th-century waterhouses, and crisp, minimalist museums, all while shopping for an expensive pair of Levi's. Below is a short list of what to look out for.

Galatasaray High School (Galatasaray Lisesi)   The school's origins date back to the 15th century, when on a hunting expedition in the area, then a thickly wooded forest, Sultan Beyazit II came upon an old man who had fought in the siege of Istanbul in 1453. At the end of this encounter, the man presented the sultan with one red and one yellow rose from his garden (the colors of the soccer team of the same name) and requested that a house of learning be built on the spot. The school was founded in 1481 as Galata Sarayı, the fourth of a network of existing palace schools. During the era of the Tanzimat, the school became a window onto the West, and much of Turkish-French relations have their origins here.

For the past 500 years, Galatasaray High School has graduated grand viziers and palace administrators, and later, prime ministers, poets, artists, and journalists. Even today, the high school continues to set the standards of learning for all of Turkey.

Istiklal Cad., across from the Fish Market (Balıkpazarı). Open with prior permission from the management; ✆ **0212/244-3666** or 0212/249-6698.

Istanbul Museum of Modern Art ✿   In a city of ancient empires, in a country whose political and economic supremacy is but a distant memory, Turkey, and in particular Istanbul, is carving itself a new niche. Only this time, it's looking forward, not back. The Istanbul Modern, opened in December 2004, occupies a crisp, utilitarian and highly functional 86,000 square feet in a former customs warehouse just outside the cruise ship docks. The collection of paintings, portraits, sculptures, and photographs serve to tell us, in some sense, what was going on in the minds of the Turks in the 20th century. Some pieces simply make you tilt your head in wonder. That alone makes this museum worth a look.

Meclis-I Mebusan Caddesi, Liman İşletmeleri Sahası, Antrepo No: 4, Karaköy (approximately 250 steps from the Fındıklı stop on the tramway, heading in the direction of Dolmabahçe Palace) ✆ **0212 334-7300.** Tues–Sun 10am–6pm (Thurs till 8pm). Admission 5YTL ($3.70), free for children under 12.

Military Museum ✿✿ (Value)   Feared, respected, and loathed for 500 years, the Ottoman warrior was the brick on which the Ottoman dynasty was built. Indeed, it was the rising influence of industry and economics over combat and conquest that contributed to the ultimate downfall of the empire. Since war plays a pivotal role in the history and culture of Turkey, no visit to Turkey would be complete without a stopover at the Military Museum. Most people breeze through without a sideways glance, hurriedly following the arrows that direct visitors to the **Mehter Concert** ✿✿✿. This startlingly powerful musical performance re-creates the traditional military band of the Janissaries, the elite Ottoman corps abolished when their power became too great. The musical arrangement is an unexpectedly organized cacophony of sounds that, preceding the approaching army, also served to instill terror in the opposing army.

The exhibit, housed in the former military academy where Atatürk received his education (the building was converted into a museum in 1993), contains a chronological and functional assemblage of artifacts of warfare from the Ottoman era through World War II. The exhibit is anything but dull, showcasing chain mail and bronze armor for both cavalry and horses, leather and metalwork costumes, hand-sewn leather and arrow bags, swords engraved with fruit and flower motifs or Islamic inscriptions, and even a petroleum-driven rifle. Not to be missed is the hall of tents, an unanticipated display of *in situ* elaborately embroidered and silk encampment tents used on war expeditions.

Askeri Müse ve Kültür Sitesi Komutanlığı, Harbiye/Istanbul (about .8km/½ mile north of Taksim along Cumhuriyet Cad.). © 0212/233-2720. Admission 1.35YTL ($1). Wed–Sun 9am–5pm. Mehter Concert 3pm (English) and 3:30pm (Turkish).

SIGHTS ALONG THE BOSPHORUS

For over 2,500 years, kings and commanders have confronted the challenge of the Bosphorus, building rudimentary bridges out of boats and floating jetties to increase the size of their empires. Mandrokles of Samos crossed on huge connecting floats in 512 B.C. Persian Emperor Xerxes built a temporary bridge, as did Heraclius I of Byzantium, who crossed a chain of pontoons on horseback. Now that several bridges connect the shores of Europe and Asia, staying on the water has become more fashionable than actually crossing it. The shores are dotted with *yalıs,* or classic waterfront mansions, built as early as the 18th century: yellow, pink, and blue wooden palaces perched along the waterfront. The surrounding neighborhoods (best visited by land) retain much of their characteristic villagey feel, in stark contrast to the restored homes inhabited by the likes of ex–Prime Minister Tansu Çillar.

Cruising up the straits is a bit easier these days than when Jason and the Argonauts sailed through in search of the Golden Fleece. A number of local tour companies organize daylong or half-day boat cruises up the Bosphorus on private boats, often with a stop at the Rumeli Fortress and visits to Beylerbeyi Sarayı. Unless you've gotten a guarantee that the tour will *not* wind up on one of the public ferries, skip the tour and hop on one of the less pristine (but serviceable) city ferries and go the route yourself.

A one-way ticket on the public ferry costs about 4.50YTL ($3.30). You can get on at either Eminönü or at the docks at Beşiktaş near Dolmabahçe Sarayı, and disembark at will, ideally planning to arrive at one of the fishing villages in time for lunch. The last stop at Sariyer is the most visited—and therefore the most touristy, but the potential for a side trip to the **Sadberk Hanım Museum** (Büyükdere Cad. 27–29, Sarıyer; © 0212/242-3813; Thurs–Tues 10:30am–6pm; admission 5.50YTL/$4) continues to make this disembarkation point the most popular. The museum, located in an old Ottoman house overlooking a section of the Bosphorus that was an old dockyard, houses a limited but excellent collection of artifacts representative of the progression of civilizations in Anatolia. If you're already up here, then it's worth a look; otherwise, you'll get a more comprehensive presentation of the same themes at the Museum of Anatolian Civilizations in Ankara.

A lesser appreciated alternative is to get off at Anadolu Kavağı instead, hike up the hill to the "Crusader's Castle"—named for a carved cross decoration dating to the crusader invasion but actually a Byzantine structure used as a Genoese Palace in the 14th century—and enjoy outstanding views of the European side.

The trip by sea from Eminönü (departures at 10:35am, winter only, and 1:35pm; the ferry makes a stop in Beşiktaş approximately 15 min. later) to the last stop at Anadolu Kavağı takes 2 hours (allow 6 hr. for the full round-trip excursion), with only two return departures leaving at 3 and 5pm. This schedule pretty much restricts the amount of jumping on and off you can realistically do in 1 day. Alternatively, you may want to take an organized tour, which provides the advantage of door-to-door transportation and usually two sightseeing destinations. *Tip:* Since *ferry schedules are prone to minuscule changes* and since they don't dally at the piers, I recommend that you pick up the most current schedule at the tourist information office, and be on time.

Leander's Tower (or the Maiden's Tower, or Kız Kulesi)   Rising from a rock at the mouth of the Bosphorus is the Kız Kulesi, built by Ibrahim Paşa in 1719 over the remains of a fortress built by Mehmet the Conqueror and the earliest original building constructed on the rock by Byzantine Emperor Manuel Comnenus I. The romance of the tower finds its root in an ancient myth along the lines of Romeo and Juliet: boy (Leander) falls in love with girl (the Aphrodite Priestess Hero); boy drowns swimming to meet girl; girl finds lover's corpse; girl commits suicide. The story originated around the Dardanelles, but was too juicy not to attach to this solitary tower. Legend also has it that the tower was connected to the mainland by way of an underwater tunnel, and that there used to be a wall between the tower and the shore—a rumor not altogether implausible considering that according to a 19th-century historian, the remains of a wall could be seen in calm water.

Since as early as the 1600s, the tower has been used as a prison and a quarantine hospital. The tower is currently in service as a panoramic restaurant and tea lounge. Take advantage of the free shuttle over and get the chance both to visit the tower and enjoy a romantic meal, but be sure to book well ahead (© **0212/727-4095;** info@kizkulesi.com.tr).

Slightly offshore south of Üsküdar, on the Asian side of the Bosphorus.

Rumeli Fortress (Rumeli Hisarı)   This citadel was built by Mehmet the Conqueror across from the Anatolia Fortress (Anadolu Hisarı) in preparation for what was to be the seventh and final Ottoman siege of the fortified Byzantine city. Constructed in only 4 months, the fortress served to cut off Black Sea traffic in and out of the city, together with the Anadolu Hisarı built by his great-grandfather across the Bosphorus

---

⸤Value See the Whirling Dervishes

The **Sufi Music Concert & Sema Ceremony** (ceremony of the Whirling Dervishes) ✺✺✺ is held on the first and last Saturday of the month at the historic Galata Mevlevihanesi, Divan Edebiyatı Müzesi, Galip Dede Caddesi, at the end of Istiklal Caddesi in Tünel (© **0535/210-4565**). From October to April the ceremony is at 3pm; from May to September it's at 5pm. Go 15 minutes early for a front-row seat in this finely decorated octagonal hall. If you miss this one, there's an alternative concert of Sufi Music and a Sema Ceremony every Tuesday and Saturday at 7:30pm in the open hall off platform no. 1 in the train station at Sirkeci (© **0216/449-9081;** www.emav.org). Tickets are 25YTL ($19); the ceremony lasts about an hour. (**Note:** please call ahead to confirm showings, as schedules do change.)

on the Asian shores. The Ottoman army eventually penetrated the city by carrying the Turkish galleons over land by way of a sled and pulley system, and dropping them into the Golden Horn and behind the city's defenses.

Tarabya Yeniköy Cad. north of Sariyer (some ferries make the stop at Rumeli Kavağı; otherwise, get off at Sariyer and take a *dolmuş* the rest of the way). (©) **0212/263-5305.** Admission 4YTL ($3). Tues–Sun 9am–5pm. By car, follow the shore road north from Dolmabahçe Palace (there is no *dolmuş* service from Taksim) through Beşiktaş, Ortaköy, Arnavutköy, Bebek, and finally to Rumeli Hisarı (the road changes names frequently).

LIBRARIES & CULTURAL CENTERS

The British Council, Posta Kutusu, Beşiktaş ((©) **0212/355-5657;** www.britishcouncil. org.tr; Tues–Fri 10am–5pm, Sat 9:30am–2:30pm), is a nonprofit cultural outreach center working for educational and cultural relations. The library is one of the best resources for multilingual information on antiquities in Turkey, as well as a great reference center for translations of Turkish literary works. There's a huge collection of English-language books on all subjects, in addition to CDs, music, and videos. The center is popular with students of the English language.

For books and historical documents on Istanbul, the Turkish Touring and Automobile Club runs the **Istanbul Library** located in one of the old Ottoman houses it restored on Sogukçeşme Sokagı in Sultanahmet ((©) **0212/512-5730;** Mon–Fri 9am–5pm).

In a forgotten ancient building across from the Fener jetty on the Golden Horn is the **Women's Library** (Kadın Eserleri Kütüphanesi; (©) **0212/534-9550;** Mon–Fri 10:30am–6:30pm; closed for religious holidays). Founded by Füsun Akatlı, a renowned Turkish writer, the library has grown into a collection of materials—mostly in Turkish but some in English—featuring female artists, photographers, directors, and artisans. There's also a section on women in Istanbul and on women in Ottoman dress.

The Istanbul Archaeology Museum, Osman Hamdi Bey Yokuşu, Sultanahmet ((©) **0212/520-7740**) has a library of over 60,000 volumes on the subject of archaeology, and will be opened upon request.

ESPECIALLY FOR KIDS

Even though Turks are notorious pushovers for their children, Istanbul isn't really a kid-friendly destination; even the most privileged and well-educated children will get bored trudging around the recesses of ancient Byzantium. Istanbul does have a series of kid-related cultural events, though, including the **Rahmi M. Koç Museum** (Hasköy Caddesi 27; (©) **0212/297-6639;** www.rmk-museum.org.tr/english), a hands-on series of exhibitions a la Smithsonian showcasing the history of human ingenuity in the areas of transportation, industry, and communications. The transparent washing machines, carburetors, decommissioned submarine bridge, trains, and aircraft will definitely push the buttons of any preteen boy (and then some), and is definitely worth a visit. Admission is 6.50YTL ($4.75) for adults and 3.60YTL ($2.70) for students, plus 3.15YTL ($2.30) and 2YTL ($1.50) for entry to the (formerly free and currently overpriced) submarine exhibit.

The **Feshane International Fair Center and Children's Playgrounds** (Eski Feshane Caddesi, Defterdar Duragı; Eyüp; (©) **0212/501-7326**) offers another option for parents and kids alike. Installed in an old Ottoman fez-making factory, this open-air park offers food and activities especially fun for kids. Adults can look forward to the Feshane market outside the fairgrounds, as long as the kids aren't too pooped.

Miniaturk (Imrahor Caddesi Sütlüce/Istanbul on the eastern banks of the Golden Horn opposite Eyüp; ℂ **0212/222-2882;** www.miniaturk.com.tr), which opened in 2003, is an open-air minimuseum sprouting models of Turkey's most-loved monuments reconstructed here at 1/25th of their actual size. The park is open from 10am to 10pm in summer (until 6pm in winter); admission is 10YTL ($7.50).

ORGANIZED TOURS

You're sure to encounter a sensory overload of city tours and out-of-town excursions once you arrive in Istanbul, because fly-by-night tour operating seems to be a highly lucrative pastime. A popular organized day trip is the cruise up the Bosphorus, which can be taken as a half-day or full-day tour. This usually includes a quick stop at the Egyptian Spice Market and a visit to the Rumeli Hisarı. But read the fine print, because if business is slow, they'll put you on the public ferry (1.35YTL/$1 each way) rather than a private boat, and charge you 40YTL ($30) for the privilege. The one advantage of the tour is that you get door-to-door transportation in clean, comfortable minibuses, and all transfers between sights.

For personal day tours of the city, I recommend nothing but the best: **Credo Tours,** Taksim Caddesi, Yonca Apt. 69/6, in Taksim (ℂ **0212/254-8175**), organizes personalized 1- and 2-day tours of the city for little more than cost. Factor in the cost of the museum admissions, the entrance fee for the *hamam,* and lunch, and you may even come out ahead (agencies negotiate lower rates for all of the above). Some of their prior requests include architectural tours of the city, Jewish Heritage tours, and art tours.

STAYING ACTIVE

Common physical pursuits in Istanbul include rambling through the streets of the Grand Bazaar and scaling one of the often-steep seven hills of Istanbul. For more traditional physical activities, most four- and five-star hotels come equipped with modern fitness centers. If your hotel has no such facilities, most major hotels allow nonguests to use their private fitness centers, which generally include use of a pool, if there is one. Five-star hotels hover around 25€ ($30) a day (weekend prices may go as high as 37€/$45), a small price to pay for spalike luxury at **The Marmara Hotel,** the **Çırağan Palace,** or the **Hyatt Regency.** (Day pool and spa facilities also available at the **Ceylan Inter-Continental** and the **Hilton Hotel.**)

Links fans should go to the **Swissôtel** (ℂ **0212/326-1100**) or **Ceylan Inter-Continental** (ℂ **0212/231-2121**), whose fitness centers include golf simulators.

Istanbul also has a number of modern, if not fashionably chic, health clubs, most of which require at least a monthly membership for use of the facilities. The young and successful go to **Vakkorama Gym,** in the Vakkorama department store near Taksim (ℂ **0212/251-1571**), where a monthly membership on the three-times-a-week plan costs about 135YTL ($100). The gym is open weekdays from 7:30am to 10pm and from 10am to 6pm on weekends. You can become a member of the **health club at the Ceylan Inter-Continental Hotel** (ℂ **0212/368-4444**) for 450€ ($550) for 3 months, or 225€ ($300) for 1 month.

SPECTATOR SPORTS

To say that **soccer** is a popular national sport in Turkey is to miss the point entirely. Soccer is closer to a religious experience; club rivalries are waged with an intensity comparable to the holy wars.

The three main soccer clubs in Istanbul are **Fenerbahçe, Beşiktaş,** and **Galatasaray,** the last of which owns its own private island club in the middle of the Bosphorus. Main matches are played on Friday, Saturday, and Sunday nights at 7pm from late August to May. (A few late summer matches are played at 8pm.) Tickets are available at the stadium the day of a match, but for more popular matches, they're a bit harder to come by and you'll have to contact the ball club directly for advance tickets. Home matches are played every other week at **Inönü Stadium,** above Dolmabahçe Palace, for Beşiktaş; at **Alisami Yen,** in Mecidiyeköy, for Galatasaray; and at **Fenerbahçe Stadium,** near Kadıköy on the Asian side, for Fenerbahçe.

6 Shopping

Perhaps it was the renown of the Grand Bazaar that put Istanbul on the map of the world's great shopping destinations. But it's the hunting grounds of Old Istanbul, the elegant boutiques of Nişantaşı, and the revival in handicraft and artwork that have kept it there.

WHERE SHOULD I GO?

Any shopping tour of the city will inevitably begin with the **Grand Bazaar** (see "What to See & Do in Istanbul" earlier in this chapter). Pay particular attention to the exclusive shops along **Kapalıçarşı Caddesi** leading up to the Nuruosmaniye entrance to the Grand Bazaar. Less overwhelming in scope but somewhat more off-putting because of the absurd prices are the shops located in the **Arasta Bazaar** and its extension along **Küçük Ayasofya Caddesi.** The **Egyptian Spice Bazaar (Mısır Çarşısı;** closed Sun) in Eminönü is another mandatory stop on any shopping tour, although its initial merchandise of exotic spices from the East has expanded to include T-shirts and that spongy Turkish delight. For handicrafts, ceramics, and gifts displayed in the historic setting of an old *medrese,* head to the **Istanbul Handicrafts Center,** Istanbul Sanatları Çarşısı, across from the Blue Mosque and next to the Derviş Tea Gardens, with former classrooms arranged around a central courtyard now displaying fine-quality hand-painted silks, Anatolian dolls, calligraphy, and miniatures crafted by local artists. There's also a quality souvenir shop with fixed prices.

Istiklal Caddesi, from Beyoğlu to Taksim, could be in any major city in the world, a bustling promenade of cafes, clothing stores, blaring record shops, and bookstores. A stroll from Tünel to Taksim Square is nevertheless an essential activity for all who visit Istanbul. Be sure to pop into the **Avrupa Pasajı** in the Balıkpazarı, located across from Galatasaray High School (a big official-looking building surrounded by gardens and a tall gate). A short taxicab ride away to the northeast of Taksim is the trendy neighborhood of **Nişantaşı,** a pleasant cross between New York's SoHo and Madison

---

Fun Fact Did You Know?

The blue-and-white evil eye *(nazar boncuğu)* has its roots in Anatolian culture, although the symbol has its variants throughout the Middle East. Turks believe strongly in the power of the evil eye (if you could only see the tattoos beneath the *hijab* . . .) to ward off negative energy, especially against young children. But the evil eye transcends this culture—just check the pyramid on the backside of your U.S. 1-dollar bill.

Avenue. Boutiques along Teşvikiye Caddesi and in the smaller side streets of the neighborhood are stocked with high-quality merchandise in elegant settings, with major names like Mudo, Emporio Armani, Vakko, and Beyman.

Istanbul also has more than its fair share of outdoor markets, selling the usual assortment of fresh produce, sweatshirts, and maybe the odd antique. A walk through one of these provides yet another opportunity to witness another facet of this complex culture. There is a **flea market** between Sahaflar and the Grand Bazaar every Sunday, in the Horhor Market located in Akisaray on weekends, and on Çukurcuma Sokagı in Cihangir daily. The **arts-and-crafts fair** on Sundays in Ortaköy has become more of an outlet for jewelry and revolutionary Turkish ideas; still it's a fun place to spend the afternoon.

WHAT SHOULD I BUY?

The first thing that comes to mind when plotting out a plan of attack for acquisitions in Turkey is a rug, be it a **kilim or tribal carpet.** Carpets, kilims, and a whole slew of related items that have lost their nomadic utility comprise an indescribably complex industry, but it is unlikely that you will get very far before being seduced by an irresistible excess of enticing keepsakes. Because the big bad city of Istanbul attracts the worst of the country's merchant opportunists, I'd recommend holding off this purchase until you get to the heartland.

Most people are unaware that Turkey manufactures some of the best **leather items** in Europe, comparable in quality to those sold in Florence, Italy (and in some stores in Florence, the merchandise *is* Turkish). Because leather items are individually produced in-house, quality and fit may vary, but the advantage of this is that you can have a jacket, skirt, or trousers made to order, change the design of a collar, or exchange an unsightly zipper for buttons at prices far less than what you'd pay back home.

The entire length of Kalpakçılar Caddesi in the Grand Bazaar glitters with precious metals from the Nuruosmaniye Gate to the Bayezit Gate, and at first it may seem that **gold and silver** are astonishingly cheap. But the cost of precious metals is fixed internationally, and the low price of gold and silver is due to the cheap cost of labor. Thanks to advanced machinery and techniques imported from Italy, the quality of workmanship in Turkey is much better than ever, but not all workshops are the same, so look your piece over carefully.

Some of the world's best **meerschaum** comes from Turkey. This heat-resistant sea foam becomes soft when wet, allowing it to be carved into playful pipes that would make a collector out of the most die-hard nonsmoker. An afternoon in a historic *hamam* will expose you to some of the most beautiful traditional **white copper** objects, available as kitchen utensils as well as bathing ones, although keep in mind that you can't cook with this toxic stuff unless the inside has been coated with tin.

As far as **antiques** go, shopkeepers seem to be practiced in manufacturing bogus certificates of origin that will facilitate your trip through Customs, but beware: The certificate may not be the only counterfeit item in the shop. Collectors should keep in mind that it is prohibited by Turkish law to export anything dated prior to and through the 19th century.

Less traditional items can easily fill a suitcase, and with clever Turkish entrepreneurs coming up with new merchandise on a regular basis, you won't get bored on your second or third visit. **Pillowcases, embroidered tablecloths, ornamental tea services, and brass coffee grinders** are just some of the goodies that never seem to get old.

> **Tips A Note About Bargaining**
>
> That old measure by which you should offer the seller half of his initial price is old hat. They've caught on to our shopping savvy, and bump up the price accordingly. I've heard that a good rule of thumb is to offer about 25% less than you're willing to pay, but in my experience, you must hold off your counteroffer for as long as you can get away with it. This method will meet with varying responses, but after a few times, you'll get the hang of it.
>
> Also, after you've narrowed down your choice to two pieces, snub your first choice and put it down (with plans to come back to it later). Negotiate on your second choice—undoubtedly one of the finer samples in the shop, and therefore one of the pricier items on sale. Once you've established that it's out of your price range, turn to your first choice with a disappointed "and what about that one."

SHOPPING A TO Z
ANTIQUES & COLLECTIBLES

Objects dating to the Ottoman period make up a popular category for roving antiquers. As a rule, all items displayed can be legally purchased and exported to your home country (unless the piece is unique, in which case you need documentation from a museum director to buy it). Objects dated prior to the Ottoman period are considered fruit from the poisonous tree. Where carpets are concerned, the cutoff is 100 years—you'll need a certificate from the shopkeeper stating the age, origin, and authenticity of the carpet. (This is standard practice anyway.) So if you're serious, your first stop should be the neighborhood along Çukurcuma in the extremely hilly neighborhood below Beyoğlu and Taksim. **Galeri Alfa,** Faikpaşa Yokuşu 47/2, Çukurcuma (© **0212/251-1672**), has limited-edition tin toy soldiers, inspired by several hundred years of the Ottoman Empire as well as by models from abroad. Galeri Alfa also deals in rare books and prints.

Ottomania, Sofyalı Sok. 30–32 (exit Tüel and walk straight through the gated courtyard; © **0212/243-2157**), specializes in high-quality old maps and engravings. To get there you'll pass by **Artrium** (Tünel Geçidi 7; © **0212/251-4362**), stocking oldish ceramics, textiles, costume jewelry, and printed matter. In the nearby **Ottoman Miniatures & Calligraphy,** Istiklal Cad. 6 (© **0212/251-1966**), pointing is going to be your best means of communication if you're in the market for rare Ottoman and Islamic prints, or a superb original framed *tuğra*.

Ziya Antiques, Utangaç Sok. 21, Sultanahmet (© **0212/638-5328**), displays an eclectic mix of old paraphernalia dating to the Ottomans, from wall hangings to traditional kilims and lace, to objects such as watch fobs, eyeglasses, and a 470YTL ($350) Russian samovar.

BOOKS

The **Book Bazaar,** on Sahaflar Çarşısı (enter from Çadırcılar Caddesi), is a wonder of the printed page. Vendors carry books on Turkish subjects ranging from art to architecture to music, both old and new. Also, some of the finest examples of Ottoman art and calligraphy can be found in this book lover's mecca.

For books in English (as well as other foreign languages), root around the many bookstores near Tünel in Beyoğlu. The Hilton Hotel in Harbiye houses an outlet of the **Dünya Aktüel Kitabevleri** franchise (© **0212/233-0094**), which stocks a small selection of Turkish-interest books along with souvenirs and international magazines. Down the street from the Galatasaray High School is **Homer Kitabevi,** Yeni Çarşı Cad. 28/A (© **0212/249-5902**), stocking a great selection of Turkish-interest books on topics of history, architecture, photography, travel, Islam, and modern issues. Farther down Istiklal Caddesi at no. 389 is the more fashionable **Robinson Crusoe** (© **0212/251-1735**), with a decent but limited selection of English-language fiction, travel guides, and books on Istanbul and Turkey. **Beyoğlu Kitabevi,** Istiklal Cad. 388C (not far from the Tünel streetcar stop; © **0212/249-8244**), stocks cassettes, videos, travel books, maps, and research materials, in addition to a good selection of English-language teaching materials for visitors looking to subsidize an extended stay.

Sultanahmet is littered with souvenir bookshops, the most notable being **Galeri Kayseri,** Divanyolu 58 (© **0212/512-0456**) with a branch across the street at No. 11, which carries every book imaginable on Turkey. **Aypa,** Mimar Mehmet Ağa Cad. 19 (across from the Arasta Bazaar in Sultanahmet), carries all the foreign papers; the owner also produces and sells souvenirs like magnets, artistic cards, and other useless-yet-must-have paraphernalia. Aypa's owner, Aykut, recently opened a branch in **Nakkas** (Nakilbent Sokak 33; © **0212/516-5222**), a veritable millionaire's warehouse of carpets, ceramics jewelry, and books (© **0212/516-0100**). Here you will find a great selection of books on Turkish art, ceramics, history, religion, and the Ottoman Empire, some rare or limited editions. **Balkaya İnşaat** (© **0212/528-0505**), located at the exit to the Yerebatan Cistern, also carries an interesting mishmash of texts and tourist publications on Turkey.

CARPETS

When in Istanbul my days are filled with powwows with carpet dealers proud to show me the thank-you letters received from Washington, D.C., insiders, foreign dignitaries, and vacationing journalists. I could easily list a handful of stores where I go regularly for a cup of tea, but that wouldn't be fair to the shop owners that I have yet to meet. And just because I gave my business card to someone as a courtesy in passing doesn't mean that I endorse his (and in the rarest of cases, her) shop.

Finding an honorable carpet seller is even more elusive than tracking down an honest car mechanic. In a country where the minimum wage produces between 80YTL ($60) and 340YTL ($250) *per month,* the business of selling carpets promises the equivalent of the American Dream, attracting the ambitious and sometimes immoral on the trail of easy money. This doesn't diminish the value of the carpets; it just creates a potentially unpleasant atmosphere for buying one.

It's not always about selling fakes, although this does happen; more often it's simply about selling a piece for the maximum profit margin. Go informed, then once arrived, be extremely suspect of any claims or "insider information" made to gain your confidence. Ultimately, you should purchase what you like, make your purchase

---

Carpet Trivia

A braided fringe on the finished end of a carpet traditionally indicates that the weaver was a virgin.

where you feel comfortable, and pay a price you feel comfortable with. (*Tip:* Leave those priceless antiques to those who really know what they're worth, and check out the carpet section in IKEA to make sure you can't get it cheaper at home.)

Dösim Turkish Handwoven Carpets Sale Center (in the Haseki Hürrem Sultan Hamamı, entrance across from the Ayasofya; © **0212/638-0035**) is a sort of collective operated by the Turkish Republic Ministry of Culture. Works by artists and craftspeople are commissioned independently and sold at fixed prices in a highly evocative setting. There are several outlets in Sultanahmet alone; the Haseki Hürrem Sultan Hamamı displays carpets, kilims, and camel bags only. The gift shop in the entrance courtyard of Topkapı Palace and the one outside the main gate stock a good variety of items, including meerschaum, kilims, pottery, jewelry, and memorabilia.

Other locations are in İzmir at the airport and at Cumhuriyet Boulevard 115 (© **0232/483-0789**); in the Göreme Open Air Museum in Cappadocia (© **0384/271-2286**); inside the Aspendos theater outside of Antalya (© **0242/735-7038**); in the Antalya Museum on Konyaaltı (© **0242/243-1604**); and in the Bodrum Castle (© **0252/316-2516**). And lately, several of the stores are stocked with an array of high-quality baubles representative of Anatolian culture, in addition to their collection of regional carpets, kilims, and tribal pieces. These reproductions of traditional tribal designs may not be silk or antiques, but if those greedy capitalists in the Grand Bazaar have either turned you off or priced you out of owning one of theirs, Dösim will leave your floors tastefully covered at (fixed) prices. Sadly, prices have almost tripled on identical items since they first opened, so it's definitely worth the effort of bargaining elsewhere.

For tips on buying carpets, see the box "*Caveat Emptor!* Carpet-Buying Tips" below.

CERAMICS

The **Istanbul Handicrafts Center,** Istanbul Sanatları Çarşısı (© **0212/517-6780**), has a choice collection of precious ceramic and porcelain reproductions from Kütahya and İznik. **Kevser,** an eye-catching boutique at Muallim Naci Cad. 72 in Ortaköy (© **0212/327-0586**), has fine ceramic pieces as well as a variety of gift items. The **İznik Foundation**'s branch at Kuruçeşme Öksüz Çocuk Sok. 14, Beşiktaş (© **0212/287-3243**), sells valuable İznik reproductions composed of up to 80% quartz and colored with true-to-the-original pigments. Prices for these pieces are slightly higher at **İznik Tiles** in the Arasta Bazaar (© **0212/517-1705**), and at **Nakkas,** located down the hill from the Hippodrome (Nakilbent Sokak 33; © **0212/516-5222**) but you'll at least save yourself the cost of transportation up to the foundation showroom.

COPPER

If you simply have to have a set of those white copper *hamam* bowls or a copper platter for a table *a la Turque,* head to **Çadırcılar Caddesi** past the entrance to the book bazaar (near the Grand Bazaar). Head to **May Galeri** in the upscale neighborhood of Nişantaşı (Süleyman Nazif Sok. Valı Konağı Cad.) for a more artistic presentation. That is, if you can't wait to get to Ankara.

CRAFTS

In another commendable preservationist project, the Touring and Automobile Club of Turkey has provided an outlet for the revival of Turkish and Ottoman crafts. Each room off the central courtyard of the **Istanbul Handicrafts Center,** Istanbul Sanatları Çarşısı (© **0212/517-6780**), formerly a restored 17th-century *medrese* on Kabasakal Caddesi (the side street next to the Derviş Tea Garden and across from the

---

Tips Vakko's Aristocratic Tearoom

Take a shopping break at the **Vakko Café**, located on the second floor (first floor in Europe) of the upscale department store Vakko (Istiklal Cad. 123–125; ℰ **0212/251-4092**). This aristocratic red velvet tearoom offers a light American-style menu: shrimp with avocado, smoked-turkey–and-bacon club, croque-monsieur (okay, French, too), salads, and pastas. Prices are reasonable—9.50YTL to 14YTL ($7–$10) for main courses, 5.50YTL–8YTL ($4–$6) for desserts, which include waffles, ice cream, crepes, and cappuccino. Open daily from 10am to 7pm.

Blue Mosque), serves as an atelier for a different craft. Here you can watch the creation of handmade treasures, including hand-painted silks, folk art dolls and puppets, gilded calligraphy and miniatures, fine porcelain reproductions, and modern examples of the art of *ebru*, or marbled paper. The center is open year-round, although you may have to knock on some doors to get a personal shopping tour during the off season. Better yet, their fixed pricing takes the guesswork out of buying. **Evihan** (Altıpatlar Sokak 8; ℰ **0212/244-0034**), in the up-and-coming neighborhood of Çukurcuma, carries handmade artistic pieces made using Turkish tiles and hand-blown glass beads.

Pasabahçe has recently begun making a name overseas for its elegant ceramics, hand-cut glass, and typically Ottoman tableware. The nationwide chain has a centrally located shop on Istiklal Cad. 314, in Beyoğlu (ℰ **0212/244-5694**).

DEPARTMENT STORES & CHAINS

So you've packed for warmer weather and the winds from the Caucasus have arrived a bit early. Head for these chains, located along Istiklal Caddesi in Istanbul, though you'll find them in major shopping areas throughout the country. **Mavi Jeans,** like a Turkish Gap, Istiklal Cad. 117 (ℰ **0212/249-3758**), and in the Akmerkez shopping center (see "Malls & Shopping Centers," below), and **Mudo,** Rumeli Cad. 58, Nişantası (ℰ **0212/231-3643**), and in Akmerkez, carry smart and casual clothes. Unlike Gap or Old Navy, however, the fabrics are *not* prewashed, so allow for shrinkage or *never* put items in the dryer. **Beyman** is a popular chain among Turks, carrying casual chic for men and women along the lines of Ralph Lauren. The Beymen Mega Store in Akmerkez (ℰ **0212/282-0380**) is more along the lines of an upscale department store, where you can find cosmetics, stationery, and even furniture. For the best designer men's and women's wear, check out **Vakko** (www.vakko.com), Turkey's answer to Barney's New York and worth a look if only for its dazzling silver embroidered scarves. Locations include Istiklal Cad. 123/125 (ℰ **0212/251-4092**), Bağdat Cad. 422 (ℰ **0216/467-4205**), and Akmerkez. The spinoff **Vakkorama,** Osmanlı Sok. 13 Taksim (ℰ **0212/251-1571**), caters to a younger clientele than the original.

FOOD

Galatasaray Fish Market, in Balıkpazarı, is a great place to stock up for an impromptu picnic meal or for a long drive into the steppes. Sure, it's a tourist trap, but as a jumble of over 25 fish and fresh-produce vendors, as well as a handful of traditional *meyhanes* and the odd seller of dashboard ornaments, it's also an undeniable hoot. Beware of anything labeled caviar; Turkey is notorious for its illegal trade in smuggled caviar, as well as for representing this lower-quality fish roe as high-quality caviar using counterfeit labels copied from reputable brands.

Follow your nose off to the left down Duduodalar Sok. 21, where you will find **Şutte** (© 0212/293-9292), a delight for your eyes and your stomach. Şutte is a chain of charcuteries with outlets all over the city, but this is the most central. Şutte carries rare pork items like prosciutto and speck as well as hard-to-come-by wedges of *parmeggiano reggiano.* You can also take out one of the many prepared sandwiches or tempting mezes. While in the Balıkpazarı, keep your eyes peeled in the various markets for vacuum-packed bunches of **sele olives**—soak them in hot water to dilute the saltiness, then serve these precious little pieces of fruit with olive oil, lemon, and a sprinkle of oregano.

The **Egyptian Spice Bazaar (Mısır Carsışı)** ✷✷✷ was established in Eminönü after the Ottoman conquest of Egypt in the 16th century as a marketplace for exotic spices arriving via sea lanes by way of Egypt. Today you can find Turkish fine linens and embroidered elf slippers in addition to the barrels of herbs and spices, pistachios soaked in honey (yet another traditional Turkish aphrodisiac and "guaranteed for five times a night"), Turkish delight, and as many varieties of saffron as your heart desires. But the best fun is in jostling your way through the streets behind the building, where the true Turkish spirit shines through in vendors proffering morsels of soft cheese, spoonfuls of spicy ezme, and samples of succulent strawberries. (While you're wandering, stop off at the Rüstem Paşa Külliyesi [opposite the bus depot that is adjacent to the bazaar], a mosque and complex built by Sinan that is one of the most enchanting places of worship, tiled top to bottom with dazzling İznik tiles painted with tulips, hyacinths, and spring flowers.)

Turkish-**coffee** addicts should head to **Kurukahveci Mehmet,** Tahmis Cad. 66, in the corner behind the spice bazaar. A producer of the infamous precious brew, Kurukahveci Mehmet is also the best-known retail outlet. For the most extensive variety of Turkish delight, stop in at **Hacı Bekir,** the legendary sweet shop with locations at Istiklal Cad. 129 (© 0212/244-2804) and Hamidiye Cad. 81–83, in Eminönü (© 0212/522-0666). **Manhattan Gourmet Store,** Güzelbahçe Sok. 14, in Nişantaşı (© 0212/225-0047), is a sophisticated American-style gourmet shop that stocks takeout sushi, Fauchon sauces, and other delicacies.

Turkey's **olive oil** really doesn't get the kind of respect it deserves—an absence of effective marketing has deprived the rest of the world of one of the country's most treasured resources. But that is changing, by the looks of the gourmet shop in the airport's duty-free area. If you've been bewitched by the flaxen temptress at the bottom of your meze bowl, pick up a bottle at any local convenience-type store. The grocery store chains carry some basic brands; opt for Komili. (A Migros grocery store franchise is near the Fındıkzade tramway stop.)

GIFTS & SOUVENIRS

The Grand Bazaar is the obvious answer to the "where to buy it" question, particularly because the last time I went, *nobody* bothered me. (Maybe I looked too poor.) The **Istanbul Handicrafts Center** (Istanbul Sanatları Çarşısı; © 0212/517-6780), next to the Yeşil Ev, provides a higher concentration of quality items in a more manageable environment. Mercifully, prices are fixed, so this is also a good place to go to arm yourself with information before heading over to the Grand Bazaar. The **Avrupa Pasajı,** in the Balıkpazarı, near Meşrutiyet Caddesi in Beyoğlu, is a narrow gallery of artsy shops selling souvenirs from antique samovars to tiny harem outfits for

Caveat Emptor! Carpet-Buying Tips

"Where are you from?" seems an innocuous enough question from a carpet dealer, but answer it, and you're on your way to being scalped. Questions like "Where are you staying" actually tell the salesperson about your economic status, as do "What do you do?" *(How much money do you earn?)*, "Where do you live?" *(Hey what a coincidence! My cousin lives near you!)*, "How much time will you be staying here?" *(How much time do you have before you have to make your final decision?)*, "What are you looking for" *(Do you even have any idea about carpets?)*, and "How long have you been here?" *(How much have you already learned about our sleazy ways?)*.

First rule of thumb: Lie about where you're staying. Take note of the name of the humblest pension near to your actual hotel, and file it away for future use. Also, they know that Americans are the biggest spenders of any other nationality visiting Turkey, so this is where fluency in a foreign language may come in handy. Above all, do your homework., and know what you like before you arrive so you don't waste precious bargaining time overpaying for the "best sample in the shop."

Visitors traveling in groups inevitably wind up at a large roadside production center. Although these are interesting from an educational and cultural point of view, don't be had: your tour guide, your tour company, and hell, the bus driver, are going to each earn a hefty commission off of your sale. (Actually, the same commission system applies to almost everything you buy.)

Once you find yourself in the shop, the seller will begin the show of rolling out one stunning sample after another, educating you in the history, cultural significance, and processes of the art of carpet weaving.

Turkish tribal rugs are divided into **kilims,** which are flat, woven rugs, and **carpets,** which are hand-knotted using a double or Gordian Knot, a technique unique to Anatolia that results in a denser, more durable product than the single-knotted carpets found abroad. Kilims are probably more recognizable, as they are inexpensive and sold abroad.

There are four types of carpets produced currently in Turkey. **Wool-on-wool** carpets represent the oldest tradition in tribal rugs. The earliest examples display geometric designs using natural dyes that were reliant on local resources like plants, flowers, twigs, and even insects, so that the colors of the carpets reflected the color of an individual region. Blues and reds are

2-year-olds (plus merchandise like brass pepper mills at prices lower than in the Egyptian Spice Market). And recognizing that packaging is everything, **Abdulla Natural Products** in the Grand Bazaar, Halıcılar Cad. 53 (© **0212/522-9078;** www. abdulla.com), stocks goods like plush terry-cloth towels, herbal olive-oil soaps, and a bath set for a home-style *hamam* (pestamal, hand mitt, and so on). As the distributor for Vakko in Japan, **The Fine Art** shop, Divanyolu Caddesi 13 (next to McDonald's; © **0212/638-9827**), carries their silk scarves, tablecloths, and other household textiles, as well as good-quality ceramics and silver jewelry.

typical of designs originating around Bergama, which derive from the indigo root and local insects. Reds seem to be dominant in carpets made in Cappadocia.

Today the business of carpet weaving has been transformed into a mass industry. Weavers have for the most part switched over to chemical-based dyes, although the trend toward organic dyes is experiencing a rebirth.

The second type of carpet is the highly prized **silk-on-silk** samples, which developed in response to the Ottoman Palace's increasing desire for quality and splendor. Silk was a precious commodity imported from China that few could afford. In the 19th century the sultan established a royal carpet-weaving center at Hereke that catered exclusively to the palace. Today silk-on-silk rugs continue to outclass all others, using silk from Bursa woven into reproductions of traditional designs. (*FYI:* Silk threads cannot hold natural dyes, so all those splendid pieces use chemical dyes.) Silk rugs are also produced in Kayseri, but these fail to attain the high standards set by the Herekes.

A more recent development in carpet production has been the **wool-on-cotton,** which, because of the lower density of the weft, accommodates a higher ratio of knots per inch, and therefore more detail in the design. **Cotton-on-cotton** is an even newer invention, duplicating the resolution and sheen of a silk rug without the expense.

Sales tactics include an emphasis on Anatolian carpet and kilim weaving as a high art. This certainly applies to rare and older pieces, which command hefty sums. But modern samples—albeit handmade copies of traditional designs—are created from computerized diagrams. Don't be brainwashed into paying the high price of art when the artist—typically a local woman—earns a shockingly low wage (and the salesperson drives a BMW or Mercedes).

For antiques: Unless you're an expert, you should avoid buying antique rugs, which cost significantly more. The bottom line is that only antique experts are equipped for a proper appraisal.

Yes, buying a carpet in Turkey can be a very daunting task. But this is not meant to diminish your admiration of the pieces, only arm you for the negotiations, which ultimately will get you an exceptional souvenir of a wonderful country and its wonderful crafts.

HOME

Moving beyond classic ready-to-wear and accessories, **Vakko Home** in the Vakko shop, Istiklal Cad. 123–125 (© **0212/251-4092**), has several floors of dazzling tabletop, linen, and textile items, from taffeta pillows 55YTL to 75YTL ($40–$55) to printed silk Ottoman designs made into anything from bed sheets to tablecloths (if you have to ask . . .). Pieces can be made to order in at least a week; otherwise, they'll happily ship abroad.

JEWELRY

The Grand Bazaar's **Kalpakçılar Caddesi** is the obvious destination for gold and silver modern pieces, but for anything appealing—like handcrafted traditional and tribal jewelry—you'll have to look elsewhere. **Urart Ateliers** in the Swissôtel (© **0212/629-0478**) and at Abdi Ipekçi Caddesi 18/1 in Nişantaşı (© **0212/246-7194**) is an upscale workshop complex of designers, artists, and craftsmen dedicated to re-creating the rich traditions of Anatolian civilizations in gold and silver. Some of their pieces are also available in the small gift shop in Topkapı Palace, in the last courtyard. **Eller Art Gallery,** Istiklal Caddesi, Postacılar Sok. 12 (© **0212/249-2364**), provides a more down-to-earth showcase for replicas of jewelry and artifacts normally seen under protective glass at Ankara's Museum of Anatolian Civilizations. For silver pendants, rings, and earrings, **Pegasus,** Muallim Naci Caddesi Yelkovan Sok. 3/B, Ortaköy (© **0212/258-7485**), is one of my favorites, and it's also gentle on the wallet.

LEATHER GOODS

SH Leather (formerly Sultan House; Yerebatan Caddesi 39, Sultanahmet; © **0212/511-3966**), has a modest selection of men's and women's leather and suede jackets. Better yet, they will craft and design to order, or you can be fitted with a tailored pair of leather or suede pants.

MALLS & SHOPPING CENTERS

You're joking, right? You'd really have to have a lot of time on your hands in Istanbul to wind up at one of these shopping centers (like me; I love each and every one of these). The **Akmerkez Mall,** in Etiler, was actually voted the best shopping mall in Europe. Other shopping malls include **Capitol Shopping Mall** in Üsküdar, **Carousel Shopping Mall** in Bakırköy, and **Galleria Shopping Mall** near the airport. **Olivium** is a newish outlet mall located halfway between the airport and Sultanahmet, where you can find various middle-of-the-range name brands at discounted prices.

MARKETS

Local markets offer a window into the vibrancy and color of the neighborhood, and provide a priceless experience in interaction with the locals. But after the umpteenth stall of fresh fruits and vegetables, rice sold in bulk, or pitiable clothing, it's probably going to be a short visit. There's an outdoor market on Wednesdays in Sultanahmet on Akbıyık Caddesi and one on Tuesdays near the Fenerbahçe Stadium in Kadıköy. There's also a Sunday crafts market in Ortaköy, where there's an abundance of lively outdoor cafes for that much-appreciated break.

MUSIC

Shops carrying traditional Turkish and modern musical instruments are bunched around the entrance to Tüel in Beyoğlu. The **Istanbul Müzik Merkezi,** Galipdede Cad. 21 (© **0212/244-5885**), sells Anatolian drums and tambourines, or you can pick up a handmade professional-grade saz for 27TYL ($20) and up. (The small souvenir-size models sell for 14YTL/$10.) If you're looking for CDs, shop to your heart's desire in one of the many record stores along Istiklal Caddesi.

TAX-FREE SHOPPING

There's an incentive for carrying that carpet home. Foreigners (and Turkish citizens with residence abroad) are entitled to a VAT (tax) refund, worth 15% of the total amount of merchandise acquired during any one purchase. To receive a refund, present the merchandise and invoices to the Customs inspectors at the point of exit within

3 months of purchase. Refunds are issued in the form of either a Global Refund check, redeemable at the İş Bankası branch on the Arrivals level, or as a credit to a credit card account. The Customs Tax-Free office at the airport in Istanbul, located in the International Departure Terminal, is opened 24 hours a day.

7 Istanbul After Dark

Don't think that because Islam prohibits its followers from consuming alcohol that the Turks are listening. (Islam, particularly in Turkey, is not heavy-handed enough to force this rule on anyone, and is, in spirit, extremely forgiving.) A typical evening will involve large amounts of food accompanied by even greater amounts of *rakı,* that aniseed-flavored spirit known as "lion's milk"—traditionally consumed in a *meyhane,* a tavern or pub where patrons gather to eat and drink. Where *meyhanes* were once the realm of men only, today it's not uncommon to find a modern mixed crowd slinging a couple back with tasty mezes in the back streets of Beyoğlu.

The *şaraphane* or wine bar is the newest nightlife trend in Istanbul, a relatively recent institution that's thrived thanks to the ever-improving quality of Turkey's wines.

Live music is a staple of Turkish nightlife, and it will be harder to find a nice quiet cafe than one with evening offerings of overamplified music. Bars and cafes in Istanbul are generally not categorized according to the type of music they play, choosing to book instead groups with different styles from night to night. A good rule of thumb is, the earlier the hour, the softer the music. Rock and pop resounds onto Istiklal Caddesi, where bars, cafes, and clubs, a few of them seedy, are too numerous to cover. Another good rule is to avoid spots with neon lights and security guards and anything with the word "nightclub" or "club" in the name, as these have the reputation of being the seedy places where bad things happen to good visitors.

Clubs that book popular musical acts may sell tickets or impose a cover charge where normally there is none, but unless the headliner is very popular, tickets to most performing arts events and concerts can be purchased at the location the day of the performance.

Hotel lounges or rooftop bars provide a relaxing alternative to wall-to-wall smoke-filled cafes. In Sultanahmet, splendidly romantic views present themselves from almost every rooftop, or you can succumb to the dubious appeal of one of the several Turkish Night shows around town.

The neighborhood of **Örtaköy** comes to life, particularly on summer evenings, when streets lined with outdoor vendors selling crafts, jewelry, and the like create a festival-like atmosphere. Waterside restaurants and coffeehouses are open till late, or you can graze through the stalls of food and gorge yourself on stuffed mussels.

GAY ISTANBUL

Separate from the bountiful public displays of affection among men in Turkey, homosexuality is alive and well in Istanbul; however, activities are less overt than in cities such as New York, London, Rome, and Paris. Although homosexuality can be traced back to Ottoman times, there's still a stigma attached to it: The worst insult used among Turks (especially at soccer games) is *ibne,* a term referring to the receiving partner in a same-sex act. Practically speaking, homosexuality is legal between consenting partners above the age of 18. Cihangir, along Sıraselviler Caddesi in Beyoğlu, is a notorious hangout for transsexuals and homosexuals, while gay clubs are centered around Taksim. General cruising takes place in Taksim Park and around the entrance to the McDonald's on Cumhuriyet Caddesi. Several *hamams* are generally accepted as

Safety for Single Men

Scenario #1: You're wandering around Taksim and pop into a bar for a quick beer or two. Before you know it, you're surrounded by lovely women and even doted on by the owner. But 2 hours and two beers later, the check arrives: $500. I wish that were a typo. Refuse to pay, and the big boys come out of the woodwork; you may even find your life and limb threatened. It's startling how many times this scenario plays out in seemingly innocuous-looking "establishments" around Taksim. One way to counter, I suppose, is to dispute the charge with your credit card carrier once the bill comes in. But the best way to handle the situation is to avoid it altogether. Stay away from anything with neon and the word "nightclub" or "club" in the sign. But sadly, there is no absolute guarantee. When in doubt, follow the advice of this guidebook, or stick to the hotel bars.

Scenario #2: You're taking an innocent evening stroll through the back streets of Sultanahmet. Suddenly, you are accosted by four young boys who identify themselves as police. Having done nothing wrong and always mindful that you are in a foreign country, you cooperate. They manhandle you (perhaps looking for ID, or even drugs), then send you packing with a shove. It all happens so fast, except that now your wallet is empty. Unfortunately, with the migration of organized crime (most likely this band of thieves was alerted by an Oliver Twist–style manager who spotted you walking earlier), nowhere is safe anymore. Don't walk anywhere alone, and avoid badly lit streets after dark.

---

gay (the men's side), including the Tarihi Galatasaray Hamamı in Beyoğlu (for hours and fees, see the section "Historic *Hamams* [Turkish Baths]" earlier in this chapter); Park Hamamı, Divanyolu, Dr. Emin Paşa Sok., Sultanahmet (no phone); and Aquarium, Istiklal Caddesi, Sadri Alışik Sok. 29 (© **0212/251-8926**). For more specific information, log onto www.istanbulgay.com.

THE PERFORMING ARTS

Built originally as an opera house, **Atatürk Cultural Center (AKM)** in Taksim Square (© **0212/251-5600**) houses the State Opera and Ballet, the Symphony Orchestra, and the State Theatre Company. Tickets are absurdly low at 4YTL to 16YTL ($3–$12), and are usually available for purchase in the month of as well as the day of the performance. During the summer months, AKM hosts the Istanbul Arts Festival but because of high demand, tickets may be hard to come by. The English-language student publication *Istanbul Classified* compiles a monthly listing of events; copies are free and available around town (try The Pudding Shop in Sultanahmet; see "Where to Dine" earlier in this chapter), or check out their website at www.istanbulclassified.com. You can also check out the government's website at www.kultur.gov.tr for the schedule of performances.

The annual **International Istanbul Festival** (© **0212/334-0700;** www.istfest.org) is organized into four separate arts festivals averaging over 50 events yearly. The festival kicks off with the Film Festival in April, including two national and international competitions. The 2003 festival screened over 175 films in a variety of venues in Beyoğlu and Kadıköy. The theater section of the festival brings companies from all over Europe and takes place in May, with one or two offerings in English. At the end of

Istanbul Biennale 2007

Istanbul has been celebrating a **Biennale** since 1987, but it wasn't until 2005, perhaps because of the anchorage of the new Istanbul Modern Museum, that the Biennale hit a home run. Artists were clustered around the revived neighborhood of Galata in venues that included an old apartment block, a tobacco ware depot, a customs warehouse, and an office building. (Previous exhibitions were housed in the Imperial Mint, in the Kız Kulesi [Maiden's Tower], on the Bosphorus P Bridge, and in Çemberlitaş Hamamı.

For information on venues, tickets, and artists, contact the Istanbul Foundation for Culture and Art (© **0212/334-0700;** www.iksv.org).

October or in early November, selected international artists come together for the Biennale, but the big to-do takes place in June/July with the International Istanbul Music Festival, representing the worlds of opera, jazz, classical music, and ballet in evocative settings like the St. Irene, and featuring world-renowned performers like Wynton Marsalis or the traditional performance of *Der Entführung aus dem Serail (Abduction from the Seraglio)* appropriately staged in Topkapı Palace. A separate Jazz Festival, sponsored by Efes Pilsen, takes place in November in various venues around town, including local jazz clubs, cultural centers, and the open-air theater above Taksim.

THE CLUB & MUSIC SCENE
TURKISH NIGHTS

In spite of mediocre food and high prices, visitors continue to insist on a "traditional" Turkish folkloric show. Inevitably there's a belly dancer and perhaps a segment resembling a Cossack dance, but aside from a few minutes of Anatolian folk dance, these shows are geared toward tourists and have more in common with former sultans' tastes for exoticism than with typically Anatolian culture. The most popular folklore show in town is the one at the **Orient Hotel,** Tiyatro Cad. 27, Beyazit (near the Grand Bazaar; © **0212/517-6163**); dinner starts at 8pm and the show goes on until midnight. The cost is 100YTL ($75) per person. Another popular venue is the Turkish night in the historic **Galata Tower** (© **0212/293-8180**). If you get bored, the wonderful panoramic view of Istanbul is sure to perk you right up. The show runs Monday through Saturday and includes dinner. The cost is 100YTL ($7, or 60YTL ($45) for the show only.

An alternative to the contrived spectacle of these "Turkish Nights" is the **Dances of Colors** ensemble, presenting authentic Anatolian and Turkic dances in a staged setting (not to be confused with the highly publicized traveling Sultans of the Dance troupe). The performance lasts 1 hour and 15 minutes with a short intermission and takes place twice weekly (Tues at 5:15pm and Fri at 7pm) in summer; in winter performances are Fridays only. At 34YTL ($25), tickets are a bit more than the show warrants, but that's the price you pay for avoiding kitsch. For information and tickets, contact the organizers through the Cordial House Hotel (© **0212/517-8692**); performances are held at the FKM/Firat Kültür Merkesi (corner of Divanyolu and Peykhane Sok. (Çemberlitaş tram stop).

There's also the nightly (in summer) sound-and-light spectacle at the entrance to the Blue Mosque in Sultanahmet Park. The show has a charming spontaneous feel, and accommodates visitors from round the globe by scheduling shows on a schedule of rotating languages. For information, see the Tourist Information Office in Sultanahmet Park (Sultanahmet Meydanı; © **0212/518-1802**).

THE BAR SCENE

Visitors to Istanbul may be surprised by the variety of bars—from seedy to SoHo chic—as well as by the stream of beer, wine, and *rakı* that flows from the taps.

SULTANAHMET & THE OLD CITY   Cutting-edge bars are not the draw in this neighborhood, where tourists wander the streets in search of authentic Turkish entertainment instead.

The torch-lit outdoor cafes on the Hippodrome provide characteristic spots for whiling away the hours and are open well into the night. (The Grand Vizier seems to enjoy some longevity, but the cafe closest to the Fountain of Wilhelm II still remains, in spite of a continuous stream of new owners.) The restaurants lining the streets of **Kumkapı** (see "Where to Dine" earlier in this chapter) provide another characteristic venue where you can combine food and fun in a lively villagelike atmosphere, where celebration and sometimes dancing accompany all the seafood you care to eat. More central and ridiculously scenic is the cluster of bars, cafes, and fish restaurants newly occupying the lower level of the Galata Bridge. Have a tea or coffee, play a game of backgammon, and ponder the sound of the evening muezzin as his melodic chant carries over the minarets and bounces off the glitter of the Golden Horn.

Just at the entrance to the Arasta Bazaar is the **Meşale Cay Bahçesi,** an outdoor collection of benches and tables perfectly placed for a balmy summer's eve or a midday tea break in the shadow of the Blue Mosque. Along with its tranquil outdoor rose garden, the **House of Medusa Restaurant Café and Bar,** Yerebatan Caddesi, Muhterem Efendi Sok. 19 (across from the police station; © **0212/511-4116**), houses some unexpected ambience where you can sink into some kilims and cushions in the third-floor *şark,* or balance on a low saddle in the fourth-floor bar. Appetizers and main courses cost from 6.75YTL to 20YTL ($5–$15).

Not far from the Grand Bazaar is the outdoor living-room-cum-tea-gardens of the **Çarşıkapı** ("market gate"), hidden in the courtyard of the old Çorlulu Alipaşa Medrese. The tree-filled garden is a perfect way to unwind, with a glass of apple tea and the essence of strawberry in your water pipe while you admire the display of carpets and souvenirs decorating the gardens of the bordering shops. The entrance to the tea gardens is on Yeniçeriler Caddesi somewhere near where the road changes names from Divanyolu Caddesi. There's another, perhaps less exotic **Café-Inn** waterpipe cafe in a hidden courtyard off Incili Çavuş Sokak (No. 23; © **0212/522-9273**), which serves aromatic hookahs for 6.75YTL ($5) and an assortment of food.

TAKSIM, TÜNEL & BEYOĞLU   Taksim is undeniably the heart of this city's commerce, while Beyoğlu brings to mind characteristic back-street cafes, atmospheric bars, and stylish restaurants. While the tourists are shuttling between Taksim Square and Sultanahmet, the residents of Istanbul are making reservations in Beyoğlu. Twenty years ago this was not so, when Istiklal Caddesi looked more like the pre-Disney 42nd Street than the open-air shopping mall it is today. But tucked inside this neighborhood of opulent 19th-century mansions and former consulates are some of the classiest bars in town. Beyoğlu is still a neighborhood in transition, and the closer you get to Taksim Square, the seedier it gets.

Babylon This is a popular venue for music concerts full of hip and cosmopolitan chain-smoking Turks in black. There are frequent live concerts with cover charges varying from 14YTL to 27TYL ($10–$20); it's a good idea to buy your ticket earlier in the day to avoid the long line. Previous artists included jazz performers Charlie Hunter, Leon Parker, and Harriet Tubman, but more often than not, the musicians are lesser-known imports playing an eclectic (even weird) fusion of music. For reservations and tickets, try to get somebody who can speak Turkish for you. Open Tuesday through Saturday 9pm to 4am. Şehbender Sok. 3, Beyoğlu (from Istiklal Caddesi near Tünel, turn onto Asmalımecit Sokagı and left onto Şehbender). ℭ 0212/292-7368. Cover 14YTL–27TYL ($10–$20), depending on the event. Closed July 20–Sept 20.

Café Gramofon Café Gramofon is a civilized music venue, where on Monday students from the conservatory take the stage, and Tuesday through Saturday the cafe is filled with the sounds of jazz, swing, and bebop. It can get pretty loud, and the crowd is sometimes mixed (read: gay/lesbian), but everyone is well behaved. During the Jazz Festival, the cover is anywhere from $12 to $15, and half-price for students with a valid ID card; otherwise, it's free. Open Tuesday through Saturday 9pm to 2am. Meydanı 3, Tünel. ℭ 0212/293-0786. Cover varies.

Galatea Restaurant & Wine Bar Atmospheric and romantic, Galatea Restaurant & Wine Bar is down some stairs in a basement cantina characterized by redbrick arches and candlelight. To find it, just listen for the magnetic Latin music emanating from below the street level. Galatea is open for lunch and dinner with a novel menu of Spanish dishes and tapas. Open Monday through Saturday noon to 2am. Asmalı Mescid Mah. Sofyalı Sok. 16. ℭ 0212/292-5431.

Harry's Bar Another popular hotel bar is Harry's Bar, in the Hyatt Regency Hotel, which attracts a mixed clientele of traveling businessmen and local yuppies. The live entertainment varies from blues, classic rock, pop, and jazz. There's also karaoke, and video screens with music, news, and sports. Open Monday through Saturday 8pm to 2am. Hyatt Regency Hotel, Taksim. ℭ 0212/225-7000.

Lokanta at Nu Pera/Nu Teras 𝒜𝒜𝒜 Nu Pera is actually the name of a renovated building in the neighborhood of Pera, now an utterly reborn neighborhood chock-full of cafes and restaurants. In summer the rooftop Lokanta Teras Restaurant offers an elegant and upscale atmosphere and views of a twinkling city—one of my favorite dining spots, actually. The blackboard "tapas" menu at the rear bar is a favorite. In winter, the party moves to more cramped quarters on the ground-floor level. Open daily noon to 3pm and 7 to 12:30am (until 4am on weekends). Meşrutiyet Caddesi 149, Tepebaşı. ℭ 0212/245-6070.

360 Istanbul 𝒜𝒜 With views as good as this, it's no wonder that Istanbul is sprouting restaurant and bar venues in what are traditionally apartment or office buildings. 360 Istanbul takes advantage of the belfry of St. Antoine and panoramic views of the Golden Horn; on a cool summer's eve, there's really no better place to be. The decor is an unexpectedly pleasing amalgam of brick, steel, glass, and velvet; tables, alfresco banquettes, and a lounge area ensure that everybody gets something he or she wants. The menu is Thai and Turkish, with appetizers and finger foods standing out. Go early for the best outdoor seating, or arrive late and mill about the wraparound terrace. Reservations are suggested for dinner. Mısır Apartment Building, Istiklal Caddesi 32/311, Beyoğlu. ℭ 0212/251-1042.

Vareli Şaraphanesi *(Finds)* Vareli re-creates the atmosphere of the Byzantine wine houses of old. Wine barrels and wooden bar tables from Bozcaada optimize the medieval feel of the place, and paving stones from the Mürefte coast, famous for its wine production, keep the cellar cool. The wine cellar stocks a wide range of Turkish wines, including Kavaklıdere's top-of-the-line Kaleçi Karası and Öküzgözü. Local and imported cheeses, French ham, seviche, and even a duck entree round out the menu, keeping your taste buds jumping from sheer pleasure. If that's not enough, there's scheduled live music nightly Monday through Saturday. Open daily 11am to 3am. Asmalı Mescit Mahallesi, Oteller Sok. 7–9, Tepebaşı (behind the Pera Palas Hotel). ℭ 0212/292-5516. Appetizers 1.75YTL–5.75YTL ($1.30–$4.30); main courses 4.75YTL–11YTL ($3.60–$8); wines 5YTL–40YTL ($3.70–$29).

V.S.O.P. Bar An elegant and upscale locale in The Marmara Istanbul, V.S.O.P. is a five-star bar for the "discerning crowd," and actually an enjoyable spot for a drink and some conversation. Open daily 8am to 11pm (later on weekends). Taksim Meydanı, Taksim. ℭ 0212/251-4696.

ALONG THE BOSPHORUS

Istanbul's nightlife succumbs to the lure of the Bosphorus in the summer months, moving alfresco and up to the seafront venues of Ortaköy and Kuruçeşme. The grande dame of after-hours entertainment is **Reina** (Kuruçeşme Cad. 44; ℭ 0212/259-5919), a veritable multiplex of popular restaurants, a handful of waterfront dance floors, and bars, including the Zagat-rated G-by-Carafe (reservations required for all restaurants). The music, as is the crowd, is eclectic; pretty much anything goes. Cover is $30 on Friday and Saturday. Almost directly opposite Reina at Muallim Naci Caddesi 119 (the street name changes) is the new **Tampa Istanbul** (ℭ 0212/236-7256), a chic nightspot attracting the really smart set. While not on the water, it enjoys magnificent views of the Bosphorus. There is no cover, and the restaurant specializes in Mediterranean fare.

Cirağan Bar & Q Club Hibernating in the cellar of the most exclusive hotel in the city in the Çırağan Palace, Q draws the cream of Istanbul society, and there's never an empty seat in the house. The venue moves on to the seaside pier during the summer, as the sound of live jazz drifts over the Bosphorus until 2am (later in summer). The evening won't be cheap but it will definitely be memorable. Open daily 6pm to 2am. Çırağan Palace, Beşiktaş. ℭ 0212/326-4646. Cover $10.

The North Shields Pub The Beşiktaş outlet of this popular pub is a favorite after-hours destination for off-duty local chefs. Thanks to the rare Scotch whiskey and English ales, there's also a huge clientele of ex-pat regulars, in for the homey atmosphere—the pub is in a late-19th-century house—and the hearty beef and ale stew. A second more centralized location is at Istiklal Cad. 24–26 (in the Fitas Sinemasi, up the steps at the entrance to the movie complex; ℭ 0212/292-9698). Open daily 11am to 2am. Akaretler Sıraevleri, Spor Cad. 13, Beşiktaş. ℭ 0212/259-1806.

8 Side Trips from Istanbul

THE PRINCES' ISLANDS

The Princes' Islands are just a hop, skip, and a jump from Istanbul, and a well-received respite from the chaos and scorching sun of the city. The islands were originally used as a place of exile for members of the royalty and clergy during the age of Byzantium. It was later taken over by the more clever residents of the city as summer homes. The atmosphere is one of pure repose thanks to the prohibition against vehicles; the only form of transportation here (besides your own steam) is the characteristic and charming horse-drawn phaeton.

Thanks to the introduction of seabuses that shorten the ferry trip by an hour, the islands are only a half-hour away, making them an accessible retreat from city life.

GETTING THERE   Ferries departing from the docks behind Sirkeci Train Station cost 4YTL ($2.90) each way and make stops at Kınalıada, Burgazada, Heybeliada, and Büyükada. From Bostancı on the Asian side, you can get a ferry direct to Büyükada. Ferries run roughly every 65 minutes between 7am and midnight (7:30am–11:30pm on weekends; return times vary somewhat; ask for a current schedule at the tourist information office in Sultanahmet). Seabuses depart weekdays from Eminönü and Kabataş and make the trip to Büyükada in under 30 minutes (fare: 5YTL/$3.70), but there are only two scheduled departures per day, one at 8:45am and the other at 6:05pm. Return boats from Büyükada with through service to Eminönü depart at 7:30am and 4:45pm. There is no service to or from Eminönü on weekends or holidays. (Call the 24-hr. hot line at ✆ **0212/516-1212** to confirm departure times.)

EXPLORING THE PRINCES' ISLANDS   Thanks to the absence of vehicles other than the horse-drawn carriage, the islands have managed to retain their old-world charm. Horse-drawn carriages serve as local taxis, charging fixed rates from 5.50YTL ($4) to the nearest beach up to $26 for a grand tour of the islands. As expected, Istanbulers inundate the islands in the summer, looking to enjoy the characteristic architecture of the many clapboard mansions along with a relaxing day at the beach.

Big Island, or Büyükada, is the largest of the five islands and the one with the most to offer, including several good beaches, diving facilities, and the old hilltop monastery of Ayayorgı (St. George) from which you can see forever. To get to the monastery, take a carriage to Luna Park and take the 30-minute uphill path to Ayayorgi Peak, where you can sip their homemade wine while enjoying the panorama at the monastery's simple restaurant on the hill. To better appreciate what the islands have to offer, organize your excursion for a weekday, when the ferries are not packed like sardine cans and you can still get a glimpse of the sand beneath the blankets of the other sun worshippers. In the fall a stroll along the deserted cobblestone lanes met by the occasional donkey cart or a friendly pack of hopeful stray dogs transports you countless years back in time.

Kınalıada was the site of a major human rights infraction—the Byzantines gouged out the eyes of and exiled Romanos Diogenes IV here for his defeat by the Selçuks in the Battle of Manzikert. The monastery built for the unfortunate general is still standing. The island was raided many times by pirates and later inhabited mainly by Armenians, but because of a harsh climate, it has attracted fewer people than the other islands. Electricity first came to the island in 1946, and it wasn't until the 1980s that the island received a water supply from the Municipality. Kınalıada is also the only one of the Princes' Islands without the services of the 19th-century phaetons.

Burgazada is the second of the Princes' Islands, originally settled as a Greek fishing village. In the 1950s the island attracted the wealthy Jews of Istanbul, who restored existing mansions or built their own. The island is also the home of a famous Turkish writer, Sait Faik, whose home has been turned into a museum. There are two swim clubs near the ferry landing, but if it's beaches you're after, you'll be better off on one of the other islands.

Heybeliada is the island closest to Büyükada and similar in character in that the natural beauty attracts boatloads of weekenders in the summer. The waterside promenade ensures a steady stream of visitors looking to avoid the crowds over on Büyükada, but aside from a few eateries, you'll have to make this a day trip or book a room on Büyükada anyway.

WHERE TO STAY   There are few experiences that top getting in a horse-and-buggy and arriving at a wooden palace. Fantasy becomes reality on Büyükada, the biggest of the islands but not so built up that you want to avoid it. The **Hotel Splendid Palace,** 23 Nisan Cad. (turn right at the Hotel Princess and drop your jaw at the white domed mansion on your left; © **0216/382-6950;** fax 0216/382-6775; double in summer 120YTL ($90); American Express, Diners Club, MasterCard, Visa), is a palatial clapboard house with views of the Marmara with peaceful gardens, a private swimming pool, two restaurants, and an on-site patisserie. It's closed November through March. The disco next door may make you think twice, though. The **Hotel Princess,** Iskele Meydanı 2 (straight up the street from the ferry landing on the right; © **0216/382-1628;** fax 0216/382-1949; double 110YTL–160YTL ($80–$120), is a more modest but gracious seaside lodge, and is open year-round. Rooms are adequate although bathrooms are a bit tight, and there's a small pool overlooking the Marmara Sea for use in the summer months.

Those undeterred by the serenity of one of the smaller islands would do well to check out the **Halki Palas,** Refah Şehitleri Cad. 88, Heybeliada; © **0216/351-0025;** fax 0216/351-0032; double from 135YTL/$100). This attractive wooden house may be isolated from civilization, but a highly recommended restaurant, an outdoor swimming pool, sauna, Jacuzzi, and garden more than make up for the loss. The hotel closes December through March.

WHERE TO DINE   Restaurants specializing in fish line the wharf to the left of the ferry landing, for breezy and atmospheric waterside dining. **Birtat Restaurant,** Gülistan Cad. 10, Büyükada (© **0216/382-1245**), is one of the first waterside restaurants that you encounter as you make your way down the wharf, and there's really no need to go any farther. **Milano Restaurant,** Gülistan Cad. 8, Büyükada (© **0216/382-6352**), just a few doors down, has been here for over 30 years, and is the most famous restaurant on the island. For a more modest meal, try the **Yıldızlar Caféteria,** Iskele Cad. 2, Büyükada (© **0216/382-4360**), actually a 100-year-old tea garden serving *döner kebaps,* grilled cheese sandwiches, and the Turkish fast-food favorite, *lahmacun.*

POLONEZKÖY

Little more than an intersection in the road, the village itself has been designated as a national park. The bucolic setting, home to several restored Polish houses set on exquisite expanses of rolling hills, makes this a fashionable weekend getaway for residents of Istanbul or foreigners with a bit of spare time.

The origins of Polonezköy go back to the mid–19th century, when the Polish exile Adam Czartoriski lobbied Sultan Abdülmecid for the creation of a colony for Polish refugees, many of whom were fleeing from the invading Russians. The sultan granted these exiles permission to build a village in a forested area on the outskirts of Istanbul. The original settlement—called Adampol after Czartoriski—had only 12 residents.

The distinctive character of the town has attracted some foreigners with impressive credentials: Franz Liszt, Gustave Flaubert, and Lech Walesa all slept here, and even Pope John Paul II stopped in for a visit in 1994.

GETTING THERE   Getting to Polonezköy is pretty much impossible unless you have a car. To get there from the European side, drive across the Fatih Sultan Mehmet Bridge north of the city and follow the highway to Beykoz, then take the turnoff for Polonezköy. It's about another 15 minutes through Turkish suburbia before you reach the winding forest road into the village; ask for directions frequently after the highway exit, as signage is sparse. (Total time from Taksim is about 30 min.)

EXPLORING POLONEZKÖY   This forested retreat is a perfect place to spend a weekend outdoors or an afternoon by the fire. A nature lover's path runs from near the Adampol Hotel through the woods, and most of the hotels have bikes for their guests. Best of all is the possibility to wander around town and negotiate the hire of a pony for an enjoyable, if not authentic, pastoral experience.

WHERE TO STAY   The recently restored **Polka Country Hotel,** Cumhuriyet Yolu 36 (© **0216/432-3220;** fax 0216/432-3042; www.polkahotel.com), is rustic and romantic. A garden swimming pool enjoys pastoral hillside views, while in cooler weather stone fireplaces in several buildings encourage guests to rekindle the romance. A dry sauna is also tempting after a windy afternoon along the forest trails. The hotel is owned and operated by Hakan Ozan, an architect whose vision for the building is simple and tasteful. All rooms have telephones and TV, but try to nab one of the two top "penthouse" rooms, made slightly more rustic thanks to slanted roofs. (These also have air-conditioning.) Rooms are 100YTL ($74) on weekdays, 150YTL ($111) on weekends.

WHERE TO DINE   Continuing the village tradition, **Leonardo Restaurant,** Polonezköy 32, Beykoz (© **0216/432-3082**), is the only restaurant in town to serve Polish food. It's also one of the few places you can get pork or even wild boar, but they also serve steaks, grills, and schnitzel at prices that hover around 14YTL ($10) per dish. The Sunday buffet lunch is a popular event as well, and costs around 18YTL ($13) per person with drinks. The restaurant is in the restored home of one of the first Polish immigrants and has a splendid outdoor garden for Indian-summer evenings.

5

Short Hops from Istanbul: Around the Sea of Marmara & the North Aegean

For centuries—even millennia—the Northern Aegean and Marmara regions attempted to defend a legacy of geographical advantage, standing helpless as empires, emperors, and armies swept through. These lands provided the first taste of Asia to those successful in crossing the Bosphorus Straits and the last obstacle to any attempted conquest of Istanbul, because an army's advancement into the Marmara region left the great city surrounded and cut off. Throughout history, each of these civilizations left its own personal mark, from Xerxes through Alexander the Great to Gazi Osman. The layers of culture superimposed over the pastoral countryside make for an enriching visit to any of the destinations outlined in this chapter. It's possible, if you're crunched for time, to make any of the destinations an overnight or weekend trip; literally hundreds of tour companies in Istanbul advertise affordable excursions with guides. (Bursa is sadly underserved in this area, but a do-it-yourself trip is just as easy.)

1 Bursa ★★

243km (151 miles) south of Istanbul; 270km (167 miles) east of Çanakkale; 380km (236 miles) west of Ankara; 322km (200 miles) northeast of İzmir

In a landscape not unlike that of Tuscany, Bursa established itself as an important center as far back as pre-Roman times, attracting emperors and rulers for its rich, fertile soil and healing thermal waters. The arrival of the Ottomans in 1326 ensured the city's prosperity as a cultural and economic center that now represents one of the richest legacies of early Ottoman art and architecture. As the first capital of the Ottoman Empire, Bursa became the beneficiary of the finest mosques, theological schools *(medreses)*, humanitarian centers *(imarets)*, and social services *(hans, hamams,* and public fountains). The density of arched portals, graceful domes, artfully tiled minarets, and magnificently carved *minbars* (pulpits) could easily provide the coursework for extensive study of the Ottomans, and without a doubt, fill multiple daylong walking tours.

Today Bursa is a thriving industrial and agricultural center, reputed for its fine silk and cotton textiles, and the center of Turkey's automobile industry. The nearby ski resorts at Mount Uludağ provide city dwellers with an easy weekend getaway, and it's not uncommon for people to make a special trip here to stock up on cotton towels. (Many just fly in on a private helicopter for a meal at Uludağ; see "Where to Dine" later in this chapter.) But many just flock here for the same reasons the Romans,

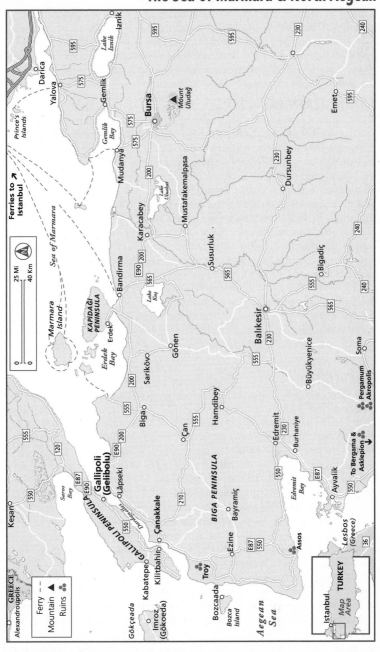

Byzantines, and Ottomans did: the indulgence afforded by the density of rich hot mineral springs bubbling up all over the region.

If you plan on just a quick architectural and historical pilgrimage, you could reasonably make Bursa a day trip from Istanbul. An overnight excursion is more realistic if you want to make it a short spa getaway and leave time to wander through the exquisite *hans* (privately owned inns or marketplaces) of the early Ottoman era.

A LOOK AT THE PAST

It was common practice for a conquering king to attach his name to the cities that he founded, so the consensus is that King Prusia of Bithynia established a kingdom on the remains of a preexisting civilization here. Prusia (say it 10 times fast and it starts to sound like Bursa) of Olympus, distinguishing it from King Prusia's other conquests, was later leagued with Rome, a colonization that is attributed to the time of Eumenes II, leader of Pergamum. Bursa thrived, thanks to Rome's influence and the introduction of Christianity by the apostle Andrew. In the 6th century Emperor Justinian constructed baths and a lavish palace in the area, taking full advantage of the region's economic and thermal resources. From 1080 to 1326, Bursa bore the brunt of more than its fair share of invasions, with Selçuks, Turks, raiding Arabs, Byzantines, and Crusaders all trying to get a hold on this prosperous center. One of the Turkic tribes broke the chain when the Osmanlı tribe of Turks, led by Osman and later his son Orhan, entered Bursa in 1326 after a 10-year-long siege. Orhan established Bursa as the first permanent Ottoman capital, building a mosque and *medrese* on the site of a Byzantine monastery in what is now the Hisar District. The city expanded and thrived under Sultans Murat I, Yıldırım Bayezit, Mehmet I, and Murad II. Bursa's importance began to wane when the Ottoman capital was transferred to Adrionople (present-day Edirne).

ESSENTIALS

GETTING THERE From the Yenikapı docks in Istanbul (© 0212/517-7137), it's a pleasant 50-minute ferry ride for 10YTL ($7.50) to Yalova, from where you will catch a bus to Bursa's *otogar* (bus station; 3YTL/$2). Ferries run every 2 hours in either direction beginning at 7:30am (last ferry: 9:30pm), and from the ferry landing it's another 50 minutes by bus to the *otogar*. The buses are lined up just outside the gates to the ferry landing—virtually all the buses go to Bursa. If you prefer to do the entire journey by land, Uludağ (© **0224/261-5533**) runs buses almost hourly from Istanbul; the 4-hour trip costs 4.50YTL ($3.30). Based in Bursa, **Nilüfer Turizm** (© **0224/444-0099**) provides the most comprehensive bus service into Bursa in Turkey. Kamil Koç will also get you there from Istanbul, which costs 17YTL ($13) on either company's bus.

Bursa's *otogar* is located more than 9.5km (6 miles) out of town, so it will be necessary to either get on a municipal bus or take a taxi into town. The bus takes about half an hour, but that 70YKr (50¢) ticket still isn't cheap enough to make me lug my heavy bags off the bus, down the road, and up the back entrance of the hotel *ever again*. A taxi is direct, quick, and cheap (expect to pay around 6YTL ($4.50) for the 15-min. ride). This is definitely one of those times when the convenience offsets the cost.

VISITOR INFORMATION The **Tourist Information office** (© **0224/251-1834;** fax 0224/220-1848) is hidden underneath Atatürk Caddesi in the center of

---

⸨Tips⸩ Turkish Towels & Such

If you're in the market for a few fluffy towels or one of those luscious Turkish bathrobes that sell for an arm and a leg in Bloomingdale's, the price for selection at Bursa's **Covered Bazaar** (see "What to See & Do" below) can't be beat. The subtlest prints and plushest linens and towels are found at **Özdilek,** with branches in both the bazaar (exit the underground passage opposite the PTT and walk 1 block in) and at Yenı Yalova Yolu 4, on the highway from the *otogar* (℮ **0224/211-5200**). Silk fabrics, such as scarves, blouses, and tablecloths, are available in shops on the upper level of **Koza Han,** the historic *bedesten* (covered market) next to Orhan Camii. For modern merchandise in a slick mall setting, the new glass pyramid–topped **Zafer Plaza** houses franchises such as Quicksilver, Vakko, Demirel, Mavi Jeans, and Polo Garage.

---

town. If you're standing with Orhan Camii on your right and the Belediye (Municipal Building) on your left, the office is straight ahead of you at 12 o'clock. The PTT (post office) is located a few blocks west (to the right) down Atatürk Caddesi on the opposite side of the street.

All of the major bus companies have ticket offices around Heykel; tickets can also be purchased through any local travel agent or at the *otogar.*

ORIENTATION   The concentration of early Selçuk-inspired architecture is clustered in the commercial center of Bursa, in the area better known to the locals as **Heykel,** after the equestrian statue of Atatürk commanding the plaza just a few blocks to the east (*heykel* means "statue" in Turkish). Again, using the Tourist Information office for orientation, to the west/right is **Tophane Park** and the **Hisar District,** where the conquering Ottoman armies set up their capital in the 15th century. The road leads into the posher **Çekirge** section, where ambassadors and statesmen flock for the hotels and thermal hot springs. The winter ski resort of Uludağ is located about 36km (22 miles) to the south of Bursa.

GETTING AROUND   In all likelihood, you will spend most of your time between the Heykel and Çekirge neighborhoods. While covering small distances on foot in either neighborhood is possible, the two are just too far apart to think about walking between them. Instead, hop on a *dolmuş*—in Bursa, *dolmuşes* are group taxis—running conveniently along the main arteries. (The street names change so many times that it's useless to mention them here.) *Dolmuşes* cost around 1.20YTL (90¢) and are distinguishable from the multiple destinations marked on the roof of the car. A taxi taking the same route will cost about 6.75YTL ($5).

WHAT TO SEE & DO

Bursa is so jam-packed with historic structures that it would be impossible to list them all here. Some are intertwined with the lives of the locals who stare curiously as visitors admire the interior courtyard facades of their workplace. In addition to the major sites named below, be sure to wander through the marketplace, spread out among open-air and covered streets. *Hans* are traditionally double-storied arcaded buildings with a central courtyard, usually occupied by an ornate fountain or pool or raised *mescit* (a small mosque). The *hans* are still used for trade, and make lovely shaded retreats to take a coffee outdoors and poke amid the local merchandise. The **Fidan Han** dates to the 15th century and has a central pool topped by a *mescit*. The **Pirinç Han** (closed) was constructed by Beyazit II to earn the revenue necessary to cover the expenses of his mosque and soup kitchen in Istanbul. The **Ipek Han** is the largest *han* in Bursa and contains an octagonal *mescit* in the center of the courtyard. The revenue from this *han* was used to pay for the construction of the Yeşil Mosque. The courtyard of **Emir Han** has a graceful marble pool with exterior faucets to allow for ablutions.

Archaeology Museum (Arkeoloji Müzesi)

Constructed with the charm of any 1972 institutional project, this museum is worth the 30 minutes it will take to get through, especially if you're strolling through Çekirge or into Kültür Park. The fact that the attendant trails you to turn the lights on and off is a bit unnerving (the museum doesn't see that many tourists), obliging you to react with an appropriate level of enthusiasm. The museum houses regional artifacts dating back to the 3rd century B.C., with crude pottery and tools from as far back as the Neolithic period. Particularly impressive is the collection of ceramic and glass objects from the Classical era, much of which has remained surprisingly intact. The extensive collection of coins displayed on the mezzanine is significant because notable figures had a habit of emblazoning their portraits on the face of the piece, providing a rare window of tangibility into the ancients.

Kültür Park. © 0224/220-2029. Admission 2YTL ($1.50). Tues–Sun 8:30am–noon and 1–5pm.

Atatürk Museum (Atatürk Müzesi)

This is one of those traditional timber mansions at which you'd love to get a closer look. The historic rooms have been left as they were when Atatürk slept here on his visits to Bursa, down to the very last particle of dust.

Çekirge Cad., next to the Çelik Palas. © 0224/236-4844. Free admission. Tues–Sun 8:30am–noon and 1–5pm.

Bursa Museum of Turkish and Islamic Arts (Türk Islam Eser. Müzesi) ⊛

Housed in the former *medrese* of the Green Mosque, built in 1419 by Çelebi Sultan Mehmet along with the other buildings in the Yeşil complex, this museum is worth a look, particularly because they've gone to the trouble of providing English translations. The exhibits are intimately displayed in small rooms around a central courtyard. There's a space devoted to dervish cult objects, a *hamam* (Turkish bath) room displaying silver clogs and silk embroidered bath accessories, and a model of a traditional Turkish coffeehouse, complete with barber's chair. The collection also includes Selçuk ceramics, inlaid wood pieces, and objects in iron, copper, bronze, and wood. A visit takes under 30 minutes.

Yeşil Cad., on the left just before the Green Mosque. © 0224/327-7679. Admission 2YTL ($1.50). Tues–Sun 8:30am–5pm.

Covered Bazaar (Bedesten)

The covered bazaar that stands on the site is a modern version of the original that was built by Yıldırım Bayezit in the 14th century and leveled in the earthquake of 1855. There's no glitz—or tourists—here, evidenced by the distressing concentration of satin embroidered towels and bedspreads. Keep your eyes open for good-quality baby clothes and knockoff sportswear, and if you're looking to stuff a throw pillow, this is the place to do it, as stalls displaying fluffy unspun cotton of varying composition and quality abound.

Enter through Koza Hanı, or follow Çarşı Cad. from Ulu Camii. Daily 8:30am–7pm.

The Great Mosque (Ulu Camii) ☙☙ When the building was erected in 1396, architects were just beginning to dabble in the problem of covering large spaces with small domes, and the result is the first example of a monumental Ottoman multidomed mosque. The 20 domes, supported on 12 stout pillars, are better admired from within, where the final result comes together in the mosque's five naves and four bays.

The date of completion (802H—H is for *hicret,* the day Mohammed left Mecca for Medina) is inscribed on the pulpit door, but several waves of renovations were necessary after the invasion of Tamerlane, with major restorations completed after the earthquake of 1855.

The wooden *minbar* (pulpit) is a masterwork of carved geometric and floral reliefs, as is the banister work and other wood details. But the main focus of the mosque is the three-tiered **ablution fountain** beneath a large light well. Although this has its practical purposes, the result is an embracing sensation of serenity, and many worshippers remain on the raised platforms surrounding the fountain for long moments of meditation.

Bursa center. Free admission. Daily dawn–dusk.

Green Mosque (Yeşil Camii) ☙ Commanding a hillside terrace above the city, Yeşil Camii takes its name from the color of the green and blue tiles in the interior. Intent on leaving his mark on Bursa, Mehmet I ordered the construction of this mosque, built entirely of hewn stone and marble, as a monument to the victorious ending of his 10-year struggle for the throne. Although an architect's inscription over the portal gives the completion date as 1419, the final decorations were ordered in 1424 on the orders of Murad II, and the two minarets were added in the 19th century.

One of the first mosques to employ an inverted T floor plan, the building signals the dawn of a new Turkish architectural tradition. The "Turkish pleat," an ingenious geometric corner detail allowing for the placement of a circular dome atop a square base, is a design device original to Turkey, while the use of multicolored ceramic tile, an influence that arrived with Tamerlane, is intricate enough to make your head spin. The high porcelain *mihrab* (a niche oriented toward Mecca) is a masterpiece of Ottoman ceramic art, difficult to miss at an understated 10m (33 ft.) high. In the center of the *mihrab* in Arabic script is the word "Allah," mounted on the wall at a later date.

The sumptuous gold mosaics and tile of the Imperial loge were probably an overstated attempt at one-upping the loggia that served the Byzantine emperors; it is flanked on either side by the servants' quarters and the harem, and a closer look is at the discretion of the caretaker.

East of Heykel at the end of Yeşil Cad. Free admission. Daily dawn–dusk.

Green Tomb (Yeşil Türbesi) ☙☙ This Selçuk-influenced tomb, representing one of the noblest of its era, has become the symbol of Bursa. If you're looking for a blue building, look no further, as the tiles of this hexagonal structure are actually turquoise, topped by a lead dome resting on a plaster rim. The construction of the tomb was ordered by the tenant himself, Sultan Mehmet I, and was completed around 1421. The color glazing of the interior tile work is an outstanding example of the art, from the window pediments adorned with verses of the Koran and *hadiths* (narrations of the life of Mohammad) in Arabic script, to the tile inscriptions on the sarcophagi. It's also worth noting the workmanship of the colors of the panels on the *mihrab,* which change color according to your perspective.

East of Heykel at the end of Yeşil Cad. Free admission. Daily 8am–noon and 1–5pm.

Koza Hanı 🏵️🏵️   Meaning "Cocoon Inn," this caravansary was built in 1490 by Bayezid II to raise funds for his mosque in Istanbul. Built on two levels, the inn provided a place for the merchants to trade the last of their goods, as this was the final stop on the Silk Road from China. In the middle of the courtyard is a small *şadırvan* (ablution fountain) 🏵️ for the small *mescit* (prayer room) poised above; in the summer the verdant space becomes a peaceful tea garden. The monumental portal decorated with turquoise tiles and carvings leads into the covered bazaar. Today the Koza Hanı continues its legacy of trading in silk with shops and boutiques stocked with scarves and fabrics at exorbitant (and extremely negotiable) prices.

Bursa Center. Free admission. Daily 8:30am–sunset.

Muradiye Complex (Muradiye Külliye) 🏵️🏵️   Constructed by Murat II between 1424 and 1426, this complex includes a mosque, a *medrese,* a soup kitchen, a bath, and a royal cemetery amid an overgrown garden of roses, magnolias, and cypress trees. Although the entrance to the grounds is open, many of the tombs and even the mosque are locked up, but the idle yet earnest ticket-window attendant will catch up with you for a private tour of the grounds, proudly locking and unlocking the royal tombs.

The Murat Paşa Mosque is a typical example of early Ottoman architecture, although the *mihrab* and *minbar* are 18th-century baroque. Reverently displayed inside on the upper-left-hand wall is an original piece from the Kaa'ba in Mecca.

To the right, beginning toward the rear of the grounds, is no ordinary cemetery. The 12 stately tombs serve as the final resting places of not only some of the first sultans, but a sobering number of members of the royal family as well, including Hüma Hatun (mother of Mehmet the Conqueror), Shehzade Ahmed (son of Beyazid II and crowned prince), Sultan Murat II, Mustafa (son of Süleyman the Magnificent), and Gülşah Hatun (wife of Mehmet the Conqueror). Because succession rights relied not on heredity but on survival of the fittest, it was standard, even expected, practice for the victorious leader to cover his back by strangling his brothers with a wire cord.

The most recognizable casualty of this practice was the son of Süleyman the Magnificent: Şehzade (Prince) Mustafa, who as object of a plot spun by Roxelana for the succession of her own son, was unjustly murdered at the hands of his father. Ironically, the tomb was built by Selim II, Roxelana's son and successor to the throne.

The recently restored opulence of the tomb and its outstanding porcelain tiling is indicative of why the technique for reproducing the superior İznik tiles is impossible. In contrast, the mausoleum of Murad I, son of Orhan and third Ottoman sultan, is elegant in its simplicity. The tomb has a domed central courtyard surrounded by the traditional ambulatory. Upon the request of the sultan, an oculus was designed in the dome to allow the rains to wash over the open tomb, symbolizing his sameness with the plain folk.

After reigning for just 18 days and living the rest of his life in exile, Cem Sultan, the youngest son of Mehmed II, was brought back to Bursa to receive a royal burial in the tomb that had actually been built for Şehzade Mustafa.

The 15th-century *medrese,* now operating as a clinic, was designed around a central courtyard accessible through vaulted arches at the entrance. No one will bother you if you want to take a quick peek, but the main use for this clinic is as a tuberculosis dispensary, so it might be better to do your admiring from the outside.

The Tarihi II Murat Hamamı next to the mosque is still in operation, with separate days designated for men and women.

Çekirge (from the town center, take *dolmuş* marked MURADIYE). Free admission. Tues–Sun 8:30am–noon and 1–5pm.

Fun Fact They Died with a Smile (or, That Joke's a Killer)

When Sultan Orhan arrived in Bursa, he immediately set out to build his mosque. He appointed a man named **Hacıvad** as supervisor, who in turn hired a local blacksmith named **Karagöz** to oversee the installation of the iron supports. Hacıvad and Karagöz used to pass the time with clever quips and witty conversation that kept the laborers in stitches. The two eventually had the workmen doubled over in hysterics, to the point that work on the mosque came to a complete halt.

When the sultan found out about the construction delays, he had Hacıvad and Karagöz hanged (or decapitated, depending on which interpretation of the oral history you hear). The decapitated version is favored, because illustrators have had a grand time depicting the two hapless jokers approaching the sultan's throne to protest with their heads under their arms. Whichever demise you choose, the outcome is the same: Orhan finds someone to relate the dialogues, until the sultan, too, is keeling over with laughter. Realizing his error, the sultan orders a local leather worker to create lifelike figures of the two, so that they can continue their legacy of comedy. This puppetlike shadow play gained momentum and grew into a popular cultural tradition, boasting as many as 200 characters in one presentation.

As you drive from the center of town toward Çekirge, ask your driver to point out the **Karagöz Hacivat Memorial,** a small but colorful representation of the two folk heroes.

Orhan Gazi Mosque (Orhan Camii) ★★ Constructed between 1339 and 1340 by Orhan Gazi, this is one of the most important early Ottoman constructions in Bursa. Pointed arches on the veranda show the beginnings of a particularly Ottoman detail, while the exterior brickwork recalls its Selçuk origins. The mosque was damaged in 1413 by Karamanoğlu Mehmet Bey and repaired in 1417 by Çelebi Sultan Mehmet. Note the star-shaped decorations representing the course of the sun, and the marble embellishments on the eastern and western facades.

The surrounding complex is one of the first in the Ottoman tradition, consisting of a mosque, *medrese,* soup kitchen, bath, and inn. The cats apparently stay there free of charge, and the whole courtyard and mosque interior have a homey feel.

Bursa town center, across from the Municipal Building. Free admission. Daily dawn–dusk.

Tombs of Osman and Orhan ★ This lovely park attracts local tourists as much for its tea gardens and stunning views as for the **tombs** of the two founders of the Ottoman Empire. The location in the *Hisar* (fortress), the oldest section of the city, which passed from Roman to Byzantine and finally to Ottoman hands, is a fitting one for the final resting places of Osman Gazi and Orhan Gazi.

According to Osman Gazi's wish to be "laid to rest beneath the silver dome of Bursa," his tomb was constructed on the chapel of St. Elie, the Byzantine monastery formerly on the site. The sarcophagus, surrounded by an ornate brass balustrade, is decorated with mother-of-pearl inlay. At one time, the building also contained the tomb of Orhan, but after it was partially destroyed by fire and then leveled by the 1855 earthquake, Sultan Abdülaziz had Orhan's tomb rebuilt separately. The Orhan tomb, slightly less ornate than his father's tomb, was constructed on the foundation of an 11th-century Byzantine church, from which some mosaics in the floor have survived.

Hisar District (inside the entrance to Tophane Park along Arka Sokağı, just west of the post office). No phone. Free admission. Daily dawn–dusk.

Uluumay Ottoman Museum   The restored architectural gem that is the Sair Ahmet Medrese rivals the museum within. Located in the Muradiye Complex, this assemblage of folk art was collected from around the Ottoman Empire, including the Caucuses, the Balkans, and the home territory of Anatolia. There's an ample ethnographic exhibition that features over 400 pieces of Ottoman-era jewelry, plus household items, saddlebags, silk scarves, and silver watch fobs. To name a few.

Sair Ahmet Paşa Medresesi, Muradiye Camisi Karşısı, Beşikçiler Caddesi, Muradiye. ℂ **0224/225-4813**. Admission 3YTL ($2.20). Tues–Sun 9am–6:30pm (closed at 6pm, Sept–Apr).

Yıldırım Bayezit Mosque (Yıldırım Bayezit Camii)   The two prominent domes, set one behind the other, represent an attempt at a design feature reminiscent of the St. Irene of Constantinople and the St. John's Basilica at Ephesus. Awkwardly juxtaposed above the three remaining domes, the larger two create a prayer hall that was to become a theme in the architecture of Ottoman mosques.

The mosque forms a part of the *külliye*, or complex, comprising a *medrese*, a *hamam*, a hospital, and the tomb of the Sultan Bayezit I, built by his son Süleyman the Magnificent in 1406.

Northeast of the town center in the Yıldırım District. Free admission. Daily dawn–dusk.

WHERE TO STAY

Atlas Hotel   A charming and economical alternative to the concrete blocks nearby, the Atlas has everything the heavy-hitting five-star hotels have, but on a smaller scale. They also have saggy beds, but at this price, your back can handle it. The hotel attempts to retain the character of a typical wooden Ottoman house by decorating the facade, lobby, and marble garden courtyard with wooden architectural features like eaves and canopies. Guests get to take advantage of one of the two private thermal *hamams*, small tiled and marble baths with miniature sunken pools. For a change of scenery, the historic thermal bath of the Kervansaray Hotel is only steps away, and the hotel is just a 5-minute *dolmuş* ride into the city center.

Hamamlar Cad. 35 (near the Kervansaray Hotel), 16070 Çekirge/Bursa. ℂ **0224/234-4100.** Fax 0224/236-4605. www.atlasotel.com.tr. 36 units. 50€ ($60) single; 75€ ($90) double. MC, V. On-street parking only. **Amenities:** Restaurant; indoor thermal pool; Turkish bath; Jacuzzi; 24-hr. room service; laundry service; dry cleaning. *In room:* A/C, satellite TV, minibar, hair dryer.

Çelik Palas Hotel 🌟🌟   Built in the 1930s under instructions by Atatürk, the Çelik Palas holds the title as Turkey's first five-star hotel. Until recently, this acclaimed Turkish icon was showing its dubious pedigree, but thanks to a recent upgrade, the Çelik Palas is once again at the top of its game. The best rooms—those facing the mountains—each combine the space of two rooms forming comfortably plush junior suites, with such luxuries as two bathrooms (one with a massage shower; the other a Jacuzzi tub), stylish furniture, and a sofa bed that increases the room capacity to four. Rooms in the annex are rarely used, making this end of the hotel great for groups. Best of all, there's the large, domed, marble thermal pool, the crowned jewel of a small wellness facility (see "Water, Water Everywhere: Turkey's Mineral Springs," below). The building of a third "annex," which has been underway for some years, has been taken over by Swissôtel and is expected to be open in 2007, adding more than 100 rooms and no less luxury than you would expect from a Swissôtel property.

Çekirge Cad. 79, 16070 Çekirge/Bursa. ⓒ **0224/233-3800**. Fax 0224/236-1910. http://bursa.swissotel.com. 241 units. 164€ ($200) double; 265€–310€ ($322–$378) suites. AE, DC, MC, V. On-site parking. **Amenities:** 2 restaurants; 2 bars; large thermal pool; spa (w/Turkish bath, Jacuzzi, and sauna); concierge; tour desk; car-rental desk; shopping arcade; salon; 24-hr. room service; massage; laundry service; dry cleaning; nonsmoking rooms. *In room:* A/C, cable TV, minibar, hair dryer, safe.

Hotel Anatolia   It's not the most opulent, nor does it have the best thermal facility. But the rooms—all recently renovated and still smelling of paint and carpet glue— are well groomed and sport burgundies, brocades, and bidets, albeit somewhat beige in style. But the unpretentious four-star Hotel Anatolia offers all the little details of good hospitality, such as in-room coffee and tea service, and service with a smile (plus rates as low as 60% below the rack rate). The hotel also has three private mini–thermal pools (8€/$10; 50% discount for hotel guests), a lovely little *hamam,* and a small swimming pool in the inner court.

Çekirge Meydanı, 16080 Çekirge/Bursa. ⓒ **0224/233-9400**. Fax 0224/233-9408. www.hotelanatolia.com. 100 units. 165€ ($200) double; 240€ ($290) suite. MC, V. Underground parking garage. **Amenities:** 4 restaurants; 2 bars; outdoor swimming pool; 3 private thermal baths; concierge; car-rental desk; 24-hr. room service; laundry service; dry cleaning. *In room:* A/C, satellite TV w/movies, minibar, coffeemaker, hair dryer.

Kent Hotel   The draw of this hotel is its location right in the center of town, which for some represents a major disadvantage. In spite of its shabby appearance (the McDonald's next door doesn't help), the Kent surprisingly has all the basic creature comforts to which we have become accustomed, including satellite TV in all the rooms. Don't expect opulence, however, and ask for a room off the avenue.

Atatürk Cad. 69, 16010 Bursa (town center next to the McDonald's). ⓒ **0224/223-5420**. Fax 0224/224-4015. www.kentotel.com. 54 units. 82€ ($100) double; 100€ ($120) suite. MC, V. **Amenities:** Restaurant; 24-hr. room service; laundry service; dry cleaning. *In room:* A/C, satellite TV, minibar, hair dryer.

Kervansaray Termal Hotel &   This is the most stylish hotel in Bursa, never letting you forget you're in a town of thermal springs. There's a decorative waterfall in the modern lobby, two swimming pools, and a renovated multidomed 700-year-old *hamam.* Most rooms have a balcony with a valley, mountain, or garden view, but, frankly, are nothing to write home about. The health club's cleverly designed swimming pool is divided by a retractable window, providing for both indoor and outdoor swimming, and the water is supplied by nearby mineral springs.

Çekirge Meydanı, 16080 Çekirge/Bursa. ⓒ **0224/233-9300**. Fax 0224/233-9324. 224 units. Summer 140€ ($170) double, 235€ ($285) and up suite; rates lower in winter. All rates include breakfast. AE, MC, V. No traveler's checks. **Amenities:** 2 restaurants; 2 bars; outdoor swimming pool; fitness room; concierge; tour desk; car-rental desk; shopping arcade; salon; 24-hr. room service; massage; laundry service; dry cleaning; historic thermal bath with separate sections for men and women. *In room:* A/C, satellite TV, minibar, hair dryer.

WHERE TO DINE

Arap Şükrü Restaurant FISH   Arap Şükrü was the first fresh-fish restaurant on Sakarya Caddesi, and eventually became an institution in Bursa. In fact, the street is better known by this name than by its actual name, having since been copied by a whole street full of knockoffs. In the summertime, when tables spill outside, there's barely enough walking space between the restaurants. Not much English is spoken here, making the point-and-choose method of ordering quite efficient.

Kuruçeşme Sakarya Cad. 4–8, Çatalfırın/Bursa. ⓒ **0224/220-6716**. Dinner 20YTL–27YTL ($15–$20) per person. MC, V. Daily 1pm–1am.

Çiçek Izgara TURKISH/KÖFTE   There's nothing worse than wandering around the center of a busy town and not knowing where to eat. Çiçek Izgara comes highly recommended by the locals, combining three floors of white linen tablecloths and impeccable service with the bright casualness of a cafeteria. Menu items include *peynerli köfte* (meatballs with cheese), *kabak dolması* (stuffed zucchini), and *cacık,* a refreshing yogurt soup.

Belediye Cad. (just after Orhan Camii on the left, 2nd floor). ✆ **0224/221-6526.** *Kebaps* and *köfte* 4YTL–8YTL ($3–$6). MC, V. Daily 10am–midnight.

Cumurcul Restaurant TURKISH/INTERNATIONAL   I have great respect and admiration for any chef who leads me into the kitchen, grabs a fish, and shows me how to make a salt-baked *levrek* (a local variety of sea bass indigenous to the Aegean and Mediterranean seas). Schooled in Germany, the chef's influences are apparent in the steamed bacon (made of beef) with pepper, tomatoes, and mushrooms.

Aside from the food, the setting is the major attraction in this former old rich man's *konak* (mansion). While the exterior is in need of a new coat of paint, rooms in the traditional Ottoman house have been converted into cozy dining areas, transforming spaces in the not-yet-renovated home into an atmospheric old taverna. The summer heat chases the restaurant into the oversize and lovely rear gardens, which after 11pm become a sophisticated nightclub.

Çekirge Cad. (across from the Çelik Palas Hotel). ✆ **0224/235-3707.** Reservations suggested in winter. Main courses 9.50YTL–20YTL ($7–$15). AE, MC, V. Daily 6pm–1am.

Kebapçı Iskender ISKENDER KEBAP   This is ground zero for what has ulti-mately infiltrated into the daily cultural life not only in Turkey but also worldwide. It was in 1867 that Grandpa Iskender tried a new way of roasting lamb; he stuck it on a vertical rotating spit (*döner* means revolving). When it was done, he sliced the meat into strips, placed them over a bed of pita with tomatoes and yogurt, and poured an alarming quantity of butter over the top—and voilà, Iskender (or *döner*) *Kebap.* The flavorful meat is spiced with aromatic thyme from Uludağ and butter from local dairy farms.

Ünlü Cad. 7, Bursa. ✆ **0224/221-4615.** All menu items 8YTL ($6) and under. No credit cards. Daily 11am–10pm.

Uludağ Kebapçısı ★★ ISKENDER KEBAPS   The best food is often found in unremarkable, even divelike places. Although Grandpa Iskender has the historical cor-ner on the *döner kebap* recipe, this place has perfected it. Located in two narrow store-fronts near the old bus terminal, the Uludağ Kebapçısı is arguably the best place in the world to eat the Iskender *döner kebap.* You can order it with decadent slices of steak *(bonfile),* surprisingly delicious kidney *(böbrek),* or what the owner called "back" *(kantıfile)*—but don't complain to me if your cholesterol levels shoot through the roof: Uludağ goes through 18 kilos (40 lb.) of butter per day. Throw caution to the wind, and top it all off with the *sütlü helva,* a heavenly milk pudding served mainly in the cooler months.

Garaj Karşısı Şirin Sok. 12. ✆ **0224/254-7264.** *Kebaps* 5.50YTL–9.50YTL ($4–$7). MC, V. Daily 11am–midnight.

A PILGRIMAGE & SOME PLATES: İZNIK ★★
To Turks, the sleepy lakeside resort of İznik provides a respite from the sweltering sum-mer sun; to Christendom, İznik sits atop modern-day Nicaea, the former seat of the Eastern Roman Empire and the site of the first and second Ecumenical Councils.

Water, Water Everywhere: Turkey's Mineral Springs

A geologic oddity-cum-spa treat with which Turkey is uncommonly blessed is the mineral spring. Thermal baths flow freely throughout the country-side, and depending on the properties and temperature of the water, are reputed to address such varied ailments as obesity, digestive problems, rheumatism, and urological disorders. Soaking in the springs and covering yourself with mineral-rich mud are some of the country's lesser-known pleasures. You can experience the thermal springs enclosed in pamper-me surroundings or in humble out-of-the-way sites. (In addition to the places listed below, see "Area Thermals" in chapter 6.)

In Bursa, history and self-indulgence go hand in hand, and no historical pilgrimage to this city would be complete without a long soak in a mineral-rich thermal pool. The **Kervansaray Hotel's 700 year-old thermal bath** 🐦🐦, Çekirge Meydanı, 16080 Çekirge (℃ **0224/233-9300**; 16YTL/$12 entrance, 15YTL/$11 kese, 15YTL/$11 for a 10-min. massage), takes advantage of the **Eski Kaplıca** thermal spring, an ancient source used as far back as Roman times. The bath was built in grand Ottoman style by Sultan Murat I in 1389, and a soak here is made all the more satisfying with its multiple domes and old stone masonry.

No one knows who originally occupied the **Yeni Kaplıca** *hamam* 🐦🐦, Yeni Kaplıca Cad. 6, Çekirge (℃ **0224/236-6968**; 6.75YTL/$5 entrance, 5.50YTL/$4 sloughing, 12YTL/$8.50 massage), built in 1555 and recon-structed for Süleyman the Magnificent by Grand Vizier Rüstem Paşa. The *hamam* (or at least, the men's side) still displays its original opulence, allow-ing wide-eyed tourists to feel like Julius Caesar for a day.

Separated from the Yeni Kaplıca building by a tea garden is the less impressive **Kaynarca**, Yeni Kaplıca Cad. 8 (℃ **0224/236-6955**; 5.50YTL/$4 entrance, 5.50YTL/$4 sloughing, 12YTL/$8.50 massage), catering to women only. **Kara Mustafa Paşa Thermal Bath,** Mudanya Cad. 10 (℃ **0224/236-6956**; 6.75YTL/$5 entrance, 5.50YTL/$4 sloughing, 12YTL/$8.50 massage), was left over from the Byzantine era and was actually the first building on the site. There are two sections, including one where you can ooze yourself into a gravelike, tile ditch full of scorching hot mud (avoid wearing a white bathing suit for this). There are also the regular bath facilities and cubicles for changing and resting. Kara Mustafa also has rudimentary hotel accom-modations. Granted, it's all rather gritty, but thoroughly worth the experi-ence. The more luxurious **Çelik Palas Hotel thermal pool** 🐦🐦, Çekirge Cad. 79, 16070 Çekirge/Bursa (℃ **0224/233-3800**; 25YTL/$19 entrance for nonguests, free for guests), rests beneath a single multiple-sky-lit dome; the hotel's facility offers opulence while the others excel in local character.

Today, İznik has once again become synonymous with Ottoman ceramic art, which reached its pinnacle in the 15th and 16th centuries during the reign of Süleyman the Magnificent. Tiles, richly decorated with floral designs and colors recalling precious gems, served as architectural decoration in the palace, mosques, tombs, and other buildings with a predominantly religious function. (The sultan was also the caliph, extending religious function into the palace.) For this reason, İznik ceramics represent one of the most important examples of Islamic art. Sadly, with the decline of the economic and political power of the Ottoman Empire, artisans and ateliers became less and less in demand, and ultimately, the techniques used to make the ceramics were lost.

Thanks to the İznik Foundation, this great artistic tradition is enjoying a slow but sure revival. The foundation, which consists of an educational facility, a research laboratory, and a commercial center, has invested an enormous amount of energy in researching the technologies necessary for achieving success in each complex step of production. One of the first challenges is the acquisition of the raw materials, as authentic İznik pieces contain a high ratio of quartz, a semi-precious stone. The remaining obstacles are technical, involving the proper ratio of quartz, the chemical composition of each pigment, and the correct application of heat (each pigment must be fired at a different temperature). Ottoman artisans labored their entire lives to perfect just one aspect of the product, with one person expert in the creation of coral red, another in cobalt blue, and yet another in maintaining accurate and consistent heat to a wood-fired kiln made of brick. The foundation's finished products are faithful copies of the originals that sell at prices competitive with the inferior products sold in Avanos (see "A Side Trip to Avanos," in chapter 8, "Cappadocia & the Interior"). The price of a plate or tile at the foundation hovers around 270YTL ($200), but remember, these are made of quartz, while the fakes are made of clay. Pottery items begin around 100YTL ($75). The **İznik Foundation,** Sahil Yolu Halı Saha Arkası, İznik (© **0224/ 757-6025;** fax 0224/757-5737; www.Iznik.com), is open to visitors and is also equipped with nine guest accommodations for those wishing to stay overnight. They also have a main office at Kuruçeşme Öksu[um]z Çocuk Sok. 14, Beşiktaş (© **0212/ 287-3243**).

The presence of such an ambitious process of cultural revival only serves to emphasize the importance of İznik as a major historical center. While you're here, you should take the time for a miniature tour of the city, with a break at one of the lakeside restaurants. The city is enclosed along the eastern edge of Lake İznik by about 5km (3 miles) of **ancient city walls** ⊛, made accessible through several ancient gates of which the **Istanbul Kapısı** ⊛ is the best preserved. In the center of town are the well-preserved remains of the **Church of Aya Sofya** ⊛⊛ (admission 2YTL/$1.50), an 11th-century church that preserves parts of the mosaic flooring and a partially exposed fresco of the Pantocrator in the niche of the left aisle. Excavations conducted in 1935, however, revealed traces of an older structure dating to the 6th century and attributed to Justinian.

Near the southwest corner of the church (across the street) are partially uncovered outdoor tile-production workshops from as early as the 15th century. Many of the **brick and mud kilns** are still intact.

The **Yeşil Cami** dates to the late 14th century and displays a minaret covered with tiles in a colorful zigzag pattern. Unfortunately, these are not originals, as the actual tiles were destroyed. Across the street is the **Nilu[um]fer Hatun Imareti,** built by Murat I and named after his mother, wife of Orhan Gazi and a Greek princess in her own right. Originally used as a charitable foundation and soup kitchen, the well-restored *imaret* (soup kitchen) now contains the **İznik Museum** (admission 2YTL/$1.50), harboring a small collection of Roman and Byzantine artifacts and remnants from nearby burial mounds. There's also a small collection of İznik tiles, as well as several ethnological items.

Thirty years of excavations have barely made a dent in the uncovering of the **Roman Theatre,** built by Pliny the Younger between 111 and 113 during his time as governor of Bythinia. Rather than building the theater into the side of a hill, the theater was constructed using vaults.

GETTING THERE & GETTING AROUND *Dolmuşes* regularly depart from Yalova from the main road that passes in front of the ferryboat landing (cross the street and hop on one headed south) as well as from Bursa. Once in İznik, buses deposit passengers on the main road in front of the church. Drivers should take the car ferry from Istanbul to Yalova. From Yalova, they should follow the road to Bursa taking the first turnoff at Orhangazi to İznik and follow the road along the north side of the lake.

İznik retains the grid plan established in its Hellenistic era. Monuments are well signposted, but without a car, you'll be pounding the pavement for the better part of a day.

2 Çanakkale ★

15km (9½ miles) north of Troy; 325km (202 miles) southwest of Istanbul; 316km (196 miles) north of İzmir; 270km (167 miles) west of Bursa

The small port of Çanakkale was of major strategic importance during World War I; at its narrowest point, it guards the entire straits of the Dardanelles. A constant reminder of its role in the war is the memorial carved into the cliff side on the opposite shore, which is visible from just about everywhere in town: "O Passer-by: The quiet earth on which you tread unaware is the place where a generation was lost. Bow and listen, for this ground is where the heart of a nation throbs." But the Great War was not the only major battle to happen in these environs. The ancient city of Troy, located just over 9 miles from here, fell several times in defense of this strategic spot.

Today Çanakkale is a quiet fishing town and tourist center, and the attractions are a mere footnote to both battlegrounds, where the action really happened.

ESSENTIALS
GETTING THERE

Buses depart for the 5- to 6-hour ride to Çanakkale from Istanbul's two main *otogars:* Harem Station (✆ **0216/333-3763**) and Esenler Station (✆ **0212/658-0036**). Bus companies also provide service from their offices along Ismet Inönü Caddesi, just east of Taksim Meydanı, which will save you a trip farther out to the *otogar*. Truva is the staple company heading out that way; fare from Istanbul to Çanakkale is 25YTL ($19). If you're heading from İzmir or Bergama, expect to pay about the same.

Most buses providing service from points around Turkey into Çanakkale have ticket offices in the main square across from the ferry docks, and will take you all the way into town. Having said that, you'll probably have my luck and get dumped at the *otogar* a few blocks east, although a fraction of the buses using the *otogar* as the end of the line have the decency to provide minibus service into town.

If you're driving from Istanbul: From the airport, take the TEM freeway toward Edirne. At Silivri exit the freeway and follow signs for Tekirdağ, which will put you on E25. Follow E25 to Keşan, then take E24 toward Çanakkale/Gelibolu (Gallipoli). Follow this road to Eceabat, where you can catch a car ferry directly into Çanakkale's ferry docks.

VISITOR INFORMATION

The **Tourist Information office** (© **0286/217-1187**) is on the main square across from the ferry docks. For emergency traveler's-check situations, thank the PTT (post office) for providing a kiosk next to the ferry ticket office.

Internet access has arrived in Çanakkale at a score of Internet cafes—virtually every one of them ingeniously named **Internet Café.** Another good bet is **Anzac House** (© **0286/217-5482**), a multiservice backpacker haven and youth hostel that caters to voyagers from down under.

ORIENTATION

The part of Çanakkale that attracts visitors is centered around the ferry docks and along the wharf, while the neighborhoods just a few blocks back retain all the charm of a factory hosting a sidewalk sale. You won't need a map for this town, and will find yourself strolling up and down the water's edge with brief detours into the hinterland. The city is divided by the somewhat commercialized Demircioglu Caddesi, which leads directly to Cumhuriyet Meydanı and the ferry docks. The clock tower, 1 block in and slightly to the west of this junction, is a good meeting point for groups. For a taste of small-town Çanakkale, pick up your diarrhea prescription at one of the pharmacies on Çarşi Caddesi, the last street before the Naval Museum.

GETTING AROUND

Çanakkale is an infinitely walkable city, and you can go from end to tourist end in under 15 minutes. Taxis for travel within the small city limits are metered; however, taxi rates are fixed according to the destination for travel beyond Çanakkale. If the rates seem blown out of proportion to you, try to negotiate a better rate with your driver. (A taxi to the Kolin Hotel will run you around 20YTL/$15; a taxi to the Tusan is 30YTL/$23). Meanwhile, ferries shuttle people across the Dardanelles every 15 minutes for 1.35YTL ($1) each way.

WHAT TO SEE & DO

Archaeological Museum (Arkeoloji Müzesi)   I'm not one to admire tchotchkes, so if bone-carved hairpins do nothing for you, skip this museum. The collection does contain an impressive exhibit of surprisingly detailed terra-cotta statuettes and well-preserved glass perfume bottles salvaged from the ruins of Greek civilizations, as well as a trifling fraction of the artifacts Schliemann dug up at Troy, along the coast.

Located about 1.5km (a mile) out of the town center, on the road to Troy. © **0286/217-3252** or 0286/217-6565. Admission 2YTL ($1.50). Tues–Sun 9am–5pm.

Naval Museum (Deniz Müzesi), Military Museum (Askeri Müzesi), and Çimenlik Castle (Çimenlik Kalesi)   The Army Museum houses various types of war paraphernalia such as uniforms, medals, and weapons, but unless you're a war geek, the most interesting part of the exhibit is just inside the main entrance. There's a model of the Gallipoli Campaign, above which are various plaques in English with attention-grabbing anecdotes and quotes of the various battleground memorials. One recounts the story of how on August 10, 1915, Atatürk received a direct hit to the heart, but a pocket watch that he was carrying shielded him from the bullet and certain death. Other sources say it was shrapnel from the doomed 57th Regiment battle, while still others say the whole story is a load of crap. According to the debatable inscription in this museum, the shattered watch is now part of Army Commander General Limon von Sander's family collection.

Next to the Naval Museum is a replica of the *Nusrat,* the minelayer that gets the credit for saving the day against invading British warships during the sea offensive. After the war, the underappreciated *Nusrat* was used as a lowly freight carrier and finally capsized in April 1990. Inside the ship is a minor exhibit of newspaper clippings with apparently significant headlines in huge block Turkish letters, as well as some diary entries and other forgettable items.

Çimenlik Castle, along with the Kilitbahir Castle on the opposite banks of the straits, was constructed by Mehmet II (the Conqueror) in the 15th century as a strategic prelude to his assault on Constantinople. The castle grounds are full of old cannons from the battles, and if you venture into one of those dark passages, you can get a glimpse of the Turkish positions, not to mention the sections of the roof that were destroyed by incoming artillery.

The park occupies a waterfront section that juts out into the sea and from which you get some of the best views in town, so if war yarns leave you cold, the grounds provide at least a pleasant diversion.

Çimenlik Park. ℭ **0286/217-1707.** Admission to museums 2YTL ($1.50), free admission to park. Museums Tues–Wed and Fri–Sun 9am–noon and 1:30–5pm. Park daily 9am–10:30pm.

WHERE TO STAY

For those hoping to squeeze in a resort experience this close to Istanbul, the arrival of Çanakkale's first five-star hotel is like a breath of fresh air. Located 2.4km (1½ miles) outside of town, the **Kolin Hotel** (ℭ **0286/218-0808;** fax 0286/218-0800; www. kolinhotel.com), in the nearby suburb of Kepez, promises its own private beach, swimming pools (both indoor and out), and all the trimmings of a hotel of this class. Another new option is the boutique-style **Ida Kale,** Mola Cad. Güzelyalı/Çanakkale, located about halfway between town and Troy (ℭ **0286/232-8332;** fax 0286/232-8832; www.kaleresort.com), owned and operated by a national tile company, a fact that plays out in the decor. At the budget end is **TJ's Hostel** in Eceabat, directly opposite Çanakkale center on the other side of the Dardanelles. The hostel is attached to TJ's Tours (see below; ℭ **0286/814-3121;** www.anzacgallipolitours.com) as well as his homey **Eceabat Hotel** (same info), with its pension feel and four-star style.

Anzac Hotel This hotel—not to be confused with the backpacker haven's Anzac House—is a welcome oasis of freshness amid a sea of tired, free-standing slabs. Sandwiched into a block just south of the main square, the hotel combines themes of Troy and Gallipoli as a backdrop for rooms that were updated in 2004. Dollar for dollar, this immaculate hotel is a great deal, but you may want to request a back room to avoid the noise of traffic and nighttime revelry.

Saat Kulesi Meydanı 8, 17001 Çanakkale (across from the clock tower). ℭ **0286/217-7777.** Fax 0286/217-2018. www.anzachotel.com. 27 units. 21€–29€ ($25–$35) single; 33€–41€ ($40–$50) double. 10% discount if you show this book. MC, V. Free parking. **Amenities:** Restaurant; roof bar; 24-hr. room service; laundry service; Internet. *In room:* A/C, satellite TV, minibar.

Otel Akol Located across the street from the city's waterfront plaza, the four-star Akol has been the choice for visitors for years. That the hotel started to show its wear and tear was beside the point until a spade of new hotels appeared and old ones took the time to renovate. The Akol finally caught up, and is now characterized by renovated rooms and bright, fresh decor. Apart from the outdoor music playing till midnight in the summer, rooms are quiet, and the balcony windows provide a stunning picture of the sun setting over the Dardanelles as well as the dawn departure of the local fishing boats. There's a cafe on the waterside promenade across the street, a nightclub on the eighth floor, and a small rectangular outdoor swimming pool that, because of the height of the courtyard walls, gets plenty of shade during those sweltering August afternoons.

Kordonboyu, 17100 Çanakkale (just beyond the government building). ℂ **0286/217-9456**. Fax 0286/217-2897. www.hotelakol.com. 138 units. 74€ ($90) double; 203€ ($150) suite. AE, MC, V. Street parking. **Amenities:** 2 restaurants; 3 bars; outdoor swimming pool; game room; concierge; tour desk; meeting room, car-rental desk; 24-hr. room service; laundry service; dry cleaning. *In room:* A/C, satellite TV, minibar, hair dryer.

Tusan Hotel   Most people visiting Çanakkale treat it as nothing but a base for day trips to Gallipoli and Troy, but if you're looking to combine a sightseeing tour with a resort-style vacation, the Tusan is the place to stay. Perched on a cliff overlooking the Çanakkale Straits yet hidden in the tree line, the Tusan is nestled in a suburban residential neighborhood. Each of the rooms has a balcony or patio and benefits from both sea and forest views. All rooms were renovated in 2002, and the bathroom tile, newly installed, gleams. During your downtime, there is a fitness room, billiards, and an assortment of private beachside terraces accessible via a footpath. The hotel serves lunch and dinner, and all meals can be taken on either the indoor or outdoor terrace. For those without a car, *dolmuşes* pass by the main road approximately every 15 minutes, or you can succumb to the taxis' exorbitant rates into town (about 32YTL/$23 each way). Otherwise, the only nuisance will be the nighttime chirping of the crickets.

Güzelyalı, 17001 Çanakkale (about 9.5km/6 miles out of Çanakkale on the road to İzmir). ℂ **0286/232-8746.** Fax 0286/232-8226. www.tusanhotel.com. 64 units. 75€ ($92) double. Rates lower in winter. Group rates available. MC, V. Free on-site parking. **Amenities:** 2 restaurants; fitness room; watersports (kayaking, windsurfing, diving); game room; 24-hr. room service; laundry service; dry cleaning. *In room:* A/C, minibar, hair dryer.

WHERE TO DINE

Çanakkale is no center of haute cuisine, but you can get a typically fresh meal at any one of the restaurants that line the harbor promenade to the north and south of the ferry landing. If you're looking for the Turkish equivalent of fast food, try one of the *kebap* houses in the neighborhood behind the clock tower, near the Naval Museum, or along Demircioğlu Caddesi.

Liman Yalova Restaurant   TURKISH   With a sunset as beautiful as the one from the rooftop terrace of Yalova, it's sometimes easy to forgive mediocre fare. There's no compromise here, however, because the fish is the best in town, and the mezes and nonfish selections are top-notch. The service is a little spotty, considering the waitstaff has to run the stairs every time a customer wants something; so if you want a glass of water with your meal, be prepared to insist.

On the quay south of the main square, entrance on Gümrük Sok. 7. ℂ **0286/217-1045.** Appetizers 5.40YTL–8YTL ($4–$6); fish by weight. AE, MC, V. Daily 1pm–midnight.

ÇANAKKALE AFTER DARK

The town enjoys a relatively civilized nightlife, except for Anzac Day (Apr 25) which commemorates the fateful landing of British, Australian, and New Zealand forces at Gallipoli. On this day, normally respectful daytime visitors shed any pretense of solemnity, fill up the bars, and empty the kegs. A quiet and tasteful alternative to the bars targeting Australian backpackers is **TNT,** Saat Kulesi Meydani 6 (ℂ **0286/ 217-0470**), right in the center of town on the water.

3 Gallipoli (Gelibolu) ⭑⭑⭑

15km (9⅓ miles) north of Çanakkale; 310km (192 miles) southwest of Istanbul

For most Americans, the name *Gallipoli* conjures up visions of a blue-eyed Mel Gibson. Australians and New Zealanders, whose combined forces formed Anzac (Australian and New Zealand Army Corps), react with a reverent hush while the British clam up out of a sense of discomfiture. For Turks, Gallipoli is a proud place, for it marks the rise to prominence of a gutsy lieutenant colonel named Mustafa Kemal (better known as Atatürk), and a turning point in the creation of their sovereign Republic.

The Dardanelles have long been a strategic point of contention—from King Xerxes of Persia, who in the 5th century B.C. created a bridge of boats to transport his troops to Greece; to Alexander the Great, who swept into Asia from the other direction in 334 B.C. Mehmet the Conqueror knew the value of the straits as well, and had two fortresses built as part of his plan to subdue Constantinople.

In the power struggle that emerged during World War I, the Russians, who up until then were forced to sail through the icy waters of the Baltic Sea, aligned themselves with the British, hoping to gain a year-round, ice-free passage via the Dardanelles and into Europe's burgeoning commercial arena. For the Allies, control of Istanbul and the straits meant exposing the flanks of Germany and Austria-Hungary, cutting off their oil supply, and forcing Turkey out of the war (and maybe getting a little caviar from the deal as well).

The fact that Vice Admiral John de Robeck's head-on attack of the Dardanelles failed was as much due to Imperial British overconfidence as to Turkish good fortune. Assuming the enemy would crumble at the sight of the great Royal Navy, the admiral sent in a fleet of 16 ships, most of which were just shy of retirement and manned with inexperienced crews. On March 18, 1915, the battleship *Queen Elizabeth* led the fleet into battle. Four of the ships were damaged or sunk by Turkish mines. After 8 futile hours, shortly before the Turkish army would have run out of ammunition, the British Navy called it a day; however, they did not give up battle for the strait.

The resulting offensive lasted 249 days. The line of attack was simple: Secure the heights, destroy the Turkish defenses, and sail on up to Istanbul. If the current hadn't swept the Anzac's landing boats a mile off course or if someone other than Mustafa Kemal had received the orders, then Turkey would probably be part of Greece right now and y'all would be reading another book. But tides were swift, communications were faulty, decisions were hasty, and watches were unsynchronized.

The Gallipoli campaign ended on January 9, 1916, when the Allies withdrew in the middle of the night. The Turks boast that not one life was lost in the pullout; the Anzacs, leaving on boats in the darkness, said about their fallen comrades, "I hope they don't hear us go."

The death toll was numbing: Roughly 86,000 Turkish forces and more than 160,000 Allied soldiers perished in the campaign. A staggeringly high number of Allied casualties were Anzac men—unfathomable losses for two countries with such small populations. Indeed, it's all but acknowledged that during the campaign, the Brits offered up the Anzac troops as cannon fodder; consequently, a trip to Gallipoli has become a grim pilgrimage of sorts for countless Australian and New Zealand tourists.

The entire peninsula is a national park. Turkish and Allied soldiers are buried side by side in 31 war cemeteries; several important monuments are grouped around two main areas. It's certainly possible to get to the highlights alone, but there's more to be gained by taking a tour. Tour groups are generally small and the information provided by the guides is informative and passionate; however, the real advantage of taking the tour is seeing the battlefields through the eyes of your Australian and Kiwi acquaintances.

ESSENTIALS
GETTING THERE
The Gallipoli Peninsula is easily accessible by ferry, but once you set foot on land, you're on your own and at the mercy of the local *dolmuşes*. Because the battlefields are so spread out, sightseeing by *dolmuş* will certainly be more frustrating than rewarding. To ensure the most efficient use of your time, either sign up for a quality tour (around 33YTL/$25) or tackle the peninsula in a private car or taxi. (Fare for a half-day will cost anywhere between 47YTL/$35 and 108YTL/$80, depending on your negotiating skills.)

Hassle Free Travel Agency, Cumhuriyet Cad. 61, in the Anzac House (© **0286/ 217-5482;** www.anzachouse.com), organizes daily tours to Gallipoli and Troy, but to experience them both by tour, it's necessary to spend the night. Separately, the Gallipoli tour costs 40TYL ($30) and the Troy tour costs 30YTL ($22).

Hassle Free also arranges overnight excursions out of Istanbul, which include the Troy and Gallipoli tours and 1 night in a hotel (the cost of the tours and a night in the Anzac House hostel is about 108YTL/$79; upgrades to other hotels are available). Tours return around 6pm and include breakfast, transportation, and museum fees. If you're looking for the grave of a particular friend or relative, they will do the research. Hassle Free can also organize underwater dives to the sites of the 1915 shipwrecks.

Although Hassle Free may be the oldest organizer of guided tours of the battlefields, their best guide, a professor and historian, now works **TJ's Tours** (© **0286/814-3121;** www.anzacgallipolitours.com). What's more, you can schedule both the Gallipoli and the Troy tour in 1 day, separated by lunch, which is included in the tour. Tours to both run daily even in winter and cost 33YTL ($25) each.

VISITOR INFORMATION
Kabatepe Information Center (© **0286/814-1297**), called Kabatepe Tanıtma Merkezi in Turkish, is 24km (15 miles) northwest of Eceabat, on a cliff overlooking Anzac Cove and the village of Kabatepe. This location—above Brighton Beach where the Anzac troops were supposed to land—is where you should begin your visit. The information center and memorial grounds claim the plateau that was the objective of the failed operation. The commanding hilltop was heavily fortified with Turkish artillery, but today remains eerily silent, with a few notable monuments and spectacular views of the cliffs.

The **museum** (admission 4YTL/$3; daily 9am–1pm and 2–6pm) houses much of the battlefield's detritus along with uniforms and old photographs. Your time is better spent outside. Visits to the battlefields are free.

EXPLORING THE BATTLEFIELDS
For the locations of the monuments and cemeteries mentioned in this section, consult our map of the Gallipoli Peninsula (p. 171).

The Gallipoli Peninsula

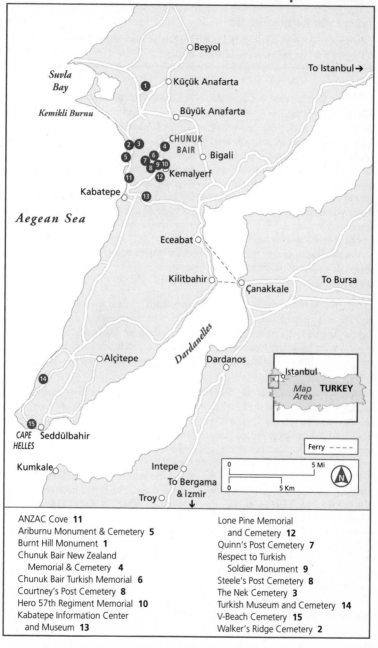

ANZAC Cove **11**
Ariburnu Monument & Cemetery **5**
Burnt Hill Monument **1**
Chunuk Bair New Zealand
   Memorial & Cemetery **4**
Chunuk Bair Turkish Memorial **6**
Courtney's Post Cemetery **8**
Hero 57th Regiment Memorial **10**
Kabatepe Information Center
   and Museum **13**

Lone Pine Memorial
   and Cemetery **12**
Quinn's Post Cemetery **7**
Respect to Turkish
   Soldier Monument **9**
Steele's Post Cemetery **8**
The Nek Cemetery **3**
Turkish Museum and Cemetery **14**
V-Beach Cemetery **15**
Walker's Ridge Cemetery **2**

Tips **Go Before You Go**

Be sure to avail yourself of the public toilets at the visitor information center; they're the last facilities you will see all day.

Arı Burnu Monument & Cemetery (Arı Burnu Anı ve Mezarlığı)   Shortly after 4am on the morning of April 25, 1915, after a long and cramped night in the boats, the Australian and New Zealand Army Corps landed—16,000 men in all—in the dark, expecting to set foot on level ground. The steep cliff that confronted them instead must have come as a horrific surprise; nevertheless, they hauled themselves up and grabbed at anything stable enough to hold them. Not expecting anyone stupid enough to stage a landing at such an unforgiving spot, the Turks were ill prepared to defend the cliff, allowing large numbers of confused Anzacs to gain higher ground. There was no defense at all in the hills, and by 8am, 8,000 heroic men had scrambled ashore, with three soldiers arriving halfway up the hill to strategic **Chunuk Bair,** 1.6km (a mile) away from the landing site.

The Arı Burnu cemetery is located at the northern end of Anzac Cove. On Anzac Day, a dawn memorial service is held here.

At the northern end of Anzac Cove.

Burnt Hill & Monument (Yusufçuktepe Anıtı)   Also known as Scimitar Hill, Hill 70, and Green Knoll, this ridge was one of the objectives of the Sulva Bay landings in August 1915. Skirmishes went on for 3 days, during which time control over the hill went back and forth. The final day of the attack was a fiasco for the British troops, who suffered the largest number of casualties—5,300—of the entire Gallipoli Campaign.

Cape Helles Landings & Seddülbahir   The Allied landing campaign was launched on two fronts: the beach at Kabatepe (which the Anzac boats overshot) and the village and medieval fortress of Seddülbahir at the toe of the peninsula. The Seddülbahir landings were carried out on five beaches simultaneously by British troops, but lacking the element of surprise and without even one cellphone among them, the advances were modest at best and fatal at worst.

After a violent bombardment of the village, and assuming that the beach (V Beach) was deserted, the 29th Division approached the shore. The Trojan horse–style landing was to have taken place using the cargo hold of the collier *The River Clyde,* which once beached, would empty itself of soldiers. Like a scene out of *Saving Private Ryan,* the operation turned into a literal bloodbath, when the Turks, waiting in ambush, opened fire on the unprepared and vulnerable British army.

The landings on the other four beaches were more successful, and the troops dug in waiting for further orders. At Y Beach, a small cove with access to the cliff tops 60m (200 ft.) up, 2,000 men, a number equal to all of the Turkish forces on the tip of the peninsula that day, landed unopposed and unaware of the carnage taking place less than 6.5km (4 miles) away. The Turks finally attacked in the night, and these troops were authorized to withdraw.

Chunuk Bair Memorials (Conkbayırı)   Atatürk's arrival on the scene marks a turning point not only in the Gallipoli Campaign but also in the history of Turkey as a nascent republic. Atatürk immediately recognized the importance of the high ground of Chunuk Bair as the key to the straits.

When Atatürk and his reconnaissance team reached Chunuk Bair, Turkish soldiers were fleeing oncoming Australians, who had gained the high ground during the fateful morning of August 25. Explaining that they had run out of bullets, the soldiers were ordered by Atatürk to lie in the grass, bayonets at the ready. Fearing an ambush, the Anzac soldiers took cover, providing the Turks with the precious time needed for reinforcements to arrive. Relentless New Zealand units briefly gained the summit, but due to an unnecessarily incompetent lack of reinforcements, the troops were either slain or forced back to a lower position.

The fateful hill, visited by thousands of pensive visitors each year, is where the main New Zealand memorial shares the crest with a statue of Atatürk as a promising young officer. The Chunuk Bair cemetery is located here, and on Anzac Day, the New Zealand service is held immediately following the Dawn Service at Arı Burnu Cemetery. Nearby are the five enormous tablets of the Turkish Conkbayırı Memorial, symbolizing an outstretched hand to the heavens, and inscribed with a narration (in Turkish) of the events from the other point of view.

The Hero 57th Regiment Memorial (57 Piyade Alayı Şehitliği)   With Anzac troops attacking Chunuk Bair, and in order to gain time for reinforcements to arrive, Atatürk gave the order to his best regiment, "I'm not ordering you to attack; I'm ordering you to die. In the time which passes until we die, other troops and commanders can take our places." Stories of the 57th regiment's courageous sacrifice, when almost 100,000 men died, are part of Turkey's proud lore, but nobody dares to touch upon the possibility that Atatürk's ambition got the better of him that day.

Oddly enough, the memorial grounds and cemetery are a fairly new addition to the national park, and it's the one place where you will run into large groups of Turks and not *one* trying to sell you any memorabilia. The lawns provide a perfect rest stop for contemplating the puzzle of war, and the ablution fountain is a welcome site for washing the grit of the trenches off of your feet.

Lone Pine (Kanlı Sırt)   The largest mass grave on the peninsula and the main memorial to the missing Australians of the campaign, Lone Pine is the final resting place of both Turks and Anzac troops, with a heavy number of gravestones reading "Believed to be buried in these trenches." About 2,200 Australians and over 4,000 Turks perished in the 3-day battle that earned Australian soldiers seven Victoria Crosses, the Australian badge of bravery and honor.

The tremendous losses at Lone Pine are even more sobering when you think that this was simply a diversionary tactic away from the main objectives of Suvla Bay and Chunuk Bair to the north. Today the hill is the site of a single pine tree rising above the scrub (the original, destroyed in a brush fire during the battle, gave seed to this one), inspiring the soldiers to name the hill after a then-current popular American hit, "On the Trail of the Lonesome Pine." Australians enter this cemetery with their heads held high, because Lone Pine embodies the spirit, character, and courage of their sons.

The Nek   Imagine the closing scene of the movie *Gallipoli*, with reinforcement after teenage reinforcement charging fearlessly into certain death. This real-life suicide mission was ordered by British Commanders on August 7, 1915, to divert Turkish troops away from Sulva Bay, where a landing attempt was being made. A break in a nearby British naval bombardment had given the Turkish army the opportunity they needed

Fact or Fiction?

The **Respect to Turkish Soldier Monument (Mehmetçik Anıtı)** commemorates what some say is an apocryphal story told in the battle's aftermath. At one point during the fighting, gunfire downed an Australian soldier in the middle of an open field, and none of his compatriots had the courage to retrieve him. A Turkish soldier got up out of his trench, and both sides froze as the Turk picked up the wounded Australian and carried him over to the enemy side. He then returned to his own trench unharmed.

to reoccupy their trenches, so when the Australian Lighthorse divisions were ordered to attack, they were summarily slaughtered.

A visit to the manicured cemetery and clean front line reveals nothing of the hardship, disease, and rotting corpses that plagued the ridge, but the wind does.

Turkish Memorial, Museum, and Cemetery (Şehitler Abidesi, Türk Şehitliği ve Müzesi) Let's not forget that a quarter of a million Turks lost their lives defending their country from invading forces. (This is the unofficial number; the official count stands at 86,000.) This somber memorial, atop a promontory at the southern tip of the peninsula, is a fitting place to pay your final respects.

Walker's Ridge, Quinn's Post, Courtney's Post, and Steele's Post These positions above Anzac Cove were gained in the first days of fighting. With the cliff to their backs and under constant heavy fire, the soldiers dug crude rifle pits, later deepening and connecting them into a network of trenches.

The confrontation in those first few days was ferocious, and the enemy lines were in some places only a few yards apart. The area between the enemy lines known as "no man's land" is now a modern road, and it is possible to spot overgrown trenches on your way to the cemeteries.

The Turks like to tell stories about the friendship that grew between two sides during the 8-month stalemate. If the Turks had cigarettes, the Anzacs provided the matches; when Anzac supplies failed to arrive, the Turks tossed tomatoes into the ditches. Despite the legends, the truth remains that a great respect between the Anzacs and the Turks grew out of a mutual sense of honor.

4 Troy ⓕ

15km (9⅓ miles) south of Çanakkale

The *Iliad* and *Odyssey* have made Troy one of the most recognizable mythological events in the world, and few can resist the chance to trod among its remains. The reality is less satisfying, however; the site for the most part is a hodgepodge of unrecognizable archaeological detritus visible from afar via a raised catwalk, some of which is blocked off by ongoing excavations. So the primary dilemma continues to be whether or not a visit is warranted. As an adjunct to a tour of Gallipoli, the trip is definitely worthwhile. But as a pilgrimage to the classical world, there are better-preserved and more representative sites on Turkish soil that are more conveniently accessible.

Until 1871, when Heinrich Schliemann decided to go dig for buried treasure, finding Troy was about as likely as finding Atlantis. There was (and to a certain extent, still is) no concrete evidence that the civilization of Homer's *Iliad* existed. One of the arguments is that the poet's epic account of the Trojan War is an amalgam of battle stories based on geopolitics of the day, with a little Aaron Spelling thrown in for flavor.

Then Schliemann, a self-taught archaeologist with an ancient-Greece obsession and an even stronger lust for buried treasure, descended upon the nearby village of Hisarlık and started poking around. His shoddy excavation resulted in significant damage to the site, and when the dust settled after his looting, there was some dispute over what it was that he actually "found" there (see "Exploring the Site" below). But there's no disputing that he began the significant excavation and reconstruction process that continues to this day.

The fact that nine civilizations were built one on top of the other is no surprise, given the strategic location. Two thousand years ago, Troy was a port city at the mouth of the Dardanelles, and it would have been surprising if a war *hadn't* been fought here. While it's anyone's guess just how heroic the goings-on were on these ancient shores, the possibility of stepping into a legend is an exciting proposition—as is climbing into the belly of a wooden horse that Walt Disney would be proud of.

ESSENTIALS
GETTING THERE
A do-it-yourself tour of Troy is a risky proposition, simply because the excavated portions of the site remain only partially labeled, and the nonexcavated portions are still just a confusing pile of rubble and stone. **Hassle Free Travel Agency,** Cumhuriyet Cad. 61, in the Anzac House (② **0286/217-5482;** www.anzachouse.com), and **TJ's Tours** (Kemalpaşa Mah. Cumhuriyet Cad. 5, Eceabat; ② **0286/814-3121;** www.anzacgallipolitours.com), both arrange half-day excursions to Troy. (Hassle Free runs their 27YTL/$20 tour in the morning; TJ schedules theirs in the afternoon; 33YTL/$25). If you're more of a solo traveler, the *dolmuş* stand for transportation to Troy is located at the entrance to the fairgrounds on Atatürk Caddesi in Çanakkale.

VISITOR INFORMATION
There is a **Visitor Information office** (no phone) at the entrance to the archaeological site (next to the Trojan Horse) where you can get an overview of the site as well as peruse reading materials written entirely in Turkish.

EXPLORING THE SITE
Stories about the young Schliemann paint a picture of a child prodigy on a vision quest from an early age. But it's entirely possible his obsession for Homer and Greek culture took root much later. It seems more likely that his main goal in life was to strike it rich; having achieved that in the California gold rush, he then set his sights on immortality.

At about 44 years old, after years of study of ancient and modern Greek and the classic epic work of Homer, Schliemann proclaimed himself an archaeologist and began digging at Pınarbaşı, which was believed at the time to be the site of Troy. Meanwhile, Frank Calvert had discovered the ruins of a palace or temple on the hill at Hisarlık, and the two agreed that this was a more likely area for the lost city.

Schliemann began bulldozing his way through the hill in 1870 and found little besides obsidian knife blades and clay tiles—which in Turkey, you can pretty much find while bending over and tying your shoe. When he finally discovered something significant—a relief of the sun god Apollo—he immediately attributed it to the ruins of Zeus's throne (and smuggled it out of the country and into his garden). It started to get interesting in August 1872 with the discovery of some gold earrings and a skeleton, and 9 months later his crew uncovered two gates guarding a stone foundation of a large building. To Schliemann, this was obviously the Scaean Gate, and the building was the palace of Priam, the last king of Troy.

Some time later, Schliemann literally struck gold, shrewdly giving the crew the day off while he and his wife dug alone. That day's findings were monumental: a treasure of goblets, spearheads, knives, and jewelry in copper, silver, and gold, including an incredible 8,750 gold rings and buttons. Eventually Schliemann smuggled the whole lot (except for a few items now in the Archaeology Museum in Çanakkale) out of the country, initially stashing a major part of the treasure with various friends around Greece, where neither Turkish nor Greek authorities could claim ownership. He also donated a portion of the treasure to a Berlin museum, but the artifacts were stolen by the Soviets during World War II and transported to Russia. Schliemann halted and resumed excavation two more times through 1890 but never came near to the findings of that first stash, now believed to have belonged to a princess around 2000 B.C.

So the question remains. Was Schliemann a lying megalomaniac with delusions of grandeur? One biographer points to the evidence. Discrepancies between Schliemann's personal letters and diary entries show that Schliemann lied with regard to his personal life. He also reported that the site of the treasure was located in Priam's Palace, when the site of the find was actually outside the city wall. The truly incriminating evidence is in the photographs he took of Priam's treasure; several of the items "found" in 1873 appear in photos taken in 1872 of earlier finds.

Maybe he was just nuts; there's evidence supporting that, too. Schliemann eventually retired in Athens, renamed all of his servants after characters in Greek mythology, and required them to deliver all messages to him in ancient Greek, a language he had taught himself. The inscription on the tomb he had built for himself seems to be his final word on the subject: "For the hero Schliemann."

Troy Open Air Museum (Truva Müzesi Örenyeri)   Over a hundred years of research have revealed that the city was reconstructed at least nine times. The first settlement, referred to as Troy I, dates back to around 3000 B.C.; it lasted 5 centuries and was destroyed by fire. Schliemann's groundbreaking discovery of King Priam's treasure was found on Level II, but later research established that this civilization would have existed over 1,000 years *before* the Troy of Homer. It is unclear what caused the destruction of the successive three civilizations, but findings from the site indicate that by Troy VI, a new culture had emigrated, probably from Mycenae, expanding on the area of preceding settlements. The year 1184 B.C. is traditionally accepted as the year in which classic Troy fell, allowing archaeologists to establish that the Troy of Homer most likely took place during the existence of Troy VII-A, which was analogously destroyed by fire around 1200 B.C. Abandoned for over 400 years, the site was resettled and invaded until the 1st century A.D., when the city was reconstructed, apparently under the orders of Julius Caesar, and given the name Ilium Novum (hence the *Iliad* in Homer's title). The prestige of the city during the Roman period is reflected in its illustrious guests: Augustus Caesar, Hadrian, Marcus Aurelius, and Caracalla all slept here.

Archaeologists estimate that Troy is actually 10 times larger than the roughly 165-sq.-m mound of ruins (1,776-sq.-ft.). A wooden walkway meanders through the excavation sites, making the discovery of the city a bit less confusing, and as the rebuilding progresses, Troy will be able to assume an honorary place among Epcot Center attractions. For now, the site is a confusing jumble of partially identified levels, punctuated by a reconstruction of the temple of Athena and sacrificial altar, a Roman theater, a *bouleterion* (senate building), and a graveyard of homeless marble columns.

Follow the road and signs in; you can't miss it. Admission 10YTL ($7.50). Summer daily 8:30am–7:30pm; winter daily 8:30am–5pm.

5 Bergama ★★

About 250km (155 miles) south of Çanakkale; 240km (about 149 miles) north of İzmir

A lack of modern accommodations has turned Bergama into a stop, look, and leave destination—that is, if visitors bother to come at all. But this modern town is worth an overnight stopover given its village feel and numerous ruins, including two of the country's most celebrated archaeological sites: the Acropolis and the Asklepion of ancient **Pergamum** ★★★ (also written as Pergamon), both listed among the top 100 historical sites on the Mediterranean.

Most of the extraordinary buildings and monuments date to the time of Eumenes II (197–159 B.C.), including the famed library, the terrace of the spectacularly sited hillside theater, the main palace, the Altar of Zeus, and the propylaeum of the Temple of Athena. The ancient city is composed of the Acropolis, whose main function was social and cultural as much as it was sacred; the Lower City, or realm of the lower classes; and the Asklepion, one of the earliest medical and therapeutic centers on record.

A LOOK AT THE PAST

The old city of Pergamum dates back to the 12th century B.C. but saw its first notable era of prosperity under Lydian King Croesus in the 6th century B.C. Pergamum briefly fell under Persian control but was wrestled back into Hellenistic hands in 334 B.C. by Alexander the Great. While Alexander was out conquering other lands, Anatolia was left in the hands of his general, Lysimachus, who had entrusted his war chest to the hands of Philataerus, commander of Pergamum. On Lysimachus's death, Philataerus founded a ruling dynasty with the late general's riches, and was succeeded by his nephew, Eumenis I. Eumenis II is credited with bringing the empire to its height, ushering in a period of economic, cultural, and artistic expansion in the 2nd century B.C. When Attalus III, the last of the ruling Attalid dynasty, died, his ambiguous testament was interpreted by Rome as carte blanche for the Romans to come in and take over. Under the Romans, Pergamum reclaimed a measure of its former greatness, but the town was all but forgotten once the Ottomans took control.

ESSENTIALS
GETTING THERE

To get to Bergama, take one of the through-buses heading to Çanakkale or İzmir. Not all buses go directly into the center of Bergama, so check when you buy your ticket if you will end up at one of the town's two bus stations or at the dusty fork in the road, about 6.5km (4 miles) out. The main bus station (© **0232/633-1519**) is near the Tourist Information office, and the second is farther up the road near the bazaar. Ask your hotel which stop is more convenient to their location. If you do get stuck at the crossroads, catch a *dolmuş,* which run daily (including Sun), or a taxi—one is usually waiting at the bus stop. Count on about a 5-hour trip by bus from either Çanakkale or İzmir, and about half that by car.

VISITOR INFORMATION

The **Tourist Information office** is located at İzmir Caddesi 54, to the right of the Government Building (© **0232/633-1862**), and is open weekdays 8:30am to 12:30pm and 2 to 5:30pm. Although the street map of Bergama is outdated, it's the only place in town that you can get site maps of the Acropolis and Asklepion, both located on the outskirts of town.

ORIENTATION

The center of Bergama, with its fruit market and carpet shops, is situated around the neighborhood of the Red Basilica, although appearances might suggest that the heart of the city lies around the town's central park and Municipal Building. The road past the Red Basilica winds up and around for about 5km (3 miles) until you arrive at the Acropolis, while the Asklepion is located closer to town behind the military camp. Frequently overlooked are the original Greek houses of Eski Bergama (Old Bergama), accessible by walking up the steep inclined streets behind the main taxi stand and carpet shops of Kınık Caddesi, and the impressive Selçuk Tower.

GETTING AROUND

There is no public transportation from Bergama to either the Acropolis or Asklepion, although the latter is a reasonable walk from the town's center. A taxi will cost about 20YTL ($15) to take you up the hill to the Acropolis; have the driver drop you off at the Asklepion on the way down. If you're looking for an uphill hike, there's a way to access the Acropolis on foot, saving the cost of round-trip taxi fare and the entrance fee all in one go. (Cross the Tabak Bridge and follow the path up and to the right toward the lower Agora.)

WHAT TO SEE & DO

The Acropolis ★★   Dominating the summit of a hill almost 300m (1,000 ft.) high, the Acropolis provides a humbling view of the surrounding plains, aqueducts, and reservoir below. The remains of this once-great empire are no less impressive, despite the fact that most artifacts are now on exhibit at the Pergamum Museum in Berlin. Here it's still possible to ramble around the Upper and Lower cities, amid the palaces, public and private buildings, and temples too large to cart away. Although only the foundation remains, the **Temple of Athena** was probably constructed, using the acropolis of Athens as a model, in the 3rd century B.C., in the earliest days of the Pergamene kingdom. Today you can see the architrave, along with fragments of columns, in the Berlin Museum.

Eumenis II's construction of the **great library** rivaled the one at Alexandria, provoking the Egyptians into an embargo of papyrus. Lacking such a basic essential, the people of Pergamum were forced to come up with an alternative, and parchment was invented. Ironically, when Pergamum came under Roman rule, Marc Antony gifted the entire 200,000-volume collection to Cleopatra, shipping the contents of the rival library back to Alexandria, where, tragically, the entire collection was destroyed in a fire. A 3m (10-ft.) statue of the goddess Athena, discovered in the area of the reading room, is now housed in the Berlin Museum.

Near the temple of Athena are the remnants of the **Palaces of the Pergamene Kings.** The smaller, northern building is believed to have been that of Attalos, while the larger palace most likely belonged to Eumenes II. Mosaics discovered in the internal courtyards of the palaces are now in the Berlin Museum.

With the Romanization of Pergamum, many of the Hellenic foundations were simply adapted to suit the arriving Roman emperors and administrators. The **Temple of Trajan** 🏛🏛 is an example of this, and because of removal or looting, the temple remains date to Hellenistic times.

The remarkable **theater** 🏛🏛🏛, built into the hillside and split into three sections of tiers, was composed of 80 extraordinary levels that seated up to 10,000 people. The panorama is awe-inspiring—a fact not overlooked by Eumenes II, who had a 240m-long (800-ft.) *stoa* (covered arcade) constructed along the upper terrace of the theater. At the northern end of the terrace promenade was the **Temple of Dionysus,** which, along with the altar, is in a fairly good state of preservation. The **Temple of Dionysus** was restored by Caracalla after a fire gutted the interior.

The largest building on the Acropolis is the **Altar of Zeus,** built during the reign of Eumenes II. Fragments of the altar were recycled in the construction of the Byzantine fortification walls, but rediscovered by Carl Humann in 1871 and later reconstructed in the Berlin Museum. The reliefs (also in Berlin) depicted the mythological battle between the Giants and the Gods—an analogy to the Pergamene victory of the Galatians.

The **Agora** and **Agora Temple** lie to the south of the Altar of Zeus. As you head down the hill to the south, you arrive at the **Lower City,** where, up until a brush fire cleared out the overgrowth, not much more than crumbling foundations remain. Ambitious types and those heading down to town on foot should keep an eye out for what's left of the **Sanctuaries of Hera and of Demeter,** the **Temple of Asklepios,** several **gymnasiums,** a **House attributed to Attalos,** and a **Lower Agora.**

Hilltop; adjacent to the Garrison. ℭ **0232/631-2886.** Admission 10YTL ($7.50). Winter daily 8:30am–5:30pm; summer daily 8:30am–6:30pm.

Archaeology Museum (Arkeoloji Müzesi) 🏛   The collection of statues, objects, and gravestones housed in this museum represents a fraction of the Acropolis and Asklepion ruins that the Germans didn't carry off. In spite of this, a visit here is a worthy complement to the site visits, and the curators have even been kind enough to create a faithful replica of Zeus's Altar, saving you from a trip to Berlin. Some other notable objects amid the artifacts include a statue of Hadrian taken from the Asklepion library, a 2nd-century-A.D. stone horse from the altar of Zeus, and the oldest statue in the museum, a 4th-century-B.C. *kuros,* an early example of the realism of the sculpted human form.

The ethnographic wing exhibits a collection of objects, costumes, and textiles from the surrounding region.

Zafer Mah. Cumhuriyet Cad. 10 (on left across from the BP gas station). ℭ **0232/631-2883.** Admission 4YTL ($3). Tues–Sun 8:30am–noon and 1–5pm.

The Asklepion 🏛🏛   This famed ancient medical center, built in honor of Asklepios, the god of healing, was also the world's first psychiatric hospital. Many of the treatments employed at Pergamum, in complement with a sacred source of water that was later discovered as having radioactive properties, have been used for centuries, and are once again finding modern application. The treatments included psychotherapy, massage, herbal remedies, mud and bathing treatments, the interpretation of dreams, and the drinking of water. The Asklepion gained in prominence under the Romans in the 2nd century A.D., but a sacred site existed prior to this, as early as the 4th century B.C.

Oddly enough, everybody who was anybody was dying to get in; patients included Hadrian, Marcus Aurelius, and Caracalla. Therapy included mud baths, music concerts, and doses of water from the sacred fountain. Hours of therapy probed the meaning of the previous night's dreams, as patients believed dreams recounted a visit by the god Asklepios, who held the key to curing the illness. Galen, the influential physician and philosopher who was born in Pergamum in A.D. 129, trained and then later became an attendant to the gladiators here.

Access is via the **Sacred Way** ⋆⋆, which at 807m (2,690 ft.) long and colonnaded, originally connected the Asklepion with the Acropolis. The sacred way becomes the stately Via Tecta near the entrance to the site and leads to a courtyard and fallen Propylaeum, or Monumental Gate. Don't miss the focus of the first courtyard, an **altar** inscribed with the emblem of modern medicine, the serpent. To the right of the courtyard is the Emperor's Room, which was also used as a library. The circular domed **Temple of Asklepios,** with a diameter of 23m (78 ft.), recalls the Pantheon in Rome, which was completed only 20 years earlier. Reachable through an underground tunnel is what is traditionally called the **Temple of Telesphorus** ⋆, which served as both the treatment rooms and the sleeping chambers, an indication that sleep was integral in the actual healing process. At various spots in the center of the complex are a total of three pools and fountains, used for bathing, drinking, and various other forms of treatment. The semicircular **Roman Theatre** ⋆ flanks the colonnaded promenade on the northwest corner of the site.

Old Pergamum. No phone. Admission 10YTL ($7.50). Winter daily 8:30am–5pm; summer daily 8:30am–7pm.

Red Basilica (Kızıl Avlu) ⋆⋆ This is one impressive pile of red brick. Built during the reign of Hadrian, and dedicated to the Egyptian god Serapis (the model for the Greek god Isis), this temple was later to become one of the seven churches of the Apocalypse. The temple was destroyed in the Arab raids of A.D. 716 to 717, and then was converted by the Byzantines into a basilica. The enormous building straddles the ancient Selinus River (today the Bergama Cayı), whose two subterranean galleries provide a canal for the water to pass. True to the ideal that holy ground is always holy ground, a small mosque resides in one of the towers.

Adjacent to the 2nd *otogar.* ☏ **0232/631-2885.** Admission 5.40YTL ($4). Winter daily 8:30am–5:30pm; summer daily 8:30am–6:30pm.

WHERE TO STAY

Tourists bypassed Bergama because of a lack of reasonable accommodations; up until now there were plenty of pensions for the backpacker crowd, but nothing decent for the travelers in search of more than the minimum level of comfort. The catch-22 is that, because there were no places to stay, nobody stayed overnight, and many hotels, even the better ones, were forced to close down. Listed here is a lone survivor and a much-welcomed newcomer.

Anıl Hotel The Anıl Hotel is the answer to Bergama's prayers: a quality hotel that caters to a more demanding clientele (if they can get past the bright pink exterior) and a reasonable address. The hotel has modern stuff like smoke alarms, fans in the bathrooms, light sensors in the hallway, and brilliant double-glazed windows to keep out street noise. The lobby has some interesting Hellenistic touches, and the rooms are tastefully decorated in bright turquoise and peach. You will practically trip over the Archaeological Museum when you step out the front door, and the rooftop solarium serves up breakfast and unobstructed views of the Acropolis at no extra charge. Their second, equally comfortable hotel, the Efsane (Atatürk Bulvarı 82; ℭ **0232/632-6350**), charges slightly less and comes with the added bonus of a rooftop swimming pool.

Hafutiye Cad. 4, 35700 Bergama (Bergama center right after park behind gas station). ℭ **0232/631-1830.** Fax 0232/632-6353. 12 units. Summer 50€ ($60) double; winter 45€ ($55) double. MC, V. **Amenities:** Restaurant; bar; 24-hr. room service; massage; laundry service; dry cleaning. *In room:* A/C, satellite TV, minibar, hair dryer.

Berksoy Hotel   More like an upscale motel, this roadside inn would be the hands-down first choice for accommodations in Bergama if it were more centrally located. Fortunately, it makes up for the distance with spotless rooms swathed in waxy loglike wood panels that, in addition to being practical, even look good in the bathroom. The other bonus is that being stranded this far out of town (okay, it's only a mile and the *dolmuş* will have you in town in no time), there's more of an excuse to hang around the fabulous pool area. The hotel mercifully has 24-hour hot water, a tennis court, lobby and terrace bars, and a rustic-looking restaurant that serves basic *kebap* fare.

19 İzmir Yolu, 35700 Bergama (about 1.6km/1 mile outside of Bergama on the road to İzmir). ℭ **0232/633-2595.** Fax 0232/633-5346. www.berksoyhotel.com. 57 units. 53€ ($65) double; 70€ ($85) suite. AE, MC, V. Free parking in lot. **Amenities:** Restaurant; 2 bars; outdoor swimming pool; concierge; 24-hr. room service; laundry service; dry cleaning. *In room:* TV.

WHERE TO DINE

Meydan Restaurant TURKISH   Tourism has ground to a halt in Bergama, and it makes you wonder how Meydan can support three locations all in the area of a mile (the third is on the road out of town). In spite of the failing local economy, Meydan manages to serve up a fresh, crisp, and tasty *pide* (flat bread) topped with chopped lamb, tomatoes, onions, and Swiss chard, all at more than reasonable prices. The usual lineup of *kebap* and cold mezes dominates the display case, and the moussaka, available only at lunchtime, shouldn't be missed.

İzmir Cad. 163 (across from park; the other central branch dominates the plaza where Doğancı Cad. meets Kasapoglu Cad.). ℭ **0232/632-4521.** All items less than 6.75YTL ($5). MC, V. Daily 10am–midnight.

Paşam Restaurant FRESH TROUT   This unassuming roadside stop is a favorite among locals and has managed to remain undiscovered by the hordes of day-trippers on tour buses clogging up the town. Outdoor tables surround a tiled pool filled with trout, the primary entree. Fried to crispy perfection, the fish is complemented by an assortment of salads and mezes marinating in the most velvety of olive oils. Try the seaweed salad or the tomato, cucumber, and parsley medley. The price goes down easy as well, at about 4YTL ($3) per person for a full meal.

İzmir Yolu (on the left as you enter Bergama, just before Kleopatra Restaurant). No phone. Whole trout about 4YTL ($3). No credit cards. Daily noon–2am.

6

The Central & Southern Aegean Coasts

For hundreds of years, the stellar ruins at Ephesus have provided voyagers all the impetus they needed to justify a trip to this stretch of scenic coastlands. And for hundreds of years, the inhabitants of the area's sprawling olive, tobacco, and fig orchards have benefited by providing room, board, and the various other services that one might need on the road. Villagers and entrepreneurs of yore were not the first to recognize the commercial value of these scenic hills and crystal waters. Historically, the central and southern Aegean coasts were crossroads for ancient trade routes. Civilization evolved out of the convergence of Eastern and Western cultures; Hellenistic settlers who fled the Dorian invasions emphasized economic expansion and forged ties with people from Egypt, Nubia, Canaan, Mesopotamia, and the Black Sea region. Welcome to the original melting pot.

At one time, the region boasted some of the most illustrious addresses in the world. The Ionian cities of Ephesus, Miletus, and Priene served as cultural incubators in the development of Western thought, home to such philosophers and scholars as Thales Anaximenes, Anaximendros, and Heraclites. Later, Mary under the care of St. John, settled near Ephesus, permanently altering the way an entire civilization perceived Christianity while contributing to the evolution of the religion itself.

The presence of the sea becomes more insistent south of İzmir, characterized by a coastline backed by olive groves, rocky crags, and pine woods. But in recent years rampant development has been the rule (as it has near any main port-cum-resort), and many of the region's characteristic fishing villages and farming towns have been bewitched, and transformed, by the irresistible lure of the euro, dollar, and yen. Nevertheless. most manage to retain at least a little of their ancestral heritage and Turkish character, especially outside the perimeter of the cities' concrete blocks.

The destinations mentioned in this chapter are all within 3 hours of one another and buses run regularly between cities. For shorter excursions, the local *dolmuşes* (minivan-type public transportation) are reliable, though they usually call it quits in the early evening, which will no doubt encourage a few leisurely overnight stays. Time can be split easily between beach activities and visiting the ancient sights. This is the place to take as much time as necessary to decompress from the worries of everyday life.

The Central & Southern Aegean Coasts

560km (347 miles) south of Istanbul; 70km (43 miles) north of Selçuk; 90km (56 miles) north of Kuşadası; 325km (202 miles) south of Çanakkale; 279km (173 miles) north of Marmaris

İzmir has come a long way since the late 1800s when the Ottoman elite christened the port city *Kokaryalı* (Smelly Waterfront). Today the city has earned the nobler designation of *Güzelyalı* (Beautiful Waterfront), and with the completion of a multi-million dollar redevelopment plan that includes the green waterside park and promenade called the **Kordon** and the restored customs house (or **Konak Pier**) built by Gustave Eiffel, the name is more than appropriate.

Little was left after the fire ignited at the tail end of the War of Independence destroyed all traces of the cultural melting pot that was once Smyrna—and there's that perilous but dormant fault line to contend with. Eighty-two years after the reconstruction began, İzmir has been reinvented as a prosperous, cosmopolitan, commercial city, more livable than Istanbul, less sterile than Ankara, and filled with wide boulevards and swaying palm trees. But with the azure waters of the Aegean and the extraordinary remains of Ephesus competing for tourist attention, İzmir sadly falls short. Despite this, I actually love the place. There's plenty to do here for anyone who would make an extended stay.

A LOOK AT THE PAST

The story of İzmir brings up yet another lineup of the usual suspects, beginning with the traces of an unidentified group dating from at least the 3rd millennium B.C. Excavations at the nearby site of Bayraklı in the Meles river valley have uncovered evidence of a primitive culture influenced by Hittite religious models; in fact, the Luwi word closely resembling "Smyrna" means "land of the holy mother." Somewhere along the way, the Amazon ruler Smyrna (or Myrina) added to the confusion of the origins of the city's nomenclature. Various civilizations referred to the city as Zmürni, Smyrne, Simirna, and Esmira; if you say them all 10 times *really* fast, the final outcome is the sound of the town you'll find on maps today.

Around 200 years after the disintegration of the Hittite Empire, waves of Ionian immigrants began to populate the region, creating a thriving metropolis comparable to the success and influence of its contemporary, Troy. The Lydians who moved in and trashed the place were no match for the Persian Empire, though they, too, succumbed to Alexander the Great's blaze of glory. In the 4th century B.C., Alex rebuilt an unmistakably Hellenistic city, relocating it on the hill of Pagos under the watchful protection of the Kadifekale citadel. İzmir was absorbed by General Lysimachos into his kingdom of Pergamum, but bad estate planning on the part of Attalus 200 years later resulted in the entire region becoming a Roman colony. Under the Romans and then the Byzantines, Ionia became a thriving center of trade and intellectual innovation, but the city was razed to the ground by a devastating earthquake in A.D. 178.

Control vacillated between the Byzantines and the Arabs until 1390, when the region was stabilized under Selçuk, then Ottoman rule.

İzmir became a flourishing center of commerce in the 15th century, nurtured by the liberal policies of tolerance practiced by the Ottomans. But there was hardly a Turk in sight. The city opened its arms to waves of immigrant Jews fleeing from the Spanish Inquisition as well as Greeks and Armenians. French and other European merchants, known as the Levantines, set up customs houses here, and each enclave left its own cultural imprint on the city. After World War I, the Treaty of Sèvres assigned Greece the administration of İzmir and the surrounding region, but the Greek occupying forces got greedy and foolishly pushed eastward. The defeat of Greek forces by Atatürk's national liberation army on September 9, 1922, was the defining moment in the establishment of national sovereignty; as the Greeks were chased off the peninsula, occupying French and British forces prudently pulled out of the regions under their protection.

Depending on who tells the story, the city was destroyed by fire either by an accident of war or by angry vengeful Turks on a rampage after their victory in 1922. The city has since been rebuilt into a modern, functional, palm tree–lined, and thoroughly pleasant metropolitan city.

ESSENTIALS

GETTING THERE

BY PLANE   İzmir's Adnan Menderes Airport is serviced by **Turkish Airlines** (see below for contact information), plus a number of private established and upstart airlines, from Istanbul. **Turkish Airlines**'s İzmir office is located below the Büyük Efes Hotel, in the plaza next to the Tourist Information office, Gaziosmanpaşa Bulv. No. 1/F (© **0232/484-1220**), and at İzmir's Adnan Menderes Airport (© **0232/ 274-2424** or 0232/274-2043). **Onur Air**, and the lesser-known newcoming, **Flyair**

İzmir

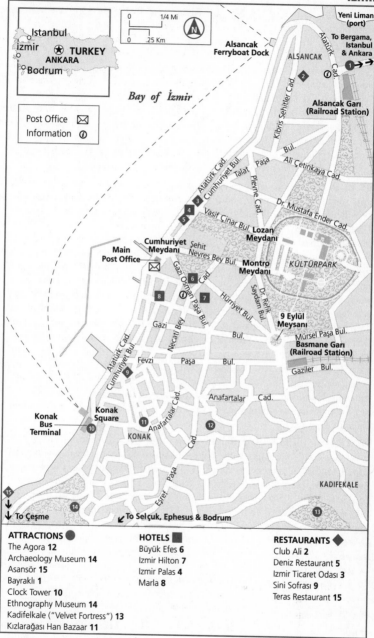

Istanbul
İzmir ★ TURKEY
ANKARA
Bodrum

0   1/4 Mi
0   .25 Km

N

Bay of İzmir

Post Office ✉
Information ⓘ

Alsancak
Ferryboat Dock

Yeni Liman
(port)

To Bergama,
Istanbul
& Ankara

ALSANCAK

2

ⓘ

1

Alsancak Garı
(Railroad Station)

Kıbrıs Şehitler Cad.

Atatürk Cad.

Bul.

Ali Çetinkaya Cad.

Paşa

Talat

Plevne Cad.

Dr. Mustafa Ender Cad.

Atatürk Cad.

Cumhuriyet Bul.

3

4

5

Vasıf Çınar Bul.

Lozan
Meydanı

KÜLTÜRPARK

Main
Post Office

Cumhuriyet
Meydanı

Şehit
Nevres Bey Bul.

Montro
Meydanı

Dr. Refik
Saydam Bul.

✉

Gazi Osman Paşa Bul.

Cad.

6

Hürriyet Bul.

8   ⓘ   7

9 Eylül
Meysanı

Mürsel Paşa Bul.

Gazi

Necati Bey

Bul.

Basmane Garı
(Railroad Station)

Atatürk Cad.

Cumhuriyet Bul.

Fevzi

Paşa

Bul.

Gaziler   Bul.

9

Anafartalar   Cad.

Konak
Bus
Terminal

Konak
Square

10

11

KONAK

Anafartalar Cad.

Cad.

12

Eşref   Paşa

KADİFEKALE

15
↓
↓ To Çeşme

14

↙ To Selçuk, Ephesus & Bodrum

13

ATTRACTIONS ●
The Agora **12**
Archaeology Museum **14**
Asansör **15**
Bayraklı **1**
Clock Tower **10**
Ethnography Museum **14**
Kadifelkale ("Velvet Fortress") **13**
Kızlarağası Han Bazaar **11**

HOTELS ■
Büyük Efes **6**
Izmir Hilton **7**
Izmir Palas **4**
Marla **8**

RESTAURANTS ◆
Club Ali **2**
Deniz Restaurant **5**
Izmir Ticaret Odası **3**
Sini Sofrası **9**
Teras Restaurant **15**

(Talatpaşa Bulvarı Dora Apt. No. 50/1 Alsancak; © **0212/444-4359**) are both represented locally by any number of travel agencies.

Havaş bus service (© **0212/444-0487**) runs daily from the airport into the center of İzmir with a drop-off point at the Turkish Airlines offices in front of the Hotel Grand Ephesus on Gaziosmanpaşa Bulvarı, next to the Hilton. Bus departure times are coordinated with flight arrivals; expect the ride into the city center to take around 30 minutes. The fare is about 9YTL ($7).

A taxi to your hotel will cost between 47YTL and 54YTL ($35–$40), depending on traffic, whether or not the meter is running, or the driver's "fixed price." If you're not sure how much to spend, try out your haggling abilities on several consecutive taxis, until you figure out how much the ride should really cost. Remember that prices are more expensive between midnight and 6am.

BY BUS Bus service is frequent and comprehensive in and out of İzmir. Service from Istanbul takes around 9½ hours; from Ankara, 9 hours; from Kuşadası, 1½ hours; from Bergama, 2½ hours; and from Bursa, about 5½ hours. As with anywhere else in Turkey, prices vary from one bus company to the next by as much as 14YTL ($10), so shop around before buying your ticket.

İzmir's main *otogar* (bus station) is laid out much like an airport, without the user-friendliness that comes with the efficient posting of signs in multiple languages. The exit to the bus station faces a busy parking lot with absolutely no indication as to where you need to go. If possible, ask the bus company that brought you if they provide free minibus service to their ticket offices in the town center. Otherwise, take a deep breath and cross the parking area toward the uncovered section and you'll spot a sleepy lineup of *dolmuşes*—none of which will take you where you want to go. Instead, get in line *before* you cross that last street to the *dolmuş* stand and wait for an antique sedan (possibly bright red) that will stuff in the first few people waiting in line. Expect to pay about 9.50YTL ($7) for the excruciating half-hour ride—through the exhaust fumes of those ahead of you—to one of the busy corners near your hotel. Keep an eye out for that urchin eyeing your luggage; he actually loads up the trunk when the *dolmuş* finally arrives.

BY TRAIN **Turkish State Railways** (www.tcdd.gov.tr/yolcu/trenler.htm) operates two trains daily from Ankara: the **Karesi Ekspresi** leaves at 7:10pm for the 15-hour trip. A seat on the train costs 18YTL ($13). You have the option of sleeping in a bed on the **Mavi Tren,** a 14-hour sleeper train that can accommodate up to three per couchette 63YTL ($47) per person for single passengers, 48YTL ($36) per person for two. A seat on the Mavi Tren costs 22YTL ($16). If you're heading north from Selçuk, hop on the **Göller Ekspresi,** which arrives in Selçuk at 5:16am on its way to İzmir (arrival at 6:56am; 13YTL/$9.60). From Istanbul, you can connect to the **Marmara Ekspresi** in Bandırma with the help of a connecting ferry from Istanbul; trains depart at 4pm and arrive in İzmir at 10:39pm. The fare is 15YTL ($11). Trains arrive into İzmir's **Basmane Garı** (© **0232/484-8638** or 0232/484-5350 for reservations), about .8km (½ mile) northeast of Konak, the town center. From Basmane Garı you will need to take a bus or taxi the short ride to your hotel.

BY FERRY In 2004, **Turkish Maritime Lines** (© **0212/249-9222**) discontinued service between Istanbul and İzmir. For transit from the Italian ports of Brindisi and Ancona, see the information in chapter 2, "Planning Your Trip to Turkey."

Those combining a visit to Turkey with a romp through the Greek islands may hop on a ferry in Chios for service to Çeşme, an hour-long bus ride from İzmir's *otogar*. Ferries run daily from July through September 15 with fewer runs off season.

VISITOR INFORMATION

Tourist information offices are located in several high-traffic areas: Gaziosmanpaşa Bulvarı 1/1 in the Büyük Efes Hotel (© **0232/484-2147**), Akdeniz Mahalesi 1344 Sokak No. 2 Pasaport (© **0232/483-6216**), and the Adnan Menderes Airport (© **0232/274-2214**). There's also an ad-hoc information booth in Konak behind the Clock Tower at the entrance of Anafartalar Caddesi. Free maps are provided at the Tourist Information office and often in your hotel room compliments of **Ramtur,** a local travel agency organizing guided excursions to Ephesus, Pergamum, Miletus-Priene-Didyma, Pamukkale, and Cappadocia (© **0232/445-9980;** fax 0232/445-7432; www.ramtur.com).

ORIENTATION

Konak, named for the Ottoman government mansion (Hükümet Konagı) located nearby, is where you'll find all the interesting stuff: a bustling seafront park, the little **Konak Camii,** and the **Clock Tower (Saat Kulesi),** the symbol of İzmir.

Just behind the tourist information booth at Konak Meydanı (the main square) is **Anafartalar Caddesi;** judging by the magnetic stream of people pouring in, this must be the entrance to the shopping district, also known as Kemeraltı. Winding through the oldest section of town are the narrow back streets of İzmir, where an unexpected 17th-century mosque, several synagogues, and a *bedesten* (privately owned market-place) cohabit an area long overtaken by inexpensive stores selling inexpensive gold chains.

To the north along the waterfront is **Konak Pier,** constructed as the Customs Building by Gustave Eiffel between 1875 and 1890 and reopened as a glossy shopping and dining destination. About a 15-minute walk farther up is Cumhuriyet Meydanı, punctuated by an equestrian statue of Atatürk, and the grassy waterfront park and promenade of **Kordon.** This neighborhood around Cumhuriyet Meydanı is home to a cluster of four- and five-star hotels, car-rental offices, and travel agencies. It's also part of the residential district of **Alsancak,** which boasts some restored homes, and another Atatürk Museum. At the northernmost tip are the harbor and ferry terminal. South of Konak Square is the neighborhood of **Karataş,** once a thriving Jewish community where you will find the Asansör and the restored houses of Dario Moreno Sokak.

Up on the hill is **Kadifekale,** the fortress established by Alexander the Great. The views are great, and the trip is free, but save yourself the hassle and have a drink in the Hilton Hotel's Windows on the Bay instead.

GETTING AROUND

Much of what might hold a non-native's interest is located in convenient little clusters at various points around the city. Unfortunately, it's all too obvious in bigger cities like İzmir that Turks are lousy at giving directions, so I suggest a taxi. Otherwise, most of your sightseeing and shopping can be done on foot in and around Konak, which includes the museums and main-square attractions, as well as the bazaar, also known as Kemeraltı. From Konak, Alsancak is reachable on foot along the scenic waterfront, but for those unable or unwilling to walk, there are municipal buses running regularly from the major bus hub at Konak (just in front of the Atatürk Cultural Center and on the street below the Archaeological Museum). If you're staying in one of the major hotels around Cumhuriyet Meydanı, you're just about dead center between Konak and Alsancak. The historic Jewish quarter, today called Asansör for the 19th-century elevator that provides access to the cliff-top residential area, is just south of Konak and also reachable by bus. The bus fare is 1.50YTL (about $1.10).

Public **ferries** crisscross İzmir's bay between Konak and the busy residential shopping area of Karşıyaka, between Pasaport (at Cumhuriyet Meydanı) and Karşıyaka, and between Pasaport and Alsancak. Fares on the ferry are about 1.35YTL ($1) each way. Purchase your jeton at the ticket window prior to boarding, and double-check the destination of the boat, particularly if you're returning to Alsancak from Karşıyaka; it's a relatively long walk from Konak Square to Alsancak if you get on the wrong boat.

The most useful **bus** line is the **no. 200,** passing by the Clock Tower at Konak on its way up and around the Bay of İzmir through Alsancak. Look above the windshield for *Teleferik-Mavişehir.*

At the risk of plowing through millennia of archaeological remains, İzmir has completed the construction of a brand-new one-line **metro,** usefully connecting Konak with Basmane Train Station and Bornova, a residential suburb known for its thermal springs. The metro runs frequently between 6am and midnight Monday through Friday; service is sparser on weekends. One ride costs 1.50YTL (about $1.10).

FAST FACTS: İzmir

Ambulance For medical emergencies, call İzmir Private Ambulance (© **0232/ 232-5955).**

Car Rentals Many agencies line the boulevard between the Hilton Hotel and Cumhuriyet Meydanı, while the major car-rental agencies have offices both at the airport and in downtown İzmir. **National Car Rental** is located both at the airport (© 0232/274-3910) and in Alsancak at Şehit Nevres Bey Bulv. 11A (© 0232/422-7107). **Hertz** is at Kultar Mahallesi, Sokak 1377 No: 8/F (© 0232/ 464-3440) and at the airport (© 0232/274-3610 for international arrivals and © 0232/349-3040 for domestic arrivals). **Avis** is located in the city center at Şair Eşref Bulv. 18D, Alsancak (© 0232/441-4417). **Budget** is located at the airport (© 0232/274-2203); the office is barely open: between 9am and noon on Saturdays and Sundays.

Currency Exchange A *döviz,* or currency exchange office, is in the international terminal of İzmir's airport. The post office (PTT) offers extremely competitive rates of exchange, while all hotels provide exchange services. Private exchange offices typically offer better rates than banks; look for the DÖVIS sign around the İzmir Hilton Hotel and in the Konak section, around Anafartalar Caddesi. Keep in mind that hotels are notorious for offering the worst rates of exchange.

Internet Access There's a small Internet cafe in the PTT next to the Mercure Hotel, open daily 8am to 11pm.

WHAT TO SEE & DO

The Agora   Constructed during the rule of Alexander the Great, the Agora is today mostly in ruins, and you'll have to walk up through a neighborhood in ruins to get there. (Call ahead to make sure it's open, and take a taxi.) What little is left remains because of Faustina, wife of Marcus Aurelius, who had the Agora rebuilt after an earthquake devastated the original in A.D. 178. On display are capitals, columns, remnants of three of the four main gates, some recognizable stalls, and some unidentifiable rubble that once composed statues of Neptune, Ceres, and Diana. The open space—impressive at about 120m×78m (400 ft.×260 ft.)—is just as efficiently seen from outside the chain-link fence as within.

East of Gaziosmanpaşa Bulv. (south of Anafartalar Cad.). ℭ 0232/425-5354. Admission 2.75YTL ($2). Daily 8:30am–noon and 1–5pm.

Archaeology Museum (Arkeoloji Müzesi) 𝒢   This place exhibits an impressive collection of ancient and Roman artifacts recovered from area excavations, including Bergama, Iasos, Bayraklı (İzmir's original settlement), and İzmir's Agora. A service path leads you to the gate of the museum grounds, which are full of wondrously oversize amphoras dating to the Hellenistic period, and columns and capitals arranged around the gardens as impromptu seating. The barren lobby contains a helpful map of Turkey indicating which regions belonged to which kingdoms—a must for understanding the historical evolution of the country and for appreciating the artifacts presented in this and other exhibits. Upstairs is a chronological exhibit of pottery, ceramics, and glass, as well as funerary objects and the reconstruction of a 3rd-millennium-B.C. tomb. Larger stone and marble statues take up the lower floor, including statues of Poseidon, Demeter, and Artemis taken from the altar of Zeus in the Agora, and a river god that ornamented a fountain at Ephesus.

South of Konak Sq. in Bahri Baba Park (main entrance up the hill from Konak Sq.). ℭ 0232/484-8324. Admission 4YTL ($3). Tues–Sun 9am–noon and 1–5pm.

Asansör 𝒢𝒢 *Moments*   The Asansör quarter is named after the 19th-century passenger elevator installed to provide access between the upper and lower levels of this hilly neighborhood. The view from the cafe, 50m (167 ft.) up, is as good as anything on the Amalfi Coast, and can be made more enjoyable over a tulip-shaped glass of tea or a meal at the **Teras Restaurant** (ℭ 0232/261-2626). At the base of the elevator is the narrow Dario Moreno Sokak, lined with old restored houses representative of the city's former Jewish neighborhood.

Dario Moreno Sok, Karataş. No phone. Elevator to the top 20YKr (15¢).

Clock Tower (Saat Kulesi)   Commanding Konak Square, this elaborately decorated clock tower has become the symbol of İzmir. Designed in a late Ottoman Moorish style, the Clock Tower was presented to the city by Sultan Abdülhamid in 1901 and stands over 24m (80 ft.) high.

Konak Sq.

Ethnography Museum (Etnoğrafya Müzesi)   This beautiful old mansion, formerly a hospital, was recovered from the İzmir Department of Public Health and put to much better use as a repository of Turkish folklore. The biggest draws are the accurate reconstruction of salons from Ottoman homes including a bridal chamber and a circumcision room. Re-created *in situ* are a number of workshops, including a pharmacy, a printing shop, a felt-making workshop, and a glassmaking atelier. Also on view is a wonderful collection of popular folkloric art, ceramics, copper utensils, and traditional costumes and decorative fabrics.

Next to the Archaeology Museum (south of Konak Sq. in Bahri Baba Park). ℂ 0232/484-8324. Admission 2YTL ($1.50). Tues–Sun 9am–noon and 1–5pm.

Kadifekale ("Velvet Fortress") Lysimachos, Alexander the Great's general, built this citadel at the summit of Mount Pagos—though given its strategic location, it was probably constructed on the foundations of an earlier civilization. It's now a seedy playground used by the underprivileged, making a stop up here often unpleasant; surely Alex would kick the butts of those pretzel-selling urchins were he alive today. Nevertheless, on a clear day you'll swear you can see as far as Greece from atop the remaining ramparts.

On the hilltop overlooking İzmir, just east of Konak. No phone. Sunrise–sunset. From Konak, take a city bus marked KALE; better yet, take a taxi.

Kızlarağası Han Bazaar ☾ This Ottoman *bedesten* has been a successful draw since its restoration, not just because few can resist a town bazaar, but also because the prices are amazingly competitive for the stocks of sumac carpets, water pipes, camel bone, and jewelry. Better yet, some of the best coffee in Turkey is served here in the shaded center courtyard.

Kemeraltı, off Anafartalar Cad. (Start asking for directions once you get close.) Daily 9am–7pm.

Konak Pier The neighborhood of Konak was another lucky beneficiary of the redevelopment of İzmir's waterfront. Along with the neighborhood's wide-open plazas, there's this restored Customs House built by Gustave Eiffel. They've turned it into a shopping mall, but if the mall at home had views like this, I'd be a lot poorer.

Atatürk Bulvarı, Konak. No phone.

WHERE TO STAY

Büyük Efes Oteli This was once İzmir's idea of a five-star hotel. It's still not a bad choice—it's steps from almost everything—but because the hotel was put up for sale in the fall of 2005, it's anybody's guess what will happen next. What's there now is an enormous monolith that takes up an entire block and encircles tended garden lawns. The traditional wood furnishings may seem a bit dated, while every room has a balcony with at least a partial sea or garden view. If you do stay here, the rooms on the seventh and eighth floors were renovated just a handful of years ago, and are nicely decorated with fabrics with a typical Ottoman tulip pattern. A glass-sided aquarium bar provides nonstop entertainment featuring anyone with the audacity to swim in the transparent pool, and the result is intriguing and playful.

Gaziosmanpaşa Bulv. 1, 35210 İzmir. ℂ 0232/484-4300. Fax 0232/441-5695. 446 units. 100€ ($82) double; 165€ ($135) and up suite. AE, DC, MC, V. Free parking on-site. **Amenities:** 10 restaurants; 6+ bars; outdoor swimming pool; fitness room; Turkish bath; Jacuzzi; sauna; concierge; tour desk; car-rental desk; shopping arcade; salon; 24-hr. room service; massage; laundry service; dry cleaning. *In room:* A/C, satellite TV, minibar, hair dryer.

İzmir Hilton ☾ Regrettably, I must give credit where credit is due and say that the İzmir Hilton is a flawless hotel, providing luxury, ease, and practicality. The hotel opened in 1992 to provide a world-class, five-star facility in a town full of wannabes. The staff is professional and dignified, the common areas sparkle, the rooms are plush, dignified, and user-friendly, and there isn't a thing the management hasn't thought of to make your stay seamless. And in typical American management style, there is a price tag on every extra little thing you do.

Gaziosmanpaşa Bulv. 7, 35210 İzmir. © **800/445-8667** in the U.S., or 0232/441-6060. Fax 0232/441-2277. www. hilton.com. 381 units. 240€ ($290) double with city view, 180€ ($219) double without view; 325€ ($396) and up suite. Breakfast 9€ ($11); 15% tax additional. AE, DC, MC, V. Parking garage free for guests. **Amenities:** 3 restaurants; 2 bars; indoor swimming pool; 2 tennis courts; health club; sauna; concierge; tour desk; car-rental desk; business center w/secretarial services (fee based); shopping arcade; salon; 24-hr. room service; massage (16€/$20/hour); babysitting; laundry service; dry cleaning; nonsmoking rooms; executive floors; free valet parking. *In room:* A/C, satellite TV w/movies, dataport, minibar, hair dryer.

İzmir Palas Oteli   Occupying a 75-year-old building, the İzmir Palas is the oldest hotel in town, still run by the same family that opened it in 1928, and one of the area's better three-star establishments. Following renovations in 2000, it's also the best bargain around. The restaurant and lobby are both casual and cozy, and its superb location, near the Kordon, makes for great views of the harbor and easy access to the best restaurants.

Atatürk Bulv., Alsancak/İzmir. © **0232/421-5583.** Fax 0232/422-6870. www.izmirpalas.com.tr. 152 units. 115€ ($140) double. MC, V. **Amenities:** Bar; 24-hr. room service; laundry service; dry cleaning. *In room:* Satellite TV, minibar.

Marla Hotel   I'm a sucker for black leather Le Corbusier chairs, so maybe this review isn't going to be as impartial as it should be, but the chairs do establish the hotel's position on good taste, and the theme runs throughout. With its stone facade and arched glass windows, the Marla Hotel is certainly more interesting than the high-rise genre of hotel. Rooms are of average size, inoffensively decorated in pinks and grays; the bathrooms are modern and utilitarian, and hot water is provided thanks to a rare old reliable: the water heater. The Atrium Restaurant should be up and running by the time this book goes to press, offering sunsets over the bay and traditional Turkish fare.

Kazım Dirik Cad. 7, 35210 Pasaport/İzmir. © **0232/441-4000.** Fax 0232/441-1150. 68 units. 110€ ($135) double; 130€ ($160) suite. DC, MC, V. **Amenities:** Bar; 24-hr. room service; laundry service; dry cleaning. *In room:* A/C, satellite TV, minibar, dataport, hair dryer, safe.

WHERE TO DINE

Ever since the completion of the waterside promenade, the **Kordon** has become İzmir's de facto center for restaurants and breezy cafes. New ones pop up practically every day. Cheap *kebap* houses and ice-cream shops line **Anafartalar Caddesi,** in the shopping area, but unfortunately, if you're feeling lazy, it's up to the hotel dining room for another overpriced plate of mixed mezes.

Deniz Restaurant   🎢🎢 FISH   Every city has the perfect place to celebrate special occasions or impress the boss. With a reputation that precedes it, Deniz easily earns the honors for İzmir's best restaurant. Their specialty is an adaptation of a meaty favorite: *Balik kavurma,* a preparation of the flakiest Mediterranean catch in a traditional earthenware pan. The fried ice cream is an unexpected delight, and the restaurant's nonsmoking room and unpretentious surroundings make the meal all the more enjoyable.

Atatürk Cad. 188/B (under İzmir Palas Oteli). © **0232/464-4499.** Reservations required. Main 3 courses 6.75YTL–14YTL ($5–$10); fish by weight from 6.75YTL–11YTL ($5–$8) per kilo and up. DC, MC, V. Daily 11:30am–midnight.

İzmir Ticaret Odası Lokali ⭐ KEBAPS   This unpretentious restaurant is a popular spot among local businessmen for lunch. There are no surprises on the menu, except for the *süt kuzu kokoreç*—a soup of sheep's intestine (tripe, essentially), a traditional remedy for hangovers. Maybe try the grills or *pides* (flat breads) instead.

Vasıf Çınar Bulv. 1 (on the 2nd floor opposite Deniz Restaurant). © 0232/421-4249. Main courses 8YTL–14YTL ($6–$10). MC, V. Mon–Fri 11am–3:30pm.

Topçu'nun Yeri TURKISH   This down-to-earth eatery is a favorite among the local businessmen, and the three side-by-side restaurants and sidewalk cafes are filled to the brim with popular national actors and artists in town for the various annual fairs. On summer days when the heat becomes too much to bear, the main section has an air-conditioned dining area on the second floor, with a TV (in Turkish, of course) for a little background atmosphere. The house specialty is *çöpşiş*, cubed beef, veal, or lamb grilled on skewers and *köfte*, the Turkish equivalent of a pressed meatball, but there is a lineup of the usual varieties of eggplant and grills on the traditional menu as well.

Kazım Dirik Cad. 3, İzmir. © 232/425-9047. Menu items under 4YTL ($3). MC, V. Daily noon–midnight.

İZMIR AFTER DARK

The redevelopment of İzmir's waterfront truly infuses new life into this city on the sea. The grassy **Kordon waterfront park,** which runs from Cumhuriyet Meydanı to the ferryboat docks of **Alsancak** and beyond, is rimmed by, at last count, 14 establishments, including restaurants, pubs, and Italian cafes, all with terrace seating, and facing the open park and promenade. According to the locals, they're "all good, all the same, all expensive." **Sera Café** (© 0232/422-1939), across from Deniz Restaurant (and below İzmir Ticaret Odası), provides live music nightly in a futuristic setting of bucket seats and streamlined bar stools.

The North Shield Pub (© 0232/483-0720) added to its portfolio of pubs by opening up a location in Konak Pier. But tables at this location are positioned as to best enjoy the serenade of the sea and the nighttime glow of the lights bouncing off the Gulf of İzmir.

The highly regarded **İzmir State Opera and Ballet** (© 0232/484-6445) and **İzmir's State Symphony Orchestra** (© 0232/425-4115; fax 0232/484-5172) perform from September to May; check with your travel agent or the official website for calendar information (www.izdob.gov.tr), but keep your Turkish dictionary handy, as you will need to know the names of the months. Tickets for performances cost from 6YTL to 13YTL ($4.50–$9.50).

2 Highlights of the Çeşme Peninsula ⭐

81km (50 miles) west of İzmir

Few foreigners make time for little ole forgotten Çeşme, located only 81km (50 miles) west of İzmir but far enough off the beaten trail to keep it out of the tourist loop. Ferries arriving into Çeşme from the Greek island of Chios have turned the seaside town into a depot rather than a destination, and passersby get only a fleeting glimpse from the bus window of the cultivated fields, windmills, and celebrated mastic gum trees of the peninsula.

But as much as Çeşme is a suburb of İzmir, it is also a beach resort in its own right, blessed with picturesque beaches that number well into the double digits. When tourists discovered the jet-set haunts of the Bodrum Peninsula, the smart set migrated north to the crystalline beaches of Çeşme. Çeşme still manages to remain relatively untarnished, offering a perfect balance between sybaritic and simple pleasures, such as the appreciation of unspoiled stretches of fertile fields of aniseed.

Most importantly, Çeşme, named after the many springs found in the area during the 18th and 19th centuries, has finally begun to harness the full appeal of its natural resources, with the opening of several luxury thermal centers.

Plan on a minimum of 3 days to explore the beaches and baste in a thermal pool. You'll want more time if you plan on sleeping late and visiting any of the culturally rich villages.

ESSENTIALS
GETTING THERE
BY CAR   A toll expressway runs the length of the peninsula and connects Çeşme with İzmir and the region beyond.

BY BUS   Buses from İzmir leave from the main *otogar* outside of town, heading westward through İzmir before getting on the highway. Therefore, if you're staying around Konak, it makes more sense to pick up the bus near Fahrettin Altay Medyanı; ask your taxi driver to take you to this secondary bus stop. Bus connections from other cities in the region must be made at the main *otogar*.

Buses arriving into Çeşme follow the main road, then loop around to leave you just at the top of the main street before continuing on to the *otogar*. Taxis are waiting at either stop.

BY FERRY   The Turkish-based **Ertürk** (© **0232/712-6768;** www.erturk.com.tr; offices located opposite the marina) operates year-round service between Chios and Çeşme (6 days a week in summer; less often in winter). Passage costs 66YTL ($49) for a one-way trip and 82YTL ($60) for a same-day round-trip passage and 99YTL ($73) for a round-trip ticket with an open return. Depending on seasonal demand, a number of other ferry companies will do the same run; for tickets, go to **Karavan Tours** (© **0232/712-7230**), located across from the marina. Turkish port taxes are included in the price; for anything longer than a day trip, a port tax of around 20YTL ($15) must be paid to the Greek authorities on arrival or departure.

Çeşme is also one of the main ports receiving ferries from Brindisi and Ancona, Italy (see p. 39 for more information).

VISITOR INFORMATION
The staff at the Tourist Information office (© **0232/712-6653**), located on the waterfront across from the castle, is ready, willing, and able to provide thorough and useful information on a wide range of subjects. If I had any influence with the local Municipality, I'd give these people a raise.

ORIENTATION
The small resort town of Çeşme is located at the extreme western tip of the Çeşme Peninsula, located about an hour's drive out of İzmir. The highway arrives from the south into downtown **Çeşme,** where several main arteries run outward to beaches, thermal springs, and ruins, passing back and forth between barren Anatolian brush land and fertile olive groves. Before arriving in Çeşme center, the highway offers a turnoff south to **Alaçatı Bay,** and about .8km (½ mile) farther, another turnoff north toward **Alaçatı** town. (There are two other approaches into Alaçatı town: one from Ilıca, the other from Şifne.)

Fun Fact **Mastic: The Truth about Gum**

The resin-producing mastic tree that grows all over the Çeşme Peninsula (and the Eastern Mediterranean) has been used for centuries in many ways: to heal stomach ulcers, to clean and polish teeth, as a sunscreen and a sunburn soother, and more. In Çeşme, mastic is used in jams, to make pudding, or as a flavoring for *rakı* (an alcoholic drink), while in the United States, the same ingredient is used chiefly as a varnish or adhesive substance. Mastic pudding, along with other cleverly bottled marmalades, is available at **Rumeli Pastanesi,** Inkılap Cad. 46, Çeşme (© **0232/712-6759**).

The road leading north out of Çeşme runs down the center of a fishtail peninsula. A turnoff onto the eastern tip leads to the small port village of **Dalyan. Ayayorgı Beach** is reachable via an earlier turnoff to the east from the Çeşme–Dalyan road.

From Çeşme heading east is the road to **Ilıca,** the thermals of **Şifne,** and, farther northeast along the coast, the ruins of **Erythrai** and the village of **Ildırı.** Yet again using Çeşme as the main hub, the road that passes southward past the marina and ferry terminal heads out into the hills and arrives at some of the finest beaches in the area, namely **Pırlanta** and **Altınkum.**

Most *dolmuş* service runs through or originates in downtown Çeşme, so getting around by *dolmuş* might require you to backtrack.

Inkılap Caddesi, Çeşme's main shopping street, leads from the highway connector to the waterfront, and *is* essentially downtown Çeşme. Inkılap Caddesi leads to the port, where a core of facilities geared at incoming ferryboat passengers includes travel agencies, ferry ticketing offices, and the Tourist Information office. The waterfront is lined with boats touting day trips to **Donkey Island,** only 1.9km (1 nautical mile) offshore. Dominating the main square is the **Genovese Castle,** which together with the **Selçuk caravansary,** is a striking sight from the sea.

Adnan Menderes Caddesi shoots off Inkılap Caddesi from the entrance to town to connect with the *otogar.* Within the boundaries of these two main thoroughfares is Anatolian suburbia, with hilly roads, narrow streets, and some open fields that on a summer night fill up with locals making music with their families and friends.

GETTING AROUND

With a car or scooter at your disposal, the peninsula will more readily reveal its special appeal, and several rental agencies can be found along the main shopping thoroughfare. For advance reservations (which are rarely necessary), call **Sultan Rent a Car & Motorbike,** Inkılap Cad. 54/C, Çeşme (© **0232/712-7395;** fax 0232/712-8259); the daily rate for a scooter is around 34YTL ($25).

Minibus service to points beyond operates from downtown Çeşme (in front of the Municipal Building or from the drop-off point where the bus from İzmir left you) to nearby beaches and sights.

There's a taxi stand (© **0232/712-6690**) next to the castle in downtown Çeşme. Taxis are metered, averaging about 11YTL ($8) to Alaçatı, 6.75YTL ($5) to Ilıca, 5.50YTL ($4) to Dalyan, and 4YTL ($3) to Ayayorgı. After midnight, fares are 50% higher.

WHAT TO SEE & DO

Built in the 14th century by the Genovese to protect wine shipments, the **Genovese Castle,** across from the ferry landing (© **0232/712-6609**), was expanded and reconstructed by the Ottoman Sultan Bayezid II in the beginning of the 16th century. It was destroyed during the wars with Venice in the 17th century, restored again in the 18th, and continued to serve as a defense system until 1833. The fortress is now the **Çeşme Archaeological Museum** (admission 2.75YTL/$2; daily 8:30am–12:30pm and 1:30–5:30pm), housing artifacts recovered during excavations of Erythrai. The mosque that was built within the castle walls is now used as the museum's administration building.

Eight kilometers (5 miles) down the road from Çeşme town through the peninsula's famous mastic tree orchards is **Alaçatı** ☆ (the village, not the bay; minibuses leave from the yacht harbor). This little inland village, which bears the mark of the Byzantines, the Selçuks, and the Ottomans, still retains much of its diverse character. The Greek-style whitewashed or stone shuttered houses are characteristic of Aegean seaside architecture. By day, these painted blue shuttered windows and doors open onto charming antiques shops, cafes, and patisseries. (Try the apple pie at **Agrilia Café Boutique,** Kemal Pasa Cad. 75; © **0232/716-8594.**) On summer evenings, modern-day cafes and restaurants spill out into the streets to give the town a wholly festive feel. A number of these houses have been converted into lovely bed-and-breakfasts targeting weekenders from Istanbul; a room at the **Alaçatı Taş Hotel** (Kemalpaşa Caddesi 132; © **0232/716-7722**; www.tasotel.com) will run from 83€ to 115€ ($100–$140) a night. Above the city on a little hill are the remnants of the typical round houses of the Selçuk period and picturesque windmills from a bygone era. The mosque in the center of town was converted from a church.

Located about a half-hour's drive (17km/11 miles) on the coastal road north from Ilıca is **Ildırı,** which enjoys the shelter of a small bay protected by a series of offshore islands. Not surprisingly, the locals, who number only about 350, make their livings on fishing boats as well as in artichoke and olive fields (and until 15 years ago, in tobacco fields, too). A number of fish restaurants line the small dock as well as the road leading to the village. On the road at the edge of town are a couple of covered shacks called restaurants—the characteristic covered, stone terraces overlook the artichoke and olive fields toward the sea. Stop here for some *gözleme* (a crepe filled with cheese, spinach, or both) and an *ayran*, or for some fish only recently pulled out of the water.

On the edge of Ildırı is the ancient Greek city of **Erythrai** ☆ (free admission, but the caretaker may ask for something; daily 8am–5pm or see the caretaker), whose remains are still mostly hidden beneath the fields of artichokes cultivated by the local villagers. Sporadic excavations conducted since 1964 have revealed a theater, dating to the 3rd century B.C. and destroyed in an earthquake in A.D. 100. There are some visible signs of a city plan including the 6th-century-B.C. Temple of Heracles (unexcavated), a 5th-century-B.C. sacrificial altar, and 2nd-century-B.C. luxury villas and mosaic stone pavement. A climb to the top of the theater and up to the summit of the hill will reveal an old basilica-style church, as well as some of the loveliest views in the region.

Day boats lining Çeşme's harbor tout excursions in the Aegean for swimming, snorkeling, or simply relaxing. A day usually includes stops at **Donkey Island** (there really are donkeys there), the **Blue Lagoon,** and **Black Island.** At 14YTL ($10) with lunch included, these tours are a good value. Stroll along the harbor the night before to inspect the boats.

If exploring the shipwrecks offshore is more your speed, or you just want to brush up on some rusty diving skills, contact **Dolphin Land** (© **0232/337-0161;** fax 0232/486-2309; www.divecesme.com) for information on their day trips around Cesme. They also offer PADI certification with English instruction.

AREA BEACHES

You'll need a car to get to **Alaçatı Bay** 🎈🎈, an expanse of water surrounded by sandy and sun-scorched hills. Thanks to year-round high winds, shallow water up to almost 450m (1,476 ft.) offshore, and wide-open space, the bay is one of the top three wind-surfing destinations in the world. Windsurfers from the four corners come here to participate in the Windsurf Turkey Cup, in which thrill-seekers compete in a stunt-filled challenge of wits and skill. The rest of the year, neophytes like us get out there and entertain the pros from the on-site windsurfing schools with our ineptitude. **B&G Surf at Windsurfers Paradise** (© **0232/716-6170;** www.alacati.com; closed Nov–Mar) makes it all possible by renting various models by the hour or by the day, with or without instruction. A 2-hour lesson will run you 82YTL ($61), including all equipment (discounts for groups of four or more). A full-day rental without lessons costs 66YTL ($49) (99YTL/$73 on weekends; wet suits and harnesses are extra (16YTL/$12for the day). To get there, just follow the Alaçatı highway out until you see a parking lot, campers, and a smattering of bamboo bungalows.

A strip of sand over 1.5km (a mile) long, **Ilıca Beach** is the longest beach on the peninsula and also the most popular. The thermal center at the Sheraton (see "Area Thermals" below) takes advantage of the scalding natural sources of the area, and also maintains the cleanest stretch of beach.

Southwest of Çeşme are two of the best public beaches the peninsula has to offer. **Pırlanta Beach (Diamond Beach)** 🎈🎈, a pristine stretch of lily-white sand, is oriented north toward the rocky coastline. **Altınkum Beach** 🎈🎈, named "golden" for the color of its sand, is a long stretch of beach wide open to the sea and facing south, making the waters slightly, refreshingly cooler than the other beaches on the peninsula. At these public beaches, the entrance is free and chairs and umbrellas rent for 1.75YTL ($1.30) per person. A minibus from the yacht harbor will take you to both beaches, a distance just under 8km (5 miles). If you're driving yourself, follow the directions for the "Ionia Hotel" at the multisigned fork in the road heading toward Altınkum/Pırlanta. (**Note:** Don't confuse Altınkum with the disappointing stretch at Tursite; follow the small black sign for PLAJ.) There's also a restaurant shack on the beach at Altınkum. There is a cafeteria/bar/restaurant on-site.

North of Çeşme, hidden amid the olive and orange groves, is **Ayayorgı Beach** 🎈🎈🎈, an intimate and secluded bay with no actual beach—just cement piers and crystalline waters, and one or two kayaks and paddle boats for rent. You'll need a car (or taxi) for the 3.5km (2-mile) ride from Çeşme to this family beach; take the road for Dalyan and follow the signs.

A day spent roaming in and out of the leather, carpet, and silver shops of downtown Çeşme doesn't have to mean you've blown your day at the beach. **Tekke Beach,** just north of the port, is the perfect escape for a quick cool-down and limited time.

AREA THERMALS

Çeşme owes its current rebirth to its thermal sources, considered sacred by the ancients. Not all the sources have been tapped, and not all that have been tapped are equal.

There may not be the luxury of the Sheraton at **Doğal Şifa Merkezi** (© 0232/ 717-2424), 3km (1¾ miles) north of Ilıca on the right in Şifne, but there's a down-to-earth sensibility in the green Astroturf runners and modest thermal pool (6.75YTL/$5 including hydro-massage). Doğal Şifa also has a thermal mud pit (the point is to mix it with the thermal water—though it was bone-dry during my visit) and an assortment of massage therapies conducted in spotless and stylish white rooms (32YTL/$24 for the works: medical, migraine/head, lumbago, esthetic, leg, and foot massages; 19YTL/$14 for a 45-min. relax massage). Vedat Akar, owner, pharmacist, and on-site physical therapist, can devise a plan of action for your healing needs. To get there by bus, change at Ilıca for a minibus to Şifne.

North of Ilıca on the tip of a small peninsula are a number of small coves, hidden in pine trees and rarely visited. In **Paşa Limanı** ✸✸ is **Vekamp** (© 0232/717-2224), which does triple-duty as a beach, a thermal, and a campsite. The long rectangular thermal pool, located at the back of the property, is partially shaded in pine, and the waters averaging 104°F (40°C) cascade down a small slide onto the pebble beach just steps below. Entrance costs 2.75YTL ($2).

The **Termalife Center** ✸✸✸ at the Sheraton in Ilıca (Şifne Cad. 35; © 0232/723-1240) was devised with nothing but sheer pleasure in mind. The Renaissance-style atrium, complete with a statue of Aphrodite, welcomes you to a full-service facility with four thermal pools, one saltwater and three highly sulfuric (of which one is a Jacuzzi and another is outdoor). The center also has a *hamam*, a steam room, a dry sauna, a solarium, and a fitness corner (access to these is 15YTL/$11 for guests; 23YTL/$17 for nonguests). Spa treatments include five types of massage, hand and foot care, Thalgo face treatments, and Thalasso therapies. Treatments cost from up to 43YTL ($32) on up to 208YTL ($154) for the Exceptional Elixir Facial, while combined use of the thermal pools costs 18YTL ($14) for hotel guests, 28YTL ($21) for outside guests.

West of Ilıca town center is the **Yıldız Peninsula;** near the point is an oddity of geology: thermal water as hot as 122° to 140°F (50°–60°C) springing forth from beneath the surface of the water. This natural phenomenon doesn't have a price tag, as there's no charge to step off the rocky point into the semi-enclosed rocky pool. (Many who have led sheltered lives come here if only to eyeball the bare flesh of women in bathing suits.) It's not uncommon either to see women submerged yet covered head to toe in full traditional dress.

WHERE TO STAY

The hotel listings below offer a choice of the best the Çeşme area has to offer. If you opt for one of the hotels in Çeşme town, you'll be trading beach access for convenience to the town center, which offers everything including car rentals, travel agencies, restaurants, and cafes. The buzz of visitors along the main drag out for the evening air also offers the people-watching you won't get in the other villages on the peninsula. Second to Çeşme as to level of activity is Ilıca, with one of the nicest stretches of beach around. The tiny village and cove of Dalyan has nothing more than a postcard-perfect marina lined with fish restaurants; to get around, you'll either have to rely on the services of the hotel concierge, or rustle up some authentic assistance by haggling at the marina. Alaçatı Bay is the most removed of the lot, and will remain so until the Süzer Paradise gets some neighbors. For the true budget watcher, try the rather sterile Şirin Villa, located in Ilıca at 5133 Sok. No. 34 (© **0232/723-4414;** fax 0232/ 723-3278; www.sirinvilla.com), where double rooms cost 33YTL (about $24).

ÇEŞME TOWN

Kervansary Hotel   If architecture and history move you, and you don't mind sacrificing some basic comforts, this 500-year-old inn is a fabulous place to hang your hat. The 16th-century caravansary was at the end of a branch of the road for the merchant caravans trekking across Anatolia to unload their goods here in Çeşme for export to Europe. In typical caravansary style, all rooms encircle a large central courtyard and are notable for the original terra-cotta tile floors, low chimneys, and monastic bed frames. The old textiles and area rugs complement the sparseness of the decoration, which is, for the most part, whitewashed and well worn. The bathroom facilities provide a crash course in intimacy for the uninitiated—there's nothing but a flimsy wooden folding screen between you and your partner's private functions. The upper rooms are accessible via the standard overly steep stone stairs, so for those with physical limitations, ask for a room on the ground floor. Because of management changes, the hotel may or may not be open in 2006. (For information, call the Tourist Information office at © **0232/712-6653.**)

Hurriyet Cad., 35940 Çeşme. Across from the Tourist Information office. © **0232/712-7177.** Fax 0232/712-6492. 32 units (all with minitub). 35€ ($43) double; 55€ ($67) suite. MC, V. Closed Oct–May 1.

Pırıl Hotel   This hotel has grown up quite a bit since we last visited, and while it's no longer that diamond in the rough we loved, the renovations—in particular the addition of a thermal center—did make us sit up and take notice. Accommodations range from standard doubles through duplex suites and on to family apartments. The modern rooms are a bit on the small side, but the balconies provide an added sense of space, soothing mountain views, and cool breezes for those hot summer nights. The older building flanks the newer one, and side by side they prove that cement slabs and glass can actually be attractive, if presented well. The hotel is located .8km (½ mile) through back streets to the main drag, a distance that makes for a lovely evening walk.

Çevre Yolu, 35940 Çeşme. © **0232/712-7574.** Fax 0232/712-7953. www.pirilhotel.com. 139 units. 38€ ($46) double; 62€ ($75) efficiency. Rates per person half board. MC, V. Free parking. Closed Nov–Mar. **Amenities:** Restaurant; bar; outdoor swimming pool; thermal center; fitness room; sauna; 24-hr. room service; laundry service; dry cleaning; nonsmoking rooms; doctor on-call; babysitting service; Internet point; free parking. *In room:* TV, minibar, hair dryer, safe.

DALYAN

Dalyan Plaza Hotel ⭐   This unspoiled stretch of beach remained undiscovered until the summer of 1999 when the Dalyan Plaza opened its doors opposite the pristine sands of Kocakarı Beach. Furnished in simple and airy Ottoman "beach style," with at least partial views of the sea (the suites get the full-on views), everything about this hotel spells relaxation. The private beach below is just a hop over the hotel's private road, while a pool perched up the hill provides sandless enjoyment of the Aegean. The hotel is also conveniently located around the bend from Dalyan's atmospheric fish restaurants and just minutes by car from Çeşme.

Akgün Sok. 26, 35930 Dalyan. © **0232/724-8000.** Fax 0232/724-9252. www.dalyanplaza.com. 46 units (all with shower). May and Sept 50€ ($61) double; June and Oct 67€ ($82) double; July–Aug 125€ ($153) double. Rates include breakfast and dinner. MC, V. Free parking on-site. Closed Nov–Apr. From Çeşme, take Dalyan Cad. about 3.5km (2 miles), following signs for Dalyan and the Dalyan Plaza Hotel. **Amenities:** Restaurant; bar; patisserie; outdoor swimming pool; fitness room; concierge; 24-hr. room service; laundry service; dry cleaning. *In room:* Satellite TV.

Sisus Hotel ★★ This is a fairly recent addition to Çeşme, and a welcome one, I might add. Public areas are a cross between A Space Odyssey and SoHo chic; rather than ask questions, I decided to concede that the formula works. All rooms enjoy a balcony, and design-wise, the architects thought to optimize the views by partitioning the bathrooms from the main room via glass walls. Sitting right on the charming cove that is Dalyanköy's Yat Limanı, rooms get either a sea or mountain view; the garden-enclosed swimming pool gets all waterfront, all the time. The hotel also provides the long list of amenities one may not want to do without, including a sufficiently sybaritic wellness center.

Yat Limani (at the marina), Dalyanköy. International bookings in Greece: ℂ **30-2810-300330**. Fax 30-2810-220785. www.lux-hotels.com/turkey/sisus. 125€–225€ ($153–$275) double; 187€–437€ ($228–$533) suite ("X" Suite 1,000€/$1,220). AE, MC, V. **Amenities:** Restaurant; 5 bars; heated outdoor swimming pool; fitness center; spa; Turkish bath; sauna; tennis court; 24-hr. room service; conference room; doctor; babysitting; hairdresser. *In room:* A/C, minibar, satellite TV, CD Player, Internet connection, coffee/tea service, hair dryer, safe.

ILİCA

Sheraton ★★ (Kids) Visually impressive, über-luxurious, and on the beachfront, the Sheraton Çeşme gives credibility to the peninsula as a major tourist destination. Still, this Sheraton has a long way to go to catch up to its own reputation. Opened in February 2001, this five-star facility boasts a top-flight thermal spa (drawing on the sources of the local Ilıca Hot Spring), which aims at nothing more than utter self-indulgence. Rooms are sizable and expectedly plush. However, despite the Sheraton's traditional reputation for efficiency and hospitality, the staff has some training issues to iron out, as many of the smaller details are still being overlooked. Also (and maybe I'm too demanding), water, coffee, and tea (at least) should be offered free of charge with dinner. Even so, the hotel is destined for greatness; it just may take a while.

Şifne Cad. 35, 35940 Ilıca. ℂ **800/325-3535** in the U.S. and Canada, 800/325-35353 in Europe, or 0232/723-1240 in Turkey. Fax 0232/723-1856. www.sheraton.com. 373 units. From 136€ ($166) double; from 360€ ($439) suites. Rates fluctuate according to market demand. AE, MC, V. Valet parking. **Amenities:** 3 restaurants; 3 bars; indoor and outdoor swimming pools; tennis courts; health club; thermal spa; Turkish bath; watersports; children's-center programs; game room; concierge; tour desk; car-rental desk; shopping arcade; salon; 24-hr. room service; massage; laundry service; dry cleaning; nonsmoking rooms; executive floor. *In room:* A/C, satellite TV, dataport, minibar, hair dryer, safe.

ALAÇATİ BAY

Süzer Paradise Hotel ★★ Although one of the first luxury thermals to spring up from the vast natural resources of the region, the Süzer doesn't go overboard. It's located on a solitary expanse of beach in the rough-and-ready landscape of Alaçatı Bay, and is perfect not only as a base for windsailing enthusiasts but also for those interested in the utter self-indulgence afforded by the hotel's Spavit spa, fitness, and beauty center (see "Area Thermals" above). The beach—more than private because the hotel stands on a solitary piece of land—is backed by lawns strewn with big cushions and lounge chairs. Hotel decor reflects Ottoman simplicity and elegance, with dark cherrywood furniture, Turkish rugs, and Santa Fe–style tile floors. Each room has a balcony, great for the constant breezes that keep this section of the peninsula cooler than the others. Both rooms and bathrooms are generous in size. The hotel was undergoing renovations as of this writing; call for updated information on rooms, amenities, and wellness center.

Alaçatı Yolu, 35940 Alaçatı. **©** **0232/716-9777**. Fax 0232/716-9762. 205 units. 90€ ($110) double; 270€ ($33) suite. AE, DC, MC, V. **Amenities:** 2 restaurants; 2 bars; patisserie; outdoor swimming pool; 2 thermal pools (1 indoor/ outdoor); 2 tennis courts (illuminated); health club; Spavit spa center; volleyball court; basketball; extensive water-sports; rentals (bike, moped, and scooter); game room; concierge; tour desk; car-rental desk; shopping arcade; salon; 24-hr. room service; massage; laundry service; dry cleaning; nonsmoking rooms; Internet connection; executive floor. *In room:* A/C, satellite TV, minibar, hair dryer, safe.

WHERE TO DINE
ÇEŞME TOWN

Kale Lokantası STEWS AND KEBAPS   This unassuming tea garden next to the castle packs up around mealtime, serving good, basic fast food at rock-bottom prices. It's much worse in the winter, when everybody has to fit into the sparsely furnished dining room. There's no menu, just steam pots full of fresh chickpea stew, vegetables with meatballs, and rice and beans. Naturally, they serve *döner kebap* (lamb roasted on a revolving spit), but no matter what you choose, a simple hearty meal couldn't be more satisfying.

Çarşı Cad. Kervansaray yanı 11, Çeşme. **©** **0232/712-0519**. All items under 5.50YTL ($4). MC, V. Daily 9am–midnight.

Körfez FISH/STEAKHOUSE   Overlooking the harborside promenade near the center of town, Körfez is one of the more atmospheric restaurants in town. The menu relies heavily on the local catch, which often includes *çupra,* a local sea bass special to Çeşme. An open *ocakbaşı,* or hooded grill, allows for the preparation of Ottoman-influenced dishes like the *borcam kebap,* a lamb dish with eggplant, tomato, crushed peanuts, and cheese, while the chef looks to the French for the steak menu.

Yalı Cad. 12 (on the waterfront). **©** **0232/712-6718**. Appetizers and main courses 6.75YTL–16YTL ($5–$12) and up for fish. MC, V. Daily noon–midnight.

DALYAN

Dalyan Restaurant "Cevat'un Yeri" *ℛℛ* FISH   This fairly elegant restaurant serves fish so fresh that its gills are still moving. The meze case presents a great variety, with items I've not seen at other restaurants, such as grilled cheese, stuffed calamari, and potato croquettes. Fish is sold by the kilo, so prices vary, with lobster tipping the scales at 38YTL to 47YTL ($28–$35) per kilo (1 kilo is approximately 2¼ lb.). The catch of the day is fished from local waters, some of it even coming from the edge of the harbor wall where you could catch a glimpse of this evening's appetizer.

At the far end of Harbor Rd., Yacht Harbor, Dalyan/Çeşme. **©** **0232/724-7045**. Reservations suggested. Appetizers 4YTL–6.75YTL ($3–$5); fish by weight 9.50YTL–16YTL ($7–$12). No credit cards. Daily noon–1 or 2am.

ÇEŞME AFTER DARK

People drive from as far as İzmir and beyond for a night out at one of the beachfront restaurant/dance clubs of Çeşme. The one with the most longevity is the **Seaside Beach Club,** Alaçatı Bay (next to the Süzer Hotel; **©** **0232/716-9899**), which has been close to the heart of Turkey's jet set (those not in Bodrum) and in-crowd. The newer open-air club at the **Hotel Grand Ontur,** Havacılar Sitesi Yanı Dalyan Mevkii (**©** **0232/724-0011**), takes advantage of the spectacular cliff-top setting and open seas. The cover for both clubs is 20YTL ($15).

Escueto   Escueto's concept is all Latin, with music and menu that are Mexican, Spanish, Tex-Mex, and Cajun (appetizers and main courses 5.50YTL–11YTL/$4–$8; MasterCard and Visa accepted). The selection of tapas goes perfectly with their frozen margaritas, and the flavors are authentic because the necessary spices (cilantro, jalapeños, and tortillas) are imported—interestingly enough, from the U.S. Daily 8am to 2am. Inkılap Cad. 8, Çeşme. © 0232/712-0696. Closed Nov–Feb.

Wine Plaza   This is a sophisticated favorite for a relaxing evening. The Wine Plaza occupies a 150-year-old house reconstructed completely from ruins. The exterior is characteristic of old Greek houses, while the interior is decorated with warm Mediterranean blues, peaches, and lavenders. An upstairs room and outdoor terrace offer cozy options to the ground-floor bar area. The wine menu is heavy on selections from Kavaklıdere and Sevilen, but includes some homemade selections. Food includes various Italian-influenced and Chilean dishes, as well as a house *kebap* (appetizers and main courses 4YTL–11YTL/$3–$8; MasterCard and Visa accepted). Musicians perform Wednesday through Saturday beginning at 10:30pm. Daily noon to midnight. Inkılap Cad. 27, Tarihi Kilise Karşısı Çarşısı. © 0232/712-0958.

3 Selçuk ★★

81km (50 miles) south of İzmir; 20km (12 miles) northeast of Kuşadası

Nobody comes to Turkey to visit poor overlooked Selçuk, relegated since ancient times to a secondary position in the shadow of Ephesus, its more illustrious neighbor. But the histories of the two cities are forever intertwined; Selçuk pre-dates Ephesus, and indeed, Selçuk *was* Ephesus.

The rise and fall of Selçuk/Ephesus, which for the purposes of this chapter refers to the combined area between and including present-day Selçuk and Mount Koressos (Bülbül Dağı; where the remains of the original city wall still stand), was directly related to the ebbs and flows of the sea. In the 7th century B.C., Cimmerian invasions relegated the Ephesians to the area around the Artemesian, at the base of Ayasoluk Hill. (Selçuk's castle occupies this hill.) Because the neighborhood of the Artemesian lies below sea level, archaeologists have been unable as of yet to excavate beyond the temple's remains. When, with the death of Alexander the Great, General Lysimachos took control of the whole of Ionia, the city of Ephesus was reestablished adjacent to the harbor. The expansion of Christianity in the 4th century A.D. saw the construction of many important religious and state buildings in Ephesus, including the castle on Ayasoluk Hill and of St. John's Basilica. The silting up of the harbor resulted in the gradual decline of Ephesus as a major commercial port, leaving it vulnerable to subsequent invasions, namely the arrival of the Selçuks in the 10th century.

Today a visit to Selçuk seems only to be a necessary sidebar to the main attraction at Ephesus, just 3km (1¾ miles) away. Nevertheless, the presence of a number of noteworthy ruins, including the representative remains of one of the Seven Wonders of the World; the nearby winemaking village of Şirince, the whole of which has been declared a historic preservation site; and a beautiful stretch of beach just minutes to the west, make Selçuk a perfect base for a well-rounded holiday.

ESSENTIALS
GETTING THERE
BY PLANE   Daily nonstop flights to nearby İzmir's Adnan Menderes Airport, Havalimanı Basmüdürlügü (© 0232/274-2424 or 0232/251-1098), arrive from Istanbul and Ankara, as well as direct from some European and Middle Eastern cities. From the airport, the bus is the easiest and most economical way to get in to town, leaving from the airport terminal every half-hour. Visitors bound for the Kalehan may want to take advantage of the 101YTL ($75) airport transfer.

BY BUS Long-distance buses from points within Turkey arrive at Selçuk's *otogar* opposite the park to the east side of Atatürk Caddesi. A simple inquisitive *"Selçuk otogar?"* directed at your bus *muavin* (driver's assistant) when you board will help you to know when you've arrived. Some long-distance buses simply dump passengers off along the main road through town in front of a small grocery; if it's late at night and there's no taxi, ask somebody inside to make a call for you. (*Note:* If you're staying at the Kalehan, ask the driver to let you off at the entrance, which is also on the main road.) Alternatively, the comfort of a taxi will run you about 47YTL ($35) for the half-hour journey from İzmir's airport. Travelers with more time to spare may choose to arrive by train, a reasonable decision at least if you're coming from İzmir.

VISITOR INFORMATION

The Tourist Information office (© **0232/892-1328**), located on the park across from the Ephesus Museum, provides free maps (and a better one for sale), as well as books on topics of local interest.

ORIENTATION

Bisecting the city of Selçuk is **Atatürk Caddesi,** which runs roughly north to south, and which doubles as the highway to İzmir once you leave the center of town. The tourist attractions are all within walking distance to the west of Atatürk Caddesi, with the castle crowning the summit of **Ayasoluk Hill.** Midway down the hill to the south are the Isabey Mosque and St. John's Basilica, both accessible via **St. Jean's Sokağı.** The train station, good for excursions to İzmir, Aphrodisias, and Denizli, near Pamukkale, is located on the eastern side of town near the end of **Cengiz Topel Caddesi** (the eastern continuation of St. Jean's Sokağı to the west). This end of town acts as the hub of Selçuk's shopping and business center, with a good concentration of banks, Internet cafes, *kebap* houses, and tea gardens.

A green park in the center of town on the west side of Atatürk Caddesi hosts the Tourist Information office; on the west side of the park is the Ephesus Museum. The road to Kuşadası heads west from the *otogar,* passing the Gendarmerie and the Artemision on the way past the turnoff for Ephesus.

GETTING AROUND

Selçuk is a pedestrian city and all of its sights are situated within a relatively small area. Taxis are available for quick hops from one end of town to the other (from the *otogar* to the Kalehan with luggage, for example) and for transportation to Ephesus, Mary's house, and the Cave of the Seven Sleepers. *Dolmuşes* leaving from Selçuk's *otogar* pass by Ephesus's Lower Gate, leaving you about .8km (½ mile) up the road.

WHAT TO SEE & DO

Ephesus Museum (Efes Müzesi) ⭐⭐⭐ The wealth of archaeological findings from the ancient city of Ephesus makes this museum one of the most important in Turkey. As in the case of many other groundbreaking sites, the first excavations were the result of a British railway engineer moonlighting as a scientist and gold digger. The British Museum became the beneficiary of the earliest artifacts, while a later Austrian expedition provided a good amount of fodder for the Kunsthistorisches Museum of Vienna. Some of the treasures actually found their way to the archaeology museums in Istanbul and İzmir, until after World War I when Turkish sovereignty was established and the Municipality retained the artifacts in a newly constructed warehouse in the center of Selçuk. By the 1970s the warehouse was bursting at the seams with a startling collection of recovered items, and an expanded and renovated warehouse morphed into the reputable institution that you see today. The museum rooms are stocked full of treasures excavated at Ephesus, so that no visit to the ancient city would be complete without a walk through here. Plan on about 90 minutes for the museum, a visit that will be made that much more rewarding *after* you've gained a point of reference over at Ephesus.

The exhibit opens with the Roman Period House Finds Room, displaying items recovered during excavations of the terraced houses of Ephesus's entitled class. Here you'll find examples of household items, including the bronze statue *Eros with the Dolphin* ★★ from a 2nd-century fountain, a 3rd-century fresco of Socrates, and finally the inspiration for all of those cheesy souvenir-shop models, the original statue of **Bes** ★★ attached to his exaggerated uncircumcised erect penis. Contrary to popular thought, Bes, actually of Egyptian origin, was not the god of the brothel, but the protector of everything associated with motherhood and childbearing. A faded fresco of Socrates recovered from one of the homes indicates the importance of philosophy in the daily life of the citizens.

During the Roman Empire, Ephesus housed an important school of medicine; here you'll also find a collection of medical and cosmetic tools (two inseparable sciences at the time) along with a wall of portraits of several famous Ephesian physicians.

Recovered from several monumental fountains are a beautiful representation of a headless **Aphrodite** ★ and a bodiless head of **Zeus** ★ dating to the 1st century A.D. Nearby is a narration of **Polyphemus**'s ★★ mythological attempt on Odysseus's life. From the Fountain of Trajan are a statue of a youthful **Dionysus with a satyr** ★, and additional statues of **Dionysus with members of the imperial family** ★. The list goes on and on. Among the mind-boggling treasures displayed in the museum, keep an eye out for the **Ivory Frieze** ★★★, discovered in an upper story of one of the Terraced Houses, which depicts the emperor Trajan and his Roman soldiers in battle against "the barbarians."

Many monumental artifacts are displayed in the **courtyards** ★★, including the **pediment** ★★★ from the Temple of Augustus (Isis Temple), reassembled with statues that had been moved to the pool of the Fountain of Pollio after the destruction of the temple; the **Sarcophagus with Muses** ★, dating to the 3rd century A.D.; and the **Ephesus Monument** ★, inscribed with the Customs regulations as issued by Emperor Nero in A.D. 62 and detailing the process of tax collection, typically undertaken by a third party, rather than as a state activity.

One of the most impressive and illuminating sections in the museum is dedicated to the mother goddess and dominated by two **colossal statues of Artemis** ★★★. Both statues are represented with rows of bull testicles, previously thought to be breasts or eggs, but all symbolically related to the idea of fertility.

The final exhibit contains numerous sculptures from Roman times, mostly overshadowed by a **frieze** ★★★ recovered from the Temple of Hadrian (sections of which are in Vienna). The frieze narrates the founding of Ephesus, the birth of the cult of Artemis, and the flight of the Amazons.

On the edge of the park near the intersection of Atatürk Cad., opposite the Tourist Information office. ☎ 0232/892-6010. Admission 4YTL ($3). Daily 8:30am–6pm.

Isabey Mosque   Built in 1375 at the direction of the Emir of Aydın and using columns and stones recycled from the ruins of Ephesus and Artemision, the Isabey Mosque is a classic example of Selçuk architecture. It is also the oldest known example of a Turkish mosque with a courtyard. It is fitting that Isabey translates into "Jesus," as the structure owes its existence to the temples of other religions, and possibly testifies to the religious tolerance exhibited by the Selçuk Turks.

Exit the basilica entrance and turn right. Free admission. Dawn–dusk.

St. John's Basilica ✸✸✸   After the death of Christ, St. John came with Mary to Ephesus, living most of his life in and around Ayasoluk Hill and spreading the word of Christianity as St. Paul did before him. John's grave was marked by a memorial, which was enclosed by a church of modest proportions in the 4th century. During the reign of Justinian, the emperor had a magnificent domed basilica constructed on the site. The tomb of St. John located under the main central dome elevated the site to one of the most sacred destinations in the Middle Ages. With the decline in importance of Ephesus and after repeated Arab raids, the basilica fell into ruins until the Selçuk Aydınoğlu clan converted it into a mosque in 1330. The building was completely destroyed in 1402 by Tamerlane's Mongol army.

The current entrance leads into the basilica through (or near) the southern transept. Originally, entry was through the oversize exterior courtyard atrium to the west of the nave, which led worshippers through the narthex and finally into the far end of the nave. The basilica had six domes.

The brick foundations and marble walls have been partially reconstructed; if they were fully restored, the cathedral would be the seventh largest in the world. More recent excavations east of the apse have revealed a baptistery and central pool, along with an attached chapel covered in frescoes depicting the saints.

Follow signs from Atatürk Cad.; the ruins are visible from the main road. Admission 4YTL ($3). Daily 8:30am–4:30pm; closes later in summer.

Şirince ✸✸ *(Finds*   Located on a hillside surrounded by apple and grape orchards is the neighboring village of Şirince. Originally settled by Greeks, the village was inhabited by the Ephesian Christians, who, displaced during the Selçuk conquests, moved up into the surrounding hills. In the Greek exchanges of 1924, Muslims from Salonica resettled here, creating a farming community highly adept at winemaking. Apple wine is a local specialty, particularly refreshing when sipped at **Artemis,** an old, restored schoolhouse converted into a wine house and terrace restaurant (on the left as you enter the village; ✆ **0232/898-3240**). Several years ago a couple of Turkish journalists and entrepreneurs restored several of the village's houses, which now rent out as guesthouses (see "Where to Stay" below). A few native villagers followed suit. Despite these developments, and because the entire village has been declared a historic preservation site, it's unlikely that the essential character of the village will change anytime soon—chickens still have the right of way on these pockmarked cobbled lanes.

By day, the village attracts tour buses and aggressive lace-peddling fiends. By night, however, the village settles down, the candles get lit, and several restaurants and wine houses open up.

6.5km (4 miles) east of Selçuk in the hills (*dolmuş* service departs from the train station every 20 min. 8am–5pm).

The Temple of Artemis (Artemision) ✸   In a marshy basin just on the outskirts of town are the pitiful remains of yet another plundered Wonder of the Ancient World. Rising out of the marsh, a lone surviving column suggests the immensity of the structure, four times as large as the Parthenon and the first monumental building to be entirely constructed of marble. As an illustration of its immensity, consider that the one remaining column stands an incredible 4m (13 ft.) *below* the point of the architrave. This ancient temple, built around 650 B.C. to the cult of Artemis, was constructed on a site considered to be sacred to the Mother Goddess, Kybele.

In 356 B.C. (the year Alexander the Great was born), a psychopathic arsonist intent on immortality set fire to the temple. Twenty-two years later, during his sweep through Asia Minor, Alexander the Great offered to reconstruct the temple. In a famous refusal related by Strabo, the Ephesians thought it unfitting for one god to build a temple to another god. The temple was eventually rebuilt remaining true to the original except for a raised platform, a feature of classical architecture adopted in the construction of later temples. By A.D. 263, the temple had been plundered by Nero and destroyed by the Goths. The temple was reconstructed in the 4th century, but the strengthening of Christianity condemned the structure to that of a marble quarry for St. John's Basilica and the Ayasofya in Istanbul. The site is best appreciated in the summer months, when the marshy waters are at their lowest, and the foundations of previous structures are recognizable.

Entrance off the road to Kuşadası, just past the Jandarma on the right, and a short walk out of town. No phone. Free admission. Daily 8:30am–5:30pm.

WHERE TO STAY

Given that Selçuk makes the perfect base for visits to Ephesus, and given that almost everyone who comes to Turkey passes through Ephesus, it's odd that there aren't more high-quality places to stay. Two nearby alternatives to Selçuk are Şirince, a pastoral village in the hills and Pamucak, a moderately developed beach town 10 minutes west of Selçuk. (In Pamucak try the beachfront **Richmond Hotel,** © **0232/893-1060;** fax 0232/893-1054; www.richmondhotels.com.) Also, **Garden Camping** (Kale Altı 4; © **0232/892-6165;** see "Where to Dine" below) added some hotel rooms to the camping facility, which are comfortable and squeaky clean.

SELÇUK

Hitit Hotel and Restaurant *Kids*   A four-star hotel is a bit unexpected in this homey little town of Selçuk, but somebody's got to accommodate all of the tour buses and visiting pilgrims passing through town. The Hitit Hotel does it sensibly, although the superimposition of black lacquer and Ottoman accents creates a bit of a style dilemma. Common areas tend to be a bit sterile, but the advantages of this are glaring in the public restrooms. A small balcony connects rooms with the countryside beyond, and rooms are pleasingly modern and accommodating, with the added bonuses of satellite TV and hair dryers. The outdoor swimming pool occupies a panoramic hill opposite the castle.

Tariş Yanı–Şarapçı Kuyu Mevki P.K. 66, 35920 Selçuk. © **0232/892-6920.** Fax 0232/892-2490. www.hititotel.com. 96 units (all with bathtub). 49€ ($60) double; 82€ ($100) suite. AE, MC, V. Free on-site parking. **Amenities:** Restaurant; 3 bars; outdoor swimming pool; shopping arcade; 24-hr. room service; laundry service; dry cleaning. *In room:* A/C, satellite TV, minibar, hair dryer.

Homeros *Value*   Homeros is essentially a backpacker pension for a young crowd; however, I include it because of the four "new" rooms and the addition of in-room bathrooms in four more. The second level of the more recent acquisition has been embellished with antique porcelain lamps and interesting old furniture, with a communal outdoor sitting "room." Homeros is also notable for its friendly rooftop terrace and family-style *şark* where Derviş's mother prepares delectable home-cooked meals, served with wine made nearby. Derviş, the young owner, likes to make his home as hospitable as possible, so expect him to slip you a nargile or glass of tea, or provide you with a free ride to Ephesus. (You can also take a bike.)

Atatürk Mah. Asmalı Sok. 17, 35920 Selçuk. © 0232/892-3995. www.homerospension.com. 12 units, 8 with bathroom. 16€ ($19) per person in room with bathroom; 12€ ($15) in room with use of shared bathroom. Breakfast 3€ ($3.50). No credit cards. Phone from the *otogar* and Derviş will pick you up. **Amenities:** Bicycles free for guests; laundry; Internet. *In room:* A/C.

Hotel Kalehan ⊛   Located just below Selçuk's castle and St. John's Basilica, the Hotel Kalehan consists of two stately stone buildings separated by a narrow trellised lane, with the rear building standing at the back of a lush, carefully tended English-style garden. The gardens enclose a raised pool area and contain wrought-iron settees, wooden lawn chairs, and the odd cartwheel for fun. Owners Ayse and Hakan, a brother-and-sister team, are avid collectors of antiques and have filled the inn with period furniture. Rooms are modest but lovely, in a monastic sort of way, and what they lack in luxury they certainly make up for in atmosphere. Recent upgrades include new mattresses in most of the rooms; special rooms are now outfitted with minibars, bathrobes, and the odd extra toiletry. The inn has a lovely rustic restaurant; the menu reflects Turkey's Mediterranean cuisine and takes advantage of the organic garden out back.

İzmir Cad., 35920 Selçuk (on the main road below the castle next to the Sunoco station). © 0232/892-6154. Fax 0232/892-2169. www.kalehan.com. 55 units (all with shower). 46€–69€ ($56–$84) double; 66€–99€ ($80–$120) special rooms. MC, V. Free parking on-site. **Amenities:** Restaurant; bar; outdoor swimming pool; boutique. *In room:* A/C, local TV, fridge.

Hotel Nilya   Owned and operated by a Turkish couple, the Hotel Nilya, located on a side street in Old Town, is easy to mistake for a private home. An imposing door with a brass plate opens onto a stone courtyard with a central fountain. Not so much as a particle of dust clutters up each room's minimalist atmosphere, where a kilim and striped cotton *hamam* (Turkish bath) cloth bedspread are the only embellishments. Spartan, too, are the bathrooms, with open shower stalls. The one "suite" is decorated a little more, and enjoys glorious sunset views, which can also be seen from the upper level outdoor lounge. The American-style kitchen is wide open to the richly furnished dining room, full of period furniture and colorful geometric-patterned kilims. The owners don't speak much English, but lots of gesturing, a peek at the calculator, and a bit of high school French will do you just fine.

1051 Sok. 7, 35920 Selçuk. © 0232/892-9081. Fax 0232/892-9080. www.nilya.com. 11 units. 33€ ($40) single; 53€ ($65) double; suite 82€ ($100). MC, V. Street parking only. Closed Nov–Mar. *In room:* A/C, no phone.

ŞIRINCE

Nişanyan Evleri ⊛⊛ *Finds*   These renovated houses at the top of Şirince's hillside offer total immersion into the daily rhythm of the village life. At the upper edge of the hillside is main Köşk (pavilion), which contains the reception area and five smartly decorated rooms with nouveau Hellenistic frescoes, fresh tubs/showers, and antique furniture. Three restored houses, standing in sharp contrast to their humbler neighbors, are accessed by a stone staircase, terraced below the Köşk. Each house sleeps a minimum of two, but can comfortably accommodate four or a maximum of six people. (Rates increase with each added person.) One features a private *hamam,* another has a semi-enclosed stone veranda, and the third contains a raised platform, canopied bed—great for the kids. A hamper overflowing with fresh eggs, village butter, jam, cheese, and bread is delivered to each house daily, saving guests the steep climb down the hillside to fetch the most basic provisions. Nişanyan also recently added a pension, where double rooms cost 48€ ($59).

Şirince (6.5km/4 miles from Selçuk and 11km/7 miles from Ephesus; watch for signs on the right before entering the village, leading to a new dirt road that stops at the main house). ℂ **0232/898-3209**. Fax 0232/898-3118. www.nisanyan.com. 3 self-catering houses and 1 house with 5 rooms. 194€ ($236) double in self-catering house, 93€–107€ ($113–$130) double in hotel. MC, V.

WHERE TO DINE

There are few restaurants in Selçuk, and just because they display the trademark of international travel guides doesn't necessarily ensure that the food will be good, or even fresh. (Be particularly wary of the mezes in the lovely garden restaurants near the train.) A good concentration of humble *kebap* houses and home-style *lokantas* (a simple eatery with pre-prepared food), many with outdoor tables, can be found in the area between the train station and Atatürk Caddesi. A safe bet is to eat at your hotel or pension, where a constant stream of guests will at least ensure fresh food and at the most, a fabulous meal prepared by the hands of someone's genius mother. If you've got wheels, head up to Şirince (see "What to See & Do" above for info).

Garden Camping and Restaurant TURKISH Set amid the peaceful green lawns of what is actually a campground, this is Selçuk's best-kept secret. A breezy outdoor garden encircles a pavilion in the shape of an Asian cone hat, with the requisite countryside trout pond for the freshest of fresh fish. All the vegetables are organically grown on the grounds, and the resulting mezes are simply divine. The stuffed grape leaves, flavored with just a hint of fresh mint, are among the best I have ever eaten, as are the crispy cheese-filled *börek*. Not many people make it into the orange groves behind the castle, so don't be put off by the absence of other guests.

Kale Altı 4 (take the road that circles behind the castle). ℂ **0232/892-6165**. Appetizers and entrees 5.50YTL–11YTL ($4–$8). MC, V. Daily 8am–11pm. The kitchen is often closed during slow seasons, so call ahead.

4 Ephesus ★★★

3km (1¾ miles) south of Selçuk

A highlight of any visit to Turkey, Ephesus is one of the best-preserved ancient cities on the Mediterranean and a major player in the birth and evolution of Christianity. Allot at least a half-day for just an overview of the archaeological site and a full day for a comprehensive visit. In the heat of the summer, it's best to avoid the midday sun when the reflection off the stones becomes unbearable.

The ancient city of Ephesus extends beyond the confines of the museum gates, and heartier (and well-watered) types can be seen walking single-file along the road between the Main Gate and the Cave of the Seven Sleepers. Meryemana is about 7km (4⅓ miles) up the hill from the Upper Gate, and therefore (at least for me) too far to walk.

A LOOK AT THE PAST

Numerous legends have been attached to the founding of Ephesus, some saying the Amazons, the Lelegians, or the Carians got here first. A favorite myth attributed to the Ionians—who had arrived here by the 10th century B.C.—says that Androclus, guided by the prophesies of an oracle regarding some fish and a wild boar, founded the city.

There must be some truth behind the legend of Croesus, king of Lydia, who upon hearing of the prosperity of the trading capital, decided it had to be his. The city fell under the sovereignty of Lydia in the 6th century B.C. and the Ephesians were displaced to the area around the Artemesian.

A century later, the city was once again the target of an empire, with the invasion of the Persians. For the most part absentee administrators, the Persians were subsequently thrown out by an Ionian uprising in the 5th century B.C., remaining in power until Alexander the Great's arrival. After his death, one of his generals, Lysimachos, reestablished the city between the slopes of Mount Koressos (Bülbüldağ) and Mount Pion (Panayır Dağı), and constructed the city's first fortifications, a defensive wall with a perimeter of 9km (5½ miles). The ruins of the archaeological site of Ephesus date to the city established at this time.

In the 2nd century B.C., the city reached its height as the most important port in Anatolia, and subsequent kings of Pergamum ruled here until the city was absorbed by Rome. The city opened up lucrative commercial opportunities with the exotic Middle East and it wasn't long before Ephesus was designated the capital of the Asian Provinces, attracting the likes of Brutus, Cassius, Antony, and Cicero. Under Julius Caesar, Ephesus was forced to submit to heavy taxation, but under Augustus's reign, the city of Ephesus once again became the most important commercial center on the Mediterranean. The final episode in the ebb and flow of Ephesus's prosperity came during the remarkable proliferation of Christianity, continuing through the rule of Justinian (6th c. A.D.). Many buildings of importance, including the castle on Ayasoluk Hill, date to this period.

Nevertheless, during as far back as Roman times, the port had begun to show signs of silting up, and any attempts at halting the process had proved unsuccessful. After centuries of sand and dirt depositing in the harbor, the port was little more than a marsh, and the citizens of Ephesus, by now an insignificant village under Selçuk control, moved farther inland. The swamp at the end of the Arcadian Way (Harbour Rd.) was once at the water's edge; it's now 5km (3 miles) inland.

GETTING THERE

Unless you're booked on a tour where transfers are included, you'll need to base yourself in Selçuk, and as well you should because some significant findings related to the ancient city of Ephesus are found there. For those who've planned on tackling this daunting historic site alone, it's important to keep in mind the logistics of a visit. Ephesus is built on the slopes of Panayır Dağı (Mt. Pion), with the state and religious buildings at the highest point and the public facilities, including the baths, theater, and Agora, down below. Obviously, it will be easier to visit the site on a downhill trajectory, so my advice would be to enter at the upper or Magnesia Gate and exit at the Lower Gate (the one nearest the turnoff from Selçuk).

From the entrance to the farthest point, the Vedius Gymnasium, it's a little over 1.6km (a mile), so if you've arrived by private car, you'll need to either backtrack the full distance or take a cab back to where you entered. (There are parking lots at both the Upper and Lower gates; the Upper Gate is private, and a nominal parking fee applies.) A taxi between the two gates costs around 8YTL ($6). A taxi from Selçuk to the site runs about 5.50YTL ($4) and as much as 20YTL ($15) for the ride up the hill to Meryemana. It's possible to grab a *dolmuş* from Selçuk; take the one headed for Meryemana and get off at the Upper Gate.

Of course, you can also book a tour, during which comfortable minibuses will shuttle you stress-free from site to site. Tours generally visit the House of the Virgin Mary, St. John's Basilica, the Ephesus Museum, and the Temple of Artemis. Lunch at

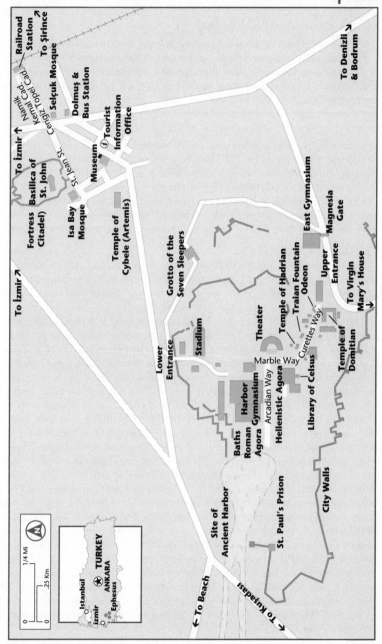

Ephesus

Railroad Station

To Şirince

To İzmir

Namık Kemal Cad.

Cengiz Topel Cad.

Selçuk Mosque

Dolmuş & Bus Station

To Denizli & Bodrum

Tourist Information Office

St. Jean St.

Museum

Basilica of St. John

Fortress (Citadel)

Isa Bay Mosque

Temple of Cybele (Artemis)

To İzmir

Grotto of the Seven Sleepers

East Gymnasium

Magnesia Gate

Temple of Hadrian

Trajan Fountain

Odeon

Upper Entrance

To Virgin Mary's House

Lower Entrance

Stadium

Theater

Curettes Way

Temple of Domitian

Marble Way

Harbor Gymnasium

Hellenistic Agora

Library of Celsus

Baths

Roman Agora

Arcadian Way

City Walls

Site of Ancient Harbor

St. Paul's Prison

To Beach

To Kuşadası

N

1/4 Mi

.25 Km

0

TURKEY

ANKARA

Ephesus

İstanbul

İzmir

209

Tips **Recommended Reading**

If you want a thorough and detailed explanation of Ephesus, complete with diagrams, maps, and photographs, go armed with Ekrem Akurgal's *Ancient Civilizations and Ruins of Turkey* (Net Turistik, 2001), available in bookstores in Turkey or through Net Turistik Yayinlar San. Tic. A.Ş. (© **0212/516-3228;** fax 0212/516-8468).

---

an adequate cafeteria-style restaurant is usually included. The day costs around 74YTL ($55) per person or up to 216YTL ($160) for a one-on-one. I recommend either booking a day tour before you go (see "Package Tours & Escorted Tours" in chapter 2) or joining one of the tour companies from the nearby towns of İzmir and Kuşadası.

It's absolutely possible to book a last-minute tour in Selçuk through one of the gazillions of local shops touting day tours to Ephesus, but these usually walk the trodden path through the center of the site, leaving some of the fringe attractions unexplored.

EXPLORING THE SITES

The Archaeological Site of Ephesus (Efes) ⭐⭐⭐   Second only to Pompeii, a visit to Ephesus is as good an introduction as one can get to ancient Roman civilization. Almost as astonishing as the site itself is that only 20% of the ancient city has been excavated.

The visit begins inside the Upper Entrance and basically follows a straight trajectory through the ancient city. You can get a fairly decent overview of the site by following the main street, but with so much of interest located in toppled buildings lining the route, you will definitely want to scramble around a bit to get a closer look. Plan on at least 2 hours for the basic overview, and double that if you're planning to really absorb all of the main sites. Add another 30 to 45 minutes in the Terraced Houses, and still more time if you're dedicated enough to trample through every last weed to the "secondary" sites off the main street. If you're visiting during the heat of the summer, begin as early as the ticket gates will allow, and bring bottled water and perhaps a snack. There are no public toilets inside the museum, so avail yourself before entering, preferably in one of the on-site restaurants, rather than in one of the overpriced and underserviced public restrooms outside the site.

Inside the entrance immediately off to the right is the **East Gymnasium** and what's left of the **Magnesia Gate,** built by Emperor Vespasian. Rather than tap into your reserves this early in the game, head straight to the **Upper Agora** ⭐⭐, specifically to the **Odeon.** To provide some context for your visit, the Upper Agora, also known as the State Agora, was the administrative center of the city and was constructed between the reigns of Augustus and Claudius. The foundations of an early temple dedicated to the goddess Isis indicate that the site was also used for religious ceremonies. Clustered around the State Agora were the **Various Baths,** attributed to Flavius Damianus. To the south of the Agora is a monumental **Fountain,** which was fed by the River Marnas (now, Dervent), via an aqueduct about 5km (3 miles) east of Ephesus.

The **Odeon** ⭐⭐, also known as the Small Theatre, functioned as a *bouleuterion* (place for meetings of the boule, or council), although it's reasonable to believe that it served as a venue for concerts and theatrical performances as well. The structure was built in the 2nd century A.D. by Publius Vedius Antoninus, according to an inscription, and was probably covered. To the north are the remains of a covered arcade, converted, according to an inscription found on an architrave, into a **Basilica** ✵ during the reign of Augustus. Excavations beneath the basilica have revealed a single-aisle colonnade. The juxtaposition of the Basilica next to the Prytaneum (see below) and Odeon lead historians to believe that even the basilica, in addition to religious purposes, held some state function. Next to the Odeon are the ruins of the **Prytaneum** ✵ or Town Hall, constructed by Lysimachos along with the **Altar of Hestia Boulaia** ✵, upon which burned an eternal sacred flame. The two famous statues of Artemis now on exhibit in the Ephesus Museum (in Selçuk) were found in this building. Part of the Prytaneum was scavenged in the 3rd century A.D. by a woman named Scholastikia, for building materials for her baths (see below).

At the corner of **Domitian Square** ✵✵ is an edifice referred to by archaeologists as the **Socle Structure,** and whose function is unknown. Just to the right of this is the **Pollio Fountain** ✵. The original structure was built in honor of C. Sextilius Pollio, architect of the Marnas Aqueduct; however, the fountain was actually added to the monument at a later date. Built in 97 B.C., the monument was ornamented with statues of the head of Zeus and the torso of Aphrodite, as well as the Polyphemos group of statues, narrating the story of Odysseus, now in the Ephesus Museum. At the far end of Domitian Street (below the southwest corner of the State Agora) is another **fountain,** built in A.D. 80 by Laecanius Bassus.

The **Temple of Domitian** ✵, the first temple of Ephesus built in honor of an emperor (A.D. 81–96) is located next to the Domitian Square. Not much remains of the temple, and what little information is available comes from the ruins of the foundation. A colossal statue of Domitian, 5m (16 ft.) high in a seated position, 7m (23 ft.) if you include the base, was the altar centerpiece in a *cella* only 9m×21m (30 ft.×70 ft.). Remains of this statue can be seen in the Ephesus Museum, while the head is on display in the İzmir Archaeological Museum (p. 189).

The **Museum of Inscriptions** takes up the underground substructure of the temple, and contains a collection of stone and marble tablets that provides a rich historical record of the official decrees, state rulings, bureaucratic matters, and civil punishments. The museum is closed more often than not, providing visitors with a good excuse to skip it altogether.

At the junction to the right stand the remains of the **Monument of Memmius** ✵, built in the 1st century B.C. in honor of the grandson of the dictator Cornelius Sulla. The figures are those of Memmius, his father Caicus, and Sulla. Next to and opposite the Monument of Memmius are two fountains: One is semicircular with a long narrow rectangular pool; the one opposite was brought here from another part of the city in the 4th century. It is decorated with garlands and a **winged Nike** ✵.

Leading away from the Upper Agora down a gently sloping street pockmarked by thousands of pounding hoofs is the famous **Curettes Way** ✵✵✵. In mythology, Curettes were demigods, a name later used by the Ephesians to designate a class of priests at first dedicated to the cult of Artemis. In Roman times, the Curettes held a place in the Prytaneum. The main thoroughfare is paved with stone and marble remnants recycled from other parts of the city, added after a 4th-century earthquake; valuable architectural elements like Doric columns and ornamental capitals are now part of the city's foundations.

About halfway down Curettes Way and blocking access to the aristocratic reaches of the Upper Agora is the **Gate of Hercules** ✵✵. Two of the columns show Hercules wrapped in lion skin.

Immediately on the right is the two-story **Trajan's Fountain** ☆☆, the point at which the star-studded section of the tour begins. Many visitors peter out because they've already spent a good portion of their time and energy before arriving at this point, so if you're resigned to the fact that you can't see everything, this is where you should begin the serious part of your tour, after having had a peek at the Odeon. Trajan's Fountain was built in the emperor's honor at the beginning of the 2nd century. The ruins have been partially restored, although only the base and a fragment of the Trajan's foot have been recovered. The fountain was decorated with statues of Dionysus, a Satyr, Aphrodite, and others, now on exhibit in the Ephesus Museum.

Located after the Trajan Fountain and running perpendicular to Curettes Way past the Baths of Scholastikia is another street, paved in some places with marble slabs. The portion leading above the theater has been excavated.

The second sacred building dedicated to a ruling emperor was the **Temple of Hadrian** ☆☆☆, one of the main attractions at Ephesus, marketed in tourist brochures almost as much as the Celsus Library. The Corinthian temple consists of a main chamber and a monumental porch; an inscription on the architrave of the porch facade indicates that the temple was dedicated to the emperor by somebody named P. Quintilius. Ornamenting the semicircular arch that rests on the two inner columns of the porch facade is a bust of the goddess **Tych,** protectress of the city. In the **entablature** ☆☆ over the main portal is a carving of a woman; some interpretations identify the figure as Medusa, symbolically keeping the evil spirits away. The temple was partially destroyed in A.D. 400, and it was during the course of restorations that the four **decorative reliefs** ☆☆ were added to the lintels of the interior of the porch. (The ones in place today are plaster casts of originals now on exhibit in the Ephesus Museum.) The first three panels from the left depict the mythological foundation of Ephesus, and show representations of Androklos chasing a boar, gods with Amazons, and Amazons in a procession. The fourth panel is unrelated and shows Athena, Apollo, Androklos, Heracles, Emperor Theodosius, Artemis Ephesia, and several other historical and mythological figures.

The bases in front of the porch facade are inscribed with the names of Galerius, Maximianus, Diocletianus, and Constantius Chlorus, indicating that at one time, the bases supported statues of these emperors.

Behind the Temple of Hadrian via a stone staircase are the remains of the **Baths of Scholastikia** ☆☆☆, constructed at the end of the 1st century and named after a rich Ephesian woman who enlarged them in the 4th. There were two entrances to the baths leading into a large main hall with niches; in one of these niches is the restored **statue of Scholastikia** ☆, in its original position. During the 4th-century renovations, the original **mosaic floor** was covered over with marble slabs; some of these can be seen beneath the level of the current floor.

The original building phase of the baths included the construction of the adjacent **brothel** and the public toilets, which allowed a bit of discreet philandering.

Bizarre in its utility, the **Public Latrine** ☆ provides more of a mental image into our humbler functions than one really needs. Men would sit side by side on these narrow stone benches above open troughs hidden under their robes and discuss current events as their waste washed away beneath them. A fountain occupies the center of the atrium, where running water would drown out the, well, sounds.

On the opposite side of Curettes Way is a colonnaded street flanked by a row of 12 shops and covered in **mosaic floor** ☆☆☆ decorated with geometric patterns. The colonnade dates to the 1st century A.D.; however, the mosaics only date to the 5th century A.D. Staircases in several of the shops indicate the existence of an upper floor, probably used as sleeping quarters for employees.

However you prioritize your time at the sight, don't miss the **Terraced Houses** ✮✮✮. Set on the hillside of Bülbül Dağı above the shops are five multichambered peristyle houses that have been uncovered in ongoing excavations. Since excavations of the site are ongoing, access is not guaranteed, so try to coax the caretaker to walk you through, and remember to tip. A separate ticket for entry is required (15YTL/$11). (***Note to visitors with physical limitations:*** As terraced housing, access is via large exterior or interior stairways, making a visit to this exhibit somewhat challenging.)

The houses were inhabited from the 1st to the 7th centuries by the richest members of society and frequently remodeled. All of the houses had running water, sophisticated heating systems, large colonnaded inner courtyards, and rich decor. One had a private basilica. Overwhelmingly they reveal the best craftsmanship the city had to offer, in monumental arched colonnades, well-preserved mosaics, and layer upon layer of frescoes. The course of tourist visits is sure to change in the coming months; but on your way through the marked passage, keep an eye out for the spectacular collection of *in situ* 2nd-century **frescoes and mosaics** ✮✮✮.

As the poster child for Ephesus, the **Library of Celsus** ✮✮✮, whose two-tiered facade reaches us in a remarkable state of preservation, is immediately recognizable. The library was built between A.D. 110 and 135 by the Consul Julius Aquila as a mausoleum for his father, Julius Celsus Polemaeanus, governor of the Asian Provinces, whose remains remain surprisingly intact under the apsidal wall.

Three levels of niches indicate that the building had three stories, the upper two levels accessible via a horseshoe-shaped gallery. Scrolls or books were stored in the rows of niches, and reading materials were dispensed by a librarian.

In the lower niches of the facade are copies of four statues personifying wisdom, knowledge, destiny, and intelligence, the originals having been taken to Vienna. The library was abandoned after a fire of unspecified date destroyed the reading room, and around A.D. 400 the courtyard below the exterior steps was converted into a pool. The facade collapsed in an earthquake in the 10th century, but was restored and re-erected by F. Hueber of the Austrian Archaeological Institute between 1970 and 1978.

Back at the top of the steps above the library begins the **Marble Way** ✮✮✮, a 5th-century street paved entirely with—you guessed it—marble. Chariot traffic on the road was high, calling for a raised lateral platform to be built for pedestrians. Carved into the marble at about halfway down the road is the **imprint** of a footprint, a heart, and a portrait of a woman, accepted by historians as an advertisement for the brothel next door. According to the rumor mill, a large underground sewage system running beneath the street—an example of how advanced city engineering was in those days—doubled as a secret passage between the library and the brothel.

The imperial arched **Gate of Mazaeus and Mithridates** ✮✮ to the right of the library was built in 4 or 3 B.C. by two emancipated slaves of Agrippa who, according to an inscription in both Latin and Greek, had the monument erected in honor of Emperor Augustus, his wife Livia, Agrippa, and Agrippa's daughter Julia. The gate, unsuccessfully named the Gate of Augustus, was designed to provide southeastern access to the Lower or **Commercial Agora** ✮✮, a space of almost 120 sq. m (400 sq. ft.) of shops and colonnaded galleries on prime waterfront real estate that is lamentably off-limits indefinitely. The Agora dates to the 3rd century B.C., was expanded and altered by Augustus and Nero, and attained its final form during the reign of

Caracalla. In ongoing excavations, the original foundation of the Agora was discovered about 6m (20 ft.) below current ground level. The middle of the Agora was studded with statues of Ephesian notables, and at the center, a *horologion,* or sundial.

The **Temple of Serapis,** located at the southwestern end of the Agora, is also closed off due to ongoing excavations. The temple was probably built by Egyptian traders, and used as a church during Christian times.

For thespians and laypeople alike, the **Great Theatre** ✸✸✸ is a dramatic spectacle to behold. Built into the slopes of Panayır Dağı (Mt. Pion), the 30m-high (100-ft.) theater (actually, 30m/100 ft. above the level of the orchestra) required 60 years of digging to clear out a space large enough to accommodate 25,000 people, estimated at only one-tenth of the city's population. The theater was begun during the Hellenistic times (some say during the reign of Lysimachos), and was later altered and enlarged by emperors Claudius, Nero, and Trajan. Even more monumentally, St. Paul delivered his sermon condemning pagan worship from the proscenium. Even if you think it'll take an additional 60 years to hoist yourself up the steps to the upper cavea, do so, or you will be missing one of the most stunning views around.

The **Arcadian Way** ✸✸ (or Harbor Rd., also closed for excavation) is the name for the triumphal marble road leading from the harbor to the base of the Great Theatre. At 600m (1,968 ft.), the promenade was flanked by two colonnaded streets paved with mosaics and lined with elegant shops that reflected the prestige of a city of the stature of Ephesus. In fact, in the ancient world, only the wealthiest cities were lit at night, a privilege enjoyed by Ephesus, as well as Rome and Antioch. The **Theatre Gymnasium** is opposite the Great Theatre, at the junction of the Arcadian Way and the Marble Road. Complete with a bathhouse, *palestra* (gymnasium), and classrooms, the Theatre Gymnasium is the largest of its type in Ephesus. You can cut through here to rejoin the path out of the site (this leads to the Lower Entrance); just before reaching the path, turn around to face the theater, and take advantage of one of the best photo ops in the region. If you've still got any blood sugar left in you (and if this portion of the site is open to visitors, which currently it is not), you can wander around the **Verulanus Sports Arena,** the Harbor Gymnasium and Baths, and the Church of the Virgin Mary, located between the path heading out of the site and the old harbor. The arena was built during the reign of Hadrian, and extends all the way to the Harbor Gymnasium, also built at this time.

The **Harbor Gymnasium and Baths** sits at the port end of the Arcadian Way and is the largest building complex in Ephesus. The building of the gymnasium is thought to have taken place during the reign of Domitian while the baths date to Constantine II. The complex has yet to be excavated.

Before exiting the Lower Entrance, follow a path and signs for the **Church of the Virgin Mary (Meryem Kilisesi)** ✸ to the left. Originally, the building was used as a Roman mercantile center, but was converted to a basilica in the 4th century. The church played an important role in the evolution of Christianity, as the first one to take Mary's name, and as the site of two important ecumenical councils in 431 and 449, in which the natures of Christ and of Mary were hotly disputed. It's a little out of the way, especially at this stage in the game, but worth the energy it'll take to trek over here (again, assuming it's not cordoned off).

A well-paved road heading east of the Vedius Gymnasium leads to **The Cave of the Seven Sleepers** ✸, about .8km (½ mile) away. According to the legend, seven young local boys (and a dog, according to one interpretation), refusing to submit to the persecutions of Emperor Decius (A.D. 249–51), fled to these caves with a group of

Roman guards in hot pursuit. In characteristic Roman fashion, the guards mercilessly sealed up the cave, putting an end to yet another heretical episode. When the boys were awakened by an earthquake that also broke the cave's seals, they wandered back into town to buy some bread only to find themselves in the 5th century and 200 years older. Evidently, times had changed and Christianity was now the state religion. After their deaths, the "sleepers" were re-interred in the cave, and it wasn't long before the site became a sacred destination for pilgrimages.

This site, one of the many caves used by Seven Sleepers throughout Anatolia (there are others, located in Akhisar, Manisa, Sardes, Tarsus, and Antakya, to name a few), is actually a grouping of small churches dating to the time of the persecutions, superimposed in the rock and containing crypts carved into the walls. The actual cave site has been fenced off, but remains a draw to die-hard pilgrims. (At the time of this writing, a hole in the fence provided access.)

No phone. Admission to archaeological site 15YTL ($11); admission to Terraced Houses 15YTL ($11) (currently under restoration). Summer daily 8am–6:30pm; winter daily 8am–4:30pm. Follow the road from Selçuk to Kuşadası, turn left following signs for the archaeological site; the official entrance (Lower Entrance) is immediately to the right; follow signs to the Cave of the Seven Sleepers and Meryemana for the Upper Entrance.

The House of the Virgin Mary (Meryemana) ★★★

According to the oral tradition of local villagers of Şirince (or Kirkince, descendants of Christians at Ephesus), Mary finished out her days in this house after migrating to Asia Minor with John. The location was "discovered" in the 19th century by Sister Anna Catherina Emmerich, a German invalid who had never left home. The discovery was in the form of a dream, from which the nun awoke with a stigmata. The site was later found as described and was visited by Popes Paul VI and John Paul II, who both verified its authenticity. The validity of the site is also supported by the oral tradition of the villagers who inhabited the village in the 19th century, as they were descendants of the early Christian inhabitants.

The house is a church nowadays, with the main altar where the kitchen was situated; the right wing was the bedroom. The site, now a national park, is a requisite stop on the itineraries of Christians, Jews, and Muslims alike, and therefore always crowded. In fact, in their religious fervor, pilgrims won't think anything of elbowing you out of the way. If you get there by 7:15am you can participate in the morning Mass (10:30am on Sun); and every year on August 15 there is a Mass celebrating the Assumption.

The park is also home to healing springs said to cure all sorts of ailments. On the way back up the path, make sure to avail yourself of the free and clean WC.

Orman Yolu. Admission to park and house 11YTL ($8). Site parking 8YTL ($6). Dawn–dusk. 7km (4½ miles) southwest of Selçuk; from both the Upper and Lower entrances to Ephesus, follow the signs to Meryemana, which is in a park and nature preserve.

5 Kuşadası

20km (12 miles) southwest of Selçuk; 95km (59 miles) south of İzmir; 220km (136 miles) west of Pamukkale; 151km (94 miles) north of Bodrum

Twenty-five years ago, when Kuşadası was discovered by the yachting set, it was a typically unspoiled community of fishermen and farmers, with barely a dirt road running through it. Have times changed. Far from the village that attracted holiday-seekers in the first place, Kuşadası has built itself up into a frenzy of tourism, leaving much of its original character in the wake of cruise ships full of tourists ready to disgorge the contents of their wallets on jewelry and carpets on their way in and out of Ephesus. Unfortunately, the local businessmen are more than willing to oblige.

On the opposite end of Kuşadası's economic spectrum are the package tourists in from England and middle-class Turks sunning themselves atop concrete hotel blocks in the center of town. The city's redevelopment of the waterfront certainly was a positive improvement, creating a stretch of sandy beach and seafront promenade. But in spite of the city's loss of innocence, the fringes of the city limits and beyond boast some of the most splendid coastline around. And if you're based pool- or beach-side, particularly at one of the hotels listed below, or on a day-boat excursion, it really doesn't matter how overdeveloped the center of town is. If you're looking for a beach holiday and a convenient jumping-off point for a visit to the surrounding archaeological sights, then Kuşadası may be just the right compromise.

A LOOK AT THE PAST

Nobody knows exactly when the city was founded, but at some point the Carians and Lelegians wandered westward from central Anatolia to find the advantages of the fertile soil and a gracious climate. With the arrival of Greeks migrating east from the islands, a historically significant melding of the two cultures occurred, producing philosophers and scholars credited with fundamental contributions to Western thought. The nearby ancient city of Panionian was the annual meeting place of the Ionian League, so when the port of Ephesus dried up, Kuşadası, then called Ania, became a more important trade center. By the 15th century, the city was dominated by Venetian and Genovese merchants and traders who gave the port the name of Scala Nuova.

After the usual parade of conquerors, the Ottomans laid claim to the city, and Kuşadası was given a new look by Öküz Mehmet Paşa, grand vizier under Ahmet I and Osman II. He erected several mosques and a caravansary and rebuilt the Byzantine fortress to secure the shores against attacks from the sea. Known as "Pirate Castle," this fortress was used as a base for the exploits of the pirate Barbarossa in the 16th century. To bolster his presence in the Mediterranean, Sultan Süleyman the Magnificent put Barbarossa in command of the Ottoman fleet against Venice and Genoa, states long covetous of access to the Eastern trade routes.

The Ottomans called the city Kuşadası or "Bird Island," a name that previously referred to the offshore island, referring to its use as a stopover for pigeons during seasonal migrations. The island was renamed Güvercin Ada, or "Pigeon Island," and today is connected to the mainland by a pedestrian causeway lined with fishermen and excursion boat captains. The shady area within the castle walls provides a respite from the blazing heat of the summer sun, and it seems that tea gardens were set in and around the ramparts to take full advantage of the tremendous sunset views of the city.

ESSENTIALS
GETTING THERE

The nearest airport is İzmir's Adnan Menderes Airport, about 97km (60 miles) away. There's no convenient transfer from the airport to Kuşadası (see section 1, "İzmir," earlier in this chapter, for information on transportation out of the airport), and a taxi will run about 95YTL ($70).

Long-distance bus service from Istanbul takes about 9 hours; 10 hours for service from Ankara. Prices vary from 38YTL ($28; Metro; © **0232/472-0222**) to 50YTL ($37; Boss Turizm; from anywhere in Turkey © **0212/444-0880** [number good in all

---

Tips Your Cruise Ship Departure Has _Not_ Been Delayed!

Warning to Cruise Ship Passengers: Unscrupulous carpet sellers have been known to waylay unsuspecting cruise ship passengers into a shop by making them believe that the ship's departure has been delayed. Don't bet on it!

---

area codes in Turkey]) from Ankara. Ulusoy's (✆ **0212/444-1888**) buses from Istanbul and Ankara have the luxury of toilets onboard. Kuşadası Koop (✆ **0256/612-6660**) provides direct service from İzmir (1 hr., 10 min.).

Kuşadası's main *otogar* is located about .8km (½ mile) out of the town center on the main road. From there, local *dolmuşes* run through the town center on the way up the shoreline, with hotels and resorts posted on the windshield. If you don't see your hotel, ask, because not all are listed. On second thought, take a taxi, because most hotel main entrances are at the end of lengthy driveways uphill from the *dolmuş* drop-off point.

Ferries from the Greek island of Samos arrive once daily into the main harbor from May to October (74YTL/$55 one-way, 91YTL/$67 same day return, 124YTL/$92 round-trip with open return ticket; prices 8.25YTL/$6 cheaper for passage originating in Turkey).

VISITOR INFORMATION

The Tourist Information office (✆ **0256/614-1103**) is located across from the main harbor at Iskele Meydanı, within handy reach of disembarking cruise ship passengers. Free maps are available, but I suggest you splurge for the better private map.

For the fastest Internet connection in Turkey and a friendly English-speaking staff, **Kısmet Internet Café** (and jewelry!), Liman Cad. 1 (across from the harbor; ✆ **0256/612-3580**), is equipped with English keyboards, AOL access, and a satellite dish, not to mention views to write home about. Its proximity to the cruise ship docks explains the higher prices—about 2.75YTL ($2) for 15 minutes. Kısmet is open from noon till late daily, but opens earlier when the ships come in.

If hotel laundry prices are getting you down, try dropping off a load in the morning at **Yat Camping,** Atatürk Bulv. 76 (across from the marina; ✆ **0256/614-1333**). Your clothes will be dry by the evening (nothing fancy, though), and all for the celebratory low price of 6.75YTL ($5) a load.

ORIENTATION

The heartbeat of Kuşadası is in the streets around the caravansary (under the Burger King icon on the free map), across from the harbor where the shore roads of **Atatürk Bulvarı** to the north and **Liman Caddesi** to the south converge. The town's commercial thoroughfare, **Barbaros Hayrettin Caddesi,** is a pedestrian mall that heads east into the area of the old bazaar. Turn left at the post office to explore the narrow streets of the old city, lined with restaurants, bars, and souvenir shops.

Just south of the main harbor is **Güvercin Ada,** with its Byzantine fortress; farther south the shore road leads to Ladies' Beach and the National Park, about 20km (12 miles) away.

GETTING AROUND

If the thought of getting on a *dolmuş* was too intimidating in the big city, in Kuşadası it's going to be your best friend. Minibuses run regularly along the shore road into and out of town, as well as south to Ladies' Beach and north to Pygale Beach, all for about 68YKr (50¢) each way.

At 41YTL ($30) a day, a scooter is an exhilarating option. A seaside jaunt up and around the nearby cliffs is a great way to get a feel for the area, and parking is never a problem. You can rent scooters at most car-rental agencies. Countless storefronts up and down Atatürk Bulvarı publicize car rentals at competitive prices. As a backup, you can contact Avis, Atatürk Bulv. 26/A (© **0256/614-4600**), or book your car through a reputable travel agent.

WHAT TO SEE & DO
AREA RUINS
No self-respecting tourist stays in Kuşadası without allotting a day for the ruins of Ephesus (see "Ephesus," earlier in this chapter, for complete information). But many people simply don't leave enough time to explore the other significant sites within easy reach.

The ancient sites of **Miletus, Priene,** and **Didyma** are three of the best-preserved Ionian settlements in Anatolia, and worth an entire day of scrambling down steps and over crumbled ruins. For the highest level of independence and flexibility, I recommend that you rent a car; at as low as 68YTL ($50) per day, the cost is actually less than hiring a taxi to do the same circuit. From Kuşadası, follow signs to Söke (where signage seems to have fallen by the wayside; just stay on the main street through to the other side of Söke), then follow the signs to Priene (38km/24 miles from Kuşadası). From Priene, it's 22km (14 miles) along the old road to Miletus, through miles of cotton fields and sadly downtrodden nomad camps. From Priene, it's another 22km (14 miles) to Didyma, from where you can either backtrack along the new road to Söke, or continue down to Bodrum (from Didyma, 139km/86 miles; follow the more modern road via Muğla).

Day tours to all three sites are available from most travel agents in Kuşadası for around 54YTL ($40) per person, depending on the tour company.

The ancient Greek city of **Priene** 🏛️🏛️, later inhabited and left relatively unchanged by the Romans, was the first city built on a grid plan. Formerly a port city and now stranded in the middle of acres and acres of cotton fields, Priene was once an important member of the Ionian League, around 300 B.C. The oldest remains here date to this time, and it's worth the short climb up if only for the **Temple of Athena,** which sits at the highest point of the city atop Mount Mykale, and a small **Greek theater.** The temple was built by the architect Pytheos, the same man responsible for the construction of the Mausoleum at Halicarnassus. The theater was used for both performances and as a meeting place for the *ekklesia*—the people's parliament. Notice the first tier of seating, which is furnished with both bench-backed and "armchair" seating designated for spectators of particular importance. Another section of similar seating, called a *prohedria,* was added to the center of the fifth tier at a later date.

One of the best-preserved buildings in Priene is the ***bouleuterion*** (**Senate House**), located south of the Greek theater. The *bouleuterion* is roughly square in shape (21m×20m/69 ft.×66 ft.) with three sides of tiered seating capable of seating a mere 640 people. The building contained both a central altar and an eternal flame. Among the many **private houses** is one occupying a whole city block, and obviously inhabited by one of the city's wealthier citizens. The house referred to as the Alexander the Great house is actually named for a small marble statue of Alexander (now in the Berlin Museum) that was found in another part of the city. Priene is open summer only daily 8:30am to 6:30pm; admission is 2YTL ($1.50).

Miletus 🔆🔆, still for the most part buried under rubble, is actually larger than Ephesus. In fact, you'll be driving over half of it on the entry road to the Roman Theatre, one of the noteworthy ruins. Having surrendered to the silting up of *four harbors,* the city's fate was much the same as that of Ephesus. In fact, the hill 6.5km (4 miles) to the west of the theater was actually the island of Lade, destroyed by fire by the Persian fleet in 494 B.C.

Miletus gave the alphabet to the classical world and was also the breeding ground for many philosophers and scientists, including Thales, who calculated precisely the arrival of the solar eclipse. The archaeological site is notable for the great **Roman Theatre** and the **Baths of Faustina,** while a surprising quantity of remnants from the city's Classical, Hellenistic, and Roman eras remains for the most part buried or overgrown with bone-dry shrubbery. Several maps and archaeological guides are available to help you walk through the ruins, including those sold at the entrance gate. (For more scholarly options, see "Recommended Books & Films" in chapter 2.) Miletus is open daily 8:30am to 6:30pm in summer, and until 5:30pm in winter; admission is 2YTL ($1.50).

The **Temple of Apollo** is really all that's left of **Didyma** 🔆🔆, but the time spent getting to and from the site is well worth it. Didyma served as a sacred sanctuary under the custody of priests called Branchids, and was connected to Miletus via a marble road, only partially excavated and visible on the opposite side of the modern road. Ongoing excavations by the German Archaeological Institute around this marble road have recently revealed an unidentified but sophisticated complex of structures; in the near future, they hope to post their findings on the organization's website, www.dainst.de.

The temple, or **Didymaion,** with columns soaring over 20m (60 ft.) high, was the largest building of its time when it was erected in the 6th century B.C. (Reconstructed in the 3rd c. B.C., the temple was eclipsed in size only by those in Ephesus and Samos.) Though burned and plundered, the temple is still an amazing and inspiring sight, and much of it remains intact. The entrance to the temple is open, revealing the site of the much-revered oracle of Apollo. Don't overlook the colossal column behind the temple, which consists of layers and layers of massive stone discs supporting each other like so many felled dominoes. Across from the entrance of the temple is the 150-year-old stone **Medusa House** (📞 **0256/811-0063;** www.medusahouse.com; 99YTL–148YTL/$73–$110 double), a nine-room inn where an overnight will allow you an after-hours stroll through the ancient site. For everyone else, Didyma is open summer only, daily from 8am to 6:30pm; admission is 2YTL ($1.50).

AREA BEACHES

Although Kuşadası built itself up around the idea of a beach resort, it wasn't until 2001 that the city took it upon itself to create an actual waterfront and beach. There's not much sand to speak of, and what little there is, is hardly worth a special trip, especially given the tourist element it attracts. Still, it's an improvement and the waterfront promenade makes for a great sunset stroll. Nevertheless, I recommend that you skip this beach and try the new **Papaz Hamamı Beach Club** to the left of the causeway to Güvercin Ada.

The town's most infamous beach, known by the locals as **Ladies' Beach** for the over-abundance of exposed boobs, draws more than its fair share of sordid macho types. This narrow stretch of sand is located about 3.5km (2 miles) south of town, easily reachable by any *dolmuş*. A bit more up to speed is the beach at **Grand Blue Sky,** which is surrounded by such resort amenities as outdoor cafes and watersports facilities.

Adjacent to Blue Sky Water Sports is **Aquaventure Diving Center** (© **0256/612-8330**), offering courses at all levels in addition to their boat, cave, and reef dives. Single dives run about 58YTL to 66YTL ($43–$49) plus a modest equipment rental (10% discount if you bring your own equipment). Aquaventure accepts American Express, MasterCard, and Visa.

The five-star **Korumar,** at the rocky north end of Kuşadası, also has a top-flight watersports and activities center. Use of the pool and beach for outside guests costs 8YTL ($6) weekdays and 14YTL ($10) on weekends.

A NATIONAL PARK

Acting as a buffer between the Greek island of Samos less than a mile offshore and the Turkish mainland, **Dilek National Park (Dilek Milli Parkı;** © **0256/614-1009**), on the Dilek Peninsula, houses a military base as well as a mountainous natural preserve that descends into the sea. A day trip to the quiet isolation of the park's beaches, where pine trees act as natural shelter for picnickers, is definitely a better alternative to the unexceptional beaches closer to Kuşadası.

To do this, you'll really need a car to make it worth your while. Although minibus service (1.50YTL/$1) leaves from the *otogar* every half-hour to take you the 20km (12 miles) to the park (*dolmuşes* also depart regularly from the *otogar;* cost 1.50YTL/$1), you still have to get to your chosen beach, which can mean up to an additional 9.5km (6 miles). Naturally, the closest beach, **Içmeler Köyü,** is the most crowded, with its sand and shady stretches located only .8km (½ mile) from the entrance. There are no public facilities at this beach. **Aydınlık Beach** and **Kavaklı Burun** are progressively less frequented (5km/3 miles and 7km/4⅓ miles, respectively, from the entrance), with nothing but pebbles between you and the shoreline. Both of these have toilet and changing facilities, along with basic snack bars. The last beach, a pristine pebble stretch opposite the Greek island of Samos, is **Karasu Beach.** Freshwater showers are available, as well as toilets and changing rooms. There are snack bars open at each of the beaches during high season. The park opens daily at 8am and closes **promptly** at 6:30pm. Admission is 1YTL (75¢) per person or 3.50YTL ($2.50) per car including passengers. For a convenient dinner spot on your way back from the park, try **Değirmen** (see "Where to Dine" below).

WHERE TO STAY

There are plenty of hotel rooms in the center of Kuşadası, and although they do offer a modicum of convenience in their proximity to the town center and harbor, few of them retain much charm. Moreover, the waterfront main drag never empties of the line of traffic.

For an extended stay in Kuşadası, I've suggested hotels with an appropriate level of comfort and amenities; close enough for an extended nighttime stroll into town for dinner, but far enough from the madding crowd to allow for a stress-free stay.

Club Caravanserail ⋆ *(Value)* Of all the caravanseries converted into modern hotels, this is one of the most elegant, and a great opportunity to soak up real Turkish culture. The rooms have been lovingly restored, the floors and furnishings glisten with wood polish, and even the alcove fireplaces found in every room are original. The success of a place can also be judged by the tenure of its staff: Many of the employees have been at this inn for 20 years, creating a warm, familial atmosphere.

A traditional Turkish folklore show is performed in the main courtyard Thursday through Saturday (see "Kuşadası After Dark" below), but the show finishes promptly at midnight so as not to blow nonparticipating guests out of their rooms with high decibel levels. (In any case, guests are bound to take in the show at least once.) For those wishing to attend, the management offers a meal plan that includes the show; also, special room rates are posted regularly on the Internet.

Atatürk Bulv. 2, 09400 Kuşadası. ℂ **0256/614-4115.** Fax 0256/614-2423. www.kusadasihotels.com/caravanserail. 26 units (all with shower). 66€ ($80) double; 131€ ($160) suite. See website for discounts. AE, MC, V. Street parking only. **Amenities:** Restaurant and folklore show; sidewalk cafe; laundry service; dry cleaning; high-speed Internet. *In room:* A/C, hair dryer.

Grand Blue Sky International (Kids)
This enormous resort complex was obviously modeled on a UFO crash-landing site, with three aerodynamic segments renovated into luxury accommodations. The 3-year-old hotel has been outfitted with every modern earthly convenience, and every room boasts a balcony and sea view, as well as a front-row seat of the playground below. Two outdoor pools, tennis courts, and the ubiquitous snack bar dot the expansive lawns, while indoor facilities include a fitness center, three restaurants, and a game room.

Rooms are modern, inoffensive, and actually quite spacious. With a private beach below, a constant flurry of organized activities, and a meal plan, you never have to leave the grounds. Two private concessions on the beach provide watersports options including diving and certification, and for after-sun hours, the management arranges nightly multilingual entertainment.

Kadınlar Denizi, 09401 Kuşadası. ℂ **0256/612-7750.** Fax 0256/612-4225. www.grandbluesky.com. 310 units (all with bathtub). Sept–June 100€ ($122) double; July–Aug 120€ ($147) double. Rates include breakfast and dinner. AE, MC, V. **Amenities:** 3 restaurants; 5 bars; patisserie; 2 outdoor swimming pools; 2 tennis courts; health club; Turkish bath; Jacuzzi; sauna; extensive watersports; rentals (bike, moped, and scooter); children's-center programs; game room; concierge; car-rental desk; salon; 24-hr. room service; massage; laundry service; dry cleaning. *In room:* A/C, satellite TV, minibar, hair dryer.

Grand Önder Otel
Although the Grand Önder has no direct access to the shoreline, the hotel provides modern and stylish facilities nothing short of what you'd get at a country club. The bright main lobby features blond parquet floors and a "fer forgé" style reminiscent of the Southwest, preparing you for the cheerfulness and comfort of the guest rooms, all of which are outfitted with showers.

An indoor restaurant opens up to the pool area below, which rests on a lower level of the hill with crisp views of the marina. Enclosing the pool are the hotel's Turkish bath, indoor and outdoor Jacuzzi, and an alcove containing just enough workout machinery to make up for those free cookies provided by the hotel at teatime.

Atatürk Bulv. Girişi Yat Limanı Karşısı, 09400 Kuşadası. ℂ **0256/618-1690.** Fax 0256/618-1689. 80 units (some with shower, some with bathtub). 80€ ($98) double; 135€ ($182) suite. AE, MC, V. Free on-site parking. **Amenities:** Restaurant; TV lounge and pool bars; outdoor swimming pool; small fitness room; Jacuzzi; sauna; Turkish bath; children's play area; game room; 24-hr. room service; laundry service; dry cleaning. *In room:* A/C, satellite TV, minibar, hair dryer.

Kısmet Hotel ⭐⭐
Co-owned by the granddaughter of the last sultan, Mehmet VI, the Kısmet Hotel indeed exemplifies elegance, simplicity, and nobility. But the hotel, lacking any recent renovations, is showing its age, especially in the bathrooms. I'd nevertheless recommend this hotel above any other in the area. The suites are amply large and boast large banistered balconies and rattan chairs, while standard doubles are more modern and less regal.

The hotel occupies a small promontory with a harborside terrace garden and restaurant on one side and the rocky cliffs of the Aegean on the other. The swimming pool, sea views, and exclusive atmosphere provide the perfect Rx for an escape from the real world. Behind the hotel, several levels of gracious cliff-side lounging are accessible via stairs that work their way down to a cement pier and the rocky water's edge. And an expansive garden overlooking the marina provides a tranquil spot for a sunset cocktail.

Akyar Mevkii Türkmen Mh, 09400 Kuşadası. ⓒ 0256/618-1290. Fax 0256/618-1295. www.kismet.com.tr. 107 units (most with bathtub, some with minitub). 123€ ($150) double; 328€ ($400) suite. AE, DC, DISC, MC, V. Parking lot on-site. Closed Nov 15–Mar 15. **Amenities:** 2 restaurants; 5 bars; outdoor swimming pool; tennis court; fitness room; Jacuzzi; shopping arcade; salon; 24-hr. room service; laundry service; dry cleaning. *In room:* A/C, satellite TV, minibar, hair dryer.

Korumar Hotel *(Kids)*   Less than a mile from the city center, the Korumar offers one of the best resort facilities around. Besides having even the kitchen sink, the hotel boasts one of the largest outdoor swimming pools on the Aegean. The hotel occupies a cliff just above the Kısmet Hotel (see above) where the coastline makes a sharp curve, providing a small sheltered pebble beach and sparkling cove just a quick dive off the cement deck to the waterline. The hotel was last renovated in 1999, with four floors again upgraded to deluxe rooms, leaving the rooms—all with balconies—freshly equipped with satellite TV, safes, hair dryers, and bidets.

Atatürk Bulv. (north of the marina), 09400 Kuşadası. ⓒ 0256/618-1530. Fax 0256/618-1110. www.korumar.com.tr. 250 units. 120€ ($146) double; 180€ ($220) and up suite. AE, MC, V. **Amenities:** 4 restaurants; 4 bars; patisserie; indoor and outdoor swimming pools; tennis courts; health club; Turkish bath; Jacuzzi; sauna; extensive watersports; dive school; children's center programs; game room; concierge; tour desk; car-rental desk; shopping arcade; salon; 24-hr. room service; massage; laundry service; dry cleaning; nonsmoking rooms. *In room:* A/C, satellite TV, minibar, hair dryer, safe.

WHERE TO DINE

Ali Baba FISH   Ali Baba's hidden waterfront location makes this restaurant the spot of choice. The catch of the day is displayed in crates on the doorstep, and just inside, the large cold case full of mezes teases you with dishes like artichoke hearts and octopus salad. Ali Baba serves meat, too, but with such a plentiful selection of seafood, *kebaps* just seem besides the point here. It's a good idea to reserve ahead, because patrons of the rear tables get the sunset views.

Belediye Turistik Çarşısı 5 (behind Anatolian Bazaar shopping center). ⓒ 0256/614-1551. Reservations suggested. Appetizers 4YTL–5.40YTL ($3–$4); fish sold by weight. DC, MC, V. Daily noon–midnight.

Avlu *(Value)* TURKISH   This *lokanta* is consistently full of locals and tourists alike, filling up on basic home-style fare. It's nothing fancy, just good hearty eggplant or lamb stews, pilaf, and endless bread.

Barbaros Hayrettin Cad. (before the PTT). No phone. Appetizers and main courses 4YTL–9.50YTL ($3–$7). No credit cards. Daily 8am–midnight.

Değirmen *(Finds)* *(Kids)* TURKISH   More than a restaurant, Değirmen is a veritable nature park located outside of Kuşadası, on the way to Dilek Milli Parkı. The restaurant proper sits at the top of a small hill surrounded by overfed rabbits and peacocks. All the food is organic, some of it grown on-site. (An olive grove provides olives for their very own olive oil, and they bottle their grapes under the Doluca label.) At your table peasant bread the diameter of a large pan accompanies such dishes as *tandır kebap* (lamb cooked in an "in-ground" oven, Anatolian style) or the special *Değirmen* *kebap* (spareribs, chicken wings, quail, and lamb chops). Try the *erişte* (homemade egg noodles) or the *içli köfte* (meat-filled bulgur balls, either boiled or fried), and finish off with a slice of the house *künefe* (cheese-filled buttery string pastry covered in syrup and served hot).

The surrounding nature complex grows out of a desire by the owner, a native of Kuşadası, to preserve a small part of the local culture. A cobbled path leads down from the restaurant to a duck-filled pond, over a dubious hanging bridge, past the chickens and sheep, and straight to the riding stables, a marvelous combination for kids. (Horseback riding available Tues–Sun at about $6 per hr.; beginners stay with a guide in an enclosed area.) The small "village store," located on the way down to the pond, is good for stocking up on basic ingredients, such as the reserve's own nuts, dried fruits, preserves, fresh eggs, olive oil, and wine. You can also buy fresh *gözleme* from a spot near the hanging bridge, or enjoy light snacks in the covered seating area down by the horses.

Davutlar Yolu (12km/7½ miles from Kuşadası on the way to the Dilek Milli Parkı). © 0256/681-2148. Reservations required to waive the park entrance fee (95YKr/70¢). Appetizers and main courses 5.40YTL–12YTL ($4–$9). MC, V. Daily noon–midnight.

Istanbul Meyhanesi TURKISH   A perfect example of those taverns you've been hearing so much about, Istanbul Meyhanesi seems to attract large groups of boisterous locals singing at the top of their lungs well into the night. The restaurant is simple: Bamboo lines the walls while lifelike ladybugs cling to layers of burlap lining the garden's stone walls. Also, the food—a recitation of the typical fare—is pretty good.

Kıçla Sok. 7. © 0256/613-1677. Reservations suggested. Appetizers and main courses 4YTL–11YTL ($3–$8.10). No credit cards. Daily 8pm–2am. Closed Nov–Mar except Sat night.

Kazım Uşta FISH   Kazım Uşta shares the harborfront with the restaurant next door, but just because the two are practically attached at the hip does not make them equal. *This* one has a charcoal grill. It also has a nonaggressive waitstaff friendly and eager to greet you, as well as a pleasant marina-side ambience. Unfortunately due to the slow tourist season, my choices for mezes were narrowed to five different varieties of eggplant. It's disillusioning, I know, but the eggplant dishes always seem to be so *outstanding*. For the main course, try the grilled sea bass to confirm what marvels an open fire will do for a fish.

Kuşadası Harbor. © 0256/614-1226. Reservations suggested. Appetizers 4YTL ($3); fish by weight. MC, V. Daily noon–midnight. Closed Nov–Mar.

Marina Restaurant TURKISH/EUROPEAN   Nothing beats the romance of a harborside terrace with views of the incoming cruise ships beneath a full moon. With atmosphere like this, who needs good food? Happily, you can have both here. In addition to a nightly buffet, dinner is served off the a la carte menu, featuring Westernized recipes such as salads, steaks, and poultry. Feeling the need for pasta, I decided to play it safe and get the *mantı,* minuscule meat dumplings swimming in a warm garlic yogurt sauce drizzled with chile oil. The only place you can expect to get better mantı is if you get a Turkish matron (with lots of free time on her hands) to make them. Also tasty was the *börek* meze, fried up Chinese style with vegetables, peas, mushrooms, and a divine chile sauce.

In the Kısmet Hotel (Akyar Mevkii Türkmen Mah). © 0256/618-1290. Main courses 5.40YTL–14YTL ($4–$10); dinner buffet $20. AE, DC, DISC, MC, V. Daily noon–3pm and 7–11:30pm.

KUŞADASİ AFTER DARK

From here, down the Aegean, Turquoise, and Mediterranean coasts, there's no way to get away from the forced partying, be it in one of the seemingly infinite clubs on **Barlar Sokağı ("Bar Street")** or in your hotel's very own discotheque.

Kuşadası's nightlife is concentrated in the old town center, in the narrow streets bordered by Barbaros Hayrettin Bulvarı and Sağlik Sokak. Kuşadası's Barlar Sokağı (walk up Barbaros Hayrettin Bulvarı, turn right onto Sağlık Sokak, and then left under the arch into the confusion) boasts more Irish pubs per square inch than Dublin. The street is swarming with ruddy-faced boys and house touts who think that dancing on the street like Amsterdam hookers in the red-light district might lure somebody in for a drink. A walk-through is great for a hoot, however.

No trip to Turkey would be complete without a Turkish Night folklore show, and the **Club Caravanserail,** Atatürk Bulv. 2 (© **0256/614-4115**), is one of the best places to do it. The entire affair is set up like an oversize wedding banquet, with lengthy tables and long lines at the buffet table. The show begins at about the time the main course arrives, and much like at a wedding, it's best to fill up on the appetizers. All in all, the mezes are adequate and the performance is fun—filled with folkloric dances from various regions, belly dancing, a spoon drummer, and the requisite lobster-red, tub-o-lard recruit for the audience participation segment. A grand finale medley of international favorites like "La Vie En Rose," "Hava Nagila," and "New York, New York" leaves no stone unturned and not a disappointed tourist in the house. Admission is 54€ ($40), but less than half that for hotel guests.

6 Pamukkale ★★ & Hierapolis ★★

75km (47 miles) northeast of Denizli airport, 25km (16 miles) northeast of Denizli; 652km (404 miles) south of Istanbul; 231km (143 miles) southeast of İzmir; 300km (186 miles) northeast of Bodrum

Until a few years ago, the cliff-side travertines that had become the poster child of **Pamukkale** were more like a slushy roadside pile of yesterday's snow. The terraces are the result of thousands of years of deposits left by calcium-rich natural springs coursing down the mountain. (In nearby Karahayıt, springs rich in iron and sulfur leave reddish metallic deposits at the point of exit.) But years of irresponsible tourism had turned this wonder of nature into a dismal theme park attraction, until finally, in desperation, the Turkish authorities called in UNESCO for backup. In an ever-evolving geological environment, it's normal that these natural springs would find new outlets, and part of UNESCO's efforts have been to divert the springs to different sections on a rotating basis to restore much-needed calcium to the upper layers of the travertines. In the 6 years since their efforts began, much of the site has been restored to its original blinding whiteness. The travertine terraces, in concert with the plateau housing the ruins of the ancient city of **Hierapolis,** now make up a national park as well as a World Heritage Site, and a visit to one would not be complete without a look at the other.

Although the cloudy white mountainside continues to act as a magnet for thousands and thousands of tourists on day excursions, the only way to really appreciate the region is to spend an afternoon basting in the local mineral-rich waters. This is a spa town, after all. For now, tourists can swim in the Sacred Pool within the courtyard of the former Pamukkale Thermal or in one of the more deluxe facilities in nearby Karahayıt. The village of Karahayıt has its own modest terraces (more like mounds), and the water over on that side of the plateau is at least 55°F (about 13°C) warmer than the pools of Pamukkale (except for the Colossae Hotel, which takes its source from Pamukkale). The best time to go is after the tour-bus season, during the crisp but gorgeously sunny days of fall, when you can still take advantage of some of the outdoor thermal pools without the unwanted company.

ESSENTIALS
GETTING THERE
All agencies offer day tours into the area from İzmir, Kuşadası, Bodrum, Marmaris, and Antalya (to name just a few), but after a 4-hour road trip each way, it's hardly worth the trouble. Plan on at least an overnight in a hotel with a thermal spring; otherwise, what's the point?

BY BUS   The only direct service into Pamukkale by bus is provided by **Pamukkale,** the ubiquitous bus line that arrives from virtually everywhere in Turkey (© **0212/ 444-3535**). Count on about 3½ to 4 hours from anywhere on the coast with fares under 20YTL/$15. The bus stops in Denizli first. Make sure when you buy your ticket that the final destination of Pamukkale is written on your ticket; otherwise, you may get stranded here. The bus arrives at the bottom of the travertines on the edge of the village, but unless you plan on sleeping in dingy quarters above one of the local eateries, you'll need to catch a *dolmuş* up to the entry of the ancient site of Hierapolis or continue on to more appealing accommodations in nearby Karahayıt.

If you've taken one of the other bus lines into Denizli, you'll need to change for a municipal bus to Karahayıt (which passes by Pamukkale village) or to Pamukkale. The distance from Denizli to Pamukkale is about 25km (16 miles), and regular bus service runs throughout the day until about 10pm. Try not to get stuck in Denizli overnight. If all else fails, a room at the four-star **Grand Otel Keşkin** next to the bus station (exit the station to the left and turn left again; the hotel is on your left), equipped with a Turkish bath, sauna, and swimming pool, will provide a morning view of why you should have left the previous night.

BY TRAIN   The train is a cheap alternative only if sitting in an upright position for 15 or 6 hours sounds appealing (12YTL/$9 from Istanbul, 5YTL/$3.70 from İzmir). A bed in a sleeper car with water basin is available on the overnight Istanbul **Pamukkale Ekspresi** train for 64YTL ($47); if you're traveling as a pair, it'll cost 49YTL ($36) per person. For more information, contact the train station in Istanbul (© **0216/336-0475,** or in İzmir 0232/484-8638).

BY PLANE   Flying into Denizli (actually into Çardak, a little over an hour away by car) is not the most convenient; it's about 90 minutes by private car over a desert expanse to Pamukkale. The Turkish Airlines bus will only get you as far as Denizli, for about 24YTL ($18). The only other way to get out is to hire a taxi for a cool 135YTL ($100), but this will only get you as far as Denizli; another taxi from Denizli to Pamukkale or Karahayıt will cost around 40YTL ($30). You may want to have a tour guide or driver waiting at the airport—you must arrange this in advance with a local travel agent. If you decide to rent a car, **Avis**, and others, will send the car to the airport.

VISITOR INFORMATION
The Tourist Information office is located at the top of the travertines (©/fax **0258/272-2077**).

ORIENTATION

The terraces lie along the base of the Çaldağ Mountains some 200m (656 ft.) above the Curuksu Plain. The upper plateau includes the ancient ruins of **Hierapolis,** a prosperous city in its heyday owing to the natural healing water sources and the local textile industry (cotton grows like weeds in these parts), the same industries that propel the local economy today.

There are two entrances to the historic and natural site, one leading from the village of Pamukkale to the southern entrance and the other about 2.5km (1½ miles) past the village up a windy road to the northern entrance. You can also walk up to the Southern Gate from the edge of the village of Pamukkale, straight uphill alongside the terraces of travertines.

If you plan to skip the necropolis (you shouldn't), the Southern Gate is more convenient because the parking lot is closer to the travertines and some of the main attractions of Hierapolis. If you're walking in from Karahayıt, you'll be entering at the Northern Gate, which will add an extra 2.5km (1½ miles) past an impressionable cemetery (the Necropolis), a bath/basilica, and the Monumental Gate before you get to the center of the site. Admission to the ancient ruins of Hierapolis (top of the travertines; where you'll find the Pamukkale Thermal and a secondary museum) is 5.50YTL ($4); admission to the enclosed archaeological museum located in the old Roman Baths is 2YTL ($1.50).

GETTING AROUND

The northern entrance of Hierapolis is only .8km (½ mile) away from the arch announcing the Karahayıt "city limits," easily walkable until you factor in the .8km (½ mile) from the hotel entrance to the city line and the additional 1.6km (1 mile) or so from the entrance to Hierapolis to the travertines (times two if you plan on going home). Even if you're driving, you'll have to leave your car in the parking lot near one of the two entrances to the site, and although the southern entrance is considerably closer to the travertines, you'll still have to backtrack the full distance on foot to see all of the ancient ruins.

You can hire a scooter or negotiate a driver in either the village of Pamukkale or Karahayıt (good for looking into the roadside textile factories); buses and *dolmuşes* serve the solitary road between the two villages and to Denizli.

WHAT TO SEE & DO

The majority of excursions to Pamukkale can be characterized by 8 hours on a bus, split in half by a quick photo op of the **travertines** *⟨⟨*, an hour of free time in the Sacred Pool, and lunch at some tourist buffet. With an itinerary like this, don't be surprised if you come away disappointed; an overnight in an inexpensive thermal hotel spa with a Jacuzzi, sauna, Turkish bath, and massage therapy seems to me the minimum requirements in a place known for millennia as a place of healing. Not only just what the doctor ordered, but it's also essential to factor in a morning stroll through the local village and a relaxed visit to the ancient ruins of **Hierapolis** *⟨⟨* after the sun has lost most of its bite.

A swim in the effervescent waters of the **Sacred Pool** *⟨⟨⟨* should be at the top of the list on any travel itinerary, but it will be eminently more enjoyable very early in the morning or during a fringe season, when the tour buses have trickled out. The Sacred Pool is the main source for the springs feeding the travertines, and naturally, some clever entrepreneur took advantage of lax governmental controls and erected a motel on the spot, oh those many years ago. The Pamukkale Thermal, the last modern structure on the plateau, has been decommissioned from a hotel, and is now essentially a historic swim club, saved from the same fate that saw the other motels razed thanks to the Sacred Pool within. The pool lies in the center of a lush garden and *çay evi* (teahouse). Scattered about at the bottom of the crystal-clear pool like so much detritus is an amazing collection of striated columns and capitals, a striking reminder of the pool's pedigree.

The thermal water maintains a relatively constant temperature of about 95°F (35°C), so that a dip in the middle of November is not out of the question. In addition to a high level of natural radioactivity, the water contains calcium bicarbonate, calcium sulfate, magnesium, and carbon dioxide, and after a swim, you should simply dry off and let the minerals do their magic.

The **Pamukkale Thermal** (© 0258/272-2024; admission 8YTL ($6) is open from 8am to 8pm daily (until 5pm in the winter) and provides basic changing rooms, but don't forget a towel.

So as not to forget that 2,000 years ago emperors and kings weekended here, the impressive remains of the ancient city-spa of Hierapolis (admission 3.60YTL/$2.70) lie all around. The city of Hierapolis was founded in 190 B.C. by Eumenes II as part of the great Empire of Pergamum and was probably named after Hiera, the wife of the legendary founder of Pergamum. Considered a sacred site for the magic of its healing waters, Hierapolis reached its peak of development under the Romans at the end of the 2nd and 3rd centuries. During the Byzantine Era, a large church was erected to St. Philip, who was martyred here in A.D. 80.

Behind the Pamukkale Thermal are the stunning remains of the best-preserved **ancient theater** ✸✸✸ in Turkey, and the third-most-impressive theater after Ephesus and Aspendos. The theater was constructed in the middle of the 2nd century by Hadrian and adapted in the 3rd century by Septimius Severus, indicating the importance of the city during both Hellenistic and Roman times. The upper section of 25 rows, added during the restoration, is constructed of stones quarried from the ancient theater to the north of the city rather than of marble, suggesting that the city hit upon financial hardships during this era. Notice the skeleton of the mechanism below the well-preserved stage. The theater comes to life in the late spring for folklore performances during the Festival of Pamukkale.

Just down the hill are the scattered leftovers of the **Temple of Apollo,** patron of the city. If you descend the incline just inside the fence and circle to the other side of the temple's stairs, you can see the **Plutonium,** a niche believed to be sacred for the noxious carbon monoxide vapors that are emitted from a nearby underground stream. Accessible via a (closed) passageway through the temple, the temple priests were the only ones with the power (or lung capacity) to emerge alive, a thesis supported by the deaths of not just a few imprudent tourists.

A pretty good hike up the hill will lead you to the **Martyrium of St. Philip** ✸, the remains of an octagonal basilica believed to have been erected on the site where Philip was martyred.

From the Martyrium you can cut down the hill toward the **Byzantine Gate** and the **Colonnaded Street.** Crossing the city on a north-south axis for .8km (½ mile), in ancient times the street ran from the Southern Gate and ended at the monumental **Arch of Domitian** ✸, a triple arch flanked by two robust cylindrical towers constructed by Julius Frontinus, the Proconsul of the Asian Provinces between A.D. 84

and 86. To the right of the gate are the pillars of the latrine, not as graphic as the toilets at Ephesus, but interesting from an architectural point of view nevertheless.

Beyond the Arch of Domitian is the **Necropolis** ✿✿✿, stretching for over 1.5km (1 mile) and ending at the northern entrance to the site. Although people traveled from all over the empire to heal their ills, it's painfully obvious from this extensive burial ground that some diseases just can't be treated by a warm bath. There are various types of sarcophagi, layers of mausoleums designed as houses for the dead, and remarkable examples of the stone cylindrical drum tumuli employed during Hellenistic times. Don't pass this up just because it's too hot.

On the paved road heading back to the southern entrance, notice the crumbling but imposing Roman bath, built around the end of the 2nd century and later converted into a **Byzantine basilica** ✿. From the looks of several of the archways, one more earthquake and this structure is road dust.

Next to the parking lot of the Pamukkale Thermal are a 6th-century **Christian basilica** and more **Roman baths** (this one for the rich folk). Dating to the 1st century, the baths were constructed in the rebuilding of the city during the reign of Tiberius after a major earthquake severely damaged the city. Now a museum, the baths house artifacts from the area, including a fairly impressive marble sarcophagus, but for the most part, you can skip the exhibit and admire the baths from the outside.

WHERE TO STAY

All of the better-class accommodations are in Karahayıt close to the Northern Gate into Hierapolis, but age and neglect in some cases may tip the balance in favor of one of the dozens of family-owned pensions in either Pamukkale or Karahayıt. In exchange for a few stars, you'll get a room for absurdly low amounts of money, and some of these even have their own thermal. Try the **Villa Lycos,** Karahayit (② **0258/271-4505;** fax 0258/271-4508; 60 units; 50€/$60 double), or **Pamuksu Boutique Hotel,** Gölyeri Mevkii Stad Caddesi 52, down near the base of the travertine (② **0258/272-2818;** fax 0258/272-2109; www.pamuksuhotel.com; 51 units; 60€/$73 double; rates include breakfast and dinner; MasterCard and Visa accepted).

Colossae Hotel Thermal   Although the lackluster and homogenous guest accommodations of the Colossae Thermal are in need of an overhaul, this five-star thermal spa and treatment center sees to it that you spend as little time as possible in the room.

Aside from the indoor thermal facility, containing a sauna, Jacuzzi, Turkish bath, and fitness center, the hotel has a state-of-the-art health, treatment, and physical therapy center offering therapies such as balneotherapy, reflexology, slimming programs, professional shiatsu, and chakra balancing massage. The center has a multilingual doctor on the premises along with highly trained professional masseuses, so that it's possible to have a course of treatment tailored to your specific ailment. Dinner is included in the price of the room, but treatment programs (packages are available) are extra, as is use of the Jacuzzi and sauna. The Colossae is lovely in the summertime, with its outdoor swimming and mud pools, extensive gardens (with tennis courts), and poolside terrace restaurant, which lights up spectacularly in the evenings.

Karahayıt Koyu, 20290 Karahayıt. ② **0258/271-4156.** Fax 0258/271-4250. www.colossaehotel.com. 230 units (all with balcony). 165€ ($200) double; 213€ ($260) suite. Rates include breakfast and dinner. AE, MC, V. Free parking on premises. **Amenities:** 6 restaurants; 6 bars; nightclub; 2 swimming pools (1 indoor thermal); 2 tennis courts (night lit); health center and thermal spa; fitness room; Turkish bath; Jacuzzi; sauna; bikes; children's playground; concierge; salon; 24-hr. room service; massage; laundry service; dry cleaning. *In room:* A/C, satellite TV, minibar, hair dryer, safe.

Richmond Hotel and Richmond Spa   Of the few acceptable thermal hotels in the area, the Richmond seems to be the preferred choice. Possessing the best thermal pool from the sulfur-rich Karahayıt source, both hotels (there are two buildings sharing a large garden) can also boast the hottest spring water in the entire region. There's both indoor and outdoor swimming and thermal pools, with the temperature of the latter at a steamy 118°F (48°C). The health center smells pleasantly of witch hazel and comes equipped with a fitness room, Jacuzzi, and sauna. Rooms are bright but a bit on the small side with the bathtub sunken treacherously low into the bathroom floor. The Richmond has a ballroom, a greenhouse, and two conference rooms, which attract businesspeople and wedding celebrations, so ask for a room away from the festivities.

Karahayıt Koyu, 20027 Karahayıt. ✆ 0258/271-4294. Fax 0258/271-4078. www.richmondhotels.com.tr. 315 units (all with bathtub). 90€ ($110) single; 120€ ($146) double; 160€ ($195) suite. MC, V. Parking on premises. **Amenities:** Restaurant; 5 bars; indoor and outdoor thermal pools; health club; Turkish bath; Jacuzzi; sauna; concierge; tour desk; car-rental desk; 24-hr. room service; massage; laundry service; dry cleaning. *In room:* A/C, satellite TV or TV/VCR or TV w/pay movies, minibar, hair dryer, safe.

WHERE TO DINE

A dinner buffet is included in the price of the hotel at all the thermal hotels, a necessary solution to the lack of alternatives in the vicinity. In many of the smaller family-run guesthouses, you'll probably be asked if you're staying for dinner (say yes!). In both villages of Pamukkale and Karahayıt, you can get a basic Turkish meal at one of the little home-style *lokantas.*

PAMUKKALE AFTER DARK

By the time evening rolls around, the temperature of the thermal pools has finally reached blissful levels of heat that suck the life right out of you, and at this point, you're way too drained to even think about going out.

The local hotels recognize this deficiency and have eagerly come to the rescue. Kayaş Wine House comes to mind (Atatürk Cad. 3; ✆ **0258/272-2267**), a charming little joint with a wall of local wines, and characteristic indoor seating on carpet-covered banquettes. There's a TV screen for endless football matches, a menu of basic fare, and a list of aromatic herbs and spices for the water pipes.

Also, few realize that the **travertines** are open 24 hours a day so you can go up at night for eerie and romantic views of the white rock. Tickets to the site are good for a full 24 hours, so save your stub from earlier in the day and sail right in.

A SIDE TRIP TO APHRODISIAS ✿✿

Just when you think you've been saturated by amazing sights, you round another bend and behold the archaeological ruins of the ancient site of **Aphrodisias** (✆ **0256/ 448-8003;** admission 6.75YTL/$5). The best-preserved example of a Hellenistic civilization in Turkey, Aphrodisias is still undergoing excavations, compliments of New York University. If you've got a car and time for a side trip, this is definitely worth your time.

There is almost no documentation on the early history of Aphrodisias, but it is commonly believed that the cult of the mother goddess was central to its origins. As early as the 1st century B.C., Aphrodisias was recognized as a sacred sanctuary, and was awarded special privileges that began with Julius Caesar and lasted through the end of the Roman Empire. Popularity in the cult of Aphrodite hung on even as Christianity took hold, but eventually waned. After raids by Selçuk and Turcomen tribes in the 11th and 13th centuries, the city was ultimately abandoned.

The site covers an area of 520 hectares (1,284 acres). Some of the highlights of the site include the **Temple of Aphrodite** ⟲, built around the 1st century B.C. and converted into a basilica in the 5th century A.D. Excavations, however, have revealed earlier structures, dating to the 7th century B.C. The immense **Stadium of Aphrodisias** ⟲, an elongated oval of 262m×59m (859 ft.×194 ft.), rivals in grandeur the stadium of Pompeii. Before it was excavated, the truly **Olympic-size pool** ⟲⟲ was originally thought to be an agora, as it was surrounded by impressive Ionic porticos and covered a vast area. The porticos were simply aimed at creating a fabulous reflection in the pool, which is laid entirely of marble. The pool is best appreciated from the top tiers of the **theater.** Nearby is the **Portico of Tiberius,** and to the west, the **Baths of Hadrian,** who had them built.

GETTING THERE   You can get to Aphrodisias by car from Pamukkale, only 1½ hours away. Also, some day tours from İzmir and Kuşadası include a stopover in Aphrodisias, on the way to Pamukkale; just comparison-shop along the main drags in İzmir, Kuşadası, Bodrum, or Antalya for a tour to fit your needs. If you're driving from Pamukkale, Karahayıt, or Hierapolis, take the road for Denizli, then follow the signs for Tavas. At Tavas, take the turnoff for Karacasu and follow signs for the site.

7 Bodrum ⟲⟲⟲

840km (521 miles) south of Istanbul; 240km (149 miles) south of İzmir; 180km (112 miles) west of Marmaris; 25km (16 miles) south of Bodrum Airport

Less than 100 years ago, Turkish writer Cevat Şakir Kabaağaçlı was sentenced to exile in the dungeon of St. Peter's Castle as punishment for his politically incorrect writings. Times under the paranoid Abdülhamid II were harsh—except the sultan apparently didn't know that the prison had been closed a decade earlier. With the help of the local governor, Cevat found a house overlooking the sea in which to live out his period of exile, enjoying a view so picturesque that it inspired him to pen piles of essays on the beauty and allure of life in what was then a laid-back fishing village.

As a probable result of this early bit of marketing, Bodrum has become Turkey's most popular seaside tourist destination, a perfect balance of whitewashed stucco hillside houses dripping in bougainvillea, magnificent vistas, historic imprints, and blowout nightlife. **St. Peter's Castle** dominates every corner of Bodrum from its spot at the middle of Bodrum's twin harbors. The crumbled yet enduring remains of the **Mausoleum,** one of the Seven Ancient Wonders of the World, also resides in Bodrum. And although Turkey's most popular "party destination," by day Bodrum is a quiet but thriving holiday beach resort. In the summertime the city's twin harbors become densely packed with hundreds of the wooden *gulets* offering trips to the nearby islands or for the *Mavi Yoluculu* (the "Blue Cruise"), Cevat's romanticized weeklong journey along the glorious coastlines of the Mediterranean. Meanwhile, Bodrum's nightlife—an all-night party organized by club owners each trying to outdo the excesses and spectacle of the other—is infamous throughout Turkey. By night the city becomes a maniacal stream of human flesh flowing through the narrow expanse of "Bar Street," which empties onto an open harbor of more outdoor cafes and bars, the whole sporadically illuminated by a laser show emanating from the famed Halikarnas Night Club. From every vantage point in town, there's St. Peter's Castle, illuminated by spotlights shining on the ramparts.

Bodrum

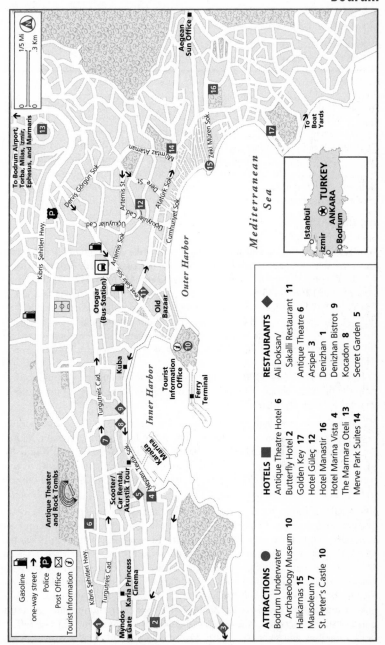

N

0 — 1/5 Mi
0 — .3 Km

To Bodrum Airport,
Torba, Milas, İzmir,
Ephesus, and Marmaris →

Aegean
Sun Office ■

Denis Görgün Sok.

Kıbrıs Şehitleri Hwy.

Artemis St.

Üçkuyular Cad.

Artemis Sok.

Mumtaz Ataman

Dere St.

Atatürk Sok.

Cumhuriyet Sok.

Zeki Müren Sok.

To
Boat
Yards →

*Mediterranean
Sea*

TURKEY

İstanbul
★ ANKARA
İzmir
Bodrum

Outer Harbor

Cevat Şakir Sok.

Turgutreis Cad.

Otogar
(Bus Station)

Old
Bazaar

Kuba

Inner Harbor

Tourist
Information
Office

Ferry
Terminal

Karada Marina

Scooter/
Car Rental,
Akustik Tour

Neyzen Tevfik Sok.

Turgutreis Cad.

Antique Theater
and Rock Tombs

Kıbrıs Şehitleri Hwy.

Turgutreis Cad.

Myndos
Gate ■ Karia Princess
Cinema

Legend

- Gasoline ▣
- one-way street ↑
- Police **P**
- Post Office ✉
- Tourist Information ⓘ

ATTRACTIONS ●

Bodrum Underwater
Archaeology Museum **10**
Halikarnas **15**
Mausoleum **7**
St. Peter's Castle **10**

HOTELS ■

Antique Theatre Hotel **6**
Butterfly Hotel **2**
Golden Key **17**
Hotel Güleç **12**
Hotel Manastir **16**
Hotel Marina Vista **4**
The Marmara Oteli **13**
Merve Park Suites **14**

RESTAURANTS ◆

Ali Doksan/
Sakalli Restaurant **11**
Antique Theatre **6**
Arsipel **3**
Denizhan **1**
Denizhan Bistrot **9**
Kocadon **8**
Secret Garden **5**

Fun Fact **High-End Mud**

Kara Ada, or Black Island, off the coast of Bodrum, is where Elizabeth Arden gets the gray mud for her line of cosmetics.

Bodrum's popularity seems to have no limits, and as fast as the Turkish jet-set can lay its claim to a secluded cove or sandy bay, tourism follows, spurring the entitled class to seek new unspoiled hunting grounds. Examples of this can be seen all along the **Bodrum Peninsula,** in the boutique hotels and beaches of Torba and Türkbükü, in the expansive seasides at **Yalıkavak, Turgutreis, Ortakent,** and **Akyarlar,** and in the poetry of the sunken ruins and waterside fish restaurants of **Gümüşlük.** Clearly, Bodrum still has quite a long way to go before becoming just another one of Turkey's overbuilt seaside resorts.

ESSENTIALS
GETTING THERE

BY PLANE   Visitors to Bodrum actually fly into Milaş, about 32km (20 miles) away and reachable in under a half-hour by way of the coastal road. **Turkish Airlines** (© 0252/536-6597 at the Bodrum airport), **Onur Air** (© 0252/523-0057), and **Flyair** (© 0212/444-4359) are all competing for your business, keeping fares around 68YTL to 95YTL ($50–$70) for a one-way flight. Turkish alone has five daily direct flights from Istanbul, as well as one direct flight from Ankara, and connecting flights from other major domestic cities. There are also several charter companies arriving from Germany and England; check with your local travel agent for information on when these are operating.

Havaş (© 0212/444-5000) provides transfer service by bus into Bodrum's bus station; the ride takes about 45 minutes and costs 13YTL ($9.25). Havaş departures are coordinated with flight arrivals.

BY BUS   Buses provide the cheapest and most comprehensive service into Bodrum, from pretty much everywhere in Turkey. The major bus companies serving Bodrum are **Pamukkale** (© 0252/315-1369), **Varan** © 0252/316-7849), and **Kamıl Koç** (© 0252/313-0468), but remember that rates vary widely from company to company. **Aydın Turizm** (© 0252/316-3250) runs service along the Mediterranean coast to Ortaca, Dalyan, Dalaman, Fethiye, Olüdeniz, and Kaş.

BY FERRY   Visitors traveling between Turkey and Greece by ferry have the option of purchasing a one-way ticket, a same-day round-trip ticket, or a round-trip ticket with open return. Prices vary (or not) according to your travel choice. For tickets purchased in Turkey, port taxes are included in the price; for tickets purchased in Greece, port taxes are around 20YTL ($15) extra. There is no visa required for entry into Greece or for excursions from Turkey with duration under 3 months. If this is your first arrival in Turkey, you will also have to pay the 27YTL ($20) entry visa.

Bodrum Express Lines (© 0252/316-1087; www.bodrumexpresslines.com) runs a daily hydrofoil service to the Greek island of Koş (15 min.) for 55YTL ($40) for both a one-way and same-day return. Hydrofoil service to Rhodes is twice weekly (Mon and Sat; 2 hr. 10 min.) for 74YTL ($55) one-way; 82YTL ($61) return.

Bodrum Express Lines also runs hydrofoils between Bodrum and Marmaris departing on Tuesday, Thursday, Saturday, and Sunday. Hydrofoils arrive in the charming town of Gelibolu (where they will complete the journey for you with a bus to Marmaris). Total travel time is 1 hour 50 minutes (the last 20 min. are on the bus); the trip costs 26YTL ($19).

The **Bodrum Ferryboat Association** (✆ **0252/316-0882;** www.bodrumferryboat. com) runs hydrofoil service (20 min.) to **Koş,** with service running once daily in July and August, and departing on an alternating schedule of 8 and 9:30am. By ferry the same journey takes 1 hour, also with a 9am departure; the fare on either boat is 39YTL ($29) one-way or round-trip. BFA also runs passenger and car ferry service to **Datça** (2 hr.) for 15YTL ($11) with a bus transfer from Korman landing to Datça town and 45YTL ($33) if you're loading a car; 26YTL ($19) will get you a round-trip ticket back to Bodrum. The ferry departs in summer daily at 9am, and less frequently in winter, possibly twice a week. All tickets for ferries and hydrofoils can be purchased either at the dock, or through any travel agent in town.

VISITOR INFORMATION
The Tourist Information office (✆ **0252/316-1091**) is open daily 9am to 6pm, good for little more than their collection of regional brochures and the latest copy of the *Aegean Sun*—a handy English-language publication with the only map available of Bodrum. Try to locate a copy of the *Bodrum Guide* as well. Stick with your hotel concierge for any significant information on Bodrum.

ORIENTATION
The white stucco town of Bodrum dots the hillside overlooking twin bays, separated by a narrow landmass from which the impressive St. Peter's Castle controlled the sea. West of the castle is the **Inner Harbor,** home to the state-of-the-art Karada Marina. **Neyzen Tevfik Caddesi** runs the length of the Inner Harbor from the marina to the castle, serving as the nucleus of a neighborhood that caters mostly to the yachting crowd, and thus is quieter and more polished than the Outer Harbor. **Cevat Şakir Caddesi** bisects Bodrum, connecting downtown Bodrum with the *otogar,* the weekly market, and the highway, ending up directly at the mouth of the old bazaar.

If there are any bargains to be found in Bodrum, it's around the **Outer Harbor,** south of the castle. This is home to Bodrum's infamous nightlife and the late-night throbbings of Halikarnas Disco, so that a basic room in a pension for $13 and a sleepless night go hand in hand.

GETTING AROUND
The narrow and one-way streets of Bodrum discourage the use of a car. Although the waterfront spreads out over two harbors, downtown Bodrum is easy to cover with a pair of comfortable shoes and a bit of stamina. A scooter is a good option, because aside from solving the parking problem, you can get away with tooling around aimlessly down side streets or weaving unexpectedly through the pedestrian traffic on the waterfront promenade. For those lodging outside the city center, *dolmuşes* provide regular service along all of the major thoroughfares through the *otogar* to the city center, and from the *otogar,* you're connected to all of the bays and villages of Bodrum's scenic peninsula. Depending on the distance, a ride will cost from 1.60YTL to 3.40YTL ($1.20–$2.50).

FAST FACTS: Bodrum

Airlines **Turkish Airlines** flies five times daily from Istanbul, and once daily from Ankara. The airline office in Bodrum is located in the Oasis Shopping Center northwest of town off the main road (© **0252/317-1203**).

Airport The general information line at Bodrum Airport is © **0252/536-6565.** THY (Turkish Airlines) has a toll-free number: © **0212/444-0849.**

Car Rentals In Bodrum the major car-rental agencies are: **Avis,** Neyzen Tevfik Cad. 92/A (© **0252/316-2333**); **National Car Rental,** Cevat Şakir Cad. 48 (© **0252/313-6110**); and **Budget,** Neyzen Tevfik Cad. 94/A (© **0252/316-7382**), all renting non–air-conditioned compact cars for as little as 68YTL ($50) per day.

Climate Bodrum's climate is Mediterranean, with temperatures rarely falling below freezing.

Embassies & Consulates The United Kingdom has representation in Bodrum, a consular agent at Kibris Şehi tleri Caddesi (© **0252/319-0093**).

Emergencies Hospitals are the best option for emergency care. The **Private Hospital (Özel Hastanesi;** © **0252/313-6566),** the **Medicare Private Clinic** (© **0252/316-7051),** and the **Karia Clinic** (© **0252/313-6233)** are open for emergencies 24 hours a day, and most duty doctors speak English.

Internet Access Internet cafes open and close quickly here. But there always seems to be one around if the wait at the hotel computer is too long.

Laundry **Fatih's Laundry Center** (© **0252/316-5081),** located next to the Merve Park Suites Hotel at Dr. Mümtaz Ataman Cad. 6, can have your laundry washed and dried in 1 hour and 15 minutes for 8YTL ($6). The laundry is open daily from 8am to 8pm.

Market Day The local market is next to the bus station and open from dawn to dusk. Thursday and Friday are the days for food; Tuesday for textiles and dry goods.

Movie Theaters The **Marina Outdoor Cinema** (© **0252/317-0001)** has a summer schedule of movies (original versions with Turkish subtitles); seating is on cushioned stones. The Karia Princess Hotel, Canlıdere Sokağı, near the Migros (© **0252/316-6272),** plays movies with the original soundtracks.

Newspapers & Magazines The *Aegean Sun* is the city's free and informative publication, with articles on life in Bodrum and current tips and trends. There's also a good map inside.

Police Dial © **155** for assistance or call the station directly at © **0252/316-8080.**

Post Office The main post office is located on Cevat Şakir Caddesi and is open 24 hours a day for phone calls and other services. The change office operates on business hours, but there are several private change windows nearby.

Shopping For upscale merchandise whose prices are fixed to the dollar (read: expensive), the Karada Marina has elegant shops with mainly nautical motifs. Local goods and souvenirs are hard to avoid in the maze around the castle.

Oasis, an outdoor shopping center located on the northwest side of town, comes complete with upscale shops, a cinema, and restaurants. Make a special trip here for the *lahmacun* (thin-crust dough topped with minced lamb, tomato, and onion) at **Öz Urfa** (⌀ **0252/317-0031**), open daily 10am to 1 or 2am, or for one of their *kebaps* or *çiğ köfte*.

Travel Agents Bodrum Touralpin, Emlak Bankası Dükkanları 6, just opposite the main post office; ⌀ **0252/316-8733;** www.bodrumtouralpin.com), is the heavy hitter in town, and where most visitors go for dealings with Turkish Airlines. **Akustik Tour,** Neyzen Tevfik Sok. 200, across from the marina (⌀ **0252/ 313-8964;** www.travelbodrum.com), is a professional, friendly and English-speaking mom and pop outfit. Check with Tolga or Özlem at Akustik before making any hotel reservations in town; they will save you a bundle. They will also direct you to the less visited archaeological sites in the region.

WHAT TO SEE & DO

Bodrum Underwater Archaeology Museum ✹✹✹   The museum is housed in **St. Peter's Castle** ✹✹✹, the easily recognizable symbol of the town. The castle juts out into the center of Bodrum's two harbors on what was once the island of Zefirya, named after Zephyros, the God of the West Wind. At the time of Mausolus, there was probably a temple dedicated to Apollo on the site, as well as a palace fortress. The land structure passed to the kingdom of Pergamum, then later to Rome before winding up in the hands of the Turks. Western sources say that the Knights Hospitalers of St. John wrenched the settlement out of Selçuk Turk hands to provide a refuge to Christians and increase their influence over the west coast of Asia during the Crusades. Turkish references say that Sultan Celebi Mehmet granted permission to the Knights Hospitalers to build an outpost. The truth remains that from their base over on the island of Rhodes, the Hospitalers' mission evolved from primarily medical to mostly military. Construction on the castle began in 1402 and became a symbol of the unity of Christian Europe against the Ottoman "infidels." According to the pope, anyone contributing to the construction of the castle would go to heaven; the naming of the **castle towers** illustrates the involvement of the various European nations, as do the presence of plaques, inscriptions, armor, and other artifacts.

After the earthquake of 1522, the Hospitalers raided the Mausoleum for building stones for repairs (some of which can be seen on the outer wall of the chapel), which apparently was not as effective as the Knights had intended, as the castle was captured by Sultan Süleyman the Magnificent that same year. Under the Ottomans, the church was converted to a mosque, adding a minaret and a public bath.

Although the castle is under the auspices of the Ministry of Culture, the museum exhibitions are overseen by the Institute of Nautical Archaeology, an American non-profit organization with bases both at Texas A&M and in Bodrum. St. Peter's Castle took on double duty in 1963 as Bodrum's **Underwater Archaeology Museum** ✹, where various shipwrecks have been reassembled for display and occupy several buildings in the castle. In the chapel, the **East Roman Ship** ✹ dates from the 7th century A.D.; the interesting display allows you to walk onto a full-scale reconstruction of part of the ship and the excavation site.

The **Bronze Age Shipwrecks** ✹ exhibit displays findings recovered from sunken trading vessels discovered by local sponge divers. The artifacts, dating to the 13th and 16th century B.C., are indispensable for understanding the late Bronze Age. Also on display is the world's oldest known shipwreck, discovered in 1982 at **Ulu Burun,** which contained a cargo of treasures, including copper ingots, tin, exotic wooden logs, hippopotamus ivory, and precious gems. In addition to Canaanite gold jewelry, one astonishing find was a solid gold scarab attributed in hieroglyphics to one-time owner Egyptian Queen Nefertiti (scarabs were often carried by sailors for good luck).

Usually, archaeologists can reassemble an object from broken pieces of glass, because many of the object's pieces are often found in the same place. Not so in the **Glass Wreck Hall** (separate admission 4YTL/$3; Tues–Fri 9am–noon and 2–4pm), which contains piles of recovered glass that defy this theory. Archaeologists deduced that the ship in question was actually transporting broken glass as cargo for recycling. This superb collection of early Islamic glass is indispensable in dating similar artifacts from other medieval Islamic sites.

The **Carian Princess exhibit** (separate admission 4YTL/$3; Tues–Fri 9am–noon and 2–4pm), also called the Queen Ada Hall, displays the tomb of what is commonly believed to be Queen Ada, a Hellenistic ruler of Halicarnassus, along with a gold crown and a few glass cases of other jewelry. The exhibit is hardly worth the added admission.

While ambling around the extensive castle grounds, home now to families of peacocks, doves, geese, and an ostrich, be sure to visit the **dungeon,** a kitschy re-creation of an amusement park horror exhibit. The castle's two main courtyards provide respite from the relentless sun. Or you can step into medieval England and sip a glass of white wine in one of the stone alcove booths in the castle's **English Tower** ⊕.

St. Peter's Castle, Bodrum center. ✆ **0252/316-2516.** Admission 10YTL ($7.50). Admission necessary for entrance to the castle. Tues–Sun 8:30am–noon and 1–7pm (last entrance at 6:30pm; closes earlier in winter).

Mausoleum of Halicarnassus Yet another plundered Wonder of the Ancient World, the mausoleum reveals only the foundations of the original masterpiece. King Mausolus of Caria ordered the construction of the 42m (140-ft.) ornate marble monument, and after his death, his wife (also his sister), Artemesia II, saw to the project's continuation. After her death the architects and artisans paid for the project out of their own pockets; it was finally completed in 350 B.C. According to historical accounts, the magnificent tomb featured pillars supporting a pyramid-shaped roof that appeared to "float" above the structure. Atop the summit was a sculpture of the king and queen riding in a chariot. In 1522, after an earthquake caused the monument to collapse, the Hospitalers used the stones from the Mausoleum as building material for the reconstruction of the castle. (Look for the greenish stones on the exterior of the chapel just beyond the entrance to the main portion of the museum.) Because of the damage caused by earthquakes, plundering, and irresponsible excavations, present-day archaeologists can only guess at the building's original appearance.

Turgut Reis Cad., up the hill off Hamam Sokağı. ✆ **0252/316-1219.** Admission 4YTL ($3). Tues–Sun 8am–noon and 1–5pm.

Fun Fact The Maltese Falcon

After Süleyman the Magnificent's conquest of Rhodes, Charles V ended the Knights Hospitalers' 8-year exile in 1530, granting them Malta and Tripoli to block Ottoman presence in the western Mediterranean. The annual fee was one falcon, the namesake of a famous American classic, *The Maltese Falcon.*

⌐*Fun Fact* **Gulets**

The crafting of a *gulet* is a tradition unique to Bodrum. The process takes about 1½ years. The type of wood doesn't matter, but it must be cut when the moon is new. Otherwise, the timber will be susceptible to worms. Completed *gulets* sell for about $133,000 without the engine. For a closer look, you can poke your nose around the workshops in Içmeler, southeast of Bodrum.

WATERSPORTS   There's nothing like a walk through the Underwater Archaeology Museum to inspire the diver in you. The waters off Bodrum are full of caverns, caves, and reefs. **Aegean Pro Dive Center,** Neyzen Tevfik Cad. 212 (© **0252/316-0737;** fax 0252/313-1296; http://aegeanprodive.com; open Apr–Oct), provides a safe and easy way to get you there. Dives with your own equipment run around 66YTL ($49), without your own equipment 82YTL ($61), including lunch. They also offer 3- and 5-day packages, group rates, snorkeling for nondiving tagalongs, and PADI certification.

It's also possible to join one of the scores of diving boats crowding the harbor just past the entrance to the castle, all of which hawk dive tours with certified divers.

If you've thrown caution to the wind (see "All About the Blue Voyage," p. 40) and decided to take a last-minute Blue Cruise, contact **Aegean Yachting** (© **0252/316-1517;** fax 0252/316-5749; www.aegeanyacht.com) or **Gino Group** (© **0252/316-2166;** fax 0252/316-5026). As the main yacht agents along the Aegean and Mediterranean, both have multiple locations along the coast, hiring out their own fleet of yachts or booking *gulet* cabin charters. Tour boats also line the harbor for sun-and-fun day trips to nearby beaches. Day tours cost about 20YTL ($15), leave around 11am, and return by 6pm.

DAY-TRIPPING
Bodrum is perfectly situated for 1-day trips to Ephesus (usually Wed and Sat); to **Pamukkale** (Mon and Fri), **Dalyan,** and **Kaunos** (Thurs and Sun). The trips are scheduled to coincide with local market days. All are easily arranged through local travel agents for 40YTL ($30) each.

If beachgoing is the main event, the surrounding bays and villages offer a combined glimpse of fantastic bays and (as of yet) authentic seaside villages. On the northern end of the peninsula and only 8km (5 miles) from Bodrum is **Torba,** where fishermen haul in their nets and you can stroll along the beach to the remains of an old Byzantine monastery. The simple hillside village and serene bay of **Türkbükü** ✸, combined with a number of extraordinary hotels, inns, and beach clubs, have attracted the jet set of Turkey. The spot is now drawing foreigners, too, as the hotels fill up with travelers looking for relaxation and the charm of a typical Turkish village. Some favorite sunspots—essentially wooden piers with ground-level cushions neatly lined up—are at **Ada Beach; Granca Restaurant, Bar and Beach; Maki Hotel and Beach; Maça Kızı Hotel;** and **Havana Beach Club,** all located on Türkbükü Bay.

The new marinas at **Yalıkavak** and **Turgutreis** are meant to fill the gap for yachters traveling between Kuşadası and Bodrum, where beaches and sheltered waterfront promenades lined with restaurants and souvenir shops make for an easy and enjoyable day out.

At the westernmost tip of the Bodrum Peninsula is the enchanting fisherman's cove of **Gümüşlük** ✸✸, site of the ancient city of **Myndos,** now partially visible just under the surface of the water. The village increases in charm in the evening, when area residents choose their favorite **waterside fish restaurant** ✸ from the many lining the cove. Thanks to its archaeological value, Gümüşlük has rejected the onslaught of "progress," and will hopefully remain as remote, charming, and scenic in the future as it is today. The remains of ancient harbor walls are scattered at the base of the headlands just to the north and west of the village; bring a snorkel to explore the site to which Brutus and Cassius escaped in 44 B.C. after having murdered Julius Caesar. Guarding the entrance to the cove and harboring its own set of ruins is **Rabbit Island,** connected to the mainland by way of a sunken ancient city wall that allows visitors to wade over from the town center. There's also an inviting beach at the far end of the village.

Other great beach destinations are **Turgutreis,** crowned by a brand-new marina; **Akyarlar,** the choice of advanced windsurfers due to the strong winds; the less windy **Ortakent Beach;** and scenic **Bitez Bay,** full of windsurfing traffic and a long sandy beach.

WHERE TO STAY

As the most popular resort in Turkey, Bodrum has been forced to expand beyond the borders of the town center. In fact, when Turkish people reminisce about Bodrum, they are often describing the heavenly bays of the Bodrum Peninsula, namely Torba and Türkbükü. But the historical and cultural importance of St. Peter's Castle draws a large share of the tourist market into nearby hotels, while creating a market for "cheap tourism" over at the charmless resort of Gümbet, or in a basic pension in the Outer Harbor. One such pension is **Baç Pension** (Cumhuriyet Caddesi 14; © 0252/ 316-1602; fax 0252/316-7917), located smack dab in the thick of the all-night body crush. But it *does* front the sea, and the windows *are* double glazed. Oh, and the pension itself is downright opulent.

ON (OR NEAR) THE WATERFRONT

Antique Theatre Hotel ✸ This enchanting sanctuary is a sophisticated yet unpretentious refuge from the stresses of daily life. The hillside location allows for truly stunning views of the castle from every room, and a view even more breathtaking from the inside of the hotel pool. All rooms connect to either a shared or private garden lined with trellises overgrown with bougainvillea. Bathrooms are suspiciously like the facilities you'd expect on a yacht, except that the ingenious marble shower basin leaves not a drop of water on the floor. Separated from the bedroom by two louvered doors, the bathroom setup is quite intimate and extremely cozy, but alas, perhaps a bit tight for those accustomed to moving around in the bathroom. The owners have taken absolute care in every detail, from the landscaping to the handmade linen bedspreads, whose creator, overwhelmed by the number ordered by the hotel, refused to sew any more when one or two regrettably wound up on a guest's plane out of Bodrum.

Kıbrıs Şehitleri Cad. 243, 48400 Bodrum (across from the ruins of the antique theater). © 0252/316-6053. Fax 0252/316-0825. www.antiquetheatrehotel.com. 20 units (all with shower). 120€ ($146) double; 150€ ($183) superior; 375€ ($460) suite. Rates lower Nov–Apr, Christmas excluded. AE, DC, MC, V. **Amenities:** Restaurant; 3 bars; outdoor swimming pool; laundry service; dry cleaning. *In room:* A/C.

Butterfly Hotel ✸ This Mediterranean villa, perched atop a hill above the inner harbor, was converted from a private home to an intimate and inviting boutique hotel.

You'll be hard-pressed to choose among this boutique hotel's six uniquely styled and plush rooms. I'm partial to the Çini Room, with its wall of Turkish tiles, and the Bahçe Room, which benefits from its own private garden courtyard. But no matter which you choose, you'll get a night's sleep like no other, thanks to the orthopedic beds and organic linens, and your choice of breakfast on your private panoramic terrace or poolside.

Eskiçesme Mahallesi, Ünlü Caddesi, 1512 Sokak No 66, 48400 Bardakci/Bodrum. (C) **0252/313-8358.** Fax 0252/ 313-83-57. www.thebutterflybodrum.com. 6 units. 82€–185€ ($100–$225) July–Aug; 74€–164€ ($90–$200) May–June and Sept–Oct. Rates even lower in winter. MC, V. **Amenities:** Restaurant; bar; outdoor panoramic swimming pool; fax service; Internet access; 24-hr. room service; laundry; dry cleaning; tour desk. *In room:* A/C, satellite TV, minibar, hair dryer, coffee/tea service.

Golden Key 🖈

This old house sits on a hill on the tip of the Outer Harbor, and as if to do justice to the fabulous garden and terrace setting, every room in the hotel is a suite. The furnishings are antique wood, some hand-painted, and the owner makes you feel as much at home as possible, with touches like wicker baskets in the bathrooms and organizers in the closet. The mansion villa is a sumptuous two-bedroom, two-bathroom triplex with shiny parquet floors, hand-painted furniture, a living room, fireplace, balconies, and a private terrace. Breakfast is served in the summer on the open terrace, while in chillier weather the warm and intimate living room provides high-back leather chairs, a stone fireplace, and a cozy fire.

Kumbahçe Mah. Şalvarağa Sok. 18, 48400 Bodrum. (C) **0252/313-0304.** Fax 0252/313-4171. www.goldenkeyhotels. com. 9 units (most with shower). 170€ ($207) double suite Apr 1–Oct 31. Closed in winter. AE, MC, V. Street parking only. **Amenities:** Restaurant; 2 bars; outdoor swimming pool; 24-hr. room service; laundry service; dry cleaning. *In room:* A/C, satellite TV, minibar, hair dryer, safe.

Hotel Güleç

Thanks to Hotel Güleç, it's still possible to get an inexpensive, clean room in Bodrum without sacrificing a night's rest. This basic pension on a back street around the Outer Harbour has simple furniture and offers a sparse breakfast. The pension hides an enormous 1,950-sq.-m garden (6,500-sq.-ft.) at the back. One of the perks is that the nearby Delphi Hotel, owned by the same family, allows guests to use its pool.

Üç Kuyular Cad. 18/A, 48400 Bodrum (from the *otogar*, turn right onto Cevat Şakir Cad., left onto Atatürk Cad., and left again onto Üç Kuyular Cad.). (C) **0252/316-5222.** 18 units (all with shower). 25€ ($30) double. Check with management regarding credit cards. Street parking only.

Hotel Manastir

Built on the site of an old monastery and set into the hillside overlooking the Outer Harbor, the Hotel Manastir commands some of the most spectacular views of St. Peter's Castle. The hotel is understated yet provides a tasteful foundation for relaxation, although its proximity to Halikarnas Night Club makes me wonder how much sleep you'll get at night. The upside of that is that the disco's laser show sets the stage for an extremely romantic summer's eve as seen from the elegant upholstered banquettes on the hillside terrace. If you're apprehensive about unwanted serenades, request a room with a courtyard patio view rather than the seemingly more desirable room with a sea view. Some bathrooms tend to be a bit small and difficult to maneuver; one suite does have a Jacuzzi. Since rooms tend to go on a first-come, first-served basis, the earlier you reserve, the bigger and better your room will be.

Barış Sitesi, 48400 Bodrum. (C) **0252/316-2854.** Fax 0252/316-2772. manastir@unimedya.net.tr. 59 units (some with tub, some with shower). 110€ ($134) double; 140€ ($170) double with sea view; 170€ ($207) and 200€ ($244) suite. Rates 30% lower Nov 1–May 16. AE, DC, MC, V. Free on-site parking. **Amenities:** 2 restaurants; 2 bars; outdoor swimming pool; tennis courts; sauna; car-rental desk; 24-hr. room service; laundry service; dry cleaning; scooter rental. *In room:* A/C, satellite TV, minibar, hair dryer, safe.

Hotel Marina Vista   Although the hotel's address on the main harbor road across from the marina may generate some suspicion as to the tranquillity of its location, the Marina Vista is nothing if not serene. The hotel is far enough from the madding crowd but within walking distance of practically everything in Bodrum. The simple design, inspired by classic Greek pediments and details, incorporates the modern conveniences of a clean, four-star hotel, most recently renovated in 1995. Only three of the hotel's guest rooms face the marina and street, while the majority of accommodations face a quiet interior courtyard with a pool. In the summertime there's a persistent layer of flower petals dusting the poolside, although because of the management's perspective on orderliness, they regularly get swept up. For romance and breathtaking scenery, the rooftop restaurant and Havana Bar offer incredible views of the mountains, harbor, and castle.

Neyzen Tevik Cad. 226 (across from the marina), 48400 Bodrum. ⓒ 0252/313-0356. Fax 0252/316-2347. 85 units (all with tub). 85€–120€ ($104–$146) double. Rates reflect season. MC, V. Street parking only. **Amenities:** 2 restaurants; 3 bars; outdoor swimming pool; fitness room; sauna; 24-hr. room service; massage; babysitting; laundry service; dry cleaning. *In room:* A/C, satellite TV, minibar, hair dryer, safe.

Merve Park Suites Hotel   Contrary to the name, this is not an all-suite hotel; in fact there are only two. But even located this close to Halikarnas Disco, Merve Park has some appeal, namely in the museum-registered artifacts decorating the small lobby, the charming rooftop garden courtyard, and the lovely sitting areas. The antiques have made it up to the rooms, which all have large bathrooms. The only downside to the hotel is its location in Downtown Outer Harbor, which translates into rooftop views of water towers and nighttime noise.

Atatürk Cad. 73, 48400 Bodrum. ⓒ 0252/316-1546. Fax 0252/316-1278. www.mervepark.com. 17 units. 110€ ($134) double; 200€ ($244) suite. Rates lower Apr–May and Oct–Nov. MC, V. Closed in winter. **Amenities:** Restaurant; bar; rooftop swimming pool; car-rental desk; 24-hr. room service; in-room massage; laundry service; dry cleaning. *In room:* A/C, satellite TV, minibar, hair dryer.

NORTH AND WEST OF TOWN

The Marmara Oteli ⚘⚘   The Marmara Bodrum is truly a feast for the eyes. Skylit hallways, white-on-white themes (including the staff's casual "uniforms"), and an eclectic mix of really cool stuff make this place seem more like an art gallery than a hotel, with a generous dose of warmth and congeniality to remind you that you're in Turkey and not on Madison Avenue. The rooms are simultaneously deluxe and sleek, with aged bamboo closet doors, made-to-order black-on-wood consoles, wrought-iron and wicker chairs, and the finest whiter than white bed linens. Every room has a balcony, but the real draw is the bathroom, a glass, marble, and chrome gallery featuring a picture window between the tub and outer room.

As if a panorama of Bodrum weren't enough, the landscaping takes advantage of the rocky hilltop, incorporating the stones into the design of the outdoor space. The poolside bar tables are crafted with İznik tiles, and the poolside lounges, chairs, and barstools are—guess what—white. Don't overlook the new spa facility, where a massage or an hour-long session relaxing in the flotation tank will leave you limp.

Yokuşbaşı Mevkii, PK 199, 48400 Bodrum (on the hilltop above the highway). ⓒ 0252/313-8130. Fax 0252/313-8131. www.themarmarahotels.com. 95 units (all with tub). 280€–385€ ($340–$470) double; 435€–900€ ($530–$1,100) suite. AE, DC, DISC, MC, V. Free parking on-site. By car from İzmir, Ephesus, Marmaris, and Bodrum airport, entering Bodrum on Kibris Sehitleri Hwy., watch for signs for the hotel entrance on the right. **Amenities:** Restaurant; bar; 2 outdoor swimming pools (1 Olympic-size); grass tennis courts; squash courts; health club; spa; Turkish bath; Jacuzzi; sauna; concierge; car-rental desk; salon; 24-hr. room service; massage; laundry service; dry cleaning; nonsmoking rooms. *In room:* A/C, satellite TV, minibar, hair dryer, safe.

IN TORBA

Queen Ada Hotel ★★ *Finds*   This might easily be Bodrum's best-kept secret, only 10 minutes from the castle yet worlds away in terms of tranquillity. The manicured lawns, backed by the ruins of an old monastery, extend practically to the pebbly water line, seductive with hazy mountain views in the distance. Surrounded by land on practically all sides, the waters of Torba Bay are as serene as those in a lake. Lounges, teak settees, and a thatch-roof bar are sparse additions to the grounds, which include a waterside raised swimming pool not far from the monastery ruins. A bi-level stone building houses the guest rooms, all with access to the outdoors via a patio or balcony. The rooms are a feast of minimalist design and the contents, including multichanneled CD systems, are nothing but the finest. While deciding whether to leave the property or not, you can make use of a small but effective fitness room and a selection of motorized watersports equipment (for a fee).

Kilise Mevkii 28, 48400 Torba/Bodrum. (C) **0252/367-1598.** Fax 0252/367-1614. www.queenadahotel.com.tr. 22 units. Apr 1–June 15 and Sept 18–Oct 31 160€–195€ ($195–$240) sea view double; June 16–Sept 17 245€–295€ ($300–$360) sea view double. Garden view rooms approximately 25% lower. Rate ranges reflect seasonal differences. AE, MC, V. Closed Nov–Mar. **Amenities:** Restaurant; bar; heated outdoor swimming pool; fitness room; watersports; bikes; concierge; 24-hr. room service; massage; laundry service; dry cleaning. *In room:* A/C, satellite TV/VCR and CD player, minibar, coffee/tea setup, hair dryer, safe.

IN TÜRKBÜKÜ

Ada Hotel ★★★ *Finds*   It's almost impossible to extract enough superlatives to describe this Relais & Châteaux property, a stunning display of understated elegance and superior taste. Fashioned like a stately country villa, the hotel was built from the ground up on a scrubby tract of land at the top of Türkbükü by the architect, Ahmet Iğdırlıgil, and designer, Hakan Ezer. Using the elements of classic Ottoman design, they incorporated such features as hand-carved stonework, outdoor living spaces, and thick stone walls. The rooms are huge and luxuriously rustic, and bathrooms are embellished with plush towels (on warmers), candles, and potpourri. Although the property has no access to the bay, the luxuriant grounds—caressed by the swaying of saz plants in the breeze—along with amenities you never thought you'd need, keep your mind elsewhere. The *hamam,* reserved by the hour for private use (outside guests pay $125 for two), enjoys views of the bay via a picture window. Two of the suites share private use of an additional terrace pool. A cinema screening room provides distractions of a large selection of films or keeps young ones occupied with a huge video-game station. And the cellar restaurant, with its velours, chandeliers, stone, and ancient wood, could easily set the stage for a scene for *Camelot.* Ultimately, the Ada Hotel is in a class all itself.

Bağarası Mah. Tepecik Cad. 128, 48400 GölTürkbükü/Bodrum. (C) **0252/377-5915.** Fax 0252/377-5379. www.ada hotel.com. 14 units. Apr–June and Sept–Oct 225€–480€ ($272–$585) double and suite; 260€–540€ ($320–$655) double and suite July–Aug. Closed Nov–Mar. AE, DC, MC, V. **Amenities:** 2 restaurants; 2 bars; outdoor swimming pool; fitness room; jaw-dropping Turkish bath; Jacuzzi; sauna; bikes; concierge; tour desk; car-rental desk; 24-hr. room service; massage; laundry service; dry cleaning; Internet connection; movie theater and video-game station; extensive movie and music library; separate waterfront beach club; library lounge. *In room:* A/C, satellite TV/DVD player, minibar, hair dryer.

Hotel Maki and Maça Kızı Hotel ★   I've combined these two unrelated properties because of their proximity and similarities. Both are stylish, relatively pricey, and waterside, although Hotel Maki does have a bouncer to guard its front gate. Rooms in both feature smart, minimalist design. The designer consciousness spills into the bathrooms, too, which, although equipped with only a shower, sport thick muslin shower curtains and high-end toiletries. Both are recommendable for a day out on the wooden deck "beaches" of Türkbükü, and as stylish alternatives to the extraordinary (and pricier) Ada Hotel (see above). A room with a view at the Maça Kızı, which is arranged in a series of buildings standing amid terraced gardens (Maki has a garden, too), might just be more desirable, given the plush window seats in the guest rooms.

Hotel Maki. Kelesharim Mevkii, 48483 Türkbükü. ✆ 0252/377-6105. Fax 0252/377-6056. www.makihotel.com. 38 units. June–Sept 200€–240€ ($245–$290) double, 270€–600€ ($330–$730) suite. Rates lower off season. MC, V. **Amenities:** Restaurant; 5 bars; outdoor swimming pool; fitness room; concierge; tour desk; car-rental desk; 24-hr. room service; massage; laundry service; dry cleaning. *In room:* A/C, satellite TV, minibar, hair dryer, safe.

Maça Kızı Hotel. Kesireburnu Mevkii, 48483 Türkbükü. ✆ 0252/377-6272. Fax 0252/377-6287. www.macakizi.com. 46 units. 150€–250€ ($185–$300) double; 275€–650€ ($335–$790) suite. Rates reflect season. Rates lower Oct–Apr. MC, V. **Amenities:** Restaurant; bar; outdoor swimming pool; fitness room; concierge; tour desk; car-rental desk; 24-hr. room service; massage; laundry service; dry cleaning. *In room:* A/C, satellite TV, minibar, hair dryer, safe.

WHERE TO DINE

The dining scene in Bodrum has been held to a higher standard than those of its Aegean and Mediterranean counterparts. Menus cater to an "international" clientele—read: international wallet. But in all fairness, the concentration of high-quality restaurants makes you empty your wallet willingly. If you're looking for a humble meal, head to the streets around the PTT (post office) near Cevat Şakir Street, a busy local neighborhood with good fast-food options such as *lahmacun* as well as pleasant little *lokantas* with large bins of fresh bread on the table.

Ali Doksan/Sakallı Restaurant TURKISH   This typical *lokanta* is a down-to-earth trucker-type place, with the food out in large pans where you can get a look at it. Fresh bread fills the plastic canisters on the tables; it's great for wrapping around a *kebap* or sopping up the tasty stews, rice, and beans. Get there before the local lunch crowd packs both the indoor and outdoor tables around 1pm.

Incı (across from the post office in outdoor pedestrian mall on the left). ✆ 0232/316-6687. Vegetable or meat dishes about 3.40YTL ($2.50). No credit cards. Daily 11am–2pm.

Antique Theatre Hotel ⭐⭐ FRENCH/MEDITERRANEAN   Hosts Selmin and Zafer Başak live in Paris, where they acquired a passion for fine food and good living, but rather than withhold their hard-won know-how, they've dedicated themselves to perfecting the dining experience at their Bodrum hotel and restaurant. Having already received accolades and a glowing review in the *New York Times,* the Antique Theatre's restaurant was recognized in 1999 by the Chaîne des Rotisseurs, the 752-year-old bastion of gastronomy.

Dinner is served poolside by candlelight or in the cozy dining room; poolside is best where the tables have been purposely arranged to take full advantage of the sparkling views of the city and of the castle. The aubergine boat filled with seafood and a Halicarnassus sauce simply whets the appetite, and just when you think you've had enough sea bass, it arrives in a sumptuous fennel-and-champagne sauce that leaves you begging for more.

Kıbrıs Şehitleri Cad. 243 (across from the ruins of the antique theater). ✆ 0252/316-6053. Reservations required. Appetizers 8YTL–18YTL ($6–$14); main courses 16YTL–32YTL ($12–$24); 4-course prix-fixe menu 58YTL ($43). AE, DC, MC, V. Open for dinner; call for hours.

Arşipel ⭐ FISH   Arşipel is set in a Greek-style whitewashed building that sits in solitude on the edge of the hillside just outside of Bodrum. In summer, beachgoers use the restaurant's waterside sun deck and make use of the kitchen for lunchtime

---

Tips Bodrum's Favorite Snacks

Locals flock to **Tatlıcı**, hidden in the maze of streets near "Meyhane Sokak" (from the Tourist Information office, follow Kale Sok., turn right into Meyhane Sok., then right again into a small passageway that will put you back onto Meyhane Sok.), for what they consider to be the best *börek* in town; by 10am, they're mostly all picked over. **Karadeniz Pastanesi** (Barlar Sokak, near the main square) has a window full of cakes, cookies, and breads, plus sandwiches and single helpings.

---

deliveries. As the sun sets, the restaurant takes on a nighttime glow that acts as a magnet for the fish below, with sea breezes adding to the romance of the spot. The restaurant specializes in the preparation of fish so fresh that several of the mezes (lagos and shrimp) are served raw in lemon, oil, and black pepper. In the cooler months, diners cozy around the fireplace in the intimate wood-beamed dining room.

Aktur Sitesi A Mahallesi (inside the Aktur Sitesi entrance, west of Bitez Beach). ℂ **0252/343-1016**. Appetizers 5.40YTL ($4); fish sold by weight according to set prices. AE, MC, V. Summer daily noon–1 or 2am; winter daily 7:30pm–1am.

Denizhan 🐾🐾 NOUVELLE TURKISH   This rustic little spot just outside of Bodrum, opened in 1998, is where you'd take a visiting ambassador. The serving style is both elegant and flamboyant, with *şiş kebaps* (skewered lamb cubes) served at the table on skewers the length of yardsticks. The preparation goes on behind a glass-enclosed kitchen in the center of the dining room, where the only thing you won't see is the chef killing the cow. Denizhan is a carnivore's delight; sample an innovative approach to cooking meatballs (fried in a cracked-wheat crust) or try the extraordinary Denizhan special (beef baked with cheese, pistachio nuts, and garlic sprinkled with sesame seeds). Find a way to get out to this restaurant.

The management recently opened the Denizhan Bistrot in downtown Bodrum (Neyzen Tevfik Caddesi), with a light menu of sandwiches, grills, pastas, and carpaccios.

Turgut Reis Yolu, about 2.5km (1½ miles) outside of town (across from the Tofaş/Fiat service station). ℂ **0252/363-7674**. Reservations suggested. Appetizers 5.40YTL–9.50YTL ($4–$7); main courses 9.50YTL–14YTL ($7–$10). AE, MC, V. Daily noon–midnight.

Kocadon 🐾 TURKISH/MEDITERRANEAN   A stone-cobbled courtyard, nestled between two traditional stone houses, is the setting for yet another of Bodrum's atmospheric quality restaurants. Start with the buffet of cold mezes, stocked with an interesting variety of salads and fritters, but don't go overboard. The kitchen puts out an ample plate of grilled calamari, and the catch of the day is prepared as you like it (try yours braised with tomatoes, peppers, and mushroom au jus). There are also some classic Ottoman dishes like the *Hünkar Beğendi* (lamb or beef stew served atop a purée of eggplant, cheese, and béchamel), which are perfectly complemented by the upper-story cumba and ancient candlelit olive press in the middle of the courtyard.

Set back from Neyzen Tevfik Cad. at the corner of Saray Sok. (near the mosque in the Inner Harbor). ℂ **0252/316-3705**. Appetizers 9.50YTL–16YTL ($7–$12); main courses 14YTL–27YTL ($10–$20). MC, V. Daily 7pm–12:30am. Closed Nov–Apr.

Secret Garden 🐾🐾🐾 MEDITERRANEAN   Dinner at the Secret Garden is one of those truly memorable meals, where by dessert, my foodie friend whispered conspiratorially, "this is *really* good . . ." The English chef, Helen, manages to re-create a seasonal menu of artistry rather than just simple food; her success was so great that the owners of the previous location hijacked the name of the restaurant. (Be sure to come to the one near the marina.) Sample delicacies include the razor clams with garlic and Parmesan au gratin, and cuttlefish in garlic, chile, soy, and cardamom. Having formidably trained a local teenage girl to hold down the kitchen fort, Helen is free to circulate in the garden, checking in every so often to ensure a seamlessly outstanding dining experience. When the evenings turn cold, diners may convene to the cozy, indoor space, and in the future, possibly to the roof terrace.

Eskiçeşme Mah. Danacı Sok. 20 (near Karada Marina; take the street between the Marina Vista Hotel and Şütte). (℃ **0252/313-1641.** Reservations suggested. Appetizers 6.75YTL–12YTL ($5–$9); main courses 15YTL–26YTL ($11–$19); 4-course dinner 37YTL ($27). MC, V. Tues–Sun 7:30pm–midnight. Closed Nov to early Mar.

BODRUM AFTER DARK

Nightlife here is legendary in Turkey, causing people's eyes to glaze over longingly whenever you mention Bodrum. The games begin behind the castle along Dr. Alim Bey Caddesi, a narrow health hazard full of crowds working their way past bars, eateries, clothing shops, and booths where you can get an exaggeratedly garish temporary tattoo. This overcrowded stretch disgorges its human contents at Cumhuriyet Caddesi, the broad walkway along the Outer Harbor thick with outdoor cafes, bars, loud music, and groups of young party-seekers conferring on where to begin. But there's a sophisticated side to Bodrum, if you know where to look. With St. Peter's Castle practically illuminating the entire bay, it's just a matter of choosing your own front seat. Several of the hotels listed above (Manastir, Mavi, Antique Theatre, Marina Vista) take advantage of perfectly sited terraces or rooftops. If you're feeling ambitious, drive out to the village of Gümüşlük for an extremely romantic seafood dinner.

Hadigari   Nestled at the base of Bodrum Castle, the Hadigari (Turkish for "let's go") occupies an old powerhouse transformed into a series of inviting intimate spaces left virtually empty on warm summer evenings, when the festivities spill out onto the quayside terrace. An early drink at a candlelit rail-side table with classic jazz playing in the background sets the mood for romance, while the subliminal revolving image of a camel does its job at filling the ashtrays. Dinner is served in the restaurant (reservations required) on the upper level from 6pm to midnight. As the hours progress, the music adapts, so that by 3am the hammering of an underground beat prevails. The Hadigari logo is also for sale in the form of an elegant tea service or on their house-brand tea and coffee. Daily 6pm to 4am. Dr. Alim Bey Cad. (℃ **0252/313-9087** or 0252/313-1960. Closed Nov–May. 24YTL ($18) cover after midnight.

Halikarnas Night Club   Vegas on the Aegean—and yes, seeing is believing. Touted as the biggest and best disco in the world, it's certainly the most infamous. This is excess at its best (and worst) and a club you love to hate, but everyone is inevitably impressed. The club's three columns tower imposingly above the harbor, a striking backdrop to the laser show later in the evening. Old and new hits from the top of the charts and nightly live shows are interrupted by the occasional appearances of famous pop singers—possibly the reasoning behind the exaggerated and self-important amount of security present in and around the nightclub. Because the nightclub has a capacity of 5,500 people, it might be a good idea to reserve one of the few tables the management holds for those with forethought, or work your way up to the upper level (and away from the fray), which is lined with cushioned banquettes and fez-covered bar stools. The club opens at 10pm but doesn't attract a soul until midnight, coaxing its clientele with theme nights like the Foam Party (every Fri and Sat), Free Beer Night (every Mon, Tues, and Thurs), and Ladies Night (every Sun 50% discount for all ladies). Daily 10pm to 5am. Cumhuriyet Cad. 178. © 0252/316-8000 or 0252/316-1237. Closed Nov–Mar. Cover 33YTL ($24).

Küba   This open-air bar is overwhelmingly popular, particularly among Turkish high society, incongruous considering the New York transplant at its helm. The atmosphere is Latin, as is the music, which even late at night isn't overwhelmingly loud. The first section of this whitewashed stone courtyard serves as the bar, full of designer aluminum chairs and tables; the rear section is dedicated to the restaurant (reservations required). Daily 9pm to 4am. Neyzen Tevfik Cad. © 0252/313-4450. Closed Nov–May.

Mavi   Bodrum's oldest cafe opens for breakfast, attracting intellectual types in silver-framed eyeglasses poring over the morning papers available on the rack. By night Mavi becomes a diminutive bar with live Turkish music, and is easy to spot by the crowd gathered around the outdoor tables. Tickets may be required for special events, but you can usually get these at the door. Daily 7am to 2am. Cumhuriyet Cad. 175 (just before the incline to Halikarnas Nightclub on the left). © 0252/316-3932. Closed Nov–May.

Mumlu Restaurant *Finds*   Mumlu is characteristic of a typical Turkish night out, combining dinner and a folk music serenade (from 9pm nightly) on two floors of a restored wooden house. The entire experience is unexpected, obscured behind lacey curtains at the end of a back alley in a maze of back streets in Bodrum's bazaar neighborhood. The food is also surprising, on a menu that includes *fıstıklı tavuk* (chicken in a pistachio-and-apricot sauce). Mezes and main courses run $3 to $7 (MasterCard and Visa accepted). When the musical portion of the evening is complete, Seyfi Bar next door continues its own live music performance in traditional Oriental-style bar-rooms. Daily 8:30pm to 12:30am. Taşlık Sokak, Taşlık Çıkmazı. © 0252/313-8462. Closed Sun in winter.

7

The Turquoise & Mediterranean Coasts

Brochures and photographs do scant justice to Turkey's exquisite southern coastline—a route familiar to caesars, saints, sultans, pirates, and at least one infamous Egyptian queen.

The Turquoise Coast which extends roughly from Antalya to Datça, is a slight misnomer because it ignores the emerald pools reflected at the base of thickets of pine trees and the rich sapphire of the open sea. To the west, the Toros (Taurus) Mountains tumble directly into the Mediterranean, making some of these rugged cliffs and shallow coves accessible only by boat. Traveling east to Antalya, rocks give way to small patches of beach, ceding completely to miles and miles of sand. And all along the length of the coastline, a short hop inland reveals long-since landlocked ancient cities that were once important trading and naval ports. The Turkish Riviera is a rich depository of layers of ancient civilizations; mentioned in Homer's *Iliad* are the Lycians, a heroic people that settled the coast from the Fethiye Bay to Antalya, while the Carians, whose origins still escape us, dominated the southwestern region from Halicarnassus to the shores of Lake Köyçeğiz.

Saul, a Greek-speaking Roman citizen and Jew from Tarsus (later known as St. Paul), spread his interpretation of the Old Testament here on his missionary journeys through the Mediterranean, laying the groundwork for some of the earliest remnants of Christianity. The legacy of these people can be found in the majestic tombs hewn into lofty cliffs, sarcophagi crowned with Gothic helmets, and ancient cities sunken beneath transparent waters. On a boat excursion into a secluded cove, it's inevitable that you will stumble upon an ancient theater, a toppled Roman bath, or the remains of a pagan temple.

Thirty years ago, the destinations in this chapter slowly began to transform from idyllic and unspoiled fishing villages into ports of call for small boats and yachts. The local population quickly caught on to the advantages of tourism, and these days, you can usually find espresso and other modern "necessities." Unlike the polished seaside resorts of the western Mediterranean or the Greek islands, however, the Turkish Mediterranean still comes with a bit of a pleasingly rugged and untamed edge.

The only problem with the destinations in this chapter is that a truly satisfying overview requires no less than 2 weeks, and that doesn't even take into account the irresistible draw of a Blue Voyage (p. 40). For those with the luxury of time, the coast should be tackled by car or *dolmuş* (minivan-type public transportation) from end to end between Antalya and Dalaman, as both are served by airports. Ideally, you'll want to avoid the winter months, because this sunny destination is best explored at its peak

The Lycian Way & St. Paul's Trail

The Lycian Way (Likya Yolu), a 500km (373-mile) footpath between Fethiye and Antalya, is the brainchild of Kate Clow, a British expatriate and advocate of the joys of Lycian Turkey. Over a period of time, she has researched, marked, and signposted a network of rural roads and mountain paths, which covers a variety of terrain through ancient sites and modern-day villages. Most recently, she's established a series of trails that follow (or closely parallel, where conditions require) the route taken by St. Paul on his three missionary journeys to Asia Minor. The latter three trails begin in Perge, Aspendos, and Egirdir, and take in not only Christian history, but also ancient bridges, aqueducts, canyons, lakes, and peaks. Covering the entire distance of a trail on foot could take a month, but the trails are set up for day excursions for independent outdoor enthusiasts, made more colorful with the help of her handbooks, *The Lycian Way* (Upcountry Ltd., 2000) and *St Paul Trail* (Upcountry Ltd., 2004); see "Recommended Books & Films" in chapter 2). Kate also conducts 1- or 2-week tours departing from either Fethiye or Antalya. For information on the trail, log on to www.lycianway.com.

(and the coastline is eerily silent in winter). For those with limited time, I recommend the chockablock destinations of the Fethiye or Kalkan/Kaş areas, although my heart is heavy at abandoning some of my most memorable moments in the seclusion of the Datça Peninsula, in the twilight calm at the fires of Olympos, and in the restorative settings of some of the coastline's more isolated lodging. But then again, I'm confident that you'll come back.

1 Marmaris & the Datça Peninsula ⓕ

590km (366 miles) west of Antalya; 165km (102 miles) southeast of Bodrum; 900km (558 miles) south of Istanbul; 185km (115 miles) southwest of Pamukkale; 120km (74 miles) northwest of Dalaman

After commissioning the construction of the castle on the hill as a preliminary to his siege on Rhodes, Süleyman the Magnificent returned from an expedition and exclaimed, *"Mimar as!"* (Hang the architect!). Locals use this story to explain how **Marmaris** got its name; and although this is another of those cute Turkish anecdotes, this one is particularly apt—not for the castle, but for what this town has become. Urban blight has stricken "ocean drive," characterized by seedy-looking signage and fast-food stands advertising baked potatoes to a high concentration of low-budget English tourists lazing about on the bleak public beach.

The local economy obviously hinges on Netsel Marina, a state-of-the-art facility that's undeniably ground zero for the yachting set and the Blue Voyage industry. In fact, the marina, the nearby wharf, and the cobblestone streets surrounding the castle are the bright spots in an otherwise charmless seaside port. It's no wonder that tour operators provide transfers from Dalaman Airport directly to the boat.

That said, the pine-covered mountains surrounding central Marmaris provide a breathtaking backdrop to the small bays, inlets, and coves of the **Datça Peninsula,** the

The Turquoise & Mediterranean Coasts

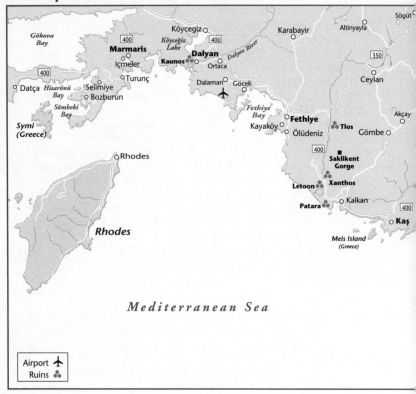

land separation between the Aegean and Mediterranean seas, which is accessible via a handful of well-worn rough asphalt roads that wind slowly through exceptionally breathtaking mountain terrain. Closest to Marmaris is **İçmeler,** a smaller seaside resort at the base of a beautifully crested, pine-covered mountain range, and home to a number of luxury resort hotels. Farther west are the azure waters of the **Gulf of Hisarönü,** and the remote and magical villages of **Selimiye, Turunç,** and **Gökova,** if forced to name just a few.

About 81km (50 miles) west across a wilderness of pine-clad mountain ranges (a little over an hour by car from Marmaris) is the oft-overlooked seaside town of **Datça,** the old Greek inland village of **Eski or Old Datça,** and farther west along a slow-going road toward the tip of the peninsula, the ancient city of **Knidos.** The Datça Peninsula still remains somewhat underdeveloped, probably because most of its visitors sail in with their own accommodations. Although this is the preferred method of travel in these parts, it's just this lack of attention that has preserved the ruggedness of the terrain and charm of the more remote fishing villages. The road west from Marmaris is in neglect, and west of Datça town it's almost nonexistent. So, if traveling by land, you may want to tackle the region of Marmaris separately from the region around Datça town—reached via ferryboat from Bodrum in under 2 hours.

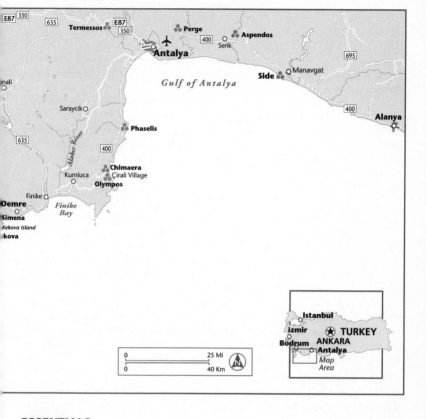

ESSENTIALS
GETTING THERE
BY PLANE **Turkish Airlines** serves Dalaman Airport year-round. Their offices in Marmaris are at Atatürk Cad. 26B (℗ **0252/412-3751** or 252/412-3752). The number at the airport is ℗ **0252/792-5395**.

Havaş (℗ **444-0487**) shuttle buses will be waiting for you at the Dalaman airport to whisk you away to either Marmaris or Fethiye (separate buses for opposite directions). The bus into Marmaris (to the *otogar*, to be exact) takes 90 minutes (85km/53 miles) and costs 21YTL ($16). There are also car-rental counters on-site, sensible if you've arrived here exclusively for a land tour. From the *otogar*, it's a 5-minute and 1.25YTL (95¢) *dolmuş* ride to the marina; taxis will also be waiting at the *otogar*. (See "By Bus" below).

BY BUS The *otogar* (station) (℗ **0252/412-3037**) is located close to the junction for the main highway, about 1.6km (1 mile) outside of the town center. If you're coming from Istanbul (14 hr.) or Ankara (10 hr.), buses depart once a day around 11pm or midnight and arrive the next day for about 45YTL ($33). Service from İzmir (4¼ hr.) is more frequent, with fares as low as 14YTL ($10) with Kamil Koç. From some towns like Selçuk or Kuşadası, you may be forced to change buses in Aydın, about halfway to Marmaris. **Marmaris Koop** bus lines (© **0252/413-5543**) runs direct, air-conditioned service to/from Bodrum (3 hr.; 9.50YTL/$7), Ortaca/Dalyan (1½ hr.; 5.40YTL/$4), Fethiye (3 hr.; 4.50YTL/$3.30), Göcek (2½ hr.; 8YTL/$6), and Antalya (7 hr.; 20YTL/$15). **Pamukkale** bus company (© **0252/412-5586**) runs year-round direct daily service to Pamukkale (4 hr.; 11YTL/$8), in addition to İzmir, Bodrum, Fethiye, Antalya, and Kaş (summers only).

Dolmuşes (minivan-type public transportation) provide regular shuttle service from the *otogar* into town. This is a good option if the bus company you arrived on doesn't provide a free minibus transfer into town. Take a taxi if you're headed to the marina and instruct your driver to take you through the gates and as close as possible to your boat, otherwise, the size of the marina may force you to walk quite a distance from the gates to the mooring.

BY FERRY   Ferries from Bodrum leave twice daily (9am and 5pm) for the 2-hour crossing to Korman, a lonesome port on the northwestern reaches of the Datça Peninsula. A one-way ticket costs 15YTL ($11) and can be purchased either at the offices of **Bodrum Ferryboat Association** (© **0252/316-0882**) just east of the castle or through any travel agent. From Korman, a shuttle bus will take you to the town of Datça, about 6.5km (4 miles) away. From there (assuming Datça is not your final destination), you can hop on a *dolmuş* for the long and alternately mountain and coastal drive into Marmaris (6.75YTL/$5; 1 hr. 15 minutes).

Bodrum Express Lines (© **0252/316-1087**) also runs hydrofoils between Bodrum and Marmaris departing on Tuesday, Thursday, Saturday, and Sunday. Hydrofoils arrive in the charming town of Gelibolu (where they will complete the journey for you with a bus to Marmaris). Total travel time is 1 hour 50 minutes (the last 20 min. are on the bus); the trip costs 26YTL ($19).

VISITOR INFORMATION

The **Tourist Information office** (© **0252/412-1035;** fax 0252/412-7277) is at Iskele Meydanı 2, across from the Atatürk statue.

ORIENTATION

As a chief point of departure for the Blue Voyage, the Marmaris seafront is where all of the action takes place. **Ulusal Egemenlik Caddesi** meets the Bay of Marmaris head-on at the main square proudly displaying the statue of Atatürk. To the east along the shore is **Atatürk Caddesi,** which forks off and changes names several times before it exits Marmaris proper and turns into a hilly country road leading into İçmeler, which is dotted with four- and five-star resorts, each with its own little cove. But before you arrive at this pine-clad paradise, you must pass through a fringe section of two-star hotels, buildings badly in need of paint jobs, and odd minor bazaars selling plastic toys.

The area east of **Ulusal Egemenlik Caddesi** is the older part of town, a cluster of old waterfront houses crowned by the castle. **Kordon Caddesi** is the pedestrian continuation of Atatürk Caddesi to the east of **Iskele Meydanı,** and where the *gulets* (wooden boats) line the wharf each Saturday night prior to their morning departure. The wharf walk makes a semicircular loop around the base of the castle, arriving at several footbridges leading to the entrance of the marina. Within the gates of **Netsel Marina** are a few pubs and restaurants with terraces overlooking the harbor, along with an upscale outdoor shopping mall.

Most of your travel-related business can be done either on Kordon Caddesi for boat-related activities, or on Ulusal Egemenlik Caddesi for general travel agencies or bus offices. Not far from Iskele Meydanı on Ulusal Egemenlik Caddesi (on the left) is the grocery store Targaş, indispensable for last-minute provisions like water and wine, which are generally not included in the Blue Voyage package.

Nighttime activities are concentrated around the harbor, with restaurants lining the wharf from Iskele Meydanı all the way into Netsel Marina. Chaos reigns on **Hacı Mustafa Sokağı,** also known as Barlar Sokağı, from Iskele Meydanı to the footbridge leading to the marina, just 1 block back and parallel to the wharf. There is a covered bazaar at the foot of the castle opposite the statue of Atatürk.

GETTING AROUND

There is one main road running the length of Datça Peninsula from Marmaris to Datça town. *Dolmuşes* run frequently from the *otogar* along Marmaris's multinamed main road via the statue of Atatürk to points west. Check the destination on the windshield if you're headed out of town; service runs as far as Datça. Consider renting a car for forays into the surrounding villages and coves, or get a scooter for ease of transportation in and around the immediate reach of Marmaris town. Ask your hotel concierge if they can help you with a rental, or even ask a bellhop, who will most certainly have a friend in the vehicle-rental business. Cars or scooters rent for as little as 33YTL ($25) day, slightly less if you plan on keeping it for only a couple of hours. Agree on a model and price by phone, and a representative will deliver the vehicle to you at no extra charge.

Several taxi boats provide service between the holiday resorts of Içmeler and downtown Marmaris. Service is more frequent when demand is up, so check with your hotel to see how often they are running, if at all, and the time of day they start/finish. The ride costs 4YTL ($3) each way.

A regular taxi from Içmeler to Marmaris costs around 8YTL ($6).

DAY TRIPS BY BOAT

Lining the wharves of most medium- to large-size towns are private captains touting day trips through neighboring waters. A typical excursion tools along the coastline to the south to Turunç, Umlu, Cadirgan, and Çiftlik bays, and to **Cleopatra's (Sedir) Island,** made famous for the pearly white sands the exotic queen had shipped over from Egypt. Day-boat excursions also leave from **Bozburun** and **Datça,** past scenery more beautiful than the last, where you can swim, snorkel, or just plain snooze, all for about 27YTL ($20), lunch included. A second itinerary out of Marmaris heads a little farther out into the Mediterranean to **Dalyan** (see later in this chapter), where, at **Iztuzu Beach,** you'll switch from your *gulet* to a motorized fishing boat for the classic tour up the Dalyan River, including a stop at Kaunos and the mud baths. Prices for this trip are a little higher, at about 34YTL ($25) per person.

Certified divers with their own boats, easily spotted by the rack of wet suits and diving equipment onboard, line the wharf near Iskele Meydanı. Diving expeditions leave early in the morning; for any day-boat trip; it's important to reserve at least the evening before. Cost of a day out is about 49YTL ($36), including equipment, insurance, guides, and lunch. There's also the reputable **European Diving Center** (www.europeandiving.com.tr), with outlets in both Marmaris (© **0252/455-4733**) and Fethiye (© **0252/614-9771**). EDC also offers a 1-day dive for beginners, a 3-day PADI dive course, and a 5-day PADI open water course.

EXPLORING IN & AROUND MARMARIS

These days, Marmaris is top-heavy with cheap tourism, and it shows. But a short drive out of town reveals the original appeal that drew visitors in the first place. Leaving their mark along the peninsula are a slew of ancient civilizations, some woven into the daily fabric of humble villages, tourist marinas, and magnificent beaches. North of Marmaris on the road to Muğla is **Gökova** ☾☾, another stop on the yachting trail, dotted with clusters of picturesque wooden houses built in the two-story Ottoman style.

Just outside of Marmaris is the lovely resort of **Içmeler,** magnificently sited in a sheltered cove at the base of rippling pine-covered mountains. The fit and ambitious may want to sample a portion of the **scenic trail** ☾☾ that runs all the way from Içmeler to Değirmenyanı, about 19km (12 miles) west. The village of **Turunç** ☾, farther south, sustains the charm of tradition and the comforts of modernity. A popular stop for yachts, it accommodates its visitors with handcrafted products such as honey, garden thyme, and sage tea. The long and winding road southwest to **Selimiye** ☾☾☾ is well worth the effort. Frozen in time, this settlement is an ideal spot for enjoying local fish, village wine, and magical sunsets following a day on Sılıman Beach. Take your time traveling south from Hisarönü, though: You can walk on water at the beach of **Kızkumu** ☾ in Orhaniye, just beyond Hisarönü, where a lengthy sand bar extends 800m (2,624 ft.) into the bay. In the heat of summer, you may want to stop off at the **waterfall** ☾ near Turgut village, stroll through the Carpet Weavers Corporation, and relax over *gözleme* (a crepe filled with cheese, spinach, or both) and *ayran* (a Turkish yogurt drink).

It wouldn't be fair to finish off this section without mentioning the **Marmaris Castle Museum** (© **0252/412-1459**), in the fortress in the old section of Marmaris. Perched above the harbor, the best access is through the bazaar behind the Atatürk statue; follow the signs through the narrow streets up the hill to the museum entrance. The exhibit isn't terribly interesting, but the views of the harbor and castle itself might be worth the 1.35YTL ($1) admission fee. The museum is open daily from 8am to noon and from 1 to 5:30pm.

WHERE TO STAY
MARMARIS

If you've done your homework, you'll arrive in Marmaris on Saturday just in time to drop your luggage on the boat and wander about for some last-minute exploration and shopping. That's not to say that Marmaris is entirely without appeal; but unless you're staying in a full-service hotel with a private beach, staying here is kind of a stretch.

There's not much in the way of accommodations in the downtown area except for noisy backpacker-class pensions. One exception is **Saryana Aparts,** 24 Sok. No. 4 (behind Netsel Marina, near the bus garage; © **0252/413-6835;** fax 0252/412-2656), offering studio rooms with kitchen facilities and a lovely garden. Doubles cost 60€ ($72) June–Aug, and 50€ ($60) Apr–May and Sept–Nov. Rates include breakfast.

About 1.6km (1 mile) or so out of the center on the road to Içmiler is the new **Hotel Almena** ⚑, Kemal Elgin Bulvarı 45 (© **0252/413-8228;** fax 0252/413-8250; www.almenahotel.com), a boutique property of 55 luxuriously decorated rooms, each with a balcony. Doubles (ask for a corner room) cost around 75€ ($92), and that includes the free movie channel.

More luxurious is the five-star **Iberostar Grand Azur Hotel,** Kenan Evren Bulv. 11 (© **0252/417-4050;** fax 0252/417-4060; www.iberostar.com), with its expansive beachfront and manicured lawns that give it a decidedly *Great Gatsby* feel. For the level of quality that the hotel strives to achieve, the rooms are somewhat disappointing; but children will love this resort for the indoor atrium kid pool, designed like a mini-jungle–water park. The adult playground is even better equipped: speedboats, jet skis, banana boats, water skis, and windsurfing equipment, not to mention the diving programs available for all levels of expertise. The rack rate hovers around 120€ ($146) for a double.

IÇMELER

The hotels of Içmeler offer a lovely alternative to Marmaris: Accessible via water taxi 2.75YTL ($2), it's close enough to take advantage of the shopping, dining, and nightlife, yet far enough away that the coastline is once again able to enchant. One difficulty independent travelers may encounter is that because these hotels work primarily with groups, they may either be booked solid for your dates or ignore you altogether. (My experience was the latter.) The most popular option is the **Divan Marmaris Mares,** Pamucak Mevkii (© **0252/455-2200;** fax 0252/455-2201 or 0252/412-1214; www.mares.com.tr), full of distractions like heated indoor and outdoor swimming pools, a fitness room, sauna, Turkish bath (fee-based), watersports, tennis, various restaurants, a patisserie, a nightclub, a shopping arcade, and even a heliport. The usual array of watersports activities is available, from diving to kayaking, or you can just relax on the narrow sandy strip. The abundance of the breakfast buffet is without equal.

The nearby **Martı Resort Deluxe Hotel** (© **0252/455-3440;** fax 0252/455-3448; www.marti.com.tr) has the more spectacular site, nestled in the cleavage of two pine-covered mountains. Built on the site of a 7th-century monastery (some of the ruins are visible out front), the Martı boasts its very own private beach, fronting an expansive playground of lawns and a duplex pool. All rooms have an outdoor entrance and a balcony. A sunken sitting area and floral decor make for a comfortable retreat, and the bathrooms are a decent size. Amenities include four indoor and outdoor swimming pools, a Turkish bath (fee-based), a Jacuzzi, a fitness room, a sauna, tennis courts, hairdresser, restaurants, and a nightclub.

WEST OF MARMARIS

Golden Key Bördübet 🏄 *Kids*   This place and the Golden Key Hisarönü (see listing below) are sister properties that sit on the edge of an undeveloped tourist frontier. What the Golden Key Bördübet lacks in waterfront, it makes up as an unmanicured garden paradise, buried deep in the pine mountains via a bumpy 12km (7½-mile) road (6.5km/4 miles of which is a rocky dirt track). The property, shaded under a forest of lemon trees and pine, is split in half by the Bördübet Stream, which, thanks to the canoes provided by the hotel, provides direct access to the sea and to the hotel's private **"island"**—a tiny slice of heaven equipped with canoes, kayaks, wind sails, lounge chairs, and a snack bar. (This beach is also accessible by land; the hotel provides a shuttle.) In contrast to the Hisarönü property, the rooms at Bördübet are updated and stylish. The guest quarters occupy several terra-cotta-colored buildings arranged around a swimming pool. Junior suites are standard rooms with balconies, while the king suites have double the space. Duplexes are actually small albeit on two levels, and enjoy small ground-floor patios. With tennis courts, bicycles at your disposal, scenic wooden bridges, a brand-new spa facility, and farm animals wandering the property, Bördübet is a great choice for parents *and* kids.

48706 Bördübet (35km/22 miles west of Marmaris). ⓒ **0252/436-9230.** Fax 0252/436-9089. 22 units. 190€ ($230) suite; 240€ ($293) king suite. MC, V. Closed Nov–Mar. **Amenities:** Restaurant; 2 bars; outdoor swimming pool; watersports; bikes; concierge; car-rental desk; 24-hr. room service; dry cleaning. *In room:* A/C, satellite TV, minibar, hair dryer.

Golden Key Hisarönü 🏄 *Kids*   A sister property of Golden Key Bördübet (see above), the hotel hugs an elevated outcropping on one of the smaller beaches of the Gulf of Hisarönü, which it shares with two teeny campsites and a family-owned restaurant. The main draw is the beachfront, backed by an expansive grassy garden strewn with lawn chairs and some kiddy paraphernalia. A swimming pool sits at the back of the property near the restaurant, along with the guest rooms, located in several buildings. At about 16 years old, the accommodations are in need of a renovation, but everything works, the beds are comfortable, rooms are large, and the private patios are great for a late-afternoon read.

48706 Hisarönü (27km/17 miles west of Marmaris). ⓒ **0252/466-6620.** Fax 0252/466-6042. 19 units. 160€ ($195) double; 380€ ($464) family suite. MC, V. Closed Nov–Mar. **Amenities:** Restaurant; 2 bars; outdoor swimming pool; watersports; children's playground; car-rental desk; 24-hr. room service; dry cleaning. *In room:* A/C, satellite TV or minibar, hair dryer.

Palmetto   Staying at the Palmetto is all about appreciating the magical little fishing village of Selimiye, located 45 long and winding mountainous kilometers (28 miles) from Marmaris on the road past Hisarönü toward Bozburun. The hotel is the creation of Dr. Erol Üçer, a Turkish-born psychiatrist who has been practicing in the United States for over 30 years, and whose love for the village prompted the initiation of this little hobby. Rooms are small, spare, and simple, with neutral tones and adequate mattresses. The floors are tiled and bathrooms have showers only. A room with a balcony overlooking the pool patio to the cove makes the most of this spot, providing a front-row seat to the waterfront's two harbors, the sheer rocky cliffs rising behind the minaret, and the ruins of an old church or monastery rising out of the center of the harbor.

48483 Selimiye (45km/28 miles southwest of Marmaris). ⓒ **0252/446-4299.** Fax 0252/446-4301. www.palmetto resort.com. 18 units (with shower only). 80€ ($100) double July–Sept. Rates lower off season. MC, V. **Amenities:** Restaurant; bar; outdoor swimming pool; 24-hr. room service; dry cleaning. *In room:* A/C, satellite TV or minibar, hair dryer, safe.

WHERE TO DINE

Marmaris isn't hiding a grand culinary tradition, and apart from the few exceptions, the best you can hope for is a baked potato at a stand along the public beach. The several restaurants and cafes in the marina offer the most appealing options. For an authentic meal with views of the marina, at rock-bottom prices, head over to the diminutive two-story **Ney Restaurant** in the castle (26 Sokak 24; ✆ **0252/412-0212**).

MARMARIS AFTER DARK

Assuming this is your first stop in Turkey, you may want to experience the excessive crowding and throbbing noise of the infamous *Barlar Sokağı* (Bar St.), characterized by an endless lineup of bars indistinguishable from the Barlar Sokağı in countless seaside resort towns along the coast. Marmaris's Barlar Sokağı is particularly narrow, so in high season it can get claustrophobic.

More sedate and infinitely more appealing are the **art house movies** shown in the open-air theater in Netsel Marina nightly in summer (✆ **0252/412-2708;** www. netselmarina.com).

SIDE TRIP TO DATÇA PENINSULA & ENVIRONS

Remote enough to weed out the riffraff, but easily accessible via ferryboat from Bodrum, Datça and its rugged surroundings are historic, peaceful, and most of all, unspoiled. The stunning coves of Palmut Bükü, Mesudiye, Domuzcukuru, Akvaryum, and Kargı boast some of the cleanest water in the Mediterranean, and with a 33% presence of oxygen in the air and a perfect Mediterranean climate, these elements combine to support the legendary longevity of the residents of Datça.

The proximity to the Greek islands of Rhodes and Simi can only suggest the richness of the Dorian civilization that passed here, but a look at the ancient ruins of **Knidos** ✿✿, whose terraced promontory rises above the site's dual harbors, certainly give us a clue. (Admission to the site is 4YTL/$3.) The lovely port village of Datça is the center of activity at this end of the peninsula; in fact, Datça is the site of the original ancient city of Knidos, which moved to its current "new" position at the extreme western point of the peninsula in about 360 B.C. More recent settlements are the villages of Eski Datça and Reşadiye, located along the road between Datça and Körmen (the ferry landing about 6.5km/4 miles to the north). **Eski or Old Datça** ✿ is a landlocked village straight out of the storybooks, a minuscule cluster of old stone houses, carved doorways, and cobbled lanes dating back to when this was a Greek town. One or two coffeehouses and a pension or two hidden behind sandy stone walls provide a respite from an already thoroughly charming visit. The village of **Reşadiye** ✿ exhibits some traditionally Turkish architecture and is worth a walk-through as well.

The road west of Datça discourages casual travel, as it is unpaved and bumpy. Not surprisingly, this end of the peninsula offers some of the most pristine bays and ancient sites, but you may want to consider arriving by boat (day excursions leave from Datça town daily; the cost is about 20YTL/$15 per person) to make the most of the peninsula's coastal wonders.

GETTING HERE & GETTING AROUND   Ferryboat service from Bodrum operates daily May through October to the minuscule port of Korman (2 hr.; 15YTL/$11 one-way; 26YTL/$19 round-trip.); a shuttle bus from the landing will take you the remaining 5km (3 miles) to Datça town. From Marmaris, it's about an hour's drive over hilly terrain; longer if you've opted for a *dolmuş.*

Finds The Olive Farm

Visitors to Turkey marvel over the superiority of the olive oil. But sheltered from the international craze for quality food products and produced by people simply unequipped to compete with an advanced marketing presence coming out of Italy, Turkish olive oil regrettably remains isolated within Turkey's borders. The **Olive Farm** (*©* **0252/712-0306**; www.olivefarm.net) will hopefully change all that. The Olive Farm (also known as Guller Dağı Ciftliği, or the Mountain of Roses Farm, named after the American couple that pioneered it) combines top-quality olives, the strictest handling procedures, and savvy marketing techniques to promote an otherwise overlooked national treasure. The Olive Farm is located only 5 minutes east of Datça, and offers tours of the mill along with tastings. If you show up on a Friday, you get the added opportunity to buy their olive bread. Bottles of oil sell on the premises for 11YTL to 24YTL ($8–$18) per liter (worth every penny). Olive Farm products are also available through their store in Portland, Oregon (*©* **888/380-8018**).

Excursion boats leave daily in season from Datça harbor to Knidos, making stops at a number of the more scenic coves along the way. By car, the road west of Datça is essentially a bumpy dirt path that leads to Knidos; the terrain is rugged and takes about 45 minutes.

WHERE TO STAY & DINE   In spite of the presence of a number of holiday resorts, the pace of this end of Mediterranean Turkey promotes a more intimate, relaxed style of lodging. Charming and tranquil hardly describes the **Dede Pansiyon** (*©*/fax **0252/712-3951;** www.dedepansiyon.com), a quiet and flowering retreat in the heart of Eski Datça. The pension is actually a renovated Greek house, complete with a swimming pool, snack bar, and a mere six rooms. Each room is faithfully decorated according to its namesake: The Chaplin room is full of movie-related objects, the Theatre room displays masks and such, and the Chagall room contains reproductions of the famous artist's works. This is a true and unencumbered retreat. All rooms have air-conditioning, and doubles cost 60€ ($72).

About .8km (½ mile) outside of Datça town is the **Marphe Hotel,** Kocatarla (*©* **0252/712-9030;** fax 0252/712-9172; www.hotelmarphe.com), set up like a Greek village, and constructed of whitewashed and natural stone. The Marphe consists of 7 apartments (bedroom, living room, full kitchen, and balcony), 7 suites, and 12 villas (2 bedrooms, 2 bathrooms, living room, full kitchen, 2 balconies, and a terrace on a huge garden property in the countryside). Prices for a suite are 75€ ($92), or 45€ ($55) in low season, including breakfast. Weekly villas rates (daily not available) range from 850€ to 1,800€ ($1,040–$2,200), or 700€ to 1,500€ ($850–$1,830) in low season. Breakfast is not included in the apartments or villas, but Marphe has an on-site restaurant, and also offers a shuttle service into town.

2 Dalyan *★★* & Kaunos *★*

110km (67 miles) east of Marmaris; 76km (47 miles) northwest of Fethiye

Dalyan offers the perfect refuge from the high-intensity holidays offered by back-to-back hotels and the constant whirring of jet-ski engines. What sets Dalyan apart from a coastline of Mediterranean powerhouses is its serene upriver location, its small-town character, the nearby natural treasure that is Iztuzu Beach, and a collection of some of the most stunning ancient monuments along the coast.

One of the last remaining major breeding sites on the Mediterranean for the sea turtle (loggerhead, or Caretta Caretta) and the green turtle (chelonia mydas), Dalyan rose from obscurity in 1986 when in protest against the development of a luxury hotel, environmental protectionists rallied to have the nearby beach declared a protected area. The publicity only served as a beacon for the first major wave of tourists, but even if every other street has a pension with the word "turtle" in it, Dalyan still remains, for the most part, a quiet river town. But even more monumental than the pristine pseudo-sandbar that makes up Iztuzu—better known as Turtle Beach—are the spectacular cliff-top temple-tombs soaring above the reeds on the opposite shores of the river. In addition to the ruins of ancient **Kaunos,** the area boasts some natural thermal sources in what has become a local ritual at the nearby mud baths. And as a delightful small village in its own right, Dalyan makes a charming base for activities such as kayaking, rafting, diving, and snorkeling; exploring village life through treks, jeep tours, and bike rides; or sailing (for days) along some of Turkey's most stunning coastline. Getting around is half the fun: River *dolmuşes* shuttle people up and down the river through an incredible maze of canals enclosed within 3m (9-ft.) walls of reeds, past mysterious Lycian cliff tombs.

ESSENTIALS
GETTING THERE
BY PLANE   Dalaman Airport lies only 21km (13 miles) southeast of Dalyan. (Count on at least 25 min. by car; see "By Plane" under "Getting There" for Marmaris, earlier in this chapter.) It is possible to get in on your own by taking the airport coach to the crossroad in Dalaman (5km/3 miles), changing for a *dolmuş* to Ortaca (9.5km/6 miles), and then changing again for Dalyan (12km/7¼ miles), an ordeal that will cost you about an hour (including waiting time) and about 4YTL ($3). Better still is to have a trusted driver waiting for you: **Kaunos Tours** (in Dalyan center, across from the post office; ✆ **0252/284-2816;** www.kaunostours.com) offers a special shuttle service for as little as 47YTL ($35) for a car that holds up to four people. See if you can get a local taxi to beat *that*.

BY BUS   There is no direct bus service to Dalyan. Buses will get you as far as Ortaca, located about 8km (5 miles) west on the Marmaris to Fethiye highway. Kamil Koç (✆ **0252/282-2045**) provides its own minibus transfer from the *otogar* in Ortaca (arriving direct from İzmir, Bodrum, and Antalya); otherwise, it's about a 15-minute *dolmuş* ride right up to the Atatürk statue in Dalyan's tiny town center. There is also limited *dolmuş* service from Fethiye (6YTL/$4.50; 1 hr. 10 min.) and Marmaris (6.75YTL/$5; 1 hr. 30 min.).

BY BOAT   A wonderful first impression of Dalyan can be had arriving by sea. You can negotiate the cost of transportation from one of the neighboring ports—Marmaris is the closest major one—or book a cheap spot on a day excursion and take it one-way only.

VISITOR INFORMATION
The **Tourist Information office** (✆/fax **0252/284-4235**) is located in the town center on Maraş Mahallesi.

ORIENTATION

Dalyan is situated on the **Dalyan River (Dalyan Cayı),** a river canal connecting the Köyceğiz Lake with the Mediterranean. At the mouth of the river is a natural sandbar protecting the canal from the open seas. Known as **Iztuzu Beach,** this beach peninsula divides the rough seas of the Mediterranean from the serene waters of the canal, and is one of the last natural breeding grounds for the loggerhead turtle.

Majestic rock-cut temple tombs hover on the cliff face, and farther upriver on the shore opposite Dalyan are the ruins of **Kaunos,** once a thriving Lycian port town and now located slightly inland. Farther north are the open-air mud baths, and continuing upriver, the thermal waters flanking the scenic **Köyceğiz Lake.** On the northern bank of the lake is the sleepy village of Köyceğiz, an alternative jumping-off point for visits to the area attractions.

The soul of Dalyan is on the river. Restaurants, waterside cafes, hotels, and pensions line the waterfront, while the business heart of the city (banks, post office, and shopping center) is located a few short steps inland. *Dolmuşes* line up next to the post office, near the statue of Atatürk.

GETTING AROUND

BY BOAT It seems that the local fishermen and their sons have figured out that it's more lucrative to run a taxi service than to get up in the middle of the night for a few pennies' worth of fish. In the summer, river *dolmuşes,* managed by a cooperative, make the 40-minute trip to the tip of Iztuzu Beach for around 2YTL ($1.50), from around 9am until slightly after midday. Upon request, they'll even pick you up at your hotel—have your hotel call ahead (© **0252/284-2094**). River *dolmuşes* run from Dalyan to Iztuzu between 9am and 1:30pm; return boats leave Iztuzu beginning at 1pm to the last run at 6pm. Don't wait till late morning to head out, though; since these are *dolmuşes,* they only leave after they've managed to pick up a reasonable number of passengers, leaving latecomers waiting indefinitely.

The cooperative's boatmen prefer to tout the more lucrative private tours to the surrounding sites, the most popular of which is an excursion that includes "Turtle Beach" (Iztuzu), Kaunos, and the mud baths upriver. Rates for a small boat cost around 82YTL ($60); a larger boat will run you 135YTL ($100) for the day, but ultimately, for that kind of money, you should be able to get the boatman to take you anywhere you want (good luck, as rates are heading skyward). The more economical option is to hook up with one of the innumerable agencies around town that offer group tours of the area; this way, the cost of the private boat rental is shouldered by all participants, and the headache of filling the boat is borne by the agency. **Kaunos Tours,** also the local representative for Europcar, runs a "Dalyan Special" for 34YTL ($25) per adult; kids 4 and older pay half-price (kids younger than 4 go free). Kaunos Tours also runs adventure trips (jeeps, horses, fishing, kayaking, diving), as well as a "Kids Club Day" tour for 60YTL ($45) adults, 35YTL ($26) kids.

There's an inexpensive and convenient rowboat shuttling those in-the-know across the river from Dalyan, at the extreme southern end of the Kordon (not far from the Dalyan Hotel) to Çandır; at only 1YTL (75¢), this service is extremely useful for those hearty and independent enough to brave the heat for the short walk up to the ruins of Kaunos, or the hour it will take to hike up to the mud baths.

BY *DOLMUŞ* *Dolmuşes* leave regularly from the town center for Iztuzu Beach (2YTL/$1.50; 20 min.), Ortaca (2YTL/$1.50; 15 min.), and Köyceğiz town (2YTL/$1.50; 30 min.). Fares quoted are one-way.

BY BIKE   Getting around on your own juice will give you the freedom to enjoy Iztuzu Beach, 18 hilly kilometers (11 miles) away, well after the excursion boats have cleared the docks. Scooters and bicycles are available for rental at Kaunos Moto across from the post office (© **0252/284-2816**) at reasonable daily rates.

WHAT TO SEE & DO
EXPLORING KAUNOS
The ancient site of Kaunos was a valuable port trading in salt and slaves that, much like other great cities of its time, eventually suffered the fate of rapidly receding waters. Lying on the Carian-Lycian border, Kaunos first entered the history books under Persian rule in the 6th century B.C., passing to Carian rule when the administration of the port was assigned to Carian governor Mausolus of Halicarnassus. From around 200 B.C., rule of Kaunos passed around like a hot potato, from Ptolemy of Egypt to Rhodes, from Rhodes to Rome, from Rome back to Rhodes, and finally back to Rome in the 3rd century A.D., when Diocletian added Kaunos to the province of Lycia. The ruins of Kaunos, especially the rock tombs, reflect this cultural jumble, including Hellenistic city walls, a Roman theater, and typical Lycian tombs.

Excursion boats moor on the river's edge amid the wooden pylons of a fish farm. The mooring is about 90m (100 yd.) from the entrance to the sight, accessible by way of a footpath. A concession near the entrance to the ruins is your last chance to buy bottled water; be sure to avail yourself of this, because there's very little shade on the walk up.

The path that forks to the right will lead you directly up to a **Roman theater** ✦, carved into the slope of the acropolis hill. Two of the statue bases that survive are inscribed with the names of Mausolus and Hecatomnos. Farther up the hill are the fairly well preserved remains of a **defensive sea wall** ✦, hard to imagine now that the sea is nowhere in sight. Take care hiking up to the top, as the terrain is pretty rugged, but evidently not too much of a challenge for the local mountain goats bleating in the distance. If you're not up for a treacherous climb, you can get comparable views of the marshlands (as well as what's left of the Great Harbor) from row 34 of the theater. Now a stagnant marshland, the Great Harbor was the cause of a seriously unhealthy malaria epidemic that stigmatized the locals for centuries.

> **Take a Break**
> The **Fruit Bar** (© **0252/284-4164**; daily 9am–1am) on Maraş Mah serves up refreshing drinks like fruit shakes, salads, and crepes.

Northwest of the theater are the **Roman baths** and a **Byzantine basilica** ✦; slightly above these are the remains of a **Roman temple,** recently identified as a temple to the cult of Apollo.

Two types of **rock tombs** ✦✦✦ are visible from the river as well as from the summit of the acropolis: those carved in the shapes of ornate Greek temples or simple chambers cut into the lower rock. The tombs were reused during Roman times, and all of the tombs at one time or another have fallen victim to scavengers. Admission to the site is 4YTL ($3).

A TRIP TO IZTUZU BEACH
One of the last and most important breeding grounds for the near-extinct Caretta Caretta (loggerhead) turtle on the Mediterranean, **Iztuzu Beach** ✦✦ came to public

consciousness in 1984 when conservationists mobilized against a local developer's plan for construction of a luxury hotel. Some good works backfire, and even though the developer never got around to building his hotel, the publicity only served to put the spot on the map. The Association for the Protection of Wildlife has established strict guidelines to benefit the turtles, among them: no distracting lights at night, no night-time visitors during the summer months, and a request that sunbathers remain behind the line of wooden stakes so as not to disturb potential nests.

There are two separate beach areas: the privately run stretch receiving the tide of excursion boats, and the less-crowded far end of the beach nearest the road, operated by the Dalyan Municipality. With the sea at your feet, the hills over your shoulder, and the calm waters and tall reeds of the river delta at your back, pristine Iztuzu is really one of the loveliest beaches in the region.

A TRIP TO THE MUD BATHS

Most commonly reached by boat, the **Mud Baths** ✿, a rough-and-ready outdoor water pool and mud bath fed by the Sultaniye Spring, is a mandatory stop on most guided excursions. Located about 10 minutes upriver and on the bank opposite Dalyan, this idiosyncratic outdoor "spa" was last dubbed "Aqua Mia," after passing through a long line of new management. There's a sign posted with instructions on the suggested procedure, which includes slapping on fistfuls of sulfur-rich mud and embarrassed waiting periods while the mud on your skin dries. Before rinsing under one of the outdoor showers, take a look in the mirror provided, and be sure to bring a camera.

There's a lonely dockside restaurant and snack bar, and the fee for individuals (admission is included in a group price) is about 4YTL, or $3. *A bit of advice:* Leave that white bathing suit at home. A few minutes away by boat to the southwest of Köyceğiz Lake is the **Sultaniye Kaplıcaları,** a thermal spring that dates to Hellenistic times with thermal water as hot as 105°F (41°C).

THE ACTIVE TRAVELER

Dalyan's accessibility makes it a good base for activity-filled day excursions. **Kaunos Tours,** across from the post office (𝄪 **0252/284-2816;** www.kaunostours.com), bills itself as "the Outdoor Specialists," offering daily adventures such as **Rafting along the Dalaman River** through narrow gorges along rapids that can reach Grade 4 (50€/$60), a **jeep safari** (40€/$50); **sea-kayaking tours** (40€$50); and **trekking** (30€$37), to name the tip of their iceberg. Lunch is included on all day tours, and children (where applicable) go along for 50% of the adult rate.

Even at the stunning natural site of Iztuzu Beach, divers and snorkelers will feel like fish out of water, because the sea floor is equally pristine below the surf—and rather boring to look at. Nearby Ekincik Bay solves that problem, with its million-year-old caves and abundance of marine life, although serious divers may want to hook up with a dive center offering day trips to the open waters around Marmaris. Kaunos Tours runs a diving trips (50€/$60 for the "discover scuba"; 25€$30 for certified divers).

WHERE TO STAY

The village of Dalyan started out as an environmentally conscious little haven that, once discovered, spawned the conversion of many local family houses into guest pensions. It was just a matter of time before more heavy-hitting hotels changed the basic character of the village; although construction hasn't quite gotten out of hand, Dalyan is no longer the untouched secret it once was. Pensions still line the main drag (for an edited listing, with rates, try **www.kaunostours.com**), but Dalyan is so small that staying in a more comfortable (and just as cheap) hotel farther inland won't make or break the holiday.

Asur Oteli Because of its environmentally sensitive design and four-star facilities, the Asur Oteli is one of the most in-demand hotels in town. The single-story octagonal units, trimmed with wood and designed to imitate the traditional architecture of the area, surround a central pool and resemble a small village of gazebos. Individual units are a bit tight and the shower basin lacks a curtain, but that shouldn't detract from the hotel's appeal. The lovely flowering garden is an oasis sandwiched between the river and the flat plain backed by hills in the distance, with a pool and restaurant as worthy distractions. The hotel also owns a neighboring (and somewhat cheaper) group of efficiency rooms.

Maraş Mahallesi (about 1km/½ mile outside of town), 48840 Dalyan. ℭ **0252/284-3232**. Fax 0252/284-3244. www.asurotel.com. 36 units (all with shower). 46€–70€ ($56–$85) double. Rates reflect seasonal differences. AE, MC, V. Closed Nov–Mar. **Amenities:** Restaurant; 2 bars; outdoor swimming pool; sauna; bikes; concierge; 24-hr. room service; dry cleaning. *In room:* A/C, satellite TV, minibar.

Club Alla Turca *(Kids)* Boasting the largest pool in Dalyan (550 sq. m/1,804 sq. ft.), this 2-year-old complex consists of four new houses. The buildings were designed to replicate traditional Turkish architectural characteristics in modern materials: wooden Ottoman *çumbas* are translated into cement, and some of the rooms are arranged in Turkish family style around an open inner courtyard. The rooms, still smelling of newness, are a delightful arrangement of greens and blues, leather accents, and inlaid marble headboards, while out-of-room amenities include an oversize TV screen, and a large children's wonderland of Fisher Price minihouses and slides. The hotel sits on a flat plain about 1km (½ mile) upriver from Dalyan's marina, but in exchange for the inconvenience, guests benefit from a clean, comfortable environment.

Gülpınar Mahallesi, 48840 Dalyan. ℭ **0252/284-4616**. Fax 0252/284-4387. www.cluballaturca.com. 60 units. 50€–74€ ($60–$90) double. Rates reflect seasonal differences. MC, V. Closed Nov 1–May 1. **Amenities:** 2 restaurants; 2 bars; outdoor swimming pool; children's pool; children's playground; game room; concierge; tour desk; car-rental desk; 24-hr. room service; dry cleaning; TV lounge. *In room:* A/C, satellite TV, minibar, hair dryer, safe.

Dalyan Hotel Both modest and sublime, the Dalyan Hotel may lack some upgraded amenities, but it's great for its small scale and outdoor access. The hotel occupies the town's most coveted piece of land—a prime piece of riverside real estate almost directly under the watchful gaze of ancient rock-cut temples. The centerpiece of the waterside garden is the circular swimming pool, encircled by two arched and arcaded room quarters. The more popular of the two has small, inviting patios looking over the pool toward the rock tombs, while the other quarters offer patios with river views and the peaceful seclusion of tall reeds and wildflowers. Each room comes with one double and single bed, both outfitted with a set of splendid pillows. So the shower drain is pathetically slow, and the staff forgets to flick the hot water switch. These are minor inconveniences, especially when considered from a relaxing spot at one of the in-pool bar stools. When full, the Dalyan provides free shuttles to Iztuzu Beach on their private boat, which is also available for private excursions at competitive prices.

Maraş Mahallesi Sok., 48840 Dalyan. ℭ **0252/284-2239**. Fax 0252/284-2240. www.dalyanotel.com. 20 units. Low season 50€ ($60) double; high season 75€ ($90) double. Children 12 and under stay free in parent's room. MC, V. Free parking. **Amenities:** Restaurant; bar; outdoor swimming pool w/views of the rock tombs; 24-hr. room service; dry cleaning. *In room:* A/C.

Sultan Palace Hotel   When two former employees unexpectedly ran off together leaving the hotel without a chef or receptionist, the manager called her mother, Özdan, to come to the rescue in the kitchen. As fate would have it, Brit native Frank Mann was staying at the hotel, having joined his family on vacation at the last minute. Three years later, Frank and Özdan were married and the proud owners of a secluded oasis of gardens and tropical plants resting at the base of a series of rocky outcroppings. The main building resembles a medieval stone tower, from which two two-story buildings radiate. The rooms are showing their age, but most of the needed improvements are cosmetic. The main detractor of the Sultan Palace is the isolated location; even though the mud baths are an easy 5-minute walk away and a hotel boat shuttles guests to Dalyan center six times a day, you may feel removed from the action. (Although Özdan's cooking is well worth the trade-off; definitely stick around for dinner.)

Horozlar Mevkii, 48840 Dalyan. ⓒ **0252/284-2103.** Fax 0252/284-2106. www.yachtcharterclub.com/sultan1.htm. 26 units. 65€ ($80) double B&B; 88€ ($107) double half board. MC, V. By car via the approach from Marmaris only; from Dalyan center, leave your car in the Denizati's restaurant lot near the hotel's boat landing for transport to the opposite side of the river. **Amenities:** Restaurant; bar; outdoor swimming pool; children's pool; croquet lawn; 24-hr. room service; dry cleaning. *In room:* A/C.

WHERE TO DINE

Nothing beats a satisfying meal while seated beneath the spectacular and awe-inspiring cliff tombs across the river, except relentless mosquitoes. Bring plenty of repellent when dining outdoors in Dalyan.

Ali Baba KEBAPS   With 22 years in the kitchen (3 in Dalyan) and a cookbook under his belt, the chef of Ali Baba provides outstanding alternatives for die-hard carnivores and people who are completely fished-out. This is also a great spot if you've got kids in tow, as the servers appear with distractions like Legos and crayons. Try their lamb chops, or throw caution to the wind and opt for the Ali Baba special: a deadly combination of chopped lamb, garlic, parsley, hot pepper, and spices on a bed of tomato sauce with yogurt, covered in melted cheese and drizzled with melted butter.

Belediye Karşısı, Davran Dükkanları. ⓒ **0252/284-4769.** *Kebaps* 9.50YTL ($7). MC, V. Daily 11am–midnight.

Ceyhan TURKISH   Ceyhan doesn't pretend to be anything other than what it is: an unpretentious assemblage of shaded tables scattered on the gravel at the water's edge. While Dalyan's other riverside restaurants are homogenous in terms of atmosphere, flavor, and price, this little gem transforms simplicity into grand appeal. The young entrepreneurs—rather, boys—who run Ceyhan have located the recipe for some of the most flavorful *yaprak dolması* (stuffed grape leaves) on the map; ditto for the decidedly unusual *fasulye* (green beans) and *patlican salatası* (eggplant salad).

Kordon Boyu (near the rowboat shuttle). ⓒ **0542/895-6730.** Main courses 9.50YTL ($7). No credit cards. Daily 8am–2am.

Riverside Café FISH/KEBAPS   The Riverside Café, set in a private garden with tables reed-side, highlights the Turkish tradition of food preparation by grilling everything, from shrimp, calamari, and a daily selection of fresh fish, to chicken and lamb, all on an oversize outdoor charcoal barbeque. Hopefully the original Riverside will transfer some of its recipes, such as the flavorful seaweed salad, the appetizer of anchovies and sardines, and the marinated calamari, over to this location. *One caveat, however:* Bring lots of mosquito repellent.

Maraş Mah. ⓒ **0252/284-3614.** Appetizers 5.40YTL–9.50YTL ($4–$7); main courses 9.50YTL–15YTL ($7–$11). MC, V. Daily noon–midnight.

Unchartered Territory: Between Fethiye & Dalyan

The most beautiful untouched bays and coves along the Turkish Mediterranean are arguably those operated as parks and campgrounds. These oases are striking enough to attract visitors but still rough enough where the music of the waves is not drowned out by air-conditioning units. The beach begins at the tree line at **Yonca Camping,** Yanıklar Köyü (℡ **0252/633-6177**), located along the coastline about a half-hour's drive northwest of Fethiye. They offer rudimentary bungalows, set back behind tents and motor homes, and a small on-site restaurant. **Katrancı Ormaniç,** Katrancı Park, Küçük Kargı (℡ **0252/612-1086**) is slightly manicured, in a Turkish national park sort of way.

For the less-earthy, there's the exclusive village of **Göcek,** recognized by the yachting community as one of the pearls of the Mediterranean, with its postcard-worthy marina, and the polish of the **Swissôtel** ⚑ at Göcek Marina (℡ **800/637-9477** in the Americas, or 0252/645-2760 local; fax 0252/645-2767; www.swissotel.com). Unlike most Swissôtels, this one is a chic and luxurious boutique village, tastefully laid out on a flat plain at the foot of the mountain range. The manicured lawns give the aura of a country club—the only thing that's missing is a golf course. Doubles cost between 82€ and 130€ ($100–$160 in low season. New in 2003 was the **Göcek Lykia Resort Hotel** (℡ **0252/645-2828**; fax 0252/645-2827; www.goceklykiaresort.com), with its pre-Classical motifs and a "real" Lycian pool. Rates from June through October are 125€ ($150); 150€ ($180) for a deluxe room. For a more home-style experience, consider the **Yonca Hotel** (not to be confused with the campsite; ℡ **0252/645-2255**; fax 0252/645-2275), a private home that's been converted into a B&B. The eight rooms have antique furnishings and cost 50€ ($60) for a double. When you're not promenading down the main street, you can swim and relax in the garden pool.

DALYAN AFTER DARK

Nighttime entertainment can be found all along Maraş Mahallesi; currently the mellower fare seems to be located farthest away from the town center.

3 Fethiye & Ölüdeniz ⭑⭑

295km (183 miles) southwest of Antalya; 170km (105 miles) southeast of Marmaris; 290km (180 miles) southeast of Pamukkale; 15km (9⅓ miles) north of Ölüdeniz

Fethiye is much more than just the Blue Lagoon, that spectacularly turquoise poster child of Turkey's Mediterranean coast. Fethiye is rocky cliffs, pine-clad mountain ranges, and offshore islets that speak of ancient civilizations. It's the quiet serenity of a sunset over the ghost village of Kayaköy. And it's the blissful solitude of a swim in one of the innumerable, unspoiled, crystalline coves, many inaccessible by land. The combination is winning: The ample natural environment inspires physical activity as much as the sun-kissed coastline encourages sloth. Scuba diving, paragliding off a mountain peak, hiking ancient mountain paths, or wading slowly through an ice-cold gorge are just a few of the activities possible in and around Fethiye. As a starting point for a Blue Voyage, Fethiye is unbeatable, offering several options for day, weekend, or weeklong charters. And of course, there's the Blue Lagoon of Ölüdeniz, one of the most astonishing natural beauties in all of Turkey.

ESSENTIALS
GETTING THERE
BY PLANE   **Turkish Airlines** services both Dalaman Airport (see "By Plane" under "Getting There" in Marmaris, earlier in this chapter) and the airport in Antalya. While there are more flights into Antalya Airport, the drive to Fethiye takes about 4 hours, so choosing Antalya will most likely be a result of fully booked flights into Dalaman, or a desire to explore the coast from east to west. Though flights are not as frequent into Dalaman Airport, it's less than 40km (25 miles) from Fethiye.

Havaş (© 444-0487) shuttle buses will be waiting for you at the Dalaman airport to whisk you away to either Marmaris or Fethiye (separate buses for opposite directions). The bus into downtown Fethiye (the marina) takes about an hour and 10 minutes and costs 16YTL ($12).

There are also car-rental counters on-site, sensible if you've arrived here exclusively for a land tour.

In Fethiye, Turkish Airlines is represented by **Lama Tours,** Hamam Sok. 3A (© 0252/614-4964; www.lamatourism.com), which also handles charter flight bookings from cities in Germany and England, and **Fetur,** Fevzi Cakmak Cad. 9/1 (© 0252/614-2034).

BY BUS   The *otogar* is about a mile east of the town center, at the turnoff for Ölüdeniz. **Ulusoy** (© 444-1888) buses run once-daily service between Istanbul and Fethiye (11 hr.; 92YTL/$68 with breakfast), and Ankara and Fethiye (9 hr.; around 67YTL/$55). **Pamukkale** (© 444-3535) connects Fethiye daily with İzmir (via Ortaca: 1½ hr.; 19YTL/$14) and Antalya (4 hr.; 15YTL/$11).

BY FERRY   Catamarans depart at 9am daily May through October for the 1-hour journey to the Greek island of Rhodes. The price of a one-way and round-trip ticket *if you return on the same day* is around 100YTL ($75). Port tax upon arrival in Greece is about 20YTL ($15) for a day excursion; more if you stay longer. Tickets can be purchased at any official travel agency. Remember in deciding whether to do this tempting trip that after traveling and waiting in customs lines, you will have precious little time to do much of anything beyond the port.

TOURIST INFORMATION
The **Tourist Information office** is located at Iskele Karşısı 1 (© 0252/614-1527), across from the harbor nearest the yacht marina.

ORIENTATION
Downtown Fethiye, along with its busy harbor and marina, sits at the southern edge of the Gulf of Fethiye. It's hard to miss the **Antique Theatre** across from the main harbor, located on the main road that cuts through town (called **Atatürk Caddesi** in the city center, Fevzi Çakmak Caddesi to the west).

Çarşı Sokağı cuts through the Old Town Bazaar perpendicular to Atatürk Caddesi, forming a triangle of shopping, restaurants, and cafes known as Paspatur. The new bazaar is located on Çarşı Sokağı, which then curves around to continue east until it meets up once again with **Atatürk Caddesi** and turns into **İnönü Bulvarı. Amyntas**

Fethiye

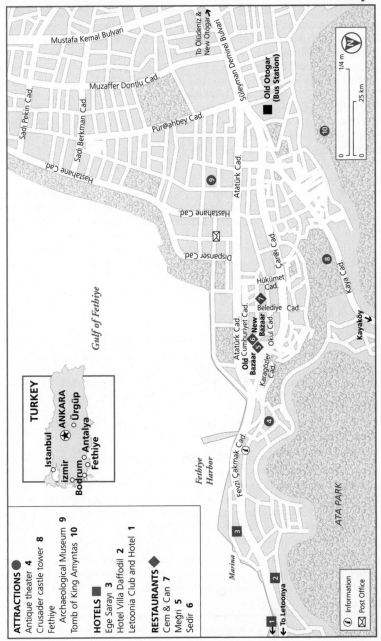

ATTRACTIONS ●
Antique theater **4**
Crusader castle tower **8**
Fethiye
  Archaeological Museum **9**
Tomb of King Amyntas **10**

HOTELS ■
Ege Sarayı **3**
Hotel Villa Daffodil **2**
Letoonia Club and Hotel **1**

RESTAURANTS ◆
Cem & Can **7**
Meğri **5**
Sedir **6**

ⓘ Information
☒ Post Office

TURKEY

İstanbul
İzmir
Bodrum
ANKARA ★
Ürgüp ○
Antalya ○
Fethiye ○

Gulf of Fethiye

Mustafa Kemal Bulvarı
Muzaffer Dontlu Cad.
Pür@ahbey Cad.
Sadi Pekin Cad.
Sadi Berkman Cad.
Hastahane Cad.
Hastahane Cad.
Dispanser Cad.
Süleyman Demirel Bulvarı
Atatürk Cad.
Çar@ Cad.
Kaya Cad.
Hükümet Cad.
Belediye Cad.
Atatürk Cad.
Old Cumhuriyet Cad.
Bazaar
New Bazaar
Okul Cad.
Karagözler Cad.
Feyzi Çakmak Cad.
Marina
Fethiye Harbor
ATA PARK
Kayaköy

To Ölüdeniz & New Otogar
Old Otogar (Bus Station)

To Letoonya

1/4 m
25 km

265

Tomb is southeast of the town center amid the barren brush, and farther east are the **Lycian Rock Tombs.** A few **lone sarcophagi** are scattered about town, one in the garden of the Municipality Building on Atatürk Caddesi, the other on Kaya Caddesi, between the old bus depot and the castle. A pedestrian promenade runs along the marina between the theater and north to Caliş Beach, and is lined with boats of all sizes touting day trips and private charters. The taxi boat to Caliş Beach is located here as well.

As you continue eastward out of Fethiye, Inönü Bulvarı intersects with the road to **Ölüdeniz,** located about 15km (9 miles) up in the hills to the south. After the turnoff for Ölüdeniz, the road arrives at Hisarönü, a characteristic town that has degenerated into a stopover for mass-marketed British groups on package tours. About 4km (2½ miles) farther is the little country village of **Kayaköy** that grew around an abandoned Greek settlement vacated in the population exchange of 1924.

Ölüdeniz, which means "Dead Sea" (but is better known as the "Blue Lagoon"), describes the beach and lagoon bearing its name and the long stretch of Belceğiz Beach. This deservedly ultra-popular seaside resort sits in a small valley at the bottom of a steep hill. Beach bums, daredevil paragliders, and at least one too many frat boys base themselves in Ölüdeniz, but with a car or scooter, you can easily make this a day trip. To the left is the public beach, enclosed by the steep slopes of **Babadağ.** The beach is tastefully lined with travel agents offering adventure tours, beach restaurants, Internet cafes, and the Club Belcekız Beach Hotel at the far end. To the right is the overcrowded natural preserve, where the lagoon of Mediterranean dreams lies, pristine and a deep shade of aqua.

GETTING AROUND

BY CAR   To really enjoy Fethiye and the surrounding areas, it's important to have your own wheels. Car-rental agencies are located near the marina, and all of the holiday resorts offer on-site car-rental services.

Europcar, at the corner of Atatürk and Çarşı Caddesis (© 0252/614-4995), and **Avis,** Fevzi Çakmak Caddesi 1/2 (© 0252/612-1385) have the highest prices. Lesser-known firms around the yacht marina and in near the Old Town Bazaar are a better bet; try **Alesta Yatcilik** (© 0252/614-1861), **Fetur** (© 0252/614-3456), or **Meğri** (© 0252/614-4444).

BY SCOOTER   This is my mode of choice, but be very careful, as the roads are gravelly and the drivers are no better at the resorts than they are on the highways. Take particular care in rounding steep hilly curves, as oncoming vehicles tend to make wide turns into your lane. Otherwise, riding a scooter through the countryside is a rare joy, a good way to maintain your suntan, and the best way to solve the parking question. Most car-rental agencies have scooters available, and there are several outfitters in downtown Fethiye that will rent you a scooter for about 35YTL ($25) for the day.

BY MINIBUS/*DOLMUŞ*   *Dolmuşes* congregate at the intersection of Atatürk Caddesi and Sedir Sokak (across from the hospital) in downtown Fethiye and provide frequent (about every 15 min.) transport to most of the sites and destinations listed

---

Fun Fact **What's in a Name?**

The ancient Greeks named every mountain higher than 2,400m (8,000 ft.) Mount Olympus.

in this section. The most useful routes leave for Ölüdeniz, Kayaköy, Tlos, and Saklıkent. A ride will cost 2YTL, or $1.50.

The Ölüdeniz Minibus Coop runs an hourly shuttle between Fethiye and Kayaköy; less frequent are the minibuses that run about six times a day to/from Fethiye to Faralya/Kabak and three times daily to/from Fethiye to Gemiler Beach.

FAST FACTS: Fethiye

Airport The information line at **Dalaman Airport** is © 0252/692-5499.

Laundry Drop off your wash with the ladies at **Şegem,** on Çarşı Caddesi (on the left where it curves; © 0252/612-5632), or at the laundry across from the Yacht Club (no phone). A wash and dry will run around 6.75YTL ($5), depending on the weight of the load.

Markets Market day in Fethiye is Tuesday. Open dawn to dusk.

Transportation The number for the *otogar* is © 0252/614-3531; the number for the **Kordon Taxi** stand is © 0252/614-4445.

FAST FACTS: Ölüdeniz

Internet Access The popular **Buzz Beach Bar & Grill** (© 0252/617-0045) has a number of computers in the back next to the bar; they charge 3.40YTL ($2.50) per hour.

Medical Assistance Most hotels make use of the services of a doctor-on-call. Dr. Öz-Ay Medical Service in the center of Ölüdeniz (© 0252/616-6456) is also on call 24 hours a day. For serious problems, call the **Likya Medical Center** (© 0252/616-6930) or **Letoon Hospital** (© 0252/612-5480), which also has an ambulance on call 24 hours a day.

Tourist Office A small information booth, located on the road into Ölüdeniz on the right before the beach, is good for area maps and assistance with finding a hotel or pension. Their number is © 0252/617-0438.

WHAT TO SEE & DO
ANCIENT HISTORY

Not much remains of ancient **Telmessos,** atop which modern-day Fethiye is built. In spite of centuries of destructive earthquakes, the cliff-side Lycian tombs and majestic sarcophagi never fail to draw a gasp.

The city was independent until Alexander the Great's arrival in 334 B.C. Three hundred years later the city came under Roman rule as part of the Lycian union.

The **antique theater** in the center of town dates to Roman times, although its open disposition on the hill indicates Greek influences. The amphitheater was picked apart for the reconstruction of the city after the devastating earthquake of 1957, and in 1994 restorations and further excavations to the site were begun. To the east of the Municipal Building is a two-story **sarcophagus** ✦ topped with a Gothic-style lid and decorated with war scenes; remains of this type of tomb are scattered about the city and hidden in private gardens.

On the hillside east of town stands the ruined **Crusader castle tower,** constructed by the Knights of St. John out of the Hellenistic and Roman stonework of an earlier acropolis.

Rock-cut tombs spot the cliff side, the most notable of which is the **Tomb of King Amyntas** ✿✿✿ in the form of a Greek temple dating to 350 B.C. The steps of the facade get a bit crowded around sunset, the favored time for a visit because of the tomb's position on the hill. Price of admission is 4YTL ($3), or free from afar.

The nearby **Fethiye Archaeological Museum,** Fethiye Müze Müdürlüğü (© **0252/ 614-1150**), is small and regrettably unimportant; exhibits consist of stones and columns from the acropolis that should have been left in place. Interesting, however, is the **stele** ✿ uncovered at Letoon, with inscriptions in Lycian, Aramaic, and Greek. It proved indispensable in cracking the code of the ancient Lycian language. The museum is open Tuesday through Sunday from 8:30am to 5pm; admission is 2YTL ($1.50).

Karmylassos/Kayaköy ✿✿✿   This haunting and magical place is the result of the population exchange between Turkey and Greece in 1924—in which the Turkish and Greek minorities in each country were repatriated to their "home countries," despite the incalculable suffering such a drastic uprooting caused. The Turkish village of Kayaköy sprouted up in the valley at the base of the abandoned hillside.

Originally the Lycian city of Karmylassos, the village was reestablished by Greek settlers as Levissi in either the 11th or 14th century. The houses that blanket the hills date to the 19th century. Today Karmylassos is a ghost town, and the remains of the 3,500 identical square stone houses, each positioned to afford the best views of the countryside, take on a haunting pinkish glow at sunset, the best time to visit. Although the churches and chapels have been scavenged in the search for buried sacred treasure, there's still enough of the original structures and ceramic mosaic flooring to make an impression.

At the top of the ghost village, a **footpath** to Ölüdeniz continues over the hill and through some spectacular scenery. For this hike you'll need a camera, a large bottle of water, and about 2 hours; leave early in the morning to beat the heat and allow an afternoon of recovery on the pearly shores of the Blue Lagoon.

A shorter trail leads to **Cold Water Bay,** a small cove fed by icy springs, and reachable in under an hour. Be sure not to mistake one trail for the other (one unscrupulous businessman diverted hikers to the latter and his restaurant; he's since been incarcerated for tax fraud)—a mistake easily avoided by picking up a sketch map of the trails at Bülent's Place, located along the Kaya road. Eager to set people on the right path, Bülent has learned the English word for "map," and will be as helpful as he can be.

The turnoff from the Fethiye/Ölüdeniz road travels through the spoiled enclave of **Hisarönü,** affectionately called Hiroshima by the locals who remember its age of innocence. If you follow this road for about 5 or 6.5km (3–4 miles) through the piney woods, the hollow stone houses will alert you to your arrival. A more inspiring entrance can be made by following the signs up and around Fethiye Castle for Kaya Village/Karmylassos. This winding back way leads through the upper edges of picturesque Kaya Valley, and if you're lucky, you'll get a glimpse of the nomad camp.

Dolmuşes make the 30-min. journey from Fethiye to Kayaköy daily for about 2YTL ($1.50). Admission is 4YTL ($3).

> ## *Tips* A Unique Shopping Opportunity
>
> In the small village of Kayaköy, a group of village women have banded together, with the help of some local subsidy, to create some remarkable carpet products. Their idea is to revive the traditional local patterns typical of carpets woven in the area, although sometimes they get bored and invent new designs. The project was initiated in the winter of 2000 to 2001 by the Halk Eğitim Merkezi Akşam Sanat Olsulu (the local community educational board), and while the selection of carpets, wall hangings, and seat covers is still small, prices are low.

Tlos ✸✸   Tlos is one of the oldest and most important cites in ancient Lycia; its position atop a rocky outpost dominates the Xanthos Valley. Hittite artifacts found here indicate the city was founded as early as 2000 B.C. After the decline of the Hittite Empire, Tlos became a Lycian city, and then was later absorbed by the Roman Empire. The city was an important bishopric during the Byzantine Era, and was finally conquered by the Turks.

The most immediately impressive feature is the severe slope of the city on the rock, carved into majestic temple-like tombs and the stone sarcophagi dotting the hillside below. A lone sarcophagus sits dramatically in the middle of a farmer's field best spotted from the stadium, located a few hundred feet up the road of the ruins near a roadside cafe graced with ice-cold springs. Take a look at the stadium first, because after the climb to the summit, it will be too much of a struggle against the heat to tack this on to the end of your tour. On the summit lie the ruins of a castle dating to the Turkish settlement, offering panoramic views of the Xanthos Valley. Excavations conducted by Antalya University have uncovered a tunnel, which seems to have provided a quick escape during times of invasion, leading to the city from the nearby village.

Follow the Fethiye/Antalya road; cross the bridge over the Esen Çay and look for indications to turn right onto the Saklıkent road. The turnoff for Tlos is before Saklıkent on the left. Admission 4YTL ($3). Daily 8am–5pm.

Yaka Park ✸✸ *Kids*   This trout farm is a wonderful place to take the kids, because after ordering your food (Yaka Park serves meat dishes as well), you can try and pet one of the finger-biting swans on the upper terrace. Yaka Park takes up several outdoor terraces on a gently sloping hill, and you can choose to sit at one of the picnic tables or under a tree in an enclosed seating area on pillows and mats. There's also a bar, whose counter has been carved out and filled up with baby trout swimming along its meandering length. The trout come right out of the central pond, and once grilled, are crispy and delicious.

Yaka Köyü, Fethiye. ☎ 0252/634-0391. Meal of trout and all-you-can-eat appetizers around 20YTL ($15). No credit cards. Daily 9am–10pm. Closed Nov–Mar. Follow the Fethiye/Antalya road and turn right to the road to Saklıkent, turn left again toward Tlos and follow the signs for Yaka Park.

THE AREA BEACHES

The coarse sands of **Çaliş Beach** lie on Fethiye Bay, 5km (3 miles) north of the downtown, and stretch for about 1.6km (a mile). Çaliş Beach is lined with the icons of mass tourism: side-by-side homogenous hotels set back behind the beachfront souvenir stands that keep visitors stocked in plastic flip-flops and their kids in cheap snorkels. A wide beachfront sidewalk extends for the length of the beach; the sight of some of the most magnificent sunsets behind the smaller islands to the west make Çaliş Beach worth a trip at least for that event. A water taxi from Fethiye's marina crosses the bay to Çaliş Beach every half-hour for 4YTL ($3) each way. Or, you can take the water taxi for about the same price to the lovely beach on **Şevalye Island** (in the middle of the bay) and stumble around the Byzantine ruins.

Çaliş Beach reclaims its innocence at the extreme north end known as **Koca Çaliş,** where the scenery returns to its pure and natural state. Taking advantage of the high winds and shallow waters of Koca Çaliş are a number of windsurfing outfitters; **Hang Loose Windsurfing & Surf Café** was the first; P.K. 170, Fethiye (© **0252/622-0753;** www.fethiyesurfcenter.com), a family-run sports center in-the-rough that focuses its energies on windsurfing lessons. Şener Aykurt, founder and windsurfing instructor (when not teaching math at Anatolian High School), teaches all levels of windsurfing, beginning with first-timers, using an on-land simulated wave apparatus. Prices per lesson, including equipment, are 100YTL ($75) for 2-hour lessons; if you're not taking the lesson, you can rent the equipment for 25YTL ($18) without. Şener's mom posts the menu of the day on a chalkboard on the walk of their beachfront shack; take advantage of real home cooking or relax in the sandy tea garden.

Only 5 minutes from the center of Fethiye town is a collection of newly established public beaches practically attached to the hip of the Letoonia Club (see "Where to Stay," below). The beaches are maybe not as breathtaking as at Ölüdeniz, but they are certainly (for the moment) less crowded.

Arguably the most beautiful beach on the eastern Mediterranean, and the smallest bay in Turkey (and probably the reason you came all this way), **Ölüdeniz** ★★★ has become Turkey's poster child because of its extraordinary beauty. Ölüdeniz Beach refers to both the long stretch called **Belcekız Beach** ★★★ at the foot of Babadağ, as well as the still blue waters of the **Blue Lagoon** ★★★, which actually takes its name from the stagnant waters behind the natural sandbar. (Ölüdeniz means "dead sea.") *Dolmuşes* leave frequently from across from the hospital in Fethiye.

The exposed **Belceğiz Beach** is ideal as a landing site for the paragliding maniacs launching themselves off the top of the mountain, although you may spot a guy flying around with a jet propulsion pack strapped to his back as well. The beach is undeveloped, the locals touting adventure trips are friendly, and the white sands and turquoise waters are hard to beat (until you walk over to the preserve).

The Blue Lagoon is tucked inside a natural preserve that requires an admission fee of 2YTL ($1.50), though if you drive in it'll be 6YTL ($4.50). From the parking lot you can either follow the sandy beach around the sandbar or take the more scenic path over the pine needles and through the woods. Families who had arrived early to stake their claim are now nestled in the shade of little pine niches, and you'll pass hundreds of these picnickers as you follow the woodsy path along the shallow section of the lagoon. Keep walking, because you'll know by the color of the water when you've arrived. If you're not sure, keep going. You might want to get here early, because by midday, the lounge chairs are all spoken for, and you may wind up piling your belongings in a heap on the pebbles and diving right in.

Make no mistake, however, the Blue Lagoon has attracted half the population of Lycia, and they've all brought their kids, so a serene afternoon of swimming and solitude is definitely out. But however overcrowded it is, this little corner of Turkey is irresistible.

With your own car, preferably a four-wheel drive, you can combine a visit to Kayaköy with a day spent tooling around **Gemiler Beach** ★★★, an undeveloped cove opposite the historic ruins of Gemiler Island and some postcard views of the mountains in the distance. Here, you can hire a local to take you over to **Gemiler Island** 🎯🎯 with the 7th-century Byzantine monastery of St. Nikola. (about 20YTL–27YTL/$15–$20; site entrance 4YTL/$3), hire a speedboat for a group ringo or banana boat ride, and feast on fresh fish over at the beachfront shack owned by the slightly creepy but ever harmless "Robinson."

Daily excursion boats offer the **"12-island tour"** 🎯🎯 (actually closer to six) around the Gulf of Fethiye, a popular diversion that can be booked directly at the dock, or through most any travel agent. In Ölüdeniz contact **Activities Unlimited** (at the Karbel Sun Hotel; 🕾 **0252/617-0601**). The beauty is impossible to describe, but for about 30YTL ($22), and even less off season, the trip provides an abbreviated taste of what a weeklong Blue Voyage would be like. Highlights of the cruise include stopovers at Hamam Bay, where you can swim above sunken Byzantine baths (erroneously called Cleopatra's Bath), and at **Gemiler Island**. There's room for a mild adrenaline rush in Turunç Bükü, where you can scale the rocks to a hanging rope and swing into the turquoise waters like Tarzan. Swimming and snorkeling around the tiny coves and bays is a high priority, and the captain is usually flexible about schedules if you decide to swim ashore to explore some medieval ruins up close.

If you haven't booked your Blue Voyage yet, and would like a taste of the Lycian Coast by sea, many agencies and boat captains offer what has now become a widely marketed 4-day, 3-night **cruise to Olympos** (if you have time, inspect the cabins of several boats before you commit), available April to mid-October. The cruise takes in some of the most stunning scenery along the coast, past Butterfly Valley, Ölüdeniz, Gemiler Island and the beach of Patara; the final leg of the trip heads by bus overland from Demre/Myra to ancient Olympos (p. 317). Prices from July 15-September 15 are £109 (about 260YTL/$193 at the time of this writing) per person, including tax and three meals, but excluding drinks. Prices go down slightly off season. (There are no cruises Dec 15–Apr 1.) Most boats provide some type of snorkeling and fishing equipment. **V-GO Tourism Travel Agency,** Fevzi Çakmak Caddesi (between the marina and the Yacht Club; 🕾 **0252/612-2113;** www.boatcruiseturkey.com), invented this trip, but my advice is to shop around and have a look at the boats.

SPORTS & OUTDOOR ACTIVITIES

EXPLORING BUTTERFLY VALLEY   A nature lover's paradise is located in **Butterfly Valley** 🎯🎯🎯, an untouched beachfront parcel named for the rare Tiger Butterfly which breaks from its cocoon in April and May and turns the skies bright red. The colorful creatures are drawn to the smell of mint, jasmine, laurel, eucalyptus, and thyme emanating from the rich vegetation. A 45-minute hike away from the beach leads to a refreshing waterfall.

Taxi boats leave from Ölüdeniz three times a day in both directions (about 16YTL/$12 round-trip)—an alternative for the adventurous and well-shod hiker is to follow the steep and rocky slope down from the upper rim of the valley, following the footpath from in front of "George House," on the road to Faralya/Kabak (gauge about 30 min.).

For those who miss the last boat out, the platform huts and tents of the on-site Butterfly Valley "pension" (🕾 **0522/818-8570;** www.zevzek.com/special/butterfly.htm) are your only alternatives. One night with all meals is around 20YTL/$15, and the basic snack bar offers the usual sparse selection of cold drinks, meatballs, and tea.

HIKING SAKLIKENT GORGE   Also known as the Canyon of the Hidden Valley, **Saklıkent Gorge** 🎔🎔 is a wonder of nature carved 480m (1,574 ft.) down into the canyon by the constant force of the waters flowing down from Akdağ (Ak Mt.). The entrance to the gorge is down an incline off the main road, surrounded by a parking lot, ticket booth, merchant stalls, and enough tour buses to make you want to turn back.

A sturdy catwalk attached to the cliff wall leads you upstream for about 150m (500 ft.) to landfall, where the gushing waters of the **Gökçesu** and **Ulupınar** springs flow down from Babadağ into the gorge. The air is unexpectedly cold at this juncture thanks to the constant roar of the icy waters, and some clever businessman knew just how to take advantage. The **Hidden Paradise Restaurant** 🎔🎔🎔 (⟨© **0252/336-8406**) is a series of cozy wooden platforms constructed over the torrents for optimal enjoyment of a meal prepared in the stone ovens and a respite from the relentless heat.

A hike up the gorge through the sometimes thigh-high waters is the highlight of the trip. Enter the gorge above where the springs gush into the creek, but be prepared for the shock of water so cold you just might have gone skiing that day. Your legs will be so numb that you won't even notice that the temperature of the water stabilizes the farther away from the spring source you get. The rock face has been sanded to a silky smoothness, creating slippery slides for kids of all ages. River shoes are advisable, especially if you plan on going the full distance of 18km (11 miles).

Small group tours by minibus or jeep safari leave for Saklıkent Gorge daily in season for around 27YTL–33YTL ($20–$25), including a stop at the ancient city of Tlos and lunch at Yaka Park. You can also get to the gorge, located about 40km (25 miles) southeast of Fethiye (about 1 hr.), by picking up a *dolmuş* at the main terminal or flagging one down on the Fethiye/Antalya road out of town (3YTL/$2). By car, follow the Fethiye/Antalya road and turn left at the road for Kemer; turn left again past Tlos and follow signs for Saklıkent. Entrance to the gorge is 4YTL ($3); parking is free.

HORSEBACK RIDING   Enjoy the scenic pine forests and mountain paths on horseback. **Activities Unlimited** (© **0252/617-0601**) and **Aventura** (© **0252/617-0314**) offer daily half-day tours, with a pickup at your hotel, for around 34YTL ($25). You can also arrange your own outing by going directly to a stable in Kayaköy. The arrival of **Perma Ranch,** Kaya Yolu (©/fax **0252/618-0182;** www.permaranch.co.uk) several years ago added two horsy Brits from Gloucestershire to the list of British expats in the area. They offer horse riding holidays (even for travelers with limited mobility!) for £295 (around $525) per person per week; ask to see if they are running their 3-hour excursion on horseback, which includes 2 hours of riding through the valley and mountains and a short stopover in the village neighborhood of Kınalı. The horses and tacking are in excellent shape, and use a sturdy English saddle.

PARAGLIDING   Thanks to the 1,950m (6,500-ft.) drop-off of Babadağ over an open body of water, and to the gentle sea breezes and stable winds, Ölüdeniz is one of the foremost sites in the world for paragliding. Professionals come from all over to prepare for international competitions, an experience that for about £70 ($125) a head is now open to the daring (and strong-stomached; if you're the type to get seasick, you may want to take a pill beforehand, or carry a zip-lock bag, just in case). Flying tandem with an experienced pilot, all of whom are certified professionals, provides a safe and easy introduction to an otherwise extreme sport.

Skysports Paragliding, located on the beach (© **0252/617-0511;** fax 0252/617-0511), is the most reputable of the dozen or so outfitters touting their flights

Tips   **Clothes Make the Woman**

Girls, listen up! Imagine a closet full of clothes designed for all occasions, all suited to you. (Clothes can be bought off the rack or made to measure.) Günsenin Günel, wife of the owner of the White Dolphin restaurant and graduate of the Chelsea School of Arts in London, is the genius behind the mannequins, which display her evening wear, trendy ensembles, and even conservative work attire tailored for real bodies. And Gün doesn't only give visiting royalty the personal-shopper experience—because when you're the only customer in the shop, it's all you. **Günsenin Boutique** is at the entrance of the White Dolphin restaurant (and therefore usually open in the evenings, beginning at 6pm; ✆ **0252/617-0068**); another more casual shop, selling jeans, cargo pants, and beach dresses (or whatever happens to be trendy at the time), is on the beach.

(although I'm told that pilots rotate among the companies regularly); they run five daily departures in high season, leaving by jeep at 9am, 11:30am, 2pm, 4pm, and 6pm for the hour climb up to the summit. Because of limited space, book at least 1 day in advance. Check out their website at **www.paragliding.net/skysports**. Other reputable organizers of paragliding jumps are **Extreme Sports** (✆ **0252/617-0018**) and **Easy Riders** (✆ **0252/617-0114;** www.easyriderstravel.8m.com). Prices are fixed among the various companies, so don't bother trying to negotiate. Be forewarned, however, human error has been known to result in fatalities, but then again, so does driving.

SCUBA DIVING   Spontaneous discovery of sunken ruins awaits you in the clear blue waters of the Gulf of Fethiye. The best in the area, with branches in Marmaris and Dalyan, is the professionally run **European Diving Center,** Atatürk Cad. 12/1 (opposite the main harbor; ✆ **0252/614-9771;** www.europeandiving.com.tr), offering a 1-day "discover scuba" course (£29/$51), a full-day snorkel trip (£20/$36) and a 3-day PADI course (£285/$506). They also offer full-day dive trips for qualified divers for as low as £22 ($39).

WHITE-WATER RAFTING   The Dalaman River is a popular spot for rafting, kayaking, and canoeing, passing remote and breathtaking canyons through Grade 4 and 5 rapids. All of the tour companies offer the same package tour that connects with a local operator in Dalaman; a day out including all transfers and professional river guides costs around £22 ($48).

WHERE TO STAY

To take full advantage of the area, you need to split your time between Fethiye and Ölüdeniz and make yourself available for nearby excursions through the forests. The accommodations listed here offer one aspect of the brightest and beautiful that the Fethiye area has to offer. Even if you're without wheels and are relying entirely on the local system of *dolmuşes* or hotel shuttles, any of these listings will do, with varying degrees of effort for your trouble.

Fethiye

Ece Sarayi 👍👍   As the crowned jewel of the Turquoise Coast, Fethiye has been sadly lacking in standout accommodations. Until now. The palatial Ege Sarayi occupies an extensive landscaped waterfront property near the western end of Fethiye's marina. Parisian-style wrought-iron balconies perch above the stunning scenery from every room. Rooms are trimmed with rosewood and embellished with the finest Vakko textiles, while bathrooms are swathed in Italian marble and come loaded with amenities such as designer soaps and plush bathrobes. The pool is surrounded by teak lounges and stunning views of the Toros Mountains. The Mrs. can while away an hour or so in the spa and wellness center (offering hydrotherapy treatments, stone therapy, and facial treatments, along with the basics), while men congregate in the terribly macho cigar room with high-backed leather chairs. The **restaurant** ⊀ will undoubtedly blow the competition out of the water (actually, there is none on this level), with a sophisticated menu that includes such specialties as filet of sea bass with couscous, semolina, wild rice, and lobster sauce, or grilled quail. Prices for entrees range from 7.40€ to 24€ ($9–$29).

1 Karagözler Mevkii (in the Marina), 48300 Fethiye. ℂ **0252/612-5005.** Fax 0252/614-7205. www.ecesaray.net. 48 units. 125€–200€ ($150–$245) double; 245€–330€ ($300–$400) suite. Rates reflect season. AE, DISC, MC, V. **Amenities:** Restaurant; waterfront cafe; 3 bars; cigar bar; full-service marina; outdoor swimming pool; fitness room; spa and wellness center; Turkish bath; Jacuzzi; sauna; small children's playground; concierge; tour desk; car-rental desk; 24-hr. room service; massage; dry cleaning; wireless Internet. *In room:* A/C, satellite TV, minibar, coffee/tea station, hair dryer, safe.

Hotel Villa Daffodil ⊀   This charming little guesthouse perched on the road across from the Gulf of Fethiye is a real attention grabber, owing to its traditional Ottoman design and wooden *cumbas* (enclosed ornamented balconies), typical of summer houses of the time. Inside, the simply decorated rooms can be rather cozy. The courtyard of the hotel doubles as an intimate breakfast and bar area, with a functioning lemon tree for a refreshing vodka tonic, and an old 19th-century horseless carriage from which you can admire the bay over the garden wall.

The owner, a retired colonel in the Turkish army, has overseen every detail of the guesthouse. The disposition of the rooms makes each type slightly different: side rooms enjoy a small balcony, others share a small inner courtyard, and upper floor rooms in the back have lots of wood and attic-style ceilings. On a back garden terrace of the hotel is a small but tantalizing pool surrounded by a lush garden, perfect for a dip after a long sweaty day out and about. The owner also maintains a six-cabin *gulet* moored in the inlet across the street for easy guest hire.

Fevzi Çakmak Cad. 115, 48300 Fethiye. ℂ **0252/614-9595** or 0252/612-5211. Fax 0252/612-2223. www.villadaffodil. com. 27 units. 40€–50€ ($50–$60) double. No credit cards. **Amenities:** Restaurant; bar; outdoor swimming pool; 6-cabin gullet for hire; sauna. *In room:* A/C, satellite TV, hair dryer.

Letoonia Club and Hotel ⊀ *Kids*   Who knew Disneyland had a branch on the Mediterranean? Until I stepped foot on the grounds of Letoonia, I had no idea. This is not fundamentally a bad thing, and actually Letoonia is more like a prefabricated paradise than a cheesy venue for Mickey Mouse.

Letoonia Club is set on a cliff-side promontory on a peninsula that juts out into Fethiye Bay, enjoying splendid seclusion and three private coves. Only the orange water slide mars the gorgeous setting of mountains and pines, but you'll be too busy taking free windsurfing lessons in one of the alternate coves to notice, although your kids definitely will. In fact, this resort caters to families not only through activities and the "miniclub," but also through the independent setup of the bungalow rooms, which are laid out with separate sleeping quarters for parents and children. To get around this massive acreage, Letoonia provides amusement park minishuttles. Although the resort sprawls over several acres, the award-winning architect saw to it that Letoonia did nothing but complement its surroundings. If you're arriving by sea, the sight of these wooden and latticed buildings emerging from the brush will take your breath away. All rooms have a balcony, and the layout of the resort ensures that 85% of the rooms get sea views. The resort provides a free hourly shuttle to Fethiye.

P.O.B. 63, 48300 Fethiye. © 0252/614-4966. Fax 0252/614-4422. www.letoonia.com. 626 units (all bungalows with shower). July–Aug 215€ ($260) double in hotel, 162€ ($198) double in bungalow; June and Sept 150€ ($184) double in hotel, 126€ ($154) double in bungalow. Rates include breakfast, lunch, and dinner. MC, V. **Amenities:** 5 restaurants; 10 bars; outdoor swimming pool; miniature golf; tennis courts; Turkish bath; Jacuzzi; sauna; extensive watersports; scooter rental; children's programs; game room; concierge; tour desk; car-rental desk; shopping arcade; salon; 24-hr. room service; massage; dry cleaning. *In room:* A/C, satellite TV, minibar, hair dryer, safe.

KAYAKÖY

Kaya Cottages ⭐⭐   This cluster of well-appointed self-catering cottages was little more than crumbling ruins until a decade ago, when a couple of ex-pats arrived, bought up what were essentially piles of stones for a song, and renovated them with a mind toward comfort, character, and sensitivity. The property has since been transferred to a new couple of British ex-pats enchanted by the authentic rural village surroundings. Each of the five houses is unique and reflects the property's original purpose as a farm. Up to three can stay in the "stables," a two-bedroom unit with a kitchen, fireplace, and secluded, walled-in terrace. The "smokehouse" sleeps four, an elegant sanctuary with high beams, a private patio, and a modern bathroom. The "granary" is rustic and enjoys its own private terraced garden. A small freshwater plunge pool was recently added for when the summer sun heats up the country mountain air.

Kaya Köyü, 48304 Fethiye. © 0537/579-2050. cdunkers@excite.com. 5 self-catering cottages for 2–4 people (most with shower, 2 with tub). £350 ($620) per cottage per week plus refundable security deposit of £100 ($178). No minimum stay. Ask for off-season rates. May–Oct. No credit cards. *In room:* A/C, kitchen, coffeemaker.

ÖLÜDENIZ

Club Belcekız Beach ⭐   Located at the very end of Ölüdeniz Beach with Babadağ as a backdrop, Club Belcekız Beach sets the stage for a perfect seaside vacation without the fuss. Owned by an architect, the Club Belcekız Beach was obviously designed by someone sensitive not only to the environment, but also to the region's heritage. The hotel buildings are painted in earth tones, Doric columns support a poolside archway, and the Cappadocian-style chimneys offer a tip of the hat to the civilizations of ancient Anatolia. Rooms are in two sections; the main garden complex and an equally nice rear garden annex. All rooms are essentially the same, with updated bathrooms and balconies or patios. The pool overlooks the beach, enjoying views of the cliffs and paragliders descending from the summit of the mountain. The on-site *hamam* and sauna are an added bonus (at £10/$18 extra), and the entire hotel grounds sprout with flowers and lush greenery. Two of the hotel's restaurants are open to the beach, one serving Indian food and the other Chinese, and there's a basketball court and tennis court on the grounds.

48300 Ölüdeniz. © 0252/617-0077. Fax 0252/617-0372. www.belcekiz.com. 160 units (some with tub, some with shower). £60—£100 ($107–$178) double. Rates reflect seasonal differences and include breakfast and dinner. AE, MC, V. Closed mid-Nov to Mar. **Amenities:** 3 restaurants; 2 bars; outdoor swimming pool; tennis courts; fitness room; Turkish bath; sauna; children's playground; game room; concierge; tour desk; car-rental desk; salon; 24-hr. room service; massage; babysitting; laundry service; dry cleaning. *In room:* A/C, safe.

Lykia World ⭐ *Kids*   The only thing wrong with this 15-hectare (37-acre) beachfront theme park that supports 2,500 guests at a time is its immensity. Built by the German-owned Robinsons' Club, visitors are ensured five-star amenities in a perfectly constructed artificial world of fun. It's a great family destination, and extremely gimmicky—the grounds shuttles are shaped like miniature Shining Time cruise ships and the pools and grounds feature reproductions of Lycian artifacts like sarcophagi. But this is nothing compared to the Children's Paradise, a wonderland of water slides, mystery caves, theme playgrounds, trampolines, and supervised activities. Adults can guiltlessly get as self-absorbed as they wish; the children's paradise also has an area for kids under 3 years, with the option of round-the-clock babysitting (at an additional fee). Then what to do? Choose one of the 17 pools. Relax on the resort's own private beach, arguably the nicest in Ölüdeniz. Or, go for broke in the health and beauty center by scheduling sessions for a high-pressure water massage, acupuncture, shiatsu, acupressure, or algae treatments.

Rooms in the Village are comfortable yet designed more for family function than those in the Residence, which have couples in mind. The biggest challenge? Finding your way back to the room.

P.K. 102 Ölüdeniz. © **0252/617-0400.** Fax 0252/617-0350. www.lykiaworld.com. 269 units in the Residence; 550 units in the Village. Online rates from 93€ ($113). Fixed-price package for kids. AE, DC, MC, V. **Amenities:** 9 restaurants; 12 bars; 17 swimming pools; golf course; tennis courts; health club and spa; Turkish bath; Jacuzzi; sauna; extensive land and watersports; rentals (bike, moped, and scooter); children's center; children's programs; children's playground; game room; concierge; tour desk; car-rental desk; business center; shopping arcade; salon; 24-hr. room service; massage; babysitting; laundry service; dry cleaning; cinema; nonsmoking rooms; executive floor. *In room:* A/C, satellite TV, minibar, fridge, hair dryer, safe.

Montabello Beach Hotel 🏵 *(Value)* Don't confuse this with the low-end Villa Beldeniz or the Hotel Montabello, all of which are under the same management; Montabello Beach Hotel is without a doubt the best of the bunch, having just recently been entirely renovated. The building is not new—an oversize three-story marginally Mediterranean-style block that's impossible to miss. But everything else is, from the new wall-to-wall carpeting, to the fresh bathrooms, to the new TV sets. The only thing wrong with it is that in your room, you could be, well, anywhere. But for this price, why not come here?

Belceğiz Beach (1 block inland on the Fethiye road next to the Olive Grove Restaurant). © **0252/617-0606.** Fax 0252/617-0598. montabello@superonline.com. 36 units. 50€ ($60) double. MC, V. **Amenities:** Restaurant; 2 bars; outdoor swimming pool; 24-hr. room service; laundry service; dry cleaning. *In room:* A/C, satellite TV, minibar, hair dryer, safe.

Montana Pine Resort 🏵 This small boutique resort was completed in 1997 and sits amid a pine forest about 1.6km (1 mile) above Ölüdeniz. The resort, a kind of complex with mini–country lodges, was built in two phases in a style that can best be described as "modern rustic." Try to stay in the newer section, placed at the back of the property far away from the poolside disco parties that blare well into the early morning hours. Every comfort has been addressed in these rooms, which sport verandas, picture windows, and spacious bathrooms. In comparison, rooms in the original section are disappointing and weary-looking, and disturbingly close to the evening festivities. The two main pools are terraced and connected by a waterfall; there's also an enchanting and cozy *şark* (Oriental seating) room, with kilims and pillows in a private little niche for pre- or post-sun relaxing. (A third pool sits behind the complex of new rooms.) The hotel provides a free shuttle service to Ölüdeniz Beach.

Ovacık Mahallesi, 48300 Ölüdeniz/Fethiye. © **0252/616-7108.** Fax 0252/616-6451. www.montanapine.com. 159 units (original section with shower, newer units with tub). 100€ ($122) double; 200€ ($245) suite. Rates include breakfast and dinner but no drinks. Rates lower for stays longer than a week. MC, V. **Amenities:** 2 restaurants;

3 bars; 3 outdoor swimming pools; miniature golf; tennis courts; fitness room; Jacuzzi; sauna; scooter rental; car-rental desk; shopping arcade; 24-hr. room service; laundry service; dry cleaning. *In room:* A/C, satellite TV, minibar, hair dryer.

Tohum ⭐ *(Finds)*   Located on 22 hectares (54 acres) of seaside cliff and brush surrounded by 140 hectares (350 acres) of forest land (the Lycian Way hiking trail passes along the road above), Tohum, which means "seed," cuts to the heart of this environmentally conscious retreat. The goal, as expressed by Turkish partners, Beti and Atila (based in Bernardston, Massachusetts), is to create a sanctuary for those wishing to reconnect with nature. A total of eight cabins dot the hillside. Half are constructed of wood beams and adobe, while the rest are made of natural wood. All are outfitted with kilims, mats, and crisp gingham sheets protected under a mosquito netting; all overlook the natural layer of brush out toward the sea. Meals are based on menus that recall the traditional Anatolian heritage. Offerings include a vegetarian selection using locally produced organic vegetables, grains, and beans flavored with the wild sage, basil, and oregano that perfumes the air. Count on leaving your idea of a deluxe vacation behind, as this is more like an upscale camping trip; however, you're guaranteed to leave here restored and ready to take on the world.

White Cape (20 min. beyond Ölüdeniz, on the dirt road to Faralya). ℂ **413/774-4140** in the U.S. Fax 413/774-4634. www.tohum.com. 508€ ($620) single in a double room; 430€ ($525) per person in a double. Rates are per person weekly and reflect full board; see website for updated prices, discounts, and shorter stays. No credit cards. Closed mid-Oct to Apr. Contact Tohum in advance for transfers from Fethiye.

WHERE TO DINE

Fethiye has its abundance of *pide* (flat bread) joints and *kebap* houses, and you certainly don't need me to point them out. Below is a small selection of the most memorable and atmospheric places in and around the three main centers.

FETHIYE

Cem & Can ⭐⭐ *(Value)* BRING-YOUR-OWN BARBECUE   Here's your chance to live abroad for an afternoon. Simply choose your fish at the fish counter (sold by weight) at the center of a bustling meat, fish, and produce market, and bring your fresh purchase over to this humble spot in the corner (nearest to Belediye Caddesi). It's as no-frills as you can get, and equally authentic.

Pazaryeri/New Bazaar (between Belediye and Hükümet Caddesis). ℂ **0252/614-3097.** Service fee, with salad and bread 5.40YTL ($4). No credit cards. Daily 8am–2pm.

Meğri TURKISH   Meğri is hard to miss with its two neighboring locations in the center of Fethiye's Old Town, an unornamented *lokanta* a few steps away, and a corner cafe. The reliability of the meals makes this hands down the most recommended restaurant in town. The main restaurant is actually two separate spaces set around the Old Town square—in summertime, tables spill out of the two stone dining rooms (one was an old converted warehouse) monopolizing the public square. Start your meal with the area's freshest, most succulent cold seafood salads with big chunks of calamari and tons of lemon, and a plateful of steamy *lavaş* on which to spread your garlic and parsley herb butter. The seafood casseroles are a local specialty, albeit a bit heavy for a sultry summer afternoon, so order your catch of the day grilled, on a şiş, or *kağıtta* (steamed in foil). The *lokanta,* Çarşı Cad. 26 (ℂ **0252/614-4047**), attracts those looking for typical food without the added price, and the new location across from the old provides plenty of pleasant outdoor seating.

Paspatur Eskı Cami Gecidi Likya Sok. 8–9 (in the center of Old Town). ✆ **0252/614-4046.** Appetizers 6.75YTL–12YTL ($5–$9); main fish dishes 11YTL–24YTL ($8–$18). AE, DC, DISC, MC, V. Daily 9am–midnight.

Sedir *Kids* TURKISH   This unpretentious restaurant and *lokanta* is a local favorite. Tables connect in the style of a long galley, seating you next to other hungry strangers; however, in summer most people choose to sit at one of the many outdoor tables. Hot tables provide a pleasing selection of stews served in such large portions that it's common and acceptable to order a half-portion, or you can choose from the traditional menu of meatballs, *pide,* fish, and mezes. Copycats have opened several carbon-copy restaurants adjacent to Sedir; so you can actually try a different one for each meal (**Şamdan,** Tütün Sok. 9, ✆ **0252/614-2868; Sofra Lokantası,** Hükümet Caddesi [at the corner outside the new food market], ✆ **0252/614-3470**).

Tütün Sok. ✆ **0252/614-1095.** Appetizers and main courses 3YTL–14YTL ($2–$10). No credit cards. Daily noon–2pm.

KAYAKÖY

Cin Bal *Finds* MOUNTAIN GRILLS   Originally a butchery, this village garden–style eatery is a well-kept secret, serving up rustic ambience and incredible food at spectacularly low prices. You can sit at one of the few tables in the slightly overgrown valley yard or on rudimentary platforms with plump pillows while a herd of goats nibble at the nearby daffodils. After choosing from a selection of meat, fish, and wild boar, all of it fresh and succulent and in abundant portions, you grill your own food on a small, tableside barbecue. The mezes are almost unnecessary with all the food that arrives, including the essential combination of onions, tomatoes, and peppers to grill alongside the meat. The local crowd of regulars tends to make an evening of it, egged on by the roving minstrels and singing increasingly off key as the night progresses.

Kaya Köyü. ✆ **0252/618-0066.** Appetizers 2YTL ($1.50); main courses by weight (about 14YTL/$10 per kilo). No credit cards. Daily 8am–2am.

ÖLÜDENIZ

Beyaz Yunus/White Dolphin *Moments* FISH   This is just the society destination that Ölüdeniz needed to detract from the overwhelming presence of frat boys and daredevil paragliders. It commands the best spot above the far end of Belceğiz Beach, on the road that leads to Faralya and Kabak, a position on dual terraces with stunning sunset views backed by a cacophony of crashing waves. Couples may want to opt for the romantic dining terrace, a quiet and candlelit spot that boasts the "G3" table, which, thanks to the best views in the house, has entertained some of the world's most privileged (Prince Charles, Elia Kazan, Tina Turner, and recently, the Bushes). Long pub tables take up the main dining terrace, with plenty of room for dishes like Mediterranean lobster and whatever the catches of the day happen to be. Mezes include the Ottoman favorite *icli köfte,* a large fried dumpling of cracked wheat surrounding a center of spiced chopped lamb, and an overwhelming variety of seafood salads. The raw whole octopus (eye included) is a house special prepared in the Greek style; or for the squeamish, there's stuffed grape leaves and other fresh cold starters. To save you the trouble of arriving sweaty in your best resort wear, the management offers a free shuttle from your hotel in Ölüdeniz to the restaurant.

On the cliff at the far end of Belceğiz Beach. ✆ **0252/617-0068.** Appetizers 5.40YTL–16YTL ($4–$12); main fish courses 24YTL ($18) or by weight. AE, MC, V. Daily 6pm–1am.

Kumsal *Kids* TURKISH/PIDES   The nearby nighttime odor of sewage might be a major deterrent, but by day, this outdoor garden deck draped in vines and dripping bunches of grapes makes a wonderful midafternoon lunch break. It's most recognized for a variety of perfectly baked and properly doughy *pide,* with choices such as spinach and cheese, meat and cheese, or all meat or all cheese. They also have a vegetarian option topped with tomatoes, peppers, onions, and mushrooms. They've also got the usual lineup of menu items, and there's an outdoor cafe/bar, which makes this a perfect stop-off when your skin is starting to get a little too crisp.

Belceğiz Beach, near the Belcekız Beach Hotel. ✆ 0252/617-0058. Main courses 4YTL–9.50YTL ($3–$7). No credit cards. Daily 8am–1am.

Oba *Value* TURKISH/PIDES   In a sea change of restaurants that pass from owner to owner, this is the one reliable and consistent dining spot (excluding Beyaz Yunus, which is in a class all its own) in Ölüdeniz. Located 1 long block away from the beach (look for Pizza Pepino), Oba makes for a quiet lunch or a lively dinner. The menu is traditional Turkish, but the food quality is excellent, and you get to choose between traditional Turkish platform seating or a table in the cool garden. *Pide* and pizza are only served in the evening hours.

From the Belceğiz Beach promenade, turn down the quiet side street once you see Pizza Pepino. ✆ 0252/617-0470. Appetizers 4YTL–6.75YTL ($3–$5); main courses 8YTL–14 ($6–$10). No credit cards. Daily 8am–1am.

FETHIYE AFTER DARK

Hotels and resorts provide the best entertainment, often drawing nonguests from the surrounding areas, with presentations of live music or some contrived line-dance activity. Look for postings around the properties for options.

The Old Town Bazaar in downtown **Fethiye** has a good number of bars, restaurants, and shops lining the ancient streets.

Hisarönü, the enclave located on the road to **Kayaköy,** turns into a fun-house festival and pedestrian market on summer evenings. The streets are lined with restaurants and boisterous bars too numerous to mention (a huge draw for the local British expats), and shops selling beach souvenirs that catch your eye under fluorescent lighting.

The promenade along Belceğiz Beach down at **Ölüdeniz,** with its handful of nightspots that play music loud and louder, is absent of any real sophistication, and utterly avoidable unless you've chosen to base yourself locally. There are two or three atmospheric locales where the daytime's paragliders congregate, but the best thing you can do for a quiet evening is to head up to the bar terrace of Beyaz Yunus/White Dolphin (p. 278). Here you can have a drink by candlelight and surf while seated in designer chairs sheltered under bougainvillea.

Buzz Beach Bar   Buzz Bar is very popular with visitors, both for the outdoor cafe along the promenade and the outdoor bar and lounge upstairs. The music is pretty good, too, albeit as loud as any other bar. You can check your e-mail with a drink in hand, as they also have an Internet corner (see "Fast Facts: Ölüdeniz" earlier in this chapter). Daily 8am to 3am. Belceğiz Beach on the promenade, Ölüdeniz. ✆ 0252/617-0045. Closed in winter.

Help Bar   Once again, the White Dolphin hit the jackpot, offering creative fun in a colorful atmosphere of odd-shaped tables (like bent dogs or bones) and hand-painted chairs named after film characters and celebrities, such as Sophia Loren and "Dirty Harry." An American-style drink and cocktail menu (read: excessively long) is complemented by light meals and starters from the restaurant's kitchen, and includes bar staples such as grilled garlic tortillas and deep-fried artichoke hearts. Daily 8 or 9am to 3am. Belceğiz Beach promenade (near the road into town), Ölüdeniz. © **0252/617-0498.** Closed in winter.

Türkü Evi *(Finds)*   Just what the doctor ordered, Türkü Evi is that perfectly characteristic Turkish pub that's so lacking in these parts. The entrance is up the exterior stone steps to the left, which lead to a softly lit pub decorated with Anatolian carpets and serenaded by a local folk guitarist. The earlier you go, the mellower the experience; after about 11pm, locals start to pile in, light up, and dance a la turque—hands raised into the air. Daily 9pm to 3am. Barlar Sokağı at Çarşı Caddesi, Fethiye. © **0542/646-1360.**

4 Kalkan ★★

81km (50 miles) southeast of Fethiye; 25km (15 miles) west of Kaş; 19km (12 miles) south of Xanthos; 18km (11 miles) east of Patara; 25km (15 miles) southeast of Letoon

When Erkut Taçkın, the famous Turkish singer from the 1960s, bought a house in Kalkan, the village's fate was sealed. For the Turkish "smart set," it had become the place to go. Ever since, Kalkan has undergone a renewal of sorts, and many of this tiny town's characteristic Ottoman and Greek structures have been brought back to life. The smart set has long moved on, replaced by Europeans (mostly Brits) looking for inexpensive vacation and retirement homes and as a result, building has sprawled almost all the way to Kalamar Bay. But while the ever-increasing influx of foreigners and visitors continues to exert pressure on this seaside village, Kalkan's terraced position below the main road prevents any palatable departure from the village's inherent small-town persona.

Contrary to its popular perception as a fishing town, Kalkan was actually settled around 150 to 200 years ago by merchants from the nearby Greek island of Meis (Castellorizo). By the turn of the last century Kalkan thrived on the production of charcoal, silk, cotton, and olive oil—it even had its own customs house. As early as the 1950s and 1960s, the town began to attract rich English yachtspeople, leading to a trend in the 1980s of transforming dilapidated houses into characteristic whitewashed homes with shuttered windows and timber balconies.

The town's population of around 1,000 swells to 8,000 in summer, meaning that Kalkan may not be putting its best foot forward in July and August. This is when the English presence in Kalkan becomes overwhelming—even disturbing. Meanwhile, two Brit-based tour operators (Tapestry and Simply Turkey) ensure that most of the town's better hotels exclusively host their clients, thus creating a shortage of rooms for the independent traveler during the main tourist season. Nevertheless, all of this attention keeps Kalkan running at full capacity, creating demand for some of the most consistent and sophisticated menus on the Turquoise Coast.

Meanwhile, services cater to a single clientele: Chips (french fries) are the unfortunate side dish to most entrees, and mobile potato kiosks are becoming a fixed part of the landscape. Price levels have been driven up to the highest level on the coast, and it shows no sign of letting up.

Kalkan's location is convenient to many historical sites—although lazy days on the beach and hours chatting with the quirky town residents are good enough reasons to base yourself here. The summertime bonus is that Kalkan is graced with the lowest level of humidity in Turkey.

ESSENTIALS
GETTING THERE
Halfway between Dalaman and Antalya airports, Kalkan lies along the southwestern coast of the Mediterranean. Unless you have your own car, there's no way to avoid the long and torturous (albeit lovely) journey by land: from Antalya it's a 6-hour, rarely air-conditioned minibus ride.

Kamil Koç (② 444-0562) provides the only direct bus service from Dalaman to Kalkan (3 hr.; 8YTL/$6), leaving daily from the bus station at 9:30am in summer, 9:30pm in winter. A taxi from the airport will run around 135YTL ($100).

From Fethiye it's an easy 11km/18 miles into Kalkan (1½ hr.; 16YTL/$12). Long-distance direct service is available with **Pamukkale** year-round from Istanbul (12 hr.; 53YTL/$39), leaving at 7pm nightly; from Ankara (10 hr.; 40YTL/$30), leaving at 10:30pm (in winter, you must change in Fethiye); and from İzmir (8 hr.; 22YTL/ $16), leaving at 9am and 9pm. **Kamil Koç** also serves these cities.

The main bus companies often send their non-air-conditioned minibuses into Kalkan. If you're headed to any of the towns along the coast up to Antalya, catch one of **Antalya Tour's** (② 0242/331-1250) air-conditioned buses (not all are equipped), and head out early in the morning—the lack of traffic can shorten your trip by up to an hour; from Antalya, it'll cost around 12YTL ($9).

Perhaps most convenient is to visit Kalkan as a port of call on a Blue Voyage. (If you're taking a Blue Voyage, it's worth trying to coax your captain into stopping in Kalkan for an overnight visit.)

VISITOR INFORMATION
There is no Tourist Information office in Kalkan. Thursday is market day.

Deniz Bank is the only bank in town, so it's a good idea to arrive in town with enough cash to get by, in case the ATM falls victim to an unexpected glitch.

At the **marina,** you can take care of the basics, such as the use of coin-operated public toilets, showers, or laundry facilities, or hire a local boat and captain for the day.

ORIENTATION
Kalkan is built on a steep hillside that descends into the bay; enclosed by rocky and rugged mountains, the village has nowhere to go but down. The main square serves as a parking lot as well as the old town center, with two or three bus company offices, some travel agencies, a barber, a PTT, and a handful of bodegas for essential refills of water. From the tiny roundabout at the entrance to the town, a connector road leads the way out to lovely Kalamar Bay. This road is at the receiving end of most of the building boom experienced here in the past 5 or so years.

In Kalkan's compact center, the crisscross of streets packed with restaurants, pensions, and shops from the main square down to the marina is known as **Yalıboyu.** Even though nobody uses a street address, it's unlikely you'll get lost. All roads lead to the harbor and marina, and you will find yourself trekking up and down the steep roads countless times a day.

GETTING AROUND
Kalkan is a pedestrian village of limited size. The main square is closed to incoming traffic, requiring automobiles to circle down to the marina, turn left at the harborfront road and left again back up the hill to the main square. If you're entering the village by car, be aware that the harbor road closes to traffic at 7pm. If you have trouble walking up and down steep inclines, Kalkan is not for you.

BY *DOLMUŞ* *Dolmuşes* leave from the main square regularly (as soon as they fill up), heading east toward Kaş or west to Patara and points beyond. *Dolmuş* service back into Kalkan ends as early as 6pm, so if you pop out of town for the day, make sure you have a ride home.

BY BUS There is a limited number of major bus companies in Kalkan, generally servicing only the longer hauls. Destinations and schedules are posted on placards outside the few minuscule ticket offices located on the main square. It's usually okay to buy your ticket at the office just prior to boarding.

BY CAR/SCOOTER It's almost impossible not to trip over a sign touting the rental of a scooter, car, or jeep. You'll find the scooters up in the main square across from the post office renting for about 27YTL to 40YTL ($20–$30), and car rentals through most travel agencies go for 67YTL ($50) and up, depending on the model.

WHAT TO SEE & DO

The distinctive features of the coastline around Kalkan and the nearby Xanthos River allow for innumerable options for day trips on or near the water. Here the jagged edges of mountains meet the sea, forming a breathtaking network of islands and coves that present endless possibilities for a day of dive bombing off the roof of a boat and swimming into eerie caves. High up on your list should be a boat trip around the island of **Kekova** and the sunken city, accessible from a number of port towns along the coast (see section 5, "Kaş," later in this chapter, for further information).

AREA BEACHES

Usually, a sign reading YACHT CLUB means members only, or more accurately, not you, thank you very much. Not so here at the Kalkan Marina, where a traveler, no matter whether the arrival was by land or by sea, can venture up and over to the other side of the breakwater, to the town "beach." Daily rental for lounges and umbrellas is around 6.75YTL ($5); the Yacht Club also has an on-site watersports concession, called Blue Marlin (© 0242/844-2783), open April through October. There's also a snack bar with competitive prices; you can also stock up at the supermarket on the harbor.

Kalkan also boasts its very own man-made **pebble beach,** at the eastern end of town, but because it's fed by the icy spring waters channeling down from the mountain, you might want to save this for a bracing sunrise dip or a refreshing cool-off at the end of a hot and dusty day.

Kaputaş Beach 🏖️🏖️ is a tiny little sandy cove at the mouth of a colossal gorge. Only 10 minutes from Kalkan, the *dolmuş* crosses a bridge between the two sides of the formation and drops you off at the highway railing, at the top of a lofty stairway down to the beach. **Mavi Mağara (Blue Cave,** named for the hue of the boulders inside) is a short swim from Kaputaş out and to the left, but as the beach is not guarded, only strong swimmers in pairs should do this.

Over at Kalamar Bay is the **Kalamar Beach Club** 🏖️🏖️ (© 0242/844-3061), comprised of an intimate series of cement patio terraces with beach lounges, backed by a restaurant and snack bar. The guys that run the concession provide free transfers from Kalkan, and make up the difference with food prices that are the highest in the area. Day rental of a lounge and umbrella is around 6.75YTL ($5), and there are also showers. Boredom is kept at bay thanks to **Aquasports** (© 0242/844-2361), the on-site provider of watersports rentals. In addition to a dive concession (see Kalkan Dive Center under "Staying Active" below), they rent jet skis and water skis (25YTL/$18 per

10 min.; lessons available for water-skiing); banana boats (8YTL/$6 per person); and 25- or 40-horsepower speed boats (100YTL/$75 per day).

Area resort hotels also make their private beaches and facilities available to nonguests for a daily fee. **Club Patara** (© 0242/844-3920) is accessible via the free water taxi to the resort's platforms, where you can take advantage of the three pools and terrace lounges for around 20YTL ($15). The water taxi pulls up to the pier next to the lighthouse, but keep in mind that the wait around lunchtime will be a bit longer—the captain goes AWOL for a bite to eat. Reservations are essential if you want to rent anything motorized.

Only 20 minutes away by *dolmuş* is **Patara Beach** 🏖🏖, the longest and certainly one of the most beautiful stretches of sand in Turkey. The beach goes on for 18km (11 miles), which makes for a pretty long surfside stroll, especially when the fierce winds are at their peak. Entrance to the beach is through the ruins of the ancient city, so if you've come by car, you'll have to pay the entrance fee of 11YTL ($8) to the site, which includes repeat visits to the beach (keep your ticket). If you've arrived on a *dolmuş*, the beach is free, but you may want to rent an umbrella. Patara Beach is also a lesser-known nesting ground for the Caretta Caretta turtle, so it is closed after dark.

The stunning scenery and sleek minimalist pool terrace at the **Harpy Hotel** at Kalamar Bay opens up its pool for a daily fee of 15YTL ($11). Although there is no direct access to the sea, the views from the pool are incomparably beautiful.

EXPLORING RUINS IN THE XANTHOS VALLEY

Kalkan is a great base for day excursions to the ancient Lycian sites of the Xanthos Valley, which includes the ancient sites of Tlos (see "Fethiye & Ölüdeniz," earlier in this chapter), Xanthos, Letoon, and Patara. All of the sites are easily accessible by car with a short detour off the main road or by *dolmuşes* that run regularly from the main square. Several travel agencies in town offer excursions to one or more of the sites as part of a day tour; contact **Kalamus Travel Agency,** Yalıboyu Mahallesi (© 0242/ 844-2456; www.kalkanturkey.com), for the most competitive rates; **Armes Travel & Tours,** at the harbor (© 0242/844-3169); or the Munich-based **Dardanos Turizm,** Hotel Dardanos Gelemiş Koyu (© 0242/843-5151).

The oldest and most important antique city of the region is **Xanthos** 🏛🏛, the ancient capital of Lycia. Homer mentions this center in the *Iliad:* It was from here that Arpedonte led his troops. More tragic is the actual history of the city: On two separate and unrelated occasions, the inhabitants of Xanthos chose collective suicide rather than submission to invading armies.

The ancient city was uncovered by Sir Charles Fellows in 1838, who had much of the city dismantled and transported to the British Museum, where ruins still reside. Nevertheless, reproductions successfully evoke the originals. On your travels through Kaş/Kalkan, pick up a free map of the site; or, you can buy a book on Lycian sites at the refreshment counter. Two unforgettable monuments are on the road from the village of Kınık—the **City Gate** 🏛🏛, dating to the Hellenistic Era, and **Vespasian's Arch** 🏛🏛, erected in honor of the Roman emperor. The **acropolis** 🏛🏛🏛 is dominated by the remains of the **Roman Theatre** 🏛🏛, flanked by the ancient city's three most memorable sites: **Harpies' Tomb** 🏛🏛🏛, named for the Persian General Harpagus through a controversial interpretation by Fellows of the tomb's reliefs; the **Lycian Tomb** 🏛🏛🏛 (one of several); and the **Roman Columned Tomb.** Farther back into the brush is a pillar tomb called the **Obelisk,** whose monumental contribution was lengthy inscriptions in both Lycian and Greek, which proved indispensable to deciphering and classifying the Lycian language (another inscription, found at Letoon and written in Aramaic, Greek, and Lycian, was also important).

The New Acropolis is located on the opposite side of the road, and is home to the **Byzantine Church** ✿, famed for the well-preserved **mosaic** ✿ flooring uncovered beneath layers of sand. Tour groups generally circle these major sites, overlooking entirely the overgrown path that leads along an ancient wall through to the **Necropolis** ✿✿, a visit that is well worth your time. Sarcophagi are scattered or overturned; keep an eye out for the **Belly Dancer Sarcophagus** ✿, named for a relief that more resembles water-bearers; the **Lion's Tomb** ✿, a sarcophagus with carvings of lions and a bull in battle; and a 4th-century-B.C. **tower tomb** ✿✿ rising above a stone-cut Roman acropolis. Admission to the site is 4YTL ($3).

Patara ✿✿ was Lycia's chief port city until the harbor silted up to form what is today an inland reed-filled marsh. If you climb to the hilltop above the **Roman Theatre** ✿, the fierce winds and unrelenting lashes of sand will give you a clue as why much of this ancient city still remains buried—a consequence that has kept the city in such an outstanding state of preservation. Founded according to legend by Patarus, son of Apollo and the nymph Lycia in the 5th century B.C., the site served during the winter months as one of the two most important oracles of the god, his winter months being spent at the temple at Delphi. Today the city gains its fame as the birthplace of the bishop of Myra, better known in northern and western circles as Santa Claus (see section 6, "Demre," later in this chapter). Little by little, ongoing excavations are beginning to reveal details above and beyond the **monumental arch** ✿✿ that rose defiantly above the meters of earth for centuries. At the time of this writing, Patara's **main avenue** ✿✿, paved with marble stone and scattered with the remains of what was probably a columned arcade, is clearly visible (albeit sometimes a bit waterlogged). Fleeting features of the **Basilica** ✿ poke through the ground, but perimeter excavations provide a cross section of the city's entombment.

The ruins can be easily explored in combination with a trip to Patara Beach; the road from the turnoff passes a saturated level of home-style pensions with varying degrees of charm and leads to the entrance of the archaeological site (admission 10YTL/$7.50). The beach is at the end of the road.

Letoon ✿, located less than 5km (3 miles) south of Xanthos, was the primary religious center of ancient Lycia. And while the buses are circling around Xanthos, you can escape here, smack in the middle of the Turkey you envisioned, along a pastoral village road, admiring the wind in the trees and the goats grazing in the archaeological site. Aren't you clever.

The ruins of **three temples** ✿✿ rise above an uneven plateau and were dedicated to the gods Apollo, Artemis, and their mother Lato, the mythical lover of Zeus for which the sanctuary was named. The foundations of the three temples are laid out parallel to each other; the **theater** ✿✿ is in better shape, and served for meetings of the Lycian Federation, religious ceremonies, and even sports events. Admission to the site is 4YTL ($3).

STAYING ACTIVE

The waters off Kalkan provide some of the best venues for **scuba diving** along the Mediterranean. It was off nearby Uluburun that sponge divers discovered a 14th-century-B.C. shipwreck. **Bougainville Travel** (www.bougainville-turkey.com) and **Armes Travel and Tours** organize group dives, or you can hook up with **Kalkan Dive Center,** a division of Aquasports over at Kalamar Bay (© **0242/844-2456;** www.kalkandiving. com), run by a couple of experienced local divers. A day of diving for beginners and pros starts at 65YTL ($50).

Canoeing along the Xanthos River is an exhilarating way to spend the day. You don't need to be a pro—the excursion organizers design tours geared toward fun rather than physical fitness. A day tour usually includes a stopover at a mud bath and a few hours of relaxation on Patara Beach. A day on the rapids runs around 55YTL ($40) per person, lunch and transfers included. These and other activities are generally planned on fixed days of the week. **Kalamus Travel Agency** and **Armes Travel & Tours** (see "Exploring Ruins in the Xanthos Valley," above) offer a reliable and exhilarating array of active trips, as does the German-based (with local presence in Patara) **Dardanos Travel** (in Germany © **49-89-489-2501;** www.dardanostravel.com). If you don't see a tour package that suits your needs, check around the main square or down by the harbor for tours organized by other outfitters.

A popular activity especially suited to the area is **horseback riding.** The Eşen Plain meets the sea at Patara where, riding through Roman ruins and sand dunes, you can imagine yourself in an ancient Greek countryside. Armes runs these trips for 65YTL ($50).

WHERE TO STAY

British tour companies have blocked out most of the best rooms in Kalkan, leaving others with sloppy seconds. Luckily, there are a few hotels and pensions in town that refuse to work with agents.

Keep in mind that while a pension or special-category hotel in the center of town will at least afford some architectural integrity, don't expect a pool. But thanks to the proximity and accessibility of nearby beaches, this should by no means be a deterrent to staying in town. If your holiday style leans more toward the plush and all-inclusive, choose one of the resorts across the bay; they are connected to the village by a water shuttle.

KALKAN

Hotel Patara Prince 🏖🏖   The grounds of the Patara Prince are nothing short of a seaside paradise, set on white stone cliffs on a backdrop of verdant gardens. The complex is constructed on the steep hillside opposite Kalkan, with facilities positioned at various altitudes connected by pure white, local stone stairways. The extremely terraced landscaping need not be a deterrent; the hotel provides a shuttle service down the service road to the waterfront.

The complex consists of more economical rooms in the main hotel; blocks of suites of varying types, smartly decorated with features like Jacuzzis, fireplaces, and bamboo-shuttered windows separating the bathroom from the living area; and villas large enough for up to six people. The villas (some loosely associated with its timeshare operation) are charming and rustic self-catering houses complete with kitchens, living rooms, multiple bedrooms, and scenic terraces.

There are three outdoor swimming pools of which one is a freshwater pool, and another is for adults only and filled with circulated sea water. Terraces for sunbathing step down the cliff side to waterfront platforms, where the watersports activities are organized. The hotel provides a free shuttle service to Kalkan.

P.K. 10, Kalkan. © 0242/844-3920. Fax 0242/844-3930. www.clubpatara.com. 60 units. 46€–188€ ($56–$230) double in hotel; 116€–338€ ($140–$410) executive and admiralty suite; 245€–2,170€ ($300–$2,950) self-catering villa. Rates reflect seasonal differences and include breakfast. AE, DC, MC, V. Parking lot on-site. **Amenities:** 4 restaurants; 4 bars; nightclub; patisserie; 4 swimming pools (3 outdoor, 1 indoor); tennis courts (2 night lit); full-service health club; extensive watersports; dive school; children's center; game room; concierge; tour desk; car-rental desk; salon, 24-hr. room service; massage; babysitting; laundry service; dry cleaning. *In room:* A/C, satellite TV, minibar, hair dryer, safe.

Hotel Zinbad Inconspicuously located down a street, Hotel Zinbad draws in passersby with a welcoming lobby and a mouthwatering lunch menu posted outside. Tiled stairs lead up to a rooftop terrace decorated with bamboo, where satisfied guests return for another delicious meal or to just hang around in the company of the hotel's owner and manager. The terrace commands views of the harbor and slender minaret from the mosque, to enjoy while dining on fresh home cooking that varies daily.

Half of the rooms (the ones facing the harbor) in the hotel were recently renovated and are clearly preferred to the less gracious ones in the back. Rooms are spotlessly clean, with a colorful kilim as the only embellishment. Hotel Zinbad also has one efficiency that accommodates up to four people.

Mustafa Kocakaya Cad. 26, 07960 Kalkan. © **0242/844-3404.** Fax 0242/844-3943. www.zinbadhotel.com. 30 units. 30€–38€ ($39–$46) double. AE, MC, V. **Amenities:** Restaurant/bar; laundry service; dry cleaning. *In room:* A/C.

Kalkan Han ✦ If the Balıkçi Han influenced the transformation of Kalkan into a tourist town, the Kalkan Han holds an important role in its architectural revitalization. As one of the pioneers of minimalism in Turkey, the interior is charming in its simplicity, with the only embellishment being the gleaming hardwood floors and whitewashed interiors. The facade retains its original character, with timber balconies topped by the traditional triangular lintel.

Each of the six suites comes with an air-conditioning unit in the sitting room and a ceiling fan in the bedroom, an essential feature in the losing battle against the heat caused by the sun blazing through the harborside windows. Rooms at the back alleviate the problem, except in the case of the standard doubles, which lack air-conditioning (but have ceiling fans), requiring you to sleep with the windows open, which lets in street noise. The roof bar is a morning oasis of beauty and calm; white muslin deck chairs and bougainvillea enclose the terrace but allow for some of the village's most magnificent sea views.

Kalkan Köy İçi, 07960 Kalkan (just beyond the main square on the left). © **0242/844-3151.** Fax 0242/844-2059. In winter contact in Istanbul at © 0212/638-1370; fax 0212/518-5060. www.kalkanhan.8k.com. 10 units. 80€–120€ ($100–$150) double. MC, V. Closed Nov 1–May 14. **Amenities:** Roof bar; laundry service; dry cleaning.

Türk Evi ✦ *Value* This guesthouse makes you feel like you've just walked into somebody's elegant country home. The Turkish and Norwegian team, along with their daughter Zirve, have created a real family atmosphere, down to the fresh farmer's butter and homemade jams. The open, farmhouselike living room, dining room, and kitchen area provide an inviting place for guests to come together, and an outdoor patio is used for family-style meals made with the freshest ingredients prepared on the outdoor barbecue (meals are for guests only). Each simple but charmingly decorated room is named after its color (the pink rooms are the ones with tubs), and the adjacent blue rooms provide a connecting balcony for families or friends traveling together. The owner has considerately hung mosquito netting over the beds, because in the heat of the summer, the windows must stay open. Nestled at the top of town in a woodsy setting, it's a bit of a steep climb up, so you may arrive back up from the waterfront a bit winded.

07960 Kalkan (behind the post office near the town center). © **0242/844-3129.** Fax 0242/844-3492. 9 rooms (2 with tub, 7 with shower). 40€ ($50) double. No credit cards. Parking near main road. Turn off the Kaş road into town;

the entrance to the guesthouse is on the road into Kalkan immediately on the left. **Amenities:** Restaurant (for guests); laundry service; dry cleaning.

Villa Mahal ✋ Having already been recognized by international style magazines, the Villa Mahal could easily be called the Jewel of the Mediterranean, offering its visitors sophisticated yet unspoiled surroundings. The large property sits in the middle of an olive grove on a steep bluff overlooking Kalkan Bay and is secluded enough that nothing man-made tarnishes the view. The actual building area takes up very little of the grounds, so the brush along the cliff side provides a good level of privacy. Hotel rooms are at the top of the bluff overlooking the sea, but at 202 steps, it's a long walk down to the waterside and much longer on the way up under the fierce heat. Characteristic waterside platforms form the "beach" where there is an array of watersports and an airy and stylish seaside cafe. Villa Mahal has a very special "honeymoon suite," a chillingly romantic secluded circular building with glass walls and its very own private terrace pool overlooking the bay. A regular water shuttle runs from the platform to Kalkan's marina every 15 minutes in high season.

P.K. 4, 07960 Kalkan. 🕿 **0242/844-3268.** Fax 0242/844-2122. www.villamahal.com. 14 units. 150€–200€ ($180–$245) double; 230€ ($280) pool room. Rates lower Apr–May and Oct. MC, V. Take the turn off the main road for Patara Club and follow signs for Villa Mahal. **Amenities:** Restaurant; 2 bars; 24-hr. room service; laundry service; dry cleaning. *In room:* A/C.

KALAMAR BAY

Harpy Hotel The good news is that from the hotel's hillside terrace, enormous enough to accommodate the heated half-Olympic-size pool, the Harpy takes full advantage of views of Kalamar Bay. The trade-off? The structure is a dull glass and cement monster that offends its more traditional surroundings through an attempt toward innovation. But still, the hotel carves out a niche. The Harpy targets a high-tech business audience with a state-of-the-art local computer network connected directly to the Internet, and individual connections in each room. There are presentation facilities, a business center, and a recreation room with a "business corner." Even the room decor screams corporate, with safe—even monotonous—furnishings and straightforward modular furniture. And ultimately, visitors looking for comfort away from the tourist hordes on one of the few unspoiled bays in the area are also heading here. All rooms have an exterior entrance, and all but four rooms enjoy a sea view thanks to large sliding glass doors to the terrace or balcony.

Kalamar Bay, Kalkan. 🕿 0242/844-1133. Fax 0242/844-1132. www.harpy.com.tr. 50 units. 45€–70€ ($55–$85) double; 60€–95€ ($73–$115) suite. Rates reflect season. MC, V. **Amenities:** Restaurant; bar; outdoor swimming pool; business center with secretarial services; 24-hr. room service; laundry service; dry cleaning. *In room:* A/C, satellite TV, dataport, minibar, hair dryer, safe.

WHERE TO DINE

The problem of choice will be a tourist's major complaint when staying in Kalkan, as this village easily has the highest ratio of quality restaurants per capita on Turkey's Mediterranean coast. The trend also is that all this great "international" food comes with price tags pegged to international currencies. Unpretentious *lokanta* fare can be had at **Ali Baba** (🕿 **0242/844-3627**), up on the main square near the post office, open 24 hours, and at the trellis-shaded **Bezirgan's Kitchen** (next to the Kamıl Koç bus office).

Many of the pensions and hotels have rooftop restaurants, and often serve some of the best meals using ingredients bought at market the same day. Whenever possible, I always opt for these. But as a nonguest, it's a good idea to reserve ahead (even by midmorning), to allow the cook to stock up on an adequate amount of food.

Be skeptical of restaurants advertising fresh fish; much of the fish along the Mediterranean arrives frozen—ask the waiter before you order if your selection was swimming anytime recently.

Korsan ✦✦ (Kids) NOUVELLE TURKISH   With its white tablecloth and candlelight, the elegant Korsan, located next to the harbor, is popular among the local community of British expatriates as well as with visitors splurging on a special meal. One glance at the menu and it's obvious that this isn't going to be another banal meal of grilled lamb and green chiles. Choosing among the many mouthwatering mezes is probably the most significant decision you will make during your vacation, with selections like chicken şiş with peanut sauce, fish cakes with pine nuts and berries, and humus with melted chile butter. By the time you fill up on the complimentary fresh-baked garlic bread and two or three appetizers, there is sadly no room for the Black Sea–style baked lamb in a pastry crust with mint or the barbecue fish *kebap*. Even the kids will be happy, with Korsan's special, less exotic, children's menu. A sister restaurant is on the rooftop of the owner's small hotel/pension, Patara Stone House (© **0242/844-3076**), located just above the harbor.

At the Marina. © **0242/844-3622**. Reservations suggested. Dress smart. Main courses 8€–16€ ($10–$19). MC, V. Daily noon–midnight. Closed Nov–Apr.

Patlican/Aubergine Restaurant ✦✦ TURKISH/OTTOMAN/INTERNATIONAL   "Harika" (Great! In Turkish), describes a dining experience at this innocuous restaurant on the harborfront. Thanks to its continued success (and the fact that harborfront restaurants are no longer permitted to set up tables on the waterside promenade), Patlican recently doubled its interior space but remains cozy and delightful. First-time guests are usually drawn to the filet of wild boar, an abundant entree served with slices of eggplant (sorry, aubergine), tomato, and vegetables, and slow roasted till tender. But leave me to the grilled prawns—flavorful and slightly spicy—and a perfectly marinated swordfish şiş any day of the week. These are just samples of the restaurant's creativity, expanded weekly in the special menu.

Harborside, Kalkan. © **0242/844-3332**. Reservations suggested. Appetizers 4.50€–9€ ($5.50–$11); main courses 8€–16€ ($10–$19). AE, MC, V. Daily 9am–midnight.

Finds Mahmut'un Yeri

About a 10-minute's drive into the mountains from Kalkan is the minuscule village of Islamlar, built on the Islamlar Spring, a freshwater source that coursed down the mountain. About 10 years ago, one young local villager had the bright idea to harness the water in a cement pool and stock it with trout, and in no time, his neighbors were standing by in disbelief as the customers began to roll into their wild and unspoiled landscape. Now there are more than a handful of imitations, all essentially identical, but **Mahmut'un Yeri** (from Kalkan, the first one as you enter the village; © **0242/838-6344**) stays ahead of the pack with a newly constructed country-style restaurant with a roof terrace that enjoys views as far as the sea. Little ones will love watching the trout leaping up out of the water, sometimes upstream through the mesh barrier to freedom and sometimes out of the pool to their death. For now, the price of a meal (trout, salad, and *ayran*) is about 6.75YTL ($5).

KALKAN AFTER DARK

Moonlight Café, which blasts its music over the collective rooftops of Kalkan well into the morning hours, is the unfortunate defining element of nightlife in Kalkan. In spite of complaints to the local *jandarma* (there's a midnight curfew), the owner arrogantly continues to exhibit a complete lack of regard for his neighbors and their guests. There's almost nowhere in town where his cafe is not audible, although an evening stroll along the marina might place enough houses between you and the cafe. Apart from that annoyance, the rooftops are a special feature of Kalkan houses, camouflaged behind small triangular lintels yet open to nighttime sea breezes.

Kleo Bar   Under the pagoda of a defunct Chinese restaurant is a sophisticated and utterly romantic spot for a quiet evening of music and conversation. An eclectic mix of lounge furniture is scattered outside at the far end of the harbor, with the most coveted spots—candlelit tables—closer to the water. Cocktails arrive with fanfare of sparklers, and live music—mostly Turkish adult contemporary—is performed nightly. Daily 9pm to 3am. Next to Korsan. No phone. Closed in winter.

Yacht Club   Candlelight and music reverberate off the water in the nighttime hours at Kalkan's main "beach." There's an outdoor bar and tables, and July through September, live music acts perform until 2am. Daily 8am to 3am. In the marina. No phone. Closed in winter.

5 Kaş ★★

81km (50 miles) southeast of Fethiye; 229km (142 miles) southwest of Antalya; 25km (15 miles) east of Kalkan; 109km (68 miles) southeast of Dalaman Airport

At only 25km (15 miles) and 20 minutes apart, Kaş and Kalkan share the same stunning coast of broken rocky coastline, so whether you base yourself in one or the other depends on your individual character and travel style (tours from one include pickups in the other). Kaş established itself as the more popular of the two in the 1960s and 1970s, first as a "hippie" hangout and later, as another ideal stopping point for yachts and *gulets* on the Blue Voyage. The town met demand by transforming itself from a small fishing village into a resort town. Yet in spite of the ebbs and flows of tourism that have left many hotels in dire need of TLC, Kaş still retains a certain small-town charm, with narrow cobblestone streets, incredible coastal views, and some of the most lovely and creative boutiques the Mediterranean has to offer. The town is built around the sparse remains of ancient **Antiphellos,** which left behind a few scattered rock tombs, a Greek theater, and an unanticipated **monumental sarcophagus** featuring four lions' heads at the upper end of one of Kaş's narrow shopping streets.

As the definition of a beach resort goes, Kaş falls somewhat short. But what Kaş lacks in proper beaches, it makes up for with rocky access to crystal-clear Mediterranean waters. Kaş is also an optimal jumping-off point for trips to Kekova, Myra, and some of the regions' best undiscovered mountain villages. The abundance of outdoorsy activities around Kaş has also helped to maintain its reputation as a relaxed, satisfying, and generally inexpensive holiday destination.

ESSENTIALS
GETTING THERE
Short of renting a car, the best (and most expensive) way to arrive in Kaş is via a travel agency transfer from either Antalya or Dalaman airport (175YTL/$130 and 170YTL/$125, respectively). Minibuses leaves regularly from Fethiye for Kalkan (2½ hr.;

6.75YTL/$5) and continue on to Kaş. The ride from Antalya takes as little as 3½ hours if you leave early in the morning, and about 4½ to 5 hours during the day when the traffic is heavier.

Kaş is a popular port of call for Blue Voyage cruises, so you may have the opportunity to arrive by boat for either an afternoon excursion or an overnight stay.

VISITOR INFORMATION

The **Tourist Information office** is located on Hükümet Cad. 2, at the marina (© 0242/836-1238). The number for the *otogar* is © 0242/836-1020. There are three taxi stands in town, Liman Taksi (© 0242/836-1489), Yat Taksi (© 0242/836-1933), and Çakıl Taksi (© 0242/836-2448).

ORIENTATION

The *otogar* is at the north end of town. From the station, the sloping street down to the town center, the harbor, and marina is called **Atatürk Caddesi.** West of the marina (turn right before the marina at the minuscule roundabout) are the ruins of Antiphellos and the well-preserved antique theater. This road makes the circuit of the Çukurbağ Peninsula then dumps you back onto the road into town.

In the opposite direction, up the hill past the marina to the east is **Hükümet Caddesi,** which leads to Küçükçakıl Beach.

From **Cumhuriyet Meydanı** at the harbor, the street that heads north, **Ibrahim Serin Caddesi,** is lined with shops, cafes, and bars. There are several travel agencies along this street, and the post office and banks are at the end of the commercial stretch. East of **Ibrahim Serin Caddesi** are beautiful craft and jewelry boutiques in converted traditional old wooden houses. A lone **Lycian sarcophagus** towers above the end of Uzun Çarşı Caddesi. Rock tombs are located high above town, obscured by the increased building at the top of the hill.

GETTING AROUND

Few places in Kaş are more than a 10-minute walk away, but if your accommodations are on the peninsula, you'll have to rely on a hotel transfer to get you there, because there is no minibus service, and taxi fares are uncommonly high.

BY BUS AND *DOLMUŞ* Minibus service runs regularly from Kaş to Kalkan (2YTL/$1.50; daily service 8:30am–8:30 or 9pm), which you can take for day trips to Kaputaş Beach, as well as to many of the surrounding sights.

BY TAXI There's a taxi stand at the marina (© 0242/836-1489) and one at the *otogar* with the following one-way rates listed (but be sure to bargain anyway): Üçağız 45YTL ($33), Demre 50YTL ($37), Olympos 120YTL ($90), Antalya Airport 150YTL ($110), Kaputaş Beach 40YTL ($30), Kalkan 45YTL ($33), Patara 65YTL ($48), Fethiye 100YTL ($74), and Dalaman Airport 135YTL ($100). In many cases, local travel agencies will provide more comfortable, air-conditioned cars or vans for lower prices (for example, the going rate for transfers to Antalya airport is 40YTL/$30, cheaper than the taxi fare).

BY BOAT Occasionally there is water-taxi service from Kaş to Üçağız (3 hr. by boat); from there you can then hire a boat to explore Kekova. Check with the Tourist Information office to find out if it's in operation when you get there, but most prefer to drive to Üçağız. If you prefer to get around independently and you know how to haggle effectively, head down to the harbor at any port village and see whether you can hire a boat yourself for a reasonable fee.

BY CAR   With everything within walking distance, you'll need a car only to go exploring out of town. You're out of luck if you expected to earn points with Avis, Hertz, National, or Europcar; only local companies rent cars in Kaş. As a consolation for lost frequent-flier miles, the rates will be lower.

WHAT TO SEE & DO

Kaş is the center for sun-and-fun boat trips to the sunken cities around Kekova Island. The surrounding protected bays, islands, and bleached coral cliffs provide some of the best opportunities for visits to the archaeological sites of the Xanthos Valley (see section 4, "Kalkan," earlier in this chapter, for details), Myra, and Demre (see section 6, "Demre," below).

Travel agencies hopefully grabbing a piece of the tourist pie line the marina and tout day excursions to the area attractions at very competitive rates. Prices range from 15€ ($18) to 15GBP ($26) for day tours to Kekova (minimum six people). More established and eminently recommendable are Bougainville Travel and Top Avenue. **Bougainville Travel,** at Çukurbağlı Caddesi, the continuation of Ibrahim Serin Caddesi (© **0242/836-3142;** www.bougainville-turkey.com), a local English-speaking, British/Turkish/Dutch partnership, is a full-service travel agency and the most well equipped outfitter for adventure travel and outdoor pursuits on the Mediterranean. They recently added mountain biking tours and canyoning excursions into the Salkikent or Kibris Canyons to their regular offerings of sea kayaking, white-water rafting, hiking, and jeep safari trips.

BOAT TRIPS TO THE SUNKEN CITY

The region of **Kekova with Kekova Island** 🐟🐟🐟 at its epicenter offers a view into an unspoiled world of picturesque undeveloped fishing villages and mysterious archaeological sites that found their way into the sea. The most visible examples of a long-gone civilization lie along the northern coast of the island, submerged beneath transparent waters. Glass-bottom boats allow you to see fleeting details of buried amphoras or other artifacts, but the most impressive relics are the city walls and private homes visible just under the waterline. Swimming and snorkeling here are prohibited to preserve the location against random disappearances of archaeological findings, and it is still a mystery as to what civilization these walls came from.

In their haste to get on a boat, many people overlook **Üçağız,** a perfect example of a sleepy fishing town, with a cluster of truly remarkable **Lycian tombs** 🐟🐟 woven into the fabric of life at the far end of the village (some visible by sea). Visits tend to ignore the ancient site of **Aperlae** as well, located west of Üçağız on the mainland and accessible by boat from the sea via the Akar Pass; the effort required to get there has ensured the preservation of another "sunken city" here, and you can plan some time on land to explore the ruins on foot.

If you're traveling independently, you may want to arrive in Üçağız by 9 or 10am, in order to negotiate the best deals with the local fishermen for a day out on their private boat. In high season and no longer pegging their rates to a sagging dollar, boatmen are now asking—and getting—hefty amounts of cash for a day out: a small private boat (capacity around 12 people) costs around 410YTL ($300). Glass-bottom boat trips from Üçağız cost 40YTL ($30) to 50YTL ($36) per person. Plan to arrive in Kaleköy (ancient Simena) by lunchtime for a scenic, relaxing, and simply marvelous meal of fresh fish. Excursions to Simena must be negotiated with the local boatmen

Finds   Kaleköy (Ancient Simena)

It's almost impossible for a fishing village to retain its innocence, but the first time I visited, time seemed to have come to a complete standstill in **Simena** *☙*. Recently, though, and even with limited access, this pastoral spot has succumbed to commercialism. The souvenir stands leading up the steps to the castle have the potential to spoil the setting with incessant offerings of hand-edged headscarves, pareos, and other superfluous accessories, but ultimately, there's still nothing like a stroll through someone's chickens and a waterside meal of grilled fish caught hours earlier.

Although it will take a little effort on your part to get to Simena, the reward will be a magical setting far removed from the modern world. There are no roads, only worn dirt paths amid the cluster of modest houses that dot the hillside. Several fish restaurants line the jetties, with comparatively excellent feasts of the freshest fish and the best location from which to stare transfixed at the one solitary stone sarcophagus poking its Gothic cap out of the bay.

Nesrin's Bademli Ev (*©* **0242/874-2170**; www.askamarine.com/bademliev. htm) is a traditional village house with three guest rooms, each with a fireplace. There are nothing but the essentials here, but all of that authenticity will run you 74YTL ($55). The hotel is closed in winter.

The **Kale Pensiyon** (*©* **0242/874-2111**; fax 0242/874-2110; www.kale pansiyon.com) is a very basic family motel converted from a Greek cottage located just above the tour boat jetty. Prices are quoted at about 47YTL ($35) a night in July and August, otherwise, it's 40YTL ($30).

The **Mehtap Pansiyon** (*©* **0242/874-2146**; fax 0242/874-2261; www.mehtap pansiyon.com) is more like a treehouse campsite, located on the uppermost part of the cliff with splendid views of the sea from its wooden platform on the rocky hillside. The rooms have something akin to a shower, and this is definitely a roughing-it experience, as most guests wind up sleeping on one of the beds arranged outside along the railing instead. A double is advertised as 82YTL ($60), but this is flexible. Mehtap also has a rustic treehouse restaurant with meals of seafood and game meats cooked by the owner himself.

to Kaleköy, based on a half-day rental. If you're planning on staying overnight, enlist your pension owner in getting transport over.

Every travel agent in town offers trips to Kekova, lunch and transfers to Üçağız included. Boats depart out of Üçağız for Kekova Island in the morning, touring the bays and islands with stops for swimming and snorkeling and exploration of some area caves. Tours usually include a stopover at the untouched village of Kaleköy for a hike up the hill to the medieval Byzantine fortress of the Knights of St. John (entrance 4YTL/$3) and a close-up of a row of sarcophagi, as well as idyllic views of the islands and bays. Sadly, these tours don't allow time for much more than that, making an all too hasty exit off this seaside village.

AREA BEACHES

At the end of the day in Kaş, you can collapse on a lounge at one of the cliff-side "beaches," where you're only a coral stone's throw away from a dip in some of the bluest and unspoiled waters this close to a major town. The best of the lot is **Çınarlar Beach** (© **0242/836-3504**) just to the east of the marina, where a private establishment of beach lounges (free) and a snack bar are set up on Küçükçakıl Beach. The rocky coast forms a small inlet, into which crazy local kids dive off the low craggy rocks.

Hidden up a small street about 100m (328 ft.) up the hill from the marina to the right, are two family-run "beaches," situated behind a corner of the craggy coast that hides any remnant of the city. The **Sahil Çay Bahçesi & Plaj** (© **0242/836-1962**) was in the process of upgrading from ad-hoc, Oriental-style wooden platforms at press time; a few steps farther is the **Elit Café & Beach** (© **0532/705-9722**), with a well-worn barroom, a nice setup of beach lounges, and food service. **Paşabahçesi,** Hastane Caddesi (© **0242/836-3180;** fax 0242/836-3082; 27YTL–40YTL [$20–$30] double, all major credit cards accepted) operates a charming garden restaurant, a water pipe cafe, and a waterfront patio all rolled into one. The grassy terrace has access to a stone deck, where, amid daisies, geraniums, and paths inlaid with shells, a day will easily fly by.

STAYING ACTIVE

PARAGLIDING   Skysports, Liman Sok. 10/A, Kaş (© **0242/836-3291;** www. skysports-turkey.com), the reputable provider of tandem flights off of Babadağ, over Ölüdeniz, runs an adjunct shop in Kaş, taking advantage of the 1,050m (3,500-ft.) summit Asaz Mountain. Pilots fly you off the ridge and over the sea, landing you safely at the marina in Kaş. A 20- to 30-minute flight (believe me, it's plenty of time) costs £70 ($124). The newcomer, **Nautilus Tandem Paragliding,** Uzunçarşı Cad. 16 (© **0242/836-2580;** www.nautilusparagliding.com), offers the same deal; both outfits are out in the town center in the evenings marketing their adventures with videos played on an oversize screen.

SCUBA DIVING   The waters off Kaş have some of the best visibility in the Mediterranean and a wide variety of sea life. Sponge divers have been navigating these reefs for decades, and it was along the coast of Ulu Burun that a 14th-century-B.C. merchant shipwreck was discovered, now displayed in the Bodrum Underwater Archaeology Museum (p. 235). Several dive outfitters with certified dive masters provide a gateway to the reefs, caves, and shipwrecks (there's even a plane wreck) for around 40YTL ($29); 50YTL ($37) if you need to use their equipment. **Bougainville Travel** (see "What to See & Do," above) is one of the better dive operators in town. They offer single dives and certification courses May through October, with prices that knock out the competition. **Barakuda Diving,** Hükümet Caddesi, on the hill above the harbor behind Mercan Restaurant (© **0242/836-2996;** www.barakuda-kas. de), offers all of the same services plus post-dive parties to follow up on a fun day or night at sea. Both outfitters will organize specialty dives and weekly (or longer) dive packages on request, and can accommodate nondivers on their boats.

SEA KAYAKING   Sea kayaking offers a low-impact opportunity to experience the magical waters of the Gulf of Kekova, past partially submerged sarcophagi and over the sunken cities. The prohibition of swimming in the waters over these archaeological sites makes this sport a superb way to enjoy unhurried close-ups of the mysterious city walls, although admittedly, you'll need some imagination to visualize those vague underwater shadows. A kayak also allows you to navigate where large craft dare not go. The day trip (63YTL/$47) is low-impact in either single or tandem kayaks, and sets off (after transferring from Kalkan and Kaş) from the docks at Uçağız. For information, contact **Bougainville Travel** (see "What to See & Do," above).

SHOPPING

Miles and miles of carpet shops, souvenir shops, and counterfeit sportswear have probably dulled your shopping instincts in Turkey, but Kaş restores the pleasures of dallying among unexpected treasures, long forgotten after your departure from Istanbul. The old wooden houses along the side streets house wonderful little boutiques in a small-village atmosphere. But however great the selection of inventory may be, you can be sure to expect equally monumental markups. Pity the poor arrival with a keen desire for a souvenir during a limited stopover, and no bargaining acumen.

Gallery Anatolia Located on the hill above Mercan Restaurant, this shop is a veritable treasure-trove of designer tableware. The *tuğra* motif coffee and tea sets are a feast for the eyes, while hand-painted cartoon-ish sea life adorn the less serious place settings. Prices start at about 8YTL ($6) and go skyward. Hükuet Caddesi 2/1. **©** 0242/836-1954.

Ipek Yolu/Silk Road Owned by a Turkish couple, this attractive shop displays an eclectic mix of souvenirs collected during their travels along the traditional Silk Road. Prices are comparatively high: Egyptian glass perfume bottles sell for pennies in Cairo's market, and those Balinese hand-painted wooden fishing cats are a dime a dozen in Indonesia, but admittedly, it would be a lot more expensive to go to the source. Gursoy Sokak, across from Barcelona. **©** 0242/836-3880.

WHERE TO STAY

Despite the density of pensions, guesthouses, and hotels that line the cliff above the beach, there's hardly a decent place above two stars in sight. True escapists of civilization have the option of lodging out on the Çukurbağ Peninsula (by car, enter Kaş's main road and turn right at the small roundabout right before the marina; all destinations on the loop road are under 5km/3 miles away), a sparsely populated collection of steep cliffs and terraced access to unspoiled waters. (Most of these hotels have been snapped up and blocked out by British-based tour operators, leaving but a handful of options for the independent traveler.) But without a car, it's undeniably more convenient to be located in the town center.

KAŞ

Gardenia Hotel Kaş is witnessing the opening of several much-needed new hotels and this is one of the more memorable of them. Rooms are unusually large compared to other hotels in Kaş and enjoy the added benefit of stunning views of the Greek island of Meis. All rooms have glass-front balconies so as to optimize the view. Actually, glass seems to be a running theme here; a chunky glass bathroom sink and console keep the bathroom both fresh looking and designer cool. The hotel serves coffee, tea, and snacks throughout the day.

Hükümet Caddesi 47, Küçükçakıl Mevkii, 07580 Kaş. **©** 0242/836-2368. Fax 0242/836-1618. www.gardenia hotel-kas.com. 11 units. 66€ ($81) double; 76€ ($93) suite. MC, V. *In room:* A/C, minibar, satellite TV, wireless Internet, hair dryer, safe.

Hotel Club Phellos *(Kids)* Sitting on the top of the hill above the beach, Hotel Club Phellos is the best option for those looking for a full-service pseudo-resort experience. The central location makes it all the more appealing—with updated rooms that have either shower cabins or minitubs. It's all a bit formalized, but that's easy to forgive when you're perched poolside overlooking the Mediterranean or melting blissfully in the tiny yet lovely *hamam*. A bright blue waterslide spills your kids into the lower children's pool.

Doğruyol Sok. 4, Kaş. © **0242/836-1953.** Fax 0242/836-1890. 81 units. 100€ ($120) double; 125€ ($150) suite. MC, V. **Amenities:** Restaurant; 3 bars; outdoor swimming pool; game room; concierge; tour desk; car-rental desk; 24-hr. room service; laundry service; dry cleaning. *In room:* A/C, local TV.

Kale Otel *Value*   This is an unexpected find: The Kale Otel offers the spartan amenities of a pension in rooms that glisten. Its position on a dead end on the hill above the ancient theater offers historical and sea views. A grassy terrace with lounges overlooking the sea makes for the perfect summertime snooze; in winter, the small sun porch offers a cozy alternative. This is also one of the recommendable hotel kitchens in town, where lawn tables are set out front like a biergarten. Prices, however, will differ if you call speaking English as I did (50€/$60 for a double) as opposed to Turkish (27€/$33) for my Turkish friend.

Yenı Camii Mahallesi, Amfitiyatro Sok. 8, Kaş. © **0242/836-4074.** Fax 0242/836-2402. 26 units. 50€ ($60) double. No credit cards. **Amenities:** Restaurant; laundry service; dry cleaning. *In room:* A/C, no phone.

Medusa Hotel   From the outside, this hotel is almost indistinguishable from the other cliff-top pensions lined up above Küçükçakıl Beach. But even though this was the first hotel to set up shop on this stretch of the beach, the regular yearly renovations show up conspicuously in contrast to its neighbors.

Like all of the hotels on this strip, the reception is located in the hotel at the top of a long stone stairway past the pool and restaurant. The lobby is clean and breezy with a kilim draped over a lattice screen and a stone fireplace for those wintry nights. Each of the rooms has a balcony and at least a partial sea view; reserve early and get a full view. The king suite has a minibar and TV. Medusa has an on-site dive school and a massage center.

Küçükçakıl Mevkii, 07580 Kaş. © **0242/836-1440.** Fax 0242/836-1441. 41 units. 50€ ($60) double; 90€ ($110) suite. Rates 40% lower in winter. MC, V. Street parking only. **Amenities:** Restaurant; 2 bars; outdoor swimming pool; dive school; massage; laundry service; dry cleaning. *In room:* A/C, no phone.

ÇUKURBAĞ PENINSULA

Otel Çapa *Finds*   This hotel overlooks the Mediterranean from the rocky coast on the north side of the peninsula, in a serene and relaxing seafront setting. The grounds are terraced down toward the seafront patio, past a shaded hammock, a postcard-perfect saltwater free-form pool, a snack bar, and a fragrant thicket of low Mediterranean brush. The painted pink main building, swimming pool, rooms, and cozy open-air bar salon sit at the top.

Each room enjoys its very own balcony or terrace overlooking the pool area to the sea, keeping them breezy, light, and airy. Rooms, and bathrooms especially, are a bit on the smallish side, but the staff makes you feel like the entire property is all yours, and the result is anything but cramped. If you ever decide to leave the property, the hotel provides a shuttle to the center of Kaş (5YTL/$3.50; taxis cost double) and tours to Kekova. Various motorized watersports are available for a modest fee.

Çukurbağ Yarımadası on the Çukurbağ Peninsula, 07580 Kaş. © **0242/836-3190.** Fax 0242/836-3192. www.club capa.com. 22 units. 60€ ($75) double. MC, V. Closed Nov–Mar. **Amenities:** Restaurant; 4 bars; 2 pools (1 saltwater); jet ski; boat rental; mountain bikes; billiards; tour desk, car-rental desk; 24-hr. room service; laundry service; dry cleaning; boat trips. *In room:* A/C.

WHERE TO DINE

As expected, the best meals in Kaş are prepared in-house, so whenever possible, take advantage of the meals at your hotel. Some of the hotels and pensions that accept dinner reservations from nonguests are **Otel Çapa,** Çukurbağ Yarımadası (✆ **0242/836-3190**), offering a four- or five-course meal with table service, and the **Savile Residence,** Çukurbağ Yarımadası (✆ **0242/836-2300**). Expect to pay 20YTL to 27YTL ($15–$20) per person.

Bahçe TURKISH   This lovely garden serves a traditional array of seafood and *kebaps,* but the real attraction here are the mezes. The meze case is overflowing with cold appetizers, making this destination a welcome alternative for vegetarians. Stuffed mushrooms, vegetable pancakes, fish cakes, and *dolmalar,* flavorful stuffed grape leaves and stuffed peppers worthy of a meal in themselves, are just a few of the items on the menu, and there are hot appetizers as well. The main dishes deviate a bit from the norm, with shrimp or a delectable plate of Turkish ravioli.

Anıt Mezar Karşısı 31 (across from the Lycian tomb). ✆ **0242/836-2370.** Reservations suggested. Appetizers and main course 5.50YTL–14YTL ($4–$10). No credit cards. Daily noon–midnight. Closed Nov–Mar.

Chez Evi 🌟🌟🌟 *Finds* FRENCH   This is the best meal you will have in Turkey, not only for the food, but also for the eccentricity of the chef. When Evy moved to Kaş and opened her own restaurant, it wasn't long before two ominous representatives of organized crime showed up. Evy wouldn't be intimidated, and chased the two away by trashing her own bar. She's quite a rich character, and she manages to pour all of that passion into her food. Weather permitting, meals should be taken in the rear garden; if the temperature outside becomes too unbearable, opt for a table in the air-conditioned *şark* dining room surrounded by years' worth of her collectibles. The menu offers crepes and salads, and one mean chicken curry. Two of my favorite dishes are the *calmars à la Provençale* (calamari in a spicy tomato sauce) and the *filet de boeuf sauce champignons* (steak in a mushroom sauce). If you really want to ingratiate yourself, order the steak rare, because she hates to overcook a good piece of meat.

Telvı Sok. 4. ✆ **0242/836-1253.** Reservations suggested. Main courses 25YTL–32YTL ($19–$24). No credit cards. Daily 7pm–midnight. Closed Nov–Mar, but owner will serve in winter with a day's notice.

Dolphin Café & Restaurant 🌟 TURKISH/FISH   Dolphin commands a dominant spot on the hill overlooking the city and marina, with views of the neighboring Greek island of Meis. But not even the best view in town can cover up for unsatisfactory food. No risk here, as Dolphin is the dining spot of choice of practically everybody in Kaş. Outdoor dining is on two rear terraces of this 100-year-old Greek house, and the patina of the original wood lends a rustic feel to the indoor area.

The selection of fresh mezes includes never-before-seen creations like crab, octopus, calamari, and shrimp salads, while the catch of the day usually includes crayfish and lobster. Factor in the candlelight, the activity below, and the boats teetering in the marina, and you've got an equation for a romantic sunset dinner.

Sandıkçı Sok. 18. ✆ **0242/836-3538.** Reservations suggested. Appetizers 5YTL ($3.50); main courses 11YTL–20YTL ($8–$15) and up for fish. MC, V. Daily 8am–midnight.

Don Quijote *Value* TURKISH BISTRO   Unceremoniously protruding from the main shopping street where it meets the main square across from the marina, this informal cafe, bar, and restaurant is the place of choice among incoming yacht and *gulet* cruisers. For such a touristy location, the food is surprisingly good and varied;

the *balık köftesi* (fish balls) are a welcomed change from the meat version, while the *pappardelle all turca* takes an Italian favorite and transforms it into a local delicacy by saucing it in minced meat and garlic yogurt. The menu also caters to westernized tastes, with an ample selection of omelets, salads, burgers, and pizzas. Top off the meal or just enjoy some people-watching while sipping a cappuccino or the more serious *espresso corretto* (with a shot of liquor).

Cumhuriyet Meydanı 1. (℃) 0242/836-1262. Appetizers 4YTL–9.50YTL ($3–$7); main courses 5YTL–15YTL ($3.50–$11). MC, V. Daily 9am–midnight.

Mercan TURKISH This friendly and popular waterside restaurant also happens to be the oldest show in town; it dates back to 1956, when the owner's father did the cooking. Fish and meat dishes are staples on the traditional Turkish menu, but Mustafa (the son) has added his own special touch, creating fragrant dishes using local herbs. The Mercan Special—a split roast lamb marinated in wine and spices—is a tender and rare treat. Try the grilled swordfish *kebap* for a lighter, but no less filling or fulfilling, meal.

Cumhuriyet Meydanı on the marina. (℃) 0242/836-1209. Reservations suggested. Main courses 6.75YTL–16YTL ($5–$12). MC, V. Daily 9am–1am.

KAŞ AFTER DARK

Kaş takes on the glow of numerous golden lights strung throughout numerous gardens and candlelight flickering from many of the town's nooks and crannies. A spot in the water pipe corner or next to the torch-lit sea wall at **Paşabahçesi,** Hastane Caddesi (℃ 0242/836-3180), is made dreamier thanks to the creative decor: garlic bunches and gourds dangle from fruit-filled lemon trees. Another waterfront spot that stays open till late is the **Elit Café & Beach** (℃ 0532/705-9722), located about 100m (328 ft.) up the hill from the marina, featuring live music nightly June 1 to October 30 from 11pm to 2:30am. Keep in mind that the bars and cafes listed below are mostly closed in winter.

Bacchus Bacchus has updated the idea of the traditional *çay bahçesi* (tea garden) and turned it into a green paradise sheltered under a thick umbrella of lemon trees. Evenings often feature a mix of favorite popular and jazz music, but you don't have to wait until the sun goes down to enjoy this wonderful spot. Daily noon to 2am. Ilkokul Sok. Across from the Monumental Lycian tomb. (℃) 0242/836-2681. Closed Nov–Apr.

Café Merhaba Catering to an international crowd, Café Merhaba is an atmospheric and cozy spot that would be inconspicuous in, say, SoHo. In Kaş, it stands out like a sore thumb, with its collection of international newspapers and magazines, in addition to the new and used paperbacks on sale. Daily 8am to 1am. Ibrahim Serin Cad. (℃) 0242/836-1883. Closed in winter.

Hi Jazz Bar It's "all jazz, all the time" at this small, bare, yet cozy bar; according to the owner, Yılmaz, the life of a New York City cab driver held no appeal, and off he went to New Orleans, where he hopped on the jazz trail. He's now here, greeting his clientele from his perch on one of the benches or small tables propped up next to the alleyway's stone wall. The music selection begins with soft jazz early in the evening, then progresses into the early hours into some hip-hop jazz. Daily 5pm to 3am. Zümrüt Sok. 3 (the street next to Bougainville Travel). (℃) 0242/836-1165.

Sun Café Located across from Mercan near the marina, Sun Café is a must-do if only to toss back a drink or have a full meal next to the Lycian rock tomb at the back.

The bar is in a pavilion-type building close to the entrance, where the team of dashing, long-haired owners keep the drinks poured and the music subtle. Daily 11am to 2am. Hükümet Cad. 3. ✆ **0242/836-1053.** Closed in winter.

6 Demre

48km (30 miles) east of Kaş; 225km (140 miles) southwest of Antalya; 25km (16 miles) west of Finike

Taking a look around Demre—situated on a fertile coastal plain 5km (3 miles) inland from the Mediterranean Sea—it's hard to imagine a flabby, local 4th-century bishop making his rounds in 105°F (41°C) weather bundled up in a big red suit. After all, there were some lovely beaches nearby and not a mammal with antlers in sight. But somewhere during the 1,650 years that followed, several national folklores got mixed up, and legends merged that would elevate old St. Nicholas, the bishop of Myra, to the jolly international hero he is today.

The ancient city of Myra lies just on the outskirts of what is now the modern town of Demre, in a region known as Kale. (The names are sometimes used interchangeably, so this can get a bit confusing.) St. Nicholas served as bishop of Myra, and earned himself a reputation of benevolence and good deeds by saving poor village girls from the fate of prostitution by dropping their dowries down the chimney. According to legend, he also rescued several village boys from the clutches of a serial killer disposed to pickling his victims in brine—but that shocking piece of history ruins the feel-good vibe altogether. The legends accumulate. Tour groups flock here for its kitsch value, while the Church of St. Nicholas continues to be a stopping-off point for religious pilgrims.

Unexpected is the **necropolis of Myra** ⊛⊛⊛, located above the ancient site and hewn into the rock like a high-rise apartment complex for dead people. This collection of rock-cut Lycian tombs is one of the best preserved and finest examples of its kind, as pale shades of fading pigment can still be made out against the fine details of the bas-reliefs.

Because the modern town of Demre is located inland, not many visitors stay here for longer than it takes to tour the necropolis and church. Hoping to change this trend, the local municipality recently closed the main road to traffic, creating the basis for what will surely become a picture-perfect pedestrian shopping mall. For now, it earns points for prettiness and charm, but still not enough to hold your interest for more than a few hours, including the area sites.

A LOOK AT THE PAST

There is not much historical evidence on Myra prior to the 1st century B.C. but rock inscriptions on the Lycian tombs date the city as far back as the 5th or 6th century B.C. We know that St. Paul visited Myra by sea on his way to Rome in A.D. 60, but Rome enters the picture officially in 42 B.C. when one of Brutus's Roman lieutenants demanded tributes for support of his civil war. The fertility of the delta and the natural protection of the river provided the city with the ingredients for thriving trade by sea, and the Romans eventually sailed past the defensive chain at the port of Andriake and, in typical style, settled into Myra permanently. The city flourished under the *pax romana,* and the fact that Emperor Germanicus and wife Agrippina paid a visit in A.D. 18 implies that this center was of major importance.

In 310, St. Nicholas was imprisoned by Diocletian for his efforts to spread Christianity but was released in 313 when Constantine ascended the throne and declared Christianity the official state religion. By the 4th century Myra had become an important

They Kidnapped the Wrong Guy

In ancient times, up until the rule of Julius Caesar, pirates ran rampant in the Mediterranean and Aegean, costing empires huge sums by blocking trade routes and intercepting ships laden with riches. Even Julius Caesar had his own run-in with these sea bandits; he was captured off the coast of Miletus, on his way back from a trip to study rhetoric in Rhodes. When the pirates told Caesar that they planned on asking a ransom of 20 talents, Caesar balked and suggested 50 would be more appropriate to his stature.

In the 6 weeks that it took for the ransom to arrive from Miletus, Caesar cavorted with the pirates, joining in their games, practicing his rhetoric, and promising to have them all crucified when the time came. When the ransom arrived, the pirates kept their promise to release him. Caesar kept his as well; upon arriving in Miletus he assembled a number of galleys, and surprised the pirates in their own lair. He had them all crucified, but ordered their throats cut first to spare them any unnecessary and vindictive suffering.

Christian center for religious and administrative affairs, and with rumors spreading of the saintly Bishop Nicholas, the town gained in popularity.

Subsequent years tell a story of Arab pirates, envious Italians coveting the sacred bones of the saint, and hidden treasure. In 7th-century pirate raids, a precious collection of liturgical gifts presented to the church by Justinian a century earlier was stolen, but was promptly reburied when the pirates in turn were attacked. In 1963, a local shepherd woman found the hoard while out with her goats; local smugglers got hold of a few pieces, which were eventually sold to the Dumbarton Oaks Museum at Harvard University for 1.35 million YTL ($1 million). Efforts to reunite the collection have been discussed between Harvard University and the Antalya Museum, but so far, the objects remain in Boston.

In 1087, hoping to redirect the flow of pilgrims back to their home, Italian merchants from Bari raided St. Nicholas's sarcophagus and transported the remains back to Italy. In their haste to get out with the goods, apparently the Barians left a few bones behind, and in 1925 the Turkish authorities were presented with a reliquary containing what was claimed to be the missing parts. Although carbon dating of the remains has proven that the bones date to the correct century, nobody knows if these are actually the bones of St. Nicholas, or where the poor guy is buried for sure. The Russians claim to have a piece of him, as does the Antalya Museum.

ESSENTIALS
GETTING THERE
BY BUS OR *DOLMUŞ* Demre lies on the road that passes by the Gulf of Finike on its way around the coastline from Antalya. Minibuses and *dolmuşes* connect with Demre from Fethiye (3 hr.; 12YTL/$9), Kaş (40 min.; 12YTL/$8.50), and Finike (20–30 min.; 6.75YTL/$5) several times a day. There's also a daily connection to Üçağız, if you're headed to or from Kekova Island. Daily bus service is frequent in summer months, allowing for the spontaneity of simply showing up at the *dolmuş* stand (usually in the town center) when you're ready to go.

ORIENTATION

The Church of St. Nicholas lies smack dab in the middle of the pedestrian mall on Müze Caddesi. A turnoff onto Alakent Caddesi before the church leads to the entrance to Myra.

Çayağzı Beach and the ancient harbor port of Andriake lie about 2km (1¼ miles) to the west of the center.

GETTING AROUND

Although the necropolis of ancient Myra is only a little over a mile from the main square and easily walkable, the unrelenting heat will surely slow you down to the point where a meaningful exploration of the small site will be impossible. Do yourself a favor and take a taxi.

Dolmuşes do exist from the main square out to the beach, although you might melt while waiting for one to pass by. A taxi will run you around 20YTL to 27YTL ($15–$20) each way.

WHAT TO SEE & DO
ANCIENT MYRA

Andriake & Çayağzı Beach   The port of Andriake at the mouth of Myra Creek (the Demre River) provided access to friendly merchant ships sailing up the river while the enclosed body of water protected Myra from direct attack by sea. Emperor Traian chose this harbor as a base for his expeditions to the East; it eventually fell into disuse as it silted up. The terrain can still be swampy at times, making the area a bit challenging to explore.

The ancient ruins straddle the river spreading around what is now Çayağzı Beach, a sleepy fishing port and boatyard. The main structure is Hadrian's Granary, built on the orders of the emperor as storage for grain prior to its delivery to Rome. The site includes a Roman bath, probably supplied by the freshwater springs, and the remains of what was probably a basilica.

The modern port is slightly grungy, in a nice way, which is perhaps the reason why it's also possible to pay a boat captain for a 2-hour tour of the Sunken City off Kekova Island 35YTL to 55YTL ($25–$40), depending on the law of supply and demand). There are a few fish stands and one restaurant from which you can enjoy wonderful sea and river views, or watch the local fishermen repair their boats.

5km (3 miles) west of Demre center (*dolmuşes* run along Müze Cad.).

The Church of St. Nicholas (Aya Nicola Kilisesi) ⍟   This church is an important mid–Byzantine Era building, even though nothing of the original remains. The first temple on the site was built for the mother goddess Artemis, but collapsed in an earthquake in the 2nd century. A Byzantine church was built over the remains of this temple, but repeated raids and numerous earthquakes destroyed the church several times. The two domed chambers were part of a 5th- or 6th-century reconstruction and form the foundation for the domed church that was later built in the 9th century. The basilica on the site today is a 1789 reconstruction using materials that date to the 8th century, and some of the early frescoes are still visible. The honeycombed mosaic stones are originals and remain surprisingly intact, as do the domes forming the roof.

Speculation continues on which, if any, of the marble sarcophagi is the one belonging to St. Nicholas. We do know the date of his death and that his body was put in a Roman sarcophagus in the central apse on the south side of the church but was believed to have been moved after the Italian and Arab raids. The one in the west apse

---

Fun Fact **The Birth of St. Nick**

Santa Claus is the invention of an American professor of divinity, Clement Clark Moore, who describes the jolly old spirit of winter in a poem: "His eyes how they twinkled! His dimples how merry! / His cheeks were like roses, his nose like a cherry . . . / He had a broad face, and a little round belly, / That shook when he laughed, like a bowl full of jelly. / He was chubby and plump, a right jolly old elf / And I laughed when I saw him, in spite of myself. / A wink of his eye and a twist of his head / Soon gave me to know I had nothing to dread."

The accouterments were introduced in an 1863 issue of *Harper's Illustrated Weekly* when the American artist Thomas Nast drew Santa in a red costume with fur trim, a cap, and a wide black belt, also replacing the various myths of horse, camel, and even dog teams with one of reindeer.

---

is believed to be that of the saint because of the reliefs of seagulls and fish scales (St. Nicholas is patron of sailors), but nobody knows anything for sure except that he's escaped to the North Pole.

Müze Cad. © **0242/871-6543**. Admission 5YTL ($3.70). Summer daily 8am–7pm; shorter hours in winter.

The Necropolis of Ancient Myra 🕸🕸🕸   Lycians believed that burying their dead high up would facilitate their rise to heaven. Until then, it seems that they expected the dead to spend some time there, as the tombs are carved to look like old wooden houses, complete with pediments, pillars, and support beams jutting out of the facade. Additional tombs are located to the west of the Roman theater, including the distinguishable carvings of a funerary rite decorating one tomb, known as the Painted Tomb.

The Roman theater, carved into the face of the mountain Greek style, dates to 141 when it was rebuilt following an earthquake. The two vaults may have been added at this time for additional support against future tremors. Columns, capitals, and ill-fated theatrical heads scatter the grounds, fallen from gracing the facade of the stage.

The entrance to the site is marred by locals who practically tow your car into the adjacent lot for "free" with hopes of selling you fresh-squeezed orange juice for about 1YTL (75¢), or some postcards. This is unavoidable, but my advice is to steer clear of the lot directly opposite the entrance to the site, operated by a particularly rude specimen.

1.6km (1 mile) north of Müze Cad., off Alakent Cad. No phone. Admission 5YTL ($3.70). Summer daily 8am–7pm; hours shorter in winter.

WHERE TO STAY

There's no reason to stay overnight in Demre, but if you get stuck, check into the **Hotel Andriake,** Finike Caddesi at the highway junction, about .8km (½ mile) south of the main square (© **0242/871-2249;** fax 0242/871-5540). The hotel has the best accommodations in town at prices around 48€ to 55€ ($60–$67). You can also brave one of the pensions on the road into the marina (Andriake).

WHERE TO DINE

Again, Demre hasn't yet fully taken advantage of the day-tripping potential. For a good-quality meal, just go where the locals go—which, in this case, is **Ipek,** Müze Caddesi, near the church (© **0242/871-5150**), a simple and unpretentious *döner* shop with indoor and outdoor tables. The *lokanta*-style steam trays display the soups, stews, and vegetables of the day, as alternatives to the meaty grills, all for under 6.75YTL ($5).

7 Antalya ⋆⋆

725km (450 miles) south of Istanbul; 467km (290 miles) southeast of İzmir; 298km (185 miles) northeast of Fethiye; 435km (270 miles) east of Marmaris; 634km (394 miles) southwest of Nevşehir

The enormous and sun-kissed region of Antalya includes seaside towns well beyond the outstretched arms of the Gulf of Antalya, as far as Kaş to the west and Alanya to the east. The beaches stretch for miles, summers are scorching, and the airport is conveniently close—a winning combination that has made Antalya the focal point of the Turkish Mediterranean in just over 10 years. Only 25 years ago, Antalya was a ramshackle fishing village huddled around a harbor backed by Roman and pre-Roman ruins and Byzantine ramparts. The arrival of the Sheraton Voyager, the first international-class, five-star hotel to build on the coastline, proved to be the anchor that would attract more visitors. It wasn't until as few as 15 years ago that the trend in Turkey toward historic preservation began to touch the historic quarter of Kaleiçi, a renaissance that, by now, is well on its way to completion. But while the renewal of Kaleiçi helped to transform Antalya from the ugly duckling of the Mediterranean to its current magical Mediterranean appeal, this ancient heart of the city—thanks to the seedy mercantile class that it has attracted—is well on its way to losing its luster. But don't cancel your trip here yet: A new renaissance is underway just to the west of the city center over at Konyaaltı, the expansive pebbly strip of prime beachfront backed by the development of a meandering, grassy promenade. Funny how it took this long for Antalya's main beach to reach the level of the Sheraton, which now shares the beach with a number of other five-star hotels (see "Where to Stay," later in this chapter). The starting point for the beach, incidentally, pretty much sits at the base of a cliff side that houses the wonderful archaeological museum.

Mostly because of Konyaaltı, Antalya vies for a position among my favorite destinations on the Turkish Mediterranean. But Antalya is much more than its beaches. It offers an escape into a world where you can (downhill) ski in the morning and swim in the afternoon, explore underwater caves, go rafting through lofty canyons, hike where St. Paul trod, or simply hide out under a straw parasol on a private beach. The city of Antalya is built on a rocky travertine plateau, formed by natural springs running down the Toros Mountains and surging off the cliffs, with the constant breathtaking silhouette of peaks and snowcaps in the distance. In addition to the wealth of outdoor pursuits, the area also has an overwhelming number of archaeological wonders. The Karain Cave, where 50,000-year-old artifacts were discovered, is the oldest human habitation in Anatolia. The ancient mountaintop ruins of Termessos continue to mock Alexander the Great's lone unsuccessful military campaign. Except in August, when temperatures go as high as 104°F (40°C), the climate always seems to cooperate, as Antalya gets no winter to speak of. Even Universal Pictures recognizes the region's promise, visible in the new 10-studio facility in the nearby town of Çandır, where the NBC miniseries *Arabian Nights* was filmed.

ESSENTIALS
GETTING THERE
BY PLANE   In **Turkish Airlines** (© **0242/243-4383**) and **Onur Air** (in Antalya © **0242/330-3432,** or in Istanbul 0212/663-9176) offer regular domestic

Antalya

ATTRACTIONS ●
Antalya Museum **4**
Clock Tower **12**
Hadrian's Gate **14**
Hıdırlık Kulesi **21**
Iskele Mosque **8**
Mevlevihane **11**
Yivli Minare **13**

HOTELS ■
Dedeman Antalya **6**
Atelya Pension **18**
Hillside Su **2**
Hotel Alp Paşa **16**
La Paloma Pansıon **22**
Marina Residence **19**
Ninova Pensiyon **15**
Sheraton Voyager **1**
Talya Oteli **5**
Tekeli Konakları **10**
Villa Perla **17**

RESTAURANTS ◆
China Garden **3**
Gizli Bahçe **9**
Kral Sofrası **7**
Marina Restaurant **19**
Sim Restaurant **20**
Stella's Bistrot **23**

connections between Istanbul and Antalya, and Ankara and Antalya. In summer **Fly-air** (© 444-4359) resumes regular service to Antalya as well.

The airport is about 11km (7 miles) outside the city center on the road to Antalya. The Havaş airport shuttle (© 444-0487 or 0242/312-2956) runs service several times a day to and from the Turkish Airlines office on Cumhuriyet Caddesi, west of Kaleiçi. Fare is 8YTL ($6). Buses are located outside the Domestic Terminal—which, if you're not laden with luggage, is walkable from the International Terminal. A taxi directly from the airport to the center of town can cost anywhere from 20YTL to 40YTL ($15–$30), depending on where you are staying; you may also want to establish the fare before you get in.

There are a number of car-rental windows in the domestic arrivals area, including **Europcar** © 0242/330-3068.

BY BUS The dual-terminal **Yeni Garaj Otogar** (© 0242/331-1250) lies 4km (2½ miles) northwest of the town center on the highway to Burdur and is almost as user-friendly as the airport—in fact, you might mistake it for the airport. An excruciatingly slow municipal bus is located outside the minibus/*dolmuş* terminal in front of the taxi stand, idling until its half-hourly departure. Tickets are cheap (around 1YTL/75¢), which is way too much for the meandering path it takes as it works its way to the center of town. A taxi from the *otogar* to Kaleiçi costs around 20YTL ($15). Buses leave frequently for direct service from most major cities; sample fares (on Varan buses) are Istanbul (12 hr.; 63YTL/$47); İzmir (7–8 hr.; 45YTL/$33) and Denizli (3–4½ hr.; 26YTL/$19). FYI: Fares for many of these destinations on Kamil Koç are approximately 30% less. For transport from the smaller towns along the coastline, either hop on one of the frequent minibuses (service is currently with Metro; © 0242/836-3033) or get to one of the major terminals listed above for full-bus service. Remember that not all of the minibuses have air-conditioning; in August, you will definitely want it.

VISITOR INFORMATION

The **Tourist Information office** (© 0242/241-1747) is about a 10-minute walk west of Kaleiçi, on Cumhuriyet Caddesi, in the Özel Idare Işhanı shopping arcade right before the intersection of Anafartalar Caddesi. It's worth a visit for fliers and brochures on upcoming events. Or, save yourself a trip and pop into one of the many travel agencies lining the cobbled streets for the same information.

ORIENTATION

The city of Antalya is built upon a limestone travertine formed from the springs that run down from the mountains, so that city meets the sea by way of breathtaking cliffs. At the center is the cliff-top fortress neighborhood of **Kaleiçi,** full of elegant garden cafes and charming ramshackle eateries, all built atop pre-Roman, Roman, and Byzantine foundations. Kaleiçi, the hassling to get you to empty your wallet notwithstanding, is a charming and characteristic area of restored Greek houses, Italian villas, and Ottoman Paşa's residences, some converted into guesthouses and hotels along narrow winding streets. At the base of the cliff is the harbor and marina, built over an ancient Roman harbor and now the center of the city's resort nightlife.

About a mile and a half to the west of Kaleiçi is the newly developed beach of **Konyaaltı,** beginning just west of the archaeological museum and extending (so far) for about 8km (5 miles). Development will continue up to the port, an extension that will simply put the icing on an already successful and crazily popular city/seaside resort destination. By day, beach umbrellas and lounges backed by cafes and green lawns are filled with sun-seekers; by night, the waterfront park gets strewn with over-size colored cushions and romantic lighting.

Beyond the inner city limits, Antalya spreads out, but in the haphazard, poured-concrete way that only Turkish towns can do. But clear waters and sandy coastlines lie within walking distance of Kaleiçi, with beaches located fewer than 8km (5 miles) to the east. Most archaeological sites and natural phenomena are within an hour of town.

GETTING AROUND

The primarily pedestrian area around the old town and harbor is very compact, and you'll have very little need to venture far from here if this is where you're holing up for the night. The Tourist Information office and the archaeological museum are to the west of the city center, accessible either by tramway or about a 20-minute walk. From Kaleiçi to Konyaaltı, it's about a 10YTL ($7.40) unavoidably meandering taxi ride; it'll be cheaper on the way back because the one-way main avenue is now working in your favor.

BY SCOOTER   Authorities seem to turn their heads the other way when you ride the wrong way down one-way streets or enter a pedestrian-only area on a scooter, my preferred mode of transportation. Among the many competing firms to try is **Cros Rent-A-Motor,** Camii Sok. 7 (© 0242/242-7017).

BY TRAM   A tramway runs parallel to the coastline from the Antalya Museum to the neighborhoods east of Kaleiçi, and is particularly convenient as a way to get from Kaleiçi to the museum, to Atatürk Parkı, and to Konyaaltı Beach. There's a hop-on point on Cumhuriyet Caddesi across from the clock tower, and the fare is about 75YKr (55¢).

BY CAR   A car in Antalya is indispensable for a thorough exploration of what the region has to offer, but within the city itself, you may want to spend your energies doing something other than sitting in traffic and making sense of the one-way cir-cuitous route through the center of town.

Although a car would be handy for a quick run to the museum, about a mile east of Kaleiçi, you'll be better off parking it and forgetting about it.

All of the major companies have offices in Antalya, both at the airport and down-town. These include **Avis,** Fevzi Çakmak Cad. 30, in the Talya Hotel (© 0242/248-1772); **National Car Rental,** Fevzi Çakmak Cad., Galip Apt. 27F (© 0242/247-0648); and **Budget** (airport only; © 0242/330-3079).

You may be able to save money by negotiating a rate with a local car-rental outfit, but even before the bartering, local car rentals are pretty inexpensive, at as low as 35YTL ($25) per day (this rate excludes gas and reflects the price of a manual com-pact car). Make sure you have the rental papers, and that the brakes and turn signals are in working order.

BY TAXI   Because Kaleiçi is a walking district, a taxi is mostly useful for getting back and forth between the marina/Kaleiçi and the museum (Konyaaltı Beach, the Shera-ton, and the Hillside Su are near the museum on the west side of town). Hiring a taxi is also an (albeit expensive) option for those unable or unwilling to rent wheels for day-tripping out of the city; because rates have gone through the roof **and** because they are quoted in a currency (the euro) that makes the dollar look like a weakling, I don't recommend this option. A tour to all of the nearby attractions will be your best bet, at this point.

FAST FACTS: Antalya

Airlines Turkish Airlines (© 0242/243-4383; airport © 0242/330-3221) is located at Cumhuriyet Caddesi in the Özelıdare Işhanı arcade.

Airport For information on departures and arrivals call the airline direct. The number for the airport is © 0242/330-3600.

Ambulance Call © 112.

Climate Antalya has four seasons: fall, winter, spring, and hell, when temperatures soar to digits even the government won't accurately report. (Everybody gets the day off when the mercury passes 104°F/40°C). Humidity can sometimes reach into the triple digits as well.

Consulates Great Britain has a Vice-Consulate at Fevzi Çakmak Caddesi, 1314 Sokak 6/8, Elif Apt. (© 0242/244-5313).

Festivals Antalya hosts the eminent Golden Orange Film Festival in October. The Aspendos Theatre has a brief shining moment in July, during the National Opera and Ballet Festival. For information on the festival schedule, tickets, or transportation, contact the **Antalya Devlet Opera ve Balesi** (© 0242/243-7640; fax 0242/243-8827; aspendosfestival@kultur.gov.tr).

Hospitals The Antalya Private Hospital (© 0242/335-0000) is at Bayindir Mahallesi 325 Sok. 8. You will also encounter English-speaking staff at the Antalya International Hospital at Kızıltoprak Mah., Meydan PTT Arkası (near the post office), © 0242/311-1500.

Post Office The PTT is open from 9am to 5pm for postal services and 24-7 for phone access. The nearest office is at the yacht harbor, on Güllük Caddesi (© 0242/241-5300 or 0242/241-5381).

WHAT TO SEE & DO
A LOOK AT THE PAST

Indigenous tribes were combating the scorching heat on the rocky coastline of Antalya since prehistoric times, until eventually the Hittites migrated off the harsh Anatolian plains in search of a more gracious climate. The Hittites were succeeded by a number of independent city-states founded in the region, and today's province of Antalya covers Pamphylia and parts of Pisidya to the north, Cicilia to the east, and Lycia to the west.

Antalya officially enters the history books in the 2nd century B.C. when King Attalus II marched in to pick up the pieces of the territorial war that broke out after the death of Alexander the Great. The city was proclaimed Attaleia after the Pergamese king, later morphing into variations of Adalia, Satalia, Adalya, and Antalya by successive cultures. The city was handed over to Rome along with the rest of Pergamum, and one of the more important events in the history of the Roman city was the arrival of Emperor Hadrian, whose visit was honored with a grand monumental gate.

Sovereignty over the region passed from the Byzantines to the Selçuks and back again, and in 1103, the port became a valuable asset to the Crusaders, allowing them to avoid the treacherous overland journey from Palestine. The decline of Byzantine influence allowed the Selçuk Sultanate of Rum to annex the region around 1207 until Antalya was finally incorporated into the Ottoman Empire.

A MARVELOUS MUSEUM

Antalya Museum (Antalya Müzesi) 🏛🏛🏛   If you do only one cultural thing in Antalya, make it this. Antalya province is endowed with one of the richest cultural heritages in Turkey, and much of it can be seen at this museum. More than 5,000 archaeological works are displayed in 14 thought-provoking exhibit halls. The **Prehistory section** 🏛🏛🏛 includes an amazing collection of artifacts recovered from the Karain Cave at Burdur—the largest inhabited cave in Turkey, with findings dating back 50,000 years and representing the Paleolithic, Mesolithic, Neolithic, Chalcolithic, and Bronze Ages. The **Gallery of the Gods** 🏛🏛🏛 gives you the chance to walk among the protagonists of classic mythology, through grand statues of Zeus, Apollo, Athena, **Aphrodite** 🏛, and the like, followed by statues of the Emperor/Gods Hadrian and Traian in the Roman Room. The **Sarcophagus Gallery** 🏛🏛 is a rich exhibition of intricately carved tombs, one of which was considerably returned by the J. Paul Getty Museum, after having found its way out of the country. The Antalya Museum devotes an entire room to coins; the chronological display represents 2,500 years of Anatolian history. Considering that this is such a rich collection, it's positively mind-boggling to realize that 25,000 to 30,000 artifacts are buried in storage.

About 1.6km (1 mile) to the west of town on Kenan Evren Bulv. ℂ **0242/241-4528.** Admission 15YTL ($11). Tues–Sun 9am–6pm. No large bags or backpacks allowed inside museum.

MOSQUES & MONUMENTS

The most outstanding monument in Antalya is **Hadrian's Gate (Hadrian Kapısı)** 🏛🏛, halfway between Cumhuriyet Caddesi and 30 Agustos Cad., built in honor of the emperor's visit to the city in A.D. 130. A classic example of a Roman triumphal arch, Hadrian's Gate is the only remaining entrance gate into the ancient city, and a great introduction to the neighborhood of Kaleiçi.

A few steps north following Imaret Sokağı is the **Yivli Minare** 🏛, built by the Selçuk Sultan Alaaeddin Keykubat in the 13th century. The fluted brick minaret stands a commanding 38m (125 ft.) high and has come to be the symbol of the city. The adjacent domed mosque (not the original) is an early example of Anatolian multidomed mosques. A small and charming cluster of souvenir stands has sprouted up in the courtyard and is at least a refreshing break from the relentless touts on the street.

The **Clock Tower (Saat Kulesi)** 🏛 in nearby Kalekapısı Square rises above the outer reaches of Kaleiçi at Atatürk Caddesi and was once a part of the old city fortifications.

Past the Clock Tower, following Atatürk Caddesi, is one of the remaining outer towers of the city fortifications, standing over 15m (50 ft.) high. Just past the tower to the left is a gracefully curving building of the former **Mevlevihane,** in use today as an art gallery (Güzel Sanatlar Gelerısı; no phone; free admission) whose stark and serene interior is worth a quick detour.

At the opposite end of the quarter of Kaleiçi and dominating the edges of the cliff is the 2nd-century **Hıdırlık Kulesi** 🏛. Also known as the Red Tower, the Hıdırlık Kulesi offers unobstructed panoramas of the sea, suggesting its original use as a lighthouse.

At the bottom of the stone steps leading down from Memerli Sokağı to the harbor is the **Iskele Mosque,** a simple stone structure set on four pillars over a spring. Unfortunately, the description lends more appeal to the site than the actual thing, because careless visitors have been using the small pool as a garbage dump.

The **Kaleiçi Museum,** Barbaros Mahallesi Kocatepe Sok. 25, Kaleiçi (ℂ **0242/ 243-4274**), takes up two buildings restored between 1993 and 1995: one a former Orthodox church, the other a traditional Turkish house. The house contains an ethnological exhibit, while the former church, built in 1863 in the name of Agios Georgios, contains different cultural and art works from the Suna-Inan Kıraç collection.

CITIES OF ANTIQUITY

The Ancient City of Aspendos

The city of Aspendos, commonly believed to have been settled by colonists from Argos, lies a few miles beyond Perge on the Antalya/Alanya highway. I suggest that you tackle both as a pair.

There's not much left of the ancient city, but the one remaining monument, the **Theatre of Aspendos** ✦✦✦, is enough to warrant a trip. Thanks to the high-quality calcareous stone and the fact that the Selçuks reinforced the structure during its run as a caravansary, this 2,000 year old theater is the best-preserved ancient theater in Asia Minor and the best example of a Roman theater in all of Pamphylia. The best way to visit the theater is to see it as it was meant to be, during the national opera and ballet festival in the summer (see "Fast Facts: Antalya," for info), but it's an awesome sight without the show.

Take the Antalya/Alanya highway east; watch for the turnoff to Aspendos on the left. ✆ **0242/735-7038.** Summer daily 8am–7pm; hours shorter in winter. Admission 10YTL ($7.40). Parking about 4YTL ($3).

The Ancient City of Perge

Three thousand years away and 11 miles east of Antalya is the ancient Pamphylian settlement of **Perge.** A clay tablet discovered in the Hittite capital of Hattuşaş shows that Perge was originally settled around 1,500 B.C. under the name of "Parha." St. Paul and Barnabas came to Perge on their first missionary journey, but St. Paul preached here only upon his return from Pisidia.

The ancient city's ruins were damaged in the early 1920s when area builders treated it like the local quarry, but the city remains an impressive site. The stadium, one of the best preserved ones of the ancient world, extends to almost 1,000 with an original capacity of around 12,000 people. It's now a modest showcase for carvings from around the city. Some finely carved marble reliefs are visible in the Greco-Roman theater, where spectacular views of the plain provide a good overview of the lower city.

Take the Antalya/Alanya highway east; watch for the turnoff to Perge on the left. ✆ **0242/426-2047.** Summer daily 8am–7pm; hours shorter in winter. Admission 10YTL ($7.50).

AREA BEACHES

A favorite beach destination for residents of Antalya is **Konyaaltı** ✦✦✦, a long stretch of pristine pebble beach backed by a meandering promenade chock-full of activities, including playgrounds and Aqualand, Antalyas's largest water park. Kids will particularly enjoy Dolphinland, where for 18YTL ($13) per person you can smile in wonder along with your little ones, and for an extra 100YTL ($75), you can swim with the dolphins. The whole complex has been dubbed **Antalya Beach Park**; at press time, it featured about 13 beach establishments—swaths of waterfront brightly equipped with lounges and umbrellas, and serviced by cafes, restaurants, changing cabins, and showers. Beach admission fees vary from about 4YTL to 10YTL ($3–$7.40) per day and includes use of the facilities. Most of the beach establishments have a watersports center, with jet skis for rent by the quarter-hour, parasailing, ringo rides, water-skiing, kayaks, sea bikes, and windsurfing, to name a few. As the sun sets, beach clubs morph into stylish outdoor nightclubs, providing cushions and lounges for lots of posing and draping, and an atmosphere of high style and frivolity. Main access to the beach is down a switchback road between the archaeological museum and the park; pedestrians can enter via a series of steps and bridges behind the Sheraton Hotel.

The sparse and sandy **Lara Beach** stretches along the coast in the opposite direction, a little over 11km (7 miles) east of downtown. Access to the beach is for the most part through the few hotel or camping establishments that dot the road eastward, and the farther out you get, the more spartan the beach becomes. The beach at the Club Hotel Sera is the jazziest, backing the hotel grounds that are literally lined with red carpets; more popular for weekend picnickers are the Erici Motel and Beach and the Adalya Beach Motel and Camping. There's a nominal entrance fee for use of private facilities at the former, and a restaurant, cafe, and bar at the latter.

Freshwater springs gushing off the mountains have found several awe-inspiring outlets in and around Antalya—a great place for a bracing, high-pressure shower. Located below Mermerli Park at the eastern end of Kaleiçi is **Memerli Plaj** ✿ (admission 3.50YTL/$2.50; entrance through the Memerli Restaurant), a miniature beach backed by the ancient sea walls. An icy spring shoots out of the rock at the end of the beach, but the narrow sandy strip is a bit unkempt and crowded. With a little more time, you'll do better to head over to the **Lower Düden Waterfalls** ✿, on the road to Lara Beach, where the waters plunge straight into the sea. Alternately, go an additional 13km (8 miles) to the **Upper Düden Waterfalls** ✿, unique because you can walk behind the cascade.

Heading west by car, Antalya's sprawl dissipates and small beaches and clusters of resort hotels dot the coastal road. The planned resort village of **Kemer,** 43km (27 miles) later, takes advantage of aquamarine calm waters backed by craggy mountainous cliffs, as waves lap through the pebbles creating a relaxing munching sound. The narrow beach is equipped with lounges and umbrellas, and the overpriced shopping strip stocks enough cash registers to keep you busy after sunning.

Just 14km (9 miles) farther west is the ancient port city of **Phaselis** ✿✿✿ (daily summer 8am–6pm; winter 8am–4pm), nestled amid the pine trees on the edge of three pristine and scenic bays. Plan to spend the day (entrance fee 11YTL/$8) to wade in the waters and wander through the main streets, agoras, baths, and temples of this enchanting ancient city.

The amazing caves and waterfalls around Antalya are accessible on 2-, 4-, or 6-hour **boat excursions** ✿; crews begin hawking the next day's tours early in the evening, or you can show up at the last minute for a boat that's about to disembark. For around 20YTL ($15), these guys will basically go anywhere you want; you can even take a night trip. Longer tours make trips to nearby beaches and may include a guided tour of the lovely and pine-shaded ancient harbor city of Phaselis.

STAYING ACTIVE

DIVING   In addition to a wide variety of colorful plant and sea life, the Gulf of Antalya is also a graveyard for several unlucky World War II fighter planes and at least one groundbreaking shipwreck. Maybe the Meltem, the winds that blow in from the Caucuses, or the rocky coastline have something to do with it, but the results are some of the most fascinating dive sites along the coast. Dive concessions are on-site at all the major hotels and resorts, and you don't have to be a guest to sign up but a day's notice is generally necessary. **Yunus Diving,** located at the base of the pedestrian bridge connecting the Sheraton to Konyaaltı Beach (ⓒ **0242/238-4486;** www.yunus diving.com), offers a 2-hour discovery dive (40YTL/$30), 2-hour licensed dives (40YTL/$30), and wreck dives (54YTL/$40); full equipment rental including the oxygen tank is an additional 27YTL ($20).

GOLF   Golf is a relatively new phenomenon in Turkey, but several clubs have created their very own sweet spot along the shores east of Antalya, in the secluded hills of Belek. To get to any of these, take the Antalya highway east and watch for signs for Belek on the right. All of the clubs and resorts are clearly signposted. You can book in advance by contacting the golf clubs individually, or by booking through **www.bookyourgolf.net**.

The **Gloria Golf Club** (© 0242/715-1520; see "Where to Stay" below) was the first and only resort to have its very own golf course. Michel Gayon designed the 18-hole Championship course; there's also a 3-hole practice course for beginners. The greens fee for the larger course is around 107YTL ($80).

National Golf Club (© 0242/725-5400; national@golfturkey.com) has an 18-hole Championship course and a 9-hole Academy course. There are a variety of watersports here, for nonputting spouses. The greens fee for a full day on the 18-hole course is 122YTL ($90).

Tatgolf International Golf Club (© 0242/725-5303; reservation@tatgolf.com.tr) has an 18-hole and a 9-hole Championship course. The greens fee for the 18-hole course is 100YTL ($75).

HIKING/CAMPING   Kate Clow, a British woman based in Antalya, turned a labor of love into a hiker's dream. She's mapped and marked a comprehensive network of ancient dirt roads and blissfully solitary footpaths. The first long-distance trail, called the **Lykia Yolu (Lycian Way)** 🟊🟊🟊, connects Antalya and Fethiye; Kate has created a companion guide to go along with it (see "Recommended Books & Films," in chapter 2). The second network of trails begins along the coast around Antalya and heads over the Toros Mountains into the Lakeland around Eğirdir and on up to Antioch in Psidia, in some cases trodding the ancient Roman roads used by St. Paul on his missionary journeys through Asia Minor. For more on the trails or for information on trekking trips, log onto **www.lycianway.com** or **www.stpaultrail.com**.

KAYAKING/RAFTING   The mountainous geography and numerous rivers in the Antalya region create exhilarating white-water rafting appropriate to all levels. The Manavgat River flows through a series of lengthy gorges but the Grades 4 and 5 rapids are accessible to experienced paddlers only.

The Köprü River, located halfway between Antalya and Side with Grade 1 and Grade 3 rapids, is no less breathtaking but a bit more suitable to beginners. This is an ideal family day out, even if you have no experience whatsoever. **Medraft Turizm,** Cumhuriyet Cad. 76/6 (© 0242/248-0083; www.medraft.com), organizes day trips for all levels, with top professional and experienced guides for about 43YTL ($32) per person with lunch.

WHERE TO STAY

Antalya is synonymous with sun and fun, and the holiday villages just couldn't resist the sandy beaches and plains ripe for development at the foot of the Toros Mountains. Several luxury four- and five-star playgrounds dot the coastline outwards from Antalya's historic Kaleiçi area and marina, while miles and miles farther out, the several become literally hundreds. If what you're after is an all-inclusive resort that you never have to leave, a better option is to seek out one of the holiday villages in the newly popularized seaside stretches of Kemer and Belek, both about a half-hour to an hour's drive from Antalya. The advantages of staying farther out are mostly a matter of seclusion, as these properties tend to take up long stretches of privatized sandy beaches. A good compromise is in the four- and five-star hotels perched on the cliffs just outside of the city's nucleus. For those sitting on the fence, the arrival of Konyaaltı's Antalya Beach Park, backed by several full-service five-star hotels, brings new meaning to the idea of a well-rounded Mediterranean holiday, without even the slightest concession to luxury, style, or location.

More attuned to the desires of the independent traveler are the hotels and pensions of Antalya proper, most notably in Kaleiçi, where hotels are housed in typical and often lovely Ottoman homes of timber or stone. The traditional Ottoman house is built around a front and rear courtyard, so that all of these hotels have at least a pool of cozy dimensions and often a serene and fragrant garden.

ANTALYA HOLIDAY RESORTS

Dedeman Antalya ⭐ *Kids*   The Dedeman is nothing you'd expect from a luxury hotel; it vibrates with activity—a perfect choice for families. One of the main attractions is the **Aquapark,** a seaside wonderland of 15 water slides, which include two river rides and a wave pool. The park is free to hotel guests (14YTL/$10 for nonguests) and also offers restaurants, cafeterias, a swimming pool, and lounges.

On the edge of the property at the bottom of the cliff is a small natural beach area, with some of the cleanest water in the city center. If you're headed off to a day of white-water rafting or deep-sea diving, the hotel provides the services of a nursery for kids up to 6 years old (for a fee). Another big plus is that the Dedeman offers extremely competitive rates to local agents that can trickle down to you. Rooms were renovated and modernized in 2000 and remain immaculate.

Lara Yolu. 07100 Antalya. 📞 **0242/321-3930.** Fax 0242/321-3873. www.dedemanhotels.com. 482 units. 115€ ($140) double; 160€ ($195) and up suite. AE, DC, MC, V. **Amenities:** 3 restaurants; 5 bars; disco; 2 swimming pools (Olympic-size outdoor, indoor); tennis courts; health club and spa; Turkish bath; Jacuzzi; sauna; extensive land and watersports; children's center; playground; water park; game room; bowling alley; concierge; tour desk; car-rental desk; shopping arcade; salon; 24-hr. room service; massage; babysitting; laundry service; dry cleaning; nonsmoking rooms. *In room:* A/C, satellite TV, minibar, hair dryer, safe.

Hillside Su ⭐⭐⭐ *Finds*   The glorious Hillside Su manages to be both futuristic and retro at the same time. Large glass sliding doors open onto an atrium lobby and lounge where four massive disco balls dangle from the ceiling. Get the idea? The Hillside Su is the most fashion-conscious beach club on the strip, offering guests the graciousness of an array of stylish day beds and lounges, *a la* Delano, in Miami Beach. Oh, and did I forget to mention that everything is white? Whitewashed floors, whitewashed walls, white linens and towels, white terry-cloth covers for everything. The whiteness of the hotel is offset by little accents of red: red (okay, orange) goldfish, red (or white) bedside tower lamps, and red lava lamps. Rooms are gracious in size, sporting king-size beds, a spacious sitting area with day bed, and twin ottomans. Every room has a balcony furnished with yet another bed; avoid the scorching heat of August and you just might spend the night alfresco. Bathrooms are industrial/functional, with a blocky half-exposed shower space (also constructed of cement) and bulky designer fixtures. Outside, the Hillside boasts a 53m (174-ft.) uncommonly narrow and exceptionally wonderful teak-decked swimming pool, flanked on two sides by a stylish double row of ground-level beds shaded by bamboo umbrellas. Beyond the second row of beds begin the lawns, which convert to a high-quality and reasonably priced fish restaurant by candlelight. Overall, the wonderful pretentiousness is mitigated by a disarmingly congenial and professional staff, and while the spare minimalism may be disarming to some, I found its clever and kitschy style to be simply enchanting.

Konyaaltı Cad., 07050 Antalya. © **0242/249-0700.** Fax 0242/249-0707. www.hillside.com.tr. 294 units. 205€ ($250) double garden view; 278€ ($339) sea view double; 290€–308€ ($355–$375) suite. AE, MC, V. Free parking on-site. **Amenities:** 6 restaurants (including sushi bar); 4 bars (including fitness bar); indoor and outdoor swimming pools; 2 tennis courts; health club; squash; Turkish bath; Jacuzzi; sauna; watersports; rentals (bike, moped, and scooter); excellent children's playground with separate kiddy pool; concierge; tour desk; car-rental desk, business center with free Internet access; shopping arcade; salon; 24-hr. room service; Balinese spa; babysitting; laundry service; dry cleaning; nonsmoking rooms. *In room:* A/C, interactive satellite TV, dataport, minibar, hair dryer, safe, toiletries bar.

Sheraton Voyager ⭐⭐ *Kids*

The beautiful landscaped gardens and luxurious brooks that snake through the property make up for the fact that the Sheraton Voyager looks like a giant concrete seagull. But it's exactly these outstretched wings embracing the property that give 80% of the rooms panoramic sea and mountain views. And every unit has a balcony from which to enjoy them. The property is perched on the cliff top, separated from the sea by a lovely shaded public park and a pedestrian bridge that provides quick, and steep, access down to the beach. (If you don't want to walk, the hotel also provides free shuttles to the beach via the access roadway.) Room decor is hotel homogenous, but the details, like large rooms, interactive TV and messaging system, bathrobes, slippers, and bathroom goodies more than make up for the blandness. The outdoor swimming pool is one of the largest in the area, with two levels and a water cascade completely surrounded by palm trees. The "wellness center" offers the health and beauty conscious a number of sybaritic reasons to stay here.

100 Yil Bulvari. © **800/325-3535** in the U.S., or 0242/238-5555. Fax 0242/243-2462. www.sheraton.com/voyager. 395 units. 103€ ($125) double; 110€–370€ ($135–$450) suite. AE, DC, MC, V. Free parking on-site. **Amenities:** 3 restaurants; 3 bars; indoor and outdoor swimming pools; adjacent golf course; tennis courts; health club and spa; extensive watersports; children's playground; game room; concierge; tour desk; car-rental desk; shopping arcade; salon; 24-hr. room service; massage; babysitting; laundry service; dry cleaning; nonsmoking rooms; executive floor. *In room:* A/C, satellite TV, dataport, minibar, hair dryer, safe.

Talya Oteli ⭐⭐

The four-star Talya Hotel, recently added to the Divan portfolio, has the comfort and character of a smaller hotel with the elegance and amenities of a five-star establishment. A six-story cement wedge, the Talya is designed in such a way that every room enjoys a balcony and direct sea views. You may never have your back to the window, but the view on the inside is of immaculate and tastefully decorated rooms. An outdoor pool, splendidly heated in the mild winter months, rests atop the cliff overlooking the sea. Steps down the cliff side is the hotel's private "beach." The fitness center, accessible past a popular Internet cafe, is one of the nicest I've seen, with a Jacuzzi, tanning salon, and fabulous Turkish bath (free to guests) designed with tile and wooden benches. If you really want to pamper yourself, reserve one of the 10 bungalow-style suite rooms down on the cliff.

Fevzi Cakmak Cad. 30, 07100 Antalya. © **0242/248-6800.** Fax 0242/241-5400. 204 units. 140€ ($170) double; 305€ ($372) suite. AE, DC, MC, V. **Amenities:** 4 restaurants; 5 bars; outdoor swimming pool; tennis courts; health club; beautifully tiled Turkish bath; Jacuzzi; sauna; watersports; concierge; tour desk; car-rental desk; shopping arcade; salon; 24-hr. room service; massage; babysitting; laundry service; dry cleaning. *In room:* A/C, satellite TV, minibar, hair dryer, safe.

KALEIÇI

Alp Paşa Some of the feedback I've gotten about this former merchant's inn restored from two 18th- and 19th-century *konaks* points to inhospitable management, but it's also true that complainers tend to give more feedback than happy campers. It's your call. I include this hotel as a shining example of sensitivity in historic preservation, which features wooden arches, carved ceilings, and massive fortresslike doors rescued from the original structures. Some of the more regal units have stained-glass windows and sea views, while all of the rooms, each one with its own special character, have elegant, even flamboyant decor. Room categories are divided among standard, deluxe, and special, the last all equipped with Jacuzzis. The standards are somewhat minuscule and disappointing when held up against the higher-level units, so you may want to upgrade if your budget allows. The main drawback to staying at the Alp Paşa is the claustrophobic pool area, squashed into the entrance courtyard and surrounded by sun lounges that are just a bit too close for comfort. The entire courtyard area must be vacated to prepare for the nightly buffet dinners, so if late afternoon poolside snoozes are an important part of your holiday, you may want to stay elsewhere.

Barbaros Mahallesi, Hesapçı Sok. 30–32. Kaleiçi, 07100 Antalya. ✆ 0242/247-5675. Fax 0242/248-5074. www.alp pasa.com. 60 units. 80€–90€ ($98–$110) double; 90€–200€ ($110–$245) special room; 100€–500€ ($122–$610) suite. Rates include breakfast and buffet dinner; rates lower in spring and winter. AE, MC, V. Limited street parking. **Amenities:** Restaurant; bar; cramped outdoor swimming pool; Turkish bath; 24-hr. room service; laundry service; dry cleaning. *In room:* A/C, satellite TV, minibar, hair dryer, safe (for a 2€/$2.50 fee).

Atelya Pension (Value)

This family-owned and -operated collection of three Ottoman-era houses offers visitors one of the neighborhood's best values. The three buildings front a large courtyard set around a fountain and decorated in traditional Turkish style. Rooms in the older building are simple with few amenities besides the original wood plank floors and loads of character; some retain decorative niches and faded original paintings. The newer building has larger rooms, modern details, and comfortable bathrooms.

Civelek Sokagı 21, 07100 Kaleiçi,/Antalya. ✆ 0242/241-6416. Fax 0242/241-2848. 21 units. 25€ ($30) single; 40€ ($50) double in old section; 70€ ($85) in new section. Breakfast not included. No credit cards. **Amenities:** Bar; table tennis; meals on request.

Doğan Hotel

This neighborhood long-timer is made up of three connected Ottoman houses, conspicuous in their restored elegance. The garden takes center stage here, surrounded by high stone walls and flanked by a soothing waterfall on one side, with a small swimming pool taking up a smaller connected courtyard. In summer, breakfast is served outside under the shade of the many orange trees. Common spaces, which include a lobby bar and "library," feature marble surfaces and touches of kilims, while rooms, which were all recently redecorated, for the most part enjoy original wide wooden plank floors and ceilings. If you request a çatı odası, you'll be happy to step foot into a room up high with a balcony and views of the harbor; try to avoid the rooms in the rear, formerly known as "pink building," because bathrooms are smallish.

Mermerli Banyo Sokak 5, Kaleiçi, 07100 Antalya. ✆ 242/241-8842. Fax 0242/247-4006. www.doganhotel.com. 28 units. Double 20€–40€ ($25–$50). MC, V. Closed Nov–Mar. Limited street parking. **Amenities:** Lobby and garden bars; cozy outdoor swimming pool; 24-hr. room service; laundry service; dry cleaning. *In room:* A/C, satellite TV, radio, hair dryer.

La Paloma Pansion

After 15 years of flying out of Germany to spend the summer in Antalya, Hans Städter decided on a more pleasurable and cost-effective option, and invested his retirement funds into the construction of this Ottoman-style house. Completed in early 2000, La Paloma still sparkles like new—not even the bright local stone used in the construction looks weathered—offering nice-size rooms, simple, tasteful decor, and ceiling fans to circulate the cooled-off air. There's the requisite swimming pool and bar, plus a children's swimming pool, in an enclosed garden courtyard. Opt for the Pavilion room and get a minibar and Jacuzzi.

Kılıçaslan Mahallesi Tabakhane Sok. 3, 07100 Kaleiçi/Antalya. © **0242/244-8497**. Fax 0242/247-4509. www. lapalomapansion.com. 12 units. 30€ ($36) double; 40€ ($50) Pavilion room. MC, V. **Amenities:** Bar; outdoor swimming pool; 24-hr. room service; massage; laundry service; dry cleaning. *In room:* A/C.

Marina Residence ⊛   This special category hotel is the closest you'll get to standard hotel amenities in Kaleiçi without sacrificing character. Three Ottoman Paşa's homes of differing styles were restored and redecorated, keeping embellishments like marble balustrades, wood beams, and polished trim. There's a long marble staircase to the rooms above in the main house, and all rooms are outfitted with bathtubs, comfortable duvets, and feather pillows. The terrace suite enjoys access to its own rooftop sun terrace, offering breathtaking views of the marina (another room gets a Jacuzzi—and twin beds). Afternoons will most certainly be spent in the courtyard, an oasis of peace with a larger-than-life aquarium swimming pool, or in the new fitness room complete with a small sauna. The Marina also has one of the best restaurants in town (p. 315).

Mermerli Sok. 15, Kaleiçi, 07100 Antalya. © **0242/247-5490**. Fax 0242/241-1765. 41 units. 125€–140€ ($152–$170) double; 225€ ($275) terrace suite. Rates lower in winter. **Amenities:** Restaurant; bar; courtyard swimming pool; fitness room; sauna; 24-hr. room service; laundry service; dry cleaning. *In room:* A/C, satellite TV, minibar, hair dryer, safe.

Ninova Pensiyon *(Value*   This modest but comfortable pension boasts the finest garden in Antalya, pleasantly overgrown with orange trees and an enchanting reflecting pond as a centerpiece. Rooms are basic and small; an additional four units on the upper floors are usually out of commission in the summer because of the oppressive heat. The longtime manager, a sweet woman from Istanbul, creates an atmosphere of warmth, encouraging guests to congregate in the TV room or the sitting area. Nights are blissfully silent, even though Hadrian's Gate and Atatürk Caddesi are only steps away.

Hamit Efendi Sok. 9, Kaleiçi, 07100 Antalya. © **0242/248-6114**. Fax 0242/248-9684. 15 units. 40€–60€ ($50–$73) double. AE, MC, V. **Amenities:** Laundry service; dry cleaning. *In room:* A/C.

Tekeli Konakları ⊛   One of the more recent restorations in the walled city, Tekeli Konakları combines six traditional Turkish houses set around a common paved courtyard with several patio levels and a small pool. The rooms—each one slightly different—are elegantly yet sparsely decorated, taking advantage of architectural features such as polished wood floorboards and carved wood ceilings. Those who appreciate attention to detail will be delighted by Kutahya ceramics fashioned into door handles, the odd antique objet d' art, and in some rooms, stained-glass, Ottoman motif artwork. ***Early-to-bedder's take note:*** The neighboring disco may intrude upon your REM time. The restaurant, which takes over the upper patios on summer evenings, has already earned a solid reputation, and a new indoor pasthane serves sweets like baklava and pudding, along with ice cream in homemade waffle cones. There's also a small boutique on the premises, stocked with high-quality textiles like embroidered tablecloths, kilims, and ceramics.

Dizdar Hasan Sok., 07100 Kaleiçi/Antalya. © **0242/244-5465**. Fax 0242/242-6714. 8 units. 100€–120€ ($120–$145) double. AE, MC, V. **Amenities:** Restaurant; bar; outdoor swimming pool; 24-hr. room service; laundry service; dry cleaning. *In room:* A/C.

WHERE TO DINE

Locals flock to the eateries in the covered walkway at the intersection of Cumhuriyet Caddesi and Atatürk Caddesi, where freshly cooked *lokanta*-style cases and *döner* stands share the pavement with tiny coffee tables. It's the Turkish equivalent of the food court, and a delicious, friendly, and economical alternative to the more tourist-minded restaurants listed below.

China Garden *Finds* CHINESE This is some of the best Asian food I've ever eaten—and I've tasted fusion foods from as far and wide as New York, Paris, London, Bali, and Manila. Located about 1.6km (1 mile) down Konyaaltı Caddesi, China Garden is hidden inside the park, down a steep hill that eventually brings you to one of those familiar, bright-red cheesy Oriental gates. A boardwalk leads down to a large and elegant dining room, thankfully devoid of plastic lanterns. The terrace sits atop a steep cliff overlooking the sea; as night falls and the glowing lanterns loosen your tensions, you can ponder the Romeo and Juliet–like stories of lovers leaping over the cliff walls.

Each entree is tastefully illustrated by a photograph on the menu. No MSG is used here. Don't pass up the appetizer of crispy prawn crackers, which arrive on a hot iron plate with a flavorful chile sauce dip. Other favorites include the shark-fin and crab-meat soup and the delectable crispy roast duck. Save room for the ice cream.

Although with plenty of good options closer to home, China Garden may seem a bit out of the way, but it's absolutely worth the trip, and it's close enough to Kaleiçi that you can walk off the meal.

Konyaaltı Cad., inside the Atatürk Kültür Parkı; take the tram from Kaleiçi to the Kültür Parkı. © 0242/248-7835. Dress smart. Main courses 6.75YTL–14YTL ($5–$10). MC, V. Daily 11:30am–2:30pm and 6–11pm.

Gizli Bahçe/Secret Garden *Moments* TURKISH/ITALIAN This restaurant combines delicious meals with a stunning environment: Choose between a table in the romantic candlelit Italianate garden, on the cliff-top panoramic patio, or next to the ancient walls with a view that peeks through the ramparts (a few choose to sit indoors in the warmer weather). The menu is pure Turkish, with some highlights of the local kitchen, including *şakşuka*, an appetizer of eggplant, zucchini, and tomato, and special selections of the chef. Try the seafood salad served on greens with an orange sauce, or the Garden Kebab Special, a plate of sirloin strips served with tomato, yogurt, and eggplant. You can also try the Secret Garden for a midday break in the new pasthane in the upper garden.

Selçuk Mahallesi, Dizdar Hasan Bey Sok., No. 1 Kaleiçi. © 0242/244-8010. Dress smart. Turkish main courses 8YTL–20YTL ($6–$15); Italian main courses 8YTL–16YTL ($6–$12). MC, V. Daily 8am–midnight.

Kral Sofrası TURKISH/MEDITERRANEAN Called the King's Table, Kral Sofrası enjoyed 20 years of success in Ankara before moving to the warmer climes of Antalya, where it was the first restaurant to open on the marina. In the summertime, meals are served on the terrace garden overlooking the rooftops and harbor, but the restaurant seems to take its name from the stately dining room inside this old Ottoman house. The Mediterranean menu offers typical Turkish harbor fare—Tygar, the owner, assures me that he rises daily at 6am to personally select the day's ingredients—with an occasional standout like the special *kiral güveç* (beef and vegetable casserole) or the spicy chile tahini dip. Pay your respects to the Elvis-like Atatürk shrine at the front entrance before you leave.

Yacht Harbor 35. © 0242/241-2198. Dress smart for indoor dining. Grilled meat and fish dishes 6.75YTL–14YTL ($5–$10). MC, V. Daily 11am–1am. Closes earlier in winter.

Marina Restaurant *FRENCH* The Marina Hotel has two restaurants—one in the garden and the other in the elegant main house—but the menu is so successful that it's the same one for both spots. Mouthwatering appetizers are presented as only French training will allow. To start, the chef has created a duck rillet with a walnut sauce mixed with orange and cognac and a salmon roll filled with prawns, Iranian caviar, and mustard-seed sauce. Entrees meld succulent mainstays with atypical flavors as in the T-bone steak with Madagascar chile sauce or the breast of duck with a vegetable soufflé and cherry sauce. The Mediterranean sole stuffed with shrimp in a saffron sauce may not be unusual, but that doesn't make it any less yummy. The meal can be completed with a selection of decadent westernized tarts, flambés, and cakes; there's even a pear poshet prepared for diabetics.

Mermerli Sok. 15, Kaleiçi. © **0242/247-5490.** Reservations suggested. Dress smart. Main courses 11YTL–34YTL ($8–$25). MC, V. Daily noon–11pm.

Sim Restaurant TURKISH HOME COOKING   The old Byzantine walls and the few tables under a bougainvillea-covered trellis make Sim impossible to resist. Multilingual graffiti decorates the downstairs walls, but if you have to sit inside, go upstairs where the dining room looks less like a men's room in a college dorm. Decor aside, this charming family-run restaurant is winning in its simplicity. Fresh vegetables line the small case, and it's a surprise to see such basic ingredients turned into things like mushrooms cooked in butter, fava bean salad, and *sigara börek.*

Kaledibi Sok. 7. © **0242/248-0107.** Appetizers and main courses under 6.75YTL ($5). No credit cards. Daily noon–11pm.

Stella's Bistrot ✦ *(Value)* MEDITERRANEAN   Far from the platforms and terraces of the tourist section, Stella's Bistrot is a welcome change from all the fish and grills. The predominantly Italian menu has been expanded to include Mediterranean dishes, but the real winner here is the authentic Italian lasagna made the way it's supposed to be, with a béchamel sauce. Salads and sandwiches are appealing alternatives for lunch, and from the sidewalk tables you can watch the tram pass by.

Fevzi Çakmak Caddesi 3/C (near end of Atatürk Caddesi). © **0242/243-3931.** Main courses 6.75YTL–11YTL ($5–$8). MC, V. Daily noon–midnight.

ANTALYA AFTER DARK

Visitors to Antalya take to the streets and hidden courtyards of Kaleiçi or along the Yacht Harbor, where an ice cream and a stroll down the jetty are accompanied by sea breezes and waterside cafes. The downside is that several slow seasons have resulted in increased hassling by those idling outside their shops.

With the arrival of **Konyaaltı's Beach Park** ✦✦✦, Antalya can now assume its place as the preeminent seaside resort on the Turquoise Coast. Stylish and tasteful cafes line the seaside beach park promenade at Konyaaltı, sharing the lawns with decadent arrays of cushions, and backed by a handful of characteristic *meyhanes.*

Meanwhile, residents looking for a quiet evening out descend on Karaalioğlu Park for a seat at one of the welcoming tea gardens dressed in bright red or for a go at a lineup of balloons with an old army rifle. When the heat and humidity become too much to bear, there's bound to be a Turkish Nights show at one of the hotels in town; standouts are listed below.

Gizli Bahçe *(Finds)*   The presence of two restaurants, four different dining environments, stunning views of the bay via the parapets, and a generally elegant atmosphere are just a few of the things that the Gizli Bahçe/Secret Garden has to offer. A polished and elegant bar area is a great option for a pre- or post-dinner aperitif, while live music is offered Tuesday through Sunday nights. Ask about their Turkish folk night, complete with buffet, usually scheduled for Wednesday night. Daily 8am to midnight. Selcuk Mahallesi, Dizdar Hasan Bey Sok., No. 1 Kaleiçi. © **0242/244-8010.** Closed Nov to mid-Apr.

Highlander   Jolly and diminutive Fazla opened this warm-hearted pub in May 2001, and owes its name to the popular series, after Fazla spotted Christopher Lambert one day on the marina. Set slightly back from the water's edge, the outdoor cafe looks suspiciously like a Fortunoff patio display, in no small part thanks to the artificial fountain set within an outdoor round bar. Indoors, however, is pure Highlander, from the leather couches, to the dartboard, to the deep manly colors. Weekends usher in live music, but early-evening hours can still be enjoyed with the house cocktail: Russian coffee with vodka and cream. Daily 8am to 3am; shorter hours in winter. Yat Limanı Iskele Cad. 2. (℗ 0242/242-4855.

Kale Bar   With wrought-iron patio chairs painted bubble-gum pink, the Kale Bar, located in the elegant Tütav Türk Evi, has the best views of the harbor from anywhere in town and some of the highest prices for cocktails of anywhere around. Daily 11am to 2am. In the Tütav Türk Evi, Memerli Sok., Kaleiçi. (℗ 0242/248-6591. Closed in winter.

La Notte   La Notte sits high above the marina with breathtaking views of the gulf. Lunch and dinner are served, and La Notte features live fasil music on Sunday evenings. Daily noon to 3am. Selçuk Mah. Iskele Cad. 1 (near the entrance to "29"), Kaleiçi. (℗ 0242/242-5550. Closed in winter.

29 Antalya 🖈 *Finds*   Antalya's most desirable and exclusive entertainment complex, 29 combines a restaurant, a spectacular open-air terrace bar, a discotheque—and a swimming pool (for daytime use only). The complex teeters on the edge of the cliff above the harbor around the centerpiece, an ancient renovated warehouse whose interior was recently redesigned with a minimalist and serene Asian theme. The terrace reserved for the late-night disco is a classy and elegant outdoor lounge of posh pillows, where in the evening, wrought-iron candelabras and the sporadic spot-lit flashes of mascot Joe Camel sliding across the wall cast an exclusive and atmospheric glow. Until around midnight, the crashing of the waves against the rocks and the sounds of samba are illuminated by the glow of candlelight; then the DJ turns into a pumpkin and blasts you the hell out of there. So much for watching the sunrise. Daily 11:30am to 3pm and 5pm to 1am. Yacht Harbor. (℗ 0242/241-6260. Reservations suggested. Dress smart. AE, DC, MC, V. Cover charge 14YTL ($10); free to diners.

EXCURSIONS FROM ANTALYA

The region around Antalya is full of superb landscapes, deep canyons, gushing waterfalls, and archaeological sites. For assistance in planning your day out, contact **Equinox Travel,** Gençlik Mah. Febzi Çakmak Cad. 1315 Sok. 1/10 (℗ **0242/247-8836;** www.equinox.com.tr), which organizes 10-day to 2-week walking tours through the Antalya region and Lake District (including Termessos), as well as a dirtbike excursion up into the Taurus Mountains. Prices depend upon the needs of the client, so consult their Web page and contact them directly.

THE "MONSTER" AT OLYMPOS

One of the highlights of a visit to the Antalya coast is the **Chimaera** 🖈🖈, near the ancient city of **Olympos** 🖈 and modern-day beachfront **Çiralı** 🖈🖈. It's a good idea to combine a visit to both the natural and archaeological sites, keeping in mind that the undisturbed—even unkempt—shoreline of Çiralı is one of the best kept natural secrets of the Mediterranean coast and a major nesting site for sea turtles.

The Chimaera, or mythical, fire-breathing monster with the head of a lion, the torso of a goat, and the rear of a snake that allegedly roams the hills is actually a series of eternal flames flickering along the rocky slopes above the ancient city of Olympos, which would account for the Lycians' worship of the fire god Hephaestos (Vulcan). But never fear: According to legend, the Chimaera was slain by Bellerophon on his winged horse, Pegasus, from his base over at Tlos. The fires are caused by the combustion of a predominantly methane gas mixture seeping out of the earth and igniting at the point of contact between serpentine and limestone rocks; though they can be extinguished briefly by covering them, they always reignite. The path up the hill to the site is at the far end of the modern village of Çıralı, about a 6- to 7km (3¾–4½-mile) hike from the beach end of the ancient city of Olympos. It's about a 20-minute hike up to the Chimaera, where a fresh pot of tea perks atop one of the flames. Although the flames are no less impressive by daylight, it's best to come at dusk, when the flames are most visible—just don't forget a flashlight.

The ancient site of Olympos hugs both sides of the Ulupınar Stream near the seashore, and dates to Hellenistic times. It's a bit overgrown and spread out on both sides of the stream, so come with a good map of the site. From 100 B.C., Olympos enjoyed the status as one of the six primary members of the Lycian League, and was later absorbed as a Roman province. During this period, the area gained renown as a place of worship for the cult of Hephaestos, or Vulcan, the God of Fire.

Admission to the ancient city ruins during daylight hours (when the booth is manned) is 11YTL ($8). There are two entrances to the site: to combine a visit to Olympos with a climb up to the Chimaera, exit the Antalya highway at the exit marked "Çıralı 7; Yanartaş 11 (Chimaera)" (Yanartaş is Turkish for "burning rock"). From here, it's a 10-minute drive along a dry stream bed bursting with Oleander, wild orchids, and lavender; you can either cross the bridge and continue straight for about a mile (don't be discouraged by the poor condition of the road during the final mile or so) until you arrive at the "base camp" for the well-marked path up to the Chimaera or turn off onto the rocky road *before* the bridge into Çıralı for access to the beach. (Walk to the right to find the beach entrance to the site of Olympos.) (The other main entrance to Olympos can be accessed from the turnoff from the Antalya road marked "Olympos 11; Çavuşköy 15".) *Dolmuşes* pass regularly along the Antalya highway, but transportation down to the beachfront via either turnoff is less reliable.

WHERE TO STAY & DINE The road that loops through the village of Çıralı is lined with small, family-run pensions with varying degrees of appeal. But until that fated day when Çıralı becomes polished and unauthentic, the best place to stay is the **Olympos Lodge** ✻✻, Çıralı, Kemer P.O. Box 38, Antalya (✆ **0242/825-7171;** fax 0242/825-7173; www.olymposlodge.net), just over the bridge into town (take that quick right). With only 12 rooms, this small slice of paradise is like a country club that's hard to get into; the parking lot is consistently full of shiny Mercedes, BMWs, and collectors' Rolls Royces. The grounds are gorgeous—a Mediterranean garden bursting with color and home to wandering chickens and peacocks abuts the beach. At 13 years old, the rooms are rather unadorned and basic, but feature old cedar wood floorboards that supposedly repel mosquitoes. The room rate of 175€ ($213) to 200€ ($245) for two people per night includes breakfast and dinner; nonguests can make dinner reservations for about 35€ ($43) per person.

When the Olympos Lodge breaks the news that it's full, the **Arcadia** ✻, Çıralı (✆ **0242/825-7340;** www.arcadiaholiday.com), located farther down the beach on a plot of land that was formerly an orange-and-lemon grove, offers four spacious and extremely comfortable wood bungalows. All were built by Ahmet, the owner, assisted by

---

Finds **Serenity East of Antalya**

An hour east of Antalya is **Villa Lapin** ✦✦, Şelale Mahallesi Küme Evler 3, 07600 Manavgat (©/fax **0242/742-9146**; www.villa-lapin.com; 95YTL ($70) double; for 68YTL ($50) they'll get you to and from the airport in Antalya), a friendly and restorative labor of love that credits the initiative of owners and newlyweds, Emin and Ria. If immersion in local living (we're talking grazing goats and some squawking chickens) coupled with an expansive riverfront garden patio gives you a travel-induced adrenaline rush, then you'll want to hole up at this hideaway for a few days. Villa Lapin rests on the banks of the serene and icy Manavgat River along a sleepy dirt road above Manavgat town. The rooms are relatively small (three compensate with balconies facing the river), but revel in local details: hand-embroidered bath towels, handmade lace curtains, and decorative seersucker bed sheets. Bikes are available for visitors. Emin's fishing boat also serves day-trippers interested in the lovely 2-hour boat ride to the harbor of Side (a magical means of arrival) at an additional charge. Emin's culinary genius of a sister, Süreyya, prepares a nightly dinner for guests.

Canadian-born Ann, a welcomed font of local information in English. Together, they've created a cozy, romantic, and rustic environment stocked with all the creature comforts, plus coffee, a tea station, and a wine rack. Arcadia has delicious on-site dining on request; eat under the beachfront pines or relax on the shady platform *köşk*. The room rate for two people is 85€ to 110€ ($103–$134) and includes breakfast and dinner.

THE MOUNTAINTOP CITADEL OF TERMESSOS

Located on a natural plateau 1,050m (3,500 ft.) above sea level, the impregnable mountaintop city of **Termessos** ✦✦ was the only settlement not conquered by Alexander the Great. The ancient site is located about a half-hour's drive from Antalya inside the Güllük Dağ Milli Parkı (© **0242/423-7416**). Alex likened it to an eagle's nest; you'll think so, too, after the steep climb up. The best approach from the plateau parking area is up the main path to the city and theater for access to the lion's share of the ruins. Rather than backtracking at the end of your visit, follow the sign toward the tombs, which follows a narrow and sometimes rocky footpath past a series of rock-cut tombs and free-standing **sarcophagi,** a path that ends about 20 minutes later in the parking lot. Although the path is shady most of the way up, be sure to carry enough bottled water, as there is no concession on-site, and it can get pretty hot. The visit on foot takes as little as 2 hours (if you're well hydrated and it's early) to as much as 4 to 5 hours, if you're sluggish and really into seeing every nook and cranny.

The most impressive of the ruins is the **Greek theater,** cut into the rock with celestial views of Antalya visible through the clouds. The ability of the city's inhabitants to withstand prolonged attacks was in no small part due to the exceptional engineering of its cisterns: five tanks fed by a duct cut into the rock. Admission to the park is 4YTL ($3) per person, plus 31YTL ($23) for your car (don't even think about walking from the ticket gate, a hefty 9km/5½ miles downhill from the plateau parking; open daily 8am–6pm in summer and 8am–4pm in winter). If you're going by car, follow the Antalya/Burdur highway north and follow signs for the park. Tours run only about 40YTL ($30) and generally include a stopover at the Duden Waterfall.

8

Cappadocia & the Interior

A stark lunar landscape. A mysterious open-air sculpture carved by Mother Nature's chisel. These common descriptions of Cappadocia really just tap dance around the subject. So let's just get this out of the way: Those fascinating "fairy chimneys" evoke nothing so much as anatomically correct erections—and circumcised ones at that. Imagine what a field day American film censors would have had if George Lucas had succeeded in his original plan to shoot *Star Wars Episode 1: The Phantom Menace* in Cappadocia.

Nobody knows who the original inhabitants of the region were, or who first hollowed out shelters in the soft rock of these sheltered ravines and odd "chimneys." But as a largely barren and desolate area, central Cappadocia was bypassed by most expansionist armies, making it a perfect refuge for the early Christians following in the footsteps of St. Paul, who established the first Christian colonies here.

The natural land formations and huge expanses of silence are just a part of the mystery of the region. As an incubator for Christian philosophy, the monasteries, cave dwellings, and feats of underground engineering are a testament to human ingenuity. Cliff walls of the valleys are riddled with innocuous-looking cavities that on closer inspection turn out to be centuries-old dwellings or chapels decorated with colorful frescoes and biblical images.

Cappadocian soil is extremely fertile, and a general tour of the region will reveal numerous vineyards in and around the valleys. Famous for its local wines, Cappadocia is a major producer; you may want to veer off at a sign for Şarap Evi (wine house) for a leisurely tasting. The creatively named Şarap Evi, in Ürgüp, has wine tastings in the evenings, but it's just as fun to drive up to any local producer and fall into the dance of local hospitality.

1 Exploring the Region

In antiquity, Cappadocia included all of central Anatolia, stretching as far as Ankara in the north and Adana in the south (see the map of Turkey's Ancient Civilizations, on p. 381). Today the region includes the area in and around a small triangle formed by Ürgüp, Avanos, and Nevşehir, where the canyons are the deepest and the pigments in the rock-cut churches are the richest.

If your time is limited, it's possible to visit the major sites of the area in 2 *full* days with either your own car or the assistance of a local tour operator. Doubtless, you'll wish you had stayed longer. Tours can be either tailor-made, and therefore more pricey, or selected from a stable of standard issues. Typical day tours include: 1) a visit to the Open Air Museums of Zelve and Göreme, overviews of the valleys from Paşabağ and Dervent, a climb up to the top of Üçhisar Fortress, and an optional pottery demonstration in Avanos, and 2) visits to the underground cities of Kaymaklı and Derinkuyu and a leisurely 4km (2½-mile) hike through the monastery-rich gorge of

Cappadocia

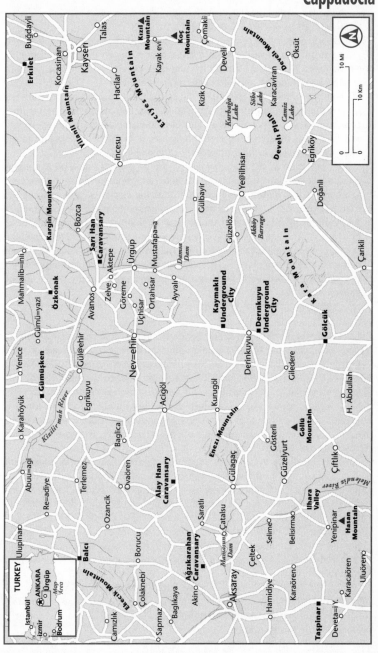

Geology 101—What's the Deal?

The erosion that carves out this fascinating topography began over 60 million years ago and can be seen in various stages even today. As the devastating 1999 earthquakes illustrated, Turkey is caught between the insistent pressure exerted from the Asian and European continental plates. The Erciyes Mountain, Melendiz Mountain, and Hasandag—all dormant or extinct volcanoes—are the result of underground forces that thrust these landmasses above water level eons ago. Recurrent volcanic eruptions blanketed the area with boulders, ash, and lava, over time creating layers of sediment, with the underneath layers more solid than the newer, softer levels of sediment.

The formation of the fairy chimneys is just an example of wind and water erosion in an extreme state. The early stages of erosion are visible in the graceful channels and dunes of the valleys. But as the elements carve away at the channels, the mass of tufa splits from its supports and forms pillars or pyramids. And without the protection of those basalt boulders caught in the balance of gravity and time, the pillars slowly whittle down to nothing, and the crowning boulder comes crashing to the ground. The precarious nature of the tufa has earned Cappadocia a place on UNESCO's list of Natural World Heritage Properties so that it receives aid for restoration and preservation of its unique environment.

Ihlara Valley. Tours may also include horseback riding; more challenging sports such as mountain biking can be easily arranged, but these are generally not advertised.

Operating with the most experience in the region is **Argeus,** Istiklal Cad. 13, Ürgüp (© **0384/341-4688;** fax 0384/341-4888; www.argeus.com.tr), which provides expert guidance on Cappadocia and Ankara, as well as destinations throughout Turkey. Regular group tours, including all museum entrance fees and lunch in a restaurant, cost 101YTL ($75) per person for groups of six or more; private tours cost 300TYL ($220) and get cheaper the more people you have. Argeus is also the local representative of Turkish Airlines.

For a more off-the-beaten track experience, contact **Cappadocia Tours,** Istiklal Cad. 19/9, Ürgüp (© **0384/341-7485;** www.cappadociatours.com), which is the companion agency to Gamirasu Hotel (see "Where to Stay" below). Led by Süleyman Çakır, tours and hotel stays will be assured the highest of quality; think visits to local village events and historical hikes lead by Süleyman or a professional archaeologist. Expect to pay 216YTL ($160) per day for between 2 and 10 passengers including the guide and driver. For an additional 34YTL ($25) per person, all entrance fees will be included (these do add up), as well as vehicle expenses and an a la carte lunch, including wine.

Aiming for the middle ground is **Stone Park Tourism,** Istiklal Cad. 19/E, Ürgüp (© **0384/341-8897;** fax 0384/341-5348; www.stonepark.com.tr), at about 88YTL ($65) per person per day. As for budget outfitters, they come and go, and vie for your business around the bus station.

THE ACTIVE EXPLORER IN CAPPADOCIA

There are few things in this world that warrant a 4:30am wake-up; usually some type of flight is involved. But chasing the sunrise above Cappadocia's spectacular landscape in a wicker basket is altogether different from boarding a 747: It's like riding on the back of a Harley with wings.

Cappadocia's climate is ideally suited to ballooning, with consistently clear summer skies and harmonious breezes. Several experienced outfitters organize hot-air balloon rides over Cappadocia. **Kapadokya Balloons** (© **0384/271-2442;** in winter call © 33-3/8681-6715 in France; fax 0384/271-2586; www.kapadokyaballoons.com) is the oldest outfitter.

A day at Kapadokya Balloons begins *well* before sunrise, when the flame bursts that fill the balloon provide much-needed warmth. Flights last about an hour and a half, offering otherworldly close-ups and stunning panoramas. Your heart will undoubtedly skip a beat several times throughout, including when they hand you the 380YTL ($281) bill (ask for seasonal rates; reservations suggested).

Göreme Balloons (© **0384/341-5662;** www.goremeballoons.com), the other game in town, has since managed to put a dent in the local market with, in addition to flights at the same price, a less expensive option of a 45-minute flight (that often stretches out to an hour) for 231YTL ($171). (Kids 6–12 fly for half price.)

Ancient Anatolian lore paints a picture of a lovelorn poet on horseback traveling through fields of irises, perpetuating the legend of Cappadocia as a "place of beautiful horses." It's still possible to replicate that equestrian journey through the region's verdant valleys and barren steppes. The new **Akhal-Teke Riding Center** (© **0384/511-5171;** www.akhal-tekehorsecenter.com) has clean, professionally run stables on the outskirts of Avanos with horses and guides for all riding levels. The charge is 34YTL ($25) per hour, and they'll accommodate any length of ride you desire—even if that ride lasts a week (prices per hour go down the longer you stay on horseback). Outdoor excursions include stays in people's homes and/or overnights in tents, with all luggage and equipment transported by van.

Kirkit Voyages (© **0384/511-3259;** www.kirkit.com), with offices in Istanbul and Avanos, organizes activities in the area, thanks to their own horse farm in the village of Güzelyurt, near the Ihlara Valley. Horseback-riding tours for all levels of experience are available with full-day treks for 66YTL ($49). Kirkit also offers 2-hour panoramic horseback rides.

For active travelers wanting to explore the lesser-known valleys and churches, there's no substitute for a privately guided hiking or mountain bike tour. Argeus's exclusive contract with REI offers reliable assurance that you'll receive optimum guides and service. Cappadocia Tours can arrange expeditions up to Mount Erciyes, led by expert trekkers and accompanied by pack mules. And Kirkit Voyages organizes winter snowshoe treks of up to a week that begin in Güzelyurt, with overnights in village homes along the way.

GETTING THERE
The arrival of Nevşehir Airport cemented the town's image as the area's transportation hub; it's already the primary destination for buses traveling from other parts of the country. Unfortunately, in 2003, Turkish Airlines suspended all flights into Nevşehir. Because Nevşehir is a town with no discernible center—or soul, for that matter—I've decided not to cover it except when referring to getting in (by bus), getting out, or getting around Cappadocia.

BY PLANE   Turkish Airlines currently has four flights daily from Istanbul (the least expensive flight, at 95YTL ($70), departs from Sabiha Gokcen Airport on the Asian side) to Kayseri, about 45 minutes by car from anywhere in Cappadocia. The German-based Onur Air (in Istanbul © **0212/663-9176,** or local rep 0384/341-7130; www.onurair.com.tr) recently added domestic service within Turkey, flying to Kayseri daily from Istanbul.

Turkish Airlines has both an office in downtown Kayseri, at Sahabiye Mah. Yildirim Cad. 1 (© **0352/222-3858**), and at Kayseri's Erkilet Airport (© **0352/338-3353**). Within the Cappadocian triangle, the official representative for Turkish Airlines is **Argeus,** located at Istiklal Cad. 13, Ürgüp (© **0384/341-4688** or 0384/341-5207).

Many local tour operators will pick you up at the airport or bus station for much less than it would cost you to take a taxi. Argeus was the first in the region to provide transfers from both airports to anywhere in the Cappadocia region in their private minivans. The fare for the 97km (60-mile) trip (1½ hr.) to/from Kayseri airport is only 9.50YTL ($7). Because of the reasonable amount of competition this presents to area taxi drivers, travelers arriving and hoping to "wing it" by jumping on the Argeus bandwagon may get some resistance from the locals. To avoid misunderstandings, travelers are encouraged to reserve space in advance with Argeus (© **0384/341-4688;** fax 0384/341-4888; www.argeus.com.tr). Also be sure to check with your hotel first—they may pick you up for free. There are no other options for transfers in and out of Kayseri.

BY TRAIN   Of all the rail connections in the country, the one between Istanbul and Ankara is the most reliable for service and comfort. Trains depart Istanbul's Haydarpaşa Station five times daily for Ankara. From there it's about a 4- to 5-hour drive to Cappadocia (6 hr. by long-distance bus).

BY BUS   All long-distance buses into Cappadocia arrive into Nevşehir, with either a quick drive-by of secondary towns or a free minibus transfer to your final destination. Through buses, like those heading to eastern Turkey, will dump you off on the side of the highway rather than make the detour into the *otogar* (bus station); insist on this basic service when you buy your ticket. As for bus companies, stick to the more dependable **Göreme** (© **0384/213-5537** in Nevşehir or 0384/341-2111 in Ürgüp), or **Kapadokya** (© **0384/214-0262** in Nevşehir or 0384/341-6233 in Ürgüp) bus lines. All have regular service to and from Istanbul and Ankara as well as frequent and reliable regional service.

By bus, expect around 4 to 5 hours from Konya, 2 hours from Kayseri, 5 to 6 hours from Ankara, and 12 hours from Istanbul. If you're headed to the Aegean Coast, you'll have to change buses in either İzmir (13 hr.) or Muğla (14 hr.); for the Mediterranean coast, you'll have to take a bus to either Antalya or Muğla, then change for minibus service to your final destination. (Certain destinations will require yet another change; for example, to Dalyan, you'll have to change in Ortaca for a *dolmuş* (minivan-type public transportation) into the center of town.)

GETTING AROUND

In most parts of Turkey, *dolmuşes* are practical. In Cappadocia, service is infrequent and at best unreliable. A local *dolmuş* follows a circuit hourly from Ürgüp bus station to Zelve, Avanos, Göreme, Üçhisar, and back; another service runs every 2 hours from Ürgüp to Avanos between 9am and 5pm.

Dolmuşes also run to the smaller villages from select main towns, so while you can get direct service from Ürgüp to say, Mustafapaşa, you'll have to change in Nevşehir if you're headed to Derinkuyu.

> ### *Moments* The Best Hikes
>
> It's hard to find a bad hike in Cappadocia, but the journey will be all the more rewarding in this ever-changing landscape of pink, yellow, and sandy colored "dunes," with nothing but the whisper of the wind for company. Wear good shoes and come prepared with a windbreaker or jacket, because whenever the sun plays coy behind a cloud, the temperature drops momentarily, yet precipitously. The best hikes are in the **Red Valley (Kızılçukur Vadisi)** from Çavuşin to the entrance of Ortahisar; in **Pigeon Valley (Güvercinlik Vadisi)** between Üçhisar and Göreme; and in the **Uludere Valley** from Uludere village to Ayvalı, where you have the option of continuing through Gomede Valley to Mustafapaşa.

A municipal bus provides service between Nevşehir and Avanos daily on the hour from 8am to 5pm.

Obviously, a day tour will solve the transportation problem (see "Exploring the Region" earlier in this chapter). For car and scooter-rental information, see "Getting Around" in the individual sections below for details.

2 Ürgüp ★★★

23km (14 miles) east of Nevşehir; 6.5km (4 miles) east of Göreme

Of the major villages in Cappadocia, Ürgüp strikes a balance between preserving its Anatolian traditions and cultivating an unobtrusive yet irresistible tourist infrastructure. To meet the rising demand, hoteliers are all too eager to create magical and otherworldly accommodations for an increasingly upscale market. Crumbled hovels are snatched up for a song, human odors of food and sweat are scraped away with the top layers of porous tufa, and perfectly charming romantic retreats materialize. Of course, one day, all of those abandoned terraced houses will sprout brand-new facades, a gentrification process that, while polished and attractive, will probably be devoid of the character that drew us here in the first place. The process has already begun, particularly in the wake of press provided by the highly popular Turkish soap opera, *Asmalı Konak*. But for now, Ürgüp remains a tranquil yet convenient corner of Cappadocia that makes an ideal base from which to explore the surrounding valleys.

ESSENTIALS
VISITOR INFORMATION
The **Tourist Information office** is in the center of town across from the police station, on Kayseri Cad. 37 (© **0384/341-4059**), and is open daily 8am to 6pm; closed Sunday in winter.

ORIENTATION
The village fans out around the bus station and a brand-new cement-block shopping gallery, which is right in the center of town. From the main square outside the bus station running northeast is **Kayseri Caddesi,** Ürgüp's main shopping street, with a wide variety of shopping options, from overstocked antiques stores to jewelry boutiques with the finest selection of lapis lazuli, handcrafted silver, and tribal items. The information office, the police station, and the hospital can be reached down this road as well. Forking east below Kayseri Caddesi is a small street of localized travel agencies,

many of which double as bike or scooter rental outfits. **Ahmet Refik Caddesi** heads northwest from the center, snaking around the base of the old village of partially collapsed and deserted rock homes to the left and **Temmenı Hill** to the right, on its way up the hill toward Göreme and Nevşehir. Buying a souvenir cluster of fairy chimneys is made all too easy along Ahmet Refik Caddesi, but once you've cleared the souvenir shops, rural life takes over. Near the top of the hill is the **Turasan winery** and the neighborhood of **Esbelli,** where you will find two hotels mentioned below. To re-enter town by car, turn left onto **Istiklal Caddesi,** which leads back into the town center.

GETTING AROUND
Ürgüp is easily walkable, but if you're staying in the neighborhood of Esbelli, you may want to know that the hill up from the center of town is quite steep. During the summer months when the Municipality fills the streets with clouds of insect repellent to combat the irritating swarms of bees that hover over your breakfast, it's best to forgo the after-dinner stroll and take a taxi up to your hotel.

Several car-rental agencies offering low daily rates of around 61YTL ($45) per day are located in the center of town, including **Avis,** Istiklal Caddesi Belediye Pasaji 10 (© **0384/341-2177**), **Europcar,** Istiklal Cad. 10 (© **0384/341-8855**), and **Budget,** Kayseri Caddesi (© **0384/341-6541**). You may also save a few dollars by working with one of the neighboring locals. Scooters and beat-up old mountain bikes are also for rent in various shops along the market from around 47YTL and 20YTL ($35 and $15) per day, respectively (hourly and half-day rates also available).

WHAT TO SEE & DO
With an easy blend of tradition and convenience, Ürgüp makes the perfect base for day excursions to the open-air museums of Göreme and Zelve, the nearby valleys, and neighboring villages.

The village is also a peaceful retreat for some quiet time, where you can walk around the old deserted section of town or enjoy the view from the lookout point atop windy **Temmenı Hill,** known as The Hill of Wishes 30YKr (20¢). A mysterious tunnel (closed; don't bother with those pestering kids) almost .8km (½ mile) long leads from around the 13th-century Kebir Camii to the Selçuk tomb of Nükrettin at the top of the hill; to this day, no one knows who built it or why. The tomb was dedicated to the Selçuk leader Kılıçarslan IV, or the Sworded Lion, and a hilltop cafe allows you to relax and take it all in.

Ayvalı ✿ This is the quintessential Anatolian village, a place where life hasn't changed for centuries. A narrow ravine cuts through the bottom of the village with the trickley Içeridere River running the length of the valley all the way to Golgoli Hill, a 6.5km (4-mile) hike away. You can fill up a bottle of sparkling fresh spring water from a source on the edge of the village, while exploring eerie, untouched caves and rock-cut churches. There's a teahouse for refreshment, and if you look enough like you don't fit in, somebody in the village will feed you. But definitely try some of the fresh seasonal fruits that sell at the morning market, the only retail establishment in town (for now). Take the road for Mustafapaşa, then turn off on the road to Ayvalı.

Paşabağ Wherever you see tour buses or souvenir stands, there's bound to be something interesting. Paşabağ, also known as Valley of the Monks, is a forest of cone-shaped fairy chimneys more shocking and lifelike (not life-size) than most. Not surprisingly, it's a popular stop for photo ops.

Ürgüp

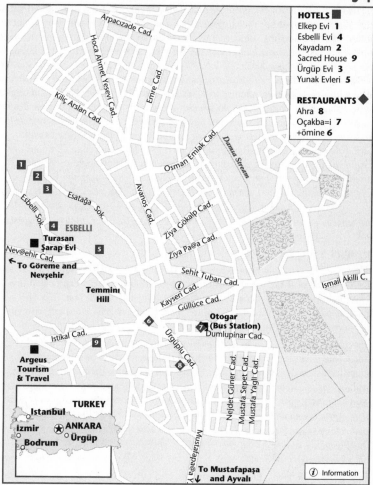

HOTELS ■
Elkep Evi **1**
Esbelli Evi **4**
Kayadam **2**
Sacred House **9**
Ürgüp Evi **3**
Yunak Evleri **5**

RESTAURANTS ◆
Ahra **8**
Oçakba=i **7**
+ömine **6**

Arpacızade Cad.

Hoca Ahmet Yesevi Cad.

Emre Cad.

Kılıç Arslan Cad.

Osman Emlak Cad.

Damsa Stream

1
2
3
Esatağa Sok.

Esbelli Sok.

4 ESBELLI
Turasan Şarap Evi
Nev@ehir Cad.
5

← **To Göreme and Nevşehir**

Temmını Hill

Avanos Cad.

Ziya Gökalp Cad.

Ziya Pa@a Cad.

Sehit Tuban Cad.

Kayseri Cad.

ⓘ

Güllüce Cad.

İsmail Akilli C.

6

Istikal Cad.

9

Ürgüplu Cad.

Otogar (Bus Station)
7 Dumlupinar Cad.

8

Argeus Tourism & Travel ■

Nejdet Güner Cad.
Mustafa Sepet Cad.
Mustafa Yağli Cad.

TURKEY
Istanbul
izmir ★ ANKARA
Bodrum ○ Ürgüp

Mustafapa@a Y.

↓ **To Mustafapaşa and Ayvalı**

ⓘ Information

The chimneys of Paşabağ harbor a number of chapels and dwellings used by Christian hermits, the most prominent of which is a tri-level chapel with depictions of the life of St. Simeon. St. Simeon the Stylite lived a life of hardship and denial in Antioch around the 4th century, high atop a 15m (50-ft.) pillar. Later hermits were inspired to do the same, initiating a "stylite" movement of isolated living.

On the road to Zelve Valley. Free with ticket to Zelve Open Air Museum.

Zelve Open Air Museum ⊛   Carved into a uniquely pink tufa, Zelve was once home to one of the largest communities in the region, inhabited by a Greek population until the 1922 population exchange, when Greeks and Turks were "repatriated" to their mother countries. When Muslims took over the valley, a mosque was hewn out of the rock, and stands near the entrance.

The first known inhabitants of the valley were monks, and although we can say for sure that they carved out the chapels, it's unclear who first began hollowing out the valley. The cave dwellings were used by local villagers up until 1952, when the structures were determined to be unsafe and the villagers were moved en masse over to nearby Aktepe, or New Zelve.

Now a national park, Zelve consists of three consecutive valleys whose walls are riddled with living quarters, blind tunnels, passageways, and traps for protection against attacks. Footholds chiseled into the smooth vertical tufa require an agility once aimed at keeping out unwanted visitors, but now present a fantastic challenge to modern-day rock climbers. Those interested in hiking should set aside plenty of time to explore the area, following a path over the mountain to Red Valley, about 4km (2½ miles) away. Exploring the caves can be exhilarating, challenging, and downright dangerous. Don't attempt anything fancy without a guide; Argeus (see "Exploring the Region" at the beginning of the chapter) offers excellent guided tours, but you can also arrange one through one of the many shops in town.

The road to Zelve Valley is accessible off the Göreme/Avanos or Ürgüp/Avanos road. ⓒ 0384/411-2525. Admission 5.50YTL ($4). Daily 8am–5:30pm.

WHERE TO STAY

There are few places on earth where you can get a good night's sleep in a cave, and Ürgüp is one of them. Besides primitive surroundings, you can expect traditionally Greek/Anatolian single-vaulted rooms with utilitarian niches cut into the rock. Because of the multilevel character of the rock, most hotels have terraces with fantastic views of the valley or of local village life.

Elkep Evi *(Finds)* Owned by an American couple from Miami, the Elkep Evi cave houses are built around a garden courtyard that enjoys views over Ürgüp. It's slightly more furnished than Kayadam, which gives it a warmer and cozier feel. An outdoor seating area is covered in kilims; rooms are simply decorated with carpets and carved wooden headboards. The hotel offers a full optional dinner based mainly on pottery-style *(güveç)* stews and vegetables for an additional 14YTL ($10) per person.

Eski Turban Oteli Arkası, 50400 Ürgüp. ⓒ 0384/341-6000. Fax 0384/341-8089. www.elkepevi.com. 14 units. 66€ ($80) double; 107€ ($130) suite. Free pickup from airport. MC, V. **Amenities:** Laundry service; dry cleaning. *In room:* Hair dryer.

Esbelli Evi *(Finds)* In keeping with the tradition of the original troglodyte home, the exterior of Esbelli Evi is unimpressive—but wait until you get inside. This is the Cappadocian inn that set the standard for all others, and it's mostly due to Süha, Esbelli's gracious owner, whose genuineness and discreet hospitality keep guests coming back again and again. Built in and around ancient cave dwellings, this hotel is a breathtaking maze of stone stairways, courtyards, and outdoor terraces. The result is an irresistible collection of rooms that, thanks to polished hardwood floors, ample modern bathrooms, and thick bright white duvets, manage all at once to be prehistoric, modern, and romantic. An unusual amenity is the communal clothes washer, a lifesaver for those with longer itineraries (and hanging out your laundry on a rock terrace will make you feel at one with the rhythm of local life).

Süha always manages to stay ahead of the pack, and has already begun renovations on a group of adjacent cave suites, each with its very own private garden, kitchen, and sitting room. They also will have Internet access, mountain bikes, and complimentary use of the swimming pool, sauna, and haman at the very nearby Club Ürgüp.

Esbelli Sok. 8, 50400 Ürgüp. ✆ **0384/341-3395**. Fax 0384/341-8848. www.esbelli.com.tr. 13 units. 70€ ($85) single; 90€ ($110) double. Inquire about rates of suites. MC, V. Closed in winter. **Amenities:** Laundry; dry cleaning; nonsmoking rooms. *In room:* Hair dryer.

Kayadam   Attilla, a geology teacher, and his wife, Rudy, a teacher of French literature and ancient languages, have created a group of comfortable pension-style cave rooms. It's less luxurious than the top-flight hotels like the Yunak Evleri, but you wouldn't know it by stepping into the bathroom, which is modern and pristine. The "tandır" room preserves the original kitchen hearth (be careful not to trip over it!), cleverly transformed into a night light. They also serve dinner on request (before noon, please!), for the reasonable price of 10€ ($12).

Esbelli Sok. 6, 50400 Ürgüp. ✆ **0384/341-6623**. Fax 0384/341-5982. www.kayadam.com. 5 units. 74€ ($90) double. V. **Amenities:** Laundry; dry cleaning; nonsmoking rooms. *In room:* Hair dryer.

Sacred House   One of the newer, upscale additions to Ürgüp's already overflowing hotel landscape is this superbly decorated and ridiculously romantic hideaway on one of the more residential back streets of town. Sacred House is the dream child of the owner of Prokopi Pub, whose passion for antiques led her to create her own storage facility. Rooms reflect a sort of medieval aristocracy in the richness of the textiles draped over heavy stone walls and invaluable antiques. Rimming an open central courtyard, each room has a slightly different theme; the cleverest (and perhaps creepiest) is the altar room, reflecting the fact that the building used to be a church. The well-appointed roof terrace offers views over town; the restaurant prepares traditional Turkish cuisine with an Armenian twist.

Karahandere Mahallesi, Barbaros Hayrettin, Sokak, No. 25, 50400 Ürgüp. ✆ **0384/341-7102**. www.sacred-house. com. 7 units. 99€–123€ ($120–$150) double. MC, V. **Amenities:** Restaurant; rooftop bar; free airport transfer from Kayseri Airport. *In room:* Jacuzzi.

Ürgüp Evi   Tucked into the village life of the neighborhood of Esbelli, this hotel is a superb alternative if Süha's place is booked up, which it is prone to be. Like many hotels in the area, the Ürgüp Evi has polished up a group of caves and magically converted them into a collection of charming guest rooms. Traditional Anatolian moldings and intricately carved alcoves were kept in the renovation of the caves, creating yet another spectacular opportunity to sleep in a modern prehistoric world. The newer section reflects the best of the lot; bathrooms are ones you'd be proud to have in your own home, with delicate little touches like herbal soap and potpourri at the ready. The owners of the Ürgüp Evi certainly make you feel at home, as they've put their kitchen and laundry facilities at the disposal of guests.

Esbelli Sok. 46, 50400 Ürgüp. ✆ **0384/341-3173**. Fax 0384/341-3173. www.urgupevi.com.tr. 19 units. 78€–172€ ($95–$210) double and suites. Free transfer from airport. MC, V. **Amenities:** Laundry; dry cleaning; nonsmoking rooms. *In room:* Hair dryer.

Yunak Evleri ✦✦ *Finds*   The Yunak Evleri feels like an old aristocratic country guesthouse. The 27 individually sited rooms, renovated from six cave houses and one mansion, are set into the base of a dramatic and soaring outcrop, much like an amphitheater. Aiming for the high end, the owner, ex–Istanbul native Yusuf Gorurgoz, outfitted his hotel with fine accessories, such as Vakko bed runners, antique furnishings, CD sound systems (deluxe and suites only), and locally made ceramics. He personally designed the bathrooms, installing Swedish multiple jet and steam showers to create a lavishness even the Four Seasons would be proud of. (The water pressure kicks butt as well!). All rooms enjoy either a private balcony or communal patio, and architectural niches in the main courts of the houses provide wonderful venues for barbecues or bonfires on crisp nights. Breakfast (included) and dinner (27YTL/$20 per person) are served on the panoramic terrace of a separate building.

Yunak Mahallesi, 50400 Ürgüp. (*) **0384/341-6920.** Fax 0384/341-6924. www.yunak.com. 17 units. 115€ ($140) double; 131€ ($160) deluxe; 164€ ($200) suite. Discounts for cash payment. MC, V. **Amenities:** Restaurant; laundry; dry cleaning; nonsmoking rooms. *In room:* Minibar, coffee/tea station, hair dryer, safe.

OUTSIDE OF ÜRGÜP

Gamirasu Hotel 🏛🏛 A few miles south of Ürgüp in the sleepy village of Ayvalı—where women still bake bread in outdoor ovens and residents still turn a blind eye to polygamy—a resident pioneer has built the handsome Gamirasu Hotel. Skeptics are advised to continue bravely past the chickens and over cow dung to the pot of gold at the end of the rainbow—or in this case, at the edge of this narrow, isolated valley.

Opened in 1999, Gamirasu is the project of one of the local villagers who through luck or fate obtained financial backing from some German investors. Undoubtedly this hotel will change the face of the village forever, but in the meantime, Ayvalı is still an untouched, unspoiled Cappadocian village with not so much as a *kebap* house or carpet shop in sight.

The hotel is built in and around the valley's caves, and enclosed within an unexpectedly elegant rose garden; if you walk along the creek a short way, you can bring back a pitcher of fresh bubbly mineral water. In keeping with the natural focus of the hotel, mattresses are handmade of 100% cotton and breakfast's bounty consists of locally dried apricots, pure village honey, and cream straight from the owner's cow. Guests can even participate in village activities like milking the cow or harvesting grapes with the residents. A local musician shows up regularly to serenade guests over dinner, and transportation to local sites is provided on request.

Ayvalı. (*) **0384/341-5825.** Fax 0384/341-7487. www.gamirasu.com. 15 units. 58€–74€ ($70–$90) double; 148€–451€ ($180–$550) suite, July 1-Aug 31 and Nov 16–Mar 15. Rates higher Mar–June and Sept–Nov 15. Rates include breakfast. AE, DC, MC, V. **Amenities:** Tour desk; car-rental desk; laundry service; dry cleaning. *In room:* Hair dryer.

WHERE TO DINE

Ahra MANTI/LOCAL HOME COOKING Whenever I'm in the region, my first thought goes to mantı—tiny delectable dumplings topped with a buttery garlic yogurt sauce. So it was no stretch that I'd wind up at Ahra soon after they opened. I wasn't disappointed. There are a number of other notable local dishes on the menu as well; I'd suggest the yağlama (lamb "pizza" drizzled in yogurt) and perhaps a plate of the house köfte. The setting gets an "A" too: a homey collection of dining rooms graced with stained-glass windows, carved fireplaces, and area artifacts.

Fabrika Cad. 66 (steps from Istiklal Cad). (*) **0384/341-3454.** Appetizers 2.75YTL–5.50YTL ($2–$4); main courses 5.50YTL–8.75YTL ($4–$6.50) MC, V. Summer daily 10am–11pm; winter daily 11am–9:30pm.

Oçakbaşı 🏛 *Value* BARBECUE/SOUTHERN SPECIALTIES Most people would turn their noses up at the thought of eating a meal in the bus station, but the only upturned noses here will be the ones sniffing out the freshly grilled food on the way up the steps to the restaurant's lovely rooftop terrace. Inside and in typical style, a "barbecue bar" circles the hooded area around the charcoal grill, or you can choose to sit farther away from the hot coals at one of the well-dressed tables in the dining room. Whole eggplants get roasted over the flames then miraculously whipped up into a delectable regional specialty, the *alinazık kebap*, which is topped by chunks of flavorful grilled meat. Don't pass up the hot appetizer, *içli köfte*, mouthwatering hush-puppy–like corn balls stuffed with meat and deep fried.

In the Ürgüp *otogar*. ✆ 0384/341-3277. Main courses 5.50YTL–12YTL ($4–$9). MC, V. Daily noon–midnight.

Şömine Café and Restaurant ★ *Value* REGIONAL TURKISH   In spite of its obvious location, this is indeed the best restaurant in Ürgüp. The marble-paved rooftop terrace overlooks Istiklal Caddesi, while on chillier evenings, you may opt for a spot inside by the cozy, fire-lit open chimney for which the restaurant is named.

The house favorite is the *testi kebap*, a lamb-and-vegetable stew cooked in a type of tandoori oven with peppers and onions. If you're leaning toward ordering this, call ahead and reserve a platter or they may be sold out by the time you get there. Another specialty is the *saç tava*, a delectable mixture of eggplant and bite-size chunks of beef prepared in an earthenware dish (ask the chef to sprinkle a layer of cheese over the top).

Ürgüp town center. ✆ 0384/341-8442. Reservations suggested during high season. Main courses 4YTL–11YTL ($3–$8). MC, V. Daily 9:30am–midnight.

IN AYVALI

Aravan *Moments* TURKISH TANDIR   In light of the success of Hotel Gamirasu, it was only a matter of time before others in the village sought to capitalize on the arrival of tourists. Aravan had a leg up, though—the owner is a cousin of Ibrahim's (of Gamirasu). Nepotism aside (what do you expect in a village of this size, anyway?), the concept is really appealing, and the atmosphere—the terrace of a renovated village home in summer and two cozy and carpeted Oriental-style dining rooms in crisper weather—is delightful. The concept of Aravan (the ancient Hittite name for the village) revolves around the *tandır*, a small cooking pit and the traditional mode of food preparation for Turks for hundreds, if not thousands, of years. The four-course meal consists of home-style recipes all prepared in the pit, from the bulgur "wedding soup," to the *kuru fasulye* (white beans in a tomato sauce), to the *güveç* (here, a succulent lamb stew). Salad and stuffed grape leaves accompany the meal, which is followed by a dessert of either fresh village apricots or local *helva*.

Ayvalı Village. ✆ 0384/354-5838. Reservations required at least 5 hr. in advance. 4-course meal 14YTL ($10). MC, V. Daily noon–11pm.

IN MUSTAFAPAŞA

Old Greek House *Value* REGIONAL TURKISH   This old Greek house in the ancient town of Sinassos (now Mustafapaşa), said to be the former mayor's mansion, is now a restaurant and pension. The owner's wife prepares delicious traditional dishes in the large kitchen off the side of the house; the traditional cave oven she uses for baking is visible from the inner courtyard. The five-course menu is essentially the same every day, and includes stuffed eggplant with lamb, *mantı* (meat dumplings topped with sauce), white beans cooked in a tandoori oven (with or without meat), *köfte* (meatballs), and potatoes. The house retains many of its original features, and guests dine either in the main courtyard, or in one of the two upper story rooms, where some impressive frescoes are still partially visible. Much of the wood paneling is original.

Mustafapaşa. ✆ 0384/353-5345. Reservations required for dinner. Full meal 18YTL ($13). MC, V. Daily noon–midnight.

ÜRGÜP AFTER DARK

Katpatuka Café & Bistro   The name means "land of beautiful horses" in Persian; just try saying it 10 times fast after a few drinks at the bar. This open-air restaurant and cafe has good food, great ambience, and appealing circular banquettes for those wishing to just relax and munch on pistachio nuts. There's also sporadic live music, which usually gets up and running after 10pm. Cumhuriyet Meydanı 4-5, Ürgüp. ⒸⒸ 0384/ 341-3002.

Prokopı Pub Bar   Opened by two city dwellers disillusioned with the rat race, Prokopı has fast become the hub of Ürgüp nightlife. The bar, which occupies the central court of a former *han* (caravansary), is unexpectedly chic, but what do you expect from an artist and a former PR executive from Istanbul? High-backed wooden stools line the island bar, but the tables for two stashed in the candlelit cave section at the back are especially romantic. There's also a breezy upper terrace, and pretty soon the cozy upstairs workshops will open as a restaurant. Summer daily 11am to 5am; winter daily 5:30pm to 3am. Cumhuriyet Meydanı 26, Ürgüp. ⒸⒸ 0384/341-4942.

Turasan Şarap Evi   This wine-production center is responsible for at least half of all the wine produced in Turkey. The Turasan has a wine cellar for free tastings of their Cappadocia reds, whites, and rosés, with other local fruits and nuts packaged up for sale, making use of all those apricots that grow naturally near grape vines. Bottles of wine cost between 2.75YTL and 20YTL ($2 and $15). May through October daily 8am to 8pm; November through April daily 8am to 6pm. On the Nevşehir road in the Esbelli section. ⒸⒸ 0384/341-4961.

3 Göreme ⒶⒶ

15km (9 miles) east of Nevşehir; 6.5km (4 miles) west of Ürgüp

With so many other charming and more characteristic villages in Cappadocia, it's a wonder that Göreme's popularity never wanes. Its name recognition is high among backpackers, particularly Australians. In the past 20 years or so, this state of affairs has led to a profusion of charmless, 7YTL ($5)-a-night dormitory-style pensions and fly-by-night bars catering to a co-ed crowd.

As occupancy in the region in general increases, young ambitious entrepreneurs are stepping up to the plate with better-endowed pensions and outright luxury hotels. For the most part, however, the magic of the horizon is marred by the presence of modern, albeit low-rise, concrete slabs.

Ultimately, I don't usually recommend Göreme as a base, but with the prices of rooms skyrocketing in places like Ürgüp and even Üçhisar, Göreme is increasingly making sense. Staying here does have its advantages. The main appeal of Göreme, besides the Open Air Museum located on its fringes, is the village's proximity to some of the most scenic valley walks. Inconspicuous early churches dot the landscape between the town and the Open Air Museum, popping up unexpectedly at the edge of a lonely corner of a valley. In Göreme itself, one of the few villages in which the rock homes and fairy chimneys have been continually inhabited, the attractions share the spotlight with the daily lives of the locals.

Gentrification has yet to push out its natives and, with it, the authenticity of the village. In Göreme it's still common to run into a donkey delivery, or stumble upon a devout gaggle of chatty women and chickens, while staying fairly accessible to food, transportation, and Internet cafes.

ESSENTIALS
GETTING THERE

Most bus companies serving Göreme stop a few blocks from the center and provide the quick minibus transfer to the *otogar,* only 2 blocks away. If you planned on taking a taxi from the *otogar* to your hotel, you may as well grab one now. An area *dolmuş* follows a circuit hourly from Ürgüp bus station to Zelve, Avanos, Göreme, Üçhisar, and back. If you're traveling by car out of Ürgüp, you can take either the road to Avanos, turn onto the road past Zelve, and take the northern approach into Göreme; or head out of town on the Nevşehir road and take the steep cobblestone road through the Göreme Open Air Museum on your way into Göreme. The difference in mileage between the two approaches is negligible. So if your purpose is to see the town and museum, then by all means, take one road in and the other out.

VISITOR INFORMATION

The **Tourist Information office** is located at the *otogar* (Terminal Içi No. 1; (℗ **0384/ 271-2124**) and mainly caters to visitors looking for accommodations. Inside is a collection of signboards of many of the pensions in town. Rates are fixed at 2.50€ to 4€ ($3 to $5) for a bed and 8.25€ to 12€ ($10 to $15) for a room. The office is open Monday through Friday from 8:30am to 7pm, but many of the pensions have signs posted outside as well. Be on the lookout for misunderstandings relating to the cost of extras; sometimes there's a big surprise when the bill arrives. Pop into one of the several travel agencies at the *otogar* for a map of the area.

ORIENTATION

If you blink your eyes, you're bound to miss it. The road from the **Open Air Museum** leads right to the center of town over a dry creek bed; turn left onto **Uzundere Caddesi** until you get to the *otogar*. Everything you need is located here or just behind the station, including tour operators, car and scooter rentals, taxis, and the Tourist Information office. The **bazaar** is located behind the *otogar* around the mosque and Roman tower.

Adnan Menderes Caddesi forks off from Uzundere Caddesi closer to the turnoff from the museum; Kapadokya Balloons is on the right and the Orient Restaurant is on the left.

GETTING AROUND

Göreme is eminently walkable, especially because much of the center of town is flat. To venture a little farther out, hook up with one of the scooter-rental shops at or around the *otogar*. They charge around 8YTL ($6) for 2 hours for a small, modestly powered Honda.

WHAT TO SEE & DO

Göreme Open Air Museum ✮✮✮   Cappadocia's main attraction and the customary starting point for an overview of what the region has to offer, the Göreme Open Air Museum is a monastic complex composed of churches, rectories, and dwellings, and one of the earliest centers for religious education.

The practice of monasticism was developed by St. Basil the Great, bishop of Caesarea (Kayseri) in the 4th century, as a reaction to his increased disillusionment with the materialism of the Church. St. Basil's definition of monastic life, based on the idea that men should live in small, self-sufficient units with an emphasis on poverty, obedience, labor, and religious devotion, took root in Cappadocia, later becoming the basis for the Orthodox monastic system.

St. Basil, his brother St. Gregory of Nyssa, and St. Gregory of Nazianzoz (St. Gregorios the Theologian), greatly influenced the course of religious thought through their writings, contributing to the development of Eastern Orthodoxy. In his extensive writings St. Basil describes the nature of the Holy Spirit as a trilogy, while St. Gregory of Nyssa wrote of the dogma of the Virgin Mary, and St. Gregory of Nazianzoz developed the thesis on Jesus as a representative of the indivisible nature of the human and divine. Because of their contributions, Cappadocia became known as "the land of the three saints," but was soon divided in two in A.D. 371 when Emperor Valens rejected Basil's thesis on Jesus as the son of God.

There are at least 10 churches and chapels in the museum area dating between A.D. 900 and 1200, each one named (after a prominent attribute) by the local villagers who were exploring these caves long before there was an entrance fee. The paintings and decoration represent a flowering of a uniquely Cappadocian artistic style, while the Byzantine architectural features of the churches, like arches, columns, and capitals, are interesting in that not one of them is necessary structurally.

The best way to approach the site is to begin in a counterclockwise direction toward a clearly marked path.

During the Iconoclastic period, many of the frescoes and paintings were damaged, while the eyes of the images were scratched out by the local Turkish population superstitious of the "evil eye."

Past a small rock tower or **Monks' Convent** ✿ is the **Church of St. Basil** ✿, whose entrance is hollowed out with niches for small graves. This is a common feature of Cappadocian churches and it's still not uncommon to reach down and come up with a knuckle bone every now and again in the more remote valleys. Another recurring theme in Cappadocian churches is the image of St. George slaying the dragon. St. George was considered a local hero, as local lore equated the dragon with a monster on the summit of Mount Erciyes. The church is decorated with scenes of Christ, with St. Basil and St. Theodore depicted on the north wall.

The **Church with the Apple (Elmalı Kilise)** ✿✿✿ is one of the smaller churches in the area, carved in the sign of a Greek cross with four irregular pillars supporting a central dome. The church was restored in 1991; however, the frescoes continue to chip off, revealing a layer of earlier paintings underneath. Paintings depict scenes of the saints, bishops, and martyrs, and to the right of the altar, a Last Supper with the symbolic fish (the letters of the word fish in Greek stand for "Jesus Christ, Son of God, the Savior"). The name of the church is believed to refer to a reddish orb in the left hand of the Archangel Michael in the dome of the main apse, although there's also speculation that there used to be an apple tree at the entrance to the church.

Santa Barbara was an Egyptian saint imprisoned by her father to protect her from the influences of Christianity. When she nevertheless found a way to practice her faith, her father tortured and killed her. The **Church of Santa Barbara** ✿✿✿, probably built as a tribute, is a cross-domed church with three apses, with mostly crudely painted geometrical patterns in red ocher believed to be symbolic in nature. The wall with the large locust probably represents evil, warded off by the protection of two adjacent crosses. The repetitive line of bricks above the rooster in the upper right-hand corner, symbolically warding off the evil influences of the devil, represents the Church.

The **Snake Church** ✿ is a simple barrel-vaulted church with a low ceiling and long nave. One fresco represents Saints Theodore and George slaying the dragon (looking suspiciously like a snake), with Emperor Constantine the Great and his mother Helena depicted holding the "True Cross." Legend has it that she discovered the cross upon which Jesus was crucified after seeing it in a dream, and that a piece of the cross is still buried in the foundations of the Ayasofya in Istanbul. Other sections of the cross are in the Church of the Holy Sepulchre and in St. Peter's in Rome. Another interesting portrait is the one of St. Onuphrius on the upper wall to the right of the entrance. The saint, a popular subject in medieval art, lived the life of a hermit in the Egyptian desert near Thebes and is usually depicted with a long gray beard and a fig leaf over his privates.

Until the 1950s the **Dark Church (Karanlık Kilise)** ✿✿✿ was used as a pigeon house. After 14 years of scraping pigeon droppings off the walls, these newly restored frescoes, depicting scenes from the New Testament, are the best preserved in all of Cappadocia and a fine example of 11th-century Byzantine art. Because light is allowed in through only one small opening, the richness of the pigments has survived the test of time. At the time of this writing, the additional 5.50YTL ($4) admission fee for entry into the church had been suspended.

Cut into the same rock as the Dark Church and accessible via a metal walkway, the **Church with Sandals (Çarıklı Kilise)** ✿✿ takes its name from the two imprints on the floor inside the entrance. In the land of truth-stretching, these footprints have been given some weighty religious significance, but the fact is, they're just footprints and all of those stories are just more creative embellishment. The church is carved into a simple cross plan with intersecting barrel vaults. The frescoes, which date to the 11th century, depict the Nativity, the Baptism, the Adoration of the Magi, and other New Testament themes.

The last thing to see before exiting the museum is the **Nunnery** or **Girls' Tower (Kızlar Kalesi)** ✿✿, a six-story convent cut into the rock with a system of tunnels, stairways, and corridors. The convent housed up to 300 nuns, whose proximity spawned rumors of a tunnel connecting the tower and the Monks' Convent to the right of the museum entrance.

About 5m (17 ft.) outside the exit to the museum site on the right is **The Buckle Church (Tokalı Kilise)** ✿✿✿, the largest rock-cut church and the one with the most sensational collection of frescoes in all of Cappadocia. Of all of the narrations of scenes from the Bible in the region, these are painted with the most detail and use the richest colors.

The Buckle Church is a complex formed of four chambers: the Old Church, the New Church, the Paracclesion, and the Lower Church. The **Old Church** dates to the 10th century, with pale hues of red and green painted in strips to represent scenes from the New Testament. Panels of rich indigo painted with pigments from the lapis stone dominate the **New Church,** carved out of the eastern wall of the Old Church and decorated with Eastern-style arches and a series of arcades. The **Paracclesion** is a chapel with a single apse, and the **Lower Church** has three aisles and a burial space or *krypto*.

The high plateau behind **Tokalı Church** brings you to Kılıçlar Valley, named "Valley of the Swords" for the jagged formations that seem to slice into the sky. This is a favorite spot for hikers because of its high cliffs, deep ravines, and vineyards, in addition to a tunnel that forms part of an old drainage system. The cliff walls are dotted with dovecotes or pigeon houses hollowed out of the rock to harvest valuable fertilizer—pigeon droppings are rich in nitrogen—by area farmers. There are several old churches in this valley, but they are closed to the public. The best way to get to the valley is to enter along an access road from the road between the Göreme Museum and the town.

Outside of Göreme Center on the road to Üçhisar. ✆ **0384/271-2167**. Admission 12YTL ($9). Daily 8am–5:30pm.

WHERE TO STAY

Göreme seems to have reached a saturation point of cheap accommodations, so if it's a bed in a squat chimney you're looking for, you've come to the right place. Head over from the bus station to the tourist office, where a cooperative formed by the local pension owners has organized its own little bulletin board. Rates are fixed and hover around 5€ ($6) for a bed in a dormitory-style room to 8.25€ to 12€ ($10 to $15) for a room in a fairy chimney with a private shower and toilet. If you're looking for something a bit more comfortable, try the **Kelebek Hotel Pansiyon** (*(*C* 0384/271-2531; www.kelebekhotel.com), formerly known as the Anatolian Cave Houses. The "regular rooms" are spare and simple, some occupying caves, and cost from 30€ to 50€ ($37–$61). The Kelebek's boutique hotel is an all-cave suites annex, taking up the spacious interiors of a number of fairy chimneys. Suites are decked out in Ottoman style and sport Jacuzzis in the bathrooms. Prices range from 85€ to 95€ ($104–$116).

Cappadocia Cave Suites   Build it, and they will come. That at least was the thought that went into the outfitting of these caves and fairy chimneys. The hotel sits on a bluff overlooking the lackluster view that is Göreme, an unfortunate downside to this otherwise handsome and well-landscaped hotel. All rooms aim for the top end and come complete with Swedish showers and kitchens (jerry-rigged into an available niche in the smaller rooms, but graciously open in the larger rooms and suites); fireplaces; and espresso machines. Antique and costly accessories like Anatolian robes, Ottoman helmets, and silk brocade table runners keep it simple yet rich, as do other decorative touches like copper radiators, carved stone beds, and the odd fireplace. Some of the rooms benefit from a terrace or balcony, and the suite even comes with a baby's cave complete with antique crib.

Gafferli Mah. Ünlü Sok. 19 (above the Anatolian Carpet Center) 50180 Göreme. (*C* 0384/271-2800. Fax 0384/271-2799. www.cappadociacavesuites.com. 18 units. 148€ ($180) double; 246€ $300 suite. Rates include breakfast and dinner. AE, DC, MC, V. **Amenities:** 24-hr. room service; laundry service; dry cleaning. *In room:* Kitchenette, fridge, coffeemaker, hair dryer.

Göreme House *(F*   This humble little guesthouse was converted from a century-old stately Paşa's mansion. A few of the rooms are cut into the rock, but the majority are the characteristic single-vaulted rooms unadorned except for a kilim and simple handcrafted Turkish linens. Two suites are perked up with the addition of en-suite Jacuzzis.

The hotel is hidden up a side street behind the shopping area and mosque, and when nobody's looking, the stone courtyard entryway seems to attract local children for the relief afforded by the house hose. Two upper terraces, one a glass-enclosed bar and TV room and the other a spectacular open balcony, offer panoramic views of the neighboring fairy chimneys and rock-cut houses, and as in many a family-run establishment, you wind up spending more time with the staff than out exploring.

Eselli Mahallesi 47, 50180 Göreme. (*C* 0384/271-2060. Fax 0384/271-2669. www.goremehouse.com. 12 units. 35€–45€ ($43–$55) double; 60€–70€ ($73–$86) suite. MC, V. **Amenities:** Restaurant; bar; laundry service; dry cleaning.

WHERE TO DINE

Alaturca TURKISH   This relatively new addition to the neighborhood infuses Göreme with a new level of style. Yet, while the atmosphere is outstanding (including the beanbag chairs on the outside lawn for partaking of tea and so forth), the food is fairly ordinary. Maybe it's best not to order the fish (duh). The restaurant, bar, and cafe serve breakfast, snacks, and meals throughout the day.

Göreme center. © 0384/271-2176. Appetizers and main courses 6.75YTL–14YTL ($5–$10). No credit cards. Daily 7am until the last person leaves.

Orient Restaurant *Kids* TURKISH The most solidly consistent restaurant in Göreme, the Orient has already succeeded in establishing itself as the town's contender. Highlights of the menu include a steak rivaling anything I've had anywhere, and an outstanding lamb rack. Orient also has an outstanding wine list that includes French imports and the best local wines (try the Okuzgozu or the Kalecik Karası). Its location at the farthest reaches of town on a decent-size plot of land could easily give you the impression of being in a country inn, but it's not so far to act as a deterrent if what you're looking for is just a quick bite to eat. There are both an outdoor patio terrace and a light and airy dining room where you can grab one of the many low-to-the-ground tables with reclining back chairs.

Göreme Center (across from Kapadokya Balloons). © 0384/271-2346. www.Orientrestaurant.net. Appetizers 4YTL–8YTL ($3–$6); main courses 6.75YTL–16YTL ($5–$12). MC, V. Daily 7am until the last person leaves.

4 Üçhisar ✶✶✶

9km (5½ miles) east of Nevşehir; 6km (3¾ miles) southwest of Göreme

The sleepy troglodyte village of Üçhisar, spread out at the base of the fortress, is a place where time altogether stands still. In the valley surrounding Üçhisar, the advancement of rock formation and erosion can be seen in all of its stages. Cresting above the valley are rocky channels that look more like pink-and-yellow sand dunes, while down below, perforating the rock face of Güvercinlik Vadisi, or Pigeon Valley, are the best examples of pigeon houses, painted white to attract the birds and their valuable droppings. The fortress of Üçhisar is the highest peak in the region, drawing tourists to its summit for panoramic views of this fascinating landscape with Mount Erciyes in the distance.

Incredibly, the tourist masses have overlooked the quiet landscape of Üçhisar, lacking the name recognition of Göreme or the advanced facilities of Ürgüp. But as the former continues to attract the backpacking set and the latter renovates itself beyond recognition, tourists looking elsewhere for the elusive and authentic Cappadocian experience may descend here in the near future.

ESSENTIALS
GETTING THERE & GETTING AROUND Regular municipal buses run from Nevşehir to Üçhisar, but the village is close enough to Nevşehir that you could take a cab without breaking the bank. If you're coming from Göreme, you can get on one of the frequent buses running to Nevşehir. Because of its quiet, isolated nature, Üçhisar is more for the independent traveler; staying here is going to require your own wheels.

ORIENTATION The village of Üçhisar is centered around the **fortress,** surrounded by a hillside of oddly shaped house-caves and neatly carved facades. Around Üçhisar is the spectacular scenery of Güvercinlik Valley, dotted with dovecotes and rolling rock dunes. A tea garden and outdoor restaurant occupy the center of town.

WHAT TO SEE & DO
Üçhisar has attracted its fair share of French, drawn by the possibility of utter seclusion in one of the exclusive cave houses of Les Maisons de Cappadoce (p. 338). Life's

frenetic pace is all but forgotten in Üçhisar, where tourists rarely venture farther than the towering rock fortress.

Üçhisar Castle   The highest peak in the region and the most prominent land formation, the Üçhisar Castle is a larger-than-life sculpture. A climb up the 120 steps to the summit of the fortress is a logical introduction to the rocky scapes of Cappadocia. In the 15th and 16th centuries, the Byzantine army took advantage of the natural elevation of three of the area's rock formations and used them as natural fortresses. Üçhisar, together with Ortahisar and a rock castle at Ürgüp (now in ruins), provided the means for an early-warning system using mirrors and lights, sending messages among the fortresses and as far afield as Istanbul. Today the outer layers of Üçhisar's rock have been washed away by erosion to reveal a honeycombed structure of tunnels and cavities, rising above the man-made facades of the modern semi-troglodyte village. Recently discovered was a secret tunnel leading to the riverbed, which provided an emergency water supply in the event of an attack.

Üçhisar. ⓒ 0384/219-2618. Admission 2.75YTL ($2). Daily 8am–sunset.

WHERE TO STAY

Les Maisons de Cappadoce 🏵   Renovated by Jacques Avizou, an expatriate French architect, these romantic cave houses look as if they stepped right out of a feature in *Maison et Jardin*. The houses are located right in the middle of a forest of fairy chimneys in the heart of the village, providing a rare opportunity for total immersion into the landscape. Closed gates and unremarkable doorways open to reveal duplex and triplex houses with breathtaking arches, stone terraces, garden courtyards, and huge fully equipped kitchens (except in the studios, which have kitchenettes). A welcome basket full of basic provisions (bread, butter, sugar, salt, eggs, and water) will be delivered on request for an additional fee. Residents are requested to provide access to the gardener or camera crews, who every now and again choose Les Maisons de Cappadoce as a location for a movie or magazine spread. The only problem with this Garden of Eden is that once you've arrived, you never want to leave. The magic of the spot is all the more evident at sunset, when the sky and chimneys turn glorious shades of red and purple.

Semiramis Aş, Belediye Meydanı 24, 50240 Üçhisar. ⓒ 0384/219-2813. Fax 0384/219-2782. www.cappadoce.com. 2 studios, 8 houses for 4–7 people. 90€–123€ ($110–$150) studio; 131€–263€ ($160–$320) house. Optional breakfast 4€ $5 per person. Flexible 4-night minimum. No credit cards. **Amenities:** Laundry service; dry cleaning. *In room:* Kitchen, fridge, coffeemaker, hair dryer.

Les Terrasses D'Üçhisar *(value)*   For those on a budget, this is the best option in town. The hotel consists of eight cave rooms, seven Anatolian-style rooms with single barrel vaults, and one family suite in a group of adjacent stone houses. The setup is typical of the area pensions—accommodations are clean, with floors of stone and tile, and ad-hoc bathroom/shower combos that you eventually do get used to. To sweeten the deal, Les Terrasses includes breakfast and walks in the valley (and maybe a stop at their friend's place?) with the room rate.

Eski Göreme Yolu, 50240 Üçhisar. ⓒ 0384/219-2792. Fax 0384/219-2762. www.terrassespension.com. 16 units. 32€ ($39) double; 70€ ($86) family suite. MC, V. **Amenities:** Restaurant; bar; tour desk; laundry service; dry cleaning.

WHERE TO DINE

Üçhisar still has a long way to go to catch up to Ürgüp or Göreme in the dining area, but remember—that's a *good* thing. As soon as commercialism rears its ugly head in

---

---

town, it'll be time to move on to another undiscovered corner of Cappadocia. Every little town has its own epicenter, and here it's the **Center Café and Restaurant,** Belediye Meydanı (© **0384/219-3117**), a leafy terrace tea garden serving standard dishes.

Elai *&* EUROPEAN/REGIONAL TURKISH   With new hotels sprouting up every day someplace in Cappadocia, it's no wonder that restaurants are beginning to follow suit. Elai, named for Kubilay, the owner, is a dressy alternative to the standard eateries that litter the town centers. Housed in the former local social club (think men, tea, and *tavla,* or backgammon), the interior has been spiffed up to make the most of a soaring space of sandstone and wood beams. Under the supervision of Kubilay's mother, the kitchen prepares a combination of European and regional Turkish cuisine, offering guests a diverse menu that includes rack of lamb, duck à l'orange, and *dolmalar* (stuffed grape leaves, stuffed peppers, and so forth). Standouts during my meal were the moussaka and the *mercemek köftesi,* mom's southeastern recipe of spicy lentil balls. Dinner or a sunset drink can also be taken on the terrace overlooking the valley and Üçhisar Castle in the distance.

Eski Greme Cad. 61. © 0384/219-3181. Reservations suggested. Main courses 15YTL–20YTL ($11–$15). MC, V. Daily 11am–11pm.

A SIDE TRIP TO AVANOS

With a tradition of pottery making that dates back to Hittite times, Avanos has made its name out of red clay. At one time, the craft so permeated the culture of the city that every household had a pottery wheel or workshop. Now the most prominent feature of the town, besides the unsightly terra-cotta sculpture in the town center, is the word "chez," as something about this particular corner of Cappadocia acts as a magnet for French nationals. As a base for explorations in Cappadocia, I couldn't recommend Avanos less. For 2 hours of poking in and out of ceramic shops, I have only slightly better things to say, if only regarding the region's distinctive terra-cotta pottery and the admittedly spectacular ceramic designs.

The city, carved into the rock like so many other ancient Cappadocian towns, sits along the banks of the Kızılırmak (Red River), the longest river in Turkey. The river takes its name from the color of the water, stained by the red clay particular to the region, an abundant source of the raw material necessary in pottery production. Currently there are about 30 pottery shops in town, most of them boasting the same techniques used by the Hittites. But although Avanos has its own homegrown brand of terra-cotta urns, a vast

The Caravansaries of the Silk Road

One of the five pillars of Islam is the Koranic obligation of alms-giving, and in the fulfillment of this obligation, the Selçuks were notorious for their commitment to public works. One of the institutions created by the Selçuks in Anatolia was the *kervansaray* or "caravan palace." Used as military bases during wartime and as inns in peacetime, these fortresses provided protection to merchants traveling along the trade routes, offering them up to 3 days of free lodging and an unprecedented system of insurance in the event of loss or injury. Caravansaries were spaced out along the trade routes at a distance of about every 49km (30 miles)—1 day's travel—and from sunset to sunrise when the main gate was closed, guests were officially under the protection of the sultan.

With control over the land trade routes and the centralization of power, Anatolia became the center of international trade under the Selçuk Empire. Thus the "Silk Road" became a great source of wealth, as taxes on overland goods continued to fill the coffers of the sultan. Spices, ivory, and fine cloth were brought from the Far East, while surprisingly, much of the trade was in slaves. The Ottoman *devşirme* system was to collect men from the Eastern lands, train them in the art of warfare, and sell them off to neighboring southern states.

Rarely did anyone travel the entire length of the route. Caravansaries also operated as marketplaces, where merchants could unload their goods, have a bath, and move on. It was unusual for anyone to stay beyond the 3-day limit, because a person's selling power was linked to the availability of new clientele, and that fizzled out after the first day. A typical journey lasted about a month before a merchant headed back home; by the time a shipment of silk brocade found its way to Istanbul, the price had been considerably marked up.

The caravansary was built according to one of three basic plans: an open courtyard, a covered building, or a combination of the two. The most opulent of the caravansaries were those reflecting the prosperity of the sultan. Called "sultanhans," these caravansaries were built on an essentially identical plan. The main portal opened onto a courtyard with a small raised mosque at the center. To the left was an arcade providing much-needed shade for protection against the scorching summer sun. On the right was a second portal leading into the apartments, which included a kitchen and *hamam*. At the back was an ornamental gate for access into the winter hall, a covered structure that shows a striking resemblance to a medieval church. The vaults in the main nave could be up to 14m (45 ft.) high, while the top of the lantern, a central domed space providing the only light in the hall, could be at a height of up to 20m (65 ft.). The walls were thick enough to provide good insulation, and tiny windows in the lantern kept out the cold. Men and camels sometimes slept in the winter section together, which combined with the smell of spices and smoke from the oil lamps and water pipes, probably required the use of a *whole* lot of incense.

While the exterior of the fortress structure was plain, the Selçuks had a tradition of richly ornamenting the *pishtaq* or portal. The pishtaq, generally limestone or marble, displayed elaborate geometrical carvings, tracery, rosettes, and inscriptions, and was hollowed out into a stalactite niche much like that of a *mihrab* (a niche that indicates the direction of Mecca).

There were also private caravansaries called *hans,* mostly located in towns that charged a fee for lodging, while the *bedesten* was typically a market-place and workshop only. These sensational structures dot the Anatolian landscape from Istanbul to Antalya and from Erzurum to İzmir, and are used as hotels, restaurants, or the dreaded discotheque; you'll probably have the opportunity to stay in one in the course of your travels.

The best conserved of all the Selçuk *hans* is the **Sultanhanı** located about 32km (20 miles) outside of Aksaray on the road to Konya. The Sultanhanı, built by Alaaeddin Keykubat I in 1229, has a highly ornamented *pishtaq* (a wide portal topped by a decorative niche) with a variety of decorative pat-terns applied in an unrelated, almost spontaneous manner.

Another fine example of a *sultanhan* is the **Ağzıkarahan,** located 15km (9 miles) outside of Aksaray on the road to Nevşehir. The Ağzıkarahan, the third largest in the area along the Silk Road, has weathered time to remain almost intact and encloses a space of over 6,000 sq. m (20,000 sq. ft.). The open section, now used to display carpets, was built by Alaaeddin Keykubat in 1231, and includes the central mosque reachable by steep and cumber-some steps. The winter section is attributed to Sultan Giyaseddin Keyhüsrev and was completed 8 years after the open section. Enormous stone vaults rise above the main aisle of the nave, flanked by raised platforms that were used for meals during the day and as sleep space at night. The camels were kept behind the raised area in the side bays. Unfortunately, the central dome has been lost.

Halfway between Aksaray and Nevşehir is the **Alay Han,** the first *sultan-han* to be built in Central Anatolia. Erected in 1192 by Sultan Kılıçarslan II, the Alay Han is threatened to become another "day facility" by the same investor who "preserved" the **Sarıhan** in Avanos. The Sarıhan, located 5km (3 miles) outside of Avanos, whose name means "yellow *han*" for the color of its stone, stands on an old trade route between Aksaray and Kayseri. Except for the mosque, which has been placed above the entrance, the car-avansary follows a traditional sultanhan plan, with massive barrel vaults supporting the arcades and side aisles of the winter hall. It now serves as a daytime cafe and an evocative setting for a nightly staging of the *sema,* or rite of the **Whirling Dervishes,** which takes place in the winter hall or sleep-ing quarters. (Sarıhan is 5km/3 miles outside of Avanos center, on the road to Kaysari; ✆ **0384/511-3795;** reservations required; admission 34YTL ($25); Apr–Oct nightly at 9pm—show starts promptly, so get there early, because there's no consideration for latecomers.)

majority of the classic İznik and Kütahya designs are mass-produced using clay from Kütahya (see "A Pilgrimage & Some Plates: İznik," under "Bursa," in chapter 5) and marketed as valuable high-quality "İznik reproductions." Sure, it's fascinating and fun to participate in a dirty demo on the kick-wheel, but it's all part of the sales pitch, as are the endless fabrications about quality—seems the art of Turkish salesmanship extends beyond the fringes of carpeting to the delicate surfaces of these ceramics. Worse, I have yet to successfully hand-carry a sample home, as many of the less expensive plates are much cheaper than the price might indicate. Charge it, and pay the bill only after the piece arrives safely on your doorstep.

What is a fair price for this pottery? At face value, many of the ceramic samples are exquisite . . . perhaps a few were even hand-painted (tiles are stamped; bowls and such are usually colored in various workshops paying their artists about 176YTL/$130 per month). But to fork over sums for everyday tableware comparable to prices paid for authentic reproductions of İznik pieces, which use precious raw materials in production, is just plain stupid. For those willing to shell out large sums of money for a piece from the "Museum Collection," why not buy the good stuff (see "A Pilgrimage & Some Plates: İznik," under "Bursa," in chapter 5)?

GETTING THERE   Avanos lies at the northern tip of Cappadocia, 18km (11 miles) to Nevşehir, 9km (5½ miles) to Göreme, and 12km (7½ miles) to Ürgüp. Municipal buses into Avanos leave from Nevşehir hourly between 8am and 5pm. There are also *dolmuşes* leaving from Nevşehir as well as from Ürgüp to Avanos every 2 hours between 9am and 5pm.

WHERE TO DINE   A welcome new addition to Avanos is **Bizim Ev,** Orta Mahallesi, Baklacı Sok. 1 (behind the Sarıhan; © **0384/511-5525;** daily 9am–midnight), offering an unusually elegant environment for Avanos, with four dining areas, including an indoor terrace, an outdoor sun patio, and an upstairs "back room" mellowed by stone, arches, and kilims. Order the *bostan kebap,* a decadent dish of shredded beef and eggplant covered in cheese and baked in a clay pot, or the uncannily juicy *tavuk şiş* (roasted chicken), all at prices too reasonable to believe (appetizers and main courses 2YTL–6.75YTL/$1.50–$5; MasterCard and Visa accepted).

WHERE TO SHOP   **Chez Galip,** PTT Karşısı 24 (2 blocks east along Atatürk Cad. in a square on the left; © **0384/511-4240;** fax 0384/511-4543; www.chezgalip.com/index.htm), is probably the best-known atelier in Avanos. In the pottery business for 39 years, Chez Galip has gained fame (infamy?) for the creepy and diabolical hair collection in one of the back caves. My advice: Keep your hair and instead fork over a wad of Turkish lira for one of the fine ceramic pieces displayed throughout the seven cave rooms.

Kaya Seramik Evi, Eski Nevşehir Yolu 18 (from Avanos center, ceramic center is just outside of town on the old Nevşehir road on the right; © **0384/511-5755;** www.gurayseramik.com.tr), now in its third generation, takes up 12 showrooms carved into the rock on the road out of town.

Sirca, Alaaeddin Camii Yanı (© **0384/511-3686**), claims to have the largest collection of ceramics in Turkey, employing more than 100 people. Sirca also has an original line of Byzantine and religious decorative designs: classical repros of vases and the like decorated with symbols from Hittite mythology or in the Greek style.

5 Derinkuyu & Kaymaklı *★**★**★*

Derinkuyu is 26km (16 miles) south of Nevşehir; Kaymaklı is 18km (11 miles) south of Nevşehir

While the idea of a prehistoric people seeking shelter in caves is not a foreign one, it's startling to have discovered a system of underground cities as sophisticated as those found in Cappadocia. Over 200 underground cities at least two levels deep have been discovered in the area between Kayseri and Nevşehir, with around 40 of those comprised of at least three levels or more. The troglodyte cities at Derinkuyu and Kaymaklı are two of the best examples of underground dwellings.

It remains a mystery as to who first started digging out the cities, although Hittite artifacts found around the caves—and the fact that many of the towns' names go back to the Hittite or Sumerian language—suggest they were inhabited as far back as 3,000 to 4,000 years ago. The early Christians probably sought temporary shelter from the persecution of Roman soldiers; and after the 6th century, these dwellings provided protection from raiding Arab tribes. The crude carving of the surface levels of rock give way to a smoother, more refined face, which indicates that the levels were carved by different people at different times.

Each rock settlement had access to the safe haven of these underground dwellings by way of a secret underground passageway that would provide swift and unseen escape in times of emergency. In fact, an access tunnel can still be found on just about every villager's property. Additionally, the underground cities of Derinkuyu and Kaymaklı, about 9km (5½ miles) apart, are believed to be connected by an underground tunnel.

Every crucial entry point into the city was either camouflaged or blocked by a keystone, a large stone wheel that once fixed in place, was immovable. Keystones were fixed at every level of the city as well. The labyrinth of tunnels and blind passageways hundreds of feet below the ground give shocking testimony to the tenaciousness of a civilization to survive and prosper by sentencing itself to months of existence deep within the earth.

GETTING THERE   Because *dolmuşes* to Kaymaklı and Derinkuyu that run out of Nevşehir require a time-consuming transfer, this is one of those times where a day tour or car rental will come in handy. The two sites are close enough to visit back-to-back, and while you're at it, you can add a side trip to the Ihlara Valley or to the evocative village of Güzelyurt.

Kaymaklı is 18km (11 miles) south of Nevşehir, with another 9km (5½ miles) south on the same road to get to Derinkuyu. Both cities can be reached by taking the Ürgüp Soğanlı road and taking the turnoff at Güzelöz.

VISITING THE CITIES

Going underground presents some uncomfortable conditions. Although passageways are well lit and even the lowest levels are ventilated, a few of the access ramps are long and narrow, requiring visitors to ascend or descend in single file, and in some cases,

---

Fun Fact **Did You Know?**

Twenty thousand people living underground produce a lot of solid waste. Lime added to cow's liver serves as a natural accelerator of the decomposition process—an important fact for those long periods underground.

hunched over. On a busy day, problems can arise for those at the lower levels, as visitors might be stuck waiting for the last of an endless group of arrivals to clear the passageway before exiting. The visit can also be strenuous: At 204 steps, the corridor from the lowest level of Derinkuyu to the surface will cause even the most physically fit visitor to catch his or her breath, and may require you to hunch over for a good part of the way.

Arrows mark the direction of the visit (red for in, blue for out). As long as you stick to the route, you should be okay, but don't wander off with a flashlight, because this labyrinth was designed to confuse intruders just like you. It's fine to veer off track in the presence of a guide—incidentally, a great and terrifying way to see how dark absolute darkness can be.

Try to avoid peak visitation hours by getting there early; tours clog the narrow one-way tunnels and cause small galleries to become loud and stuffy. Curious about the possibility of a power outage, I was told that in the event that the lights go out, a backup generator would kick in after 10 seconds.

Those with claustrophobic tendencies have mixed reactions to visiting these sites: Some find going underground to be a walk in the park, while others don't do as well. It's really up to the individual to decide his or her own level of tolerance. For those concerned with claustrophobia or physical limitations, a good alternative to the Derinkuyu and Kaymaklı underground cities is the more modest **Mazıköy Underground City and Roman Graves** (4YTL/$3; daily 8am–6:30pm; if the ticket window is closed during open hours, go find a local to track down the ticket taker). The underground complex is actually built *up* into the rock formation; the entrance is at ground level. More adventurous explorers should check this one out as well; access to the upper levels will require some rudimentary rock-climbing skills, a dusty experience described by friends as "epic."

Derinkuyu Underground City (Derinkuyu Yeraltı Şehri)

The underground city at Derinkuyu, aptly translated as "dark well," is the largest known example of troglodyte living in Cappadocia. Eight of the levels are open to the public, with the lowest level at a depth of 54m (180 ft.). The complex is an organized and functionally advanced public space for galleries, rooms, chapels, access tunnels, water wells, and air shafts for when the communities had to dig in for the long haul. A long raised mound surrounded by trenches is thought to have been used as a school, while the stables occupied the extreme upper floors.

Only about 10% to 15% of the city's total area is available to the public, and it is thought that the city goes much farther down. Like many of the underground cities, the passageways and cavities at Derinkuyu were used as storage by local farmers until 1964, when the complex was opened to the public.

Derinkuyu. ✆ 0384/381-3194. Admission 10YTL ($7.50). Daily 8am–5pm.

Kaymaklı Underground City (Kaymaklı Yeraltı Şehri)

Where the sheer vastness of the underground city at Derinkuyu makes it an impressive example of a troglodyte complex, the functional nature of a subterranean complex is more easily appreciated at Kaymaklı. On the four levels that have been cleared out since 1964, kitchens, stables, and a winery have been discovered, as well as a chapel with a confessional. The complex, believed to go down 20m (65 ft.), was home to approximately 15,000 people at a time, with air shafts, water wells, and storage spaces capable of supporting the population for several months.

Practical considerations, including protection, survival, and revelry, were given to many facets of living underground. In the face of an attack, keystones were quickly moved into place; these blocked access from the outside and sealed off the various levels. Small holes were carved into the floor and used to communicate with the level above or below, so even when the keystone was pushed back, residents were saved from taking the long way around to pass on messages. The engineering of air shafts that extend beyond the lowest level and exit just below ground level provide an efficient and impressive level of air circulation that even succeeded in emptying the tunnels of the black smoke from the kitchen hearths. Because the same flues were used for communication and for water wells, the shafts did not extend all the way to the surface; this protected the water supply from contamination. Other interesting details are the grape presses that allowed for the grape juice to drain into a stone tank below. Wine was an important consideration in daily life, and probably used in religious rites as well.

Kaymaklı. ✆ **0384/218-2500**. Admission 10YTL ($7.50). Daily 8am–5pm.

6 The Ihlara Valley ✦

97km (60 miles) southwest of Nevşehir; 49km (30 miles) southeast of Aksaray; 15km (9 miles) southwest of Güzelyurt

Only 49km (30 miles) south of Nevşehir, the barren steppes of the Ihlara Valley split open to reveal a 15km (9-mile) fissure carved by the Melendez River. A hike through the canyon is an opportunity to see another face of Cappadocia. In contrast with the dusty expanses of the rest of Cappadocia, the bottom of the canyon, nourished by the riverbed, is a valley full of vegetation, supporting village life much as it did centuries ago. Local women wade along the banks of the river, their traditional baggy trousers trailing in the river's edge as they do the day's washing. Life in the canyon goes back much farther, however. Early Christians were just as drawn to Ihlara's canyon fertility as residents are today. The canyon is home to over 100 carved churches and an estimated 4,000 dwellings, hidden in the cliff walls or behind a landslide.

The canyon descends over 90m (300 ft.) in some places, twisting and turning at the beckoning of the river along wide trails lined with poplars and pistachio trees or narrowly navigable paths. There are a number of official entry and exit points along the canyon, past modest yet viable troglodyte villages. Official entry and exit points at the villages allow for either full-day or abbreviated hikes, but you should leave time for detours to the area churches and to pet the donkeys tied to a tree along the river's edge.

ESSENTIALS

GETTING THERE & GETTING AROUND   If you come by private car, you'll probably have to leave it in the parking lot at the main entrance, which doesn't do you much good way over at the opposite end of the canyon in Belisırma or Selime. An easier way is to take a guided tour; this will make seeing the valley a whole lot richer, giving you the background information necessary to appreciate the rock churches, rather than taking just a lovely walk through the gorge. Not to be overlooked is the bonus of having someone waiting for you at the end of the canyon, thus saving you the long hike back. (You can also hike up and out to the main road and catch a rare *dolmuş* back to the main entrance.) Guides can be expensive, though, so if you've got the stamina, then by all means, go it alone.

It's a 1½-hour drive from central Cappadocia to the Ihlara Valley. From central Cappadocia you will need to get to Nevşehir, then get from Nevşehir to Aksaray, then from Aksaray to the village of Ihlara. The traditional hike begins at the main entrance about 1.6km (1 mile) away, but to get there, you'll need to get on yet another mode of transportation, either a *dolmuş* or taxi. See what I mean about the ease of a guided tour?

Dolmuşes that run between Aksaray and Ihlara village pass Selime and the turnoff for Belisırma, so theoretically you could descend into the canyon or exit at any of the three main entrances. *Dolmuş* service for Ihlara village also leaves from Güzelyurt, a charming forgotten village of semi-troglodyte houses with its own tradition of monasteries and churches that date back to the life of St. Gregory of Nazianzoz.

ORIENTATION The main entrance to the valley is a little over 1.6km (1 mile) north of the village of Ihlara. There's a parking lot, a snack shop with great cheese toasts (for added strength), and the main gate leading to the long stairway down. The cliff walls are dotted with churches and abodes on both banks of the river, with most of the sites of interest clustered around the wooden footbridge at the base of the main entrance and over near the village of Belisırma. The 3.5km (2-mile) hike from the main entrance to the village of Belisırma is a relatively easy one, and many people choose to have lunch at the restaurant near the riverbed and call it a day. It's also possible to begin the hike at the village of Ihlara following the left bank of the river, adding on about 3km (1¾ miles) to the total. If it's an isolated outdoor experience you're after, there are campgrounds and shack-style restaurants at both Belisırma and at Selime, an additional 11km (7 miles) or so away. The shorter hike takes about 1½ to 2 hours, depending on your level of fitness and how many pistachios you choose to crack open and eat along the way, while a hike up the entire canyon will take about 5 hours.

EXPLORING THE IHLARA VALLEY

Ihlara Canyon The most common starting point to a hike into the valley is the southern entrance near the village of Ihlara, down an endless man-made serpentine stairway 400 steps to the bottom. About 3.5km (2 miles) away, over sometimes-rough terrain, is the village of Belisırma, an ancient center of medicine before Selçuk Sultan Kılıçarslan II transferred the school to Aksaray. The process of mummification was extensively practiced in this part of the valley; a mummy of a woman found here is on display in the Niğde Archaeological Museum.

The churches, some of which are difficult to reach, date from the 8th or 9th century while the decorative frescoes date to a later post-Iconoclastic period, somewhere between the 10th and 13th centuries. The styles of the churches are generally grouped into two categories: those with an Egyptian or Syrian influence mainly found around the main entrance, and those reflecting a typical Byzantine style, bunched around Belisırma.

The first church encountered at the bottom of the steps from Ihlara is **Ağaçaltı Kilisesi** ✹✹✹ or The Church Under the Tree, also known as the Church of Daniel or the Church of Pantassa. Designed on a Greek cross plan, the interior, which has succumbed quite a bit to the elements, may appear a bit primitive at first, but a closer inspection reveals a strong Eastern influence, visible through the use of checker patterns, medallions, and rosettes. An interesting detail is in the depiction of the Nativity; notice that the Magi are seen dressed in Phrygian-style caps. The scene of the Dormition of the Virgin recalls the mosaics of St. Savior in Chora in Istanbul, with a depiction of Jesus holding the soul of Mary in the form of an infant.

Other churches in the vicinity of the Ihlara entrance and worthy of note are the **Pürenli Seki Kilisesi (the Church with Terraces)** ✹✹, and the **Kokar Kilisesi (the Church that Smells!)** ✹✹, both to the right of the steps as you descend into the canyon.

Considered the oldest church in the valley, the **Eğritaş Kilisesi (the Church with the Crooked Stone)** ✹✹ was probably a funerary chapel. The vaulted chapel has a single apse and a burial chamber below, much of which has been damaged by erosion and rockslides. The badly decaying frescoes, depicting scenes from the life of Christ, are distinctive for a style that recalls Eastern pre-Iconoclastic art.

On the other side of the river over a wooden footbridge is the **Yılanlı Kilisesi (Church of the Serpents)** *ⓡⓡ*. The church is named for the scene on the western wall, showing serpents in the act of punishing four female sinners. Women as the source of evil is a common Eastern theme taken up by later monks, and in this case, the representations probably symbolize the sin of adultery, disobedience, and slander. The most graphic of the punishments shows the fourth female sinner with two snakes biting her nipples, probably for her failure to feed her children.

Back on the left bank of the river heading in the direction of Belisırma is the **Süm-büllü Kilisesi (The Hyacinth Church)** *ⓡⓡ*, distinctive for its ornate facade of pillars and arched niches carved directly into the rock. A set of steps leads up to the church, passing the wild growths of hyacinths that give the complex its name. The church is actually a monastery complex hollowed out of the cliff; there are spaces for both living and worship. The few surviving frescoes include a well-preserved Annunciation and a Dormition.

Kırk Damaltı Kilisesi (the Church of St. George) *ⓡⓡⓡ*, one of the latest of the region, is interesting from a purely social aspect. A portrait of the donor, a female in Byzantine dress, is pictured with her husband, a man in typical Selçuk costume. The inscription reads: "This most venerable church . . . decorated through the assistance of the lady Thamar, here pictured, and of her Emir Basil Giagoupes, under his Majesty the most noble and Great Sultan Masud at the time when Sire Andronikos reigned over the Romans." It is thought to be an expression of Christian gratitude for the religious tolerance of the Selçuk Turks and dates the church to the late 13th century.

Take the Nevşehir/Aksaray road and turn off on the road south for Ihlara; the road leading into the canyon is signposted before the entrance to the village. *ⓒ* 0382/453-7084. Admission 5YTL ($3.70); parking 6.75 ($5) extra. Daily 8am–7pm.

A CHARMING VILLAGE DETOUR

Only 15km (9 miles) away is peaceful **Güzelyurt** *ⓡ*, a small village on the outskirts of Ihlara Valley with cave dwellings and underground cities that date to prehistoric times. Güzelyurt, which means "beautiful homeland," embodies all of the characteristics of Cappadocia: open fields and pastures, troglodyte houses, underground cities, and monastery complexes all within smelling distance of the villagers' freshly baked bread. The present-day village of Güzelyurt was settled by the early Christians under the name of Gelveri, probably after the hill of Calvary in Jerusalem. The village grew during the life of Gregory of Nazianzoz, where less than 1.6km (1 mile) away in Monastery Valley, over 50 rock churches have been found. According to one story, Emperor Valens was in such opposition to the Christian faith that after exiling St. Basil, he sent women disguised as nuns into the valley to seduce the monks. An insult in local vernacular that means "son of a nun" probably refers to this questionable episode. Several rock-cut mosques from Ottoman times have been found in the valley as well.

In the village is the St. Gregory of Nazianzoz church. It was probably built by St. Gregory with the support of Emperor Theodosius in the 4th century, although the pulpit dates to the 18th century, when it was donated by Czar Nicholas I. Built with a similar architectural structure to that of the Ayasofya in Istanbul, the church, now whitewashed and converted into a mosque (Kilise Camisi; admission 4YTL/$3), is the subject of a proposal to restore the interior to its original state. A spring in the courtyard, considered to be holy, attracts pilgrims as well as those with prayers for the healing of loved ones.

It is possible to visit the many underground cities in Güzelyurt, particularly the one near the Kilise Camisi. The entrance is different than the sloping tunnels of Derinkuyu and Kaymaklı; the one here is more like a well.

There are several lookout points and cliffs from which to survey the village and the parade of passing cows, and as Güzelyurt is famous for its hospitality, it's more than likely you'll get stopped to share a pot of tea. To get there, start from the main entrance to Ihlara Valley (the entrance with the parking lot) and follow the access road out to the road to Aksaray. Once you're on the main road, follow signs for Gelveri/Güzelyurt.

WHERE TO STAY

If you've come to the valley to hike the entire length, you're probably prepared to take advantage of one of the campgrounds on the banks of the river at Belisırma and Selime, all of which have some kind of adjunct restaurant. If it's a bed you're after, ask whoever's running the campground for a recommendation of a pension in town, and he will probably set you up with a room in a private home. Otherwise, I recommend that you head over to the village of Güzelyurt and stay in **Otel Karballa** (Güzelyurt; ✆ **0382/451-2103;** fax 0382/451-2107; www.kirkit.com), operated by Kirkit Voyages. Originally a 19th-century Christian girl's school, the Otel Karballa has done time as a school, a police station, and a movie theater. When the current management team, a Turkish/Israeli couple, came in, they invited the architecture department of Yıldız University to develop a plan for restorations. The original building, with its enormous stone barrel-vaulted rectory, now used as a dining area, contains four family rooms. A second building, completed in 1913 in the Byzantine style, was converted into guest-room space by splitting the elevation into two levels so that the upper rooms are framed by a vault, while the lower rooms have a flat wooden ceiling. Both levels share a single oversize window. The property, organically overgrown with brush and vines, benefits through the addition of an inconspicuous bi-level swimming pool that overlooks the steppes. All units have central heat. Doubles are 34€ ($42), and all major credit cards are accepted.

7 Kayseri ⨀

316km (196 miles) southeast of Ankara; 770km (478 miles) southeast of Istanbul; 102km (63 miles) northeast of Nevşehir

Today little more than a religiously conservative and industrialized town, Kayseri's biggest draw is its rich legacy of Selçuk monuments. During the reign of Alaaeddin Keykubat, the Selçuk Empire briefly became the world's most powerful and culturally advanced state while showing a singular tolerance to the Anatolian people. Through a cooperation, even a merging, with the Anatolian people, the Selçuks developed a unique form of art, architecture, and culture.

Kayseri has contributed other great things to the cultural mosaic of Anatolia. As an important stop on the Silk Road and even today recognized for its textiles, Kayseri is still one of the leading producers of carpets and kilims in Turkey. Finely woven silk carpets have earned Kayseri a reputation second only to Hereke, and the colors and patterns of the local wool and cotton carpets rival the beauty and quality of Anatolia's oldest weaving traditions. However, the town's current, most celebrated exports are *mantı,* tiny meat-filled ravioli topped in a garlicky yogurt sauce, and *pastırma,* a spicy cured beef flavored with red pepper, lots of garlic, and fenugreek seed. (No trip to town would be complete without one or the other.)

Few visitors venture into Kayseri's city center, motivated instead to reach their final destination, Cappadocia, after a late evening flight. Having endured the indignity of tourism's equivalent of the cold shoulder, local shopkeepers have responded by targeting the more intrepid with insistent, relentless, and bothersome sales tactics. And, sadly, it's this persistence that has made Kayseri infamous throughout Turkey. To appreciate the town, you have to have both an enthusiasm for Selçuk architecture and a thick skin. As religious zeal pervades the air, it might be a good idea to dress modestly as well. Plan to spend half a day seeing the sights and another couple of hours extricating yourself from the clutches of the local "tag men."

ESSENTIALS
GETTING THERE
BY PLANE   There are two flights daily from Istanbul on **Turkish Airlines** into Kayseri's Erkilet Airport (© 0352/338-3353), approximately 6.5km (4 miles) outside the city center, and one flight daily from Istanbul on **Onur Air** (in Istanbul © 0212/663-9176). As of this writing, Turkish Airlines provides a minibus shuttle to their offices in the center of town, or you can take a municipal bus (marked CENTRUM or ŞEHIR MERKEZI) or *dolmuşes* (marked ŞEHIR) for under a dollar. A taxi into town costs around 8YTL ($6).

If you're just passing through Kayseri on your way to Cappadocia, **Argeus Tourism & Travel** (© 0384/341-4888; inform@argeus.com.tr) will pick you up at the airport in one of their private minivans and transport you right up to the doorstep of your hotel for 9.50YTL ($7). (Actually, they'll also drive you into Kayseri, if that's where you're headed.) Other agencies and hotel owners have caught on to this practice, in fact, many hotels and pensions will pick you up for free.

BY BUS   As a major crossroads, Kayseri is another one of those cities whose *otogar* functions much like an airport. Located about 1.6km (1 mile) northwest of town, you'll need to hop on either a city bus (marked CENTRUM or ŞEHIR MERKEZI) or *dolmuş* (marked ŞEHIR).

BY TRAIN   Trains service Kayseri from both Istanbul and Ankara. The **Doğu Ekspresi** departs from Istanbul's Haydarpaşa station (© 0216/336-0475) daily at 8:35am and Tuesday through Sunday at 8:30pm and arrives into Kayseri at 1:17am the following morning (18YTL or 26YTL/$13 or $19 for a single bed in a couchette). From Ankara (© 0312/311-0620; 8.75YTL/$6.50 for a seat; 18YTL/$13 for a bed), take the **Erzurum Ekspresi** train; it leaves at 1:30pm and arrives at 8:20pm. The Kayseri train station is about .8km (½ mile) north of Düvenönü Meydanı at the end of Hastane Caddesi. Train service takes longer than the bus, so unless trains particularly turn you on, seek out alternative transportation.

VISITOR INFORMATION
The **Tourist Information office** (© 0352/222-3903) is located right in the town center across from the Citadel and next to the Hunat Hatun complex at Kagnı Pazarı 61. If you're standing in Cumhuriyet Meydanı facing the castle, the information office is up ahead on your left.

Turkish Airlines's Kayseri office is on Sahabiye Mahallesi Yıldırım Cad. 1 (© 0352/222-3858), 1 block north of Sivas Caddesi. The number at the airport is © 0352/338-3353.

ORIENTATION

All roads into town eventually lead to the **Citadel**—you just have to drive past some industrial blight to get there. Smokestacks, flat-topped warehouses, and car dealers fade away the closer you get to the city center. A good place to get your bearings is under the clock tower in **Cumhuriyet Meydanı,** right before heading across the traffic square to the Hunat Hatun Mosque and Medrese complex. The Great Mosque, or Ulu Camii, is obvious in its grandeur, and on your way over you will inevitably get sidetracked into one of the three main bazaars.

Several examples of the cone-topped octagonal **Selçuk tombs** are located on or around the center island on the road to Mount Erciyes, with the Archaeological Museum located not far from the Döner Kümbet. A close inspection will require a little effort, but you won't be sorry, especially if you take a cab back.

GETTING AROUND

Most of what Kayseri has to offer an outsider is centered around Cumhuriyet Meydanı and the Citadel. Some Selçuk tombs spread out around the roads out of the town center, but are for the most part reachable in less than 15 minutes on foot.

WHAT TO SEE & DO

The Selçuks were way ahead of their time, introducing social programs and advancing studies in the sciences. Centers of higher learning, or *medreses,* blossomed under Selçuk rule, not only as centers of theology but also for the study of law (based on Koranic principles), astronomy, mathematics, and geography. Selçuks also attributed much importance to the medical sciences, opening the first medical school in Anatolia here in Kayseri. Often a hospital was part of the complex of mosque, *hamam,* and *medrese,* and in the case of the Çifte Medrese, it is both.

Of special importance was the *türbe,* a cylindrical or polygonal tomb with a conical roof whose geometric design was uniquely Selçuk. Selçuk art and architecture were a result of the merging of Anatolian traditions with Persian styles and classical Arab Islamic forms, cultures with whom the Selçuks kept in continued contact. Unlike the Persian Selçuks and Byzantines, the Anatolian Selçuks preferred stone to brick, developing great skill in the art of stone carving.

If your sightseeing already hasn't been interrupted by a new "friend" who refuses to unstick himself from you, now's the time to give in and follow him back to the marketplace. Continuing a long tradition of commerce, Kayseri has three covered markets in the center of town, clustered around the Ulu Camii (Great Mosque). The **Bedesten,** a work of art in deep hues of gray and brown, began as a market for clothing and textile merchants. Now carpets are a backdrop for the huge windowed domes and massive vaulted arches, and definitely worth a look. The **Vezir Hanı,** which was originally a caravansary constructed of gray lava stone, now sells raw textiles such as wool and cotton on the lower floor and carpets upstairs. The recently restored **covered bazaar** has over 500 shops selling the usual amalgamation of gold, sweatshirts, and leather or woven handbags. There are also plenty of stalls around the Citadel and inside the walls to slow you down. For a look at some really fabulous handmade carpets, check out the Ulu Camii, the focal point of the city center, with its mosaic tile minaret.

Archaeological Museum   Twenty-one kilometers (13 miles) north of Kayseri is the archaeological site of Kültepe, a large mound (the name means Mound of Ashes) on the site of the ancient city of Kanesh. A satellite colony of Assyrian merchants called a *karum* dates to 2000 B.C. Except for the mound, there's nothing much to see, as all of the excavated artifacts have been moved to the Kayseri Archaeological Museum, with some findings exhibited at the local Kültepe Museum and the Museum of Anatolian Civilizations in Ankara.

Artifacts from Kültepe include Assyrian tablets used for recording commercial transactions, as well as some Hittite findings from the area. A couple of Roman and Byzantine statues top off the collection, but don't trip over yourself to get to this one.

Gültepe Mahallesi Kışla Cad. 2. ⓒ **0352/222-2149.** Admission 2YTL ($1.50). Tues–Sun 8am–5pm.

Çifte Kümbet 🏛 Definitely off the beaten track, the Çifte Kümbet was the final resting place of the second wife of Alaaeddin Keykubat, the mother of the chosen heir. She and her two sons were murdered by Keyküsrev II, son of Hunat Hatun, who ascended the throne after clearing out the competition and poisoning his father at a banquet. Called the "twin tomb," only one has survived.

Sivas Cad, 6km (3¾ miles) east of the Citadel.

Çifte Medrese 🏛 The Çifte Medrese brought the Persian Selçuk tradition of medical instruction to Anatolia as the first school of anatomy and the first of its kind in Anatolia. Çifte, meaning "twin," refers to two practically identical *medreses,* both of the open courtyard type, connected by a barrel-vaulted passageway. One was actually a hospital and not a *medrese,* and is believed to have been built by Gevher Nesibe Hatun, sister of Sultan Giyaseddin Keyhüsrev, who is thought to have built the medical school. The buildings are now part of Erciyes University and house the Institute of Medical History, with a fascinating collection offering a window into medical practices of the 13th century.

Gevher Neshibe Mahallesi, in Mimar Sinan Parkı Ici. North of Park Cad. in the Mimar Sinan Parkı. ⓒ **0352/231-3565.** Admission 2YTL ($1.50). Tues–Sun 8am–5pm.

The Citadel The best example of a Selçuk military complex, the Citadel stands at the heart of the city, its dark basalt stones carved out of the volcanic rock spewed from Mount Erciyes looming in the distance. As heir to a fortress built by Justinian in the 6th century reputedly built on the site of a church erected by St. Basil, Selçuk Sultan Keykubat I reinforced the Citadel in 1224, building over the foundations and adding 19 seemingly invincible towers and inner walls almost 3m (10 ft.) thick. The contrast between the crude Byzantine stones and the carefully cut Selçuk ones is a clear indication of the passage of time. The Citadel was later repaired by Mehmet the Conqueror, who added the small Fatih Camii over a previous prayer hall near the northwest corner of the inner courtyard. The inner court and outer walls now bustle with, not surprisingly, a bazaar.

City Center, Cumhuriyet Meydanı. Daily dawn–dusk.

Döner Kümbet 🏛 Although the tradition of monumental tombs spread first through Persia, the Anatolian Selçuks adopted and adapted the custom by constructing them out of stone and sticking a conical dome hat on top. Speculation on the origins of the shape refer back to desert Turkoman nomadic tents, while the geometric patterns and foliage designs may have been influenced by the indigenous Anatolian cultures.

The 12 sides of the Döner Kümbet are said to give the illusion of movement, thus the name, "Revolving Tomb," although with a stony appearance more like a rocket ship, this thing isn't going anywhere. The tomb was built in 1276, for Şah Cihan

Hatun, daughter of Sultan Keykubat, although there's nothing inside except an old dusty broom and some paper refuse. Instead of peering inside, take a close look at the intricately carved reliefs, particularly the arabesques and palms and a tree of life crowned by royal eagles' heads.

On the center island of Talas Cad., about 15 min. from the Citadel by foot.

Ethnographic Museum ✿ You get a two-for-one bang out of the ethnographic collection now that it's been moved from the Hunat Hatun Medrese to the inside of this Ottoman Paşa's mansion. This beautifully restored home, with its Eastern-style wooden beams, original timber ceilings, and lattice screens, is one of the few examples of vernacular architecture surviving in Kayseri. The house was built between 1417 and 1419, with a traditional harem for the women and a *selamlık* section for the men added at a later date. Islamic tombstones are on display in the gardens.

The exhibition rooms are on an upper floor reachable through an exterior staircase. Collections are small, containing jewelry, robes, arms, and Ottoman currency, with the most striking pieces being the exquisite tiles taken from the Hunat Hamamı and the 13th-century minaret. The museum has the requisite Turkoman nomadic tent setup, and wax figures in displays of the various uses of an Ottoman home.

Güpgüpoğlu Konağı, Cumhuriyet Mahallesi Atatürk Evi Karşısı. ✆ **0352/222-9516**. Admission 2YTL ($1.50). Tues–Sun 8am–4:30pm.

Hunat Hatun Complex ✿✿ Hunat Hatun—called *Mahperi,* or Fairy Moon by her husband—was the daughter of Kir Ford, Christian governor of Alanya. When the Selçuk Sultan Alaaeddin Kaykubat conquered Alanya, the treaty included his daughter's hand in marriage. The Hunat Hatun Külliyesi, built in 1237 in honor of Hunat Hatun, was the first mosque complex to be built by the Selçuks in Anatolia. The complex is comprised of a mosque, a *medrese,* a tomb, and a public bath.

The Selçuk tradition of the *medrese* was a way to ensure the purity of the Sunni faith, which was being challenged by the Shiite Fatimids. There are many examples of Selçuk *medreses* in Kayseri, but this one deserves a closer look. It's possible that the *medrese* was built before the mosque and that it was constructed by the sultan and not his wife. The building, entered through a magnificent monumental portal with stalactite carvings, is an open court with a double antechamber at each end, and 16 identical rooms opening up to a courtyard. Above the *medrese* up a dark and secretive staircase (remove your shoes) is the octagonal tomb of Lady Mahperi Hatun, buried alongside her granddaughter and another unidentified grave. The exterior of the tomb can be admired from inside the mosque.

Cumhuriyet Meydanı, next to the Tourist Information office. Free admission. Daily dawn–dusk.

WHERE TO STAY

You don't want to stay here overnight. But somebody is. Hilton just built another member of the chain in town (Cumhuriyet Meydani Istasyon Cad. 1; ✆ **0352/207-5000;** rates fluctuate wildly and go as low as 70€/$85). Even the evening Turkish Airlines flight arrives in plenty of time to get you picked up by Argeus and transported back to more pleasant and memorable accommodations among the weird and wonderful formations of Cappadocia.

If you've got an early flight out of Kayseri's airport, and have no choice but to overnight here, plan to arrive the afternoon before; you'll have adequate time to explore the architectural highlights.

Grand Eras Hotel   Located halfway between the city center and the airport, this four-star property is unfortunately more than a stroll away from the Citadel. Nevertheless, it's shiny and new, and will most certainly help keep prices reasonable at the Hilton which opened in 2003. All suites come with a Jacuzzi.

Barbaros Bulv. İnönü Mah. 6, Melikgazi/Kayseri. © 0352/330-5111. Fax 0352/330-5129. www.granderashotel.com. 110 units. 74€ ($90) double; 99€ ($120) suite. MC, V. **Amenities:** Restaurant; bar; concierge; tour desk; car-rental desk; 24-hr. room service; laundry service; dry cleaning. *In room:* A/C, satellite TV, minibar, hair dryer.

Hotel Almer   A 5-minute walk from the Citadel and only 5km (3 miles) from the airport, the Almer provides a clean and reliable option for a quick layover in town.

Osman Kavuncu Cad. 15, Düvenönü Meydanı. © 0352/320-7970. Fax 0352/320-7974. www.almer.com.tr. 77 units (all with minitub). 62€ ($75) double. AE, MC, V. **Amenities:** Restaurant; bar; concierge; tour desk; car-rental desk; 24-hr. room service; laundry service; dry cleaning. *In room:* A/C, satellite and cable TV, minibar, hair dryer.

WHERE TO DINE

Well, you won't starve in Kayseri, but don't expect a culinary extravaganza. The narrow and congested streets behind the Citadel, between Kaleönü Caddesi and Turan Caddesi, are full of fast-food *pide* places, but keep your eyes peeled for signs for fresh *mantı*, Turkish ravioli in a spicy garlic yogurt sauce, which is a scrumptious specialty of the region.

This is also a good opportunity to try your hand in the local shops or to stock up on provisions at the Migros Supermarket on Cumhuriyet Caddesi for a picnic in the park. Check out the deli meats, particularly the locally cured *pastırma* and the varieties of Turkish salami for which Kayseri is famous.

Beyaz Saray KEBAP HOUSE   Fronted by a fast-food counter on the street level, the Beyaz Saray, which has a pleasant enough dining room upstairs, is consistently recommended by the locals. Beyaz Saray offers a good selection of local specialties, including plenty of grilled meats and *pide.* The selection of mezes is limited, but at least you'll have plenty of room for one of the desserts listed on the special ice-cream menu.

Millet Cad. 8. © 0352/221-0444. Main courses under 5.50YTL ($4). MC, V. Daily noon–midnight.

Mantı Restaurant ✦ MANTI HOUSE   Somehow this *mantı* house has succeeded in creating a reputation for itself, tempting visitors in Kayseri to take the detour for a good meal. There are other items on the menu such as the mandatory offering of grills and some local dishes, but if you've come this far, there's no excuse for skipping the pasta dish. Ask for extra chile oil and stick around for the live music on Saturday night.

Located in the Toyota Dealer Plaza at Ambar Mahallesi, Zafer Cad. 4 on the road to Ankara. © 0352/326-3075. Main courses 4YTL–8YTL ($3–$6). AE, MC, V. Daily 11am–midnight.

CAPPADOCIA TO THE COAST: A VISIT TO KONYA

Konya elicits images of religious fanatics. It's a rare hotel or restaurant that serves alcohol, and the mosque entryways turn into traffic jams at prayer time. But like Turkey itself, Konya is a city of contradictions. Although the reputed spiritual center of Turkey and one of the most conservative towns in Anatolia, Konya has the highest rate of consumption of alcohol anywhere in the country. Rebellion takes many forms, and in a city with 50,000 students, it's in the lipstick and rouge peeking out of headscarves and in skirts with slits as far up as the knee—probably Konya's version of a pierced nose.

Most travelers come here to make a pilgrimage to the tomb of Mevlana, founder of the venerable Sufi sect of Islam that preaches love, charity, humility, equality, and tolerance, among other elemental principles. Members of the sect seek union with God through a meditative ceremony called the *sema,* a ritual whirling symbolizing the liberation from earthly bonds and a connection with the heavens. Ironically, all Sufi sects were banned by Atatürk in the 1920s in his far-reaching opposition to religious extremism. But Mevlana's ideals have nevertheless survived, and in recent years have gained a popular following not only among Turks, but also internationally.

GETTING THERE   By Bus   Countless bus companies run hourly service from Antalya (5 hr.). The most reliable of these are Kontur, Meram, Kontaş, and Özkaymak. These and other major bus companies offer repeated daily service from Istanbul (9 hr.), Ankara (3 hr.), Antalya (5 hr.), and İzmir (8 hr.). Bus rates range from 14YTL to 41YTL ($10 to $30); from Nevşehir (4 hr.), the fare is around 15YTL ($11).

A taxi from the *otogar* will take about 20 minutes and cost around 6.25YTL ($4.60), but if you don't have a lot of luggage to carry around, you may want to take the tramway (exit the main entrance, walking left along the main road toward the main intersection; the tramway is on the right corner), which takes about 45 minutes and costs 1YTL (75¢). Get off at Alaaddin Hill in the center of town; from there, the Otel Hüma is just across the street; the Balıkçılar is about a 10-minute walk down Alaaddin Caddesi in the direction of the Mevlana Museum. Also from the *otogar,* a *dolmuş* takes half the tramway's amount of time and costs about the same 1YTL (75¢).

By Car   It's an easy and scenic 3 hours over the Taurus Mountains via the excellent three-lane highway from Antalya to Konya (via Seydişehir). The road via Beyşehir, passing by Lake Beyşehir, is more scenic, but takes longer. From Nevşehir, it's an easy 3 hours through flatlands past Aksaray; the highway is one big speed trap so remember to stay at 90kmph (55 mph)—you're allowed a 10% margin of error.

WHERE TO STAY   Given that the bulk of visitors pass through Konya on tour buses for a quick stopover at the Mevlana Museum, there's little incentive or economic basis for hotels to do much more than coast. This may change with the opening of the new Hilton Hotel, Istanbul Yolu, Selcuklu near the university (© **0332/221-5000;** www.hilton.com). For mediocre accommodations in the center of town, try the **Balıkçılar,** Mevlana Karşısı 1, 42020 Konya (© **0332/350-9470;** fax 0332/351-3259). The hotel overlooks the majestic and monumental Selimiye Mosque and Mevlana complex, so that you won't even mind that from the exterior, this hotel is an eyesore. Along with the outstanding location, the hotel has a Turkish bath and sauna (open in the rare case when the hotel's occupancy is up), a billiard table, and a couple of old exercise machines. All rooms have air-conditioning, minibars, and satellite television. Rack rate for a double is 88€ ($107). Otherwise, the eye-catching, two-story **Otel Hüma,** Çifte Merdiven Mahallesi Alaaeddin Bulv. 8, 42020 Konya (© **0332/ 350-6389;** fax 0332/351-0244), across from Alaaeddin Hill, is one of the few hotels in town that doesn't turn its back on local vernacular architecture. It may not fool anyone into thinking it's an authentic caravansary, but the main entrance—modeled after a traditional Selçuk portal—and the conical tower are a nice touch. All rooms have a minibar and television (local stations); the rack rate for a double is 40€ to 60€ ($49 to $73).

WHERE TO DINE   Downtown Konya has its fair share of *kebap* joints and *lokantas,* but **Hacı Şücrü,** Isaniye, Behşehir Yolu (near the Municipality; no phone), seems to be the place to try Konya's signature dish, the *fırın kebap* (a greasy slab of lamb slow cooked in a clay *tandır* oven; called *etli ekmek* when served on a grease-soaked *pide*). Adjacent to the Mevlana Museum is the **Mevlevi Sofrası,** Civar Mahallesi Şehit

Nazımbey Cad. 1 (© **0332/353-3341;** no credit cards), which gives the tourists what they want: traditional food and ambience, several outdoor roof terraces overlooking the Mevlana Museum gardens, two indoor rooms with traditional Oriental seating, and a *sema* show nightly at 9pm.

A popular spot among the local student crowd is the **Nargile Kahvesi,** Osmanlı Carşısı, Ince Minare Sokak (behind the Ince Minare, next to Tömer language school; © **0332/353-3257**), an utterly atmospheric teahouse and cafe located in an old, converted wood house, with coal/wood stoves, low stools, and divan benches. The top floor has three separate *şarks* (Oriental-style dining areas, with pillows and kilims), and even a tiny prayer room in a corner closet. There's a barber in the basement, and a bunch of water pipes, which smell like spices.

WHAT TO SEE & DO   The history of Konya dates to at least the 8th century B.C.; some of the most important archaeological findings belonging to the earliest stationary civilizations known to man were discovered at nearby **Çatalhöyük,** while Hittite artifacts have been discovered in the regions east of Konya.

Known as Iconium during the Roman and Byzantine eras, the city was the location of one of the earliest church councils. After the Selçuk victory over the Byzantine army at Malazgirt (also called Manzikert) in 1071, the Selçuks migrated west, establishing a capital on Alaaeddin Hill, and setting their sights on an empire that would rival Rome—called the Sultanate of Rhum. Some of the foundations of this early Selçuk Empire are still standing on Alaeddin Hill, including the **Selçuk Palace** built for Sultan Kılıç Arslan II between 1156 and 1192, now for the most part a crumbled stone wall sheltered beneath a concrete tripod arch—the unfortunate symbol of the city. The **Alaaeddin Mosque,** also built during the reign of Alaaeddin Keykubat, dates to 1221; note the *minbar* (pulpit) ✿ and the *türbe,* containing the remains of eight of the ruling Selçuk sultans. The Alaaeddin Hill is also an attraction in itself, home to five lovely tea gardens.

At the opposite end of Alaaeddin Caddesi and about a 10-minute walk is the **Mevlana Müzesi** (Mevlana Mahallesi; © **0332/351-1215;** daily 9am–6pm), the original *tekke* or lodge of the Mevlevi Dervishes. The complex was built by Beyazit II and Selim I successively at the end of the 15th and beginning of the 16th centuries. The *tekke* includes a *semahane,* where the ritual *sema* or whirling ceremony takes place, a *şadırvan* for ritual ablutions, a library, living and teaching quarters, and the mausoleum housing the **tomb of Celâleddin Rumi** ✿✿, founder of the sect and later awarded the honorable title of Mevlana. The mausoleum room is highly ornamented with Islamic script and enameled bas-relief, and contains the tombs of several of the more important figures of the dervish order. The main tomb enclosed behind a silver gate crafted in 1597 is that of Mevlana. The tomb of his father, Bahaeddin Veled, is upright and adjacent to his son's, a position that signifies respect.

The adjoining room, or the *semihane,* is now a museum of Mevlana memorabilia displaying musical instruments and robes belonging to Mevlana, along with Selçuk and Ottoman objects like gold-engraved Korans from the 13th century. Among the fabulous ancient **prayer rugs** ✿✿ is the most valuable silk carpet in the world. The museum is open daily 9am to 6pm; admission is 5.50YTL ($4).

As in all Muslim holy places, you must remove your shoes to visit the Mevlana Müzesi, but here, the floor is bare parquet, so wear socks. Since overnight groups schedule their visits for first thing in the morning, you may want to stagger your visit

The "Whirling" Dervishes

Dervish sects began appearing in Islamic countries around the 9th century, with beliefs and customs as fantastic as stiletto-pierced body parts and snake eating. Some dervish sects required their followers to maintain absolute secrecy to discourage members from joining for hypocritical reasons. Others required their followers to wander through lands or to dress in bizarre costumes as part of their orders.

The Mevlevi order of the dervishes arose in Turkey with the spreading of Islam, and is based on the philosophies of Mevlana Celaleddin-i Rumi, who was born in Balkh, the first capital of the ancient Turkish territory of Khorasan (Afghanistan) in 1207. An invitation extended by Sultan Keykübad I to his father, a man of great learning and a respected spiritual leader, brought Celaleddin to Konya at the age of 21, the -i Rumi being added upon his migration into the heart of the Selçuk Rum Empire.

The mystical order is based on the principles of universal love and the oneness of creation, which states, "to love man is to love God." While the concepts of the sect were set forth by Celaleddin-i Rumi (the *Mevlana*—Arabic for "lord"—was added to his name as a title of respect), the rites and rituals associated with the order were consolidated by his son, Sultan Veled ("sultan" here used to designate spiritual leadership). The Mevlevi philosophy eventually gained the respect of the Ottoman sultans, and Selim II, Mahmud II, and Mehmed V, were among its members.

The Mevlevi ritual takes the form of the *sema*, a ritual "whirling" dance whose purpose is to create a sphere of divine reality. The Mevlevi believe that purity of heart, peace with self and the universe, and the search for perfection through ritual dance bring them closer to God. The positioning of the body during the ritual has great symbolic significance: Outstretched arms with one hand facing the heavens and the other facing the earth symbolize man as a bridge between the two spheres. The white robes worn during the *sema* are symbolic of shrouds.

Although this and other brotherhoods were officially outlawed by Atatürk's sweeping reforms, the order continues to exist. The Konya order opens the ritual *sema* to a rare public viewing every December 17 in Konya, a celebratory gathering marking the death of Mevlana Celaleddin-i Rumi.

to Konya by arriving here a little later. (The end of the day is a good time, as most tour buses have already left.)

Near the entrance gate of Mevlana Müzesi, one of the buildings has been converted into a shopping arcade full of quality objects created by local artisans. Reviving the traditional art of felt making is Mehmet Girgiç (✆ **0332/350-7551**); you can pick up a tall dervish hat for 68YTL ($50), a *kepenek* (outdoor felt overcoat), or a *yurt* (Anatolian tent). He also sells a few carpets at what seem to be reasonable prices. Mehmet hosts felt-making workshops in the United States and abroad.

On an overnight stay, there are several other sites in Konya worth a look. The **Karatay Medrese,** built during the reign of Sultan Keykavus II in 1251 by his grand Vezir Celâleddin Karatay, houses the **Ceramic Museum (Alaattin Meydanı; © 0332/ 351-1914;** admission 2YTL ($1.50); daily 9am–noon and 1:30–5:30pm). The museum displays a small but noteworthy collection of faience with representations from the most important centers of early ceramic arts in Anatolia. Most impressive are the 13th-century Selçuk tiles, also employed to embellish the interior space. Notice the exterior portal (street side), typical of the restrained ornamentation of Selçuk architecture. The nearby **Ince Minare** is another fine example of the ornamental use of Selçuk tiles. Admission is 2YTL ($1.50); the minaret is open daily 9am to noon and 1:30 to 5:30pm.

Next to the Mevlana Museum in the park is the stately **Selimiye Mosque** *, a clas-sic Ottoman building constructed between 1558 and 1587 when the future sultan Selim II was governor of Konya.

9

Ankara

Unlike Istanbul, vulnerable for centuries to neighboring countries with imperialistic motives, **Ankara** ✿ lies deep within the heartland, protected and insulated from uninvited guests. Atatürk deliberately chose Ankara for his new republic; while Istanbul was the seat of an imperial and dissolute empire, he saw Ankara as the clean-slate capital of an entirely new Turkish state. In the 80 years since Atatürk rode in on a dirt road and literally lifted Ankara out of the ashes, the city has established itself as the political and cultural center of Turkey. Ankara is almost exclusively geared toward sustaining a wide-ranging population of foreign ambassadors, visiting dignitaries, local politicians, and politically minded business enterprises. If you're looking for a good English pub, then you've come to the right place. It also boasts a number of prestigious universities and technical colleges, as well as the largest library in the country. Ankara is a center for opera, ballet, jazz, and modern dance, and is home of the Presidential Symphony Orchestra, the State Theatre, and the State Opera and Ballet.

But while Ankara buzzes with the everyday business of keeping house, you can't compare Ankara to cities like Washington, D.C., or London, even if the brilliant Museum of Anatolian Civilizations is worth a special detour. It's not that there's nothing to do here: The short list of worthy monuments and museums includes Atatürk's mausoleum, a handful of Roman-era sites, and as mentioned before, the archaeological museum. There's a predictable concentration of statues of Atatürk, and dotting the parks and avenues are monuments to inspire a strong sense of nationalism. The **Victory Monument,** in Ulus Square, honors the heroes of the War of Independence, while the **Monument to a Secure and Confident Future,** in Güvenlik Park, reminds Turks to "be proud, work hard, and have self-confidence." The **Hatti Monument** ✿, an oversize replica of a bronze solar disc, is hard to miss on Sıhhiye Square and stands as a constant reminder of the country's Anatolian roots. If none of this sounds too convincing for a stopover in the country's capital, I have to admit that the choice of whether to stop here is a dilemma borne by many. Most people choose to skip Ankara in favor of a direct transfer to Cappadocia, but, if you're this close, you should stop at least for a visit to the Museum of Anatolian Civilizations and a stroll in and around the ancient citadel. A longer stay, however, will allow for a little exploration and perhaps a poke around the copper workshops at the base of the citadel.

1 Orientation

454km (282 miles) southeast of Istanbul; 544km (338 miles) northeast of Antalya; 582km (362 miles) east of İzmir;
277km (172 miles) northwest of Nevşehir

GETTING THERE

BY PLANE Ankara's **Esenboğa International Airport** is a major hub for domestic
flights on Turkish Airlines (© **0312/398-0100** at the airport). Direct international
flights arrive from Vienna, Moscow, and Munich, as well as some other German cities,
with increased service in the summer.

The Esenboğa International Airport is 32km (20 miles) from the city center. **Havaş**
provides bus transportation to the city, leaving from the main bus terminal with a stop
at the train station. The ride costs 8YTL ($6). (Buses to the airport also arrive
at/depart from 19 Mayıs Stadium, Gate B, in Altındağ). Departures coincide with the
landing schedules of the flights. (Claim your luggage quickly, because they only wait
around 30 min. after landing time.) Otherwise, a taxi into the city will run from about
27YTL ($20) to Ulus and 34YTL ($25) to Kavaklıdere. For information on Havaş
buses back to the airport, call the bus station (© **0312/310-6584**).

BY BUS Virtually every city in the country, no matter how small, has at least one
bus company with service to Ankara, offering almost as many fare options as buses.
For example, Varan (© **0312/224-0043**) runs 10 buses daily from Istanbul (travel
time 6 hr.; 53YTL/$40); Pamukkale (© **0312/433-0470**) runs buses from virtually
everywhere in western Turkey, including from Istanbul (7 hr.; 27YTL/$20); Özkay-
mak (© **0312/224-0055**) and Kent (© **0312/224-0138**) operate buses from Kayseri.
To get to town from Ankara's **AŞTI Otogar,** hop a cab—about 13YTL ($10) to the
city center. There is a metro station just outside the bus entrance, but whoever
designed it didn't think of travelers with luggage; you must navigate an insurmount-
able number of steps to get to the platform.

BY TRAIN Of all the Turkish National Railroad trains in the country, the modern,
air-conditioned, and dependable **Ankara Ekspresi** night train from Istanbul's Haydarpaşa train station to Ankara is the most reliable for service and comfort. A bunk in
one of the sleeper cars costs 65YTL ($48); two beds cost 45YTL ($33) per person. Cabins sleep (tightly) up to three passengers, and they don't penalize you for taking up the
whole cabin as a single traveler. (There's also a 1.35YTL/$1 "conductor fee" collected
by the car attendant at the end of the journey; this is a legal and modest surcharge.)
You'll need a reservation for a spot on this train, so don't leave your ticket purchase until
the last minute. The train departs nightly at 10:30pm (travel time: 9 hr. 40 min.).

There are nine additional daily departures of slow trains heading to points east,
with fares around 22YTL ($16), depending on which train you take. Tickets and
information are available at both Istanbul's Haydarpaşa (© **0216/336-0475**) and
Sirkeci (© **0212/511-5888**) train stations. You can also get automated information
for the sleeper train (© **0216/336-4470**) and the regular train (© **0216/336-0475**),
but because the recordings are in Turkish, you'll want to enlist aid from your concierge.

Remember that all trains to Ankara leave *from Haydarpaşa Station on the Asian side*
(ferries depart from Karaköy to Kadiköy every half-hour for the 15-min. trip;
5.40YTL/$4). If you're wondering what to do in the hours prior to the departure, the
restaurant in the Haydarpaşa Station is a popular rest stop.

Father of Turkey: The Man Called Atatürk

It's impossible to overstate Atatürk's hold on this country, nearly 70 years after his death. His presence is unavoidable, his legacy everywhere. Children are taught from near birth to revere the heroic, ambitious, revolutionary figure who single-handedly forged a united Turkish state from the tattered remains of the Ottoman Empire.

On May 19, 1919, Mustafa Kemal Pasha landed in the Black Sea port of Samsun, officially launching the War of Independence. Less than a year later, the Grand National Assembly convened, prompting the sultan to condemn Kemal to death. But Kemal's savvy military campaign did not falter, and 2 years later, liberation armies succeeded in clearing the mainland of all foreign presence.

Born Mustafa Kemal in Salonica in 1881, he channeled his energy into a military career at an early age. In 1905, while in the service of the sultan, he co-founded a secret organization to fight the Ottoman ruler's despotism. But unlike some power-hungry despots, Kemal's efforts resulted from a zealous love for his culture, and a refusal to see his country's sovereignty compromised. He gained widespread attention in 1915 for his pivotal role in turning back Allied forces during the long, brutal battle at Gallipoli, and emerged from that campaign with the makings of a hero's reputation. At the close of World War I, Allied victors appeared ready to move in and carve up the Ottoman Empire, to the apparent indifference of the sultan. This galvanized Kemal, and he moved to harness nationalist sentiment and recruit an organized resistance.

VISITOR INFORMATION

There's a **Tourist Information office** at the airport (© **0312/398-0348**) as well as downtown at Ismet Inönü Bulvarı (© **0312/212-8300** and Gazi Mustafa Kemal Bulv. 121, Tandoğan (across from the Maltepe subway entrance; © **0312/229-2631**). The latter location doubles as a cute museum-type souvenir shop.

If you're here for an extended stay, why not think about Turkish language classes? **Tömer** offers courses at two locations: Ziya Gökalp Cad. 18, in the neighborhood of Kızılay (© **0312/434-3090**), and Tunalı Hilmi Cad. 97, in Kavaklıdere (© **0312/426-2047**), or check out their website at www.tomer.ankara.edu.tr.

CITY LAYOUT

The city's major thoroughfare, suitably named **Atatürk Bulvarı,** runs the length of Ankara from north to south, from the Equestrian Statue of Atatürk at Ulus Meydanı all the way down to the Presidential Mansion in Çankaya, about 5km (3 miles) away.

The area around Ulus Meydanı forms the oldest section of the city. To the north of the open statued square are remnants of ancient Rome. Immediately west of the statue runs **Cumhuriyet Bulvarı,** home to several museums and monuments to Republican Turkey. **AŞTI,** Ankara's *otogar* (station), is located southwest of Ulus at the end of the metro line. The **train station** is more centrally located closer to Ulus

That military victory was just the beginning, for Kemal intended no less than a societal revolution to follow. "We shall strive to win victories in such fields as culture, scholarship, science, and economics," he declared, adding that "the enduring benefits of victories depend only on the existence of an army of education." With blackboard and chalk in hand, he traveled to every corner of the country, breathing new life into this withering nation.

In his 15-year presidency, Atatürk drew his country into the 20th century through drastic and sweeping changes, not the least of which were the adoption of the Western alphabet and the insistence on a complete separation of church and state. He abolished many of the institutions that lay at the heart of Turkey, thus forcing the country to reject its Ottoman heritage. He created a new national identity, a sense of unity and pride that endures to this day. In 1934, when a law establishing surnames was instituted, the parliament gave him the name *Atatürk*—Father of the Turks. He died in 1938, 18 years after becoming president and utterly transforming his homeland.

Atatürk's influence on modern Turkey has not been without criticism, although much of this must be discreet, because *it has always been illegal to slander the Father of the Republic.* Fundamentalist critics argue that Islam as a way of life provides for all the legal needs of the country; for highly observant Muslims, the separation of mosque and state has gone too far. But Atatürk recognized that a march into the future was inevitable, and his vision lives on in a prosperous and modernizing Turkey. In his words: "Proud is he who calls himself a Turk."

at the southwestern end of Cumhuriyet Bulvarı. Not surprisingly, the closer you get to the transport hub, the seedier it gets.

At the base of the fortress hill, located about a 5-minute walk uphill on Hisarparkı Caddesi east of the Atatürk statue, is where you will find the **Museum of Anatolian Civilizations**. A detour from Hisarparkı Caddesi onto **Çıkrıkçılar Yokuşu** will take you through the market; eventually, all roads uphill lead to the old fortress, a living, breathing mix of modern Turkey and the Turkish heartland. The neighborhood directly opposite the main entrance is undergoing a stunning transformation; here you'll find the newly preserved **Çengelhan,** a Caravansaray dating to 1522 and housing the new Rahmi M. Koç Museum, along with a number of newish cafes and teahouses.

South of Ulus along Atatürk Bulvarı is the modern section of **Kızılay,** a bustling zone of modern shopping, outdoor cafes, and bookstores. On the south side of Gazi Kemal Bulvarı is the neighborhood of **Yenişehir,** or "New City," the modern business heart of Ankara; here you'll find airline and bus ticket offices, restaurants, and a few recommendable three- and four-star hotels.

Still farther south on Atatürk Bulvarı is **Kavaklıdere,** an old vineyard now home to the Sheraton, Hilton, residential housing, and easy living. The cluster of neighborhoods that includes Kavaklıdere, Çankaya, and Gaziosmanpaşa is where you'll find most of the foreign embassies.

Ankara Accommodations, Dining & Attractions

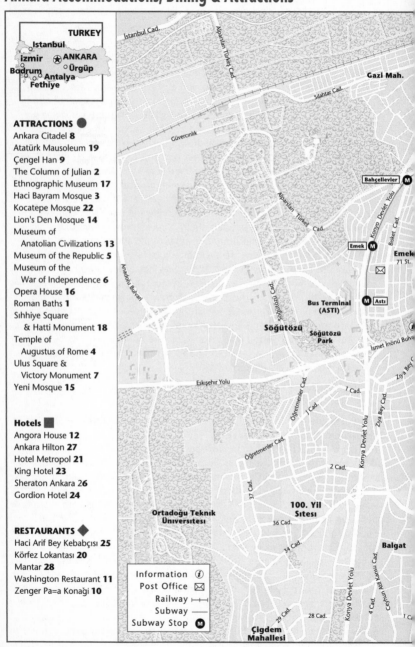

TURKEY

Istanbul
İzmir ★ **ANKARA**
Bodrum ○ Ürgüp
Antalya
Fethiye

ATTRACTIONS ●
Ankara Citadel **8**
Atatürk Mausoleum **19**
Çengel Han **9**
The Column of Julian **2**
Ethnographic Museum **17**
Haci Bayram Mosque **3**
Kocatepe Mosque **22**
Lion's Den Mosque **14**
Museum of
  Anatolian Civilizations **13**
Museum of the Republic **5**
Museum of the
  War of Independence **6**
Opera House **16**
Roman Baths **1**
Sıhhiye Square
  & Hatti Monument **18**
Temple of
  Augustus of Rome **4**
Ulus Square &
  Victory Monument **7**
Yeni Mosque **15**

Hotels ■
Angora House **12**
Ankara Hilton **27**
Hotel Metropol **21**
King Hotel **23**
Sheraton Ankara 2**6**
Gordion Hotel **24**

RESTAURANTS ◆
Haci Arif Bey Kebabçısı **25**
Körfez Lokantası **20**
Mantar **28**
Washington Restaurant **11**
Zenger Pa=a Konaği **10**

Istanbul Cad.
Alparslan Turkeş Cad.
Gazi Mah.
Silahtar Cad.
Güvercinlik
Alparslan Turkeş Cad.
Bahçelievler Ⓜ
Konya Devlet Yolu
Basket Cad.
Emek Ⓜ
Emek
71 St.
⊠
Anadolu Bulvarı
Söğütözü Cad.
Bus Terminal (ASTI) Ⓜ Astı
Söğütözü
Söğütözü Park
İsmet İnönü Bulvarı
Eskişehir Yolu
Öğretmenler Cad.
J Cad.
1 Cad.
Ziya Bey Cad.
Ziya Bey Cad.
Öğretmenler Cad.
2 Cad.
37 Cad.
Konya Devlet Yolu
Ortadoğu Teknik Üniversitesi
36 Cad.
34 Cad.
100. Yil Sitesi
Balgat
4 Cad.
Ceyhun Atıf Kansu Cad.
29 Cad.
28 Cad.
Konya Devlet Yolu
Çigdem Mahallesi

Information ⓘ
Post Office ⊠
Railway ├┼┤
Subway ──
Subway Stop Ⓜ

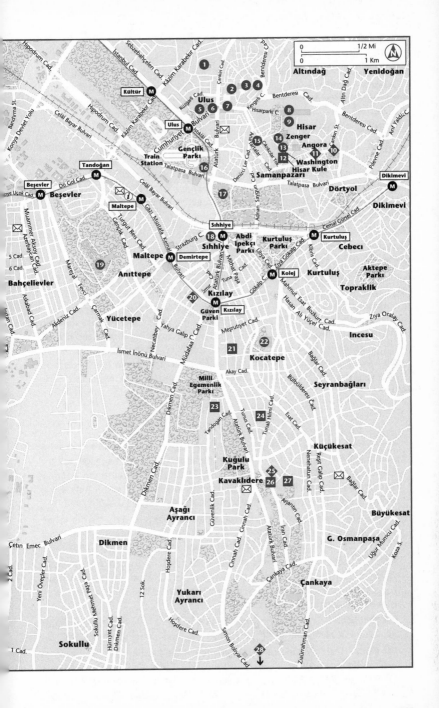

Altındağ   Yenidoğan

1

Kültür   **2** **3** **4**

Ulus   Ruzgari Cad.   Bentderesi Cad.

5 **6** **7**   Kengiri C.   Bentderesi Cad.

Ulus   Hisarparki C.   **8**

   9 Hisar
   Zenger

Cumhuriyet   **14** **15** **13** Angora   **11**
Train   Gençlik   **12**   **10**
Station   Parki   Washington
   16   Hisar Kule
   Samanpazarı

Tandoğan   Dikimevi
Beşevler
   Dörtyol   Dikimevi
Beşevler   **17**

Maltepe   Sıhhiye

5 Cad.   **18**   Kurtuluş   Kurtuluş
   Sıhhiye   Abdi   Parkı
6 Cad.   İpekçi   Cebeci
   Parkı
Maltepe   **19**   Demirtepe   Kolej   Kurtuluş   Aktepe
Bahçelievler   Anıttepe   Parkı
   Toprakli

   Kızılay
   20
Yücetepe   Güven   Kızılay   İncesu
   Parkı

   Meşrutiyet Cad.
   21   **22**
   Kocatepe   Seyranbağları
   Akay Cad.

   Milli
   Egemenlik
   Parkı
   23   **24**

   Küçükesat

   Kuğulu
   Park   **25**
Kavaklıdere   **26** **27**

Aşağı   Büyükesat
Ayrancı
   G. Osmanpaşa
Dikmen

   Çankaya
   Yukarı
   Ayrancı

Sokullu

   28
   ↓

363

Tips **Convenient Airport Check-In**

Turkish Airlines allows you to complete the check-in process for flights out of Ankara from the Havaş bus terminal before boarding the bus for the airport.

GETTING AROUND

BY CAR   The Anatolian highway system is uncomplicated enough that a visitor can easily make his or her way to the greater Ankara area. Problem is, once you get there, one-way streets and avenues wind around until you unexpectedly pass your destination in a no-turn lane. And the population boom has resulted in an absence of adequate parking. If you'll be navigating by car, get your hotel to spell out the route in advance—or leave the car at the hotel in lieu of a taxi.

BY TAXI   Taking taxis makes the most sense in Ankara, especially for short stays. Gasoline costs less here and taxi fares are slightly lower than in Istanbul.

BY PUBLIC TRANSPORTATION   Ankara's metro system is a fast and easy way to get around. The only problem is that stops aren't in areas where a tourist would want to go. The north-south line provides the most obvious access, from Kızılay to Ulus, but the metro stop is still a bit of a distance from the Roman ruins and the citadel. One single ride costs around 1YTL (75¢), but if you buy a pack of five, you save about 30%.

Metropolitan buses and *dolmuşes* depart from Güven Park in Kızılay and from Ulus to all points around the city, usually for under 1YTL (75¢). But if you're trying to catch a bus somewhere along the middle of a route, the system can be perplexing. Unless your stay here is extended, it's not worth wasting the time to decipher the local system.

FAST FACTS: Ankara

Airline Information   For information on flight arrivals or lost baggage, call the Esenboğa Airport information line (© **0312/398-0100**). Because the information line is in Turkish, have the hotel concierge call for you. Turkish Airlines has a downtown office at Atatürk Bulv. 154, Kavaklıdere (© **0312/428-1700**).

Ambulance   The national number for an ambulance is © **112**, but for emergency assistance from a private company, call Bayındır Hospital Ambulance (© **0312/287-9000**) or Özel (Private) Ambulans Servisi (© **0312/425-1565**).

American Express   Turk Ekspres at Cinnah Cad. 9/4, in Çankaya (© **0312/467-7334**), is the local travel service representative of American Express in Ankara. For customer assistance, you must contact the Istanbul number (see "Fast Facts: Istanbul" in chapter 4, "Istanbul").

Bus Companies   Companies include **Kamil Koç** (© 0312/417-3936), **Pamukkale** (© 0312/433-0470), **Ulusoy** (© 0312/440-1468), and **Varan** (© 0312/426-9753).

Car Rental   The following car-rental agencies have locations at the airport, as well as downtown (Kavaklıdere) offices: **Avis,** Tunus Cad. 68/2, Kavaklıdere (© 0312/467-2313); **Europcar,** Koza Sok 142/17, Gaziosmanpaşa (© 0312/448-2747); **Hertz,** Tahran Cad, 18 (© 0312/446-5048); **Budget,** Tunus Cad. 39/A

(© 0312/417-5952) and the Turkish company, **De-Car,** Tunus Cad. 77/1 (© 0312/426-9737) as well as in the Dedeman Hotel. Don't underestimate the need for an English-speaking sales representative, and compare your receipt with your credit card bill when it arrives.

Courier Services **DHL Worldwide** (© 0312/318-6800), **FedEx** (© 0312/442-2686), **TNT** (© 0312/285-7394), and **UPS** (© 0312/318-6729) all have locations in Ankara, and offer convenient pickup services.

Currency Exchange Rates at foreign currency exchange offices are better than those at the banks and hotels. There are several in Kızılay at Mesrutiyet Cad. 2/91, Mesrutiyet Cad. 3/25, Mesrutiyet Cad. Kok Han 2/90, and Atatürk Bulv. 73. In Çankaya you'll find offices at Çankaya Cad. 6/1, Çankaya Cad. 6/B, and in the Atakule Tower.

Embassies & Consulates See "Turkish Embassies & Consulates," p. 23.

Hospitals Among the private hospitals in town are **Çankaya Hospital,** Bulten Sok. 44, Kavaklıdere (© 0312/426-1450); **Başkent University Hospital,** Fevzi Çakmak Cad. 10, Sok. 45, Bahçelievler (© 0312/212-6868); and **Bayındır Hospital,** Kızılırmak Mahallesi 28, Sok. 2, Sögütözü (© 0312/287-9000). The last also has a dental clinic on the premises.

Post Office The main post office is located in Ulus on Atatürk Bulvarı. There is another branch in Kızılay Square and countless others around town, all open from 8:30am to 5:30pm, Monday through Friday.

Telephone Dial © 115 for an international operator (and remember to dial 0 before a city's prefix). For calling cards and collect calls via ATT, dial © 00/800-122-77.

Turkish Railways The number for Ankara's Gar or train station, located at Talatpaşa Bulvarı at the bottom of Cumhuriyet Bulvarı, is © 0312/0312-6708. For information on schedules and trains, call © 0312/311-0620; for tickets and reservations, call © 0312/310-6515. You can also check out their website for information and schedules (in Turkish only) at www.tcdd.gov.tr/yolcu/trenler.htm.

2 Where to Stay

Until recently, Ankara hadn't witnessed the opening of a new hotel since the advent of the republic—probably due to the fact that no one wanted to spend the night here. It's not uncommon for people to fly in, spin through the museum, then drive the 4 to 5 hours to Cappadocia. But with the opening of the Angora House, which occupies a characteristic house in the citadel, and the Gordion Hotel, a handsome boutique-style hotel in Kavaklıdere, an overnight in Ankara is no longer a necessary evil.

ULUS

Angora House ✪ *Finds*   This restored former home of Şakir Paşa, a member of Atatürk's first parliament, provides visitors to Ankara with the only opportunity to live amid the city's early history, smack dab in the historic citadel. Virtually unscarred by tourist overdevelopment, the citadel is literally steps away from the archaeological museum. The hosts like to look after their guests (Ahmet might even play some folk music come nightfall), and each room has the character of a guest room in a private

---

Tips   Five-Star Workouts

Even if you're not staying in a five-star hotel, you can still pay to use its gym, which usually includes a swimming pool. Try the **Sheraton Ankara,** Noktalı Sokagı, Kavaklıere (© **0312/468-5454**), or the **Ankara Hilton,** Tahran Cad. 12 (© **0312/468-2888**). Or try the more affordable private gym, Tivolino, on Tunali Hilmi about 4 blocks south of the Sheraton.

---

home. Of the scant six rooms, it's hard to say which is best: an antique Assyrian wardrobe stands in no. 18; no. 16 gets a latticed wooden ceiling and the only bathtub in the house; no. 22 (one of the suites) has a spacious bathroom in a hidden niche and a stunning gold-leaf ceiling; and no. 20 (the other suite) enjoys a view of Ankara from the shower. Antiques are scattered about, architectural highlights such as original prayer niches remain in place, and an inner courtyard offers the perfect opportunity for you to avail yourself of host Muammer's considerable knowledge, eke out a quick Turkish lesson, or bum a cigarette.

Kalekapısı Sok. 16, 06240 Ankara (in the citadel; instruct the taxi driver). © **0312/309-8380.** Fax 0312/309-8381. 6 units. 70€ ($85) double. MC, V. **Amenities:** 2 bars; laundry service; dry cleaning.

KIZILAY

Hotel Metropol   Located down a quiet street near the Kocatepe Mosque, this 13-year-old cement block is one of the best buys in Ankara. Mercifully painted brick red, the interior is decorated more inventively, with marble details in the lobby and a charming stained-glass panel of a Turkish village in the dining area. The rooms are clean and comfortable, decorated in deep blue, brick, and rusty hues, but the lack of air-conditioning might make you think twice before holing up here in the height of summer. The hotel is nestled amid restaurants, coffee shops, and Internet cafes, but you'll have to take a taxi to visit most of the major sights.

Olgunlar Sok. 5, Bakanlıklar (just below Kızılay). © **0312/417-6990.** Fax 0312/417-6990. 32 units. 100€ ($120) double; 123€ ($150) suite. Breakfast 3.25€ ($4) extra. AE, DC, MC, V. Free parking available. **Amenities:** Restaurant; bar; 24-hr. room service; laundry service; dry cleaning. *In room:* Local TV.

King Hotel *Value*   At first glance the King, in the neighborhood west of Kavaklıd-ere, may be considered a less than convenient base (unless your destination is the American Embassy). But the hotel makes up for the distance with two on-site restaurants, a pool, a sauna, and a lovely garden. Rooms are tastefully simple without being banal, offering more than an average amount of space. The bathrooms cover all of the comfort bases, with tub/shower combos, en-suite telephones, and plenty of indigenous marble. The slightly nobler sister hotel (Piyade Sokak 17, Çankaya; © **0312/ 440-7931**) costs only a few dollars more and is convenient to the UN House and to Mantar restaurant (see below).

Güvenlik Cad. 13, 06700 Aşağı Ayrancı/Ankara. © **0312/418-9099.** Fax 0312/417-0382. otetas@kinghotel.com.tr. 36 units. 50€–60€ ($60–$75) double. MC, V. **Amenities:** 2 restaurants; 2 bars; outdoor swimming pool; sauna; health club; fitness room; business center; laundry service; dry-cleaning; 24-hr. room service; wireless Internet. *In room:* A/C, TV, dataport, minibar, hair dryer, safe.

KAVAKLIDERE

Ankara Hilton *⑧*   The Ankara Hilton delivers the impeccable service and creature comforts that business travelers and tourists alike expect from the chain. Renovated in

2004, new multi-functional rooms sport Murphy-style beds to create a meeting environment, and an entire floor of studio suites caters to long stays. Rooms are crisp and comfortably outfitted in the inoffensive and reliable decor that Hilton is so famous for. An unfaltering American management style has provided for cable TV, laptop connections in all of the rooms, and morning delivery of the English language *Turkish Daily News.*

Tahran Cad. 12, 06700 Kavaklıdere. ℂ **800-HILTONS** or 0312/455-0000. Fax 0312/455-0055. www.hilton.com. 324 units. 238€ ($290) double on standard floor; 280€ ($340) double on executive floor; 315€ ($385) and up suite. AE, DC, MC, V. **Amenities:** 2 restaurants; bar; indoor swimming pool; fitness center; Turkish bath; Jacuzzi; sauna; concierge; tour desk; car-rental desk; business center w/secretarial services; shopping arcade; salon; 24-hr. room service; laundry service; dry cleaning; executive floor. *In room:* A/C, satellite TV w/movies, fax, dataport, minibar, hair dryer, iron/ironing board, safe.

Gordion Hotel 🌟🌟   For those who prefer the intimacy of a small hotel but can't do without five-star amenities, this is the place. With its earthy tones and leather and brass detailing, the decor is a bit masculine for your typical boutique hotel. Or maybe I'm just partial to plants and silken textiles. Still, I'd stay here in a heartbeat, not least of all for the in-house beauty center and spa-like pool setting. The location is also dandy: right off the main shopping/eating district in the heart of Kavaklıdere. All rooms are wired for Internet access, and laptops, cellphones, and even PlayStations are available for rental—great for keeping kids busy during dad's business meeting.

Büklüm Sokak 59 (just off of Tunalı Hilmi), Kavaklıdere. ℂ **0312/427-8080.** Fax 0312/427-8085. www.gordionhotel. com. 44 units. 65€–115€ ($80–$140) single; 82€–148€ ($100–$180) double; 165€–255€ ($200–$310) suite. Rates include breakfast but exclude tax. MC, V. Indoor parking. **Amenities:** 2 restaurants; bar; indoor swimming pool; fitness center; steam room; sauna; meeting room; salon; massage; 24-hr. room service; laundry service; dry cleaning; nonsmoking rooms. *In room:* A/C, interactive Internet TV; dataport, minibar, hair dryer, safe.

Sheraton Ankara 🌟🌟   I was determined not to like the Sheraton Ankara, with its tower surging arrogantly into the Ankara sky (a visual companion to the obtrusive nearby Hilton). But the bright atrium lobby, tastefully smattered with an eclectic mix of traditional and designer furniture, immediately won me over. The trendy yet inviting touches include plum-colored leather bucket chairs with stainless steel feet and a mezzanine lounge that doubles as an art gallery.

The rooms are what you'd expect from a Sheraton, and even a little more, with spacious Turkish marble bathrooms and plush room decor. There are a few "smart" rooms for business travelers equipped with high-tech phones and faxes; modem lines have been installed in every room. The rooftop sun deck transforms itself into a movie theater on summer nights, and the hotel even serves Sunday brunch.

Noktalı Sok., Kavaklıdere. ℂ **800/325-3535** or 0312/468-5454. Fax 0312/467-1136. www.sheratonankara.com. 307 units. 213€–233€ ($260–$285) double in the hotel; 262€ ($320) in the towers; 439€–902€ ($535–$1,100) suite. Breakfast may or may not be included in rate; ask for special packages. AE, DC, MC, V. Free parking in outdoor lot. **Amenities:** 3 restaurants; 3 bars (only 2 in winter); outdoor swimming pool; tennis court; squash; health club; Turkish bath; Jacuzzi; sauna; concierge; tour desk; car-rental desk; business center with secretarial services; shopping arcade; salon; 24-hr. room service; massage; laundry service; dry cleaning; nonsmoking rooms; executive floor. *In room:* A/C, satellite TV w/pay movies, minibar, hair dryer, safe.

3 Where to Dine

If you're in Ankara overnight, I recommend eating dinner in one of the restaurants converted from an old Ottoman house in the citadel. Alternatively, seek out an inexpensive to midrange *kebap* joint around Kızılay or step out in style at one of the trendy restaurants along Abjantin Caddesi in Kavaklıdere or in Çankaya. Don't forget to grab a mid-morning snack of sımıt, a crispier version than what you'd find in Istanbul, smothered with soft cheese (found at stands everywhere in the mornings).

AROUND ULUS

Washington Restaurant TURKISH   An institution in Ankara, the Washington Restaurant was established in 1955 with the money the owners raised while working at the Turkish Embassy in Washington, D.C. The restaurant remained in Kızılay until 1992, when it reopened in its present location in the citadel. Sadly, they've gone back to Kızılay, but the new owners have installed a solid traditional menu of quality favorites. The 400-year-old timber-framed house, restored by the Municipality, makes use of a huge outdoor dining terrace (open in summer only), which capitalizes on hilltop views of Ankara and the bell tower next door.

Doyran Sok. 5–7, in the citadel. © 0312/311-4344. Appetizers and main courses 3.40YTL–11YTL ($2.50–$8). AE, DC, MC, V. Daily 11:30am–midnight.

Zenger Paşa Konağı *(Kids* TRADITIONAL TURKISH   If you haven't yet tried *mantı* (Turkish ravioli), do it here. These minuscule dumplings are made on the premises right before your eyes, and served in a warm spicy garlicky yogurt sauce (sadly, it's available at lunchtime only). There's a brick oven for crunchy *pide* (flat bread) as well as the ubiquitous *gözleme*, a hearty but light crepelike treat with a selection of fillings. The *kebaps* arrive on a piping-hot tile. The brick and timber house has a back porch for a romantic twilight supper and spectacular views of the hillside below. The topfloor dining room will get you views of Ankara and the serenade of a live guitar player. Before you leave, be sure to have a look at the small collection of Turkish and Ottoman memorabilia.

Doyran Sok. 13, in the citadel. © 0312/311-7070. Appetizers and main courses 3.40YTL–7.40YTL ($2.50–$5.50). MC, V. Daily 11am–midnight.

KIZILAY

Körfez Lokantası TURKISH   This no-frills but popular spot isn't in all the books for nothing; excellent food at reasonable prices is a guarantee at Körfez. Besides the fish and grills and a lineup of great mezes, Körfez has a special menu of the day—the way to go if you want to ensure freshness and divert your palate from the items you've been eating day after day. Try the specialty of the house, Körfez's fried anchovies.

Bayındır Sok. 24, Kızılay. © 0312/431-1459. Fish courses 11YTL ($8) and up; *kebaps* 6.75YTL ($5). No credit cards. Daily 11am–midnight.

KAVAKLIDERE AND ÇANKAYA

Hacı Arif Bey Kebabçısı KEBAPS   If you're looking for a special place to dine, it's unlikely that you're going to seek out another *kebap* place in this neighborhood. Too bad, because this restaurant comes highly recommended. One of the more established places in the area, Haçıçı Arif Bey Kebabçısı has managed to maintain a loyal clientele by consistently serving perfectly cooked grilled meats and an incredible sticky-sweet baklava every time.

Güniz Sok. 48, Kavaklıdere. © 0312/467-6730. Appetizers 3.40YTL–4YTL ($2.50–$3); main courses 6.75YTL–12YTL ($5–$9). AE, MC, V. Daily noon–11pm.

Mantar TURKISH HOME-STYLE   A hit with the locals as well as a lunchtime favorite of UN employees down the road, Mantar serves grub that is good enough to bring you back again and again. Thought you'd have an outstanding hunkar begendi or yaprak dolmasi (stuffed grape leaves)? Try the ones here. They also serve some dishes I'd never seen elsewhere. My favorite is the karamanmaraş köftesi (delectable balls made of semolina); another is the irmik dessert (more semolina) with chocolate sauce.

4. Cadde 4/A Yıldız. ⓒ 0312/440-0978. Appetizers and main courses 5.40YTL–11YTL ($4–$8). MC, V. Daily 11am–midnight.

4 What to See & Do

In spite of Ankara being one of the top three cities in Turkey for work and play, my unofficial subtitle for this section is, "Give Me One Good Reason to Spend the Night in Ankara." Like any capital city, Ankara offers an endless selection of cultural institutions, activities, and events, but let's be realistic—you didn't come all this way to check out the Museum of the Centennial of History of Sports and Education now, did you? But you did come to see the Museum of Anatolian Civilizations, and you won't be disappointed. The question is, then what?

Although the Atatürk Mausoleum (Anıtkabir), set on the western side of the city, deserves a look, most of your free time should be spent in and around the citadel; it's the most picturesque and typical neighborhood of old Ankara, with some of the best views.

THE TOP ATTRACTIONS

Ankara Citadel (Hisar) ⓖ   The Hisar presides over an outcropping in the oldest settled part of the city. It's believed to have been built by the Galatians, but no one really knows for sure. The fortress has an inner and outer wall, the outer added during the Byzantine occupation of the city. The castle in its present state was most recently restored by the Ottomans, and dates to the Selçuk period.

Today the citadel retains much of the flavor of a small Anatolian village; from its narrow winding streets, you can catch a fleeting glimpse of the home life within. If there's any architecture worth a gander in Ankara, it's within the walls of the fortress. Many of the traditional wood-beamed houses, complete with large courtyards and gardens, have been restored and converted into marvelously atmospheric restaurants. One such establishment is the And Café, a welcomed characteristic rest-stop just beyond the stone arched entrance to the outer citadel (with your back to the Angora House, walk right to the end; the arch is on your left; the And Café is on the second floor).

Ulus. (Follow Cumhuriyet Bulv. past the statue of Atatürk, and continue along Hisar Parkı Cad.)

Atatürk Mausoleum (Anıtkabir) ⓖⓖ   The Turkish psychological equivalent of the John F. Kennedy Memorial at Arlington National Cemetery in Washington, D.C., Anıtkabir draws reverent Turks from all over the country to pay their respects to the founder of the republic. Built in 1944 atop a hill overlooking the city, the memorial complex stands starkly unadorned except for the vast mosaic courtyard and the mausoleum itself, the inside of which is covered in gold leaf. Outside, soldiers are present at every corner, and if you time it right, you can witness the severe, imposing Changing of the Guard. The courtyard arcade permits entry into various rooms including the gift shop and the recently installed **Atatürk and War of Independence Museum** ⓖⓖ. The museum extends the entire circumference of the courtyard (lower level), and honors the founder of Turkey and the republic with sound and light dioramas of the War of Independence campaigns, portraits and period artwork, and various exhibits highlighting the history of the republic.

Entrance on Akdeniz Cad., Anıttepe. ⓒ 0312/231-7975. Free admission. Tues–Sun 9am–5pm.

Museum of Anatolian Civilizations (Anadolu Medeniyetleri Müzesi) ✹✹✹
This is the finest archaeological collection in all of Turkey and the primary reason
Ankara is worth a stopover. Housed in a **15th-century caravansary and covered
bazaar** ✹ constructed under the reign of Mehmet the Conqueror, the museum contains a remarkable record of every civilization that passed through Anatolia as far back
as the caveman.

The exhibit begins with artifacts believed to date to the Paleolithic Age, and follows
the progression of time throughout the museum. The most impressive Neolithic Age
findings are an **8,000-year-old wall** ✹✹, clay and ceramic representations of **bulls'
heads** ✹, images of a fat and misshapen Mother Goddess called **Kybele** ✹✹✹ (later
Cybele, forerunner of Artemis and probably the Virgin Mary), and **wall paintings
from Çatalhöyük** ✹, man's oldest known stationary civilization. The collections illustrate the first time that man tills the soil, builds homes, and takes it upon himself to
decorate his surroundings. The Neolithic section gives way to artifacts recovered from
Hacılar, the center of the Chalcolithic Era, and includes a large collection of stone and
metal tools and decorative jewelry.

The Hatti tribes dominate the Bronze Age display with an abundance of **solar
discs** ✹, **deer- and bull-shaped statuettes** ✹✹✹, and an evolved (and much thinner)
version of the Mother Goddess ✹✹. Loads of **gold jewelry** ✹ give a rare look into
the daily and religious practices of this ancient people.

Findings from the Assyrian trade colonies discovered at Kültepe, near Kayseri, are
represented in the southern hall. (The Assyrians are credited with the introduction of
the written word into Anatolia, much of which records transactions, receipts, and
business agreements.) Over 20,000 **clay tablets** ✹✹✹, inscribed in Assyrian
cuneiform, have helped reveal a priceless amount of information on this period.

The highlight of the Great Hittite Empire exhibit is the famous **relief of the God
of War** ✹✹✹ taken from the King's Gate at Hattuşaş, but the bronze statues of fertility gods, bulls, and deer are not to be overlooked. There are various fruit bowls and
vases with animal shapes, and an infamous **vase** ✹✹ that depicts a wedding ceremony
along with the popular coital position of the time. Of major significance is the Akka-
dian-inscribed **tablet** ✹ (1275–1220 B.C.)—a correspondence between Egyptian
Queen Nefertari (identified here as Naptera), wife of Ramses II, and Hittite Queen
Puduhepa, wife of Hattuşili III, written after the treaty of Kadesh.

Around 1200 B.C. the Hittite Empire collapsed and left a vacuum in which the
foundation of new city kingdoms formed. The Phrygians were one of the more important of these civilizations; most of the artifacts in this section were found in the **royal
tumulus at Gordion,** the kingdom's capital. The tumulus measured 300m (984 ft.)
in diameter and 50m (164 ft.) in height. A reproduction of the **ancient tumulus** ✹
(burial mound) in which the tomb of King Midas was believed to have been found is
on display here; recent disputes have fueled speculation as to whether the tomb and
tumulus are actually those of Gordius. The Phrygian section also includes carved and
inlaid wooden furniture, hinged dress pins, ritual vessels in pottery and metal, and
depictions of powerful animals such as lions, rams, and eagles.

Displays in the central vaulted building are rotated, but generally contain **monumental statues** ✹ from the various collections.

On the lower lever (entrance located past the Chalcolithic display; save this for the
end of your visit, circling back around to the Neolithic section and taking the stairs
down) is a newer section of artifacts dating from the classical period plus a collection

of objects recovered from around Ankara. The small exhibition contains some marble statues, jewelry, decorative vessels, and coins.

Near the citadel entrance, Ulus. © **0312/324-3160**. Admission 10YTL ($7.50). Daily 8:30am–5:30pm.

OTHER ATTRACTIONS

The Column of Julian   The column, popularly known as the Belkıs Minaresi, or Queen of Sheba monument (for reasons unknown), was erected to commemorate a visit by the Emperor Julian in A.D. 362. The Corinthian capital dates to the 6th century; the stork's nest, a permanent crowning feature, is of more recent vintage.

Near Hükümet Meydanı, Ulus. Free admission.

Hacı Bayram Mosque (Hacı Bayram Camii)   Constructed in the 15th century for the founder of the Bayrami dervish sect, a Sufi poet and composer of hymns, the Hacı Bayram Mosque is one of the most important mosques in Ankara. The mosque was built in the Selçuk style and later restored by Sinan. The ceiling is made entirely of ornamental wood, punctuated by a single hexagonal rosette, and floral and plant motifs are found throughout the mosque. The decorative Kütahya tiles were added in the 18th century.

The **Hacı Bayram Mausoleum** attracts the faithful who visit the tomb of the Sufi mystic for prayer and inspiration. The mausoleum, with its marble facade and a sturdy lead dome over an octagonal drum, was completed a year after the mosque and borders the *mihrab's* exterior wall. The tomb's original wooden exterior and interior entrance doors are now part of the collection of the Ankara Ethnography Museum.

Ulus (from Ulus Meydanı follow Hisar Parkı Cad., turn left onto Hükümet Cad. and take the right fork). Free admission. Dawn–dusk.

Kocatepe Mosque (Kocatepe Camii)   Commanding the hill of Kocatepe, this mosque is the newest and the largest in all of Ankara, earning its place as a modern city landmark. The traditional Ottoman-style mosque was completed in 1987 and is ornamented with marble and gold leaf, stained-glass windows, decorative tile, and an enormous crystal chandelier. Enclosed in a booth in the center of the mosque is a model of the Mescid-I Nebevi mosque at Medina, presented to the Turkish President Demirel by King Fahd B. Abdulaziz of Saudi Arabia in 1993. Practicality reigns supreme in Islam, accounting for the superstore that has been opened in the cavernous basement area below.

Best access is from Olgunlar Sokagı, Kocatepe (southeast of Kızılay). Free admission. Dawn–dusk.

Lion's Den Mosque (Aslanhane Camii)   Named after the lion statues embedded in the wall of the tomb complex, the Aslanhane Mosque is another fine example of Selçuk architecture, with its polychrome ceramic mihrab. The rows of wooden support columns are unusual, all the more because they are topped off with recycled marble Corinthian capitals.

Off Kadife Sok. (near the entrance to the citadel), Ulus. Free admission. Dawn–dusk.

Museum of the Republic   This stone building was built from 1923 to 1925 to house the Grand National Assembly, after it was transferred from its original home base just down the road. The building was abandoned from 1961 until 1982, when it was renovated to accommodate the Museum of the Republic.

The center Assembly Hall is surrounded by corridors with access to exterior rooms, and constructed entirely of timber. The hall's two stories are decorated in typical

Selçuk and Ottoman style, housing a minor display of documents from the early days of the republic. The exhibit is labeled exclusively in Turkish, indicating that this museum is more a class-trip destination, but if you're in the neighborhood, it's worth a look for the Republican style of the building itself.

Atatürk Bulv., Ulus. © 0312/310-7140. Admission 2YTL ($1.50). Tues–Sun 8:30am–5pm.

Museum of the War of Independence (Kurtuluş Savaşı Müzesi)

This modest but dignified two-story building served as the first official seat of the Turkish Grand National Assembly. The exhibition includes documents, pictures, weapons, and objects from the War of Independence up to the founding of the republic, set in the original hall with desks straight out of a classroom scene from *Little House on the Prairie*. Lining the walls are wax figures of all of the presidents, an unusually grotesque custom of veneration repeated in the Atatürk Mausoleum.

Ulus Meydanı, Ulus. © 0312/310-4960. Admission 2YTL ($1.50). Tues–Sun 8:30am–5pm.

The Roman Baths

The baths were constructed during the time of Emperor Caracalla in honor of the god of medicine, Asklepios. The unusually large complex has three main divisions: a *frigidarium* (cold room), a *caldarium* (hot room), and a *tepidarium* (tepid room). The frigidarium had a pool and changing rooms; the caldarium contained a washing area and a *sudatorium* (sweating area); and the tepidarium was used primarily as a room for relaxing. There are also courtyards, hearths, service areas, and storage in the complex, although today only the foundations of the heating system and service section are visible.

Çankırı Ave. (just west of Cumhuriyet Bulv.), Ulus. No phone. Admission 2YTL ($1.50). Daily 8:30am–noon and 1–5:30pm.

The Temple of Augustus and Rome

The temple was built by the Galatians in A.D. 10 as a tribute to Augustus during the emperor's lifetime, and later reconstructed by the Romans in the 2nd century. In anticipation of his own death, Augustus prepared a total of four documents (a list of his lifetime deeds, a financial and military accounting of the state of the empire, orders for his funeral, and his last will and testament) with instructions that the documents be dispatched and publicly displayed throughout the Roman Empire. Copies of the four documents have been found throughout ancient Rome; this temple displays the best-preserved copy of the *Res Gestae Divi Augusti*, or Deeds of Deified Augustus (written in both Greek and Latin), which represents an invaluable historical resource. Unfortunately, millennia of seismic activity and exposure to the elements have taken their toll on the temple, which is encased in decayed and rusted scaffolding and closed to the public. Inclusion in 2002 on the World Monument Fund's list of most endangered sites has afforded it renewed attention—an ambitious study for restoration is currently underway by a joint project with the University of Trieste in Italy and the Middle Eastern Technical University in Ankara.

Attached to the Hacı Bayram Mosque, Ulus. No phone.

Yeni Mosque (Cenab Ahmet Paşa Camii)

This mosque was built in the 16th century by Sinan, the royal architect to Süleyman the Magnificent. It is the largest Ottoman mosque in Ankara and constructed of local red porphyry. The regal looking *mihrab* and the *minbar* (pulpit) are of white marble.

Ulucanlar Cad. and Çankırı Sok. (just east of the citadel), Ulus. Free admission. Dawn–dusk.

ESPECIALLY FOR KIDS (OF ALL AGES)

If scrambling around the old streets of the citadel wasn't enough to turn your kids on, the Ankara location of the **Rahmi M. Koç Museum** (Çengelhan, Sutepe Mahallesi, Depo Sokak 1, across from the entrance to the citadel; © **0312/309-6800**) will definitely do the trick. The museum, new as of April 2005, is housed in the freshly restored Çengelhan—an Ottoman-era Caravansaray standing at the center of what was a major commercial crossroad during the 16th and 17th centuries. The exhibits, which include thematic areas such as engineering, road transport, scientific instrumentation, medicine, and maritime pursuits—will appeal particularly to fans of "The Way Things Work"; many are interactive. Both the Divan Café (think gourmet chocolates and baklava) and Divan Brasserie have locations here; the latter sits in the atmospheric courtyard. The museum is open Tuesday through Friday 10am to 5pm; Saturday and Sunday 10am to 7pm. Admission is 3YTL ($2.25) for adults; students pay 95YKr (70¢).

The **Atatürk Farm and Zoo (Atatürk Orman Çiftliği),** 6.5km (4 miles) south of Ankara along the road to Bursa, was originally commissioned by Atatürk to demonstrate to a skeptical populace the possibilities inherent in an apparently barren land. Thanks to his initiative, and the latest agricultural techniques (ca. 1920), the farm and zoo has become a popular afternoon picnic destination, with its wide-open green spaces, cafes, and restaurant. The fact that the land does in fact yield fruit is proven by the excellent beer, old-fashioned ice cream, yogurt, and milk that visitors can sample. There's also an on-site replica of the house where Atatürk was born.

5 Shopping

In the bazaar area along **Çıkrıkçılar Yokuşu,** near Ulus, the strange sensation of being left alone permeates the air. In all of your travels around Turkey, you can bet that this is the *one* place you will not be accosted, hassled, harassed, or even approached. This might be due to the fact that this bazaar sees few foreign visitors. But even in the face of satin bedcovers, floor-length coats, and plastic shoes, a quiet stroll gazing at the local linens and essential items of daily life in Ankara is a lovely way to spend an afternoon.

At the end of Çıkrıkçılar Yokuşu is **Bakırcılar Çarşısı,** a characteristic street of local shops displaying a basic mix of handcrafted copper, kitchen, and hardware items. (Prices for trays and urns begin at around 47YTL/$35.) Heading left up the hill to the citadel gate is a street with a village feel and lined with spices, dried fruits, and nuts, all set out in bulk outside the shop entrances. There's also a good amount of wicker items and copper up this way as well, until you reach the gate of the citadel, where handicrafts give way to chintzy souvenirs.

Ankara has no shortage of modern shopping centers. Upscale shops like **Burberry's, Beymen, Calvin Klein,** and **Polo** can be found in the **Karum Iş Merkezi,** the shopping mall near the Sheraton and Hilton hotels. For those looking for more ready-to-wear, step outside Karum Iş Merkezi onto Tunali Hilmi Caddesi (the street running north-south between Kocatepe and Kizilay). Don't bother with the **Atakule Tower** in Çankaya; most of the shops are of low quality or closed altogether.

In **Kızılay,** where Gazi Kemal Bulvarı and Atatürk Bulvarı meet, is a busy intersection swarming with students and office workers on their lunch breaks. The **Gima** department store offers low-priced essentials and groceries, and is a useful marker to aid you in crossing the wide boulevard over to the streets between **Tuna Caddesi** and **Gazi Mustafa Kemal Bulvarı (Ziya Gökalp Caddesi** west of Atatürk Bulvarı).

Opposite the Gima is the more upscale **Yeni Karamürsel,** and interspersed among the outdoor cafes and beer houses around **Sakarya Caddesi** are a number of new- and used-book stores, most with a selection of titles in English, along with a passable number of Internet cafes.

If you've got a car, head out to where most of the better shops have transferred—to the Armada Shopping Center, located off the eastbound side of the road to Eskisehir or the Mudo megastore on the Konya road.

Even without the slightest intention of buying a sack of potatoes, it's still fun to take a walk through one of the many neighborhood *pazars* **(local markets),** where you're likely to find Polo or Banana Republic overstocks, as well as other necessary and not-so-necessary goods. The largest market is located in the center of Ankara behind the Abdi Ipekçi Park in Sıhhiye. The market operates on Wednesdays and Saturdays, and like other local markets, is open from dawn to dusk. Also on Wednesday is the covered bazaar in Aşağı Arancı, down the hill off Hoşdere Caddesi near Tomurcuk Sokak. On Mondays the **Maltepe Pazarı** spreads out behind the Maltepe Mosque, and on Fridays, the **Bahçelievler Pazarı** takes over 10 Sokak near Azerbaycan Caddesi in Bahçelievler. The **Ankara Halı** is a chaotic permanent market in Ulus, saturated with stalls of fresh fish, fruit, and vegetables. Farmers gather here in summertime to sell their own produce. The area is also full of butcher shops and charcuteries. Assembling a picnic meal of fresh cheese, meats, olives, and dried fruits is a tempting prospect; if you walk along Hisarparkı Caddesi (Fortress Park Ave.) up the hill toward the citadel, you can picnic on the grass or sit on the wall at the base of the fortress.

6 Ankara After Dark

Ankara may be a happening cultural center for the highbrow arts, but because most travelers pass through at a brisk pace, few get to actually take advantage of these events. Many do have time for a drink, though, and can select from a laundry list of pubs, wine bars, and chic cafes catering to the hefty consular population, or, at the other end of the scale, lowbrow diversions for the resident students. Most hotels have live music to offer as well; even Ahmet over at the Angora House will pull out his *fasıl* and perform some folk songs.

As an alternative, you may want to head over to the local cinema, as most films are shown in the original version with Turkish subtitles. If you're staying around Kızılay, head over to the Sheraton's rooftop-terrace cinema for nightly movies in summer, or check out the **Derya,** Necatibey Cad. 57 (© **0312/229-9618**); the **Kızılırmak,** Kızılırmak Sokagı (© **0312/425-5393**); or the **Metropol,** Selanik Cad. 76 (© **0312/ 425-7478**), which occasionally shows classic movies. The **Akun,** Atatürk Bulv. 227 (© **0312/427-7656**), and the **Kavaklıdere,** Tunalı Hilmi Caddesi (© **0312/426-7379**), are both in the Kavaklıdere neighborhood.

THE PERFORMING ARTS
With Ankara's designation as capital of the new republic, the city had the responsibility of becoming a cultural capital as well. Rising out of the dust of an old village, Ankara has surpassed the other cities in Turkey to become the most active cultural center in the country.

Ankara is home to the prestigious **Presidential Symphony Orchestra,** the **State Opera and Ballet,** and a large number of theaters that feature the work of Turkish authors. The Presidential Symphony Orchestra performs twice weekly on Fridays and

Saturdays during the October-to-May season, showcasing classical music by Turkish and foreign composers. Monthly programs for the State Opera and Ballet are listed in the Sunday edition of the *Turkish Daily News,* as well as on their Internet site (www. devtiyatro.gov.tr; in Turkish). Tickets can be purchased at the Opera House (© **0312/ 324-2210**), in Opera Meydanı, Ulus up to a month in advance of a performance.

FESTIVALS The capital also nurtures the arts by hosting several festivals throughout the year. Ankara's **International Film Days,** in March, and the **Sevda Cenap International Arts and Music Festival,** in April and May, attract the best of Turkish and international musicians. The **Children's Festival** is held in April, with groups of children from all over the world arriving to take part in this colorful, lively event. On August 30, Ankara celebrates Victory Day with pomp and circumstance appropriate for the Capitol City. Ankara also organizes a series of fairs throughout the year in **Altın Park,** attracting families for an afternoon of cotton candy, piping-hot *gözleme* fresh off the cart, and the occasional kiddy ride. See "Visitor Information," earlier in this chapter, for Ankara tourist offices and information about the festivals.

THE CLUB, CAFE & BAR SCENE

Much of Ankara's nightlife is geared toward the diplomatic community, with cafes, jazz clubs, and the odd English pub clustered at the south of town. A more youthful crowd, predominantly from the nearby university, congregates in the outdoor beer gardens around Sakarya Caddesi in Kızılay. A few restaurants at the citadel offer nightly music. In the neighborhood of Kavaklıere, just off Tunalı Hilmi on Abjantin Caddesi, is a lineup of smart looking, candlelit bistros; there's even a Starbucks for those of you feeling homesick.

The Lord Kinross Much more than just a pub, The Lord Kinross is Ankara's official dart center and a popular hangout for a crowd of regular expatriates. If the clubby feel of the place doesn't intimidate you into heading out the front door, the dart league will at least provide a bit of mealtime entertainment. The menu is typical pub food, with hearty cuisine like chicken-and-mushroom pie, big steaks, homemade pork sausages, and wild boar. The Lord Kinross also serves a rib-sticking full English breakfast on Sunday; a vegetarian version is also available. Open Monday through Saturday from 6pm to midnight and Sunday from 10am to noon and 6 to 10pm. Cemâl Nadir Sok. 18, Çankaya. © **0312/439-5252.**

The North Shield Pub This is the Anatolian branch of a popular national chain of pubs. Patrons frequent the place as much for its imported whiskeys as for its international menu. Daily noon to 1am. Güvenlik Cad. 111, Ayrancı. © **0312/466-1266.**

7 A Side Trip to the Hittite Capital of Hattuşaş ⟨★⟩

Center of the great Hittite Kingdom for almost 500 years, the ancient site of **Hattuşaş** constitutes one of the most important archaeological sites in Turkey. Having imported cuneiform script from Mesopotamia and the Assyrian trade colonies, the Hittites recorded the most minute details of their civilization. Exhaustive archives of public, political, and religious life have been found in several repositories throughout Hattuşaş, and thanks to the work of a Czech linguist who succeeded in deciphering the Hittite alphabet in 1915, a wealth of information on one of the most important ancient civilizations of Anatolia is now available.

Hattuşaş was not only the Hittite political capital but the religious one as well. The site is located at the summit of an imposing and rocky terrain high above the fertile valley of the Turkish village of **Boğazköy**. About 1km (¾ mile) to the northeast is the cliff temple of **Yazılıkaya** ⟨★★⟩ (the access road takes a slightly more circuitous route), spectacular for the exceptional reliefs carved into the rock. If you find yourself debating whether to go on or not, here's my take: Don't come all this way just to skip the best part.

GETTING THERE   All but the most intrepid and unscheduled travelers will need a car for this trip, easily 2½ hours away from Ankara through rolling Anatolian hills. The highway winds through a desolate and amazing land—but be sure to fill up the tank, because the farther out you go, the less likely you'll find a station with anything other than diesel. The good news is that you can drive through the site on a road that circles through the city, stopping at will to get a closer look at the highlights, which have been obligingly signposted.

To get there by car, take highway 200-E88 out of Ankara and follow the signs for Samsun. Take the turnoff for Çorum, following past Delice and Sungurlu, and begin looking for signs for Boğazköy and the archaeological site.

To get there from Ankara by public transportation, take a bus to the *center* of Süngürlü, where you'll be changing to a *dolmuş* for the remaining 14-mile ride into Boğazköy. Taxis from Süngürlü run around 40YTL ($30); clients of the Hattuşaş Pansiyon or Baykal Hotel can get a pickup for free.

VISITOR INFORMATION   The only available information is a rough topographical map placed outside the ticket booth that won't do you any good once you drive away. The Hattuşaş Pansiyon has a good map of the site and the town; see **www. hattusha.com**.

There may be an "employee" at the booth offering his services or, more innocently, asking for a ride through the site, but don't be fooled—this is a local posing as a guide for tips. Although some of the locals can be knowledgeable, you'll have to weigh the fact that you'll be relinquishing your right to silence and self-discovery as you attempt to absorb the enormity of the place. All of the significant sites are signposted, so you don't have to worry about missing them.

EXPLORING THE HITTITE SITES OF HATTUŞAŞ ⟨★★★⟩

A natural stronghold situated atop an impregnable area of steep rocky terrain, Hattuşaş had been inhabited as far back as the 3rd millennium B.C. The Hatti, an

---

Hattuşaş: City of a Thousand Gods

In Hittite documents, Hattuşaş is referred to as the "City of a Thousand Gods," indicating the importance of religion in daily life. In their roles as high priest and priestess, the king and queen would often consult the appropriate god before making decisions on even the most minor of questions. Excavations, begun in 1932 on behalf of the German Archaeological Institute (archaeological surveys began much earlier), have already revealed the remains of over 75 temples.

As equal-opportunity worshippers, the Hittites appropriated foreign deities of the civilizations they had conquered, adding them to the Hittite anthology of gods and offering prayers and gifts to keep them appeased. Each god or goddess became the focus of a cult, so that much of the calendar was taken up with duties associated with ritual ceremonies.

Anatolian people of unknown origin who set up a dominion of independent kingdoms, settled here as early as 2500 B.C. Later, around 1800 B.C., King Anitta of Kushara (an ancient kingdom of undetermined origins and whereabouts) invaded and set fire to the city, pronouncing it accursed, then moved on.

King Labarnas, a descendant of Anitta of Kushara, returned several generations later to reconquer and rebuild the city. Labarnas called the city Hattuşaş, or "Land of the Hatti," and changed his name to Hattusilis. Hattusilis I is accepted as the true founder of the Hittite kingdom.

From 1650 to 1200 B.C., the Hittites ruled most of Anatolia, succeeding in spreading out as far as northern Syria—much to the dissatisfaction of the Egyptian pharaohs. Tensions came to a head at the historic Battle of Kadesh, which in essence ended in a stalemate. For the first time in the history of mankind, a written treaty was drawn up between the two warring factions. A copy of the treaty was discovered in the Hattuşaş Palace Archives and is now in the Archaeology Museum in Istanbul.

The Hittites were the undisputed power in western Asia from 1400 to 1200 B.C., but a period of struggle over the ascendancy left the empire weak and vulnerable. Around 1200 B.C. the city was burned and razed by the Phrygians, and abandoned soon after. The Phrygians returned sometime between the 9th and 7th centuries B.C. to establish a fortified city, and rebuilt much of the city that stands today. Minor settlements were later set up by the Galatians, Romans, and Byzantines.

The ancient site lies within an area of a little over 1.5 sq. m (about 1 sq. mile), behind fortified walls 6km (3¾ miles) in length. The city was open to the north, sheltered by the natural protection of steep cliffs and rugged terrain.

The city was accessible through several monumental stone gates carved with reliefs of lions, sphinxes, and gods, which stand now in various states of erosion. Many of these original reliefs and statues have been moved to the Museum of Anatolian Civilizations (p. 370) in Ankara.

Today there is one main entrance to the site. The first set of ruins you pass is the **Büyük Tapinak.** Located at the center of the Lower City and surrounded by a wall, this temple was the most important, consecrated to the Storm God and the Sun Goddess of Arinna, who were identified with their Hurrian equivalents, Teşup and Hepatu. The temple was constructed during the reign of the last great Hittite king, Hattusilis III (1275–1250 B.C.). The ruins of the foundations show an ample presence of storerooms, offices, and workshops; this indicates the temple was an important public building in addition to a sacred one. In some of the corners, you can still find the remains of large pottery receptacles. The actual temple is in the center, isolated from the outer sections; only the king and queen, in their roles as high priest and priestess, could enter it.

From the Büyük Tapinak, follow the road up to where it forks. Take the left fork and you will encounter the **Büyükkale (Great Fortress).** The royal residence occupies the highest point of a naturally rocky crest enclosed by a network of defensive walls. The palace also housed the high guard, with public rooms for the state archives, a large reception hall, and some sacred areas. Not much detail can be discerned from the remaining foundations—invisible from a lower elevation amid the grassy terraces—but a stopover at this point can provide a visual overview of the invincible position of the city.

Farther up the path on the right is **Nişantepe** ✦, an artificially smoothed rock outcropping that bears an almost 9m-long (30-ft.) inscription. Badly weathered and only partially deciphered, the inscription is most likely an accounting of the deeds of Şuppiliumus II, last of the Hattuşaş kings. Across the road to the left is a path leading to **Hieroglyphic Chamber no. 1** 🗝 and the **Southern Fort,** erected several centuries after the collapse of the Hittite Empire. The Hieroglyphic Chamber dates to 1200 B.C. and is built into the side of an artificial dam. (The other end is part of the fortress.) On the back wall is the figure of a man in a long cloak. The figure, probably a god, carries a sign similar to the Egyptian *ankh* ("life") and is possibly representative of an entrance into the underworld. On the wall opposite the figure are hieroglyphics. Few remains were found in **Hieroglyphic Chamber no. 2,** which is visible from the road but was inaccessible as this book went to press.

The best-preserved city gate at Hattuşaş is the **Kralkapı** 🗝🗝🗝, or King's Gate, flanked by two towers with both an inner and outer portal. To the left of the inner doorway is a replica of the famous relief of the Hittite God of War, dressed in a short skirt and a horned helmet, and bearing a battle-ax in his right hand. It's a stunning sight to see the relief *in situ,* even if the original is in the Museum of Anatolian Civilizations (p. 370) in Ankara.

On the road up to **Yerkapı,** over 28 temples have been uncovered. Yerkapı, which means "Earth Gate," or "Gate in the Ground," is better known as the **Sphinx Gate** 🗝🗝 and is the highest elevation in the area. You can either climb the stone steps to the top of the 15m-high (49-ft.) artificial bank and reenter the city through the tunnel, or take a deep breath and tackle the tunnel first. The 69m (226-ft.) tunnel is an excellent way to grasp the impenetrable appearance of the city to potential invaders. During times of peace, the tunnel provided a quick, easy point of entry to the city. In wartime, the exterior stone embankment, constructed in the shape of a truncated pyramid, probably served to discourage attacks. Once outside the tunnel, follow the path to either the right or the left and climb the outer set of monumental steps to the sphinx at the top. The gate was named for four great sphinxes that guarded the inner gate, two of which were reconstructed from fragments and reinstalled on-site. The two remaining great sphinxes are keeping watch over the Museum of the Ancient Orient (part of Istanbul's Archaeological Museum) and a museum in Berlin. The four additional bas-relief sphinxes that were carved into the portal of the outer embankment were unfortunately not spared this end; all that remains of the originals is one badly chipped and barely distinguishable image on the western wall.

A recurring theme in Hittite and Mesopotamian architecture is the image of a lion with an open mouth and staring eyes. The **Aslanlıkapı (Lion's Gate)** displays one of the best-preserved artifacts remaining on-site at Hattuşaş—the frontal portions of two lions carved directly into stone blocks, which symbolically ward off evil spirits. There's a hieroglyphic inscription above the head of the one on the left, but unless the sun stands at high noon, the inscription is invisible.

No phone. Admission 2YTL ($1.50); car 1.35YTL ($1) extra. Tickets good for sites of both Hattuşaş and Yazılıkaya. Daily 8am–sunset.

A NEARBY SITE

Yazılıkaya 🗝🗝 This shrine, formed by two natural ravines, is the largest known Hittite rock sanctuary. The purpose of the shrine remains a mystery, although we can speculate that it was used for annual cult celebrations or even as a royal funerary site. There was probably a processional road leading down from the royal residence at Hattuşaş, and the presence of a nearby spring may have played a part in the selection of the site as a sacred spot.

In the large rock-enclosed court of **Chamber A** ✸✸✸ are some of the most incredible treasures of the Hittite architectural legacy. Hewn from one end of the rock enclosure to the other is a representation of a sacred procession of deities, all of which are of Hurrian origin. Hurrian gods were given prominence by the Hittite Queen Putuhepa, wife of Hattusilis III, who was herself of noble Hurrian or Eastern origin. The cylindrical domed headdress is a symbol of divinity of Mesopotamian influence. The deities are oriented to the main scene on the back wall where the Storm God Teşup and the Sun Goddess Hepatu meet. The Storm God Teşup and Sun Goddess Hepatu, also of Hurrian origin, became the two most important deities in the Hittite pantheon, the accepted counterparts of the Hittite Storm God and the Sun Goddess of Arinna. Towering above the main scene and standing over 3.5m (12 ft.) high is a large relief of King Tudhaliya IV, son of Hattusilis III and Puduhepa. The existence of three depictions of Tudhaliya (there are two others in Chamber B) at the exclusion of all other Hittite kings leads scholars to believe that the sanctuary dates to his reign (1250–1220 B.C.), although the sanctuary's construction was probably begun by his father.

To the right passing through a narrow rock crevice is **Chamber B** ✸✸, probably a memorial chapel to King Tudhaliya IV, son of Hattusilis III and Putuhepa. The reliefs in this chamber were buried until the end of the 19th century, so they are better preserved than the ones in Chamber A. The largest relief is of King Tudhaliya IV, on the main wall next to a puzzling depiction of a large sword formed by two extended lions with a divine human head for a handle. This possibly represents the God of Swords, or Nergal of the underworld. The relief on the right wall depicts a row of 12 gods bearing sickles similar to the ones in the other chamber. The number 12 as a sacred number is first seen here and repeated many times in subsequent civilizations—there were 12 gods of Olympus, 12 apostles, 12 imams of Islamic mysticism, 12 months in a year, 12 days of Christmas, and 12 to a dozen. The three niches carved into the far end of the chamber are believed to have contained the cremated remains of Hittite royalty.

Follow signs to the right after exiting the grounds of Hattuşaş. Admission included in ticket to Hattuşaş. Daily 8am–sunset.

WHERE TO STAY AND DINE

Located 50m (164 ft.) from the entrance to the site is the motel-style **Asikoglu Hotel** (Çarşı Mah. 9, Boğazkale; ✆ **0364/452-2004;** fax 0364/452-2171), with its 33 rooms all with balconies, kitchenettes and (weak) hair dryers for 78€ ($95) double. There's also a restaurant on-site.

The recently restored (2004) **Hattuşaş Restaurant and Pansiyon,** on the main square (✆ **0364/452-2013;** fax 0364/452-2957; www.hattusha.com), offers simple rooms for 12€ ($15), including breakfast. The family also owns the **Hotel Baykal** (same address and contact info), with double rooms for 30€ ($37). The **Hattuşaş Restaurant and Pansiyon** has basic meals adjacent to the owner's carpet shop for about 6.75YTL ($5). For that matter, any of the campgrounds or "pansiyons" will feed you if you're hungry—and so will the locals, if you hang around long enough.

Appendix A:
Turkey in Depth

The history of Turkey reads like the history of mankind. Virtually every major Western civilization—Hittite, Greek, Roman, Byzantine, Selçuk, Ottoman—fought for control of this land and its surrounding waters. The result is a fascinating cultural and historical amalgam, and a land with countless archaeological treasures still waiting to be discovered. It's not uncommon to hike through the countryside and literally trip over a 2,000-year-old chunk of marble or the head of a statue unearthed by a farmer going about his daily business—almost too much history for one country to contain.

1 History 101

IN THE BEGINNING

In the beginning, Noah's Ark landed on Mount Ararat, or so recovered fossilized wood and boatlike support beams might indicate. Actually, the beginning in Turkey was much earlier; archaeological findings in central Anatolia indicate the presence of cave dwellers as early as 10,000 B.C., living a crude nomadic existence. The oldest documented tribe in Anatolia was the Hatti, a nameless, faceless civilization that seems to have established small city kingdoms in central Anatolia and ruled there for about 500 years. Cuneiform tablets discovered in the regions to the east of Kayseri evidence a thriving trade between these indigenous settlers and Assyrian merchants, who appear on the scene around 2000 B.C. With the arrival of the Hittites, an ancient tribe of uncertain mixed Indo-European origins, all evidence of the Hatti seems to dissolve, while commerce between the Assyrian merchants and now-ruling Hittites continues.

THE HITTITES (2000–1100 B.C.)

Around 2000 B.C., central Anatolia was invaded by an "Indo-European" people migrating from either Europe or Asia, who subdued the indigenous Hatti kingdoms, appropriating their language, customs, and women. The Hittites assumed Hatti names and adopted the practice of worshipping multiple deities, usually in the form of animals or representative of a force of nature. Even the term "Hittite" derives from the Hittite expression for "people in the land of the Hatti." The Hittites were also the first known literate civilization in Anatolia, having adopted a cuneiform script imported from Mesopotamia.

The Hittites built an empire of city-states in this manner, the most important of which was Hattuşaş ("Land of the Hatti," in the Hittite language) outside what is now Bogazköy. By the mid–13th century B.C., the Hittites had taken control of a large part of Anatolia, and under Suppiluliumas I managed to extend their borders to the south and east. Persistent invasions by Hittite successors created border tensions with Egypt, leading to the historic battle of Kadesh (ca. 1300 B.C.) between Hittite Emperor Muwattalis and Egyptian Pharaoh Ramses II. The Hittites are famed for their military prowess, and their deployment of the three-wheeled chariot probably gave them a huge advantage. Although historical accounts of the battle are contradictory (both sides claimed victory), the

Turkey's Ancient Civilizations

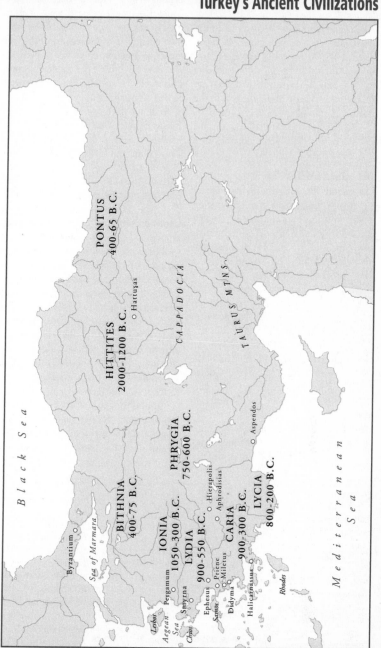

Hittites continued their hold on Syria. Later, and for the first time in the history of mankind, a written treaty between the two countries was concluded, between Hattusil III, Muwattalis's successor, and Ramses II (ca. 1284 B.C.), who eventually married two of Hattusil's daughters to seal the pact. A copy of the treaty is in the Istanbul Archaeology Museum (p. 107). The Hittite Empire soon fell into decline and was finally destroyed by the invasion of a "Sea People."

THE HELLENIC AGE

The period following the destruction of the Hittite Empire saw the immigration of and invasion by a number of civilizations. In Anatolia the Hittite Empire, now destroyed, fractured into independent principalities. The **Phrygians,** who were probably the "Sea People" or migrants from Thrace responsible for the destruction of the Hittite Empire, became the dominant Anatolian power in the 8th and 9th centuries B.C.

The demise of the Phrygian Kingdom came during the reign of King Midas, the last Phrygian king (and of the Golden Touch of mythology fame). He succumbed to invasions by the **Cimmerian** nomadic people around 725 B.C. The **Hurrians,** a native Anatolian mountain people, gave way to the **Urartians,** who, up until around 850 B.C., occupied the eastern region around Lake Van; they constructed walled citadels and an elaborate system of escape tunnels for their own defense. The **Lycians,** probably survivors of a nation of sailors or pirates—and possibly one of the Sea Peoples who caused the fall of the Hittite Empire—settled along the southwest coast.

At about the same time the Phrygians rose to power, several Hellenistic tribes fled Greece to escape the invading Dorians. This group, the **Ionians,** migrated to the Aegean islands and into the central west coast of Anatolia (although the term Ionia often refers to the entire west coast). Ephesus, Miletus, and Priene are among the settlements formed during this migration; around 850 B.C., Smyrna (now İzmir) was established as their center. Originally an agricultural civilization, Ionia developed an advanced artistic and literary tradition, taking its influences from other, more advanced groups in Anatolia as well as from contact with Egyptians, Assyrians, and Phoenicians. Miletus became a vibrant center for the exchange of scientific ideas, and here you find a foundation for modern-day mathematics, geometry, astronomy, and philosophy.

Around the 7th century B.C., the **Lydians** appeared on the coast, establishing their capital at Sardis and inhabiting the inland district of western Anatolia. The

Dateline

- **ca. 10,000** B.C. Cave deposits in Antalya and surface discoveries around Ankara and Hatay regions suggest earliest cultures.
- **ca. 1940–1780** B.C. Assyrian merchants from Mesopotamia establish trading colonies in central and eastern Anatolia; Indo-European people arrive, assimilating with existing Assyrian colonies.

- **ca. 1750** B.C. Indo-Europeans conquer Hattuşaş, establishing the Old Hittite Kingdom.
- **ca. 1300** B.C. The battle of Kadesh between Muwattalis and Ramses II; both sides claim victory.
- **ca. 1284** B.C. Hattusilis III and Ramses II sign peace treaty.
- **ca. 1200** B.C. Invasion by the "Sea Peoples" destroys

Hittite power in Anatolia; the Trojan War.
- **ca. 1200–700** B.C. Migration of Greeks to Aegean coastal regions; establishment of Phrygian, Ionian, Lycian, Lydian, Carian, and Urartu kingdoms.
- **ca. 546** B.C. Persian King Cyrus the Great conquers Croesus of Lydia.
- **ca. 499** B.C. Persians drive out the Greeks.

Lydians were the first to coin modern money, mixing gold from the rich Pactolos Valley with silver and thus immortalizing the (apparently very rich) King Croesus. The Lydians also claim to have invented the game of dice.

Under Croesus, Lydia conquered and incorporated Ionia into its kingdom, but in 546 B.C., it was defeated and captured by Cyrus the Great of Persia, who was consolidating Persian power in Asia Minor. Cyrus the Great's successor, Darius I, crossed the Bosphorus and incorporated Thrace and Macedonia into the Persian Empire.

The **Carians,** mostly known as mercenaries, settled along the southwestern coast, having been chased off the Aegean islands by invading Greeks. They established, among other cities, Halicarnassus. In the 6th century B.C., Caria was incorporated into the Lydian kingdom, but later it, too, succumbed to the Persian Empire. Carian kings continued to rule as subjects of Cyrus the Great, maintaining some degree of autonomy. But 200 years of Persian domination created feelings of resentment toward Eastern ways. Many Ionians, including most of the philosophers and artists, migrated back to either Athens or Italy. The remaining Ionians regained their freedom by joining the Delian League, a federation of Greek city-states formed in 478 B.C. as security against the renewal of Persian aggression.

In the summer of 334 B.C., **Alexander the Great** began his war on the Persian Empire, retaking Thrace, crossing the Dardanelles, and confronting the Persian armies near Troy. He succeeded in annexing all of Anatolia under **Macedonian/Greco** rule. Alexander showed an unprecedented tolerance toward the Eastern world: He took Persians for wives and permitted Persian nobles to retain their land in exchange for loyalty. Alexander the Great's untimely death, in 323 B.C., was the catalyst for internal conflict among his generals, resulting in generations of clashes over the division of his territories.

During the 3rd and 2nd centuries B.C., several independent Greek states emerged in western Anatolia. The city of **Pergamum** was established and, under Eumenes II, enjoyed its greatest period of prosperity, earning itself a privileged position with Rome.

ROME & THE EASTERN PROVINCES

When Attalus III, the last of the ruling Attalid dynasty of Pergamum, died without a successor in 133 B.C., the Romans interpreted his ambiguous bequest in their favor and claimed the city, beginning the **Roman Empire**'s mass penetration into

---

- **334 B.C.** Alexander the Great drives Persians out of Anatolia.
- **323 B.C.** Alexander dies; Generals Lysimachos and Seleucus divide the Anatolian Empire.
- **133 B.C.** Attalus III dies, leaving Pergamum to Rome; Pergamum becomes the province of Asia with its capital at Ephesus.
- **40 B.C.** Mark Antony and Cleopatra marry in Antioch.

- **A.D. 47–57** St. Paul establishes first Christian community in Antioch.
- **284** Diocletian reforms Roman administrative system.
- **313** Edict of Milan establishes official tolerance of Christianity.
- **330** Constantine establishes his capital at Byzantium, renaming it New Rome, then Constantinople.

- **476** Fall of the Roman Empire; Constantinople emerges as sole religious and cultural capital of the Eastern Roman Empire.
- **527** Justinian ascends the throne.
- **726** Leo III rejects the idea of icons.
- **1054** Catholic and Greek Orthodox churches split.
- **1071** Selçuks defeat Byzantine army at Malazgirt.

Gordius, from Pauper to Prince

Legend has it that the Phrygian elders, seeking a leader to mediate quarrels and to gain status with their neighbors, consulted a local oracle for advice on how to select a king. The oracle responded that the next person to pass his shrine riding in a cart should be king, and soon enough, a farmer named Gordius rode by in his oxcart on the way to market. Gordius was proclaimed king, and the capital (near present-day Ankara), assumed his name, Gordion.

The expression "Gordion knot," which refers to a highly complex problem, takes its name from Gordius as well. Apparently, Gordius was quite proud of the fittings on his oxcart—particularly of the unusual knot he used to tie the cart's pole to the axle. He challenged all potential passersby to untie it, but the knot remained intact long after his death. When Alexander the Great arrived in Gordion more than 500 years later, he carefully studied the knot, then decisively severed it in two with his sword, before continuing on to more challenging conquests.

Asia Minor. The Romans claimed Pergamum and effectively absorbed the independent states of Bithynia, Cappadocia, and Pontus. Except for sporadic conflict—most notably with Mithridates of Pontus, who between 88 and 63 B.C. massacred over 80,000 Romans at Ephesus—the Asian Provinces enjoyed a relatively long and prosperous period of peace. It was during the 1st century A.D. that **St. Paul,** advocate of the Christian faith, began his missionary travels through Anatolia. (He was even briefly imprisoned at Ephesus.)

In A.D. 284, **Emperor Diocletian** instituted a doomed system of governmental reform, dividing the empire into two administrative units, both to be ruled by an emperor (an *Augustus*) and a designated heir (or *Caesar*). It was a system destined to collapse into civil war; but the long-term effect was a more theological schism, as Christianity grew and took hold. In the wake of Diocletian reform, **Constantine** emerged to establish his capital at the Greek town of Byzantium, rebuilding the city to equal if not surpass the splendor of Rome. Six years later, in 330, its architectural eminence realized, the city was baptized "New Rome," then renamed Constantinopolis (or Constantinople, now Istanbul) in honor of the emperor.

- **1204** Crusaders sack Constantinople.
- **1243** Mongol invasions destroy Selçuk power.
- **1261** Michael VIII Palaeologus reclaims Constantinople.
- **1326** Ottoman capital established at Bursa.
- **1453** Mehmet the Conqueror takes Constantinople.
- **1481** Reign of Bayezid II begins.
- **1492** Columbus discovers the New World.
- **1512** Reign of Selim I begins.
- **1517** Selim I captures Cairo and proclaims himself caliph.
- **1520** Reign of Süleyman begins.
- **1521** Süleyman captures Belgrade and takes Rhodes; releases surviving Knights of St. John.
- **1566** Reign of Selim II begins.
- **1570** Turks capture Cyprus.
- **1571** Turks defeated at battle of Lepanto.
- **1574** Reign of Murad III begins; Tunis is captured.
- **1622** Osman II assassinated by the Janissaries; Ahmed I restored to throne.
- **1687** Reign of Süleyman II begins.
- **1699** In the Treaty of Karlowitz, the Ottoman Empire relinquishes territory for the first time.

By the time Constantine had established imperial Roman power in Constantinople, his acceptance of Christianity was complete, having publicly espoused the faith in the Edict of Milan in 313, which mandated the tolerance of Christianity within the Roman Empire. Under **Theodosius,** paganism was outlawed and Christianity, by this time already widespread, was made the official religion of the state. By Theodosius's death in 395, the eastern and western provinces had grown apart ideologically, and the Roman Empire was divided in two. When Rome fell in 476, Constantinople emerged the dominant capital of the empire. But although predominantly Greek and Christian in culture, citizens of Byzantium considered themselves Roman, and the leadership maintained a thoroughly Roman administration.

THE AGE OF BYZANTIUM

The reign of Emperor **Justinian** and his Queen **Theodora** (527–565) inaugurated a period of great prosperity in Anatolia. Justinian reconquered the West, and eventually regained North Africa and Italy. His construction of the majestic Ayasofya (Church of Holy Wisdom) established Constantinople as the spiritual center of Christendom. Justinian commissioned new buildings and conducted restorations all across the empire—an undertaking so vast that it thrust the empire into economic crisis after his death. His primary legacy was the **Justinian Code**—his attempt to codify and organize the ancient system of Roman laws—that ultimately became the foundation for many modern Western legal systems.

Around the end of the 9th century, a rivalry emerged between the Orthodox Church and the Papacy over the veneration of icons. The worship of idols was first condemned by **Emperor Leo III** in 726 and then reiterated by successive emperors. In 1054, over this and other theological disagreements, the pope severed any ties that had united Byzantium with the West.

Distracted by religious and bureaucratic disputes, the Byzantines were unprepared for the arrival of nomadic Turkish warriors raiding lands in the east. The Turks (from the Chinese "Tu-Kiu") had migrated south and west from Mongolia during the 7th or 8th century. They had assumed Islamic practices, influenced by encounters with Arab tribes centered around Baghdad, home of the caliphate. By the 10th century, the bulk of Turks—still nomads and warriors by nature—had accepted Islam as their religion, although some Turks, such as the **Selçuks,** subscribed to the orthodox Sunni form,

- **1711** Defeat of Peter the Great at Prut River.
- **1774** Reign of Abdülhamid I begins; Treaty of Küçük Kaynarca follows defeat by Catherine the Great.
- **1789** Reign of Selim II begins; education becomes obligatory.
- **1826** Janissary massacred and corps abolished; medical and military schools opened; and Tanzimat Reforms.

- **1839** Reign of Abdülmecid begins; establishes parliamentary system and laws.
- **1854** Britain and France support Ottomans against Russia in the Crimean War.
- **1856** Treaty of Paris; Ottoman Empire accepted as a European state.
- **1861** Reign of Abdülaziz begins.
- **1875–85** Loss of most European territories, Tunisia, Egypt, and East Rumalia.

- **1876** Reign of Abdülhamid II begins, establishes first constitution; then, frustrated with parliamentary gridlock, imposes an autocracy.
- **1878** The "Sick Man of Europe" progressively deteriorates; Britain occupies Cyprus.
- **1881** Mustafa Kemal born in Salonika.
- **1908** Coup d'état led by Young Turks; Abdülhamid is deposed.

while others, such as the **Turkomans,** accepted the splinter Shiite sect.

These *gazi* tribes, or "warriors of the faith," marched north from Baghdad, conquering lands in the name of Islam and penetrating deep into the heart of Anatolia. The Selçuks marched northwest in a campaign to expand their territory and a desire to control the Turkoman tribes. An accidental encounter with the Byzantine army resulted in a Selçuk victory in the **Battle of Malazgirt in 1071,** opening the door to a mass Turkish migration into Anatolia.

In response to the growing Turkish presence, Byzantine Emperor **Alexius Comnenus** turned to the Christians of western Europe for aid against the increasing threat of the Turks. The first Crusade saw the recapturing of Jerusalem and the regaining of control of most of Anatolia.

The Selçuk Turks triumphed over the second Crusade in 1147, eventually setting up **The Sultanate of Rum** at Konya and achieving significant cultural growth and territorial expansion. The Selçuks revived the classical Islamic system of education, attracting philosophers, poets, and craftsmen to the court. One of the most influential arrivals was the scholar Celaleddin i-Rumi, who founded the Order of the Mevlevi (or "Whirling")

Dervishes. The Selçuks laid the foundation for modern-day Middle Eastern government with the implementation of a bureaucratic hierarchical system. They are also credited with the development of a system of way stations called **kervansarays** (caravansaries), designed to meet the need of merchants traveling on behalf of the state, and established insurance for the loss of tradesmen.

But the Crusades were by no means a cure-all. Tensions arose because the Crusaders had no specific mandate from the pope, little sympathy toward the Greek Orthodox religion, and no agreement on the nature of their association with the Byzantine Empire. Allied with Venetian merchants who had an eye on the riches of the East, the Crusaders sacked and plundered Constantinople in 1204 in the fourth Crusade, creating the Latin Empire of Constantinople and widening the schism between the churches of the East and West. Driven from Constantinople, the Byzantines established a small empire in exile at Nicaea, creating a balance of power with the flourishing Selçuk Sultanate of Rum.

Michael VIII Palaeologus, ruler of the empire in exile, succeeded in reclaiming the city of Constantinople in 1261. Though their territory was drastically reduced, subsequent Byzantine emperors

- **ca. 1908–09** Mehmed V installed as lame duck sultan.
- **1914** Ottoman Empire enters World War I as ally of Germany.
- **1915** Under leadership of Mustafa Kemal, Turkish forces successfully repel Anzac forces at Battle of Gallipoli.
- **1918** Reign of Mehmed VI begins; Turks surrender; Allied forces enter Istanbul.
- **1919** Mustafa Kemal leads national resistance for

sovereignty; occupational Greek army lands at Smyrna.
- **1920** Grand National Assembly created in Ankara with Mustafa Kemal as president.
- **1922** Greeks driven from Anatolia; sultanate abolished; Abdülmecid named as caliph only.
- **1923** Treaty of Lausanne, Mustafa Kemal establishes the modern Republic of Turkey; Kemal is elected

president; Ankara replaces Istanbul as capital.
- **1924** Caliphate abolished.
- **1924–38** Mustafa Kemal Atatürk institutes programs of modernism, secularism, and reform.
- **1934** Voting rights established for women.
- **1938** Atatürk dies in Dolmabahçe Palace; Ismet Inönü becomes republic's second president.

Selçuk Sultans—The Rum Line

Sultan	Reign
Tugrul I Beg	1037–63
Alp Arslan	1063–73
Malik Shah I	1073–92 (battle for throne)
Süleyman I ibn Qutalmïsh	1078–86 (battle for throne)
Kılıç Arslan I	1092–1107
Malık Shah II	1107–16
Meşud I	1116–56
Kılıç Arslan II	1156–92
Giyaseddin Keyküsrev I	1192–96
Süleyman II	1196–1204
Kılıç Arslan III	1204 (child)
Giyaseddin Keyküsrev I	1204–10
Kaykavus I	1210–20
Alaaeddin Keykubat I	1220–37
Giyaseddin Keyküsrev II	1237–46

(Selçuks conquered by Mongols in 1243 and become vassals; a fight for succession of the sultanate ensued.)

Kaykavus II	1246–57
Kılıç Arslan IV	1248–65
Kaykubat II	1249–57
Kaykusrev III	1265–82

(Meşud II and Kaykubat III clash for control of throne 1282–1307 until Meşud II is deposed by Mongols in 1307.)

repeatedly tried to reunite the Orthodox and Catholic churches against the threat of invading Turks. This proved futile, and in 1453, the Ottoman Turks conquered what little remained of the Byzantine Empire and made Constantinople their capital.

- **1945** Turkey declares war on Germany.
- **1946** Turkey becomes charter member of United Nations.
- **1950** Inönü's Republican People's Party defeated in first free election. Adnan Menderes's Democratic Party takes over.
- **1952** Turkey joins NATO.
- **1960** Military coup overthrows Menderes, who is executed the following year.
- **1961** Army restores parliamentary government.
- **1964** Turkey granted associate member status in European Union.
- **1965** Demirel's Justice Party wins elections.
- **1971** Demirel resigns after army intervention.
- **1973** Republican People's Party wins elections; Bulent Ecevit becomes prime minister.
- **1974** Turkey sends troops to northern Cyprus.
- **1980** Military coup d'état; General Kenan Evren leads government.
- **1983** Turgut Özal elected prime minister.
- **1989** Özal elected president.
- **1991** Süleyman Demirel elected prime minister.
- **1993** Özal dies; Demirel becomes president; Tansu Çiller becomes Turkey's first female prime minister.

OTTOMAN BEGINNINGS

Numerous independent Turkish principalities occupied the frontiers between the Selçuk Sultanate and the Byzantine Empire. These mercenary warriors traded battles and loyalties for grants of land, aiding the Selçuk rulers in their struggles against the Christians, while selling their services to hopefuls vying for the Byzantine throne. The **Osmanlıs,** whose geographical proximity to the Byzantine Empire incited an instinct for plunder, were successful in rousing the surrounding *gazis* (fighters for Islam) to do the same. After the Selçuk defeat at the hands of the Mongols in 1243, the Osmanlıs, under their leader **Osman** and his son **Orhan,** began a rapid expansion.

The Osmanlıs entered Bursa in 1326, where they set up their first permanent capital. Heading northwest, they rapidly conquered the Marmara shores, crossing the Dardanelles to establish a second fortified base at Gallipoli, in 1354.

Orhan was the first Ottoman leader to assume the title of sultan (formerly an honorary title that caliphs granted to chiefs of Islamic-influenced territories to emphasize their role as spiritual leaders). For the Ottomans, the title had military and political connotations as well. "Sultan" became the standard designation for those in power who answered to no superior other than Allah.

Orhan's son **Murat I** enjoyed one military success after another. He established a European presence at his new capital of Adrianople (now Edirne), and then directed his armies east into the Turkish emirates as well as west into the Balkans, Albania, and Bulgar territories. By this time the Byzantine emperor, isolated except for sea access, became a vassal of the sultan, and aided the Ottomans in their conquests of the East.

Murat I defeated a Serbian coalition at the Battle of Kosovo, though he was killed in that campaign. Murat's son **Bayezid** continued his father's expansionistic tendencies, striking both west and east and earning himself the nickname of *Yıldırım,* Turkish for "lightning" or "thunderbolt." The Ottoman advance to the west began to alarm the pope, who was unable to galvanize a proper offensive, except for two dismal attempts by the French and Hungarian armies during a lull in the Hundred Years' War. The Ottomans defeated the French army at Nicopolis on the Danube in 1396, and again on the Black Sea in 1444. But their continued campaigns into the west left their eastern flanks vulnerable. The Mongols, led by **Tamerlane,** emerged as a major threat in the east, supported by

- **1996** Çiller steps down as prime minister.
- **1999** Bulent Ecevit elected prime minister again. Kurdistan Workers Party (PKK) leader Abdullah Ocalan captured in Kenya, convicted of treason, and sentenced to death. Two major earthquakes rock northwestern Turkey in August and November, killing an estimated 18,000 people.
- **2000** Former prime minister Necmettin Erbakan sentenced to 1 year in prison for challenging Turkey's secular rule.
- **2001** Turkish troops assist American military operation in Afghanistan.

Turkish emirates inflamed by Bayezid's warring on his Muslim brothers—an act expressly forbidden in the Koran. Bayezid was eventually imprisoned by Tamerlane, who restored the independent territories. Bayezid died in prison, leaving behind a 10-year power vacuum in which his sons would fight for control.

Mehmet I was the sole survivor, and he and his son **Murat II** are credited with consolidating the Ottoman territories and absorbing, either by force or by marriage, the Turkish emirates to the east. Nonetheless, they were unable to either penetrate Constantinople's defenses or cut off the city's sea routes.

Mehmet II set a nasty royal precedent by strangling his infant brother in order to solve his own problems of succession. He eventually sanctioned fratricide by law: Whoever got acclaimed first was ruler and all his brothers had to die— ostensibly assuring the ascension of the most capable son.

Mehmet II set his sights immediately on Constantinople, and in 1453, in a brilliant strategy, circumvented the Byzantine defenses of the Golden Horn by carrying his fleet, ship by ship (by means of a brilliantly engineered "moveable path") over land, behind the Byzantine navy. After centuries of decline and decay, the Byzantine Empire had come to an end.

THE OTTOMAN EMPIRE

With his victory over Constantinople, Mehmet II acquired the title of *fatih,* or conqueror, and established his new capital, naming the city Istanbul, probably after having heard the Greeks say *"eis ten polin"* (to the city). His troops were permitted 3 days of looting and pillaging, and then the city—by now practically unpopulated—was restored to order. He immediately began reconstruction, converting churches into mosques and repopulating the city with artisans, merchants, and farmers from all over the

empire. The importance of sea power was not lost on Mehmet, who established control over the Black Sea and managed to capture some of rival Venice's islands in the Aegean. The city's importance as a naval and trading center was confirmed. Istanbul quickly became an international city with a mixture of cultures as Christians, Greeks, Armenians, and Jews all were welcomed by the sultan. After all, these diverse peoples brought with them a wealth of knowledge as well as new tax revenues.

Having removed the final obstacle to the unity of his empire, Mehmet the Conqueror resumed his Holy Wars, dreaming of a world united under Islam. Soon the empire extended into Europe, with conquests of the Balkans, Greece, Albania, Serbia, and Bosnia. The Turks had suddenly become a major European presence, influencing the balance of power to the west.

Bayezid II continued his father's expansion eastward against the Safavid dynasty in Iran, a Shiite presence that would challenge the Ottoman's legitimacy for centuries. Bayezid's son **Selim the Fierce** (known as Selim the Grim in the West, for his cruelty), impatient with his father's lagging military campaigns, assassinated him and slew his brothers, along with any other possible contender for the throne. He ruthlessly conquered and subjugated the heretic Safavid dynasty of Iran, then subdued the Mamluk Sultans of Syria and Egypt. The guardian of the holy cities of Mecca and Medina wasted no time in recognizing Selim as the new spiritual leader of Islam, and he promptly proclaimed himself caliph.

The long reign of Selim's son **Süleyman** was the golden age of the Ottoman Empire, distinguished by military successes, administrative organization, economic prosperity, social order, and cultural greatness. The empire flourished

The Ottoman Sultans

Sultan	Reign
Osman I	1290–1326
Orhan	1326–59
Murat I	1359–89
Bayezid I Yıldırım (the Thunderbolt)	1389–1402
Mehmet I	1402–21
Murat II	1421–51
Mehmet II (*Fatih,* the Conqueror)	1451–81
Bayezid II	1481–1512
Selim I Yavuz (the Grim)	1512–20
Süleyman I (*Kanuni,* the Magnificent)	1520–66
Selim II	1566–74
Murat III	1574–95
Mehmet III	1595–1603
Ahmed I	1603–17
Mustafa I	1617–18
Osman II	1618–22
Ahmed I (restored)	1622–23
Murat IV	1623–40
Ibrahim	1640–48
Mehmed IV	1648–87
Süleyman II	1687–91
Ahmed II	1691–95
Mustafa II	1695–1703
Ahmed III	1703–30
Mahmud I	1730–54
Osman III	1754–57
Mustafa III	1757–74
Abdülhamid I	1774–89
Selim III	1789–1807
Mustafa IV	1807–08
Mahmud II	1808–39
Abdülmecid I	1839–61
Abdül Aziz	1861–76
Murat V	1876
Abdülhamid II (the Damned)	1876–1909
Mehmed V	1909–18
Mehmed VI	1918–22
Abdülmecid II (Caliph only)	1922–24

under his direction; the population grew, road and caravansary networks were extended, trade prospered, and his military machine enjoyed success after success.

He expanded on the Turkish and Persian traditions of justice to protect the lowest members of society from unfair governmental practices or excessive taxation; state decrees were posted publicly to discourage officials from instituting fraudulent or arbitrary laws. The people responded by hailing him as Süleyman the Lawgiver.

OTTOMAN ADMINISTRATIVE STRUCTURE

The Ottoman ruling class was organized into five Imperial Institutions, the most important of which was the military. Almost as important as the military were the scribes, or "men of the pen," whose primary function was the collection of revenue, in addition to their formidable duties in general record keeping. Religion and culture were the dominion of the *ulema,* Muslim leaders educated in theology and law assigned the task of religious leadership, education, and justice. Finally, the Inner and Outer Palace Services took care of the general day-to-day administration of the palace and care of the sultan.

In theory, all lands belonged to the sultan, who by divine right could claim all titles, revenues, and property. The actual administration was bureaucratic, and the sultan's newly acquired territories were controlled through a *timar* system adapted from the Selçuks and Byzantines. A *timar* was a province assigned to a military administrator who, in exchange for the land and its revenue, provided military services and assistance in the administration of the territory. With time and expansion of the empire, the *timars* were converted into tax-paying farm units, and one-fifth of all property, goods, and captives became royal possessions.

In contrast to the Christian policy of lands passing along generational lines, *timars* were assigned according to merit. Christians and prisoners provided the sultan with a steady supply of loyal subjects under the *devshirme* (literally, collection), where teams were sent to conquered territories in search of the best and most promising young boys. Families often hid their children, but on the whole, the opportunity for a distinguished career of service to the sultan was appealing, especially since slaves acquired the social status of their master. Candidates between the ages of 8 and 15 were selected and sent to Istanbul, where they were converted to Islam and educated in the palace school. The finest of the *devshirme* were chosen for continued education and placement in high palace positions while the majority of the trainees entered into the elite military corps of Janissaries. By 1700 the Janissaries (*yeniçeri;* literally "new troops") had swelled to over 100,000 from 12,000 during the reign of Mehmet the Conqueror, ultimately becoming more powerful than the government they served and inciting frequent rebellions.

The Turkish aristocracy, comprised of Muslims, Turks, Arabs, and Iranians, shared the rank of *askerî,* with the newer *devshirme* class of Christian converts making up the ruling class. During Süleyman the Magnificent's reign, this internal rivalry was expertly maneuvered to ensure honesty and obedience.

From the time of Mehmet II, sultans attended sessions of the Imperial Council, a meeting of the sultan's viziers, judges, and department heads (seated on a cushioned platform later simply known as the *divan*) in Topkapı Palace. At meetings 4 days a week, all government business was conducted; public petitions and complaints were heard in the morning and executive issues were addressed in the afternoon.

Driven by the *gazi* guiding principle of *jihad* (struggle), the Ottomans had transformed themselves from plunderers into conquerors.

THE OTTOMAN DECLINE

Several factors, both foreign and domestic, contributed to the progressive deterioration of the Ottoman Empire over the subsequent 2½ centuries. Although Süleyman left a legacy of territories on

Süleyman the Magnificent: Pragmatic Statesman

In 1520 Süleyman ascended to the Ottoman Empire throne and immediately launched invasions into Europe. In 1521 he gained control of Belgrade and the Danube. He then turned his attention to Rhodes, the last Crusader stronghold and bastion of the Knights of St. John—the island that stood between him and his Egyptian territories, not to mention Mecca and Medina. Süleyman triumphed after a 145-day siege, and mercifully released all the Knights and mercenaries, thus gaining the admiration of much of Europe (though he'd come to regret this act later in his career). Eight years later the Knights were granted Tripoli and the Island of Malta in a charter sealed by Holy Roman Emperor Charles V to thwart movement of Ottoman fleets in the Mediterranean.

Süleyman insinuated himself into the politics of Europe and attempted to destabilize both the Roman Catholic Church and the Holy Roman Empire; he believed that any power in those hands was a threat to Islam. Urged on by Francis I of France, Süleyman defeated the young Hungarian king, Louis II (nephew of Charles V), in 1526 at the battle of Mohács. In 1529, at the request of the appointed king of Hungary, he returned to confront Archduke Ferdinand of Austria. Süleyman drove Ferdinand back to Vienna but was unable to penetrate the city's defenses—a failure that would become a recurrent theme for the Ottomans.

Although Süleyman's reign was characterized by almost constant war, he brought peace to the lands that he conquered. Süleyman was said to have embodied perfectly the characteristics of *adale* (justice), much like his namesake, King Solomon. Conquered lands often fared better once he took over. Looting was forbidden, and the sultan gained respect by placing provisions

three continents and the splendor of an empire without equal, he also left behind a scheming widow—Roxelana, the Circassian-born concubine he took as his wife and trusted advisor. Roxelana manipulated her husband, his sons, and the court with sometimes fatal results. Roxelana orchestrated events culminating in the murder of Süleyman's favorite sons, Mustafa and Bayezid, thus clearing the path of ascension for her utterly incompetent son, Selim II. Nicknamed Selim the Sot, he preferred the pursuits of physical pleasure to governing the empire, and left his grand vizier in charge of decision making. The grand vizier assumed more responsibility, but simultaneously set an unfortunate precedent of bribery, favoritism, and corruption. And taking a page from Roxelana's book, members of the harem (that is, mothers of prospective heirs) exerted more and more control over the workings of the government; this culminated in the mid–17th century with an era recognized as "The Sultanate of Women."

The abandonment of the traditional practice of fratricide contributed to the weakening of the system as well. Rather than kill off all potential heirs and risk the endangerment of the line, sultans, beginning with Mehmet III in 1595, adopted the practice of imprisoning their sons and heirs instead of assassinating them. Iso-

along the route of a carefully planned military campaign so as not to take anything from the local peasants along the way. Kings were retained as vassals of the sultan, and as long as the tributes (taxes) were sent to Istanbul, life continued as before.

Above all, Süleyman was a pragmatic statesman. In 1536 he signed a treaty with Francis I of France, conceding commercial privileges to the French in exchange for an informal alliance against their common enemy, the Hapsburgs. With these "Capitulations," the French were exempt from Ottoman taxes and were permitted to fall under French jurisdiction. In response to this French-Turkish cooperation, the Hapsburgs urged the Persians to wage war against the sultan. Turning his attentions East, Süleyman wrestled Iraq from Persian control, arriving as far as the Persian Gulf. Here the Portuguese dominated trade with the East—a presence he was never able to repress.

The Mediterranean Sea was another source of annoyance; despite Süleyman's conquest of Tripoli in 1551, the Knights of Malta (including many of the Knights released after the sultan's victory over Rhodes) were aggressively cutting off Ottoman sea routes. Süleyman began his siege of Malta in 1565, but the Knights fought back ferociously, the battle dragged on to winter, and Süleyman was forced to stand down.

The Ottoman armor was beginning to show weakness, provoking Süleyman, at age 72, to reassert his empire's superiority by taking Vienna once and for all. But he died in his tent during the campaign on the Danube. According to tradition, his heart is buried in Szigetvár on the spot where he passed away.

lated from daily life, inexperienced in the ways of the government or military, accustomed to excess, they either went crazy or emerged completely unprepared for the demands of leadership.

Meanwhile, in the Janissary Corps, celibacy had long been abandoned, and Selim II decreed that sons of Janissaries—who were born free Muslims—could enroll. Eventually this paved the way for other free Muslims to join, and by the mid–17th century the Janissary Corps had swelled to 200,000, squeezing the state for the payroll to support the increase in numbers. The purchasing of office undermined the merit system, and although the palace school continued to function, the *devshirme* was abandoned. During times of peace, without a paycheck, with no active duty and no prospects of conquest or booty, the Janissaries would often turn to moonlighting or to the looting of their own locally governed lands. Already feared by the state structure, they continued to exert an influence on politics to further their won financial interest. Osman II recognized this threat in 1622, but was assassinated by the Janissaries after an effort to control them. Nevertheless, the internal deterioration of the Corps was inevitable as was the weakening of Ottoman military might.

The organization of the *timer* (feudal-like system of government) was not left unaffected by this internal degeneration. To meet the needs of an expanding empire, the *timer* system was converted to a tax-based system of farm units, requiring administrators to send a portion of their tax revenues to Istanbul. Local administrators treated the land as private property, siphoned tax monies, and removed any incentive for the peasant population to produce. The effects were not only economically disastrous, but this weakening of the centralized government also encouraged local bandit raids and peasant revolts, consequences that the government was ill-equipped to control.

With the government decentralized, corrupt, and morally hollow, the Ottomans were unable to deal effectively with outside threats, at their northern and western borders, nor could they absorb the economic pressures of a Europe in Renaissance. Vasco da Gama's circumnavigation of Africa opened up new trade routes to the east; the East India Company of London could therefore sell their goods in Istanbul for less than the Ottomans would pay for direct trade with India. And with new sea trade routes, merchants no longer paid levies for passage through Ottoman territory. Meanwhile, a Western industrial revolution produced cheaper goods that flooded the Ottoman market, thanks to those Capitulations (see "Süleyman the Magnificent: Pragmatic Statesman," above). Silver and gold mined in the Americas drove up prices, the cost of living rose, and peasants abandoned their villages, which had disastrous effects on agricultural production.

Obviously not all sultans and administrators proved to be indifferent, ineffectual, and corrupt, but those who weren't were the exceptions. Although a technically inferior Ottoman navy was defeated by a coalition of Western states at Lepanto in 1571, the Ottoman navy was able to reestablish its naval presence by taking Cyprus from Venice later the same year.

The gradual decline was arrested later that century with the reign of **Murat IV** and his grand vizier, **Köprülü,** who maintained a policy against corruption and a return to the more centralized system of government. The *gazi* spirit was reignited, inspiring decades of new campaigns toward further expansion. Köprülü was so effective that the position of grand vizier was handed down to his son and his grandson, Kara Mustafa; this was the first dynasty associated with the post.

The Ottomans were determined to capture Vienna, and in 1683 **Kara Mustafa** led the army's second doomed attempt to take the Austrian capital. The Ottomans were no match for new European artillery and were soundly defeated by an alliance of European forces—a miscalculation that Kara Mustafa paid for with his life. The army's retreat was met by ambushes and further defeats, ending in the 1699 **Treaty of Karlowitz,** which granted Austria the provinces of Hungary and Transylvania, and marked the first time in history that the Ottoman Empire actually relinquished territory.

The 18th century was, for the most part, characterized by wars with Austria and Russia. Victories against the Austrians served to stabilize borders along the Danube, but the Russians were pushing into Muslim territory in an attempt to become a Black Sea power. In the first half of the century, the Ottoman military met with many successes, not the least of which was the defeat of **Peter the Great** at the Prut River in 1711. Nonetheless, two additional clashes with Russia culminated in the **Treaty of Küçük Kaynarca,** which followed a 1774 victory by Catherine the Great. (She, as champion of the Christian Orthodox faith, actively encouraged revolt in Ottoman territories.) The treaty was an enormous blow to the Ottomans, demonstrating that the Ottoman Empire was no longer the great power it once was. In addition to annexing European territories, the Treaty of

Küçük Kaynarca granted the Russians extensive commercial privileges in the Black Sea, a diplomatic presence in Istanbul, and the protection of the Orthodox Christian faith on Turkish soil. The desire for territorial and economic dominance, along with the trafficking of loyalties, would characterize the Russian-Turkish conflict well into the 20th century.

REFORM ATTEMPTS

It was obvious to Selim III that reform was needed. Inspired by the American and French revolutions, he created a new corps, the *nizam-i jedid* ("the new order"), on Western models, even adopting European-style uniforms. Threatened by a loss of power and privilege within the system, the Janissaries revolted, and in a conciliatory gesture that cost him the throne, Selim dissolved the *nizam-i jedid* in 1807. In the next few years, the Janissaries executed many of the reformers as well as Selim's successor, Mustafa IV; **Mahmud II** was spared only because he was the sole surviving Ottoman prince. Proceeding with caution, Mahmud's first action was to deal with the anarchy that had taken root in the provinces, selecting more obedient governors. Meanwhile, nationalistic sentiments were the cause of revolts in Serbia, Greece, Algeria, and Romania; Serbia gained autonomy in 1829, while Greek rebels, aided by Russia, were able to secure independence by 1830. Faced with a series of defeats, it was clear that the Janissaries were of little use in the defense of the empire, allowing Mahmud to gain enough support to finally have the corps destroyed. The corps was abolished on June 15, 1826, in a staged massacre, and a new army trained in European techniques by German military advisors was formed.

Finally rid of the Janissaries' influence, Mahmud II, followed by his successor, **Abdülmecid,** was able to embark on significant modernization that would last for 40 years. The period of **Tanzimat** (literally, "reordering") was ushered in, aimed at strengthening the power of the government while encouraging an economic and social structure similar to that of Europe.

Influential during this period was the arrival of telegraph lines into Istanbul in 1855, facilitating a literary renaissance that would develop into an incubator for new nationalistic ideas. Supporters of this patriotism were called "New Ottomans," whose objectives of preserving territory and limiting autocratic rule would be attainable through the adoption of a constitution. Considered dissidents, many of these supporters were forced to flee, pursuing their nationalistic aims from posts abroad.

The reforms, however, failed to alleviate a worsening financial crisis brought on by a flood of foreign products, ending in a Franco-English monopoly on tobacco, salt, alcohol, silk, and other essentials. Loans to foreign banks were bankrupting an empire that had come to be known as "the Sick Man of Europe." European powers used this weakness to manipulate political balances. This foreign domination was no more evident than in the Ottoman participation in the Crimean War (1854–56), when the Ottomans granted the Catholic French the right to protect Christian sites in the Ottoman-held Holy Land. The Orthodox Russians found the excuse they needed to further their territorial ambitions and declared war on the Sultanate. Britain and France entered the conflict to protect their commercial interests, and the Russians were ultimately defeated. Even though the outcome was territorially favorable to the Ottomans, the empire was demoralized, having gone from imperial power to political pawn in less than 300 years.

Abdülhamid II succeeded in temporarily reinvigorating the failing empire, but it was too little too late. In 1875 he was confronted with a rebellion by a pan-Slavic movement in the Balkans that was united under Russian protection. Battered, and driven back almost to Istanbul, the Ottomans were forced to sign the disastrous **Treaty of San Stefano** in which much of the Ottoman's European territory was lost. Anti-Russian powers swiftly united behind Britain to force a modification of the treaty in 1878 at the Conference of Berlin. Nevertheless, the damage had been done. European imperialism was costing them more losses: Tunisia to the French in 1881, Egypt to the British in 1882, and East Rumalia to Bulgaria in 1885.

Abdülhamid II responded by reaffirming his designation as caliph and beginning a policy of reinvigorating Islamic unity. With nationalistic tendencies developing among the Arab groups and Albanians, he hoped to create a sense of solidarity geared at holding the empire together.

Succumbing to external and internal pressures, he reluctantly instituted the first written constitution establishing a parliamentary system modeled on those in the West. For the first time in the history of the empire, absolute Ottoman rule had been relinquished, but as a condition to accepting the document, Abdülhamid insisted on retaining the right as final arbiter on unresolved issues. When the opposition became too outspoken in 1877, he simply neglected to reconvene the parliament, essentially shutting down the constitution and ruling autocratically for the next 30 years. Harshly criticized for repression, censorship, and paranoia of conspiracy, he was nevertheless effective in his Westernization of the empire, concentrating on public works, economic development, education, and communications. The telegraph, which provided access to information from beyond the empire's borders, was also useful to his network of spies, providing Abdülhamid with a means for controlling potential insurgencies from within.

The strengthening of the ideal of nationalism, both within the empire and among the provinces, had important negative consequences. Armenian revolutionary groups were springing up in response to a new sense of national identity. Concerned with another separatist movement and suspicious of an Armenian allegiance with European powers, Abdülhamid suppressed these insurgencies in a series of brutal massacres in which an estimated 300,000 Armenians were killed. (This number is disputed.) More separatist movements arose: Greeks in Crete demanding unification with Greece rebelled, resulting in the loss of the island, while Bulgar aggression in Macedonia was inciting unrest among the Greeks there.

European response to Abdülhamid's regime was less than positive, but the Ottomans continued to receive consistent support from the Germans, who, along with the concessionary rights to a Berlin-to-Baghdad railway, enjoyed substantial commercial privileges.

Abdülhamid's crushing policy of censorship was unable to staunch the flow of new ideas. In the late 1880s an organized movement called the Committee for Union and Progress (CUP), made up primarily of military officers and rebels in Macedonia, was organized. In the name of "Liberty, Justice, Equality, and Fraternity" these **Young Turks** orchestrated a successful nonviolent coup d'état in 1908 designed to reinstate the constitution. Abdülhamid was deposed and his brother **Mehmed V** was released from prison as token head of state.

THE YOUNG TURKS

The constitution once again in place, the Young Turks, led by a triumvirate dominated by **Enver Pasha,** had gained control but lacked a clear objective other than controlling autocratic rule and territorial integrity. Ottomanism was no longer a viable ideology given the rise of nationalistic tendencies in the troubled provinces. Solidarity based on a policy of **Pan-Islamism** was especially popular as a way to cement people across national lines, but proved to be too racially narrow. The ideal of **Pan-Turkism,** the uniting of all Turkish-speaking peoples, gained popularity but gave way to **Turkism** as the new national identity, which merged a modernized Islamic tradition with European cultural influences. In spite of these parliamentary disagreements, the effects on administration were significant: a political structure based on European models; a transformation in the role of the press; the engagement of European advisors in agricultural, law, and military matters; increased public works; and the establishment of individual and women's rights.

The social effects of these institutions were lasting, but internal conflict was seen as an opportunity by foreign powers. In 1911 Italy seized Libya and the Dodocanese Islands. Even more devastating was the loss of the remaining European territories in the first Balkan War to an alliance among Bulgaria, Serbia, Greece, and Montenegro. Some European territory was regained 2 years later in the second Balkan War, but the situation was enough for the CUP to mutate into a military dictatorship controlled by a triumvirate of Enver Pasha, Mehmet Talat, and Ahmet Cemal.

WORLD WAR I

Although the Turks favored neutrality in the conflict germinating between the Central Powers of Germany and Austria and the allied countries of England, France, and Russia, Enver Pasha, who declared himself war minister in 1914, favored cooperation with the Germans. Business is business, however, and two battleships were commissioned from the British, destined to restore pride to an outdated navy. Fearful of Turkish entente with their adversaries, the British withheld consignment of the ships, and the Germans shrewdly came to the rescue with the delivery of two battleships, the *Göben* and the *Breslau,* complete with a German crew sporting fezzes.

In the summer of 1914, Enver Pasha signed a secret peace treaty with the Germans promising naval assistance in the face of Russian aggression in the Black Sea. Two months later, flying the sultan's flag, the *Göben* and *Breslau* attacked Russian ports and the Ottoman Empire was dragged into a war. The Russians retaliated by land through the Caucuses, while the British had successfully organized Arab revolts in the eastern provinces, leaving the Turks surrounded by hostile forces. Mustafa Kemal Atatürk's legendary defense of Gallipoli in 1915 succeeded in saving the Straits, and therefore Istanbul, from invasion. Nevertheless, Turkish forces were no match for Allied tanks, automatic weapons, and airplanes and on October 30, 1918, the CUP government agreed to an armistice with England and France. Two weeks later British and French troops were occupying the sultan's palace. Enver Pasha, Mehmet Talat, and Ahmet Cemal fled the city on German warships, leaving the Allied forces to decide how to divide up the empire's few remaining territories.

Under the Treaty of Sèvres, all of the European territory was lost except for a small area around Istanbul. Armenia and Kurdistan gained autonomy, Greece was assigned the administration of the region around İzmir, and French and Italian troops were left to occupy portions of the rest of Anatolia. The Capitulations, suspended shortly before the war, were restored and control of Turkish finances was taken over by the Allies. The government of **Mehmet VI** signed the treaty August 20, 1920.

THE NATIONALIST MOVEMENT

Spurred on by defeat and foreign occupation, nationalists established pockets of resistance called "Defense of Rights" groups. **Mustafa Kemal** (the name Kemal, meaning "perfection," was given to Mustafa by a school instructor for his exceptional achievement; "Atatürk" was added later) was already an active nationalist, having taken part in the CUP overthrow of 1909. He had subsequently distanced himself from the CUP, but his outspokenness had made him many enemies. Mustafa Kemal was sent to Samsun on May 19, 1919, with nebulous military orders, but instead began organizing various nationalist factions, formally resigning from military service shortly after. His goals in leading the resistance were inflexible: the recognition of a national movement and the liberation of Anatolia from foreign occupation.

That same year two important nationalist congresses were convened at Erzurum and Sivas, forming the basis for the **National Pact.** The first conference called for an independent Turkish state, while the second defined the objectives of the movement. Presiding over these meetings, Mustafa Kemal called for the rights to all remaining Ottoman territories, control of Istanbul and the Straits, the guarantee of minority rights, and rejection of foreign intervention in Turkish affairs. Unwilling to alienate the loyalists and conservatives, Mustafa Kemal reasserted the movement's allegiance to the sultan-caliphate, maintaining that until the sultan was free of foreign control, the committee would act on behalf of the people. In response, the sultan declared Mustafa Kemal a rebel, and a *fetva*—the killing of a rebel as a religious duty—was issued. Mustafa Kemal and his followers established themselves in Ankara, far from the reaches of their enemies, voting on August 23, 1920, for the creation of the **Grand National Assembly.**

In the fall of 1919, the Greeks got greedy and began moving inland, arriving as far as the Sakarya River (about 81km/50 miles west of Ankara). Troops led by **Ismet Paşa** (General) beat the Greeks back to İzmir, and in several decisive victories, Mustafa Kemal succeeded in driving the Greek troops completely off the peninsula. This last victory in the war for independence earned Kemal recognition by foreign governments as de facto leader of the Turks. The Soviet Union was the first power to sign a treaty with the nationalists in 1920, establishing set boundaries between the two countries. As nationalist troops approached Thrace, France begged off a confrontation with a complete withdrawal of French forces. Although the British remained in Thrace, they were unwilling to get caught up in a battle on behalf of the Greeks and instead arbitrated the Armistice of Mundanya, requiring the Greeks to retreat behind the Maritsa River. Kemal had succeeded in retaking possession of Istanbul, the Straits, and Thrace, essentially nullifying the Treaty of Sèvres, and it was clear that a new treaty would have to be drawn up. The Allies invited both the Ottoman government and the Grand National Assembly to participate in the creation of the **Treaty of Lausanne,** but fearing that divided representation would only weaken his cause, Kemal declared the sultanate abolished and sent Ismet Paşa as sole representative of Turkey. Mehmet VI was smuggled to Malta on a British ship where he remained in exile, putting the final nail in the coffin of the Sick Man and ending 6 centuries of an empire. The role of caliph was given to his cousin Abdümecid, heir to a defunct Ottoman dynasty.

In 1923 the Treaty of Lausanne recognized Turkey as a sovereign nation. The nation's borders as proposed by the National Pact were established except for the concession of Mosul to Iraq and that of Alexandretta and Antakya (now the Hatay) to France as part of a Syrian mandate. The treaty also called for Greece and Turkey to exchange their respective minority populations, excluding those in Istanbul and western Thrace. This was meant to improve relations between the two countries in the long run, but tragically uprooted almost two million people from their adopted homelands.

Success at Lausanne was immediately followed by the Grand National Assembly's proclamation of the Republic of Turkey and the election of Mustafa Kemal as president.

MUSTAFA KEMAL ATATÜRK & THE REPUBLICAN PERIOD

At the beginning of the war for liberation, Kemal saw a country in ruins. Kemal's vision for the republic was Westernization, modernization, solidarity, secularization, and equality for all Turks. Kemal governed as an inflexible yet benevolent autocrat, asserting that a transitional period was necessary in securing effective reform. To this end he formed the Republican People's Party (RPP), which became the exclusive political vehicle for his programs. When Abdümecid indicated a desire to expand his role as caliph into the political sphere, Kemal, wary of opposition from anti-reformers and traditionalists, succeeded in having the caliphate abolished, going so far as to banish all members of the house of Osman.

In 1924 the Grand National Assembly drew up a constitution establishing guaranteed civil rights and a legal framework for the government. Elected president by the assembly, Kemal selected Ismet Paşa as his prime minister, handpicked his cabinet, and set out virtually unobstructed on a path of brisk modernization.

To Kemal, secularization was essential in a modern system and vital in dealing with a European world. He ordered all religious schools secular, and closed the religious courts. His rapid reforms were not without opposition—both from those who wanted a larger role for Islam in the government as well as those who grew disillusioned with Kemal's pervasive cult of personality. The Progressive Republican Party (PRP) was formed from an opposition consisting of former supporters and associates. Kemal, in a willingness to experiment with open dialogue, admitted the party into the system, even replacing Ismet Paşa with the PRP's Fethi Bey.

An uprising in the southeast put a hasty end to this experiment. An insurgency led by Sheikh Said of the Nakshbendi Order of the Dervishes in the Kurdish southeast had broken out, intent on restoring the caliphate. Kemal responded by invoking an emergency law (the Maintenance of Order Law), reinstated Ismet Paşa as prime minister, and swiftly crushed the rebellion. The sheikh was condemned and hanged along with more than 40 other rebels; newspapers were closed down, journalists arrested, and the PRP outlawed.

Years earlier on a trip to Europe, Kemal had been the brunt of ridicule for his tasseled red felt hat; so, in 1925 the fez, symbol of Ottoman oppression, was outlawed. Stating that "civilized men wear civilized hats," Kemal chose to wear the more modern Panama hat, much like how Mehmet the Conqueror had replaced the turban with the more "modern" fez.

Dervish orders were outlawed (but not completely suppressed). The praying at tombs was prohibited. Honorary titles were abolished. It seemed to the people that Kemal was determined to sever all ties with the past and with tradition, and the people in the outlying regions rioted. Mindful that a drastic measure such as banning the veil would enrage his critics, he opted for discouragement instead. Women in Istanbul and in the other cities began to appear in public without the veil, but the practice caught on less quickly in the rural areas.

The legal code was overhauled, taking its examples from the Swiss, Italian, and German systems. Civil law, previously the dominion of the religious leaders, was secularized, which had a particularly profound effect on women's rights. In a move toward equality, polygamy was outlawed and marriage became a civil contract, depriving husbands of the absolute right provided by Islamic law to divorce for any reason. Women were also granted equal rights in matters of custody and inheritance, while education for women on the secondary level was recognized as equal in importance to that of men. By 1934, women's rights had extended to universal suffrage, and Turkey won the distinction of being the first country in the world to have elected a woman to the Supreme Court.

Kemal's flurry of reform angered many Muslims, and in 1926 a plot to assassinate the president was uncovered (although it is unclear whether or not the plot was actually contrived by Kemal himself to rid himself of his opponents). Fifteen conspirators were hanged, including members of the extinct Peoples' Republican Party and a former deputy, while others were either tried and exiled or acquitted. In 1928 a constitutional provision declaring Islam as the state religion was deleted, completing the secularism of the Republic of Turkey.

A census, which was the first systematic accounting of the people of Turkey, brought to light gaping holes in the needs of the population. Only 10% of the people over the age of 7 were literate while even a smaller percentage of children were even in school, prompting significant reforms in education in the next few years.

Kemal's next task was aimed at both engendering Turkish pride and uniting his polyglot nation under one tongue. By the 1920s, Arabic, Persian, and French words made up 80% of language use, and Kemal ordered his scholars to the task of constructing a pure Turkish language purged of foreign influences. Arabic script was replaced with Latin characters. To quiet the voice of his critics, Kemal personally traveled around the country teaching the new alphabet in public squares when necessary. Not even Islam was spared: In 1932 the state made it mandatory for the traditional call to prayer to be broadcast from the loudspeakers in Turkish instead of Arabic, the language of Islam.

All this modernization and bureaucratic reorganization only served to underline yet another need for change. Keeping track of all these Mohammeds, Mahmuts, and Mehmets was getting confusing, and it was obvious that a better method of identification would be necessary. Up to this point, villagers were called by their first names; now, the people were ordered to select a last name, lest they be assigned one less imaginative. Mustafa Kemal was given the name Atatürk ("father of the Turks") by the Grand National Assembly. Ismet Paşa (the Paşa meaning "general") adopted Inönü, the site of one of his victorious battles, while others selected surnames from the less original Bey ("Mr.") to something more creative along the lines of "slayer of mountains." Old habits die hard, however, and even today it is common practice to address a person by his first name, followed by the respectful "Bey."

Atatürk's presidency was characterized by six guiding principles later to be known as the "Six Arrows." In addition to the three early principles of Republicanism, Nationalism, and Secularism, Atatürk worked toward emphasizing the ideals of Populism, Reformism, and Etatism. Populism was based on the principle that all (men) were equal, but just as important was that all men were Turks, emphasizing the sovereignty of the people over their nation. Reformism confirmed their responsibility toward rapid modernization, while Etatism embraced the government's role in economic development. "Political and military victories cannot endure unless they are crowned by economic triumphs," said Kemal, and in 1934 a 5-year plan for achieving economic sovereignty was inaugurated. The Ottoman economic legacy was one of agricultural stagnation and little public confidence in the quality of Ottoman products. A British saying went, "If you want to hang yourself, do it with English rope." Kemal reversed these trends by developing agricultural and industrial production, raising Customs tariffs to protect the local industry, buying up the foreign railroad concessions, and determinedly avoiding the foreign debt trap. Nevertheless, growth was slow and the people began complaining of a low standard of living. The labor law of 1936 set up provisions for the rights of workers: Strikes were outlawed but a method of arbitration was set up. A state insurance program providing for accidents, for unexpected death, and for seniors was established, furthering the government's support of the labor force.

Atatürk fostered a policy of peaceful foreign relations, subscribing to his enduring ideal: "Peace at home, peace abroad." For the first time in Turkish history, antagonism and warfare were not central to the government's approach to its borders. He signed pacts with Greece, Romania, Yugoslavia and the Balkans, Iran, Iraq, and Afghanistan, and entered into friendly status with the Soviet Union, the United States, England, Germany, Italy, and France. In 1932 Turkey became a member of the League of Nations and in 1936, in response to Mussolini's aggression in Ethiopia, Atatürk successfully lobbied at the Montreux Convention for Turkish fortification of the Straits.

In 15 years of presidency, Atatürk had transformed a feeble dictatorship into a modern, reasonably democratic, forward-thinking republic. On November 10, 1938, his efforts finally took their toll, when, after years of drinking, he died of cirrhosis of the liver, but not without naming Inönü as his successor. The League of Nations offered tribute at his death by calling him a "genius international peacemaker." Atatürk's legacy lives on and even to this day, the time of his death is always observed with a minute of silence.

FOREIGN POLICY & WORLD WAR II

Having served as prime minister from the beginning, having fought alongside Kemal in the war of independence against the Greeks, and having represented Turkey at the Lausanne Conference, Ismet Inönü's appointment to the presidency by the Grand National Assembly the next day was a mere formality. But no sooner did Inönü take office than he was confronted with an international crisis of unprecedented proportions.

The Soviet Union's relentless lusting over the Bosphorus Straits made it a continuous threat, while Hitler's menacing of the Balkans boded badly for Turkey. Sandwiched by two great powers, Turkey entered into a "declaration of mutual guarantee" with Britain followed by a treaty of nonaggression with France. The Nazi-Soviet pact of nonaggression signed in August 1939 presented a difficult problem for Turkey, now that the Soviets had taken sides against Britain and France. Turkey sent an envoy to the Soviet Union in an attempt to secure a peace treaty with them, but none was forthcoming. Betting on security in numbers, Turkey entered into a "treaty of mutual assistance" with Britain and France stipulating that no action would be required of Turkey that might lead to an eventual involvement in war with the Soviet Union. The arrival of the Germans on Turkey's doorstep with the invasion of Greece prompted Turkey to initiate a preemptory nonaggression treaty with Germany, stipulating nonaggression with either Britain or France. Four days later Germany invaded the Soviet Union, an almost irresistible turn of events for the Turks, given their historically acrimonious relationship with the Russians. Nevertheless, Inönü never permitted German access to the Straits or passage on or over Turkish land, maintaining his assertion that the Germans could not win the war. After Germany's defeats in Egypt, North Africa, and Stalingrad seemed to confirm this position, Inönü relented at a meeting with Roosevelt and Churchill in Cairo to a request that Turkish military facilities be made available to the Allied forces.

Inönü's fence-sitting allowed Turkey to maintain its neutrality at least until February 1945, when a declaration of war on Germany became a prerequisite for admittance into the San Francisco Conference (the precursor to the United Nations, of which Turkey was one of the original 51 members).

Nevertheless, war took its toll on the Turkish economy. During the war years, inflation rose significantly, and to feed the war debt, the government imposed a capital levy on the Turkish people. Contrary to the government's posture of absolute equality, the levy was applied arbitrarily and mercilessly, and was particularly biased against rich Greek, Armenian, and Jewish merchants. Deadlines for payment were often harsh, and default was punishable by property seizures, arrest, and deportation into forced labor. To this day, Turkey acknowledges this as a shameful episode in its history, attributable to the extraordinary pressures of war.

There were postwar problems to address as well. The discovery of wartime documents revealed the Soviet Union's enduring desire for control of the Bosphorus and the Dardanelles. Historically a European issue, the United States joined with Britain to support Turkey against Cold War pressures, expanding Turkey's scope of "Europeanization" to now include the United States. The Truman Doctrine of 1947 confirmed a United States–Turkish friendship with the United States' contribution of $400 million toward strengthening the security of Turkey and Greece against Soviet aggression. Turkey later demonstrated its support of Western policies by sending an infantry brigade to Korea to serve under United Nations command in the 1940s and 1950s.

In a postwar desire for political stability and national security against Russian aggression, Turkey pursued a policy of friendship with its neighbors, signing the Greece-Yugoslav Alliance, the Turkish-Pakistani Mutual Security Pact, and the Baghdad Pact, in addition to its membership acceptance by NATO. Turkey's recognition of Israel provoked outrage among its Arab neighbors, but because Arabs still had the stigma of being Ottoman subjects, they were simply ignored.

MUSICAL CHAIRS IN TURKEY'S POLITICS

Pressure mounted in postwar Turkey over the state's increasingly authoritarian rule. Responding to spreading dissension, Inönü yielded to his critics and authorized multiparty activity, permitting access to a democratic process. In 1946 four of the dissenters, Jelal Bayar, Adnan Menderes, Refik Koraltan, and Fuad

Koprulu, founded the Democratic Party, which gained unexpected popularity in the general elections. Despite bribery, scare tactics, and even suspicious ballot handling, the Democratic Party won 61 out of 465 seats in the assembly, and consequently an official, if not modest, voice in the decision-making process. By the election of May 1950, the Democratic Party had attracted enough of the displaced minorities to win a sweeping majority, appealing to private business owners, Islamic reactionaries, and the struggling rural population. In a first-time stunning example of Turkish democracy at work, Inönü stepped down peacefully to lead the minority People's Party. Bayar was elected president, Menderes was chosen as prime minister, and a period of relative prosperity was inaugurated. Economic initiatives were taken to relax government controls and to encourage private enterprises, and Menderes' alliance with the United States resulted in the arrival of American aid, agricultural assistance, equipment, and countless John Deere tractors. In a move to appease their Islamic supporters, the Democratic Party approved the reinstatement of religious instruction as an optional educational program and reversed Atatürk's decree requiring Turkish as the language of the call to prayer.

Despite a brief period of progress in the early 1950s, Turkey's economy took a nosedive. To finance its poorly managed reforms, the government was forced to take out foreign loans, and Turks began seeking employment beyond their borders. Meanwhile, in a move to return to a one-party system, Menderes began undermining his opposition by banning political meetings, invoking censorship, and creating a special Democratic Party to "investigate political activity," a sufficiently vague mandate for random arrests. Although Menderes maintained a high degree of popularity, the military elite

and the foreign-educated intelligentsia began to sow the seeds of rebellion. In response, Menderes imposed martial law. Within a week, students were demonstrating in the streets and cadets from the military academy were staging protests. Cemal Gürsel, a commander of the ground forces and one of the leaders of the movement, decided it was time to act, and in spite of a lack of a clear plan, set the military machine into motion. On May 27, 1960, in a nonviolent coup d'état, the armed forces arrested President Bayar, whose later sentence of death was changed to life in prison. Menderes was hanged on charges of treason, along with hundreds of members of the Democratic Party. The Committee of National Unity, composed of high-level military officials who had participated in the coup, dissolved the Democratic Party government and took over. The people, jubilant of the overthrow, were rewarded with a new constitution; Gürsel was elected president of the Assembly, and former President Inönü, 37 years after his first appointment as prime minister, assumed the position again, along with the task of constructing the Second Republic.

Four political parties offered candidates in the 1961 election, of which only four won seats: the Atatürk-influenced Justice Party, led by Süleyman Demirel; the social democrat RPP; the right-to-moderate Turkish Workers Party; and the communist Confederation of Progressive Trade Unions. Despite Inönü's popularity, the RPP lost ground, while the JP, plumped up by displaced members of the late DP, made gains. Nevertheless, neither was able to summon a majority and legislation was paralyzed. After a year and a half, the military handed over control of the state to civilian rule but maintained a watchful eye on the government in the ensuing years, even failing in two attempted coups later in the first half of the decade. In 1965 the JP was successful in acquiring a majority in the Grand National Assembly, sidelining the RPP for the first time since 1961 and providing Demirel with enough votes to end the coalition-style government in favor of a cabinet.

MODERN TURKEY & THE THIRD REPUBLIC

In spite of the new structure, bickering, crossing of party lines, and splinter groups plagued the political machine. Confidence in the system plummeted, as did the value of the Turkish lira, resulting in unemployment, poverty, hunger, and ultimately social repression. The social and economic situation deteriorated so much so that in 1971, in what became known as the "coup by memorandum," Demirel was forced by the military to resign.

The 1970s were a reactionary time in Turkey, much as the 1960s were in the United States, with Marxist and Leninist doctrines clogging impressionable minds. It wasn't long before antigovernment organizations turned to violence in order to further their cause. The left-wing Turkish People's Liberation Army resorted to political assassinations, kidnappings, and fantastic bank robberies, while the Grey Wolves, the terrorist arm of the Islamic-minded National Salvation Party, made standing in a bus line a fatal risk. By mid-1979 the death toll attributed to terrorist violence had reached 20 people a day.

The military coup of 1980 led by army Chief of Staff General Kenan Evren was greeted with relief by the general population as well as by concerned members of NATO. Two years later, just as they did after previous coups, the military restored civilian government, although they did only offer one candidate for president: Kenan Evren.

The new government found a secure identity in the Motherland Party, led by Turgut Özal, an economist with a proven track record in economic policy. Atatürk's policy of étatism was removed in favor of private enterprise. Unfortunately, two particularly volatile situations impeded Özal from achieving significant progress in building a free market and boosting foreign trade. Tensions in the east were mounting among the Kurdish nationalists, while Turkey's involvement in the Korean War only further drained the country's resources. Expecting to have received some type of recognition or economic support for its participation in the war and having received none, the Turks reacted with violence on military facilities and a decidedly anti-American opinion.

Prior to the 1987 National Assembly elections, the bans against opposition parties and politicians were lifted, with the only restriction being that only parties with more than 10% of the national vote would gain a seat. Only three parties exceeded the 10% requirement: Özal's Motherland Party (Anavatan Partısı or ANAP), which gained a meaty 36% of the vote; the Social Democratic Populist Party (or SHP, which combined the Sosyal Demokrat Partı or Sodep, with the Populist Party, or HP) led by Inönü's son Erdal; and the True Path Party (Doğru Yol Partısı or DYP), reconstituted from the JP and headed by Demirel. Özal succeeded in making headway in areas of foreign policy and economics, despite the impediments of additional political parties and messy clusters of changing coalitions. Nevertheless, some of Turkey's nouveau riche got accustomed to the excesses of the 1980s, although not always by legitimate means. Upon Özal's death in 1993, Demirel made yet another political comeback as Turkey's seventh elected president.

TURKEY AT THE TURN OF THE 21ST CENTURY

Although Turkey has been vigilant in guarding its secularism, it has not been without a constant struggle. An increasingly corrupt government was bound to

Cyprus 101

Cyprus is another one of these divisive territorial issues not entirely dissimilar to the Northern Ireland, Palestinian, or Kashmir conflicts. Situated 65km (40 miles) off the Turkish coast, Cyprus was a part of the Ottoman Empire for centuries, with sizable migrations of Muslim Turks adding to the Orthodox Christian Greek inhabitants of the island. The island became a British colony in 1878 in exchange for support of Turkey against Russian aggression. Anti-British terrorism by Greek Cypriots in the mid-1950s incited riots in Istanbul; Turks were fearful that Greek ownership of the island would be a threat to Turkish national security. The London agreement, negotiated by Britain, Greece, and Turkey, established the independent republic of Cyprus in 1960, with a Greek president, a Turkish vice president, and a fair proportion of representatives in the government.

This bi-communal state functioned for only 3 years, as militant Greek Cypriots (backed by Greece) ousted the Turkish Cypriot members, which resulted in a series of brutal attacks on both Greek and Turkish villages. Once again, it is a case of finger-pointing about who threw the first punch. For the next 10 years, the Turkish Cypriots lived as refugees, during which time Turkey unsuccessfully sought support from a U.S. government unwilling to intervene on behalf of either the Greeks or the Turks. A Greek coup aimed at annexing the island and aided by local Greek Cypriot forces in 1974 called Turkey to action. A Turkish expeditionary force was deployed, occupying the northern third of the island, which in 1983 proclaimed itself the Turkish Republic of Northern Cyprus. Greek inhabitants of the northern territory fled south.

The United Nations has called for a unified state made up of two politically equal communities, and in 2005, Turkey voted yes for reunification. But the Greek Cypriots voted no. There have been no further attempts at negotiation as the international community pretty much waits for the dust to settle. Meanwhile, the United Nations still does not recognize the northern republic and UN peacekeeping forces continue to patrol the border zones between north and south. Now that the E.U. has cleared the way for accession talks with Turkey, it remains to be seen how much Cyprus will remain a thorn in the side of Turkey.

---

provoke resistance, and a return to traditionalism gave credibility to Islamic activity. Educational and welfare programs made possible through endowments from Saudi Arabia gave rise to religious fanaticism, reinforced in the wake of the 1979 revolution in Iran. By 1995, with pro-Islamic sentiment on the rise, the Islamic partisans, having formed the Welfare Party, had gained enough votes in the parliamentary elections to make the coalitions stand up and take notice. With Necmettin Erbakan at the helm, the Welfare Party obtained legitimacy through a coalition with the True Path party, an alliance that most factions had tried to avoid. Erbakan was appointed to serve alternating years as prime minister with the current prime minister, making him the first Islamic leader in the history of the Turkish Republic.

Erbakan's participation as prime minister was an outright affront to the 1982 constitution's prohibiting of "even partially basing the fundamental, social, economic, political, and legal order of the state on religious tenets." Erbakan was widely criticized, especially by the military, which

The Kurdish Question

So who are the Kurds, these people without a country? History books pinpoint their origins to western Iran, but it's more accurate to say that the Kurds have roots in many different lands. Over time, the Kurds have developed a distinctive culture, and today the Kurdish population spreads over eastern Anatolia, northeastern Iraq, Syria, and western Iran.

In the wake of World War I, Kurdish demands for an independent state were met in the Treaty of Sèvres (1920), but the treaty was nullified by Atatürk's victories over foreign occupation and replaced by the Treaty of Lausanne (1923). This new treaty made no mention of the Kurds. The Kurds have been struggling for independence ever since, suffering from repression not only in Turkey but in other countries in the region. In the 1980-to-1988 Iran-Iraq War, entire Kurdish villages were annihilated due to Iraq's use of poison gas; as a result the Turkish government allowed 100,000 Iraqi refugees to flow over the border into Turkey.

In 1978 Abdullah Öcalan formed the PKK as an organized separatist movement, accusing the Turkish government of oppression, repression, torture, and censorship. The Turkish government labeled the PKK a terrorist organization with a limited following intent on destabilizing the Turkish nation and threatening its sovereignty. Turkey considers its Kurdish population Turkish citizens, although in practice, many of the predominantly Kurdish territories, typically in remote regions, are impoverished and lack basic public services.

The PKK took up arms in 1984, and the violence persisted until Öcalan's capture in 1999. In the 16-year armed conflict, the Turkish government estimates that over 30,000 people lost their lives, although this estimate is probably a modest one. At the end of Öcalan's trial, the PKK leader was sentenced to death; since that time, Turkey has abolished the death penalty and Öcalan can expect to live out his days in a Turkish prison.

The PKK, now known as KONGRA-GEL (People's Congress of Kurdistan), declared an end to the cease-fire in 2003, and since then, sporadic assassinations, attacks, and counterattacks have been reported in the Southeast. But this time around, Turkey has the support of the U.S. and the international community in designating the organization as a terrorist one, leaving the Kurdish fighters with dwindling resources and increased opposition to their cause. Meanwhile, the average Kurd in Turkey is very much weary of the unnecessary killing, leaving the insurgents with fewer and fewer recruits. At the same time, the Güneydoğu Anadolu Projesi or Southeast Anatolian Development Project, the massive regional sustainable development plan, promises to lift the Southeast out of poverty while integrating the Kurdish population into the Turkish national experience. For those whose livelihoods are bound to improve, the GAP is a godsend. For others, who have been displaced by the project or who have focused their lives' energies on the creation of an independent Kuristan, this is an anathema to be resisted at all cost.

later forced him to resign. The Welfare Party was accused of being antisecular and was banned in 1998 along with Erbakan, who was prohibited from participating in politics until 2003. The Justice and Development Party (Adalet ve Kalkınma Partısı or AKP in Turkish), formed in August 2001, took over where the Welfare Party left off, claiming a new, moderate stance and a willingness to work within the secular system. The AKP was propelled into power in 2002 with more than 34% of the vote, in no small part as a result of the ineptitude of the government in power to handle the 1999 earthquake, which claimed the lives of over 20,000. It is a well-publicized fact that much of the destruction caused by the earthquake could have been avoided had adequate building methods been employed, and that poorly constructed buildings were a result of corrupt business practices. The vote was also seen as a backlash against institutional corruption as well as dissatisfaction with the crumbling Turkish economy. Reccep Tayıp Erdoğan, the former mayor of Istanbul whose leadership of the party was delayed as a result of incendiary remarks he had made in 1997 (*"Mosques are our barracks, domes our helmets, minarets our bayonets, believers our soldiers"*), has been at the helm since 2003, and apparently, the Turks are more than satisfied with his performance. In 2004, the AKP received an unprecedented 44% of the vote. And in the years since, Turkey has experienced a historic level of economic stability and progress. Erdoğan has also been at the forefront of Turkey's push for full admittance into the E.U. In September 2005, E.U. member states voted to begin accession talks with Turkey, a process that will take at least a decade.

2 Arts, Culture & Music

First impressions of Turkey reveal a society much more European than one expects, but echoes of a strong and proud heritage shine through in the arts, culture, music, and folklore. Tourists flock to those "Turkish Nights" shows expecting to cram in a few hours' worth of "authentic" folklore. But while a belly dancer in a glittery harem hat may seem the epitome of exoticism, this ritual crowd-pleaser is anything but a Turkish invention.

Turkish culture developed by absorbing the artistic traditions of conquered lands, so more than any one defining style, Turkish art is characterized by layers and layers of civilizations. From the time the Turkish tribes spread through Anatolia in the 11th century until the end of the Ottoman Empire, the Turks had incorporated decorative and architectural styles from the Sassanids (a pre-Islamic Persian dynasty), the Romans, the early Christians, the Byzantines, and Renaissance-era Europeans.

ARCHITECTURE

The architectural and decorative arts of Turkey are closely linked to the Islamic faith, which gave major importance to mosques, *medreses* (theological schools), and mausoleums. Almost all mosques follow the plan of Mohammed's house, which was composed of an enclosed courtyard surrounded by huts, with a building at one end for prayer and an arcade to provide shade. Whereas in Mohammed's time the call to prayer was sung from the rooftops, minarets were added later for convenience and style.

The main objective reflected in Selçuk architecture was the proliferation of the purist Sunni orthodoxy, which was achieved by concentrating its efforts on the construction of *medreses* and other public works such as mosques and baths. To provide a means of safe passage for trade as well as the means for communication from one end of the empire to another, the Selçuks built a network of fortified caravansaries. Although Rum Selçuk architecture at first reflected the influences of the Iranian Selçuks, over time they developed a distinct style, incorporating features like pointed arches from the Crusaders and lofty arched spaces from Christian Armenians and Syrians employed under the sultan. They also developed the squinch, a triangular architectural device that allowed the placement of a circular dome atop a square base, laying the groundwork of what was later to become an outstanding feature of Ottoman mosque architecture. The Selçuks also combined traditional Arabesque styles with indigenous Anatolian decorative motifs that literally flowered into a unique style of geometric architectural ornamentation.

A defining feature of Ottoman architecture became the dome, a form that expanded on earlier Turkish architecture but was later haunted by the feat of superior engineering accomplished in the soaring dome of the Ayasofya. As the Turks conquered Christian lands and churches were converted into mosques, traditionally Byzantine ideas were crossing cultural barriers and finding their way into the Selçuk and Ottoman vocabulary.

Ottoman architecture reached its zenith in the 16th century under Süleyman the Magnificent, in the expert hands of his master builder, Sinan. In the service of the sultan, Sinan built no less than 355 buildings and complexes throughout the empire, including the Süleymaniye, whose grand and cascading series of domes has become not only a defining feature of the Istanbul skyline but also a pinnacle in Ottoman architecture. (Sinan succeeded in surpassing the Ayasofya with the Selimiye in Edirne, a destination not covered in this guide.)

ART

Whereas Byzantine art featured elaborate religious interiors and the use of luxury materials like gold and silver, Islamic

hadith frowned on the use of luxury items in its mosques, favoring instead unpretentious items like ceramics, woodcarvings, and inlay. Additionally, because of the Islamic prohibition against the representation of religious images of living creatures, Turkish decorative arts were channeled into alternative features like flowers, geometric forms, and Arabic script.

The Selçuks introduced the use of glazed bricks and tiles in the decoration of their mosques, and by the 16th century, the Ottomans had developed important centers of ceramic production at İznik and Kütahya. Ottoman tiles incorporated a new style of foliage motifs, and used turquoises, blues, greens, and whites as the dominant colors. Spectacular uses of tile can be seen all over the country, in mosques, palaces, *hamams* (Turkish baths), and even private homes.

Woodworking and mother-of-pearl or ivory inlay were primarily used in the decoration of the *minbar* (pulpit), but this craft extended to the creation of Koran holders, cradles, royal thrones, and even musical instruments.

Calligraphy is intimately related to the Islamic faith and dates back to the earliest surviving Koran manuscripts. Over the centuries, different styles of calligraphy emerged, with one of the basic requirements being that the text is legible. The Selçuk period brought about a more cursive graceful script, while the earlier Arabic script was more suited to stone carving. The ornamentation of holy manuscripts became an art in itself, as seen in pages that are gilded with gold leaf or sprinkled with gold dust, and in script whose diacritical marks are accented with red ink.

Besides the use of calligraphy in religious manuscripts, under the Ottomans the application of an imperial seal or *tuğra* (pronounced *too*-rah) on all official edicts became customary. The earliest example of a *tuğra* can be traced back to Orhan Gazi on a 1324 endowment deed, with each successive sultan creating his own distinct and personal representation. Today these seals are significant works of art, bearing price tags that stretch into the hundred- or even thousand-dollar ranges.

The art of marbled paper is another traditional Anatolian art that flourished under the Ottomans. Known as *ebru*, the art of marbling calls for natural dyes and materials, and a precise hand to create a collection of one-of-a-kind designs.

The art of carpet weaving has a complex heritage that goes back for thousands and thousands of years based on the necessity of a nomadic existence. As tribes migrated and integrated, designs and symbols crossed over borders as well. Carpet designs parallel those of the other artistic media, with geometric patterns a common feature of the 13th century. Turkish carpets became one of the more coveted trappings of status in Europe, appearing in the backgrounds of many a Renaissance artist such as Giovanni Bellini and Ghirlandaio. But for the traditionally nomadic Turks, their carpets had more practical functions: warmth and cleanliness. Wool carpets provided warmth for the harsh winters, while kilims, also placed on the ground, provided coverings for cushions in a *şark-* (Oriental-) style setting that could later be used to transport the contents of the tent. Prayer rugs, identifiable by a deliberate lack of symmetry (the "arrow" will always be lain in the direction of Mecca) continue to be one of the more beautiful categories of traditional Turkish rugs.

MUSIC

Much like the art, architecture, and even food of Turkey, Turkish music blends a wide range of styles and cultures, from Anatolian troubadours on horseback

---

Fun Fact Nasrettin Hodja, a Turkish Treasure

Nasrettin Hodja is a folk hero of larger-than-life dimensions—not only for images that depict him as a sizable man atop an unfortunate donkey, but also for his humorous and positive outlook on life that has touched the collective funny bone of the nation. Born sometime during the 13th century, this irrepressible humorist and prankster is still Turkey's most popular story character. Turks continue to add to his ostensible repertoire by creating and updating stories in which he is the protagonist. Some of the anecdotes don't translate across cultures; nevertheless, UNESCO proclaimed 1996 the year of Nasrettin Hodja, for his universal commentary on human nature and weakness.

Sample tale: One day Hodja went to a *hamam*, but he was dressed poorly, and the attendants didn't pay him much attention. They gave him a scrap of soap, a rag for a loincloth, and a worn-out towel. When Hodja left, he gave each of the two attendants a gold coin. Considering the poor service, the two attendants were surprised. They wondered if treating him better might have gotten them an even larger tip. So when Hodja showed up the next week, they treated him like royalty—massaged and perfumed him, gave him embroidered towels and a silk loincloth. As Hodja left the bath he handed each attendant the smallest copper coin possible. "This," said Hodja, "is for the last visit. The gold coins were for today."

Nasrettin Hodja's tomb is located in Akşehir, near Konya. It is fronted by a great padlocked gate with no walls—Hodja always did get the last laugh.

Local Lingo

Walking through a bazaar or past a restaurant entrance may elicit a *"buyurun"* or *"buyurun efendem,"* both of which are expressions of courtesy. *Buyurun* has no English equivalent; it's used as an invitation to "Please feel free" (to look, to come in), or as a "You're welcome," much like the Italian *prego*. *Efendem* is a highly polite gender-neutral form of address that also means "Pardon?"

bringing messages of love, to the commercially successful tunes of arabesque at the top of the charts. Different combinations of styles and genres have given rise to countless new sounds that despite being modern still sound unfamiliar to a Western ear untrained in Eastern modes. An irregular meter called *akşak,* typical to Turkish folk music that originated on the Asian steppes, may sound strange to ears trained on the regular cadences of double, triple, and 4/4 time.

This style was kept alive by lovelorn troubadours singing the poetic and humanistic words of folk icons like Yunus Emre or Pir Sultan; only recently was the music written down. Folk music endures in the rural villages of Turkey, coming to life for wedding celebrations, a circumcision ceremony, or as an amalgam in a nightly folkloric show.

Classical Turkish music began as the music of the Ottoman court, and in an empire composed of a patchwork of cultures, the top composers were Greeks, Armenians, and Jews. Turkish classical music has its origins in the Persian and Arabic traditions, and eventually, the music of the Mevlevi became a major source as well.

Military music had an important role in the successes of the Ottoman Empire, with its thunderous use of percussion aimed at demoralizing an enemy before battle. The Janissary band influenced 18th- and 19th-century European music, in *alla turca* movements written by Mozart and Beethoven, and operas written by Lully and Handel.

The "Europeanization" of the Ottoman Empire in the 19th century brought many foreign musicians to the court, including Giusseppe Donizetti, brother of the more famous Gaetano Donizetti, who was given the position of head of the Imperial Band in 1831.

Pop music took hold of Turkey in the 1950s and 1960s, much as it swept the Western world. But pop in Turkey took on a different form, first with the popularity of the tango in the 1950s, and then with the re-recording of Western favorites using Turkish lyrics. It wasn't long before Turkish musicians began composing their own forms of pop. In the 1970s, as the rural population began to migrate to the cities in search of their fortunes, a widely disparaged form of music called *arabesque* swept the nation off its feet, with the sounds of unrequited love, sentimentality, and even fatalism. Arabesque was a fusion of the new pop, folk, and traditional music that developed into a new and highly commercial style; today, these both exotic and catchy phrases blare from every taxicab, long-distance bus, and discotheque.

LANGUAGE

Turkish is the official language of Turkey, uniting not just its citizens, but also a diaspora of Turkish-speaking peoples throughout Asia. The Turkish language originated in the highlands of the Altay Mountains of Central Asia and is heavily spoken in lands stretching from Turkey to China, including Azerbaijan, Turkmenistan, Özbekistan, Turkistan, Kazakistan, Kirgizistan, Tajikistan, and Northern Cyprus. At the height of the

Ottoman Empire, the Ottoman language was a mélange of outside influences heavily infused with Arabic, the language of religion and law; Persian, the language of art and diplomacy; and French, well, just because it's French. Pure Turkish, spoken by the lower classes and the illiterate, was considered vulgar and its usage was discouraged.

Atatürk was convinced that pride in one's language was critical in instilling a sense of nationalism in a people, and one of his landmark reforms was the purging of foreign influences from the Turkish language and the introduction of the Latin alphabet. Words of Arabic origin still maintain a tremendous presence in daily usage, especially concerning religious matters, and knowledge of some foreign languages will nevertheless come in handy in places like the *kuaför* (coiffeur), the *asensör* (elevator, in French), or the *likör* (liquor) store. English is slowly creeping into the language, particularly in the area of technology, with words like *telefon, Internet,* and the less high-tech *seks.*

Turkish is an agglutinative language, which means that words (and sometimes whole sentences!) get formed by tacking stuff on to the root. Each suffix has some grammatical function but also provides for a discreet amount of flexibility in shades of meaning. To make matters worse, the suffix must follow rules of spelling and phonetics, so that there are eight ways of expressing the word "of."

In 1924, when Atatürk introduced the mandatory use of the Latin alphabet, Turkish became a phonetic language, and is pronounced exactly as it is written, making it relatively easy to read. Is it hard to learn? Compared to what? Will a novice's pronunciation be any worse than an American's attempt at getting his lips around French? Probably not. But Turks are so uncommonly adept at languages that in all likelihood your contact with Turkish will be kept to a minimum. In most major tourist areas and many secondary ones, the local merchant population speaks English, along with French, German, Spanish, Italian, Danish, and even Russian.

Even so, it's absolutely the minimum of courtesy to put yourself out there in an attempt to communicate a few words in the native land of the country you are visiting, and knowing a few basics will help you feel less isolated and helpless. See appendix B, "A Glossary of Useful Turkish Phrases," for a glossary of common phrases and terms, with a pronunciation guide.

3 Food & Drink

As nomads, the Turks were limited by what the land offered and by what could be prepared over a crude open fire, so it's not a stretch to understand how *kebaps* and *köfte* became the centerpieces of Turkish cooking. Turkish food today concentrates on simple combinations, few ingredients, and fresh produce.

With access to vast cupboards stocked with ingredients from the four corners of the empire, the palace chefs developed a more complex cuisine. The majority of these recipes, recorded in Arabic script, were regrettably lost in the language reforms. Some Ottoman favorites have made it to us nevertheless, like the

You'll Never Count Sheep Again

Bus drivers in Turkey abide by an unwritten rule never to eat *cacık*—a salad of yogurt, cucumber, and garlic, often served as a soup—while on duty. The dish is believed to be a surefire, and natural, cure for insomnia.

hünkar beğendi (the sultan was pleased), *imam bayaldı* (the priest fainted; Barbara Cartland might have likened it to a woman's "flower"), and *hanım göbeği* (lady's navel), a syrupy dessert with a thumbprint in the middle. These have become staples in many run-of-the-mill restaurants, but true Ottoman cuisine is difficult to come by. Several restaurants in Istanbul have researched the palace archives to restore some of those lost delicacies to the modern table, providing a rare opportunity to sample the artistry and intricate combinations of exotic flavors in the world's first fusion food. The Turkish kitchen is always stocked with only the freshest vegetables, the most succulent fruits, the creamiest of cheeses and yogurt and the best cuts of meat. But, unless you're a pro like the chefs to the Sultans, whose lives depended on pleasing the palate of their leader, it takes a lot of creativity to turn such seemingly simple ingredients into dishes fit for a king.

A typical Turkish meal begins with a selection of mezes, or appetizers. These often become a meal in themselves, accompanied by an ample serving of *raki* (see the "Drinks" section, below), that when taken together, form a recipe for friendship, laughter, and song. The menu of mezes often includes several types of eggplant, called *patlican; ezme,* a fiery hot salad of red peppers; *sigara böregi,* fried cheese "cigars"; and *dolmalar,* anything from peppers or vine leaves stuffed with rice, pine nuts, cumin, and fresh mint.

The dilemma is whether or not to fill up on these delectables or save room for the *kebaps,* a national dish whose stature rivals that of pasta in Italy. While *izgara* means "grilled," the catchall phrase *kebap* simply put, means "roasted," and denotes an entire class of meats cooked using various methods. Typical *kebaps* include lamb "shish"; spicy *Adana kebap,* a spicy narrow sausage made of ground lamb; *döner kebap,* slices of lamb cooked on a vertical revolving spit; *patlican kebap,* slices of eggplant and lamb grilled on a skewer; and the artery-clogging *Iskender kebap,* layers of *pide,* tomatoes, yogurt, and thinly sliced lamb drenched in melted butter. Turks are equally nationalistic over their *köfte,* Turkey's answer to the hamburger: flat or round little meatballs served with slices of tomato and whole green chili peppers. But even though signs for *kebap* houses may mar the view, Turkish citizens are anything but carnivores, preferring instead to fill up on grains and vegetables. *Saç kavurma* represents a class of casseroles sautéed or roasted in an earthenware dish that, with the help of an ample amount of velvety Turkish olive oil, brings to life the flavors of ingredients like potatoes, zucchini, tomatoes, eggplant, and beef chunks. No self-respecting gourmand should leave Turkey without having had a plate of *mantı,* a meat-filled ravioli, dumpling, or *kreplach,* adapted to the local palate by adding a garlic-and-yogurt sauce. *Pide* is yet another interpretation of pizza made up of fluffy oven-baked bread topped with a variety of ingredients and sliced in strips. *Lahmacun* is another version of the pizza, only this time the bread is as thin as a crepe and lightly covered with chopped onions, lamb, and tomatoes. Picking up some "street food" can be a great diversion, especially in the shelter of some roadside shack where the corn and *gözleme*—a freshly made cheese or potato (or whatever) crepe that is the providence

A Punishment Worse Than the Crime?

In Turkey, tripe soup, called *İşkembe Çorbası* or *Korkoreç,* is a widely accepted remedy for a hangover.

Fun Fact **Caffeined Out**

As a result of the Ottoman's second unsuccessful siege on Vienna, many of the army supplies were left behind in the retreat, including sacks and sacks of coffee beans. Believing them to be sacks of animal waste, the Viennese began to burn the sacks, until a more worldly citizen, aware of the market value of the bean, got a whiff and promptly saved the lot. He later opened up the first coffeehouse in Vienna.

---

of expert rolling pin–wielding village matrons—are hot off the grill.

Desserts fall into two categories: *baklava* and milk-based. Baklava, a type of dessert made of thin layers of pastry dough soaked in syrup, is a sugary sweet bomb best enjoyed around teatime, although several varieties are made so light and fluffy that you'll be tempted to top off dinner with a sampling. The milk-based desserts have no eggs or butter and are a guilt-free pick-me-up in the late afternoon hours, although there's no bad time to treat yourself to some creamy *sütlaç* (rice pudding). The sprinkling of pistachio bits is a liberal addition to these and many a Turkish dessert, while comfort food includes the *irmik helva,* a delicious yet simple family tradition of modestly sweet semolina, pine nuts, milk, and butter (okay, I lied about the guilt-free part).

So what's the deal with Turkish delight? Otherwise known as *lokum,* this sweet candy is made of cornstarch, nuts, syrup, and an endless variety of flavorings to form a skwooshy tidbit whose appeal seems to be more in the gift giving than on its own merit.

DRINKS

Rather than the question, "Would you like something to drink?" Turkish hospitality leaps immediately to the "What?" Tea, called *çay* (chai) in Turkish, is not so much a national drink as it is a ritual. Boil the water incorrectly and you're in for trouble. Let the tea steep without prior rinsing and you've committed an unforgivable transgression. What's amazing is that so many tea drinkers manage to maintain white teeth, and as you'll see, some don't. Tea is served extremely hot and strong in tiny tulip-shaped glasses, accompanied by exactly two sugar cubes. The size of the glass ensures that the tea gets consumed while hot, and before you slurp your final sip, a new glass will arrive. If you find the tea a bit strong, especially on an empty stomach, request that it be *"açik"* or "opened," so that the ratio of water to steeped tea is increased.

The coffee culture is a little less prevalent but no less steeped in tradition. Early clerics believed it to be an intoxicant and consequently had it banned. But the *kahvehane* (coffeehouse) refused to go away, and now the sharing of a cup of coffee is an excuse to prolong a discussion, plan, negotiate, or just plain relax. Turkish coffee is ground to a fine dust, boiled directly in the correct quantity of water, and served as is. Whether you wait for the grinds to settle or down the cup in one shot is entirely an individual choice, although if you leave the muddy residue at the bottom of the cup, you may be able to coax somebody to read your fortune.

There are two national drinks: *rakı* and *ayran.* Rakı is an alcoholic drink distilled from raisins and then redistilled with aniseed. Even when diluted with water, this "lion's milk" still packs a punch, so drink responsibly! *Rakı* is enjoyed everywhere, but is particularly complementary to a meal of mezes.

A Restaurant Primer

The idiosyncrasies of a foreign culture can create some frustrating experiences, especially when they get in the way of eating. In Turkey, dining out in often boisterous groups has traditionally been the province of men, and a smoke-filled room that reeks of macho may not be the most relaxing prospect for a meal. A woman dining alone will often be whisked away to an upstairs "family salon," called the *aile salonu,* where—what else—families, and particularly single women, can enjoy a night out in peace and quiet. Take advantage of it, and don't feel discriminated against; it's there for your comfort.

Restaurants are everywhere, and although the name *restoran* was a European import used for the best establishments, nowadays practically every type of place goes by that name. Cheap, simple, and often charming meals can be had at a family-run place called a *lokanta,* where the food is often prepared in advance *(hazır yemek)* and presented in a steam table. A *meyhane* is a tavern full of those smokin' Turks I mentioned earlier, whereas a *birahane* is basically a potentially unruly beer hall. Both are said to be inappropriate for ladies; however, recently, some *meyhanes* have morphed into civilized places for a fun and sophisticated night out.

Now that you've picked the place, it's time to sit down and read the menu, right? Wrong. Not all restaurants automatically provide menus, instead offering whatever's seasonal or the specialty of the house. If you'd feel more comfortable with a menu, don't be shy about asking, and politely say, *"Menüyü var mı?"* Mezes (appetizers) are often brought over on a platter, and the protocol is to simply point at the ones you want. Don't feel pressured into accepting every plate the waiter offers (none of it is free) or into ordering a main dish; Turks often make a meal out of an array of mezes. When ordering fish, it's perfectly acceptable to have your selection weighed for cost; if the price is higher than you planned to pay, either choose a less expensive fish or ask the waiter if it's possible to buy only half.

Ayran is a refreshing beverage made by diluting yogurt with water. Westerners more accustomed to a sweet-tasting yogurt drink may at first be put off by the saltiness of *ayran,* but when mentally prepared, it's impossible to dismiss the advantages of this concoction, especially after a dehydrating afternoon trudging through shadeless, dusty ruins.

4 An Overview of Islam

Images of car explosions and hostages come to mind when confronted with the idea of a country that is over 98% Muslim; but, without a basic knowledge of the religion and a sense of how secularism has affected Turkey, these types of sweeping characterizations are unfair.

The history of Islam dates to the beginning of the 7th century in the city of Mecca, in today's Saudi Arabia. At the time, Mecca contained what was believed to be the first holy shrine built by Adam and Eve. Later, after Abraham was spared the task of sacrificing his only son, he rebuilt a temple on the same spot and dedicated it to the One True God. This shrine, constructed in the shape of a simple cube (hence the word *Kaaba*), attracted the devotion of a host of pagan cults and, by the end of the second half of the first millennium, contained over 360 statuettes and cult objects. Pilgrims representing a broad range of cults flocked to the city, and the wealthy and influential members of the community were delighted with the revenue that these pilgrimages brought.

Mohammed was born in Mecca around A.D. 570 (or CE, for "Common Era") and grew up in a monotheistic family tradition. A naturally pious man, Mohammed often headed off into the hills for moments of isolated contemplation and prayer. On one of these occasions, Muslims believe that the angel Gabriel appeared with a message from God, a revelation that is accepted as the first verse of the Koran (*Koran* means "The Recitation"). The Koran forms the foundation of the Islamic faith, and is believed by Muslims to be the direct word of God.

In a world of inequality, poverty, and misery, Mohammed's preachings of purity of heart, charity, humility, and justice gained a devoted following well beyond the borders of Mecca. The tribesmen of Mecca grew alarmed and hostile at these developments, eventually forcing Mohammed and his followers to leave Mecca in fear for their lives. The town of Yathrib welcomed Mohammed and gave him an honored position as leader, changing its name to Madinat al-Nabi or "the town of the Prophet." The town was later to become known simply as Medina.

Many of the misconceptions of Islam come from models that are related to culture and not religion. The basic principles of Islam are quite admirable, and every requirement has a practical purpose. The act of prayer sets specific time aside for the recognition of a greater power, and the act of physical prostration is a constant reminder of one's humility and man's equality. Practically speaking, regular prayer develops a sense of peace and tranquillity, of punctuality, obedience, and gratitude. Furthermore, the setting aside of 5 minutes 5 times a day for introspection and meditation can only have positive effects on one's overall health, especially in the face of the stresses that the modern world has to offer. The month of ritual fasting, or Ramadan (*Ramazan* in Turkish), reinforces principles of discipline and teaches people to appreciate what they have and to understand what it's like to do without. Ramadan also brings families and communities together in a feeling of brotherhood and unity.

Islam is a socially conscious religion that attends not only to inner growth but to external affairs as well. The concept of charity is implicit in Islam, which calls for a specific contribution to be made to those less fortunate (2.5%) unless doing so would cause undue hardship to the giver.

Sadly, people tend to dwell on the concepts of polygamy, unequal treatment of women, and terrorist activity associated with the Islamic idea of *jihad,* concepts which when looked at in context have roots in purity but have been manipulated by self-interest and justified as a cultural interpretation. (The idea of multiple wives gained ground at a time when wars were creating an abundance of widows whose only alternative for survival would have been prostitution.)

Islam preaches modesty, and in many societies, particularly in Saudi Arabia and Iran, this concept has been taken to extremes, requiring women to wear a black chador in public. Ironically, there is absolutely nothing in the Koran or any of the hadiths that requires a woman to wear any specific garment. In fact, the requirement of modesty applies to men as well. To force or coerce a women (or anyone) in matters of religion goes against the true spirit of Islam.

A divisive issue in Islam dates back to the death of Mohammed and relates to the succession, an area of disagreement that spreads into ideology. **Shiite** Muslims believe that the true line of *imams* (or spiritual leaders) is one based on genealogy, and that the rightful representatives of Islam descend from Ali, Mohammed's cousin and son-in-law. Shiites believe that part of the imam's inheritance is divine knowledge, which has resulted in blind adherence, because these imams are believed to be infallible. **Sunni** Muslims interpret Mohammed's ideology more democratically, and acknowledge the line of succession as one based on merit and "the consensus of the community."

Turkey, whose Muslims are predominantly Sunni, is the only Muslim country in the world to allow its citizens the freedom to decide their own level of observance. While the political atmosphere in Turkey represents both liberal and conservative extremes, Atatürk's reforms on secularism provided the country with the basis for personal freedoms not available to other Muslim countries where national law is based on the *shariah* (the way of Islam).

The universal reaction of Westerners arriving in Turkey is the revelation that Islam is a religion, not a political cause. While it's true that throughout the history of Islam (and Christianity, and others . . .) religion has been manipulated for political purposes, it's edifying to learn that Islam represents a generosity of spirit, a gentleness of heart, and the practice of good, clean altruistic living. The Anatolian influences in Turkish culture add some rich traditions and folklore into the mix, the result being that many Turks have found a way to adapt to the contradictions inherent in a changing world.

Appendix B: A Glossary of Useful Turkish Phrases

1 Pronunciation Guide

VOWELS

a like the "a" in f*a*ther

â like "ya" (the circumflex adds a diphthong)

e like the "e" in b*e*d

i like the "i" in *i*ndigo

ı like the "e" in th*e*

o like the "o" in h*o*pe

ö like the German "ö" or like the "u" in the English word f*u*rther

u like the "u" in super

ü like the French "u" or like the "u" in the English word f*u*neral

CONSONANTS

c like the "j" in *J*upiter

ç like the "ch" in *ch*urch

g like the "g" in *g*ather

ğ is silent and indicates that the preceding vowel should be elongated (*dağ* becomes "daaah," meaning "mountain")

h is **always** aspirated (pronounced without the "h," the proper name Mahmut means "big elephant!")

j like the "s" in plea*s*ure

s like the "s" in *s*imple

ş like the "sh" in *sh*are

2 Basic Vocabulary

NUMBERS

1	bir	8	sekiz
2	iki	9	dokuz
3	üç	10	on
4	dört	11	onbir
5	beş	12	oniki
6	altı	20	yirmi
7	yedi	21	yirmibir

30	otuz	100	yüz
40	kırk	101	yüzbir
50	elli	200	ikiyüz
60	altmış	1,000	bin
70	yetmiş	2,000	ikibin
80	seksen	1,000,000	birmilyon
90	doksan	2,000,000	ikimilyon

DAYS OF THE WEEK

Sunday   **Pazar**

Monday   **Pazartesi** (literally, "the day after Sunday")

Tuesday   **Salı**

Wednesday   **Çarşamba**

Thursday   **Perşembe**

Friday   **Cuma**

Saturday   **Cumartesi** (literally, "the day after Friday")

MONTHS OF THE YEAR

January   **Ocak**

February   **Şubat**

March   **Mart**

April   **Nisan**

May   **Mayıs**

June   **Haziran**

July   **Temmuz**

August   **Ağfustos**

September   **Eylül**

October   **Ekim**

November   **Kasım**

December   **Aralık**

EXPRESSIONS OF TIME

1 hour   **bir saat**

Afternoon   **Öğleden sonra**

Morning   **Sabah**

Night   **Gece**

Today   **Bugün**

Tomorrow   **Yarın**

What time is it?   **Saat kaç?** (literally, "how many hours?")

Yesterday   **Dün**

USEFUL SUFFIXES

ci, cı, çi, çı, cu, cü, çu, çü   indicates the seller of something

i, ı, u, ü   indicates "of something" (an "s" is added after a vowel)

ler, lar   makes a word plural

li, lı, lu, lü   indicates the presence of something; "with"

siz, sız, suz, süz   indicates the absence of something; "without"

USEFUL WORDS & PHRASES

Check, please!   **Hesap, lütfen!**

Cheers! (drinking)   **Şerefe!**

Closed   **Kapalı**

Do you have any dishes without meat?   **Etsiz yemek var mı?**

Excuse me   **Pardon** (French pronunciation) or **Afadersınız**

Gate (travel)   **Kapı**

Hello   **Merhaba**

Goodbye   **Güle güle** (said by the one staying); Allahaı   **Smarladık** (said by the one leaving)

Goodbye   **Hoşça kalın** (an all-purpose goodbye)

Good day   **Iyi günler**

Good evening   **Iyi akşamlar**

Good morning   **Günaydın**

Good night   **Iyi geceler**

How are you?   **Nasılsınız?**

How much?   **Kaç para?** (literally, "how much money?") or **Ne kadar?**

I'm fine, thank you.   **Iyiyim, teşekkür ederim.**

Is there . . . ?   **Var mı . . . ?** (question of availability)

Is there any meat stock in this dish?   **Içinde et suyu var mı?**

No   **Hayır** *(higher)*

One ticket, please   **Bir tane bilet, lütfen**

Open   **Açık**

Please   **Lütfen**

Pleased to meet you   **Memnun oldun**

Thank you (formal)   **Teşekkür ederim** (try to remember: "tea, sugar, a dream")

Thank you (casual)   **Sağol**

Thank you   **Mersi**

There isn't any; no; none   **Yok**

Very beautiful   **Cok güzel** (said also when the food is good)

Welcome!   **Hoş geldiniz!** (response: **Hoş bulduk**)

Well done!   **Bravo!** or **Aferin!**

Where? Where is it?   **Nerede?**

Where's the toilet?   **Tuvalet nerede?**

Yes   **Evet**

3 Glossary of Terms

Acropolis   Highest part of a Greek city reserved for the most important religious monuments

Ada(sı)   Island

Ağa   Arabic title given to commanders in the Ottoman military

Bahçe(sı)   Garden

Bayanlar   Ladies

Baylar   Gentlemen

Bayram   Arabic term meaning "feast" denoting several of the Muslim holidays

Bedesten   Covered inn or marketplace

Bey   Turkish title of courtesy following a man's first name meaning "Mr." as in "Mehmet bey"

Bulvarı   Boulevard

Büyük   Big

Caddesi   Avenue

Caldarium   Hottest section of a Roman bath

Caliph   Literally "successor" to the prophet Mohammad; in the past, the title was held by the religious leader of the Islamic community and was known as "commander of the faithful"

Cami/camii   Mosque; derived from the Arabic *jama* meaning "place of reunion"

Caravansary   A fortified inn; Turkish spelling is *kervansaray*

Çarşı(sı)   Market; bazaar

Celebi   Nobleman

Çeşme   Fountain

Cıkış   Exit

Cumhuriyet   Republic

Cuneiform   Linear script inscribed into tablets; used by the ancient Mesopotamians and in Asia Minor

Deniz   Sea

Dervish   A member of a mystical order of Islam

Divan   Word used to refer to the Ottoman governmental administration

Dolmuş   Minibus, minivan, or any car that operates as a group taxi

Döviz   Foreign currency

Eczane   Pharmacy

Efendi   Turkish title of courtesy following a first name meaning "sir" or "ma'am"

Emir   Arabic title for a military commander or governor of a province

Ev/evi   Home, house

Fatih   Conqueror

Frigidarium   The cold room of a Roman bath

Gar   Station

Gazi   Literally, "warrior"

Giriş   Entrance

Gişe   Ticket window

Hadith   Traditions based on the words or actions of Mohammad

Hamam(ı)   Turkish bath

Han(ı)   Inn or caravansary

Hanım   Address of respect meaning "lady"

Harem   Women's quarters of a house (literally: "forbidden")

Havaalan(ı) or **hava liman(ı)**   Airport

Hegira   Literally, "the emigration"; *see* hicret

Hicret   The date in 622 when Mohammad left Mecca for Yathrib (Medina) to escape local hostilities; this event marks the beginning of the Islamic calendar.

Hijab   From the Arabic *hajaba* meaning "to conceal"; used to mean any modest covering worn by a Muslim women

Hisar   Fortress

Iconoclasm   8th-century Christian movement that opposed all religious icons

Imam   Literally "leader"; an educated religious guide

Iskele(sı)   Wharf, quay, or dock

Janissaries   The select corps of the Ottoman army

Jihad   Literally, "struggle" or "striving" (Arab; in Turkish: *cihad*)

Kaaba   Muslim sacred shrine in Mecca

Kale(si)   Castle or fortress

Kat   Floor (of a building)

Kervansaray   *See* caravansary

Kilim   Flat weave rug

Kilise   Church

Konak/konağı   Mansion

Koran   The holy recitations of the Prophet Mohammad; Muslims believe that these revelations are the direct words of God

Küçük   Small

Kule   Tower

Külliye(sı)   Religious and social complex consisting of mosque, school, and buildings for public use

Kümbet   Literally, "cupola" or "dome"; synonym for *türbe*

Liman(ı)   Port

Mahalle(sı)   Neighborhood

Medrese   Muslim theological school

Mescit   Small prayer space; mini-mosque

Mevlana   Title of respect meaning "Lord" (Arabic)

Meydan(ı)   Public square

Meyhane   Tavern, pub, or rowdy restaurant

Mihrab   The niche in a mosque oriented toward Mecca

Minaret   The towers of a mosque from which the müezzin chants the call to prayer

Minbar Pulpit

Müezzin The Muslim "cantor" of the call to prayer

Necropolis Ancient Greek or Roman cemetery

Oculus Round "skylight" in the top of a dome

Oda(sı) Room

Otogar Bus station

Pansiyon Pension, guesthouse

Paşa Title given to commanders in the Ottoman army (close to general) and to governors of provinces

Ramadan Islamic month of ritual fasting; Ramadan (*Ramazan* in Turkish) follows the lunar calendar, so that the festival is not confined to one season

Şadirvan Literally, "reservoir"; used for ablution fountains

Şarap Wine

Saray(ı) Palace

Şarcüteri Delicatessen

Satrap Persian governor of a province

Şehzade Crowned prince

Selamlık In a traditional Turkish house, the part reserved for the men and the reception of guests

Sema Mystical dance of the Mevlevi order of the dervishes

Seraglio Sultan's palace

Sokak/sokağı Street

Stele Ancient tombstone

Sublime Porte Originally the main door of the palace where meetings of the divan were held; the term was eventually used to refer to the government, and the entire Ottoman Empire in general

Tepidarium The tepid room of a Roman bath; used for relaxation

Tuğra Sultan's imperial seal

Türbe(si) Turkish monumental funerary tomb

Ulu Great

Yalı Traditional wood Ottoman house, usually a secondary residence, built on the sea

Valide Sultan Turkish title equivalent to Queen Mother

Yol(u) Road (karayolu: highway or autobahn)

Yurt Nomadic tent, traditionally made of felt

4 Menu Guide

WHAT IS IT?

Alabalık Trout	**Barbunya** Red mullet
Ananas Pineapple	**Beyin** Brain
Ançuez Anchovy	**Bezelye** Peas
Balık Fish	**Biber** Pepper (kara biber: black pepper)

Bıldırcın Quail

Bonfile Filet of beef

Çam fıstığı Pine nut

Ciğer Liver

Çilek Strawberry

Çorba Soup

Çupra Sea bream

Dana Veal

Domates Tomato

Domuz Pork

Dondurma Ice cream

Ekmek Bread

Elma Apple

Enginar Artichoke

Erik Plum

Et Meat

Fasulye Bean

Havuç Carrot

Hindi Turkey

İspanak Spinach

Istravrit Mackerel

Jambon Ham

Kabak Squash (zucchini, pumpkin, and the like)

Kalkan Turbot

Karides Shrimp

Karnıbahar Cauliflower

Karpuz Watermelon

Kavun Melon

Kayısı Apricot

Kaz Goose

Kefal Gray mullet

Kılıç Swordfish

Kiraz Cherry

Köfte Meatball

Kuzu Lamb

Lağus Grouper

Lavaş Grilled unleavened bread

Levrek Sea bass

Limon Lemon

Lüfer Bluefish

Mantar Mushroom

Marul Lettuce

Meyva Fruit

Meze Appetizer

Mezgit Cod

Mısır Corn

Mürekkep balığı Squid

Muz Banana

Ördek Duck

Palamut Bonito

Patates Potato

Patlıcan Eggplant/aubergine

Peynir Cheese

Pide Flat bread

Pilaf (pilâf) Rice

Piliç Chicken

Portakal Orange

Salatalik Cucumber

Sardalya Sardine

Şeftali Peach

Şeker Sugar

Sığır Beef

Soğan Onion

Som Salmon

Sosis Sausage

Tarak Scallop

Tatlılar Sweets

Tavuk Hen (for stewing)

Tereyağı Butter

Ton Tuna

Torik Large bonito

Tuz Salt

Un Flour

Üzüm Grapes

Yumurta Eggs

Zeytin Olive

Zeytinyağı Olive oil

HOW IS IT PREPARED?

Buğulama Steamed

Çevirme Meat roasted on a spit

Çiğ Raw

Doğranmış Chopped

Dolma Stuffed

Ezme Paste

Fırın Roasted or baked; oven

Füme Smoked

Guveç Earthenware dish; casseroles cooked in this pot

Haşlama Cooked, boiled

İzgara Grilled

Islim Braised

Kavurma Fried or roasted

Kebap Roasted

Pane Breaded and fried

Püre Purée

Rosto Roast meat

Saç Iron griddle for cooking over wood fires

Sahanda Fried

Şiş Skewer

Sote Sauté

Tandır Clay lined oven

Taşım Boiled

Tava Fried

DRINKS

Ayran Yogurt drink made by the addition of water and salt

Bira Beer

Çay Tea

Kayısı suyu Apricot juice

Kiraz suyu Cherry juice

Kola Cola

Maden suyu or soda Carbonated mineral water

Meyve suyu Fruit juice

Portakal suyu Orange juice

Rakı Alcoholic drink made of aniseed and diluted with water

Şarap Wine

Şekerli With sugar

Şekersiz Unsweetened

Şişe suyu Bottled water

Soğuk içecekler Beverages

Su Water

Süt Milk

Suyu Juice

APPETIZERS

Ara sıcak Hot appetizers (translated literally, "in the middle hot")

Arnavut ciğeri Spicy fried liver with onions

Beyin haşlaması Boiled brain

Beyin kızartması Fried brain

Börek Flaky pastry, either baked or fried

Cacık Salad of yogurt, cucumber, and garlic; often served as a soup

Çiğ köfte Spicy raw meatballs

Çoban salatası Salad of tomatoes, peppers, cucumbers, onions, and mint in olive oil and lemon

Ezme salatası Spicy relish of chopped tomatoes, cucumbers, peppers, hot green chile peppers, onion, and parsley

Fesuliye piyası White bean with onion salad

Havuç salatası Carrot salad

Hibeş Spread of chickpeas, red pepper, onion, and yogurt

Humus Chickpea purée

Patlıcan salatası Purée of roasted eggplant (also served warm; also refers to eggplant sautéed with tomatoes and peppers

Sigara böreği Fried filo "cigar" pastry filled with cheese

Soğuk mezeler Cold appetizers

Su böreği Baked filo filled with meat or cheese

Talaş böreği Puff pastry filled with meat

Yalancı dolması Stuffed grape leaves (no meat)

Yaprak dolması Stuffed grape leaves (sometimes with meat)

SOUPS

Balık çorbası   Fish soup

Domatesli pirinç çorbası   Tomato and rice soup

Et suyu   Consommé

Ezo gelin çorbası   Red lentil soup with bulgur and mint

İşkembe çorbası   Tripe soup (also kokoreç)

Mantar corbası   Mushroom soup

Mercimek çorbası   Lentil soup

Sebze çorbası   Vegetable soup

MEATS & KEBAPS

Adana kebabı   Meatballs of spicy chopped lamb flattened and grilled on a skewer

Böbrek   Kidney

Çöp kebabı   Same as çöp şiş

Çöp şiş   Small lamb cubes grilled on a skewer; also called Çöp kebabı

Döner kebap   Thin slices of lamb roasted on a vertical revolving spit

İçli köfte   Corn or bulgur balls stuffed with minced lamb (boiled or fried)

Iskender kebabı   Sliced *döner kebabı* served on a layer of pide, tomatoes, and yogurt, and covered with melted butter

Izgara köfte   Grilled meatballs

Kadın budu köfte   "Lady's thigh," meatballs of lamb and rice, deep fried

Karışık izgara   Mixed grill

Kuzu budu rostosu   Roasted leg of lamb

Kuzu pirzolası   Grilled lamb chops

Şiş kebabı   Marinated lamb cubes grilled on a skewer

DESSERTS

Aşure   Thick sweet pudding of whole wheat, mixed fruits, and nuts

Baklava   Flaky pastries soaked in syrup or honey

Çukulatalı pudding   Chocolate pudding

Fırın sütlaç   Baked rice pudding

Hanım göbeği   Honey-soaked flour pastry

Helva   National favorite of semolina, sesame paste or flour, sugar, and nuts

Kaymaklı kayısı tatlısı   Poached apricots stuffed with cream

Krem karamel   Crème caramel

Künefe   Butter-soaked pastry filled with melted cheese, soaked in syrup, and served hot

Muhallebi   Milk pudding

Revani   Honey-soaked semolina

Sütlaç   Rice pudding

Tatlılar   Sweets or desserts

Tavukgöğsü   Sweet chicken pudding

OTHER FAVORITE DISHES

Damat dolması   Squash stuffed with ground lamb and nuts

Domates doması   Stuffed tomatoes

Etli biber dolması   Stuffed green peppers

Gözleme   Folded savory pancake filled with potato, cheese, or meat

Hunkar beğendi   Eggplant purée topped with lamb cubes (literally, "the sultan was pleased")

Imam bayıldı   Stuffed eggplant (literally, "the imam fainted")

Lahmacun   Fast food of thin crust dough topped with minced lamb, tomato, and onion

Mantı   Meat dumplings topped with warm sauce of yogurt, garlic, and chile oil

Menemen   Wet omelet of beaten eggs, tomato, and green peppers

Musakka   Casserole of eggplant, vegetables, and ground lamb

Peynirli tost   Grilled cheese sandwich (also called tost)

Simit   Sesame seed–coated soft pretzel

Index

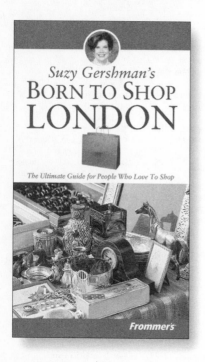

FROMMER'S® COMPLETE TRAVEL GUIDES

Alaska
Amalfi Coast
American Southwest
Amsterdam
Argentina & Chile
Arizona
Atlanta
Australia
Austria
Bahamas
Barcelona
Beijing
Belgium, Holland & Luxembourg
Belize
Bermuda
Boston
Brazil
British Columbia & the Canadian Rockies
Brussels & Bruges
Budapest & the Best of Hungary
Buenos Aires
Calgary
California
Canada
Cancún, Cozumel & the Yucatán
Cape Cod, Nantucket & Martha's Vineyard
Caribbean
Caribbean Ports of Call
Carolinas & Georgia
Chicago
China
Colorado
Costa Rica
Croatia
Cuba
Denmark
Denver, Boulder & Colorado Springs
Edinburgh & Glasgow
England
Europe
Europe by Rail

Florence, Tuscany & Umbria
Florida
France
Germany
Greece
Greek Islands
Hawaii
Hong Kong
Honolulu, Waikiki & Oahu
India
Ireland
Italy
Jamaica
Japan
Kauai
Las Vegas
London
Los Angeles
Los Cabos & Baja
Madrid
Maine Coast
Maryland & Delaware
Maui
Mexico
Montana & Wyoming
Montréal & Québec City
Moscow & St. Petersburg
Munich & the Bavarian Alps
Nashville & Memphis
New England
Newfoundland & Labrador
New Mexico
New Orleans
New York City
New York State
New Zealand
Northern Italy
Norway
Nova Scotia, New Brunswick & Prince Edward Island
Oregon
Paris
Peru

Philadelphia & the Amish Country
Portugal
Prague & the Best of the Czech Republic
Provence & the Riviera
Puerto Rico
Rome
San Antonio & Austin
San Diego
San Francisco
Santa Fe, Taos & Albuquerque
Scandinavia
Scotland
Seattle
Seville, Granada & the Best of Andalusia
Shanghai
Sicily
Singapore & Malaysia
South Africa
South America
South Florida
South Pacific
Southeast Asia
Spain
Sweden
Switzerland
Texas
Thailand
Tokyo
Toronto
Turkey
USA
Utah
Vancouver & Victoria
Vermont, New Hampshire & Maine
Vienna & the Danube Valley
Vietnam
Virgin Islands
Virginia
Walt Disney World® & Orlando
Washington, D.C.
Washington State

FROMMER'S® DOLLAR-A-DAY GUIDES

Australia from $60 a Day
California from $70 a Day
England from $75 a Day
Europe from $85 a Day
Florida from $70 a Day

Hawaii from $80 a Day
Ireland from $90 a Day
Italy from $90 a Day
London from $95 a Day

New York City from $90 a Day
Paris from $95 a Day
San Francisco from $70 a Day
Washington, D.C. from $80 a Day

FROMMER'S® PORTABLE GUIDES

Acapulco, Ixtapa & Zihuatanejo
Amsterdam
Aruba
Australia's Great Barrier Reef
Bahamas
Berlin
Big Island of Hawaii
Boston
California Wine Country
Cancún
Cayman Islands
Charleston
Chicago

Disneyland®
Dominican Republic
Dublin
Florence
Las Vegas
Las Vegas for Non-Gamblers
London
Los Angeles
Maui
Nantucket & Martha's Vineyard
New Orleans
New York City
Paris

Portland
Puerto Rico
Puerto Vallarta, Manzanillo & Guadalajara
Rio de Janeiro
San Diego
San Francisco
Savannah
Vancouver
Venice
Virgin Islands
Washington, D.C.
Whistler

FROMMER'S® CRUISE GUIDES

Alaska Cruises & Ports of Call

Cruises & Ports of Call

European Cruises & Ports of Call

FROMMER'S® DAY BY DAY GUIDES

Amsterdam
Chicago
Florence & Tuscany

London
New York City
Paris

Rome
San Francisco
Venice

FROMMER'S® NATIONAL PARK GUIDES

Algonquin Provincial Park
Banff & Jasper
Grand Canyon

National Parks of the American West
Rocky Mountain
Yellowstone & Grand Teton

Yosemite and Sequoia & Kings
  Canyon
Zion & Bryce Canyon

FROMMER'S® MEMORABLE WALKS

Chicago
London

New York
Paris

Rome
San Francisco

FROMMER'S® WITH KIDS GUIDES

Chicago
Hawaii
Las Vegas
London

National Parks
New York City
San Francisco

Toronto
Walt Disney World® & Orlando
Washington, D.C.

SUZY GERSHMAN'S BORN TO SHOP GUIDES

Born to Shop: France
Born to Shop: Hong Kong, Shanghai
  & Beijing

Born to Shop: Italy
Born to Shop: London

Born to Shop: New York
Born to Shop: Paris

FROMMER'S® IRREVERENT GUIDES

Amsterdam
Boston
Chicago
Las Vegas
London

Los Angeles
Manhattan
New Orleans
Paris

Rome
San Francisco
Walt Disney World®
Washington, D.C.

FROMMER'S® BEST-LOVED DRIVING TOURS

Austria
Britain
California
France

Germany
Ireland
Italy
New England

Northern Italy
Scotland
Spain
Tuscany & Umbria

THE UNOFFICIAL GUIDES®

Adventure Travel in Alaska
Beyond Disney
California with Kids
Central Italy
Chicago
Cruises
Disneyland®
England
Florida
Florida with Kids

Hawaii
Ireland
Las Vegas
London
Maui
Mexico's Best Beach Resorts
Mini Las Vegas
Mini Mickey
New Orleans
New York City

Paris
San Francisco
South Florida including Miami &
  the Keys
Walt Disney World®
Walt Disney World® for
  Grown-ups
Walt Disney World® with Kids
Washington, D.C.

SPECIAL-INTEREST TITLES

Athens Past & Present
Cities Ranked & Rated
Frommer's Best Day Trips from London
Frommer's Best RV & Tent Campgrounds
  in the U.S.A.

Frommer's Exploring America by RV
Frommer's NYC Free & Dirt Cheap
Frommer's Road Atlas Europe
Frommer's Road Atlas Ireland
Retirement Places Rated

FROMMER'S® PHRASEFINDER DICTIONARY GUIDES

French

Italian

Spanish

HE NEW TRAVELOCITY GUARANTEE

EVERYTHING YOU BOOK WILL BE RIGHT, OR WE'LL WORK WITH OUR TRAVEL PARTNERS TO MAKE IT RIGHT, RIGHT AWAY.

To drive home the point,
we're going to use the word "right" in every single sentence.

Let's get right to it. Right to the meat! Only Travelocity guarantees everything about your booking will be right, or we'll work with our travel partners to make it right, right away. Right on!

Here's a picture taken smack dab right in the middle of Antigua, where the guarantee also covers you.

The guarantee covers all but one of the items pictured to the right.

For example, what if the ocean view you booked actually looks out at a downright ugly parking lot? You'd be right to call – we're there for you. And no one in their right mind would be pleased to learn the rental car place has closed and left them stranded. Call Travelocity and we'll help get you back on the right track.

Now, you may be thinking, "Yeah, right, I'm so sure." That's OK; you have the right to remain skeptical. That is until we mention help is always right around the corner. Call us right off the bat, knowing that our customer service reps are there for you 24/7. Righting wrongs. Left and right.

Now if you're guessing there are some things we can't control, like the weather, well you're right. But we can help you with most things – to get all the details in righting,* visit **travelocity.com/guarantee**.

*Sorry, spelling things right is one of the few things not covered under the guarantee.

I'd give my right arm for a guarantee like this, although I'm glad I don't have to.

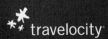

travelocity
You'll never roam alone.